Global Medical Device Regulatory Strategy

Edited by Michael Gropp and Peter A. Takes, PhD, RAC, FRAPS

Copyright © 2016 by the Regulatory Affairs Professionals Society.
All rights reserved.

ISBN: 978-0-9969491-3-2

Every precaution is taken to ensure accuracy of content; however, the publisher cannot accept responsibility for the correctness of the information supplied. At the time of publication, all Internet references (URLs) in this book were valid. These references are subject to change without notice.

RAPS Global Headquarters
5635 Fishers Lane, Suite 550
Rockville, MD 20852
USA

RAPS.org

Contents

Chapter 1	Development and Implementation of Regulatory Strategies for Medical Devices	1
	By Mark A. Chipperfield, MSc and Thomas R. Hutchinson MS, RAC, FRAPS	
Chapter 2	Core Development Teams	5
	By Pamela J. Weagraff, MBA, RAC and Chie Iwaishi, RAC	
Chapter 3	Components of Regulatory Strategy—The Basics	27
	By Melissa Walker, MS, RAC, FRAPS	
Chapter 4	Setting Up a Quality Management System	37
	By Matthew D. O'Donnell, PhD, and Ann Goodall, PhD	
Chapter 5	Strategy for Risk Management in the Device Design and Development Process	59
	By Susan R. Hibbeln and Tony C. Chan, DRSc, MBA, MSQA	
Chapter 6	Global Medical Device Labeling Strategies	73
	By Elisabeth George and Michael A. Siano	
Chapter 7	Manufacturing	85
	By Melissa R. Gaynor, MS, RAC and Penny Northcutt, RAC, FRAPS	
Chapter 8	Nonclinical Laboratory Testing	91
	By Dorota Grabowska, PhD, and Peter A. Takes, PhD, RAC, FRAPS	
Chapter 9	Global Medical Device Clinical Strategy	103
	By Dawn Norman	
Chapter 10	IVDs	109
	By Jocelyn Jennings, MS, RAC and Nobuko Nakajima, MS, RAC	

Chapter 11	Combination Products	121
	By Allyson B. Mullen and Jeffrey N. Gibbs	
Chapter 12	Global Regulatory Processes	131
	By Xianjun Chen, Manuel Urena and Brian Young	
Chapter 13	Global Regulatory Process—Third-Party Point of View	147
	By Gert Bos	
Chapter 14	Regulator's View on Global Device Strategy Trends	157
	By Raymond Chua, MD, MSc and Rama Sethuraman PhD, RAC	
Chapter 15	Use of Standards in Medical Device Global Regulatory Strategy	169
	By Prithul Bom RAC, Michelle Wu and Michael Morton	
Chapter 16	Global Medical Device Marketing Strategy	185
	By Maria Shepherd, MBA	
Chapter 17	Global Postmarketing Regulatory Strategy	201
	By Scott D. Dickerhoff	
Chapter 18	Regulatory Resources for Strategy Development	215
	By Gretchen Parker, PhD, RAC, CIP and Philip E. Sax	
Chapter 19	Borderline Regulation of Stem Cell Technologies: Therapies, Devices and Combination Products	237
	By James A. Smith, Sue Dopson, Benjamin M. Davies, Karolina Wartolowska, Andrew J. Carr and David A. Brindley	
Chapter 20	Patents and Intellectual Property	249
	By Joanna T. Brougher, Stanley F. Chalvire, Sean D. Detweiler, David A. Fazzolare and Lisa M. Warren	
Chapter 21	Software	261
	By Taranjit Samra, DRSc, MSEE and Stewart Crumpler, MSPH, CSQE	
Chapter 22	Reimbursement	283
	By Amit Kukreja, MBA	
Index		295

Figures

Figure 3-1.	Target Market Approval Timelines	33
Figure 4-1.	Basic Process Model	37
Figure 4-2.	PDCA Cycle in Resource Management	38
Figure 4-3.	Mandatory Procedures and Documents for ISO 13485:2003	39
Figure 4-4.	Sample Schedule for QMS Implementation	42
Figure 4-5.	QMS Documentation Defining Responsibilities	43
Figure 4-6.	Typical QMS Document Hierarchy	44
Figure 4-7.	Iterative PDCA Cycle	45
Figure 4-8.	ISO 17021 QMS Certification Cycle	47
Figure 4-9.	Design Process	51
Figure 4-10.	ISO 13485:2016—Potential Timings	56

Figure 5-1.	FDA's View on Managing Pre- and Postmarket Product Risks	64
Figure 5-2.	FDA's Role in Medical Product Risk Management	65
Figure 5-3.	Framework for Environmental Health Risk Management	66
Figure 6-1.	Example of Orthopedic Implant Label for US and EU	74
Figure 8-1.	Strategy for Performing Animal Studies	97
Figure 12-1.	Data integrity verification process outline	136
Figure 14-1.	Rollout of the Medical Device Regulations in Singapore	160
Figure 14-2.	Medical Device Lifecycle	166
Figure 14-3.	Lifecycle Approach to Medical Device Regulatory Framework	167
Figure 15-1.	Document Hierarchy	173
Figure 16-1.	Estimated Cost of Medical Device Regulatory Approval by Country	188
Figure 21-1.	Details of Scrum Methodology (Agile for All, 2011)*	271
Figure 21-2.	Software Development Lifecycle Tools for DHF Documentation and Other Artifacts*	274
Figure 22-1.	Market Access Key Stakeholders	284

Tables

Table 2-1.	Example—Development Phases	8
Table 2-2.	Regulatory Pathway Assessment Elements	16
Table 2-3.	Regulatory Strategy and Plan Elements	18
Table 2-4.	Ebb and Flow of Core Team Member Involvement	23
Table 3-1.	Simplified Global Regulatory Strategy Element Table	28
Table 3-2.	Simplified Example of the Expanded Element Table	32
Table 3-3.	Regulatory Submission Requirements	34
Table 3-4.	Summary of Regulatory Risks	35
Table 4-1.	Key Differences Between ISO 9001 and ISO 13485	38
Table 4-2.	Applicability of ISO 13485 in Various Global Jurisdictions	40
Table 4-3.	Benefits and Barriers to Certification	46
Table 4-4.	Certification Body QMS Assessment Objectives, Scope and Criteria	47
Table 4-5.	Audit Duration for Medical Device ISO 13485 Audits Based on Staff Numbers	48
Table 4-6.	Factors That May Increase or Reduce Audit Durations	49
Table 5-1.	Risk Mitigation Strategies	62
Table 8-1.	The Universal Elements of GLP	92
Table 8-2.	Examples of GLP violations from FDA Warning Letters	93
Table 8-3.	Sources of Device Risk	94
Table 8-4.	Biocompatibility Tests	95
Table 8-5.	Medical Device Classification Based on the Nature of Body Contact and Contact Duration	95
Table 8-6.	Basic Animal Study Protocol Elements	96
Table 8-7.	Animal Models for In Vivo Medical Device Assessment	96
Table 8-8.	International Animal Research Laws, Policies and Guidelines	98
Table 8-9.	Useful Web Resources for Planning and Conducting Animal Studies in Accordance With the 3Rs Principles	99
Table 8-10.	Questions a Company Should Consider When Selecting a CRO	100
Table 12-1.	Global Submission Planning and Prioritization Process	133
Table 12-2.	Considerations for Selecting In-Country Agents	142
Table 14-1.	Risk Classification of Medical Devices in Singapore	161
Table 16-1.	Example of a CV Medical Device Company Product Development Matrix	186
Table 16-2.	Country-Specific Information from the Handbook of Pharma and MedTech Compliance	189
Table 16-3.	High-Level Marketing and Advertising Information for Countries in Asia-Pacific	190
Table 16-4.	High-Level Marketing and Advertising Information for Countries in Europe	191
Table 16-5.	High-Level Marketing and Advertising Information for Countries in Latin America and South America	192

Table 18-1.	African and Middle Eastern Regulatory Agencies	218
Table 18-2.	Asia/Pacific Regulatory Agencies	220
Table 18-3.	European Commission Competent Authorities	220
Table 18-4.	Eastern European Agencies	222
Table 18-5.	Latin American Regulatory Agencies	223
Table 18-6.	North American Regulatory Agencies	223
Table 18-7.	Global Regulatory Professional Trade Organizations	224
Table 18-8.	Miscellaneous Resources	228
Table 18-9.	African/Middle Eastern Intelligence Resources	230
Table 18-10.	Asia/Pacific Intelligence Resources	231
Table 18-11.	European Commission Intelligence Resources	232
Table 18-12.	Latin American Intelligence Resources	233
Table 18-13.	North American and Other Critical Intelligence Resources	234
Table 19-1.	Summary of Select Revenue-Generating Cell Therapy Products Currently on the Market	238
Table 19-2.	Definitions of Manipulations Considered Minimal (US) or Not Substantial (EU)	240
Table 19-3.	Summary of Regulatory Routes and Documents Applicable to Stem Cell and/or Device Products	241
Table 22-1.	Original Purposes and Principal Purposes of DRG Systems in Europe	285
Table 22-2.	Names of Selected DRG Coding Systems and Numbers of Codes	286
Table 22-3.	Main Types of US Reimbursement Coding Systems	287
Table 22-4.	Types of Economic Evaluations	290

Acknowledgments

The Regulatory Affairs Professionals Society would like to thank the following individuals for sharing their expertise in this book:

Editors

Michael Gropp
Chair
RAPS Global Advisory Council

Peter Takes, PhD, RAC, FRAPS
Principal Consultant
Regulatory Intelligence Associates LLC
Adjunct Instructor
Washington University School of Medicine

Authors

Prithul Bom, MBA, ASQ-CSQE, RAC
Senior Director, Scientific Affairs
Medical Devices & Diagnostics
Chiltern International Ltd.

Gert Bos, PhD
Executive Director & Partner
Qserve Group

David Brindley, FRI, FRSA, MEng
Research Fellow in Regenerative Medicine Commercialisation
Nuffield Department of Orthopaedics, Rheumatology and Musculoskeletal Sciences
The University of Oxford

Joanna T. Brougher, Esq., MPH
Biotechnology, Pharmaceutical and Medical Device IP Attorney

Andrew Carr, ChM, DSc, FRCS, FMedSci
Director
Botnar Research Centre
University of Oxford

Stanley F. Chalvire, PharmD, JD
Senior Attorney
Morse, Barnes-Brown & Pendleton PC

Tony C. Chan, DRSc, MBA, MSQA
Principal Consultant
Advanced Global Scientific Management Inc.

Xianjun Chen, MS, RAC
Senior Regulatory Specialist
Smith & Nephew Inc.

Mark A. Chipperfield, MSc
Principal Consultant
Corvus Device Ltd.

Assistant Professor Raymond Chua, MD, MSc
Group Director,
Health Products Regulation Group
Health Sciences Authority

Stewart Crumpler
Principal Life Sciences Consultant
Quality and Compliance Services
Quintiles

Benjamin M. Davies
Research Associate
CASMI Translational Stem Cell Consortium

Sean D. Detweiler, Esq.
Member/Partner
Morse, Barnes-Brown & Pendleton PC

Scott D. Dickerhoff
Director of Regulatory Affairs – Acoustic Implants
Cochlear Ltd.

Sue Dopson
Professor
Said Business School
University of Oxford

David A. Fazzolare, Esq.
Registered Patent Attorney
Ward and Smith, P.A.

Melissa Gaynor, RAC
Consultant, Quality Systems and
    Regulatory Affairs
REGSolutions LLC

Elisabeth M.-v.d. M. George
VP Global Regulations & Standards
Philips Healthcare

Jeffrey N. Gibbs, JD
Director
Hyman Phelps & McNamara PC

Ann Goodall, PhD
Medical Devices
British Standards Institution

Dorota Grabowska, PhD
Research Scientist
Washington University

Susan R. Hibbeln
Director of Quality and Regulatory
    Affairs

Tom Hutchinson, MS, RAC, FRAPS
Vice President Regulatory Affairs
Davol Inc.

Chie Iwaishi, RAC
Vice President, Regulatory Affairs
    Asia Pacific
Alere Inc.

Jocelyn Jennings, MS, RAC
Deputy Director, Regulatory
    Coordination
bioMérieux Inc.*
*current affiliation, Grifos Therapeutics Inc.

Amit Kukreja, MBA
Global Market Access Specialist

Michael C. Morton, PhD
Vice President, Corporate Regulatory
    Affairs
Medtronic

Allyson B. Mullen, Esq., RAC
Asssociate
Hyman, Phelps & McNamara PC

Nobuko Nakajima, MS, RAC
Manager, Regulatory Affairs
Roche Molecular Systems Inc.

Dawn N. Norman, MS
Executive Vice President
MRC-X

Penny Northcutt, RAC, FRAPS
President & CEO
REGSolutions LLC

Matthew O'Donnell, MEng, PhD
Scheme Manager/Product Specialist
Orthopaedic & Dental Devices
BSI Group

Gretchen Parker, PhD, CIP, RAC
Advisor/IRB Co-Chair
Pearl Pathways

Sethuraman Rama
Deputy Director, Medical Devices
    Branch
Health Products Regulation Group
Health Sciences Authority

Taranjit S. Samra
Head of Quality Assurance
Verily

Philip E. Sax
Adjunct Assistant Professor
Master of Regulatory and Quality
    Assurance Program
Temple University

Maria Shepherd
President
Medi-Vantage

Michael A. Siano
Senior Global Regulatory Specialist
Emergo Group

James Andrew Smith
DPhil Candidate
Nuffield Department of
    Orthopaedics, Rheumatology
    and Musculoskeletal Sciences
University of Oxford

Peter Takes, PhD, RAC, FRAPS
Principal Consultant
Regulatory Intelligence Associates
    LLC
Adjunct Instructor
Washington University School of
    Medicine

Manuel Urena
Regulatory Affairs Director,
    Emerging Markets
Smith & Nephew

Brian Young
Principal and Chief Regulatory
    Consultant
Parenteau BioConsultants LLC

Melissa Walker, MS, RAC, FRAPS
President & CTO
Graematter Inc.

Lisa M. Warren
Managing Partner
Morse, Barnes-Brown & Pendleton
    PC

Karolina Wartolowska, MDD, DPhil
Botnar Research Centre
University of Oxford

Pamela J. Weagraff, MBA, RAC
Director, Medical Device &
    Diagnostics Regulatory
Quintiles Advisory Services

Michelle Wu
Director of Quality
Ximedica

Foreword

Around the world, the scope of products deemed "medical devices" is growing. Historically, "devices" largely were capital equipment (e.g., x-ray machines, MRIs), surgical tools (e.g., scalpels, drills, bone saws), assist devices like wheelchairs and the odd in vitro diagnostic (IVDs; e.g., chemistry analyzers, hematology stains, Elisa's). But worldwide, the diversity of medical devices has expanded at a pace rivaling or exceeding that of pharmaceuticals. Technologies such as software, implants (e.g., pacemakers, neurostimulators, IUDs and joint replacements), robotic surgical systems, advanced home use medical interventions and more refined laboratory and home use IVDs (e.g., immunohistochemistry, various fertility tests, lateral flow and multiplex tests and PCR) have broadened the need for regulatory oversight. Increasingly, medical devices are manufactured in jurisdictions other than the US, EU, Japan and Canada. They often are intended for use by persons other than trained health professionals. In parallel, the complexity of the regulatory schemes to be followed by professionals with primary responsibility for establishing, engineering, and managing strategies toward successful medical device development, regulatory clearance and/or approval, and eventual commercialization has expanded.

The questions raised are seemingly endless:
- Is this product regulated as a medical device?
- If so, where; in every corner of the globe?
- How is this medical device classified under different regulatory systems?
- What is required to demonstrate device quality, safety, effectiveness and performance?
- What clinical evidence and evaluation are required?
- What is the role of standards in device development and which apply?
- How do the answers to these and many other questions evolve into a cohesive regulatory strategy?

The "how-to's" already exist on the Internet and in various publications and books. In addition, they often change rapidly and will do so over time. Therefore, this RAPS publication is not simply a summary of technical requirements, but rather is intended to help readers analyze and apply regulatory requirements in support of a business strategy. Authors guide the reader in framing discussions within an organization (particularly with management) about choices required to develop a cohesive and comprehensive applicable regulatory strategy with a high probability of success.

Although, by necessity, certain chapters address specific medical device types, this book's general context is not specific to a particular device category. Rather, this information is intended to be applied to any device class or type, in markets large and small, with technologies advanced or less so and assuming a worldwide regulatory scope. *Global Medical Device Regulatory Strategy* is designed carefully as both a textbook for the novice regulatory professional and a reference and guidebook for the most experienced medical device regulatory expert.

Peter A. Takes, PhD, RAC, FRAPS
Principal Consultant
Regulatory Intelligence Associates, LLC

Michael Gropp
Chair
RAPS Global Advisory Council

Development and Implementation of Regulatory Strategies for Medical Devices

By Mark A. Chipperfield, MSc and Thomas R. Hutchinson MS, RAC, FRAPS

Globalization

A global regulatory approach to the entire medical device lifecycle has been evolving in recent years and at an apparently increasing rate. Effective and strategic medical device development must integrate the changing regulatory environment with associated current business practices. It is essential the regulatory professional understand the regulations and successfully convey that understanding within an organization to implement the design and execution of an effective medical device regulatory strategy.

The Global Harmonization Task Force (GHTF) was initiated in 1992 by the regulatory agencies in the US, EU, Japan, Australia and Canada, with representation from the medical device industry. Specific committees, such as Study Group 1—Premarket evaluation and Study Group 5—Clinical Safety/Performance, developed harmonized recommendations for members to consider when promulgating regulations in their respective markets. Regulatory professionals closely monitored these regulations' development and implementation. Other regional organizations, such as the Association of Southeast Asian Nations (ASEAN) and Pan American Health Organization (PAHO), observed GHTF activities and developed similar recommendations for their member countries.

The release in 1997 by the US Food and Drug Administration (FDA) of 21 CFR Part 820, Quality System Regulations (QSR), with specific provisions for fundamental quality system requirements for medical device design, was an alignment process with the device development and design requirements inherent in the EU medical device directives 90/385/EEC, 93/42/EEC, of 1990 and 1993, respectively, and subsequent amendments. An important element of regulatory requirements for medical device product development in the EU approach in these directives has been to reference system standards, such as ISO 46001 and subsequently EN ISO 13485 and EN ISO 14971, as processes to use to demonstrate product development resulting in safe and effective medical devices. Many of these have reached consensus standard status across Europe and other regions and have been reviewed and acknowledged officially by FDA to become 'Recognized consensus standards'—furthering harmonization and providing subsequent benefits.

In 2011, GHTF was dissolved and superseded by the International Medical Device Regulators Forum (IMDRF), with current membership consisting of the original GHTF members, with the addition of Brazil, China and Russia, and the World Health Organization (WHO) in observer status. Medical device industry representatives are invited to participate in open forums during global meetings.

Through these various regional and global organizations and initiatives, some progress has been made toward harmonizing and aligning medical device product development process and system elements. The objective is to promote the development and marketing authorization of safe and effective products to address clinical needs while helping minimize the overall societal cost of healthcare delivery.

Key concepts of medical device product design development have emerged and have been reflected in global market authorization requirements:

- design control (or some form of structured product development process)
  - design planning
  - design input (clinician and patient needs)
  - design output (clinically relevant product performance specifications)
  - design review
  - design verification (to ensure the final product design meets the specifications)
  - design validation (to ensure the product meets clinician and patient needs)
  - design transfer (manufacturing scale-up and consistent compliance to the product design)
  - design review (overall review and management of the process by appropriate functions)
  - design history
- risk management
  - risk management planning
  - risk analysis (intended use, hazard identification, risk estimation)
  - risk evaluation
  - risk control (options, implementation, residual risk evaluation, benefit-risk analysis)
  - overall risk acceptance
  - risk management reporting
  - post-production information (product information and market surveillance)
- human factors
  - application specification
  - user interface design and implementation
  - task analysis and use-related risk assessment
  - usability verification
  - user interface design development and testing
  - usability validation

Regulatory agency interest continues to increase in using clinical information in medical device marketing authorization and postmarketing risk management processes. The proposed revisions to the various EU medical devices directives (adopted by the European Parliament 22 October 2013 and under further final review) include requirements for clinical data analyses for all medical device submissions and centralized reporting of both clinical trial information and adverse event information in the centralized Eudamed database. FDA increasingly has issued orders for postmarket data analysis as authorized by Section 522 of the *Food, Drug, and Cosmetic Act*—17 studies in 2009, 142 in 2011 and 111 in 2012. While in subsequent years the 522 orders have been reduced—47 in 2013 and only three in 2014—the 522 regulation remains a potent FDA regulatory option. Also, the China Food and Drug Administration (CFDA) is in the process of publishing a catalog of devices that may be exempt from clinical trial requirements; the devices are being assessed based on risk, although how risk is assessed is not yet codified. In 2014, Japan revised the *Pharmaceutical Affairs Law* (*PAL*) to separate the regulation of medical devices from pharmaceutical products, add new requirements regarding medical device design center quality system certification, and is assessing a revised approach to postmarket study requirements.

The elements of medical device design control, appropriate manufacturing quality system, risk management and clinical evidence or other form of postmarket clinical information now have been accepted generally on a global basis. In the evolving worldwide medical device industry, how these concepts are implemented in different organizations and then demonstrated to and reviewed by regulatory agencies for market authorization is an essential requirement for the regulatory professional to understand and master. Regulatory professionals must navigate both the regulations and the organizational approaches to medical device product development successfully to support potential global market authorizations for products and their organizations.

Medical Devices Versus Medicinal/Pharmaceutical Products

It is important to understand some basic differences between medical devices and medicinal/pharmaceutical products, as more and more frequently, these products are being combined to provide new therapeutic options to clinicians and patients.

Medical devices interact with the human body in physical or mechanical modalities and do not principally interact through metabolic, immunologic or pharmacologic molecular or chemical mechanisms. In fact, FDA defines a medical device as: "intended to affect the structure or any function of the body of man or other animals, and which does not achieve its primary intended purposes through chemical action within or on the body of man or other animals and which is not dependent upon being metabolized for the achievement of any of its primary intended purposes."[1] Consequently, medical device development and manufacturing systems have been derived from mechanical engineering approaches applicable to discrete mechanical manufacturing. Medical device development and manufacturing controls are intended to identify and control unit-to-unit variability to permit consistent reproducible medical device performance in the hands of a broad spectrum of clinicians and the intended patient population.

Medicinal/pharmaceutical products interact with the human body through physiologic means, and product development and manufacturing systems are based on chemical engineering and pharmaceutical engineering controls for continuous or homogeneous batch processes. Lot uniformity is essential to provide the same product dose for each clinical situation, and product development and manufacturing control requirements have developed to support this need.

Evolving Technologies

Technology advances include not only various combinations of devices with drug substances and biologic agents but also the incorporation of software, data analysis and communication systems as overall product components. Regulatory agencies have been issuing regulations and various guidance documents to address these new products. An example of this is FDA's Request for Designation to determine a new product's appropriate review pathway.[2]

As in all other medical device regulatory affairs areas, being informed about these developing regulations is a key regulatory professional challenge and responsibility, as they assess potential implications for medical device regulatory strategy and provide guidance to the organizations they support during medical device development. A medical device may require its own market approval (CE, 510(k), PMA, etc.) or may be reviewed as part of the pharmaceutical product. A combination product may be regulated as a medical device in one market and a pharmaceutical product in another. The implications of these and other scenarios include not only the regulatory submission pathway and mechanism but also manufacturing quality systems, clinical trial requirements, product labeling and adverse event reporting requirements. Potential regulatory challenges in managing a product as both a device and a pharmaceutical, for example, can have impact organizational resources significantly.

In personalized medicine and new individual digital healthcare sensing and monitoring technologies, regulations are evolving rapidly. Software validation and data integrity regulations continue to evolve with the emerging technologies. FDA's *Guidance on Mobile Medical Applications* is just one recent example of this.[3]

Current Global Regulatory Dynamics

The regulatory environment's rate of change is significant, with proposed, new or updated legislation, regulation, industry standards and guidance documents being issued constantly. A few examples of the rapidly changing landscape are:

- As described above, with IMDRF's establishment, global transparency across regions and countries and information sharing among regulatory agencies are increasing. Internet and regulatory agency websites publish regular updates regarding product performance problems and field actions. Recent high-profile medical device performance issues (PIP breast implants, metal-on-metal hip replacements, pelvic floor surgical mesh products) have been communicated quickly around the world, resulting in increased public caution and focus on regulated devices' lifecycle management.
- In efforts to minimize rising healthcare costs, outpatient surgical centers, clinics and home-care-based technologies continue to develop. This results in greater emphasis on the design and development of medical device human factors analysis to include nonclinically trained individuals to ensure appropriate product performance levels with minimum risk to patients.[4] Reimbursement systems are being implemented focusing on clinical-outcomes-case-management results and not just any one medical device's specific contribution.
- Information sharing on a global basis is accelerating due to the planned implementation of the Unique Device Identifier (UDI). This information is cross-referenced to the Global Medical Device Nomenclature (GMDN) database used by regulatory agencies, industry and healthcare institutions since 1992.

Understanding global regulatory dynamics, such as the few examples noted above, and providing guidance and interpretation within an organization, are key strategic skills a successful regulatory professional must develop and improve constantly. Successful medical device product development, market authorization and ongoing compliance and risk management across the complete product lifecycle are dependent on the regulatory professional's knowledge and interpretation skills.

This book provides extensive information about tasks that need to be performed, suggestions around how the regulatory professional can perform these tasks as an effective contributor within an organization and some guidance on when to involve a regulatory body.

Chapter Topics

Chapters in this book can be grouped broadly by subject matter into the following categories:
- Strategy—Components of a Regulatory Strategy (Chapter 3), Global Labeling Strategy (Chapter 6), Global Regulatory Processes (Chapters 12, 13 and 14)
- Technical elements—Device Design and Development Process (Chapter 5), Manufacturing (Chapter 7), Nonclinical and Laboratory Testing (Chapter 8), Clinical Trials (Chapter 9), Use of Standards (Chapter 15)
- Commercial—Marketing (Chapter 16), Postmarketing (Chapter 17), Patents (Chapter 20), Reimbursement (Chapter 22)
- Organization—Core Development Team (Chapter 2), Setting up a Quality Management System (Chapter 4), Regulatory Resources (Chapter 18)
- Special technology areas—IVDs (Chapter 10), Combination Products (Chapter 11), Stem Cell Technology (Chapter 19), Software (Chapter 21)

The regulatory professional will find extensive information in this book to develop and implement an effective regulatory strategy to support global medical device development.

References
1. Is the Product a Medical Device? *Food, Drug, and Cosmetic Act* Section 201(h), 21 USC §321(h). FDA website. http://www.fda.gov/medicaldevices/deviceregulationandguidance/overview/classifyyourdevice/ucm051512.htm; Accessed 9 November 2015.
2. 21 CFR Part 3 "Request for Designation"
3. *Mobile Medical Applications: Guidance for Industry and Food and Drug Administration Staff* (9 February 2015). FDA website. http://www.fda.gov/downloads/MedicalDevices/DeviceRegulationandGuidance/GuidanceDocuments/UCM263366.pdf). Accessed 9 November 2015.
4. *Draft Guidance for Industry and Food and Drug Administration Staff - Applying Human Factors and Usability Engineering to Optimize Medical Device Design* (22 June 2011). FDA website. http://www.fda.gov/medicaldevices/deviceregulationandguidance/guidancedocuments/ucm259748.htm . Accessed 9 November 2015.

Core Development Teams

By Pamela J. Weagraff, MBA, RAC and Chie Iwaishi, RAC

Introduction

New scientific discoveries or novel ideas often are at the root of innovative medical device development—whether the product is a transformative technology, a modified version of an already marketed model or a novel application of existing tools or scientific approaches. Most new medical devices are developed or conceived as a solution to an unmet clinical challenge, many of these in academic centers.

The first phases of a device's total product lifecycle revolves around product development, from concept to marketing. After discovery and ideation, further development to achieve regulatory approval and market launch requires a cross-functional team. In this chapter, the team formed to bring a medical device from concept to market is defined as a core development team (CDT).

A CDT's goal is to meet project milestones in a timely and efficient manner while maintaining regulatory compliance. Forming and supporting robust CDTs is a strategic competency of any medical device company, from the very small to the very large. High-functioning CDTs create momentum in realizing strategies for smart product development, accelerated time-to-market and medical devices with rapid early adoption. Less efficient CDTs can induce project rework, project delay to market and ambivalent early adoption by key customers. CDT performance also can have an immediate impact on the organization.

CDT Fundamentals

CDT Purpose and Function

A CDT creates an environment for cross-functional experts to focus on achieving goals for highly collaborative and complex projects. In contrast, less-complicated, short-term projects, e.g., implementation of design changes to an existing product, may not require a CDT. Even so, CDTs offer several inherent advantages.

First, a CDT makes the decision-making process efficient, particularly in mid- to large-size companies organized in traditional functional vertical structures. A CDT typically is organized horizontally under a project or program team lead. A CDT allows a cross-functional management approach and can be viewed as a dual-reporting (matrix) relationship, solid line to the CDT member's manager and dotted line to the CDT project or program lead. In a well-functioning cross-functional CDT, planning, discussing and resolving issues and implementing decisions as a unit creates great efficiencies and has proven to decrease time-to-market. Critical project decisions still should be expected to involve various functional line managers, and significant business and financial decisions would be expected to be subject to executive management oversight during phase review or milestone meetings.

Another CDT benefit is creating a project history and product knowledge portal. Because individuals from different functions are working in close cooperation, CDT members learn the value of sharing information to achieve common goals. In effect, a CDT becomes a valuable resource for project information.

In a CDT, each team member brings specialized knowledge about his or her function to the team. Ideally, the CDT decision-making process proceeds in a balanced, pragmatic manner, leading to high-functioning teams. This approach also serves as a great employee motivator since team members have more opportunities to voice ideas and concerns directly, as well as influence day-to-day decisions.

Identification of Projects Suitable for CDT Structure

Typically, a company's design control program provides guidance on which projects require design and development planning for conformance with regulatory requirements and achievement of business efficiencies and, thereby, benefit highly from CDT formation. CDT structure may not be appropriate for certain projects. In small companies, the design control program should allow enough flexibility for CDT formation to avoid inefficiencies. Also, less-complex projects, e.g., design changes to existing products, may not warrant CDT formation.

Product portfolio or product management leads should be well versed in balancing business needs when selecting projects and securing sufficient funding so the CDT, once formed, can move forward with great clarity concerning project scope, objectives and goals. A classic impediment to timely project execution is ambiguity, which can result in "back-tracking" to re-scope the project and secure requisite funding.

Roles and Responsibilities of CDT in the Organization

Medical device product development calls for untold numbers of decisions across all functional areas, from conception through market launch, in the postmarket environment, through product obsolescence. These decisions need to maintain the equilibrium between regulatory design control and risk management program requirements, and business and financial goals and objectives. The CDT also must lay the foundation for handover to full production, market release and post-launch performance monitoring.

The CDT's cross-functional structure is intended to focus on business and financial goals and objectives as well as maintain appropriate regulatory compliance. In an ideal balanced system, regulatory compliance requirements inform the project strategy but stop short of driving it. The team should exercise considerable autonomy in decision making, consulting with the executive management team for business or financial strategic decisions leading to project phase review or milestone meetings.

The interdependencies are the "glue" holding the CDT together and, when functioning well, can instill great executive management confidence. Again, a robust design control program should include well-defined roles and responsibilities for each team member, including involvement in decision making at all levels, with respect to patient and healthcare provider needs, business and financial goals and regulatory compliance requirements.

Essential Considerations

When forming a CDT, several things should be considered:

System and Process Feasibility

When project goals call for developing innovative or higher-risk products than the company has developed previously, the CDT must assess the existing quality management system's (QMS) adequacy, particularly design control and risk management programs, to support project goals. QMS requirements allow a company to establish a system commensurate with the nature and level of risk presented by the products to be designed, developed, manufactured and distributed. However, innovative technology and/or a high-risk device may require QMS upgrades to ensure processes and practices are robust enough to address heightened requirements.

For example, if a company that historically has developed legacy medical devices with mature technologies decides to enter a new market segment where new requirements may apply, e.g., device/drug combination products, the company must assess its QMS in view of combination product requirements, i.e., 21 CFR Part 4. Similarly, a company that historically has made single-use disposable devices would have to reevaluate its QMS before starting to develop electromedical devices.

For a small company moving from research into product development, it is imperative to establish first those QMS elements necessary to support product development activities. A small company may implement a QMS in a staged manner, establishing quality system elements required for product development first, followed by implementation of quality system elements pertaining to later postmarket activities. Small companies also must understand investigational devices are expected to have been designed and developed in the context of a design control and risk management program, and the Essential Requirements (assures devices' safe function for their intended use)[1] have been met via some level of design verification and/or design validation testing. This is an explicit US requirement, implicit in all other countries, for the investigational device to have an assurance of safety before use in patients. The manufacturer also must be able to demonstrate via design controls that clinical evidence, if any, gathered with early-stage devices reasonably represents the devices' expected clinical performance once they are released to the market.

The QMS infrastructure requires company investment and executive management commitment, but without appropriate policies and procedures in place, the impact on downstream efforts to develop product registrations and ultimately commercialize the product can be detrimental.

Global Strategy and Submissions

A new product or change to an existing product intending to fulfill an unmet clinical need could be local, but in today's world, is more likely global in scope. The rapid pace of innovation in the past few decades has been far-reaching and has transformed the medical device industry and drastically affected regulatory environments and market dynamics. Target markets for projects under consideration, whether attractive due to their market size or strategic competencies, should be identified early so the CDT can be staffed appropriately to meet global launch projections.

Even with the strong focus on harmonizing regulatory requirements, significant differences still exist in technical requirements for product registrations, QMS inspection and audit methods and such postmarket surveillance activities as adverse event reporting.

It is not unusual for mechanical performance testing results acceptable under the EU *Medical Devices Directive* (*MDD*) to be unacceptable in some Asian countries due to differences in lifestyle, medical practice or device accessory supply shortages. First learning about differing requirements at submission or during regulatory review has deleterious effects, leading to rework and overall project delays. Advance understanding of global regulatory requirements and associated nuances ensures the CDT and its *ad hoc* members can address preclinical or clinical data requirements, inspection or audit requirements expeditiously and efficiently, and expedites product registration workflows.

Product registrations in most countries require local representatives. Without well-defined processes to support global product registrations, e.g., information flow for product registrations and response to local regulatory authority questions, CDTs can be consumed by local demands. Some mid- to large-size companies may rely on an internal international regulatory function to support global project registrations. However, mid- to small-size companies more often rely on CDT members to support global registrations. Identifying key markets and incorporating their testing and registration requirements early in a project plan is critical for a successful global product launch. Developing tools and procedures for submission dossiers and certificates and responding to regulators' questions may be necessary if simultaneous product launch in multiple markets is planned. A CDT also should consider building consensus with management and international partners in advance on what accessibility level to proprietary information is given to distributors in contrast with direct affiliates.

Challenges

While a CDT structure provides essential elements for meeting project milestones, potential challenges extend beyond the immediate goals and objectives. One common issue is navigating the direct reporting relationship with a manager and the indirect reporting relationship with a CDT project lead. Mixed messages can lead quickly to inefficiencies, not to mention present very real obstacles to efficient decision making. Organizational clarity regarding reporting structures and decision authority is especially critical to CDT functioning.

CDT members need to be agile and able to adjust to change rapidly to advance the project. As the project progresses, the impact of a change increases exponentially, in the form of rework and the impact on the project's schedule. Lines of communication need to be open at all times so adjustments can be made to any necessary changes in a fluid manner across all affected functions.

Last but not least, resource planning needs to take into account the ebb and flow of CDT member involvement (see section on Ebb and Flow of CDT Member Involvement).

Composition of CDTs—Context is Everything

A CTD's composition depends on the project's goals, objectives and complexity. In addition, CTDs in large and small companies will vary given the differences in available internal versus external resources. Without some context, it is difficult to grasp the exact extent to which CDTs can make or break a project. This section assumes the following development phases, as described below and illustrated in **Table 2-1**.

Many process approaches exist for managing product development, all of which are acceptable, provided, in the US for example, the process approach ensures design control requirements according to 21 CFR §820.30 are

Table 2-1. Example—Development Phases

Phase 1—Requirements	Phase 2—Design	Phase 3—Verification and Validation	Phase 4—Commercialization	Phase 5—Product Maintenance
Input: Market requirements based on market research; proof of principle based on market requirements and test results; reassessment of business case; regulatory pathway and initial strategy; reassessment of IP	**Input**: Project management plan and supporting plans, design requirements, product specification, risk analysis	**Input**: Updated project management plan and supporting plans, design requirements, product specification, risk analysis, prototypes	**Input**: Updated project management plan and supporting plans, design requirements, product specification, risk analysis, verification and validation results for production equivalent prototypes; information for regulatory submission(s) available	**Input**: Request for design change, e.g., to the device, its packaging or labeling or to the DMR; request for product obsolescence
<ul><li>Develop project management plan and supporting plans</li><li>Develop design requirements, based on market requirements, risk analysis, regulatory requirements and information on comparable, commercially available medical devices</li><li>Translate design requirements into initial product specifications</li></ul>	<ul><li>Update project management plan and supporting plans as needed, and conduct activities as called out in plans</li><li>Finalize the product specifications with identification of Essential Requirements for the device and convert to development prototype</li><li>Optimize design as needed</li></ul>	<ul><li>Verify specified product in the form of development prototype, meet the design requirements prior to the start of design validation activities, readiness to conduct clinical studies</li><li>Validate technical and clinical performance to user requirements under simulated or actual use conditions</li></ul>	<ul><li>Transfer design output to manufacturing, including validation of any required manufacturing processes</li><li>Execute plans for order generation, distribution, installation and service</li></ul>	<ul><li>Review request for design change, determine which aspect of design control and risk management are applicable and manage accordingly</li><li>Review request for product obsolescence and develop plan to execute obsolescence activities</li></ul>
Output: Project management plan and supporting plans, design requirements, product specification, risk analysis	**Output**: Updated project management plan and supporting plans, design requirements, product specification, risk analysis, prototypes	**Output**: Updated project management plan and supporting plans, design requirements, product specification, risk analysis, verification and validation results for production equivalent prototype; information for regulatory submission(s) available	**Output**: Completion of actions per project management plan and supporting plans; design transfer activities complete; adequate quantity of product available for shipments to customers; regulatory registrations in place; order generation, distribution, installation and service processes in place	**Output**: Completion of actions per design change request and release as effective for use; completion of activities per product obsolescence plan, with all affected customers notified and adequate replacement parts for installed base product
Phase Review: Approval of phase 1 outputs	**Phase Review**: Approval of phase 2 outputs	**Phase Review**: Approval of phase 3 outputs	**Phase Review**: Approval of phase 4 outputs results in release to manufacturing and readiness to ship commercial product to customers	**Phase Review**: Approval of phase 5 outputs results in release of the design change as effective for use or results in obsolescence of product per requested timeline

fulfilled in a manner commensurate with the product to be marketed.

Phase 1—Requirements

Once management approves formal transition from research to development and assigns a project manager, that individual initiates development activities by asking functional managers to assign representatives to serve on the CDT. The project manager begins phase 1 by planning design and development activities in the form of a project or design and development management plan and assigning supporting plan development responsibility to CDT members by function.

Documenting design and development planning activities helps develop supporting project documents, e.g., design requirements, product specification, design plans (electrical, mechanical, software, etc.), regulatory strategy, clinical development, etc. Timing associated with these project documents is discussed in the section on Ebb and Flow of CDT Member Involvement.

Key activities for phase 1 typically include but are not limited to:
- developing design requirements, based on market requirements
- conducting initial risk analysis
- defining specific regulatory requirements
- providing supplementary information on comparable, commercially available medical devices
- translating design requirements into initial product specifications
- conducting and documenting design review(s); note: design reviews typically are specific, focused reviews and differ from phase reviews because the focus is on a design document, e.g., design requirements or product specification, but do not include business-related concerns with regard to project costs, project timelines, etc.
- conducting phase review according to phase 1 exit readiness checklist

Phase 2—Design

During phase 2, the project manager updates the project plan to reflect activities completed in phase 1, including the phase 2 design list of deliverables and readiness checklist and monitors updates to the supporting plans with the designated "owners," i.e., individuals responsible for the activities. Typically, the project manager assigns a manufacturing plan owner who also monitors the design transfer checklist during phase 2.

Key activities for phase 2 typically include but are not limited to:
- converting initial specifications into development prototype components
- integrating development prototype components into a development prototype system
- optimizing design as needed
- finalizing product specifications by identifying the device's Essential Requirements
- converting final specifications into production prototype components, representative of the commercial product
- integrating production prototype components into production prototype system
- conducting and documenting design review(s)
- conducting phase review according to the phase 2 exit readiness checklist

Phase 3—Verification and Validation

The project manager updates the project plan to reflect activities completed in phase 2, including the phase 3 verification and validation list of deliverables and readiness checklist, and monitors updates to the supporting plans with the assigned owners.

Key activities for phase 3 typically include but are not limited to:
- developing and documenting verification and validation test protocols according to the verification and validation plan, for production prototype components, separately, and as an integrated production prototype system
- executing verification test protocols and documenting results; verifying product specifications in production prototype components, separately, and integrated production prototype system meet the design requirements prior to starting design validation activities (At minimum, essential design requirements, i.e., affecting user or patient safety, must be verified before performing validation activities.)
- for design verification of non-essential design requirements performed concurrently with validation activities, design changes implemented as a result of design verification results may require repeating some validation activities
- executing validation test protocols and document results; validating production prototype component technical and clinical performance characteristics, separately and, as an integrated production prototype system, to market or user

requirements under simulated or actual use conditions
- based on verification and validation activities' results and, according to the project regulatory plan, finalizing regulatory application(s) and submitting to the appropriate regulatory authority as required, e.g., 510(k) Premarket Notification or Premarket Approval (PMA) for US; Technical File (submission not required) or Design Dossier for EU; Medical Device License for Canada, etc.
- conducting and documenting design review(s)
- conducting phase review according to the phase 3 exit readiness checklist

Note: Regulatory application requirements may specify preclinical animal studies and/or human use studies as part of design validation activities or to support the regulatory application. If human use clinical studies are required, additional regulatory requirements may apply depending on the type of clinical study or studies and country or countries in which the study may be conducted.

Phase 4—Commercialization

The project manager updates the project plan to reflect activities completed in phase 3—verification and validation—and phase 4, commercialization's list of deliverables and readiness checklist, and monitors updating the supporting plans with the assigned owners.

Key activities for phase 4 typically include but are not limited to:

- ensuring all design transfer activities have been completed per the manufacturing plan and records are on file
- confirming new product release audit is complete, confirming compliance to applicable quality standards per the project regulatory plan and record is on file
- verifying regulatory registrations and third party test certifications are received and archived per the regulatory plan
- ensuring product launch activities related to order generation, distribution, installation and service (if applicable) have been completed and records are on file
- conducting and documenting design review(s)
- conducting phase review according to the phase 4 exit readiness checklist

Phase 5—Product Maintenance

Depending on how the company manages postmarket design changes, e.g., via R&D or a manufacturing engineering function, the activities essentially would be the same and would follow requirements for implementing a design change request. For product obsolescence, a design change request may be used as a mechanism to organize and execute activities for affected functions.

Key activities for phase 5, design change implementation, typically include but are not limited to:

- design changes considered to be changes that could affect an existing product, its packaging or labeling or Device Master Record (DMR) after release to manufacturing, e.g., change to product specification, change to quality test method, change to manufacturing product, or other design-related activities
- identifying applicable design control phases in the design change request based on the scope of the design change, the impact on the device risk profile (e.g., review of the most current risk management report, complaints, adverse events, recalls, etc.), resulting requirements for design verification and/or validation implemented following the company's design control procedures, and involving cross-functional representatives according to design control procedure requirements
- incorporating the design change request in the company's change control process or a stand-alone process; assessing design changes with respect to validation or, where appropriate, verification (If validation and/or verification are required, the activity must be completed before implementation of the change.)
- including or referencing resulting documentation associated with the design change request in the applicable DMR

Key activities for phase 5, product obsolescence, when managed as a design change request, typically include but are not limited to:

- identifying applicable design control phases in the design change request based on the scope of the product obsolescence project, the impact on postmarket risk due to the product no longer being available, e.g., adequate spare parts inventory to cover the obsolescence period
- developing a marketing plan for customer communications

- developing a regulatory plan for notifying regulatory authorities where the product is registered
- developing a manufacturing plan for deactivating affected, dedicated production areas

With the development phases' context established, this section proceeds to explore CDT members' roles and their respective expectations of the regulatory CDT member.

R&D

In the majority of medical technology companies, whether small or large, the R&D function serves as the project lead; however, if the project is not specifically design-driven—e.g., adding a new indication for use to an existing product or introducing significant manufacturing process changes—the assigned project manager could come from marketing or manufacturing, respectively.

The underlying assumption in this section is the project manager will be an individual assigned from either the R&D function or a dedicated project or project management function.

The project manager and/or R&D team member rely on the regulatory member to provide advance notice of regulatory or other requirements derived from applicable guidance documents and recognized standards. Delay in providing this information can result in significant design and development rework and substantial schedule delays.

Typical project management activities include but are not limited to:
- recommending CDT member assignments to management team for approval
- managing the project management plan and coordinating development of remaining supporting plans
- ensuring generation of:
    - design and development (project or program) plan, including but not limited to:
        - identifying the design being developed
        - identifying design phases to be followed
        - identifying project team members and responsibilities
        - establishing the communications mode (meetings, minutes, etc.) between team members, including conflict resolution
        - developing project schedule listing high-level tasks and deliverables in the remaining phases including, at a minimum, task start and end dates, responsibilities and task descriptions
        - identifying expected design review topics
    - project verification and validation plan
    - risk management plan with traceability to design requirements and user needs

Note: The project manager may assign a designee to generate these plans.
- tracking all project plan deliverables, updating the plan as the project proceeds through the development cycle
- ensuring the project is executed according to the company's documented quality system

If the project manager is the CDT R&D representative, he or she also may be responsible for the following activities:
- creating a development plan—a description of the methods, tools and standards applied, including plans for activities relevant to hardware, software, mechanical/industrial design, labeling design and packaging design
- developing design requirements, specifications, detailed design and necessary production processes
- providing supporting documentation to regulatory for inclusion in the regulatory application(s)
- interfacing with component suppliers and/or external partners, if applicable
- executing and documenting verification and validation activities
- transferring the design to manufacturing

In all cases, the project manager will rely on the regulatory team member to provide necessary input to the project management plan and design requirements. Although not involved as directly in establishing product specifications, the regulatory team member should participate in a review and approval capacity for all project-related documents.

Small Company Perspective

In a small company, the project manager often fills dual roles as both the project manager and the R&D team member on the CDT. The R&D team member may elect to outsource all or some of the design- and development-related project activities to move forward as efficiently as possible. Given the multiple responsibilities, it is imperative for the regulatory team member to try to anticipate information needs so the project manager/R&D team member can proceed with R&D-related activities.

Large Company Perspective

In a large company, the project manager may come from R&D or a dedicated project or program manager function. In either situation, project management responsibilities would be the same. Depending on the project's complexity, the R&D team member may lead a dedicated design team consisting of R&D experts in areas such as electrical design, mechanical design, industrial design, software, etc., and represent this design team on the CDT. Outsourcing some design- and development-related project activities also may be a consideration for a large company, depending on the type of expertise required and available resources.

For either a small or large company, the R&D team member should qualify any external resources, e.g., consultants, in accordance with the company's supplier selection and qualification process. The R&D team member also should ensure responsibilities for design control and risk management are documented clearly in the supplier agreement. The regulatory/quality assurance team should ensure, in addition to the supplier agreement, a separate quality agreement exists when appropriate, particularly for a contract design service supplier.

Marketing

The marketing and regulatory team members need to be closely aligned regarding performance and clinical or technical claims. These claims will drive the device's intended use and indications for use and serve as pillars of the regulatory strategy and plan. The marketing team member often develops and executes the following project activities:

- provides clarification of user (user types and needs) and market requirements
- participates in review of and comment on design requirements, specifications and other design outputs, e.g., risk management activities
- supports design output user assessments
- develops and executes marketing support plan(s), including but not limited to: market opportunity; customer needs results; outcomes, costs, productivity; competitive analysis; product positioning; claims; production introduction plan and criteria; sales forecast; pricing and merchandising; field training; distribution channels; customer follow-up; demo plans; futures; technical marketing requirements; product documentation and training materials; sales and customer training; and marketing communications, e.g., advertising and promotion
- manages key opinion leader (KOL) program—identifying and managing KOLs may fall under marketing or clinical affairs' responsibility or be a shared responsibility; in either case, close interaction with regulatory and/or legal can ensure continued compliance with current conflict of interest and healthcare compliance standards

Small Company Perspective

In a small company, the marketing function either may consist of a single individual or may have not been established. If there is no marketing function, marketing-related activities may be assumed by another CDT member with some marketing knowledge. The marketing and regulatory team members need to be closely aligned regarding the performance type, clinical or technical claims. If a marketing function exists and is limited to a few members or a single individual, the marketing team member may explore outsourcing options.

Large Company Perspective

Much like the R&D representative in a large company, the marketing representative may lead a dedicated marketing team, consisting of individuals from product management, product marketing, technical marketing, marketing communications, etc., and serve as the dedicated marketing team representative to the CDT. Outsourcing marketing-related activities still may be a consideration, depending on the type of expertise required and available resources.

For a small or large company, the marketing team member should qualify any external resources in accordance with the company's supplier selection and qualification process. The marketing team member also should ensure responsibilities for the outsourced activities are documented clearly in the supplier agreement.

Manufacturing

The manufacturing team member will look to the regulatory team member to understand any regulations, guidance documents and/or applicable recognized standards requirements that could affect manufacturing-related project activities.

The manufacturing team member often develops and executes the following project activities:

- strategy for process engineering and assembly and manufacturing test and product release criteria
- process failure modes and effects analysis (FMEA) and process validation
- identified manufacturing risks and contingencies; facility planning; major capital equipment

needs and production test equipment requirements; production materials selection
- Device Master Record (DMR) structure
- production scheduling, including production prototypes, capacity analysis, logistics planning and production personnel training

Small Company Perspective

It is not unusual for a small company to outsource manufacturing completely to an original equipment manufacturer (OEM). In this case, the assigned OEM project representative may serve as the CDT manufacturing team member. Alternatively, the R&D team member also may serve as the manufacturing team member liaising with the OEM project representative, relying on the OEM project representative to plan and execute the manufacturing-related project activities.

Large Company Perspective

In a large company, manufacturing-related project activities may be distributed over a number of different functions, depending on the company's organization and the project's complexity. As with R&D and marketing, the manufacturing team representative may lead a dedicated manufacturing team and serve as the CDT representative. Depending on the product's nature, a large company also may opt to outsource some manufacturing-related project activities, e.g., shipping container design, etc.

For a small or large company, the manufacturing team member should be the contact for an OEM or supplier of a subset of manufacturing-related project activities in accordance with the company's supplier selection and qualification process.

Given the criticality of relying wholly on an OEM for manufacturing, it is paramount the manufacturing and quality team members collaborate on OEM selection and qualification. A detailed and comprehensive quality agreement specifying responsibilities for the outsourced activities should be included in the supplier agreement.

Clinical Affairs

Although clinical data may not be required for all target countries, the EU and countries using the conformity assessment process will require a clinical evaluation. This often is the case for Class II and, certainly, Class III devices in the US as well. The clinical team member works closely with the regulatory team member to ensure clinical development plans support regulatory objectives.

The clinical team member often develops and executes the following project activities:

- activities relevant to the clinical study design, i.e., investigational plan, site selection, set-up and management
- clinical study planning to support regulatory submissions, third-party payer objectives, feasibility testing and/or actual use testing, e.g., human factors testing, clinical data acquisition and analysis, proposed clinical sites and clinical study objectives
- KOL program; identifying and managing KOLs may fall under marketing or clinical affairs' responsibility or be a shared responsibility

Small Company Perspective

In a small company, the project manager may look to an external KOL to serve as the clinical team representative, but KOL accessibility and availability and potential conflicts of interest often may prohibit this level of involvement.

As an alternative, a regulatory team member with expertise in clinical study development and execution may serve double duty by representing clinical affairs' interests, relying heavily on a consortium of KOLs and a Clinical Research Organization (CRO) to establish a clinical development plan, execute any required clinical studies, conduct clinical data analysis and develop the final clinical study report.

Large Company Perspective

In a large company with an established clinical affairs function, the clinical team member may lead a dedicated clinical team and serve as representative to the CDT. Large companies often differentiate between clinical-related project activities representing unique activities, e.g., site selection, qualification and initiation, clinical study design, etc., versus routine activities, e.g., monitoring activities, study start-up and close-out activities.

As with all outsourcing activities, the clinical team member should qualify any CRO in accordance with the company's supplier selection and qualification process and also ensure the CRO agreement clearly documents responsibilities for the outsourced activities.

Quality Assurance/Quality Engineering

The quality and regulatory team members often work in tandem since both are focused on ensuring project-related activities conform to design control and risk management requirements as well as recognized process- or product-specific standards.

The project manager often looks to the quality team member to coordinate and lead risk management activities and coordinate master design verification and validation plan development. The quality team member also may be tasked with coordinating, scheduling and executing third-party testing, e.g., biocompatibility, transportation testing, etc., as required by the master design verification and validation plan.

Both the quality and regulatory team members may provide independent oversight for the CDT, as checks and balances; however, this responsibility often is assigned solely to the quality team member. The quality team member also works closely with other CDT members to qualify new suppliers and usually takes the lead when formal supplier qualification is required pursuant to the company's QMS requirements.

The quality team member often develops and executes the following project activities:
- planning quality assurance or quality engineering elements underlying product development and product support, postmarket launch
- project management in accordance with quality system requirements
- serving as an independent participant in design reviews; reviewing and approving design verification and validation protocols and plans and reports of test results
- lead preapproval inspection (PAI) preparation activities and host regulatory authorities during PAIs, if applicable

Small Company Perspective

In an early stage start-up or small company, the quality function's importance may be underestimated. Typically, early stage start-up companies are focused on activities perceived to hold the greatest business risk—e.g., intellectual property portfolio strength, addressable market size, proof of technology feasibility and the regulatory pathway—and tend to overlook the need to establish at least some of the critical quality system elements to support formal product development, such as design controls, risk management and document controls. In the rush to first-in-human studies, early stage start-ups may encounter unnecessary delays by not having established these early quality system building blocks and/or not being appropriately attentive to such requirements.

For small companies, it is not unusual for the quality function to be understaffed, resulting in the valuable check and balance oversight being stretched too thin to be effective.

An early stage start-up may elect to engage a qualified consultant to cover the quality function by planning and implementing quality system elements. Another alternative would be to have the regulatory team member, assuming sufficient understanding of quality system requirements, serve double duty by representing quality interests but rely primarily on a qualified consultant to carry out quality-related project activities.

Another issue often encountered by early stage start-up or small companies is the presumption that conformance to *ISO 13485:2012 Medical Devices—Quality management systems—Requirements for regulatory purposes* is the same as compliance with FDA's Quality System Regulation, Title 21 CFR Part 820 (QSR). It is important to note while FDA's QSR is similar to ISO 13485 in some respects, there are significant differences in emphasis. FDA's QSR is intended to ensure manufacturers can provide safe and effective medical devices consistently, whereas ISO 13485 emphasizes consistently meeting customer requirements (including regulatory requirements). As a result, FDA's QSR requirements are more prescriptive for management controls, design controls and risk management, and corrective and preventive action. The quality function plays a crucial role in educating CDT members regarding the level of detail required specifically for design control and risk management activities.

Large Company Perspective

Although a large company will have a dedicated quality function, management commitment can dilute the effectiveness of the check and balance oversight role. Under cost-cutting pressures, the quality function may not be as protected from downsizing measures such as R&D or some other functions.

Quality-related project activities may be distributed in a large company, depending on the area of focus, e.g., software quality assurance, quality engineering, etc. As in other functions, the quality team member may lead a dedicated quality team and serve as representative to the CDT.

The quality team member may decide to outsource some quality-related project activities to conserve internal resources, e.g., supplier audits for qualification of new suppliers.

In outsourcing any quality-related project activities, the quality team member should qualify the external resource in accordance with the company's supplier selection and qualification process and also ensure the supplier agreement clearly documents responsibilities. Suppliers' performance also should be assessed periodically, e.g., in the regularly scheduled QMS management review.

Ad Hoc Participants in CDTs

Depending on a project's scope and complexity, the project manager may designate *ad hoc* participants to join the team at various points. For example, business development, supply chain, finance, legal or public relations may not be part of the team throughout the product lifecycle but represent important functions and stakeholders in product development. The project manager, in discussion with CDT members and corresponding functional managers, should determine when an *ad hoc* participant should be included in team meetings and the extent of the *ad hoc* participant's involvement in project team activities, particularly for design reviews.

Business Development

If the project's basis is external, the company's business development function may be involved until a project is defined, formalized and a CDT lead and cross-functional team have been assigned. Business development works with potential partners with the aim of purchasing a company, licensing technology or other business transaction. Business development processes often require due diligence by members of R&D, quality, regulatory or other functions. Knowledge acquired during this exploratory period can be transferred readily to the CDT and other appropriate internal departments. Once business development secures the transaction, marketing often assumes CDT responsibilities for business and marketing considerations.

Supply Chain

Supply chain management's primary responsibility is to capture product demands in all target markets and feed this information back to manufacturing. Some medical devices have very complicated supply chains, and the role of the supply chain CDT member may be to improve product supply and pricing efficiencies. The regulatory CDT member must maintain excellent communication and collaboration with the supply chain to support production planning and optimize business opportunities. Product registrations often are approved at different time points and may result in the ability to ship product to some markets but not others, awaiting product registration approval.

Communication

Psychologist Bruce Tuckman first came up with the memorable phrase "forming, storming, norming, and performing" in his 1965 article, "Development Sequence in Small Groups."[2] Tuckman used this phrase to describe the path most teams follow on their way to high performance.

Later, a fifth stage was added, "adjourning" (sometimes known as "mourning").

- Forming—In this stage, most CDT members are positive and polite. Some are anxious, as they do not understand fully what work the team will do. Others simply are excited about the task ahead.

  The CDT project or program lead plays a dominant role at this stage, because team members' roles and responsibilities are not clear.

  This stage can last for some time, as CDT members start to work together and make an effort to get to know their new colleagues.

- Storming—Next, the CDT moves into the storming phase, where team members start to push the boundaries established in the forming stage or challenge inputs provided by other CDT members. Mastering this phase, or not, lays the foundation for success or failure.

  Storming often starts where there is a conflict between CDT members' work philosophies or management or communication styles. Although there may be a solid basis for a particular approach to a problem, these differences can give rise to unforeseen problems, frustrating and discouraging other team members.

  Another aspect of storming is challenges to the CDT project or program lead or "positioning" for greater influence. Clear definitions of how CDT members will work together and communication channels can ease individual team member anxiety.

  Some CDT members may not be invested fully in the project goals and objectives and resist cooperating with others in the team or in completing assigned tasks.

- Norming—At gradual and, sometimes, differing paces, CDT members move into the norming stage. CDT members find approaches to resolve differences, gain appreciation for other team members' contributions and support and respect the CDT project or program lead's role. At this point, CDT members will provide constructive criticism more readily and develop the commitment level necessary to execute the project successfully.

- Performing—The team reaches the performing stage when difficult issues can be resolved relatively easily to achieve a positive outcome and allow the project to move forward efficiently and expeditiously.

  The CDT project or program lead may

Table 2-2. Regulatory Pathway Assessment Elements

Inputs	Contributor	Outputs
Technology overview	R&D	Discussion from the regulatory authorities' perspective by target country: • intended use/indications for use • technological characteristics • expected product classifications • potential commercially available devices, i.e., comparable devices likely to confirm classification • expected device classification and associated regulatory application type • potential regulatory authority concerns, e.g., indications for use/intended use or technological characteristics
Intended use and indications for use	R&D/marketing/clinical affairs	
Description of standard of care, commercially comparable technologies and/or products	Marketing/clinical affairs	
Peer-reviewed publications concerning technology, intended use, indications, disease or condition to be diagnosed, treated or monitored	R&D/marketing/clinical affairs	
Review of common nonconformances and complaints (if own product); reportable adverse events, recalls, etc.	Regulatory/quality	Discussion from the regulatory authorities' perspective by target country
Proposed design specification for any research prototypes, if available	R&D	
Initial risk analysis, if available	R&D/quality	
Initial target countries	Marketing	

share more responsibilities with team members, delegating certain tasks and, overall, the CDT works smoothly.

- Adjourning—At the end of a project, typically at a transition from product development to product support, many companies disband the CDT, transitioning product support activities to manufacturing. This stage can present difficulties if CDT members lose focus before the transition is complete. Attention to detail is required of all CDT members until the project is completed.

Communication Within the CDT

One key characteristic of a strong design control program is embedded communication requirements. Communication vehicles such as regularly scheduled CDT meetings, one-on-one meetings and written or electronic communications keep team members updated on project-related topics, including celebrations of successful team accomplishments. Team members working well together should not be considered a given team value; it requires careful nurturing, cultivation and sincerity.

Communication With Management and With the Company Organization

Another challenge is communicating with company management—a "no surprises" approach for critical project decisions bodes well for a CDT in winning and keeping management support. Company management anticipates risks and mitigates them before the crisis occurs. Succinct and timely CDT communication to company management cannot be overemphasized.

Communicating with the larger organization is important in companies of all sizes. Providing regular comprehensive updates can minimize distraction when a project encounters a setback, as it inevitably will. Updates to the broader organization also can achieve general "buy-in" to what the CDT is trying to achieve.

Communication With International Partners

In aiming for global development, CDTs work with international partners in market research, incorporating quality and regulatory requirements in project plans, coordinating submissions, planning supply and conducting postmarket surveillance. In that work stream, CDTs need to navigate cultural differences and communication styles. The differences could come from punctuality expectations or word choices in an email, particularly from those whose primary languages differ.

Many textbooks and seminars are available on communicating in multi-cultural settings. In global product development, where all stakeholders share ultimate goals of speed to market with quality products, setting ground rules and expectations can be a more immediate and effective solution. One of the most common frustrations for international partners is not getting registration information or prompt responses from a CDT.

Since CDTs need to work through priorities, they may not be able to give immediate attention to international registration requests. Creating simple ground rules at the project start, such as the CDT acknowledging receipt of a request within 48 hours, with an estimated completion time, and communicating it to the affiliate or distributor regulatory representative, would reduce email traffic. It also helps affiliates and distributors plan their launch timing. Larger companies may benefit from creating IT solutions to capture requests and disseminate registration dossiers. The feasibility of developing such systems should be determined based on the balance of improving efficiency and investment.

Understand the Key Regulatory Interactions With CDT Members

CDT effectiveness and a team's ultimate success in launching a new product on schedule can be achieved only when CDT members understand and respect one another's value-added contributions. Regardless of the development project's scope, from a project involving a significant design change to a marketed medical device to a project involving new, innovative technology, cross-functional dependencies demand each function has a voice in project discussions and actively participates in project decisions.

This section discusses key regulatory interactions with fellow CDT members, specifically focusing on typical inputs and outputs CDT members may require from regulatory. Conversely, the typical inputs and outputs the regulatory team member would require from other CDT members also are described. These inputs and outputs are the essence of moving the project seamlessly through product development and on to a timely market launch. In each case, both the small and large company perspectives are offered.

Regulatory

The regulatory representative's role on the CDT most often includes the following responsibilities:
- developing and executing the regulatory strategy and plan, including preclinical and clinical testing requirements (Note: also may include market adoption clinical studies, as directed by marketing, or clinical studies to support reimbursement for third-party payers)
- managing formal and informal communications with regulatory authorities
- assuring and confirming continued regulatory compliance throughout the process

To be an effective CDT member, it is imperative the regulatory team member be equipped with substantive understanding of regulatory requirements for the countries where the product will be marketed as well as design control and risk management requirements,[3,4] and the company's design control process and risk management program.

It is not unusual for the regulatory member to have developed a high-level regulatory pathway assessment prior to formal transition to product development. If this is not the case, the regulatory pathway element assessment can be incorporated readily into the regulatory strategy and plan.

Typical inputs for a regulatory pathway assessment and the resulting output are illustrated in **Table 2-2**.

If a regulatory pathway assessment has not been documented prior to formal transition to product development, as a first outreach action to other team members, the regulatory member should communicate the input requirements to CDT members so a regulatory pathway can be established for each target country.

As with all design and development planning documents, e.g., project plan and supporting plans, the regulatory strategy and plan evolves over the course of the development project. During phase 1—requirements, the regulatory team member should expect a number of particulars concerning the project and the device to be developed to be unknown or in initial form and necessarily will become more specific.

Assuming the regulatory team member has acquired the information to determine the regulatory pathway by target country, the next step during phase 1—requirements would be to establish the initial draft of the regulatory strategy and plan. Typical inputs for a regulatory strategy and plan and their resulting output are illustrated in **Table 2-3**.

Upon completion, the regulatory team member should submit the initial regulatory strategy and plan for formal change control according to the company's change control system, with the requisite review and approval.

Small Company Perspective

For a small company, developing and executing a complex regulatory strategy and plan can be a daunting proposition.

Key considerations should focus on the project's complexity, the regulatory function's skill and experience and resources needed to accomplish regulatory-related project tasks effectively and efficiently. In some cases, a

Table 2-3. Regulatory Strategy and Plan Elements

Inputs	Contributor	Outputs
Regulatory pathway assessment	Regulatory team member	Note: if the regulatory pathway assessment was not established prior to formal transition to product development, the regulatory team member should request the inputs described in **Table 2-2**.
- Project plan - Detailed design plan - Initial design requirements document - Initial risk analysis - Marketing plan	Regulatory team member	Purpose: communicate regulatory strategy and plan to CDT members; describe regulatory elements underlying product development strategy from concept to product obsolescence: - identifies and describes the regulatory requirements for all elements - Includes responsibilities for specific regulatory tasks and deliverables, and the associated milestones - Regulatory strategy and plan to be updated, reviewed and approved at the end of each development phase to ensure any changes in regulatory requirements are captured and communicated to the CDT
- Project plan - Detailed design plan - Initial design requirements document - Initial risk analysis - Marketing plan - Manufacturing plan	R&D, marketing, manufacturing, clinical affairs, quality	Scope of Project: device; configurations of device, if applicable; target countries, in order of expected product launch; communicate scope of regulatory strategy and plan to CDT members: - applicable pre- and postmarket product and process regulations, recognized standards and regulatory guidance documents - target countries intended for product launch in priority order - device that is the subject of the development project, to include all possible configurations, accessories, instructions for use, on-product labels, packaging labels and packaging - considerations for outsourcing key business activities, e.g., manufacturing, third-party testing, distribution, etc. - company's regulatory status with respect to device, e.g., manufacturer and specification developer for FDA, legal representative for other countries of interest
- Initial design requirements document - Initial risk analysis - Marketing plan	R&D, marketing and/or clinical affairs	Intended use and indications for use Note 1: the intended use and indications for use are central to determining the device classification under most regulatory schemes, e.g., risk-based classification for the US, rule-based classification with embedded risk considerations for the EU, Australia, Canada and many other countries. Therefore, it is imperative to maintain and control a single source of "truth" concerning the intended use and indications for use statements. The regulatory strategy and plan serves as the most appropriate controlled vehicle to accomplish this. An alternative approach to including the intended use and indications for use statement in the regulatory strategy and plan would be to maintain the intended use and indications for use as a separate controlled document, which requires formal change control when modifications are required.
		Note 2: intended use is specific to the US 510(k) premarket notification program, whereas indications for use are specific to the US Premarket Approval (PMA) program. The rule-based, embedded risk classification system used by the EU, Australia, Canada and many other countries considers different criteria such as the "duration of contact with the patient, the degree of invasiveness and the part of the body affected by the use of the device. Intended purpose is defined in Article 1 paragraph 2(g) of Directive 93/42/EEC.[a] - Conformity assessment is the method by which a manufacturer demonstrates its devices comply with Directive 93/42/EEC's requirements. The medical device's classification will impact the conformity assessment route the manufacturer should follow to affix a CE Mark on the medical device. - Regardless of device class, all medical devices must meet the Essential Requirements, including those regarding information to be supplied by the manufacturer (Annex I of the Directive 93/42/EEC) and are subject to the medical device vigilance system's reporting requirements. Elements of the intended use/indications for use statement: - Intended Use: general purpose of the device or its function; encompasses the indications for use,[b] expressed as an over-arching statement describing: manufacturing, labeling, technical or performance specifications and materials that determine the device's diagnostic, therapeutic, monitoring or measuring function. - Indications for Use: refers to a description of the "disease or condition the device will diagnose, treat, prevent, cure, or mitigate, including a description of the patient for which the device is intended."[c]

Inputs	Contributor	Outputs
- Project plan and supporting plan[d] - Design requirements - Product specification - Risk management - Master design verification and validation plan	All CDT members	Definitions, acronyms, company-specific terminology: consistency and clarity are of the utmost importance in design control and risk management documentation as well as in any design and development planning documents that may be distributed to external parties, e.g., regulatory authorities, third-party test laboratories and suppliers and sub-contractors. As with the intended use/indications for use statement, it is advisable to develop a cross-functional list of definitions, acronyms and company-specific terminology as a single source of "truth" that can be referenced by CDT members in developing their assigned project documents. The regulatory strategy and plan can serve as the controlled vehicle for this purpose since the definitions, acronyms and company-specific terminology generally are included in regulatory applications. It is important to note that regulatory authorities are prone to interpret different terms for the same item or paraphrased definitions as distinctly different from each other, resulting in unnecessary requests for clarification or additional information.

- Project plan and supporting plans
- Design requirements
- Product specification
- Risk management
- Master design verification and validation plan
	All CDT members	Applicable regulations, directives, guidance documents and recognized standards: for each target country anticipated for product launch, the regulatory team member, assisted by other CDT members, identifies the applicable regulations for all project aspects; this may include but not be limited to product and process.
		- Regulations: codification of legislation that has been signed into law, e.g., Title 21 CFR Part 814 Premarket Approval.
		- Directive: framework for a common regulation for legal market access to the EU, including uniform rules for all Member States; EU legislative act that requires Member States to achieve a particular result without dictating the means of achieving that result. It can be distinguished from EU regulations, which are self-executing and do not require any implementing measures, i.e., transposition into Member States' national laws, e.g., *Medical Devices Directive 93/42/EEC*. Member States may add requirements upon transposition. Unlike the US, it also is important to note the EU,[e] Canada, Australia and many other countries differentiate between:
		- Medical devices: any instrument, apparatus, appliance, software, material or other article, whether used alone or in combination, including the software intended by its manufacturer to be used specifically for diagnostic and/or therapeutic purposes and necessary for its proper application, intended by the manufacturer to be used for human beings for the purpose of:
		   o Diagnosis, prevention, monitoring, treatment or alleviation of disease
		   o Diagnosis, monitoring, treatment, alleviation of or compensation for an injury or handicap
		   o Investigation, replacement or modification of the anatomy or of a physiological process, control of conception
		- In vitro diagnostics (*IVD Directive*): medical device that is a reagent, reagent product, calibrator, kit, instrument or system, intended by the manufacturer to be used in vitro for the examination of specimens derived from the human body principally for the purposes of providing information about the state of physiological conditions, health, disease, congenital abnormalities or compatibility and therapy monitoring
		- Active implantable devices (Active Implantable Devices Directive): intended to be totally or partially introduced, surgically or medically, into the human body or by medical intervention into a natural orifice, and intended to remain after the procedure
		- Active medical devices: any medical device operation that depends on a source of electrical energy or any source of power other than that directly generated by the human body or gravity and that acts by converting this energy. Medical devices intended to transmit energy, substances or other elements between an active medical device and the patient without any significant change, are not considered to be active medical devices. Standalone software is considered to be an active medical device.

Review of publicly available information from regulatory authority websites and international and national standards development organizations	Regulatory	Impending changes to regulations, guidance documents or recognized standards in target countries: provide overview of impending changes that could affect the project with respect to preclinical, nonclinical and clinical testing for the respective regulatory applications.
Project plan and supporting plans	All CDT members	Responsibilities: define regulatory activities to be performed internally or to be outsourced, if applicable

Inputs	Contributor	Outputs
- Project plan (product launch timelines) and marketing plan (target countries of interest) - Review of publicly available information from regulatory authority websites - Regulatory intelligence from in-country regulatory experts	All CDT members	Regulatory strategy by country of interest: for each country, the regulatory team member may elect to develop: - A single country-by-country strategy or plan for required registrations to minimize the number of control documents - Individual country strategy or plan for required registrations in the most critical countries (tier 1 countries) and a separate country strategy or plan for less critical countries (tier 2 countries), to allow the detail granularity level to ensure successful execution of the regulatory strategy or - Individual country strategy or plans for required registrations in each country of interest - Due to time and resource constraints and the press of achieving time to market objectives, the regulatory team member will be challenged to find a balance between the appropriate level of planning and plan granularity and time/resource efficiency. Regardless of the selected approach, the regulatory team member will need to identify the regulatory requirements and deliverables, including owners and timelines for each country.
- Regulatory authority requirements, e.g., device specific or technical guidance documents - Project plan and supporting plans - Design requirements - Product specification - Risk management - Master design verification and validation plan	All CDT members	Preclinical testing: identification of required preclinical testing; sterilization/shelf-life, biocompatibility, software, electromagnetic compatibility and electrical safety, device-specific bench testing, packaging testing, etc.; preferred test methodologies, test set-up and sample size, if known
- Regulatory authority requirements, e.g., device-specific or technical guidance documents - Project plan and supporting plans - Design requirements - Product specification - Risk management - Master design verification and validation plan	All CDT members	Nonclinical testing (animal): identification of required animal testing, preferred animal model, test methodology, preferred sample size, etc.
- Regulatory authority requirements, e.g., device-specific or technical guidance documents - Project plan and supporting plans - Design requirements - Product specification - Risk management - Master design verification and validation plan	All CDT members	Clinical testing (design validation; human factors,[f] regulatory application): identification of specific types of clinical studies, e.g., early feasibility, pilot and pivotal studies; preferred study designs, expected inclusion and exclusion criteria, sample sizes if known, acceptable primary and secondary endpoints Note: the clinical plan should provide detailed information concerning how the study will be designed to meet the requirements set out in this regulatory strategy and plan. In other words, the regulatory strategy and plan describes the studies that will be required, whereas the clinical plan describes how the studies will be designed and executed.
- Design requirements - Product specification - Risk management - Master design verification and validation plan	R&D, egulatory, quality	Traceability: The regulatory team member should identify formal traceability (design inputs to design outputs, design outputs to user needs and intended use and indications for use) requirements. Note: a traceability matrix may be accomplished using a validated software tool or manually via a spreadsheet and is typically a task assigned to R&D or quality.
- Regulatory authority requirements, e.g., device-specific or technical guidance documents - project plan and supporting plans	R&D, manufacturing, regulatory, quality	Preapproval Inspections (PAIs): The regulatory team member should identify whether any PAIs will be required, including the PAI's expected timing and scope

Inputs	Contributor	Outputs
- Regulatory authority requirements, e.g., device-specific or technical guidance documents - Project plan and supporting plans	All CDT members	Regulatory authority communication (informal and formal): the regulatory team member should describe the type and frequency of communications with regulatory authorities. These will be dictated by the technology's novelty or complexity. Mature technology for moderate-risk devices may not warrant any regulatory authority communication prior to registration, whereas novel and/or complex technology generally warrants early and frequent communication with a regulatory authority. The expected purpose and content of the communication, the desired outcome and timing should be included.
Project plan and supporting plans	All CDT members	Regulatory strategy and plan milestones: the regulatory team member should extract the relevant milestone dates from the project plan and align the high-level regulatory plan milestones to support efficient execution of project-dependent activities. Country-specific regulatory strategy and plan should include more-detailed milestones that align with the overarching regulatory strategy and plan milestones.
- Regulatory authority requirements, e.g., device-specific or technical guidance documents - Marketing plan - Master design verification and validation plan	Marketing, regulatory	Localization requirements: the regulatory team member should include any requirements for local languages in the country-specific regulatory strategy and plan. In some cases in the US, local language may be optional, but for customer satisfaction purposes, the marketing plan may stipulate the need for local language. Localization verification and validation should be included in the master verification and validation plan to confirm (1) the labeling has been correctly translated into the target foreign language (verification), and (2) a user who is fluent in the target language can operate the device according to the translated labeling (validation)
- Regulatory authority requirements, e.g., device-specific or technical guidance documents - Project plan and supporting plans - Design requirements - Product specification - Risk management - Master design verification and validation plan	All CDT members	Labeling requirements: the regulatory team member should identify general and special labeling requirements for investigational and commercial purposes. The regulatory team member should include all labeling, i.e., on-product labels, packaging labels, instructions for use and training materials, and installation and service documentation if applicable. For software as a medical device, software user interfaces, the text available for user viewing also is considered "labeling." - Investigational use: if clinical studies are to be conducted or devices are to be shipped to third parties for preclinical or nonclinical testing, the regulatory team member should provide specific wording of statements as called out in the applicable regulations or guidance documents for the destination country, as well as any labeling requirements for manufacturer name, address, etc. - Commercial use: as with investigational device labeling, the regulatory team member should provide specific wording of statements as called out in the applicable regulations or guidance documents. Please note regulatory submissions should serve as the source of "truth" for commercial device labeling. Text derived from regulatory submissions should be subject to review and approval by the regulatory team member prior to external use to ensure technical and clinical claims are consistent with the regulatory registration for the target country. Note: since labeling is part of the device, it should be subject to change control with appropriate levels of review and approval.
- Regulatory authority requirements, e.g., device-specific or technical guidance documents - Project plan and supporting plans - Design requirements - Product specification - Risk management - Master design verification and validation plan	All CDT members	Country-specific issues: the regulatory team member may address country-specific regulatory issues in the high-level regulatory strategy and plan or in a country-specific regulatory strategy and plan. For example, although Italy, as an EU Member State accepts CE marking, there are national requirements to import product into Italy for investigational or commercial purposes. Turkey, although not an EU Member State, recognizes CE marking but has a number of national requirements that must be fulfilled to import investigational or commercial devices into the country.

Inputs	Contributor	Outputs
- Regulatory authority requirements, e.g., device-specific or technical guidance documents - Project plan and supporting plans - Design requirements - Product specification - Risk management - Master design verification and validation plan	All CDT members	Unique device identifier requirements: at present, unique device identifier requirements have been rolled out only in the US, with compliance dates phasing in over the next several years. Requirements for UDI label, GUDID, date format for Class III devices became effective as of 24 September 2014. Requirements for direct marking (permanent) UDI on product will go into effect for Class III—life-saving or life-sustaining as of 24 September 2015, etc.[g] - Device label or package of medical devices distributed in the US must include a UDI that is readable in plain text and by automatic identification and data capture (AIDC) technology - All required product information must be submitted to FDA's GUDID (Global Unique Device Identification Database) Note: IMDRF issued a guidance document, *Unique Device Identification (UDI) of Medical Devices*, 9 December 2013, which likely will be adopted by most IMDRF members, with the exception of the EU. The new EMDR will require a UDI program, but some EU Member States are reluctant to adopt the IMDRF proposal. Other countries likely are to develop national UDI programs, e.g., China and Russia.

a. Medical Devices: Guidance document (MEDDEV 2. 4/1 Rev. 9, June 2010), *Classification of Medical Devices*
b. FDA, *The 510(k) Program: Evaluating Substantial Equivalence in Premarket Notifications [510(k)], Guidance for Industry and Food and Drug Administration Staff* (28 July 2014).
c. PMA Regulation, 21 CFR 814.20(3)(i).
d. Supporting plans include but are not limited to: detailed design, marketing, manufacturing, regulatory, clinical and quality
e. The EU *MDD* is being revised and will be converted from a directive to a new European Medical Device Regulations (EMDR); publication of the proposed regulations as final has been delayed and is not expected to be published as final until late 2015 or early 2016. The EMDR will phase in over time beginning with the highest-risk Class III devices, and lower-risk devices would be phased in over a three year period.
f. AAMI/ANSI HE75:2009, human factors engineering—design of medical devices
g. FDA. *Unique Device Identification System: Small Entity Compliance Guide: Guidance for Industry and Food and Drug Administration Staff* (13 August 2014).

small company may not have established a regulatory function yet. In either case, the project manager and/or regulatory team member should assess project complexity and time-to-market requirements carefully as a guide to determining the optimal resourcing approach. Options include but are not limited to outsourcing the regulatory function to a qualified consultant, subcontractor or consulting organization, or partially outsourcing regulatory-related project activities. When considering regulatory outsourcing options, it also is important to consider the benefits and risks of selecting a consultant or a consulting organization. If outsourcing this function, companies must be cognizant of the fact they ultimately are responsible for the decisions made, and be certain they consider consultant recommendations fully.

For a cash-flow sensitive small company, a consultant often is an attractive option from a cost perspective, but may not be as efficient when deep expertise is needed or many target countries are involved. If this is the case, a consulting organization with an expert staff and offices located in target countries may appear to be more expensive but, in fact, could be less expensive overall due to time efficiencies. In all cases, the regulatory team member should qualify external resource in accordance with the company's supplier selection and qualification process.

Large Company Perspective

For the regulatory team member in a large company, rather than exploring extensive regulatory outsourcing options, required resources may be identified internally. In some cases, outsourcing regulatory-related project activities may be a better option, depending on the required skill set or expertise and the extent of internal resources. The regulatory team member also should consider the value of engaging an appropriate external regulatory consultant who can serve as an independent sounding board for complex regulatory issues or, if necessary, assist in preparing for key meetings with regulatory authorities, e.g., a PMA Advisory Panel meeting.

For a small or large company, the regulatory team member should qualify any external resources in accordance with the company's supplier selection and qualification process, and ensure the consulting agreement clearly identifies responsibilities.

CDT Member Involvement and Interaction Ebb and Flow Throughout the Product Lifecycle

On a truly cross-functional team, each CDT member's involvement level will vary over the product development lifecycle's course. For the regulatory team member, it is

Table 2-4. Ebb and Flow of Core Team Member Involvement

Core Team Function	Phase 1 Requirements	Phase 2 Design	Phase 3 Verification and Validation	Phase 4 Commercialization	Phase 5 Postmarket
Project Manager	Project management plan	Update		Close-out to DHF	Application of design controls and risk management to be commensurate with scope of design change to product (device, packaging or labeling) or process (affecting product quality)
R&D	Design requirements	Update		Transfer to DMR	
	Design strategy and plan	Update		Close-out to DHF	
	Execute design strategy and plan, e.g., nonclinical testing	Physical design activities	Nonclinical design verification and validation activities	Close-out to DHF	
	Start product specification	Finalize product specification, e.g., mechanical drawings, software code, component selection, labeling, packaging, etc.	Update	Update and transfer to DMR	
	Start verification and validation plan	Finalize verification and validation plan	Update	Close-out to DHF	
	Execute verification and validation plan	Execute design verification activities as design activities progress, e.g., inspection, measurement, analysis, test	Execute final design verification activities on "frozen design" (production-equivalent)	Close-out to DHF	
			Execute simulated use design validation acitvities		
Marketing	Marketing strategy and plan	Update		Close-out to DHF	
Marketing, cont.	Execute marketing strategy and plan, e.g., user needs assessments, focus group assessments of design concepts	Continue to update user needs via focus group assessments and key opinion leaders of critical design concepts		Execute market launch activities	Application of design controls and risk management to be commensurate with scope of design change to product (device, packaging or labeling) or process (affecting product quality)
	Develop and execute key opinion leader strategy and plan	Update		Close-out to DHF	
Regulatory	Regulatory strategy and plan	Update		Close-out to DHF	
	Clinical study submissions	If actual use design validation or clinical data for product registrations is required, prepare required documentation	Provide regulatory documentation to support clinical trial applications, e.g., IDE for US	Close-out to DHF	
	Product registration	Conduct meetings with regulatory authorities per regulatory strategy and plan	Prepare product registrations per regulatory strategy and plan	Close-out to DHF	

Core Team Function	Phase 1 Requirements	Phase 2 Design	Phase 3 Verification and Validation	Phase 4 Commercialization	Phase 5 Postmarket
Clinical	Clinical study strategy and plan	Update		Close-out to DHF	
	Execute clinical study strategy and plan	Select and qualify clinical study sites; prepare clinical trial applications (CTAs)	Submit required documentation to ethics committees (EC)/institutional review board (IRB)	Close-out to DHF	
	Conduct studies to support product registrations/actual use design validation		Conduct clinical studies, monitor sites and records; adverse event reporting; close-out clinical sites, final data analysis	Close-out to DHF	
Quality	Quality strategy and plan	Update		Close-out to DHF	Application of design controls and risk management to be commensurate with scope of design change to product (device, packaging or labeling) or process (affecting product quality)
	Execute quality strategy and plan	Provide quality oversight for design activities	Continue to provide quality oversight for design activities	Transfer to DMR / close-out to DHF	
			Review/approve design verification and validation protocols and reports of results	Conduct new product audit prior to phase 4 checkpoint review (device release for customer shipments)	
			Conduct readiness audit prior to shipment of investigational devices for third-party testing or clinical use	Close-out to DHF	
			Prepare for pre-approval inspection (PAI) if applicable	Close-out to DHF	
Manufacturing	Participate in project planning	Start manufacturing plan	Finalize manufacturing plan	Close-out to DHF	
		Execute manufacturing plan		Transfer to DMR	
Core team members	Risk management plan	Update		Transfer to RMF	
	Execute risk management plan activities	Update		Transfer to RMF	

very important to serve as a sentinel, alerting the CDT to impending regulation changes and their potential impact on project activities. The regulatory team member also should communicate related changes that may affect registration times in countries or regions, such as changes in regulatory staff for international affiliates or distributors and/or a change in distributors. The marketing CDT member also serves a sentinel function in communicating evolving market and user needs.

At a project's outset, all functions should be involved equally in planning project activities and, in subsequent phases, depending on the project's scope, each team member's respective activities will ebb and flow in interactions and shifts in emphasis. **Table 2-4** illustrates CDT members' "busy" versus "less busy" periods. Each CDT member must advocate and be in a position to navigate the company's organization while building consensus and support. The most notable CDT members can be described best as "doers," individuals who know how to work within the company's organization, can communicate effectively back to their respective functions and to management and remain engaged even during quiet periods.

The CDT member involvement ebb and flow throughout product development phases will not be appreciably different for a small organization versus a larger organization. Significant differences are very likely in how resources may be allocated and/or applied. In a small company, a single CDT member may represent multiple functions or an external consultant may be engaged to participate as a CDT member. In a large company, as stated previously, it is possible a CDT member is assigned to a project with a functional support team.

Conclusion

This chapter presents CDT fundamentals and the environment or context in which they operate. A robust design control program and inclusive company culture valuing and respecting diversity can foster optimal performance even when a CDT is up against seemingly insurmountable challenges. Human nature prevails in the CDT, and the project or program lead must concentrate in the early stages on team member bonding. Each CDT member plays a vital role at some part of the product development cycle, appreciating the ebb and flow of a CDT member's involvement, interactions and interdependencies.

References

1. *Medical Device Directive (MDD)* Annex I: Essential Requirement means "the devices must be designed and manufactured in such a way that, when used under the conditions and for the purposes intended, they will not compromise the clinical condition or the safety of patients, or the safety and health of users or, where applicable, other persons, provided that any risks which may be associated with their intended use constitute acceptable risks when weighed against the benefits to the patient and are compatible with a high level of protection of health and safety."
2. Tuckman BW. "Developmental sequence in small groups." *Psychological Bulletin*, Vol 63(6), Jun 1965, 384-399.
3. FDA's "Design Control Guidance for Medical Device Manufacturers." 11 March 1997.
4. ISO 14971:2012, Medical devices - Application of risk management to medical devices.

Recommended Reading

Kaplan AV et. al. "Medical device development, from prototype to regulatory approval", *Circulation* 2004; 109:3068-3072, doi:10.1161/01.CIRf0000134695.65733.64.

Sobelman N. "Beyond compliance: medical device product development, Balancing product development effectiveness with regulatory compliance." Originally published 10 March 2010, Kalypso white paper. Kalypso website. http://viewpoints.kalypso.com/uploads/files/Beyond_Compliance_Medical_Device_Whitepaper_1.pdf. Accessed 9 March 2015.

3 Components of Regulatory Strategy—The Basics

By Melissa Walker, MS, RAC, FRAPS

Introduction

A strategy is defined as, "a careful plan or method for achieving a particular goal usually over a long period of time." The end goal of a regulatory strategy is to get safe and effective products to patients in need. To do that as quickly and efficiently as possible, multiple factors must be considered. This chapter assumes a global regulatory strategy is needed for a new product. Where does a regulatory professional start? As the King said to the White Rabbit in *Alice in Wonderland*, "Begin at the beginning, and go on till you come to the end: then stop."

For a global regulatory strategy, the beginning is the patient need and the company's plan to meet that need. The end comes when the product is no longer used or on the market. During the product's lifecycle, the regulatory strategy must be updated constantly to adjust to shifting requirements of patients, physicians and regulatory agencies. Why start with the product plans? These are the boundaries for the strategy. The countries selected, resources available and market timing will drive the final strategy.

Gather Information

The regulatory professional should remember the information gathered will be helpful for both the global regulatory strategy (GRS) and the regulatory plan. Think of the strategy as the overall approach to getting the product to market. The GRS should include a top-level summary of what needs to be accomplished to get the product to healthcare professionals and patients. The regulatory plan should be much more detailed, offering direction and requirements to the project team. More discussion of the difference between the content of these two documents is found in the "Communication" section of this chapter.

Before gathering information, the regulatory professional should make a list of the elements to be included in the GRS and the regulatory plan. The circumstances surrounding any project can be very different. The GRS content should reflect the project's nature. This content list should guide both the research and analysis efforts. Other stakeholders' questions, priorities, timing and outcomes should be incorporated in the research efforts. Why include this? When assembling the strategy, it is highly likely some elements will not meet the project team's ideal outcome. These points will need to be defended when the strategy is reviewed. The length of the debate can be minimized if each variation from the ideal is well supported by data.

The GRS elements and the needed information should be identified, including a brief statement on project plan expectations. The research methodology to fit each element best must be considered. Some elements will require an exploration of something in particular (qualitative research), while others may start with a hypothesis (quantitative research). Some elements may require both. At this initial stage, the regulatory professional should do his or her best to identify the type of research and data needed. If there is a specific expectation for the result, that should be listed in the table as well, as it could be the hypothesis for a quantitative research activity. This list frequently needs adjustment as the research process

Table 3-1. Simplified Global Regulatory Strategy Element Table

Element	Expectation	Research Methodology	Data Needed
Review times	90 days	Quantitative Qualitative	• Published review times for similar products (if available) • Regulatory network resources—individual submission experiences
Available standards	Yes	Qualitative	• International standards list • Standards accepted in previous submissions • Accepted standards declarations (country-specific)
Clinical study needs	None	Qualitative	• Guidance documents • Previous submissions for competitive products
Environmental trends	None	Qualitative	• Review public meeting schedules (past and present) • Guidance documents planned or pending • Public health issues • Legislative activity

moves forward, so it should be readily available and edited accordingly.

A simplified example is shown in **Table 3-1**. It is very tempting to jump into a previously assembled strategy and follow its pathway. Time is precious, and every minute that can be "saved" is a valuable commodity. However, it is important to remember the path followed previously may not lead to the same conclusion. The regulatory environment is fluid. Requirements can change quickly. These questions should be asked before proceeding to document the strategy:
- Is the clinical application understood?
- Are the business and market objectives understood?
- Are the technology and engineering aspects understood?
- Is the competitive landscape understood?
- Are existing products' regulatory and compliance history understood, in all desired national markets?
- Are the clinical evidence or clinical trial requirements understood?
- Are there regulatory or clinical practice trends that will affect the product?

If the answer to any of these questions is "no," time should be taken to do more research. With the advent of the Internet, online searches for product information can lead to many sources. Even though there is almost too much information to sift through, it is worth the effort. The regulatory professional should compile notes on the various research areas. While not everything found during research may go into the regulatory strategy document, it can be very valuable for future research efforts.

This sounds like a lot of research to perform before even starting to assemble the GRS and may take more time than the regulatory professional would prefer, but will pay off in the long run. The more thorough the research, the better the GRS and regulatory plan will be, reducing the number and impact of "surprises" that often show up over the course of a project.

Product Plan

Questions to answer:
- What device(s) is/are the subject of the plan?
- What countries does the product plan target?
- What is the desired timeframe for each proposed market introduction?
- Is the device new to the company, or is it an improvement/iteration of an existing device?
- What are the plan's key assumptions?
- What are the key regulatory risks (and associated schedule risks) in the plan?

To create a regulatory strategy, the regulatory professional first must understand what the product is, its use and the targeted countries. Every organizational segment wants to be in every available market as quickly as possible. In reality, however, each country will have its own requirements and timing. The costs of obtaining and maintaining a marketing authorization may mean entry into every country desired may not be reasonable given a particular product's sales potential. It is important to prioritize the various countries.

Every plan is made with certain assumptions. It is critical to understand which assumptions, if shown to be false, would result in the project's failure. For example:

A known competitor will be in the EU within one year. The product's success depends on getting to the market first. The product is similar to an existing one, but changes are needed. Development can proceed quickly, and the product can be ready in 9–10 months. The plan assumes product modification will not require prior Notified Body review. Any additional time due to a review will mean the market window has closed.

Another example is:
An adverse inspection has resulted in closure of the competitor's facility. The company that can increase production to cover the product volume can lock in a multi-year supply contract. The product is a Class III product in the US and several other markets. To cover demand for the product, a company must expand production to a new facility. The plan assumes regulatory approval in one of the major markets (US, EU or Japan) must be received within six months. Without the multi-year supply contract, the project is not financially feasible.

Other types of limitations also will affect the GRS. Product plans for the same product may be very different based on the company's size and nature. For example, how would a GRS differ for a:
- small company (fewer than 50 people, venture-funded, no currently marketed products)?
- large company (more than 10,000 employees, profitable, fully developed product lines currently marketed)?

Small, venture-funded companies often have scarce time and resources. The first product may have enough features and capability to get into the clinic; getting a product's first iteration on the market can mean the organization's continued viability. Larger companies are not as sensitive.

The variations are virtually endless. Unless the regulatory strategy takes the plan's limitations into account, the project is destined for failure.

Clinical Application

Questions to be answered:
- What clinical conditions apply to the device?
- Who will be using the device?
- Where will the device be used?
- How will the device be used?
- What other devices will be used with the device?
- Are there off-label uses for the product?

To understand the answers to these questions, the regulatory professional needs to understand the clinical condition being treated. This information can come from internal experts in the marketing, R&D and/or clinical groups. To be fully informed, it also is necessary to look at outside sources. To understand how regulatory agencies view treatments, it is important to look for clinical summaries or disease-specific guidance published by regulatory agencies.

For example, in the US, current clinical practice summaries are published by both the Agency for Healthcare Research and Quality (AHRQ) and the Centers for Medicare & Medicaid Services (CMS). AHRQ publishes clinical guidelines and recommendations for healthcare professionals, as well as clinical condition reports for consumers. The UK's Medicines and Healthcare products Regulatory Agency (MHRA) produces educational modules on the use of various device types at http://www.mhra.gov.uk/ConferencesLearningCentre/LearningCentre/Deviceslearningmodules/index.htm. These modules are aimed at educating healthcare professionals on the use of specific devices.

Many peer-reviewed clinical publications, such as the *New England Journal of Medicine* (*NJM*) or the *Journal of the American Medical Association* (*JAMA*), are available on the Internet, but often are pay-per-view. These publications are good sources for understanding evolving research and scientific explorations around a particular clinical condition or treatment. Regulatory professionals should have a solid understanding of current clinical practice before embarking on a detailed review of published literature. The US National Library of Medicine's MEDLINE/PubMed service provides a broad spectrum of resources.

It is important to remember standard practices for treatments may vary from country-to-country or region-to-region. These differences can be minor or major, based on the devices or drugs currently approved or available to local healthcare providers.

Where the device is used affects its development and even classification. For example, a cardiac defibrillator is used to terminate cardiac dysrhythmias. If this device will be used by physicians in a catheterization lab, the design considerations are very different than if it will be placed in a high school gym for use in emergencies by the general public.

Even if a regulatory professional believes he or she has a good understanding of the clinical condition being treated, it is always a good idea to find resources that provide the most up-to-date information about the condition.

Technology and Engineering

Questions to be answered:
- Is this a new technology?
- Is this a new application of an existing technology?
- Is the technology used in other devices?
- What materials are used in the device?
- What problems have been reported with existing devices using the same technology?
- Does the technology' application pose any new questions or risks?

Regulatory professionals come from a wide variety of backgrounds. From biology to engineering to psychology, it is important to establish a broad base of understanding across multiple disciplines. Medical devices' technology and engineering aspects range from simple to complex. A handheld instrument's engineering and design are much different than those of a robotic radiosurgery system. A clear understanding of a device's scientific principles is a necessary piece of a thorough GRS.

Device technologies often appear in multiple clinical specialties. A technology that begins in one area (e.g., radiofrequency probes for cutting and coagulating tissue in general surgery procedures) can expand to additional clinical specialties (e.g., intracardiac ablation to treat cardiac arrhythmias). Often, relevant similarities exist in technical requirements or risk factors. Technical risks and failure modes for one clinical application easily can apply to another application. Ultrasound can be used for imaging or coagulating/ablating tissue. A failure mode for either device can present risks to the system's safety and effectiveness.

Examining risks and failure modes of devices using the same technology also will provide insight into how a regulator may perceive the new device. Regulatory professionals should remember regulators have a much broader visibility into a technology's clinical uses than any one company. Problems seen in other clinical applications easily can lead to additional questions about a new use. Thoroughly analyzing the technology's existing clinical uses is time well spent.

Regulatory History

Questions to be answered:
- Are similar devices already in (or out of) the target marketplace(s)?
- What data were required for the existing device's clearance or approval?
- How long were the review processes?
- Who manufactures or distributes similar devices?
- Have the existing devices' manufacturers had findings or observations during regulatory or conformity assessment bodies' inspections (those who make audit or inspection reports publicly available)?
- Were clinical studies required?
- How long was the review process?
- Have there been any recalls of existing devices?
- What guidance documents or performance standards are available?
- Does the device have any other uses not part of the targeted indications?

Researching a medical device's regulatory history can be time consuming. This is especially true when multiple countries are included in the project plan. It is simpler if the GRS is for an extension of an existing product line in the same target countries. If there is no internal product history, research will be necessary for each country. Countries publish varying amounts of information about a particular product's review and compliance history.

In this exercise, the regulatory professional is assembling a puzzle but may not have all the pieces from "official" sources. Not all the required important information will be found on websites or in written guidance. Often, the critical information needed will be found in other regulatory professionals' experience. Leverage the experience of company colleagues, consultants, distributors or attorneys. The recent growth of such social media outlets as RAPS Regulatory Exchange and LinkedIn makes it easier to access a broad range of expertise. There also are useful blogs that address particular topics and can be searched online.

The device's classification in each country should be identified first. Classification schemes have much in common and use a risk-based approach but can be different in important ways. For example, Japan has four classifications (I, II, III and IV), while the US has three (I, II and III). Under the EU *Medical Devices Directive*, there are four classes with six subclasses (I, I Sterile, I Measurement, IIa, IIb and III). What is considered a Class II device in the US may be Class III in the EU due to differing definitions within each device class. The submission type required within a particular class also may be different. In Japan, the application type depends on whether the device is "new," "improved" or "me-too." International standards' applicability also can influence the required application type. This level of detail should be captured in the research.

Information about competitive devices and their manufacturers generally is available from various stakeholders within the company. Because the US publishes a significant amount of information on devices and their manufacturers, researching FDA websites is a good starting place. Identifying the US product code (or codes) enables a search of the 510(k) or PMA databases. This will provide a list of manufacturers and sponsors with a US regulatory history with the device or technology. Using the company and trade names enables a search of individual regulatory agency websites.

Any regulatory agency website search will have limitations. For example, only portions of the needed information may be available to the general public. Only a few countries have a process for obtaining information by request (e.g., the US *Freedom of Information Act*). Search terms need to be broad enough to capture what is needed but narrow enough to limit the results to a manageable number. Company names and trade names also can vary from country to country, leading to missed references under an alternate name.

Often, the competitor's website will be a good source of product information. Many companies publish labeling content and list the markets where products are sold. Product information also may be available through a customer service request.

The estimated review time is a key GRS element. If specific data already are available for similar products through the regulatory process, a range can be established based on prior experience. The regulatory professional should be cautious when assembling GRS estimates. Multiple factors influence the final review time. Even within device types (same generic name), there can be significant differences in the devices' nature. For example, a "diagnostic programmable computer" may be a device intended for collecting ambulatory heart rhythms or producing complex cardiac electrical maps during invasive catheterization procedures. The technology's complexity, inclusion of clinical data, need for additional test data and even the time of year (holidays can mean longer timeframes) can influence review time. It generally is best to consider the most recent reviews of similar devices for the estimate.

Anticipating the need for clinical trials is a key GRS element. A thorough GRS will examine the need for pre- or postapproval studies. The need for clinical data can vary significantly from country to country. There may be specific patient population reasons for a clinical data requirement. It also may be related to the device's classification. Regulatory agencies may publish summaries of safety and effectiveness data provided in regulatory submissions, including clinical studies. Clinical studies also are described in either medical or scientific publications or on websites like clinicaltrials.gov, providing a significant amount of valuable insight for the GRS. Over time, types of devices that initially required clinical data may not do so for subsequent approvals. As clinicians, sponsors and regulators become familiar with a device type, preapproval clinical trials may be unnecessary.

Product recall records are available on many regulatory agency websites. The records may be in a database specific to a particular product, or found in summary form within annual reports from the regulatory agency. These records can provide information on several GRS aspects. Products frequently associated with recalls may be subject to more regulatory scrutiny. Understanding the types of recalls (and the reasons for them) reported for similar products also will contribute to review time estimates, risk analyses and overall regulatory environment surrounding the product.

The GRS should include a review and assessment of device "problem" reports and safety alerts. These types of reports are available on regulatory agency websites. A review of these reports will provide failure modes and use errors for the development team. The regulatory professional should put himself in the role of a regulator, which provides insight into the problems that may arise.

Environmental Influences

Questions to be answered:
- Are there any ongoing public health issues associated with the condition being treated or devices currently on the market?
- Are there any public meetings (previously held or planned) relevant to the device or its clinical use?
- Are new guidance documents planned, or have any been issued since the last product?
- Are revisions to relevant existing standards (national or international, mandatory or voluntary) under consideration or in the works? Are new standards being developed?
- What are the relevant trends in the clinical literature, e.g., changing clinical practice standards, such as adjunctive therapies used with devices?
- Are there ongoing discussions of, or work on, legislative or regulatory framework changes in key markets of interest?

Environmental changes come in all shapes and sizes. They can have a positive or negative impact on industry, clinical practice or patients. Such changes can be related to a particular product, as when a new performance standard is published. Regulation changes commonly come through agency announcements analyzed and debated in the public arena. Perhaps a device is "down classified," reducing the regulatory requirements and opening the

Table 3-2. Simplified Example of the Expanded Element Table

Element	Expectation	Research Methodology	Data Needed	Analysis Result	Presentation
Review times	90 days	Quantitative Qualitative	• Published review times for similar products (if available) • Regulatory network resources—individual submission experiences	180 days	Graphic
Available standards	Yes	Qualitative	• International standards list • Standards accepted in previous submissions • Accepted standards declarations (country-specific)	Six relevant standards	Statement (GRS) Listing (regulatory plan)
Clinical study needs	None	Qualitative	• Guidance documents • Previous submissions for competitive products	Performance standard available. No clinical data required.	Statement (GRS) Provided (regulatory plan)
Environmental trends	None	Qualitative	• Review public meeting schedules (past and present) • Guidance documents planned or pending • Public health issues • Legislative activity	Issues identified with technology in a different clinical use	Description (GRS) Details for risk mitigation (regulatory plan)
Resources	None	Qualitative and Quantitative	• Format and content for filings in each country • Available staffing levels	Simultaneous submissions require additional regulatory staff	Graphic or tabular (GRS) Details for each filing (regulatory plan)

door to the entry of new competitors into the space. New guidance documents or standards can be posted for weeks, months or even years prior to implementation. A public meeting held to discuss a particular issue reveals a regulatory agency's perspective. These types of environmental changes are fairly visible and generally happen over a manageable period of time.

Other environmental changes may happen quickly. Generally, these are in response to a very visible public health issue. A series of recalls may trigger a change in a performance standard. Insurance reimbursement changes result in the abandonment (or adoption) of a particular device or clinical use. Postmarket event analysis can lead to a safety alert followed by product approval withdrawal. A class action lawsuit may be filed on an entire product type. All these scenarios can contribute to shifts in both the regulatory and clinical practice environments.

If a public health issue arises, it is likely some regulatory change will occur. This is particularly true when the issue has a significant risk for harm, affects a significant number of people and is highly publicized. How quickly the regulatory change can occur is dependent on its nature. Changes requiring legislation can take considerable time. Debates and discussions within legislative bodies often require months to years. Reviewing or monitoring legislative activities becomes key in both generating a GSR and executing the strategy. Health issues significant enough to trigger a change in one country are highly likely to trigger similar actions in other counties. In most instances, legislative activities generate mounds of documentation and public visibility. Information regarding these activities generally is available.

If a change requires regulation or guidance modification, implementation time can vary from months to years. As is the case with legislation, many regulatory authorities follow a process that provides an opportunity for public review and comment on proposed changes.

A change in practice, however, can come very quickly, with no advance notice or warning. Regulatory authorities have a clear view of the presence and cause of product problems. This knowledge can affect many aspects of similar products' reviews and requirements, without prior signals to sponsors. Anticipating these types of changes—identifying the invisible "regulatory risks"—is an important aspect to consider in both GSR generation and regulatory plan execution.

Figure 3-1. Target Market Approval Timelines

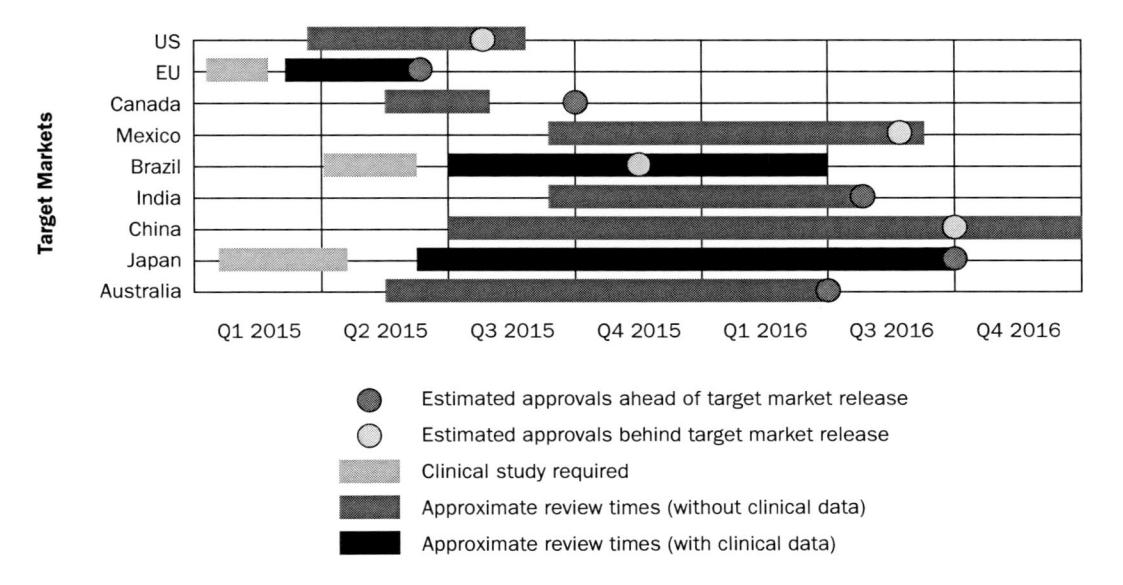

- Estimated approvals ahead of target market release
- Estimated approvals behind target market release
- Clinical study required
- Approximate review times (without clinical data)
- Approximate review times (with clinical data)

This can be the most difficult element of a GRS. Keeping current on environmental changes is a huge challenge for the regulatory professional, who should utilize his or her network and available public information. Combining these resources provides the best support for the strategy.

Resources

- What regulatory resources are needed to support the GRS?
- What expertise is needed?
- Can the project be supported by external resources?
- What in-country resources are available to support registrations?

GRS creation and execution require considerable time and effort. While the focus often is on what happens following the submission, submission creation and organization are not small tasks. This is particularly true when the schedule calls for simultaneous submission dates. It often is easier for stakeholders to understand the need for an additional engineer than for more regulatory staff. Thus, the GRS resource section is critical to project success.

Many methods exist to estimate the resources needed to execute the GRS successfully. Project management software programs can be helpful, and a spreadsheet program can be used to determine where resources may be constrained. Requests for additional resources will be scrutinized closely. The GRS should make a solid case for additional support.

Regulatory staff often are spread over multiple projects and responsibilities. Each project has its own timeline and milestones. As a shared resource, regulatory staff must balance their workload around each team's schedule. This should be taken into consideration when the resource section is developed. Project teams focus on their projects and make them their first priorities. Sufficient time should be allowed for submission preparation, review and editing. Even final submission preparations (e.g., electronic format, multiple paper copies) take time and should be included in the plan.

Some project aspects may require areas of expertise not available within the organization. This applies to regulatory and other functions. For example, if the project is the first to require a clinical trial, study design, statistics or US IDE, submission expertise may be required. If the project incorporates a new software program, expertise in this area may be needed. It is necessary to determine whether this resource should be a permanent staff addition or an external resource.

Even adding a consultant will take time to identify and familiarize the person or firm with the project. This also should be considered in the resource analysis.

Assemble the Strategy

- What elements comprise the GRS versus the regulatory plan?
- What types of analyses are needed?

Chapter 3: Components of Regulatory Strategy—The Basics

Table 3-3. Regulatory Submission Requirements

Country	Classification	Type of Submission	Clinical Data	Estimated Review Time
US	II	510(k)	No	5 months
EU	III	Design dossier	Yes	4 months
Canada	II	MDL application	No	2 months
Mexico	II	Equivalency review	No	8 months
Brazil	III	Cadastro registration	Yes	9 months
India	Listed Device	Device registration certificate application	No	8 months
China	II	Registration dossier	No	15 months
Japan	III	New device, clinical data required	Yes	12 months
Australia	III	Design dossier and application audit	No	10 months

- What if analysis results differ from the product plan?
- What resources are needed to execute the strategy successfully?

Various stakeholders' interests will depend on the project's nature, as well as the regulatory research results. At minimum, the GRS summary should address:
- brief device description and indication statement
- list of countries (in order of market preference)
- for each country
  - regulatory path
  - particular points of regulatory concern
  - clinical trial requirements
  - approximate review time
- regulatory risk areas
- regulatory areas to be monitored as the project proceeds
- required resources

The regulatory plan should detail GRS topics, since it is the development team's guideline. This plan also will be the basis for regulatory project management.
- key milestones
- design and testing requirements
- clinical data requirements
- relevant guidance documents and standards
- risk analysis elements
- resources used for the plan (e.g., websites, publications)

Using the information collected, the relevant data for each element identified in the content list should be analyzed, paying careful attention to those elements that do not appear to meet the project team's needs (or desires). These elements may require more supporting data than those matching project team assumptions.

For example, the product plan often underestimates a particular market's review time. The project team will want the review to be as quick as possible. Team members may have previous experience with a similar product and mental benchmarks on the review time length or may have misinterpreted relevant published data. If review time data are available for similar products, experienced regulatory personnel should analyze other products' reviews over an appropriate time period. Providing an answer based on proper data interpretation rather than individuals' experiences will lend credibility to the estimate and decrease the opportunity for debate when the GRS is presented.

The element table should be reviewed before starting research. Two new columns can be added: Analysis Result and Presentation. Analysis results drive both the presentation's nature and how it is incorporated into the GRS and regulatory plan.

A simplified example of the expanded element table is shown in **Table 3-2**.

Communicating the Strategy

Once the information to create a regulatory strategy has been collected and analyzed, it must be communicated clearly. The audience is likely to be different company stakeholders. Not all audience members will want to review a 25-page report. Summarizing conclusions on the first couple of pages will make the information easier to understand and absorb. Graphic presentations also are simpler to understand quickly. References should be added to show data sources and provide greater credibility.

Table 3-4. Summary of Regulatory Risks

Country	Risk	Description	Mitigation
US	Potential need for clinical data	Clinical data have been required for some existing products but not all. FDA may not accept a rationale for why clinical data are not necessary.	Request a presubmission meeting to discuss the project and ascertain the agency's opinion.
EU	Device description changes within the directive	Recent events have triggered a review of the rules relevant to this type of device. There is a potential for a change in testing or design requirements.	Monitor the discussions and guidance published by regulators.
Canada	None identified	NA	NA
Mexico	Slower clearance in the US will delay initiation of the Mexico submission and review	Based on the regulatory plan, clearance in the US is required prior to submitting in this market.	Prepare to utilize an alternate regulatory path by engaging a distributer with existing product approvals for a similar product.
Brazil	Laws and regulations currently are fluctuating	Requirements are likely to change over the course of the project, resulting in the need for additional test data and the possibility of a clinical study.	Monitor legislative and regulatory activities. Engage a local, in-country consultant to monitor and report on changes as they occur.
India	None identified	NA	NA
China	Delays in market entry	Identifying an in-country representative is necessary before submission and commercialization.	Identify the representative by the end of January.

Summary Presentation

The Device

A summary should describe the device briefly, including any features or benefits critical to the product's success.

The Big Picture

To present an overview of each country's review process timeline, a presentation like the one in **Figure 3-1** can provide an easily understood comparison with each target market's release. This presentation style also is useful for reporting strategy updates.

Should any particular country's review time not meet the product plan's original expectations, a graphic data presentation should be considered to determine approximate review times.

Regulatory Submission Requirements

Regulatory classification, submission type, clinical data requirement and estimated review time overview is helpful. Usually, a tabular presentation works well (see **Table 3-3**).

Regulatory Risks

This GRS should address only those risks outside typical development and regulatory risks. These risks may surface due to a lack of information on a particular topic or direct knowledge of changes in the regulatory environment. **Table 3-4** shows one way to summarize the possible risks detected during research.

Areas to Monitor

Every strategy operates under assumptions based on research results. The regulatory professional should make a list of these assumptions and decide how they should be reverified during the project. These areas will need regular review. Naturally, the items cited in the regulatory risks section also will be included in a monitoring plan.

The monitoring frequency for each area should be integrated into the regulatory plan and assigned to appropriate team member.

Resources Required

If the analysis finds additional resources will be required, careful attention must be paid to the presentation for this GRS element. The GRS stakeholder audience will not necessarily understand the effort required to manage the project's regulatory elements effectively.

The timing and resources needed to accomplish the product plan should be presented. If there is resistance to adding the needed resources, the regulatory professional should be prepared to offer an alternative option using available resources, showing the consequences of fewer resources in understandable terms. Often, this means shifting market introduction timing (for this project or others), which will reduce the revenue generated within that country or region.

Credibility is a major factor in this presentation. The regulatory professional must provide a thorough, data-driven analysis of why added resources are needed to make a credible argument.

General Recommendations

Following are some key points for developing a great GRS:
- A checklist of all needed information should be developed, starting with business objectives. The questions provided here are not intended to be all inclusive. They should be used as a guide and tailored according to the project's nature and subject.
- Some countries have more expedient approval processes if the device has an EU CE Mark, an FDA clearance or approval and/or marketing authorization in the country of origin. This should be taken into consideration when assembling the strategy.
- A complete strategy should consider potential changes during plan execution. A process should be created for both developing and monitoring all regulatory strategies.
- Any "new" elements in a device deserve special attention. Although many potential changes can occur during device development and marketing, a new element can offer the most unknowns. Regulatory authorities understandably are cautious when faced with a new technology or clinical application. Unexpected questions may arise during the review, as reviewers need to be comfortable with the new device. Careful attention to a device's new element(s) can mitigate much of this risk.
- Generating a GRS is a team activity and should involve the project team or stakeholders. This keeps them involved and manages their expectations of the output. During research, some twists and turns may arise. Working closely with the project team allows a focus on what is important for the project's ultimate success.

4 Setting Up a Quality Management System

By Matthew D. O'Donnell, PhD, and Ann Goodall, PhD

Introduction to QMS: ISO 9001 and ISO 13485

Management system standards make best practices available to organizations of all sizes in all sectors. Any organization can implement a system to improve efficiency and effectiveness and manage "its way" of doing things by:
- ensuring nothing important is omitted
- clearly defining who is responsible
- describing what to do, why, when, how and where
- ensuring people are not just "doing their own thing"
- ensuring the organization goes about its business in an orderly way

Quality management is the set of coordinated activities to direct and control an organization with regard to quality. Quality management systems (QMS) are central to the medical device regulatory process in many countries to ensure safe products perform as intended on entering the market. ISO 13485:2003 *Medical Devices—Quality Management Systems—Requirements for Regulatory Purposes* is a QMS standard based on ISO 9001 *Quality Management Systems Requirements*. The ISO 9000 series originally was published in 1987, based on the British Standards Institution's (BSI) BS 5750 series of standards. ISO 9001 covers both product quality assurance (providing confidence quality requirements will be fulfilled) and enhanced customer satisfaction. The standard can be applied to all products and services. ISO 9001 is based on the eight quality management principles:
1. process approach
2. system approach to management
3. continual improvement
4. factual approach to decision making
5. mutually beneficial supplier relationship
6. customer focus
7. leadership
8. involvement of people

The ISO 9001 family of standards, including ISO 13485, promotes the process approach. A process is an activity using resources and managed to transform inputs into outputs (**Figure 4-1**). The process approach applies a system of processes and the processes' identification and interaction and their management.

The process approach emphasizes the importance of:
- understanding and meeting requirements
- looking at processes in terms of added value
- obtaining process performance results
- continual process improvement

Figure 4-1. Basic Process Model

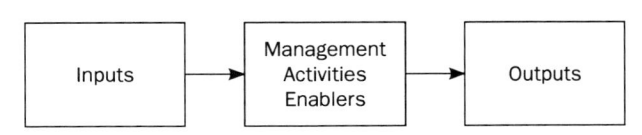

Inputs → Management Activities Enablers → Outputs

Figure 4-2. PDCA Cycle in Resource Management

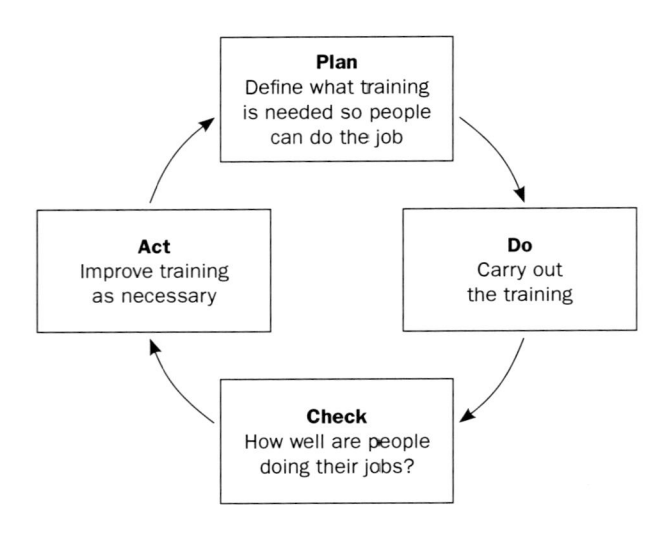

Plan: Define what training is needed so people can do the job
Do: Carry out the training
Check: How well are people doing their jobs?
Act: Improve training as necessary

Plan-Do-Check-Act (PDCA) (**Figure 4-2**) applies to all processes. Each ISO 9001 main clause starts with a 'planning' activity, has a 'doing' activity, has a 'checking' activity (measurement may be implied) and has an 'acting' activity (improvement may be applied).

EN ISO 13485:2012 is the latest harmonized European publication (August 2012) used by organizations wishing to implement a QMS in conformance with the EU *Medical Devices Directive* (93/42/EEC, *MDD*), *Active Implantable Medical Devices Directive* (90/385/EEC, *AIMDD*) and *In Vitro Diagnostics Directive* (98/79/EC, *IVDD*). The standard is applicable to manufacturers placing medical devices on the EU market. For the rest of the world, ISO 13485:2003 remains the applicable standard. The two versions have the same requirements. The 2012 version includes annexes detailing the ISO 13485 sections, where the Notified Body focuses on the directives' additional requirements for CE marking. The standard is used to assess medical devices' and related services' ability to meet customer and regulatory requirements. It is not intended to imply uniformity in the QMS structure or documentation. The standard is complementary to product and technical requirements. Some requirements in the standard apply to named groups of particular products, such as implantable or sterile devices. ISO 13485 is a standalone standard based on ISO 9001, containing all of the ISO 9001 clauses except, primarily, continuous improvement and customer satisfaction. ISO/TR 14969 gives guidance on implementing ISO 13485. ISO 13485 is not intended to include requirements specific to other management systems (e.g., environmental or health and safety), but it allows an integrated approach with those standards (e.g., ISO 14001). ISO 13485 specifies requirements for organizations that:

a) design, develop, produce, install or service medical devices

or

b) design, develop or provide related services

ISO 13485 certification is available to organizations producing products regulated as medical devices in at least one country in the world (ISO 13485 certificates should not be issued to pharmaceutical or cosmetic product manufacturers); for example, human tissue, although not medical devices in the EU, are covered under Japanese MHLW Ministerial Ordinance 169 and could be covered by an ISO 13485 QMS. Examples of related services that can be certified to ISO 13485 include contract sterilizers and packers, manufacturers of significant medical device components (e.g., machining implants) and warehouses.

Exclusions and non-applications to ISO 13485 should be listed and justified in the organization's quality manual. Exclusions are limited to design and development controls, Clause 7.3 (regulations may be a justification, e.g., 93/42/EEC, Annex V). Parts of Clause 7 may not be applicable due to the medical device's nature (e.g., a non-sterile, non-implantable, non-active device).

The standard is structured as follows (Clauses 4 to 8 are the auditable requirements and are shown in more detail):

Table 4-1. Key Differences Between ISO 9001 and ISO 13485

ISO 9001	ISO 13485
6 documents	27 documents
Aims for customer satisfaction through continuous improvement	Does not include customer satisfaction and continuous improvement as objectives
Covers all products	Different requirements for different types of products
Basis for voluntary certification	Basis for regulatory certification

0. Introduction
1. Scope
2. Normative references
3. Terms and definitions
4. Quality management system
    4.1 General requirements
    4.2 Documentation requirements
5. Management responsibility
    5.1 Management commitment
    5.2 Customer focus
    5.3 Quality policy
    5.4 Planning
    5.5 Responsibility, authority and communication
    5.6 Management review
6. Resource management
    6.1 Provision of resources
    6.2 Human resources
    6.3 Infrastructure
    6.4 Environment
7. Product realization
    7.1 Planning of product realization
    7.2 Customer-related processes
    7.3 Design and development
    7.4 Purchasing
    7.5 Production and service provision
    7.6 Control of monitoring and measuring devices
8. Measurement, analysis and improvement
    8.1 General
    8.2 Monitoring and measurement
    8.3 Control of nonconforming product
    8.4 Analysis of data
    8.5 Improvement

Key differences between ISO 9001:2008 and ISO 13485:2003 are shown in **Table 4-1**.

The documentation level required for an ISO 13485 QMS is higher than that for a typical ISO 9001 QMS due to the risk of products an ISO 13485 system covers (medical devices) and the traceability requirements if there are issues with the products once placed on the market. Mandatory procedures and documents for an ISO 13485-compliant system are shown in **Figure 4-3**.

An ISO 13485-certified QMS can support regulatory compliance in a number of jurisdictions, as shown in **Table 4-2**.

The data to support regulatory submission depend on properly trained and qualified personnel performing tests, standard operating procedures, properly calibrated test equipment, documentation and configuration control of test articles, design controls, etc.—all QMS elements.

Figure 4-3. Mandatory Procedures and Documents for ISO 13485:2003

4.2	4.2.1 Quality manual, quality policy and quality objectives
	4.2.3 Control of documents
	4.2.4 Control of records
6	6.2.2 Competence, awareness and training*
	6.3 Infrastructure
	6.4 Work environment
7.1	Planning of product realisation
7.3	Design and development
7.4	Purchasing
7.5.1	7.5.1.1 Production and service provision-Control of production and service provision
	7.5.1.2.1 Cleanliness of product and contamination control
	7.5.1.2.2 Installation activities
	7.5.1.2.3 Servicing activities
7.5.2	7.5.2.1 Validation of processes for production and service provision**
	7.5.2.2 Particular requirements for sterile medical devices
7.5.3	Identification and traceability
7.5.5	Preservation of product
7.6	Control of monitoring and measuring devices
8.1	General***
8.2	8.2.1 Feedback
	8.2.2 Internal audit
	8.2.4 Monitoring and measurement of product
8.3	Control of nonconforming product
8.4	Analysis of data
8.5	8.5.1 General (advisory notices and adverse events)
	8.5.2 Corrective action
	8.5.3 Preventive action

*National or regional regulations might require the organization to establish documented procedures for identifying training needs.

**The organization shall establish documented procedures for validating computer software applications (and changes to such software and/or its application) for production and service provision affecting the product's ability to conform to specified requirements. Such software applications shall be validated prior to initial use.

***National or regional regulations might require documented procedures for implementation and control of the application of statistical techniques.

Table 4-2. Applicability of ISO 13485 in Various Global Jurisdictions

Australia	Requires an audited quality system. ISO 13485 meets those requirements.
Canada	Requires an ISO 13485 registered system for CMDCAS certification for Class II or higher devices. Allows permissible exclusions depending on class of device.
EU	A QMS is required for CE marking that must accompany any medical device sold in the EU. A registered ISO 13485 system is recognized as proof of a QMS for CE marking when the certificate is issued by a Notified Body.
Japan	Requires establishment of a QMS that conforms to MO No. 169, which is similar to ISO 13485. ISO 13485 is an option but not a requirement.
Taiwan	The GMP requirements for Taiwan are based on ISO 13485.
US	Medical device companies are required to establish a QMS that conforms to FDA Quality System Regulations. ISO 13485 is an option but not a requirement (and does not connote full conformity with the QSR).

This is an ongoing process with links between the QMS and postmarketing surveillance (PMS). From an ISO perspective, PMS is one of the key QMS activities in Clause 8 linking to Corrective and Preventive Action (CAPA), complaint handling and adverse event/vigilance reporting, etc. At some point, changes driven by CAPA may require a new regulatory submission.

Regulatory requirements for the region where products are being sold would be part of ongoing certification body assessment as part of the assessment of an organization that has ISO 13485 certification.

ISO compliance is assessed by a certification body, and CE marking, where required, is assessed by a Notified Body (NB). These entities are regulated differently: NBs by Competent Authorities and QMS certification by an accreditation body, e.g., United Kingdom Accreditation Service (UKAS) and the Standards Council of Canada (SCC). The scope of the QMS certificate and CE certificate are dependent on the organization's activities and must be demonstrated by the organization before they can be included in the certificate's scope.

Implementing an ISO 13485 QMS

To implement an ISO 13485 QMS (or any kind of QMS, voluntary or mandatory), the following steps may be followed (discussed in more detail below):
1. gain top management commitment
2. appoint implementation team
3. promote awareness
4. perform gap analysis
5. develop an implementation plan
6. approve the implementation plan
7. implement the plan
8. operate and assess the system
9. continually improve the system
10. certification and registration

Gain Top Management Commitment

Top management must provide a commitment to develop, implement and maintain an effective QMS. Management is responsible for ensuring customer requirements are determined and met. Management also is responsible for creating the organization's quality policy and ensuring it is appropriate, effective, complete, communicated and maintained. In addition to the policy, management should set measurable quality objectives consistent with the policy. Management also should ensure adequate resources are available during planning to meet requirements and the company's objectives, including changes to the QMS. Top management should establish the responsibilities, authorities and relationships within the organization.

- Top management should appoint a management representative to manage the QMS, report on performance, promote QMS awareness within the organization and interact with regulatory bodies.
- Management should establish internal communication procedures, including those about QMS effectiveness and changes. It also should review the QMS at planned intervals (management review) to determine whether the QMS is effective and fit for its purpose.
- The management review has required inputs and outputs that must be documented (e.g., new regulatory requirements, resource needs and internal audits).

Before implementing the QMS, management must make the decision and commitment to consider:
- Why ISO 13485?
- What is the business need?
- What are the expected benefits?

- How much employee time is necessary?
- What is the operational impact?
- What is the estimated cost?
- Is certification to ISO 13485 required and/or desired?

At this stage, management is making a commitment to proceed with planning, and the plan itself is subject to approval or revisions before a final implementation process decision occurs. Management must commit resources to the implementation effort, which could include the following:
- assigning a manager as a project lead
- developing a high-level implementation plan
- ensuring adequate project resources
- approving ISO 13485 and related training requirements
- classifying implementation as a high-priority project
- communicating the decision and plan

To gain commitment and support, the organization's top management must understand the implications of their decisions and the need for continued personal involvement. One way to demonstrate commitment is to assign a key management member, perhaps the management representative, to lead the project. Management should be given an initial estimate of the people, time and costs (resources) expected for the project, and should be provided with a more accurate estimate after the plan is developed (before final approval). Resources should be assigned to implement the QMS and maintain its effectiveness and ability to meet customer and regulatory requirements. Personnel performing work affecting product quality must be competent and have the relevant education, training, skills and experience for the jobs they are performing, and this should be recorded and maintained. The infrastructure (e.g., IT systems, manufacturing equipment) needed to operate the QMS and ensure product conformity also must be determined. Environmental requirements (e.g., cleanliness and contamination controls) to achieve product conformity also must be outlined.

Appoint Implementation Team

Most organizations will require more than one person to fulfil the implementation initiative successfully. Implementation team members should be trained to ensure they understand the standard's requirements. The project lead typically will be the management representative (who is often the company's quality manager) and should have sufficient organizational influence. Duties may include:
- developing and managing the implementation plan
- ensuring all needed processes are established
- promoting awareness of customer and regulatory requirements
- monitoring QMS performance
- identifying any needs for improvement
- reporting on performance to top management
- communicating with external parties (e.g., suppliers, customers, regulatory bodies) about the QMS

Team members, particularly the project lead, should review and familiarize themselves with guidance documents (e.g., International Medical Device Regulators Forum (IMDRF), International Accreditation Forum (IAF), EU medical devices directives (MEDDEVs), US Food and Drug Administration (FDA)), guidance on ISO 13485 (ISO/TR 14969) and related standards such as ISO 19011 (principles of auditing).

Promote Awareness

To promote awareness within the organization, the implementation team should inform employees of the intent to implement the standard, including its benefits to staff, the organization and customers. Top management ensures communication throughout the organization by:
- announcing implementation plans
- describing benefits to the company
- explaining benefits to the employees
- developing a communications plan
- making progress visible
- conducting an ISO 13485 overview
- encouraging wide participation

It would be a mistake for the implementation team to proceed in near secrecy to avoid interfering with current business activities. Employees should be informed of the plan, why it is happening, how it will them, who is involved and scheduled key activities. If employees are kept in the dark about the project, they will be less supportive when their help is needed to implement required practices. Another mistake would be to announce the project and not communicate the status. Employees should be kept informed of progress and how they might be needed. Keeping the project visible, with plans for regular project updates, will ensure management support and encourage everyone to keep to the schedule. Ongoing personnel training is key to the success of any QMS.

Figure 4-4. Sample Schedule for QMS Implementation

1–2 months	3–4 months	5–6 months	7–8 months	9–10 months	12+ months
• Training • Planning • Define QMS • Gap analysis	• Documentation • Certification body selection • Implementation	• Implementation • Operation • Evidence	• Pre-assessment • Internal audit • Management review • Corrective actions	• Stage 1 audit • Stage 2 audit • Corrective actions • Certification	• Audit follow-up • Surveillance audits

Perform Gap Analysis

During this stage, the current system should be reviewed, compared with the standard's requirements, and any gaps should be identified. Gap analysis should be a cross-functional activity. Every organization will have a management system in place at some level. The current system should be understood before defining the new system. The current system may not be documented and defined to the degree required by the standard. Processes, responsibilities and resources should be identified, and risks and opportunities considered. Every organization will have existing policies, procedures and processes already compatible with the standard's requirements. Others may require amendment, and some potentially may be redundant. When reviewing the current system, the following should be addressed:
- define processes to meet objectives
- identify process owners
- establish process inputs and outputs
- identify resources to meet objectives
- define methods for process measures
- include processes to maintain effectiveness

Gap analysis outputs may include:
- an inventory of current documents and records
- current quality objectives
- current monitoring and measurement methods
- gaps in ISO 13485 requirements
- missing documents, records and practices
- implementation plan deliverables and activities

QMS implementation assists in providing controls to mitigate risks, which should be among the main drivers for introducing a QMS; as a result, risks and opportunities should be reviewed when performing the gap analysis (see ISO 14971 for guidance on risk management throughout product realization). It is good business practice to determine the day-to-day risks and decide what controls are required to reduce them to the financially appropriate extent.

Develop an Implementation Plan

Once the gap analysis determines what has to be achieved, an implementation plan can be developed. In developing the plan, key activities, responsibilities, costs, schedules and resources should be estimated and refined. The following activities should be considered when developing the plan:
- establish system scope and objectives
- assign roles and responsibilities
- determine training needs
- identify development areas from gap analysis
- define and schedule activities
- develop system implementation project plan
- establish budget and approve plan
- review progress, update plan and communicate status
- manage project using practices in standard

The plan may change over time due to unforeseen events, so it should be designed for easy maintenance. At minimum, the plan should list key activities, estimated start and finish dates and responsibilities. Any assumptions and dependencies should be listed to confirm the plan's foundation. The responsibilities identify activity ownership. An overall plan owner must be established to manage the plan's day-to-day aspects. Top management will review and approve the plan. The plan owner will inform management of actual results compared to the plan. Another important consideration is maintenance of the current system's integrity while planning and implementing the modified system (Clause 5.4.2 of ISO 13485). The following paragraphs and **Figure 4-4** demonstrate a sample schedule, which can be shortened or lengthened depending on the organization's size, existing gaps and system status.

The first one to two months typically are spent organizing, training, planning and performing the gap analysis. The next few months are allocated to corrective actions for any nonconforming practices, preparing the necessary documents and selecting the certification body (certification body selection considerations may include costs, scope of activities, resources and timelines).

After five to six months, it is time to implement the system and make it operational. Records should be kept as evidence of conformity, and conformity must be documented in writing. The next few months are used for pre-assessment to take any corrective actions and undergo the certification audit. After the certification audit, the implementation team responds to any findings, and the QMS is certified and listed in public registries of certified systems. After being certified, the organization prepares for its first surveillance audit by the certification body. Internal audits are conducted to verify closure of identified issues and examine selected system parts defined in the company's internal audit program.

When developing the implementation plan, costs to be considered include: certification body (onsite audits and offsite reviews), training (external and in-house), consulting and other internal resource costs. The budget should be agreed with top management.

When identifying resources, committed people should be selected for the implementation team. The workload should be shared across the organization to reduce the impact on other business activities and raise awareness. Management should support resourcing and understand team members' time demands to minimize any changes to the team at a later date that could cause delays and impact the project. Responsibilities and authorities should be defined clearly. The organization already may have job descriptions that define roles, responsibilities, education, experience, training and skill requirements; these may need to be developed, revised or created as part of the implementation process. All of the standard's elements should have a process owner within the organization (**Figure 4-5**).

Approve the Implementation Plan

Top management will decide whether to proceed with the implementation plan or send it back to the project team for revisions. Before requesting approval, the plan should cover:
- assumptions and dependencies
- intermediate milestones
- start and completion dates
- activities and deliverables
- responsibilities and authorities
- resources and estimated costs
- tracking and reporting methods
- expected benefits and returns

Figure 4-5. QMS Documentation Defining Responsibilities

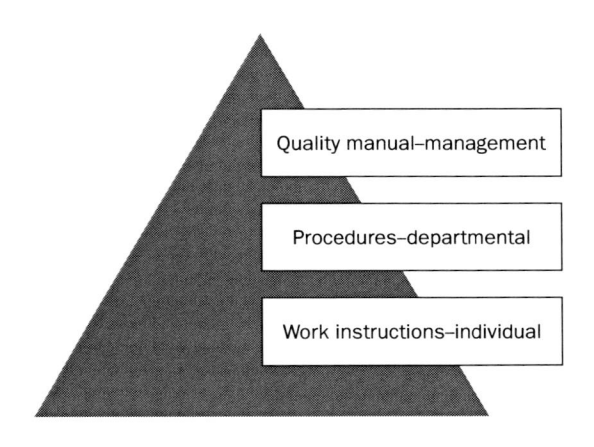

- Quality manual–management
- Procedures–departmental
- Work instructions–individual

The implementation plan should be clearly defined and formally agreed by top management. The plan may need revisions before finally gaining approval.

Implement the Plan

Implementation is where the work to meet the standard's requirements takes place. It is not unusual for the management system to be implemented in stages. The approved plan should be carried out, and training should be provided when needed. The implementation team should be given the resources and support needed to complete assigned activities successfully. Progress should be monitored frequently (not just at the points defined in the plan), and encouragement and assistance should be offered. Tracking data should be collected to report to top management. Some activities will be dependent on earlier activities. If delays are anticipated, the impact on later activities should be considered to minimize problems. Documentation is important at this stage, so policies can be created, procedures developed and records kept.

Training on ISO 13485 should be conducted early in the project to aid in planning. Managers and other employees should be included, as appropriate, to ensure staff are aware of the standard, the importance and relevance to their jobs and how the standard is applicable to the organization's products and services. Expertise should be developed to assist and guide implementation activities. The training budget should cover needed courses and travel, and records should be maintained as evidence. Further training will be needed as the QMS is implemented and procedures and policies are developed.

The QMS should be documented, including:
- quality policy and objectives

Figure 4-6. Typical QMS Document Hierarchy

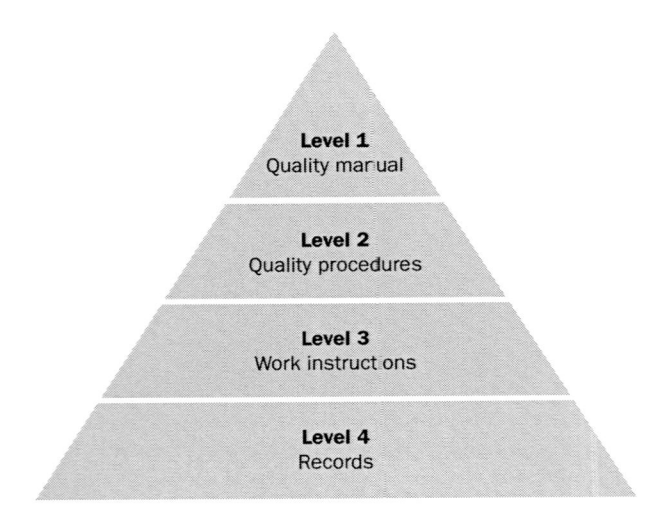

- Level 1: Quality manual
- Level 2: Quality procedures
- Level 3: Work instructions
- Level 4: Records

- quality manual and documented procedures
- necessary planning operation and control documents
- required records, including regulatory

Documents and records required by the QMS should be controlled and maintained. A typical QMS document hierarchy is shown in **Figure 4-6**.

The quality manual describes the QMS in accordance with the company's policies and objectives. Procedures define interrelated processes and activities (who, what, why, when and where). Work instructions and other documents needed to plan, operate and control processes are the detailed work documents (how). Records are the evidence of results achieved and activities performed.

The draft quality policy should now be formalized to ensure it is communicated and understood within the organization and reviewed for continuing suitability. Objectives also should be formalized along with measures. The quality manual should include the QMS scope, details and justification for any exclusion or non-applications, documented procedures (or references to them), description of interaction between QMS processes and an outline of the QMS documentation structure. The manual's format is a decision for each organization and will depend on the organization's size, culture and complexity. A small organization may find it appropriate to include a description of the entire QMS within a single manual, including all the documented procedures required by the standard. Large, multi-national organizations may need several manuals at the global, national or regional levels, and a more complex hierarchy of documentation. When implementing the plan, the following should be considered in relation to the documentation:

- What is the value?
- What is required?
- What is needed to support the QMS?
- How extensive should it be?
- What is the format?
  - procedures
  - flow charts
  - work instructions
  - forms
  - electronic
  - hard-copy

ISO 13485 has 50 references to required records, generated by executing a process and providing evidence of conformity. Examples of records are completed forms, audit reports, meeting minutes and test data.

The project team should report to top management on the project's overall status from the plan owner, and progress should be reported by process owners (so the project does not appear to only be a quality department initiative). The project tracking data can be used to share a high-level summary of completed activities, show progress, maintain interest and keep the project visible. Involving management ensures the project remains a priority and demonstrates management's ownership and commitment to the system.

During implementation, the certification body typically is contacted if certification is sought. Three to six months of records and metrics usually are required for the certification body to assess and certify the QMS. A few months of lead-time should be factored into the schedule before the certification process is initiated.

Operate and Assess the System

Once the system is operational, it should be assessed continually by monitoring and measurement, documentation, internal audits and management reviews to evaluate whether the QMS is working as intended and is achieving defined goals and objectives. Processes can be implemented as they become ready for release as long as users are trained and ready to operate their parts of the system. Not all processes need to be implemented concurrently, only those with certain interdependencies. It is important to control documents and records as required by ISO 13485 and internal procedures. Records pre-dating QMS implementation will not be considered by auditors except to check record retention times. Typically, at least three months of evidence of the management system's operation will be required for the certification body to assess conformity before the initial audit.

It is important to determine what to measure, how to measure, who will be responsible and the frequency of measurements to be performed. The implementation project team can begin monitoring and measuring activities. Suitable monitoring methods should be applied. Where applicable, process measurements then can be used as evidence of the processes' ability to achieve planned results. Top management can use the implementation project team to begin its QMS reviews. The tracking meetings probably will not qualify as management reviews, as they may not meet all of the requirements of the relevant regulation clause (Clause 5.6), but they will be good practice in setting agendas, identifying issues, taking actions and recording minutes. Regular review meetings can be the precursor to management review meetings and system reviews. Meetings with core team members should be held frequently to review progress. The review meetings should be short and feedback schedules agreed with top management. Progress and achievements should be communicated to top management. Monitoring and measurements should be performed as soon as processes are in place, with processes reviewed and updated as needed during implementation.

Internal audits also are used to monitor and measure the system. The internal audit program should conform to planned arrangements (implemented and maintained effectively) and meet ISO 13485, organizational, customer and regulatory requirements. Ideally, the majority of the QMS should be implemented before internal audits are initiated.

The word 'audit' may have negative connotations in some organizations because it often is associated with financial audits. However, audits (a team might be more receptive to the term "inspections") can have great benefits to an organization, its product, services and employees, and this ideally should have been communicated in the earlier promotion of implementation project awareness. Audits help an organization investigate any quality problems and verify solutions are implemented effectively. Management needs factual information to make informed decisions. Audits provide impartial, objective results for management action. Periodic audits keep the quality awareness level high and foster improved internal communication.

Internal audits are expected to examine all areas and shifts, some areas more often based on previous results (a risk-based approach), and show audit scope (coverage) as part of the schedule. Internal audits should be conducted by properly qualified staff members who are independent from the areas being audited (i.e., not auditing their own work) and impartial. Many auditor training and

Figure 4-7. Iterative PDCA Cycle

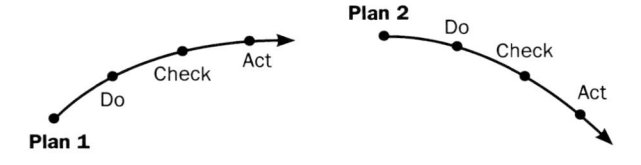

certification programs are available and recommended for personnel responsible for this task. Programs provided by recognized quality standards organizations (e.g., the American Society for Quality's (ASQ) "Certified Quality Auditor" (CQA) proficiency qualification) should be considered. Other organizations also train and certify auditors to specific ISO regulations.

Internal audits must follow a documented auditing procedure (Clause 8.2.2). The organization must follow its documented corrective action procedure to resolve any findings in audit reports. A follow-up audit verifies actions taken and reports the results (see ISO 19011 for guidance).

Management reviews should be conducted to ensure continuing QMS suitability, adequacy and effectiveness. New or revised regulatory requirements should be included in the review. Opportunities for improvement to maintain QMS effectiveness and QMS changes, including policy and objectives, should be assessed in the management review. Such meetings can be used to review implementation process activities and make immediate improvements. Review outputs should include resource needs and product improvements related to customer requirements. Review records must be controlled and maintained. The reviews analyze a number of metrics, including audit results, customer feedback and process performance and product conformity.

Based on the system review, improvements or corrections may be proposed. This may result in taking appropriate corrective or preventive action, improving products or processes and determining resource needs or changes. These improvements then should be implemented, communicated and fed back into the next planning stage. Improvements should follow the documented procedure for corrective action and the results recorded (Clause 8.5.2). In addition to initiating the corrective action process, quickly identifying any findings in one area potentially can help remaining areas avoid a similar problem (and reduce the number of reported nonconformities).

Continually Improve the System

Organizations must recognize the management system will need continuous improvement to keep meeting

Table 4-3. Benefits and Barriers to Certification

Benefits	Barriers
Expanded access to world markets	Difficulty identifying and creating new processes for the system
Ability to bid for contracts	Developing the necessary documented procedures and instructions
Use as a market differentiator	Lack of visible and demonstrated management commitment and support
Display of the certification mark	Personnel not following the prescribed procedures per their training
Independent audits by professionals	Resistance by some employees to change (e.g., providing process measurements)
	Conflicting interpretations within the organization and by the certification body

quality expectations. ISO 13485 requires organizations to improve their Quality Management systems continuously; these are audited by the certification body as part of ISO13485 certification. The system can be improved in a number of ways, including:

- QMS auditing
- monitoring processes, products and services
- collecting customer feedback
- monitoring customer complaints, nonconformances, other inputs to CAPA
- monitoring supplier performance
- reviewing required competencies
- reviewing training needs
- reviewing training effectiveness
- maintaining QMS effectiveness

The Plan-Do-Check-Act (PDCA) cycle is an iterative process that is refined continuously as the QMS evolves (**Figure 4-6**).

The regulatory professional's role in establishing and maintaining a QMS will depend on how the organization is structured. In some organizations, QMS compliance is under regulatory, but many manufacturers leave the responsibility with the quality function. Responsibilities should be organized to ensure there are no conflicts of interest. In some organizations, quality assurance reports to operations or manufacturing, with a separate regulatory function reporting elsewhere. Within ISO 13485, Clause 5.5 relates to independence, and 8.2.4 talks about planned arrangements to ensure those releasing product are authorized to do so, but there is no reference to quality being a separate function. A close working relationship between the regulatory professional and the QMS group is always required to understand and "interpret" the QMS regulatory requirements.

Certification and Registration

The first steps an organization seeking certification should consider are planning for the external audits, performing the pre-assessment and undergoing Stage 1 and 2 (initial) audits (the certification body audit process is described in more detail below). Formal certification is achieved only through external (third-party) assessment; certified bodies are accredited to conduct such QMS audits. A number of factors can influence the choice of a certification body, such as cost, timelines and the scope of the certification body's activities. Qualified auditors will be assigned to evaluate the total QMS. They will provide a plan and a written report. Benefits and barriers to certification are listed in **Table 4-3**.

The Stage 1 audit usually is a one-day, on-site audit of the partial system: QMS documentation, management review and internal audits. It also is intended to determine readiness for the Stage 2 audit (typically one to two months later, but ideally no more than six months). Internal audits are good practice for the external audits to ensure everyone onsite is ready, has a chance to explain their personal involvement, emphasize the business value of audits, give advice on interview behavior and arrange logistical audit support. The Stage 2 assessment is a multi-day, on-site audit of the full system scope. This audit is to evaluate QMS implementation and effectiveness and to examine evidence of conformity to requirements. The certification body will audit links between requirements, policies, objectives, responsibilities, competence, procedures and performance.

The next steps for organizations seeking certification, following the Stage 1 and 2 audits, are to take corrective action if any nonconformities arise, receive the certificate and then maintain and improve the system. The corrective action plan submitted to the certification body should address root cause(s) of all nonconformities, and the organization must await approval of corrective action(s) from the certification body. The audit team only recommends certification (or not). They do not grant the certificate. That comes later, after the certification body's headquarters reviews the team's audit report and makes the final decision. After the final decision, it is time to notify customers, suppliers and other interested parties of successful certification. Some implementation team members may deserve special recognition for their efforts. The certification body guidelines should be followed on the use of the certification mark to publicize ISO 13485 certification.

Receiving the certificate is not the end of the quality process; it is an important and valuable milestone. The system must be maintained and improved continually. The company has embarked on an ongoing process of optimizing the business outcomes across the organization.

ISO 13485 Audits by a Certification Body

Just like the organizations they certify, certification bodies have their own management systems. These systems are assessed and accredited by the accreditation body in the country in which the body is based (e.g., UKAS and SCC), who are members of the International Accreditation Forum (www.iaf.nu). The general requirements for bodies certifying management systems are given in ISO/IEC 17021:2011 "Conformity assessment—Requirements for bodies providing audit and certification of management systems." This section focuses on ISO 17021 Clause 9, which applies to audit process requirements.

The standard states the audit program should include a two-stage initial audit, surveillance audits in the first and second years and a recertification audit in the third year prior to certificate expiration (**Figure 4-8**).

The three-year cycle begins with a certification or recertification decision. A plan must be established and documented for each audit identified in the program along with objectives, scope and criteria (**Table 4-4**).

The audit plan, which is communicated to the client in advance, includes at minimum the audit's objectives, scope and criteria as well as the audit's dates, duration and the audit team's roles and responsibilities. Audit team selection will be based on the auditor's competence to achieve the audit's objectives, certification requirements (e.g., the applicable medical device regulatory background), language requirements and impartiality. The audit team also may be supplemented by technical experts, translators and interpreters.

The audit's duration is based on the following guidance: IAF Mandatory Document for the Application of

Figure 4-8. ISO 17021 QMS Certification Cycle

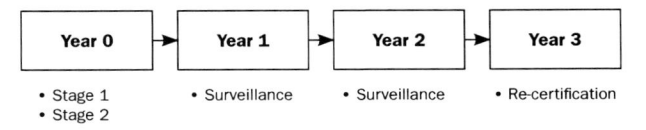

Year 0 → Year 1 → Year 2 → Year 3

- Stage 1
- Stage 2
- Surveillance
- Surveillance
- Re-certification

ISO/IEC 17021 in Medical Device Quality Management Systems (ISO 13485) - IAF MD 9:2011. This document suggests the number of audit days based on the organization's size (number of personnel) and provides a number of factors that may be used to increase or reduce the number of audit days (**Tables 4-5 and 4-6**). The duration includes offsite planning and reporting activities.

ISO/IEC 17021 allows sampling of multi-site organizations; however, IAF MD 9:2011 does not allow sampling of sites performing design and development and manufacturing.

Once the auditors are onsite, the audit starts with a formal opening meeting, where the audit's objectives, criteria and scope are confirmed. Communication during the audit is through the audit team leader to the main site contact (typically the management representative). Observers can be present as part of the audit team, but their presence should be communicated and agreed prior to the audit. The manufacturer needs to provide guides for the audit team; the number should be based on the audit agenda and the number of auditors to meet the audit plan objectives. The auditors will employ a number of methods to collect and verify information, including observing processes, interviews and reading documentation. The audit team will identify and record audit findings during the course of the audit (typically by handwritten notes) and produce a formal report at the end of the audit or shortly thereafter.

Before the closing meeting, the auditors will require some time to prepare their conclusions, to determine whether the audit's objectives have been accomplished and whether to recommend certification (initial audit), continued certification (surveillance audit) or re-certification (re-assessment audit). During the meeting, an audit summary will be provided, including any findings

Table 4-4. Certification Body QMS Assessment Objectives, Scope and Criteria

Objectives	Scope	Criteria
Conformity of QMS with criteria	Physical locations	Normative QMS documents (e.g., ISO 13485)
Ability to meet applicable requirements	Organizational units	
Effectiveness to meet objectives	Activities	Defined processes and documentation in QMS
Areas for improvement	Processes	

Table 4-5. Audit Duration for Medical Device ISO 13485 Audits Based on Staff Numbers

Effective Number of Personnel	Audit Duration Stage 1 + 2 (days)	Effective Number of Personnel	Audit Duration Stage 1 + 2 (days)
1-5	3	626-875	15
6-10	4	876-1175	16
11-15	4.5	1176-1550	17
16-25	5	1551-2025	18
26-45	6	2026-2675	19
46-65	7	2676-3450	20
66-85	8	3451-4350	21
86-125	10	4351-6800	22
126-175	11	5451-6800	23
176-275	12	6801-8500	24
276-425	13	8501-10700	25
426-625	14	>10700	Follow progression above

Source IAF MD9:2011

(observations and nonconformities) and agreed actions. A corrective action plan will be required for any identified nonconformities to be corrected within the certification body's defined time period. The corrective action plan should contain a number of elements, including traceability to the original nonconformity, the correction and containment to address the nonconformity initially, the nonconformity root cause analysis and investigation, the corrective action to be implemented, preventive action (if applicable), responsibilities, timelines and how the corrective action's effectiveness will be verified.

Additional audits may be required outside the surveillance cycle (e.g., to close a major nonconformity, verify critical or significant suppliers or perform a scope extension for new products or processes). Once the audits have been performed and corrective action plans accepted, the certification body reviews the auditors' recommendation independently before making the final certification decision. The certification body also reviews the contract with its client to ensure that when the initial application is received by the certification body, the required assessments can be delivered in terms of resources and competence. The initial audit comprises Stage 1 and 2 audits as described above. Stage 1 is an on-site documentation check to ensure the company has the basic and mandatory element in its QMS and to confirm readiness for Stage 2. The Stage 2 audit then will be performed (typically one to six months later to ensure there is adequate design and production documentation and the management review, CAPA and internal audit processes have generated auditable documented evidence). The Stage 2 audit covers applicable parts of the standard. The recertification audit again covers applicable parts of the standard, with the objective of recommending recertification (typically about three months before the end of the three-year certificate life). In surveillance audits, not all standard clauses typically will be audited, as the audit's duration will be shorter than the initial and recertification audits.

FDA has conducted unannounced inspections for a number of years. A relatively new development is Notified Bodies performing unannounced audits under the EU *Medical Devices Directive* (*MDD*) (always a provision in the *MDD* but a requirement under the new *Medical Device Regulation*). These are in addition to scheduled audits and focus on assessing ongoing production of CE-marked devices and linking devices in production to technical documentation and specifications. Taking this into consideration, companies need to have in place one or more Standard Operating Procedures (SOPs) defining their structures, considerations and roles in handling audits, whether anticipated or unannounced. These SOPs should include responsibilities for handling the audits, accessing and tracking documentation and communication within the organization regarding audit initiation and continuation.

Quality System Regulation (QSR), 21 CFR Part 820 (US FDA)

The QSR defines quality system requirements that must be fulfilled to place medical devices on the US market. This section does not detail the requirements but provides an overview of some key aspects to be considered when setting up a QMS to meet QSR requirements. Setting up a QMS that meets QSR requirements is the same as for an ISO 13485 QMS, but consideration must be given to ensuring QSR requirements are included.

The QSR was developed to ensure medical devices used in the US are safe and effective, which is the regulation's prime goal. The regulation has evolved over the years.

- In 1906, the *Pure Food & Drug Act* was enacted following poisoning related to drugs.
- In 1911, adulterating foods or drugs was made illegal.
- In 1938, the *Federal Food, Drug, and Cosmetic Act* was enacted, making it illegal to sell unsafe drugs.
- The law was amended in 1962 to include drug effectiveness, following the Thalidomide scandal in Europe.
- In 1963, the first drug Good Manufacturing Practices (GMPs) were adopted.
- The *Medical Device Amendments* began in 1976 and were published in 1978.
- The *Safe Medical Devices Act* was enacted in 1990.
- In 1996, the Quality System Regulation was published, incorporating ISO principles, becoming effective in June 1997. The design control requirements took effect in June 1998, replacing the 1978 GMP requirements and based on ISO 13485:1996. All of these changes focused on ensuring safe and effective drugs, and then included medical devices to ensure they caused no harm.

The QSR provides a basic framework for manufacturers, but these requirements are not prescriptive. The manufacturer is responsible for determining how it will meet the requirements. This enables both large and small organizations to meet the requirements and covers the broad and diverse range of medical devices, technologies and manufacturing processes.

Among other factors, the QMS should be developed to accommodate the risk of devices of any complexity, taking into account relevant manufacturing processes and organizational complexity and size. The QSR outlines basic elements for inclusion. Additional details may be required as device complexity and potential risk increase.

Subsystems of a Quality System

As in ISO 13485, QSR requirements can be segmented around subsystems.

Table 4-6. Factors That May Increase or Reduce Audit Durations

Increase	Decrease
Large range of devices	Reduced product range
Device complexity	Reduced design processes
Cannot demonstrate supplied processes' and parts' conformity	Reduced production processes
Poor regulatory compliance	

Source: IAF MD9

Management

An organization's management needs to demonstrate its understanding, support and leadership for implementing and maintaining a QMS that complies with QSR requirements. This should be demonstrated by a QSR assessment.

The organization's quality policy outlines its aims and how they are fulfilled regarding regulatory requirements as defined by management. It is important to include FDA quality system requirements as part of the policy.

The organizational structure has to be defined. The independence of those responsible for product quality (the quality unit) and product release to customers must be defined clearly; they must be autonomous from influence by those in the organization not responsible for product quality. Typically, product quality responsibility within an organization is a different reporting line from that of those responsible for product research and development, manufacturing, sales and/or marketing.

Management review is the opportunity for executive management to confirm the quality system remains effective. Clearly defined inputs, usually in the form of metrics for each subsystem, should assess how the system is functioning while ensuring the metrics demonstrate products remain safe and effective. It is important to follow through on any actions (may be via the CAPA system) resulting from the management review. The intervals at which management review occurs must be defined and scheduled on a regular basis. The review must take place annually, at a minimum; however, reviews typically are quarterly. Annual reviews are not sufficient to ensure quality system effectiveness.

The management representative's role is key within the organization. Executive management appoints the management representative and documents it in writing. The QSR defines the management representative's responsibilities in ensuring the QMS is established and maintained effectively and requires the representative to report on QMS performance to executive management.

This is done primarily through regular management review meetings.

Quality audits are key elements of any QMS. They are the means by which an organization can assess QMS 'health' and look to areas needing changes. It is important to have an annual audit program covering all QSR aspects. The program is not static; changes may be implemented to address problem areas. The internal auditors must be independent of the areas they are auditing. Further, as noted above, auditors must be trained appropriately (e.g., ASQ CQA).

Internal (and external) audits can be difficult for small organizations where "independence" often is not defined clearly, especially for auditing QMS quality and regulatory aspects. Typically, small companies engage external consulting auditors to fulfill both internal and external audit functions. Any issues (nonconformities) identified by internal audits should result in corrective actions. There should be clear input from internal audit results to management review, and equally clear actions and justification for those tasks.

The QSR also includes personnel requirements. There should be sufficient resources for the organization's activities, and the personnel should be educated or trained appropriately for their roles. Organizations must have job descriptions for each position, which must be linked to individual training plans. The QSR has specific requirements for training personnel to recognize defects that could occur in relation to the product. This should be an element of personnel training, and the link between the potential defects and training to those issues should be documented. This includes personnel performing verification and validation activities.

Document and Record Control

When setting up a QMS to meet QSR requirements, once management has determined the system's scope, the document and record control support processes should be established.

This should include document review and approval authority and how documents are made available to all personnel who use them. Changes to the documents also must be controlled and approved, at minimum, by the same function or personnel approving the original document.

The procedure for records needs to include how they are completed to become permanent records, their retention period in relation to the device's life, and how to prevent their destruction. The record control system must recognize the various types of records listed in the QSR.

CAPA

The CAPA system is an important QMS element that the organization must establish and maintain to meet 21 CFR 820 requirements.

Organizations usually have one CAPA system for action with one procedure.

Organizations can implement very complex systems, usually based on databases to manage CAPA, but for smaller organizations, a simpler approach may be possible. It is important the system inputs come from all parts of the quality system, not just those related to product, which often is the focus.

The CAPA processes have defined wide-ranging inputs to cover all QMS parts. Nonconformity or other potential quality problem causes that are system inputs must be investigated and identified in a timely manner. CAPA processes to prevent recurrence must be planned. It is necessary to ensure any actions taken will not have an unanticipated impact on the finished medical device.

CAPA should be linked clearly to management review. An overview of the issues that are inputs to CAPA, ensuring they have been implemented effectively, provides management a real indication of the health of the QMS for which it is responsible.

Nonconforming product needs to be identified and controlled to prevent its unintended use or delivery. The process controls and responsibilities for nonconforming product must be defined in a documented procedure. This should include nonconforming product identification, segregation and disposition.

The product must be segregated in a timely manner to ensure it cannot be used, for example, either by having the product under lock and key or using a stock control system to ensure no one can take the material and use it as a medical device or component thereof.

If an organization reworks nonconforming material, the rework must demonstrate the medical device still meets the product's defined specifications.

Elements that need to be included in the control process for nonconforming product should be defined. These should include how the product is identified and controlled, so it is not used inadvertently.

Personnel responsible for deciding on the disposition of nonconforming product must be identified and documented. If the nonconformity is detected during finished medical device testing, the disposition decision probably would be made by more senior personnel, so the quality and regulatory impact can be considered by those with the widest knowledge of the organization.

A formally designated complaint unit should be responsible for the specific requirements relating to

Figure 4-9. Design Process

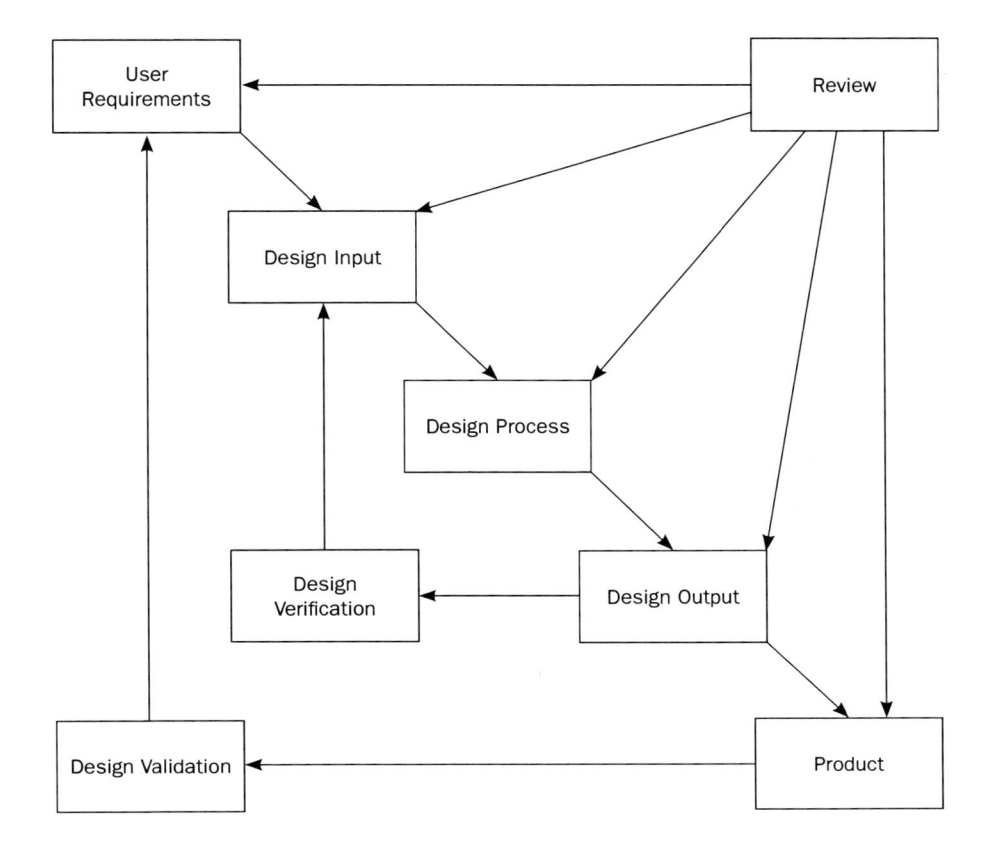

complaint files. All complaints have to be documented, including those received verbally by phone or received by other members of the organization who normally would not receive complaints.

There is a defined timescale for assessing all complaints to determine whether they are medical events under the requirements of 21 CFR Part 803 (Medical Device Reporting). The period from receipt of a complaint to its review must be within the timescale.

If a service report is a medical event, this would be included in the reporting system the manufacturer must have in place. In the system, the manufacturer has to ensure service report review to determine whether they are medical events.

21 CFR Part 806's requirements relating to corrections and removals also must be included in organization procedures. In addition, the organization must ensure the procedure can be implemented at any time, even on a public holiday.

A Medical Device Tracking regulation (21 CFR Part 821) requirement that needs to be built into the quality system, states the manufacturer or importer is responsible for devices that fall under the regulation. This will be covered in an FDA assessment. The organization must ensure it can locate the device in a timely manner, so the customer can be contacted in the event the device is subject to a correction or removal.

There should be procedures in place for any statistical techniques used in the QMS.

Design Control

Design and development include all aspects of bringing the medical device to the customer. This ranges from determining the design inputs and ensuring they are in line with the user and regulatory requirements through product availability and customer service. It also includes managing design changes.

QSR requirements identify various ways to approach this:

- planning
- inputs
- outputs
- review

- verification
- validation
- transfer
- design changes
- Design History File (DHF)

Design control procedures are required, including some specified in the QSR. Each device must have a DHF. This may include all the documents relating to the device's development and should include any change(s) made once the device has been placed on the market and throughout its lifecycle. There should be clear traceability, linking inputs to outputs that demonstrate the input has been achieved. This usually is managed using a trace matrix. These matrices often use databases to ensure clear linkage of the requirements, especially for a complex device. The DHF also will include evidence of the design reviews that took place during the device's development, and key decisions made. The design review must include an independent review by someone not involved in the device's development but with sufficient knowledge to assess the device's safety and effectiveness and ensure the design is appropriate for its intended use. This often occurs at two levels: assessing the device development process and ensuring user and product requirements are met; and, at a management level, assessing the decisions made allowing the device to move from one design control phase to the next. The reviews should consider whether the device is on track to be safe and effective. Often linked to the reviews, the device risk analysis will be revisited to ensure risks remain as expected for the development stage, and no unresolvable new risks have been introduced.

Figure 4-9 demonstrates these linkages. The inputs are the user requirements, which also include regulatory requirements, with the device as part of the output.

Production and Process Control

Production and process control, equipment and facility control and material control cover how the device is manufactured or supplied in a controlled way and all the processes bringing the device to the customer. These include purchasing materials and services, production and manufacturing and device delivery, the facility and calibration and maintenance of equipment used in these processes.

Purchasing

Requirements for purchasing materials or services include identifying, evaluating and managing suppliers.

Supplier management is part of the purchasing process and includes selecting, evaluating and monitoring (re-evaluating) suppliers.

The amount of control required for suppliers depends on the risk and nature of the product or service being supplied, e.g., control over the supply of a catalogue item like a simple chemical will be very different from a critical medical device component. New products or services or a product or service change would need to be considered during the design and development process or change control process.

The Global Harmonization Task Force (GHTF) guidance, GHTF/SG3/N17:2008 *Quality Management Systems—Medical Devices—Guidance on the Control of Products and Services Obtained from Suppliers*, describes the process of establishing controls for products and services obtained from suppliers and includes a process flow detailing more information related to the six phases of working with suppliers throughout a medical device's lifecycle.

Traceability and Identification

Traceability and identification are linked: identifying the materials and equipment used to provide a product or service makes traceability possible. Identification comprises the product lot number or material status.

The QSR documents procedures for identification throughout product realization, from the organization's receipt of materials through finished device delivery and customer use.

The QSR requires an organization to have a documented traceability procedure. Often, organizations have a combined traceability and identification procedure. Where traceability is required, the organization must have a record of the item's identification. The traceability record will need to be maintained for the device's lifetime, and normally the organization's manufacturing system maintains batch records that provide lot identification as required in the DHR.

FDA now requires finished, high-risk medical devices to have unique identification numbers (UDIs).

The facility must be appropriate to maintain the device's quality. When a manufacturing facility is being established, considerations should include:
- how the facility is constructed
- how the equipment is installed
- proper equipment maintenance
- facility cleanliness
- how the product will flow through the facility to ensure segregation
- facility, utilities, equipment and cleaning qualification

- work environment influences on product quality—how the work environment is established, the process equipment used and the personnel working within that environment, relating the work environment to the product, the impact the environment can have on the product and the impact of the health of the employees on the medical device
- equipment and facility calibration and maintenance

Process validation is separate from design validation and demonstrates the manufacturing processes are capable of consistently producing the device. Verification confirms by examination and objective evidence the specified requirements have been fulfilled. Where a process cannot be 100% verified, it has to be validated. Manufacturers validate many processes to maintain high quality without endless testing.

Process validation demonstrates processes' ability to meet the planned results. A validation protocol or plan has to be established and must be approved before starting validation. This protocol or plan must include defined criteria the process must meet for successful validation, including:
- approval of equipment and personnel qualification
- use of specific methods and procedures
- records requirements
- revalidation

A validation master plan is useful in defining the validation approach for a site or product range as well as individual processes. For complex or large systems, a plan can be used to define what processes require validation and what validations will be performed (installation qualification (IQ), operational qualification (OQ), process qualification (PQ) or software). A validation master plan often will include details of the organization's approach to validation, setting out the types of facilities and equipment and the approach to process and test method validation. It will define whether a process is to be validated or verifiedtsand spreadsheets can be used to prioritize the processes and/or equipment requiring revalidation or requalification.

Acceptance activities include incoming, in-process and final activities and acceptance status.

A system is required to accept purchased materials and services and define the type of inspection, testing or checking used to ensure they meet the organization's needs. Labeling must be inspected by designated individuals before release to storage.

The component manufacturing process must ensure the requirements are met. Usually, there also are defined requirements for final acceptance activities. Throughout all these stages, the materials' or device's status has to be clear to ensure only devices meeting requirements are supplied to customers.

During handling, storage, distribution and installation, traceability and identification processes must be maintained, and the product must be stored and handled so its quality, e.g., temperature and sterility, is not affected. All processes, from research to dispatch and label storage, must be designed to prevent mix-ups.

The QSR includes specific requirements for labeling and packaging control. Processes must be in place to ensure labeling integrity (labels and package inserts) is maintained and all labeling can be accounted for fully. Examples of the labels used for each batch must be kept in the DHR. Device packaging must be appropriate to maintain the device's quality during processing and distribution.

QSR vs. ISO 13485

QSR and ISO 13485 requirements are fundamentally the same, so a QMS can fulfill the requirements of both FDA and ISO 13485. ISO 13485 supports implementing QMS systems fulfilling regulatory requirements in many countries, and the QSR establishes US regulatory requirements.

The differences include areas where FDA includes prescriptive requirements for records, documents and labeling. The QSR is used for enforcement purposes. The QSR's purpose is to ensure a medical device will be safe and effective, and its application is a regulatory and legal requirement. This differs from ISO 13485, which is a voluntary standard supporting regulatory requirements in a number of regions, including the EU and Canada.

Some QSR aspects that differ from ISO 13485 are:
- definitions of corrective and preventive action
- defined complaint file requirements
- requirements for specific types of records, including device master record, device history record, quality system record
- requirement for an approved supplier list
- training to handle potential product defects
- enhanced requirements for controlling nonconforming product to prevent inadvertent use
- design transfer requirements
- risk management is mentioned only in the QSR preamble; risk management is expected to be used as it is in an ISO 13485 QMS
- purchasing controls specify consultants as well as other suppliers

FDA does not have access to internal audit reports and management review records, although it can access any CAPA actions resulting from internal audits and management reviews. Manufacturers must show evidence internal audits and management reviews have taken place. This could be from the internal audit schedule and a statement saying the audits have been completed; for management review, it could be a list of attendees and the agenda to show the items discussed. Notified Bodies for CE marking have access to internal audits and management review minutes, which differs from FDA practice.

With the proposed changes to ISO 13485 published in 2015, the two QMS systems' requirements are expected to be more aligned than those in the current published standard.

Vendor Quality Systems

Management of suppliers and their materials or services can affect product quality and services the organization provides to its customers. Without good supplier management of appropriate materials or services, an organization will not be able to deliver its product or services. Supplier management and purchasing controls are emerging topics of interest, and inadequate supplies can result in unintended consequences, some very serious. The manufacturer has the ultimate responsibility and cannot delegate it. Supplier management is of increasing importance, and a systems approach to supplier quality can help reduce unintended consequences. Manufacturers should remember suppliers are an extension of the company's business. Within the medical device industry, subcontractors frequently supply critical components or complete products. In recent years, issues have resulted that point to the need for greater control over subcontractors; counterfeit electronic components and contaminated heparin have been high-profile examples of supplier issues impacting medical device safety. Regulatory expectations for purchasing controls and acceptance have increased due to these issues.

GHTF published *GHTF/SG3/N17:2008 Quality Management Systems—Medical Devices—Guidance on the Control of Products and Services Obtained from Suppliers*, which provides a good basis for any supplier and material or service purchasing control system.

How to Audit Suppliers

The manufacturer should assess potential suppliers' ability to meet selection criteria, which could include various methods, such as a questionnaire or an audit. It is not be possible for any organization to audit all its suppliers, so this is where risk management should be applied, where the evaluation's depth and methods used are related directly to the product or service's risk.

How the Process Differs From Internal and Third-Party Audits

An audit is a systematic, independent, documented process for obtaining evidence and evaluating it objectively to determine the extent to which audit criteria are fulfilled. This definition is taken from ISO 19011: 2011 Clause 3.1. ISO's *Guidelines for auditing quality management systems* is a helpful framework for an organization setting up an internal audit program or conducting supplier audits. It also includes information on third-party audits when an organization is audited by a certification body.

Third-Party Supplier Audits

In certain situations, an organization my hire a third party to conduct supplier audits.

Strategic Considerations and Customizing a QMS

All companies differ in size, maturity, culture, products and many other factors. Following are important QMS considerations for any organization:
- Engage in discussions with the certification body as early as possible to ensure the certification body has the right competency and resources to deliver audits and reviews, and there are no significant issues with QMS plans.
- Ensure the QMS, regulatory projects and design and development activities are resourced adequately and have top management's commitment.
- Personnel involved in the QMS should have relevant, documented background and training. Any gaps can be addressed in training plans.
- The QMS should be the remit of not only the quality department but also should have the involvement, understanding and commitment of staff from virtually every part of the business: quality, regulatory, research and development, engineering, production, sales, marketing, HR, top management and administration.
- There are many documentation and record requirements due to medical devices' high-risk nature. Record retention based on device lifetime also is an important consideration.

- What are the environment and infrastructure considerations to ensure product conforms to requirements and how are these documented?
- Exclusions or non-applications should be documented in the quality manual. Just because a process is outsourced does not mean it can be excluded or not applied in the QMS; it may need to be covered in supplier agreements and audits.
- The company's assignment of responsibilities should be clearly documented, e.g., through an organizational chart and job descriptions.
- The internal audit program should allow all processes to be covered in a reasonable time period. This can be adapted based on the organization's size and particular processes' risk and importance in the QMS.
- Management review frequency and format, like the internal audit program, will depend on the organization's size and maturity. A monthly meeting onsite may be appropriate for a small organization; for a larger organization, each site may dial into a meeting chaired by the corporate site.
- A reasonable amount of objective documented evidence must be in place before the initial audit. Ideally, a batch or lot of medical devices will have undergone the entire production process and be documented (this can be prototype product).

Common mistakes and areas of nonconformities under ISO 13485:2003 include:
- not fulfilling the internal audit schedule or setting unrealistic internal audit plan (8.2.2); the schedule can be adjusted over time if this is documented with a reasonable rationale
- not following up on CAPAs in timely manner (8.5); extending CAPAs for various reasons may be acceptable, but repeatedly missing CAPA deadlines indicates the CAPA process is not effective, and the process may need to be amended and addressed
- not following up on previous audit nonconformities (8.5); again, this indicates an ineffective CAPA process, and the certification body likely will upgrade the nonconformance to a major nonconformance, requiring immediate attention
- not reporting adverse events (8.2, 8.5) often is a major nonconformance due to the manufacturer's failure to fulfill its regulatory obligations
- document/record retention time not based on device lifetime (4.2) when clinical data indicate device lifetime is longer than that defined
- incomplete training records (6.2); no personnel training records verifying individuals are trained and competent for their defined roles and responsibilities
- training effectiveness not verified (6.2) and documented
- CAPA or internal audit findings not verified (8.2, 8.5) and documented
- change process does not contain provisions for informing regulatory authorities or Notified Body of significant changes (7.5)
- changes implemented but not verified and validated (7.5)
- no documented environmental control or condition requirements (6.4)
- product regulatory requirements not considered (7.2), including product-specific standards and requirements
- inadequately defined team roles and responsibilities (7.3)
- no design and development plan (7.3)
- undocumented or poorly defined design inputs and outputs (7.3)
- product placed on market or progressed to design transfer stage before verification and validation completed (7.3)
- process risks not considered in addition to design and clinical risks (7.1)
- no evidence of new or revised regulatory requirements considered in management review (5.6)
- inadequate supplier control in terms of audits, contracts, monitoring and evaluation (7.4)
- limited or no process and product monitoring (8.2)
- instruments calibrated, but with reference materials not calibrated themselves (7.6)
- inadequate segregation or marking of nonconforming product (8.3)
- quality manual does not list and justify non-applicable or excluded clauses (4.2)
- quality objectives not measurable or are inconsistent with quality policy (5.4)
- document changes and approvals or reviews not clear in revised documents (4.2)
- internal auditors not independent from areas being audited (8.2)
- customer property requirements not fulfilled even though the organization retains customer

Figure 4-10. ISO 13485:2016—Potential Timings

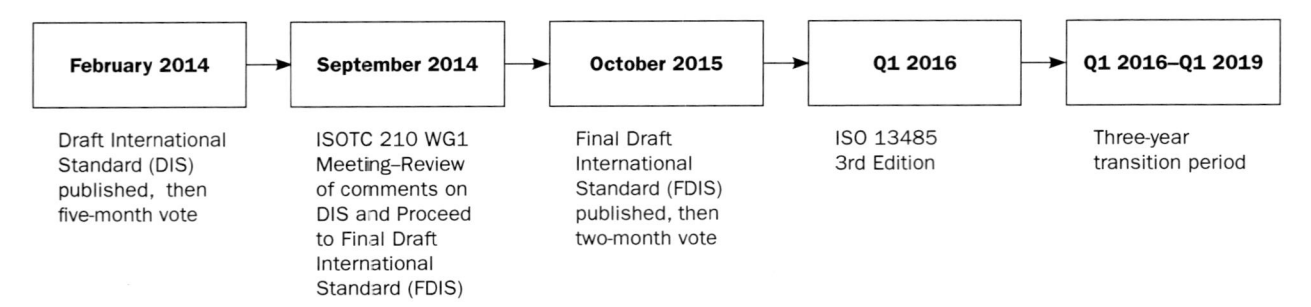

February 2014 → September 2014 → October 2015 → Q1 2016 → Q1 2016–Q1 2019

- **February 2014**: Draft International Standard (DIS) published, then five-month vote
- **September 2014**: ISOTC 210 WG1 Meeting–Review of comments on DIS and Proceed to Final Draft International Standard (FDIS)
- **October 2015**: Final Draft International Standard (FDIS) published, then two-month vote
- **Q1 2016**: ISO 13485 3rd Edition
- **Q1 2016–Q1 2019**: Three-year transition period

property, such as intellectual property, patient records, designs and drawings onsite (7.5)

The Future—ISO 13485:2016

ISO 13485:2016 was published 26 February 2016. The standard has many additions, some new requirements, some expansions and clarifications, and provides increased clarity on the interrelationships among clauses and requirements. There is an increased focus on meeting regulatory requirements and the number of definitions. There also have been changes to sub-clause numbering to facilitate alignment with the Medical Device Single Audit Program (MDSAP).

National regulatory authorities, including US FDA, will have to consider what, if any, the effects of revisions to ISO 13485 will have on their national regulatory schemes.

Significant changes to each auditable clause are summarized below.

QMS

Clause 4 now includes requirements for a risk-based approach when developing QMS processes and documenting organization roles, with regulatory implications for those in the supply chain, such as manufacturers, authorized representatives or distributors. There also are new requirements for keeping records to demonstrate compliance with regulatory requirements and for monitoring and controlling outsourced processes commensurate with risk. A significant addition is a requirement to validate QMS computer software (in addition to software used in the product) prior to initial use and following any changes; this includes software used in production, design and development, testing, inventory control, labeling, distribution, calibration, maintenance, CAPA, data management and complaints handling. Clause 4 now includes a detailed list of the technical documentation contents that could be used to meet regulatory requirements, including product description, classification, preclinical testing, clinical evaluation, user information (e.g., labels and IFU), standards applied and risk management documentation.

Management Responsibility

Clause 5 requires top management to communicate the importance of meeting customer and regulatory requirements within the organization (previously, this was explicitly the management representative's remit). There also is a new requirement to document authorities and responsibilities. Action item identification and implementation to meet quality objectives are required, along with documentation of progress and any revisions. The management representative's liaison with external parties now includes regulatory authorities. Management review frequency and a rationale also should be documented. An additional management review output is improvements needed to respond to new regulatory requirements.

Resources

Clause 6 now specifies organization personnel working at all levels in product quality, process fulfilment, regulatory requirements and QMS compliance shall be competent on the basis of education, training, skills and experience. Staff competence should be maintained, and training effectiveness verification must be commensurate with the risk of the work for which the training is provided. A documented process now is required for staff competence processes.

If maintenance activities can affect product safety or performance, documented procedures must exist for that equipment. Additionally, if the work environment can affect product safety or performance, the organization must document the requirements and have procedures in place for monitoring and measuring the work environment.

Product Realization

Clause 7.1 requires a risk management process be established, with specified criteria for product and product acceptance: verification, validation, revalidation, monitoring, measurement, inspection, test activities, handling storage and traceability. Clause 7.2 requires the organization to determine user training needs and develop provisions for protecting confidential health information. There also is a new clause with requirements on communicating with regulatory authorities.

In addition, the updated standard contains more details on design planning, with an emphasis on decision points and further details on transfer activities (to ensure design outputs have been verified before transfer to production occurs). There are more details on verification and validation (V&V) requirements. V&V activities require a specific plan, with details on methodology, sample sizes and acceptance criteria. The standard also contains a new clause on design transfer, specifying planning activities for suppliers, personnel, materials and equipment. Another new clause relates to file contents for design and development records.

Clause 7.4 contains specific requirements on approving (including planning and evaluating) and monitoring suppliers and maintaining records; a risk-based approach is required (including the extent of purchased product verification).

Clause 7.5 has a number of new requirements and clarifications for implementing defined labeling and packaging operations. Processes that cannot be verified should be validated. There also are specific requirements for packaging validation and planning and documentation. A UDI system is specified if required by relevant regulatory requirements. The standard also contains specific requirements for device packaging and product preservation during distribution.

Measurement, Analysis and Improvement

Clause 8 has a feedback process requirement for risk management and statistical analysis, tools and techniques to be used in determining the need for feedback data to be escalated into CAPA. This clause also contains further details on minimum complaint handling requirements. There is a new requirement for equipment and personnel to be identified and recorded for product monitoring. The standard contains more detailed nonconforming product requirements, depending on whether the nonconformity was detected before or after delivery, and considerations for escalating to CAPA. Corrective actions should be commensurate with the risk and taken without undue delay. Process and product data should be reviewed to identify inputs to the CAPA process. Analysis should be an input to management review.

In summary, the revised standard contains emphasis and new requirements on:
- regulatory requirements emphasized throughout the standard at all levels of the organization and product lifecycle
- risk management used throughout the standard, with actions and decisions commensurate with risk
- planning activities required for more processes
- additional design verification, validation and transfer requirements
- more-detailed requirements on outsourced processes and supplier control
- feedback analyzed statistically to determine escalation to CAPA
- additional nonconforming product requirements and CAPA escalation considerations
- specific design and development file contents and technical documentation

5 Strategy for Risk Management in the Device Design and Development Process

By Susan R. Hibbeln and Tony C. Chan, DRSc, MBA, MSQA

Introduction

Medical device design and development face many changes, challenges and opportunities. A new world of potential threats from information insecurity, technological integration and regulatory convergence are realities a device company should strategize to overcome and should overcome to thrive.

Medical devices using advanced information technology have become an integral part of modern society. Some of these amazing healthcare technologies have become realities, but they also have introduced a new world of risks once thought as implausible as Hollywood fiction. For example, hacking into electronic pacemakers or insulin pumps from a few hundred feet away has shown practical and possible fatal acts of intentional harm to those in positions with local, national or global responsibilities. These smart medical technologies expose a new world of risk not just to patients or users but also to the innovative companies creating these products, through legal, regulatory, liability and financial risks. Professional liability insurers have focused on financial losses passed on to the innovators. Regulatory agencies are moving rapidly to implement new regulations to control these new medical technologies. Devices like medical device data systems (MDDS), mobile medical applications and various types of electronic health record (EHR) systems that may or may not connect with other medical device software have been a hot topic over the last several years for many regulators concerned about these devices' continual safety and effectiveness, cybersecurity and data integrity.

Another potential challenge is technological integration driven by the constraints of cost pressures, patient and user demands, population aging and technological advances. To combat this, different medical technology industry sectors are integrating their strengths to deliver economical, easy-to-use and prompt responses to medical solutions. According to the Drug Information Association (DIA), an estimated 30% of all new healthcare products under development today are combination products. The technological convergence of combination products presents many challenges to be overcome to ensure the innovations are both safe and effective. Thus, regulatory agencies such as the US Food and Drug Administration (FDA), European Medicines Agency (EMA) and others are gearing up new regulatory approaches to address developments in the emerging combination products market.

Regulatory agencies need to develop a comprehensive understanding of these technologies and how they are integrated, whereas medical product manufacturers need to take a proactive approach to working with the agencies on premarket reviews, clearances and submissions. In addition, as attractive as the rewards might be, making technological convergence successful is easier said than done. Success relies on making sure all the risks that come with the convergence opportunity are mitigated or minimized. Among these risks, not only should the technological risks be addressed, but the organizational and human aspects also should not be overlooked. Often, the growing demand for a product creates partnerships between or among companies. When coming together, these companies should address knowledge sharing and team building. Trust and respect become major difficulties in bringing together the different parties' various viewpoints, practices and experiences. These ventures' successes depend on the level and intensity of collaboration and risk mitigation from all involved parties. The regulatory professional acts as a liaison among these groups and communicates directly with the regulatory agency. It is important for this individual to understand the product, team, partners, regulators, competition and any gaps to communicate appropriately and provide strategic guidance to all parties.

The third challenge is the recent development of regulatory convergence. Since 2007, the US and EU have been constructing a market of more than 800 million people with converging regulatory schemes. They plan to set a benchmark for the global market through the Transatlantic Economic Council (TEC). The TEC aims to achieve "increased regulatory co-operation." Both sides agreed the convergence of new technology regulations should be backed by "a science-based approach," and product deployment should be based on "risk assessment."

In April 2013, a joint US-EU industry trade group, represented by the Advanced Medical Technology Association (AdvaMed),[1] European Coordination Committee of the Radiological, Electromedical and Healthcare IT Industry (COCIR),[2] European Medical Technology Industry Association (Eucomed),[3] European Diagnostic Manufacturers Association (EDMA)[4] and Medical Imaging & Technology Alliance (MITA),[5] initiated three priorities (these have been promoted to the International Medical Device Regulators Forum (IMDRF)) for the medical technology sector:
1. single audit of medical technology manufacturer quality management systems
2. single harmonized standard for marketing application format
3. unique device identification

While the first two priorities offer potential opportunities to streamline compliance and product submissions, all the business risks may be concentrated in one basket and not diversified as necessary for local markets. In a global company, design and development teams tend to diagnose risks globally and simultaneously. Depending on local standards, the product itself, its classification in various markets, its integration with other devices and non-devices (and their classifications in various markets) and local standards, the regulatory professional must remember and communicate the impracticality of a complete one-size-fits-all approach to the global marketplace. The last priority, now officially implemented for certain products on the US market, will need to be followed closely as it is introduced to other global jurisdictions. The uncertainty as to how this initiative will be adopted in other key jurisdictions may pose a global risk if an incident occurs.

The use of a risk management approach to address these emerging risks as early as possible can be essential for a device manufacturer not only to survive but also to thrive. Further, a fully integrated risk management strategy should address both the threats and opportunities present throughout the entire product and business cycle. Consequently, successful implementation of such a strategy can neutralize the significant constraints and pressures posed by technological challenges and regulatory convergence, allowing a company to achieve maximum business potential. It, therefore, is important for a medical device company to address these risks as early as possible, i.e., by utilizing a total lifecycle approach during a medical device's design and development stage.

A Strategic Approach to Meet Challenges—Total Lifecycle Risk Management for Design and Development Using Recognized Standards and Harmonized Guidance

Until 1996, the primary tool for ensuring product safety was the regulation requiring Good Manufacturing Practices (GMP). In the mid-to-late 1980s, it became apparent that such an approach had limitations. FDA discovered more than 40% of medical device postmarket product problems came from design flaws rather than manufacturing issues.[6] These design problems were one of several reasons a new regulation, 21 CFR 820—Quality Systems Regulations, was published 7 October 1996, embracing a design control strategy with a broader focus on the whole product lifecycle.[7]

One of the stipulations of FDA's current Quality System Regulation (QSR) is a requirement for risk analysis. A specific comment (#83) in the regulation's preamble further identifies the need to perform risk analysis according to ISO's 14971-1 standard,[8] *Application of Risk Analysis to Medical Devices*.[9] The preamble also states medical device manufacturers should update their systems as this particular risk-related standard evolves over time.[10] As of 9 March 2010, a second edition of the ISO 14971 Standard, ISO 14971:2007, was adopted.[11] The standard was further enhanced in 2012 and since has been adopted by industry. As part of this standard, regulatory expectations have evolved, so the standard no longer focuses on risk assessment but rather embraces a wider system of risk management for the entire product lifecycle.[12] In related news, the ISO committee on quality management and corresponding general aspects for medical devices—TC 210—has finalized another revision of the Quality Management System standard for medical devices in early 2016. Medical device companies will be required to implement a risk-based Quality Management System (ISO 13485, Section 4.1.2).[13] This is not a new requirement in the US and is consistent with the FDA's QSR.

It is challenging for companies to move to a comprehensive, action-oriented and problem-solving risk management system from a simple analysis program. Since 1996, regulatory expectations in managing medical device risks throughout the product lifecycle have increased significantly. It is evidenced by the aforementioned need for risk management during the design and development phase.[14] The company also is expected to integrate risk management into the quality management system[15] and, in addition, into such activities as outsourcing[16] and corrective and preventive actions (CAPA).[17]

Therefore, it is not clear what constitutes "usual practice" or "best practice" for risk management across a spectrum of companies. In addition, the recognized and harmonized EN/ISO 14971 standard has provided the framework for acceptable industry practice for more than 10 years, a long enough period for companies to develop reasonably mature practices and operational experience. However, there is not a systematic approach to understanding what methods are used to conduct risk management activities, what issues are most problematic in achieving good results or what elements not captured by the ISO standard framework, which can impact the company's success in avoiding safety problems with the products it produces.[18]

Device Design and Development—Planning for a Global Strategy

"There is no longer any sustainable competitive advantage to be gained through technology, but only through making better judgments on whether each opportunity has the right amount of risk, neither too much nor too little."[19,20]

This quote on technology applies well to medical device design and development, particularly in a global market with a multi-national supply chain. It would be unusual for a medical device company not to consider the risks of globalization when designing and developing its products. When a company begins working with partners that do not share the same culture or language and are oceans apart and, in many cases, have completely different motivations, potential risks and opportunities for misunderstanding are high.

The 2012 Axendia Medical Technology Globalization Report[21,22] summarized executive management concerns as follows:
- intellectual property protection
- product, raw material or service quality
- product, raw material or service delivery as promised (on-time and within budget)
- maintaining consistent quality standards across internal and external sites
- changes without corporate/executive approval
- product theft, diversion or counterfeiting
- inadequate visibility into in-process parametric quality information
- outsourcing partners becoming competitors

Axendia's report recommends medical technology companies consider the three following major issues when managing the new globalization "normal:"
1. holistic governance, risk management and compliance
   Medical technology companies should be concerned about holistic governance, risk management and compliance, from receiving initial regulatory marketing approval throughout the product lifecycle to maintain consistent value chain quality standards and ensure device safety and effectiveness.
2. enhanced visibility
   Medical technology companies should be able to obtain relevant information about the product at the appropriate time to enable decisions with a high degree of confidence based on contemporary data analysis.
3. improved collaboration
   Medical technology companies should demand full collaboration from international partners. Cross-continental partnerships require working effectively in groups (internal and external) as peers with mutually shared accountability. Companies should implement commands and controls to overcome global and outsourced environment barriers.

These are not the only issues to which medical device companies need to pay attention in a globalized business environment. The convergence of information technology, communication technology and Internet capabilities has given rise to a new information communication technology (ICT) industry. In addition, the pharmaceutical technology, biological technology and medical technology industries—the life science industries—have converged and created a new breed of hybrid products: combination

Table 5-1. Risk Mitigation Strategies

Risk	Mitigation Strategy
Vendor reliability	Develop specific contractual agreements, or assess and approve more than one vendor
Material shortages	Increase stock of materials during prototype build
Equipment issues	Maintenance and repair program/back-up approved equipment
Employee turnover or illness	Mentoring and back-up systems at company

medical products. These technological convergences add to not only device design and development process complexity but also to the acceleration of looming changes when regulatory and compliance expectations are ever increasing.

Medical technology advances have expedited the combining of product types in the medical technology industry. These are combinations of device-drug, device-biologic or drug-biologic products providing therapeutic or diagnostic utilities to patients or caregivers. A single definitive product risk assessment type cannot apply to combination products. Because combination products involve components regulated under different regulatory schemes and authorities, risk assessment approaches and documentation can impact regulatory processes in all aspects of product design and development.

Moreover, regulatory strategy must align with the organization's overall strategy. Planning is required not only as part of design and development controls but also is a necessity for businesses to function. Creating the project team is one part of planning, but strategic planning goes beyond the project team. Good advice on tackling project risks includes but is not limited to:
- risk identification and prioritization
- risk mitigation
- risk trigger point determination
- contingency plans[23]

Risk identification and prioritization involve the risk itself, how quickly the risk could occur and whether the risk actually will occur. For example, the design team needs to have prototypes ready for biocompatibility testing by a specific date. Some risks that could prevent on-time delivery of the prototypes are vendor reliability, material shortages, equipment issues or even employee turnover or illness. Risk mitigation involves the steps taken to prevent the risk from occurring. A formal risk mitigation strategy with assigned responsibilities can help teams avoid a crisis situation. To use the same example of prototype biocompatibility testing, a team might consider the mitigation strategies in **Table 5-1.**

The trigger point is when despite the risk identification, prioritization and mitigation strategy, the team knows the risk is going to occur and needs to act. The contingency plan is the action taken when a risk cannot be avoided. For example, the design team experiences a trigger point when an act of nature, like a tornado or hurricane, shuts down the project team's approved strategic supplier. In this example, the design team approved a secondary vendor during risk mitigation strategy activities. The contingency plan is now to get that secondary vendor up and running as soon as possible to ensure the design team still meets its testing due date.

Anticipating and combating business risks is a necessary part of global strategic planning. These four steps need to be reviewed and repeated throughout the project lifecycle and updated as new information arises.

Medical device companies also should embrace comprehensive total lifecycle planning to keep current and manage not only technical risks but also regulatory and other risks during the device design and development process that encompasses preclinical testing, clinical investigation, marketing applications, manufacturing, quality assurance, adverse reporting, promotion, advertising and postapproval changes. This planning should occur as early as possible and evolve during product design and development. The Association for Strategic Planning reported "strategic planning has high impact on overall organization success." For example, project teams might think they are developing a strategic worldwide commercial product launch plan. The regulatory professional knows there is no worldwide submission and must guide the project team to understand a practical launch plan that aligns with business objectives. The term "worldwide" has many layers in requirements, language barriers, registration lead-times and critical markets.

Benefits of early risk management planning are many, including predetermined risk responses and mitigation strategies, fast responses to incidents and contingency, understanding of interdependencies through early communications, etc. See the section on Risk Analysis in Design Control for a few commonly and globally acceptable models of risk management. Following these models, medical device companies should consult and plan according to their own needs and resources.

Device Design Requirements—Safe and Effective Design in a Global Convergent Environment

For a medical device company to claim its products are safe and effective, full comprehension of user needs, clear articulation of the device's intended uses, concise delineation of design requirements and thorough determination of design specifications are indispensable. The company should record its earliest efforts in designing and developing its products. These records can appear in formal documents capturing the rationale and interpretation methods for all or any combinations of its customers', patients' and users' needs and wants. These needs and wants (e.g., the device should be portable) are translated into design requirements (e.g., a device hand-held by the intended users—age 16 and above) and then formal design specifications (e.g., 4" x 6" x ¼" in dimensions and 4 oz. in weight), providing standards for accurate and consistent fabrication.

However, there are many challenges in understanding user needs, articulating intended use, delineating concise requirements and creating thorough specifications in a global convergent environment. A few examples of the particular challenges for designers addressing the ergonomic needs of users include accommodating left-handed and right-handed use, reading from the right and left, inverted digital display issues, etc.

Design requirement delineation from user needs and wants is particularly important in technologies used to design and develop nonprofessional use devices, i.e., self-help or self-care (without the help of a professional caretaker); for example, home-use medical devices. These requirements should be scrutinized extensively in areas related to social, physical and technical environments.[24,25] These environments shape risks for tasks and demonstrate ways self-care devices can be mi-used. These risks' complexities should be addressed considering the additional dimension of cultural differences in various markets around the world. Therefore, global medical device companies not only should understand but also should articulate a device's intended use well, delineate design requirements precisely, fabricate accurately according to specifications and assure the technology's safe and effective use by nonprofessionals in various markets early in the design and development process. A later section in this chapter discusses human factors, ergonomic design and medical device usability in more detail.

Therefore, fully comprehending user needs, clearly articulating product intended use, precisely delineating design requirements and creating thorough product specifications helps a device company provide evidence supporting its claims the product as manufactured is safe and effective for its intended use.

Design and development efforts can continue through evidence collection during verification and validation activities after a prototype (pilot design) is fabricated according to product specifications.

Device Verification and Validation—Safety and Effectiveness Demonstrations in a World of New Risks

The merging of new and existing technologies, product types and global regulations create many new risks for medical device companies. These challenges require nontraditional and outside-the-box practices to determine and implement countermeasures. Traditional verification and validation strategies alone may not be comprehensive enough to face these challenges. For example, instead of testing a pilot design to its specifications in the traditional approach, test it to its extremities and look for hardware and software failures and vulnerabilities, which can be beneficial in understanding product behaviors and user environments to prevent hazards and accidents early in design and development. Traditional verification and validation approaches may be too late and too expensive for corrective and improvement actions.

Moreover, a level of confidence should be achieved to demonstrate user fee fulfillment without safety concerns through the actual use environment or clinical assessments, including a comprehensive usability risk study. The collected data quality and quantity may be categorized, stratified and codified from all clinical assessments.[26,27] The cumulative data could provide valuable information for analyses when future incidents occur. A medical device company should establish a risk information system to record and retain codified incident information[28,29] before any verification and validation activities begin. A well-established risk information system could close the loop for the entire device design and development lifecycle and also provide valuable assistance in all other device surveillance efforts.

Another area of concern is the verification and validation strategic focus. A medical device company should avoid confirmation bias and compliance-only exercises[30] when conducting verification and validation activities. These activities should emphasize not only demonstrating the device is safe, but instead showing it is unsafe.[31,32] Because design engineers already have made sure the design is safe and effective, it usually is the quality or reliability engineers' job to challenge the design. A mindset independent from the designers is necessary to find safety

Figure 5-1. FDA's View on Managing Pre- and Postmarket Product Risks

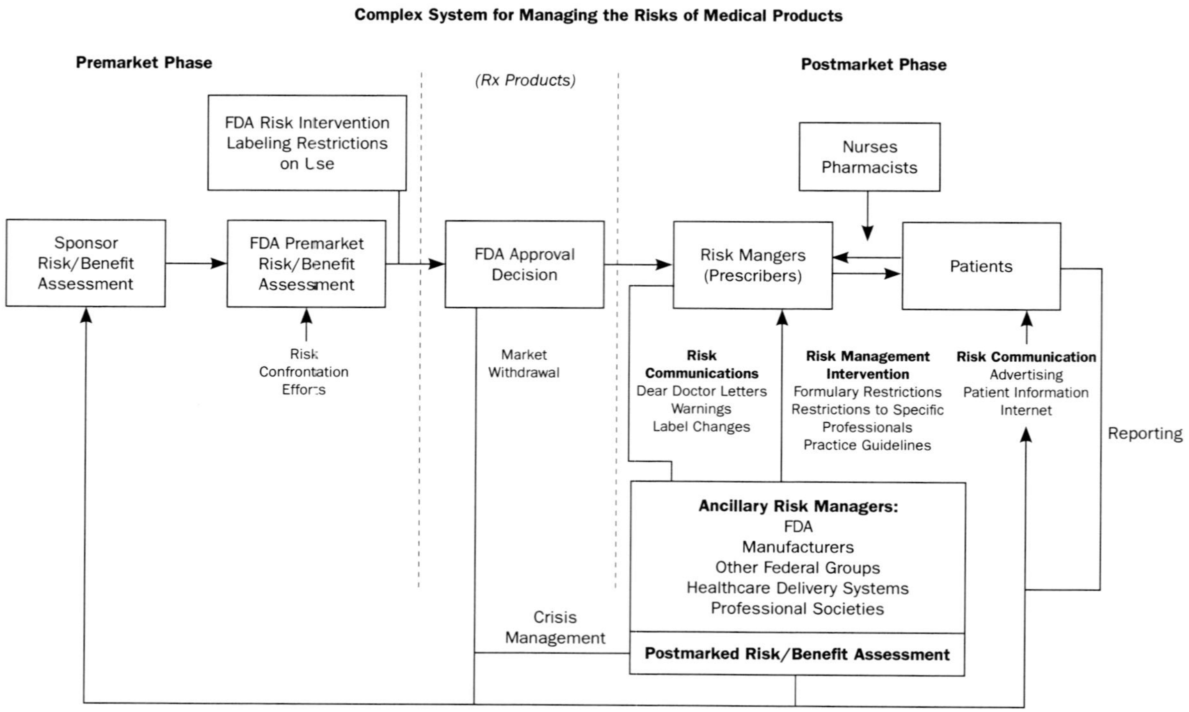

Complex System for Managing the Risks of Medical Products

Source: US Department of Health and Human Services, Managing the Risks From Medical Product Use

faults and ineffective performances. This demonstration strategy can elevate the product to a higher level of safety and effectiveness assurance and to a practicable reality level. To achieve this reality level, verification and validation should predict the unpredictable and prevent the unpreventable events traditional approaches that would not have been precipitated.

The verification and validation strategies should include:

- These activities are useful only if they can influence design decisions. Therefore, they should be conducted as early as possible in the design and development process.
- Design and operating environment changes, drift or creep should be analyzed, understood, remedied and documented.
- These activities should not be a one-time effort but should continue throughout the product lifetime; particularly when design changes occur.
- As changes occur, hazard and safety analyses should be revisited from a system perspective and not in a silo.

- All analyses should consider worst cases, not just the likely or expected cases, because accidents and incidents can occur beyond normal operations or unexpected situations.
- Analyses should be comprehensive. They should include not just device failures and operator errors but also management structure and decision making. The entire system of operation involves both device and human interaction behaviors and capabilities.
- Qualitative and verifiable quantitative information should be used, not just probabilistic system models. Subject matter experts should be consulted and involved in product evaluations and reviews.
- An integrated system should be considered, not just isolated consideration of a hazard or component.
- Personnel involved should be experienced and qualified. They should accept responsibilities and have appropriate authorities. One or more independent observers or experts will add value to these activities by challenging not only the

Figure 5-2. FDA's Role in Medical Product Risk Management

FDA Role in Medical Products Risk Management
(Rx Products)

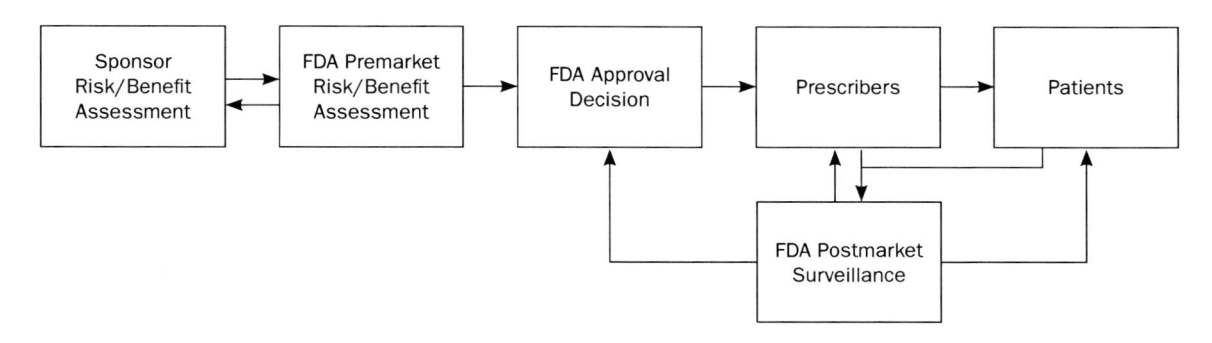

Sponsor Risk/Benefit Assessment → FDA Premarket Risk/Benefit Assessment → FDA Approval Decision → Prescribers → Patients; FDA Postmarket Surveillance feeds back to FDA Approval Decision, Prescribers, and Patients.

Source: US Department of Health and Human Services, Managing the Risks From Medical Product Use

product's technical aspects but also the potential blindness of group thought.

Safety and effectiveness should be designed into the device at the beginning of the design and development process and not become the subject of an argument at the end of the verification and validation process. Objective scientific evidence should support those arguments and conclude the previously declared claims and the discovery of unsafe and ineffective scenarios are demonstrated and properly managed during the design and development process and proven at the verification and validation stages. Comprehensive safety and effectiveness demonstrations require hazard and accident analyses and control plans showing how hazards and accidents are identified, considered and mitigated, i.e., prevented, eliminated or controlled. The process should include documenting the limitations of what was done and the uncertainties and assumptions underlying hazard and accident analyses and procedures used. Efforts should not be just for the sake of analyses but should focus on how risks should be managed continuously.

Device Risk Analysis From Design Control to Global Engagement

In a world of growing convergences, the demand for safe and effective use of medical devices has neither relaxed nor remained at the status quo but is becoming an ever-pressing priority. Moreover, the rise of emerging markets and the increased flow of information have led to the growing complexity of regulations. The consequence of these trends is not only phenomenal growth of opportunities in the medical device sector but also rapid increase of risks, including legal, regulatory, liability, and financial, and their impacts to a device company. Globally sourced materials flowing through multiple steps of the product design and development processes and converted into finished devices have made it difficult for device companies to ensure all players along the supply chain fulfill their safety and effectiveness promises. These compromised contracts can lead to more sophisticated threats of fraud, product adulteration and even terrorism. A simple and straightforward product risk analysis (e.g., using a single tool such as Failure Modes and Effects Analysis to address risks) in design control will not be sufficient for the sustainable survival of a medical device company.

A medical device company cannot disengage due to the rising pressure to lower costs, improve productivity and increase efficiency while global engagement poses all the aforementioned risks. A medical device company must implement a comprehensive risk management approach that covers the entire product design and development lifecycle and is integrated with other business operations.

Before a medical device company implements a risk management plan, it is beneficial to explore risk management frameworks that express the thinking and expectations of regulatory agencies. The US Food and Drug Administration (US FDA) formed a committee that issues a report titled "Managing the Risks From Medical Product Use,"[33] suggesting the need for a systemic framework to structure the risk management of medical products. **Figure 5-1** shows this framework and indicates how various stakeholders should be involved in managing medical product risks.

The report also describes the roles of all participants in the medical product development lifecycle and delivery system (**Figure 5-2**). The ultimate aim of clearly defined

Figure 5-3. Framework for Environmental Health Risk Management

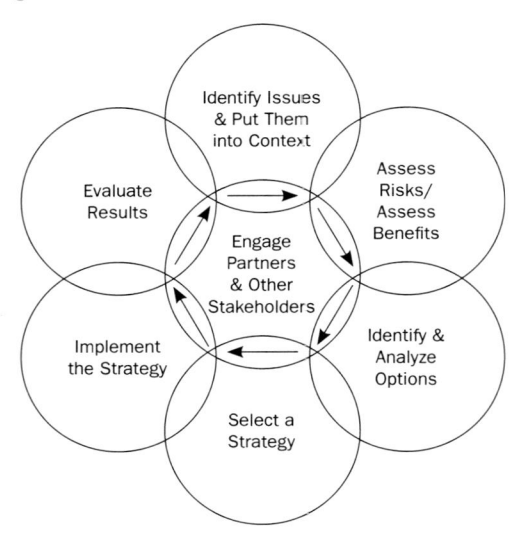

roles was seen to maximize benefit and minimize risk. Every participant in this process would have a clearly defined role and a shared responsibility to safeguard a threshold in which benefits outweighed risk. This goal was to be achieved by ensuring medical products were evaluated for risk throughout their lifecycles to improve patient health, i.e., through development, testing, manufacturing, labeling, prescribing, dispensing and usage.[34]

An original comprehensive risk management framework related to public health, authored by the US National Research Council, contributed to the 1997 report of the US Presidential/Congressional Commission on Risk Assessment and Risk Management. This framework emphasizes a dynamic risk communication process involving the ongoing engagement of stakeholders, whereas ISO 14971 is the medical device-specific risk management framework used to identify hazards, estimate and evaluate risks and establish risk control measures, including design, production and post-production risks. The process was named "The Commission's Framework for Environmental Health Risk Management."

The framework developed by the Presidential Commission, illustrated in **Figure 5-3**, was designed to help all types of risk managers, including government officials, individuals employed by private sector businesses and members of the public, make good risk management decisions when dealing with any type of environmental health risk. This framework is broad enough to apply to many situations, including those in which the degree of effort could be scaled to the importance of the problem, and can be used to evaluate the potential severity and economic impact of the risk, the level of controversy surrounding the risk and resource constraints. The framework is intended primarily for risk decisions related to setting standards, controlling pollution, protecting health and cleaning up the environment. However, it is generally applicable to medical device companies' risk decisions. Three key principles are important for the successful implementation of this framework:

1. adopting a broad context for risk assessment instead of evaluating single risks associated with single agents in a single environmental medium
2. involving stakeholders at all phases of the process
3. adopting an iterative approach, so that any new information or perspectives that may emerge are taken into account by revisiting early stages of the process

The development of these frameworks and associated principles and guidelines has brought an element of clarity to the field of risk assessment and risk management. Risk management principles can be of value in assigning priorities to important risk issues competing for attention and resources, in reaching decisions in the face of scientific uncertainty about the level of risk associated with health hazards, in balancing benefits and risks and in acknowledging social and cultural considerations in risk management.[35] Without such guidance, risk management decision-making can be highly complex, raising difficult questions to which there are often no easy answers.[36]

To assist in the development of a more specific framework for medical device risk management, many risk managers looked both to FDA and international organizations, particularly to standard-setting bodies such as the International Organization for Standardization and the International Medical Device Regulators Forum (successor to the Global Harmonization Task Force).

A medical device company needs to determine an appropriate model of risk management. The following additional frameworks are widely accepted and available for reference:

- International Convention on Harmonization ICH Q9 Harmonized Tripartite Guideline – Quality Risk Management[37]
  This is a document providing guidance on the principles and some of the tools of quality risk management that can enable more effective and consistent risk-based decisions, by both regulators and industry, regarding the quality of drug substances and drug products across the product lifecycle. This guidance is not intended to create any new expectations beyond the current regulatory requirements.

- International Organization for Standardization
  ISO 31000 Risk Management – Principles and Guidelines[38]
  This International Standard recommends that organizations develop, implement and continuously improve a framework whose purpose is to integrate the process for managing risk into the organization's overall governance, strategy and planning, management, reporting processes, policies, values and culture. It provides the principles and guidelines for managing any form of risk in a systematic, transparent and credible manner and within any scope and context.
- International Electrotechnical Commission
  IEC 80001-1:2010 Application of Risk Management for IT-Networks Incorporating Medical Devices[39]
  Recognizing that some medical devices are incorporated into IT-networks to achieve desirable benefits (e.g., interoperability), this international standard defines the roles, responsibilities and activities that are necessary for risk management of IT-networks incorporating medical devices to address safety, effectiveness and data and system security.
- Committee of Sponsoring Organizations of the Treadway Commission
  COSO Enterprise Risk Management—Integrated Framework[40]
  COSO introduces a framework that is usable by management to evaluate and improve an organization's enterprise risk management. It provides key principles and concepts, a common language and clear direction and guidance to satisfy an organization's internal control needs and emphasizes a move toward a fuller risk management process that encompasses all the operational aspects of an enterprise.

Assessment of Human Factors in Medical Device Design and Use

Murphy's Original Law
If there are two or more ways to do something, and one of those ways can result in a catastrophe, then someone will do it.

Murphy's Law
If anything can go wrong—it will.

Murphy's First Corollary
Left to themselves, things tend to go from bad to worse.

Murphy's Second Corollary
It is impossible to make anything foolproof because fools are so ingenious.

Quantized Revision of Murphy's Law
Everything goes wrong all at once.

Murphy's Constant
Matter will be damaged in direct proportion to its value.

The Murphy Philosophy
Smile...tomorrow will be worse.[41]

Murphy simplifies why consideration of both human factors and medical device usability testing are so important. Human factors' assessment occurs throughout the product lifecycle but is most visible during design controls, risk management, verification and validation, user feedback and design change control. According to ISO 14971, risk management is a process to analyze, evaluate, control and monitor risks systematically; usability engineering considers, assesses and mitigates risks associated with human factors.[42]

When usability testing is performed during design, usability test engineers may discover use issues prior to release of a device on the market. As a result, the use issue then can run through the risk management process to determine next steps, such as design changes. When no usability testing is performed, there is a greater risk of postmarket use error that could lead to complaints or recalls, legal issues, severe injuries or even loss of life.[43,44] Thus, integrating risk management and usability testing during the development process can result in better controlling potential risks that otherwise could go unidentified.

Medical device use error's potential risk increases across different cultures and languages. During the design and development process, the risk management team might analyze labeling translation's potential risk. For example, the instructions for use labeling for a device to be used in South America contained a translation error. The Spanish version read "Es imposibe," (It is impossible), while the correct English instructions, "It is possible" is the complete opposite. Using this same example, the usability team, however, would look at how the user interprets the correct instructions, and whether any issues result from the direction of "it is possible" in the instructions for use regardless of language.

Device labeling is integral to medical devices' correct and safe use. Thus, design teams must include human factors when creating and validating device labeling. It is essential they consider impacts and interactions arising from how, who, where, with what and why devices will be used. When a physician interprets a laboratory test result, manufacturers must ensure the physician can interpret the test the same way as a laboratory professional. If a nurse receives an alert on a mobile device from a patient monitoring device, manufacturers must consider the user interactions with monitoring and mobile devices. For example, what happens to the medical mobile application when the mobile device's manufacturer has a software update?

FDA has the comprehensive guidance on human factors,[45] which should be consulted for US strategies and can be helpful for global strategies. Two of these guidance documents, *Human Factors Principles for Medical Device Labeling*[46] and *Write It Right, Recommendations for Developing User Instruction Manuals for Medical Devices Used in Home Health Care*,[47] are helpful in creating and validating device labeling in various use settings. In addition, two standards, *ANSI/AAMI HE75 Human Factors Engineering—Design of Medical Devices*[48] and *IEC 62366-1 Medical Devices—Application of Usability Engineering to Medical Devices*, focus on human factors engineering throughout the device lifecycle.

As the main purpose of device regulation is to ensure medical devices' safe and effective use, human factors are an essential part of design and development risk management. Even those requirements can cause confusion in different markets. For example, Universal Laboratories (UL) recently notified manufacturers that safety, warning and caution language must be bilingual for devices in Canada.[49] It is not enough just to implement the requirement. This requirement's impact on users in Canada and other cultures now must be assessed. Will French and English language be confusing in Spanish-speaking countries? Should other language's markings be added? Will the additional markings cause more clutter and result in a label unreadable by end users? Does the manufacturer need to customize labels by country? How does customization impact the device master record? Could customization lead to manufacturing errors and subsequent use errors? These are just some of many questions related to human factors needing to be answered during the design and development process and throughout the device's lifecycle.

Today, globalization, ever-changing technology, increased automation, software and systems' interaction and professional use settings' expansion like point-of-care (POC) have increased challenges associated with human factors. Thorough risk management and usability validation go hand-in-hand and are an essential part of successful device design and development, which must continue throughout a device's lifecycle.

Managing Design Transfer for Global Product Launches

Managing design transfer in one region is complicated enough. The complexity increases exponentially when planning for a global product launch. According to the US FDA QSR preamble, design transfer occurs when the device "properly performs according to the intended use and user needs." Depending on the region or culture, the interpretation of intended use and user needs can be different. Teams must plan carefully and coordinate global design transfer activities. Risk management and standards may result in less-stringent testing than dictated by certain regulatory authorities. For example, a company initiates packaging studies based on risk management, packaging materials' history and current industry standards. While some countries accept this test methodology, others want additional testing requiring delay in design transfer. Still other countries may insist on performing their own testing to validate the intended use and claims. Or, they may rely on specific country approvals before allowing the device in their own country.[50]

Despite the best intentions, global transfer activities can be impacted by unforeseen events like FDA shutdowns.[51] What happens when FDA closes, and other jurisdictions are waiting on a certificate to foreign government (CFG) before allowing the product in their markets? Some countries require specific translated information outside global labeling standards on systems and instruments. A requirement like this can impact a global launch greatly if there is only one product configuration. One design project may have multiple launches, as claims, test studies, translations, unforeseen events and other project steps are finalized.

Like other project design phases, global design transfer includes having the right people at the right place at the right time. There is much more to design transfer than handing over specifications to manufacturing and marking a design transfer checklist. A US company cannot expect to transfer a design project to gain approval in Australia if the project only delivers FDA requirements and does not consider Australian Therapeutic Goods Administration (TGA) requirements. For effective design transfer, manufacturing and design team members need to communicate early and throughout the design phases and design transfer.[52]

Multi-Jurisdictional Product Technical File

As more countries formalize medical device regulations, international regulatory and quality systems professionals must refine their internal processes continuously for developing and registering medical device products. Tailoring the medical device submission to each specific country's requirements can be a complicated process and is becoming more complicated. Global companies trying to market products in regions as diverse as Brazil, Canada, Europe and the US may have to undergo four separate quality system audits and may have to create four different submission packages before being allowed to sell one product in these countries. Providing clear scientific communication to a multitude of health authorities is critical in obtaining timely market approvals. When compiling a global technical file, a team must anticipate questions from various regulators carefully and prepare documented evidence with credible arguments supporting a product approval decision. Overall, the goal of a multi-jurisdictional technical file is to convince regulatory authorities and other stakeholders a product is safe and effective and complies with relevant regulatory requirements. To do this, a project team must present arguments with accurate scientific conclusions based on evidence. It is difficult to do this without performing risk management throughout product design and development. For example, a company is designing two medical devices with different marketing scopes. One country may have fewer regulatory requirements than another. The project team cannot look at country requirements alone. The team must balance the country requirements with risk management conclusions to ensure the device's safety and intended use.

Failure is the Mother of Success— Lessons Learned From Risk Management Failure

"Failure is the Mother of Success."—A Chinese Proverb

Having a framework to analyze risk is not always sufficient to ensure no problems occur. Much can be learned about current risk management approaches' limitations and challenges by looking at recent history, when hazards were managed inadequately and resulted in serious negative outcomes despite the presence of a seemingly robust risk management system. To gain insight into other risk management aspects that also might be important to a risk management program's success, learning why risk management failed and what other elements or attributes would have led to a successful program is indispensable.

Conclusion

"Experience: that most brutal of teachers. But you learn…"
—*C. S. Lewis*

This chapter has explored important risk management system elements and proposed the following strategies for meeting the design and development challenges a medical device company faces.

Enabling Technological Integration

Not only should technological risks be addressed; but organizational and human aspects should also not be overlooked. Rely on traditional practices as might be appropriate, and search for new ideas like a total lifecycle program and a proactive approach with regulators to predict the unpredictable and prevent unpreventable events that would not have been detected by existing or current approaches.

Enacting Convergence of Global Regulatory Expectations

Fulfillment should be backed by "a science-based approach," and product deployment should be based on "risk assessment."

1. Operating principles should be accepted globally or based on harmonized and recognized standards and practices, such as the Common Submission Dossier Template (CSDT), Summary Technical Documentation (STED), Regulated Product Submission (RPS), etc.

Engaging Emerging Markets—The New Normal of Globalization

1. Establish integrity governance to manage corporate risks and compliance.
2. Acquire timely access to information and trustworthy partnerships.

Enhancing Safe and Effective Design in a Global Convergent Environment

1. Begin with full comprehension of user needs, clear articulation of product claims and intended uses, concise delineation of design requirements and thorough determination of design specifications.
2. Emphasize not only demonstrating the device's safety but also understanding worst-case scenarios.
3. Establish hazard and accident analyses and control plans to show how hazards and accidents are identified, considered and mitigated.

4. Establish a risk information system that closes the loop of the entire device design and development lifecycle to provide valuable assistance to all device surveillance efforts.

Embracing Risk Management at the Root Level

1. Learn from others' failure experiences.
2. Avoid confirmation bias and compliance-only exercises.

As a key interface with teams, executives, partners and regulators, the strategic regulatory professional must guide, instruct, lead and build relationships continually to foster an organizational culture beyond minimal compliance while pioneering methods to meet business and regulatory objectives.

A medical device company's survival in an era of technology, product and regulatory convergences may not favor the focus on the "how-to's" of medical device design, design control and development. The consequential risks arising from these convergences are not easy to foresee, but diligent deployment of methodological efforts could help face these challenges. To meet these future challenges, a device company should explore and adopt state-of-the-art practices, adapt to the ever-changing geopolitical and technological environments and search for new, nontraditional approaches providing innovative solutions. These solutions are not always technological. Previous failure experiences have shown organizational and human aspects often play significant and influential roles in solving the challenges and preventing potential mishaps.

Medical device companies should always consult and use globally harmonized and recognized approaches such as national and international standards or acceptable trade practices in the device design and development process. However, a total lifecycle approach may help device companies excel and thrive.

References

1. AdvaMed represents medical device and diagnostics manufacturers in the US.
2. COCIR is the voice of the European radiological, electromedical and healthcare IT industry.
3. Eucomed represents the medical technology industry in Europe.
4. EDMA is the industry association representing the interests of the in vitro diagnostic industry throughout Europe.
5. MITA is the collective voice of medical imaging equipment, radiation therapy and radiopharmaceutical manufacturers in the US.
6. "Device recalls: A study of quality problems." FDA. Rockville, MD, US Department of Health and Human Services. Available from National Technical Information Service. NTIS website. https://www.ntis.gov/Search/Home/titleDetail/?abbr=PB90181272. Accessed 19 January 2016.
7. Chan TC. "Risk Management and Opportunity: 'Two Sides of the Same Coin.'" *PDA Letter* 2004, XL(October): 1, 10-16.
8. *ISO 14971 Medical Devices—Application of risk management to medical devices.* Geneva, Switzerland, International Organization for Standardization.
9. "Commission communication in the framework of the implementation of Council Directive 93/42/EEC of 1 June 1993 in relation to medical devices and Directive 98/79/EC of the European Parliament and of the Council of 27 October 1998 on in-vitro diagnostic medical devices." *Official Journal of the European Communities* (C182).
10. "21 CFR Parts 808, 812, 820; Medical Devices: Current Good Manufacturing Practice (CGMP) Final Rule; Quality System Regulation." *Federal Register*, Vol. 61, No. 95.
11. "Commission communication in the framework of the implementation of the Council Directive 93/42/EEC concerning medical devices, European Union." *Official Journal of the European Union* (C186).
12. Chan TC. "A HACCP Framework for Risk Management in Bio-Pharmaceutical Processes." *PDA Letter* 2005, XLI(March): 1, 14-19.
13. *ISO 13485 Medical Devices—Quality Management Systems—System requirements for regulatory purposes.* Geneva, Switzerland, International Organization for Standardization.
14. *Design control guidance for medical device manufacturers* (March 1997). FDA, US Department of Health and Human Services. FDA website. http://www.fda.gov/RegulatoryInformation/Guidances/ucm070627.htm. Accessed 18 January 2016.
15. *GHTF/SG3/N15R8 Implementation of risk management principles and activities within a Quality Management System* (May 2005). Global Harmonization Task Force. IMDRF website. http://www.imdrf.org/docs/ghtf/final/sg3/technical-docs/ghtf-sg3-n15r8-risk-management-principles-qms-050520.pdf. Accessed 18 January 2016.
16. *GHTF/SG3/N17R9 Quality Management System—Medical Devices—Guidance on the control of products and services obtained from suppliers*, December 2008. Global Harmonization Task Force. IMDRF website. http://www.imdrf.org/docs/ghtf/final/sg3/technical-docs/ghtf-sg3-n17-guidance-on-quality-management-system-081211.pdf. Accessed 18 January 2016.
17. *GHTF/SG3/N18 Quality Management System—Medical Devices—Guidance on corrective action and preventive action and related QMS processes*, November 2010. Global Harmonization Task Force. IMDRF website. http://www.imdrf.org/docs/ghtf/final/sg3/technical-docs/ghtf-sg3-n18-2010-qms-guidance-on-corrective-preventative-action-101104.pdf. Accessed 18 January 2016.
18. Chan TC. "Implementation of Risk Management in Medical Device Companies: A Survey Analysis of Current Practices." 2012, School of Pharmacy, University of Southern California. Los Angeles, CA. 174.
19. A respondent's comment from MacMillan's study on quantitative methods.
20. Hubbard DW. *The Failure of Risk Management: Why It's Broken and How to Fix It.* 2009, John Wiley & Sons, Inc., Hoboken, NJ.
21. Axendia's research report is based on a survey of 125 individuals from 89 different companies from 16 countries. The research was guided by a 12-member "Executive Advisory Council."
22. Axendia. "Walking the Global Tightrope: Balancing the Risks and Rewards of Med-Tech Globalization." 2012, Axendia, Inc., Yardley, PA.
23. Saunders R, Ju R. Risk Mitigation Planning. RA 705 Project management Planning Lecture. 2012, San Diego State University.
24. A model "Home As Living Space" proposed by Venkatesh and Mazumdar at the 30th Annual Conference of the Environmental Design Research Association in 1999.

25. Venkatesh A. "The Home of the Future: An Ethnographic Study of New Information Technologies in the Home." 2001, *Advances in Consumer Research* XXVIII: 88-96.
26. Johnson provided a comprehensive overview of a reporting system on adverse health care events. He explored the architectures, form designs and how human factors influenced and biased analyses.
27. Johnson CW. "Human Factors Engineering of Health Care Reporting Systems." *Handbook of Human Factors and Ergonomics in Health Care and Patient Safety*. 2012, P. Carayon, CRC Press.
28. Chan advocated using the Medical Device Reporting Coding Scheme to integrate risk management and CAPA information.
29. Op cit 7.
30. Leveson N. "The Use of Safety Cases in Certification and Regulation." *Journal of System Safety* (Nov/Dec 2011).
31. MIT Professor Leveson argued the certification of safety-critical systems usually is based on evaluation of whether a product reduces risk of specific losses to an acceptable level at a one-time effort. She emphasized product safety was a continuous operation involving users, operators and environments that changed over time. Therefore, product safety should be evaluated from a dynamic system perspective involving human and machine interaction behaviors and changing operating environments during the entire product life in a continuous manner. She also suggested hazard and accident prevention using system dynamics models as an alternative approach to safety in complex systems.
32. Leveson N. *Engineering a safer world: systems thinking applied to safety*. 2011, The MIT Press, Cambridge, MA.
33. *Managing the risks from medical product use: Creating a risk management framework*. May 1999, FDA, Rockville, MD, US Department of Health and Human Services. FDA website. http://www.fda.gov/Safety/SafetyofSpecificProducts/ucm180325.htm. Accessed 18 January 2016.
34. Op cit 18.
35. Ibid.
36. Krewski D. "Risk Assessment, Risk Management." *Encyclopedia of Public Health*. 2008 Springer Science+Business Media, LLC.
37. ICH (2006). *Q9 Quality Risk Management* (November 2005). ICH website. http://www.ich.org/products/guidelines/quality/quality-single/article/quality-risk-management.html. Accessed 18 January 2016.
38. *ISO 3100 Risk Management—Principles and Guidelines*. Switzerland, International Organization for Standardization. 2009.
39. *IEC 80001-1:2010 Application of Risk Management for IT-Networks Incorporating Medical Devices*. 2010, IEC, Geneva, Switzerland.
40. Enterprise Risk Management—Integrated Framework. 2004, Committee of Sponsoring Organization of the Treadway Commission Jersey City, NJ.
41. Götz A. *The Ultimate Collection of Murphy's Laws* (30 July 2012). Ultimate Collection website. http://murphyslaws.net/. Accessed 18 January 2016.
42. Story MF. FDA Perspectives on Human Factors in Device Development. RAPS webinar presentation given 7 June 2012.
43. Op cit 10.
44. *Strategic plan for regulatory science*. 2011, FDA website. http://www.fda.gov/ScienceResearch/SpecialTopics/RegulatoryScience/ucm267719.htm. Accessed 18 January 2016.
45. *Applying Human Factors and Usability Engineering to Medical Devices*. FDA website. http://www.fda.gov/ucm/groups/fdagov-public/@fdagov-meddev-gen/documents/document/ucm259760.pdf. Accessed 5 February 2016.
46. *Human Factors Principles for Medical Device Labeling* (September 1993). FDA website. http://www.fda.gov/downloads/MedicalDevices/.../UCM095300.pdf. Accessed 18 January 2016.
47. *Write It Right, Recommendations for Developing User Instruction Manuals for Medical Devices Used in Home Health Care* (August 1993). FDA website. http://www.fda.gov/downloads/MedicalDevices/.../ucm070771.pdf. Accessed 18 January 2016.
48. *ANSI/AAMI-HE75 (2009). Human Factors Engineering—Design of Medical Devices* (2009). AAMI. Arlington, VA.
49. UL Mark Integrity Program. Canadian Certification Requirements for Bilingual Safety, Warning and Caution Markings.
50. Packard R. Which countries require CE marking of medical devices (27 September 2013). Medical device academy website. http://medicaldeviceacademy.com/which-countries-require-ce-marking-of-medical-devices/. Accessed 18 January 2016.
51. FDA issued a notification of impacts of the government shutdown on October 1, 2013.
52. Gagliardi J. *Controls: Design Transfer, Changes, and the Design History File* (30 December 2010). Bonezone website. http://www.bonezonepub.com/component/content/article/233-design-controls-design-transfer-changes-and-the-design-history-file. Accessed 18 January 2016.

Bibliography

Asian Harmonization Working Party (AHWP). *Comparison between the GHTF Summary Technical Documentation (STED) formats for Medical Devices and In Vitro Diagnostic Medical Devices and Common Submission Dossier Template (CSDT) format*, 2013. AWHP website. http://www.ahwp.info/sites/default/files/ahwp-files/7_Documents/7_Final_Documents/Final_AHWP_WG1a_F004_2013.pdf. Accessed 15 January 2016.

Chan TC, Wong J, Tong R. (2013). Chapter 13, "ISO 14971: Application of Risk Management to Medical Devices." *Handbook of Medical Device Regulatory Affairs in Asia*. 2013, Pan Stanford Publishing: 145–161.

Chan TC, Bills E. "Exploring Post-Development Risk Management." *Medical Device and Diagnostic Industry*. May 2004.

Committee on Shuttle Criticality Review and Hazard Analysis Audit, S. A. B., Commission on Engineering and Technical Systems, National Research Council (1988). *Post-Challenger Evaluation of Space Shuttle Risk Assessment and Management*. Washington, DC, The National Academy Press.

"Commission communication in the framework of the implementation of Council Directive 93/42/EEC of 1 June 1993 in relation to medical devices and Directive 98/79/EC of the European Parliament and of the Council of 27 October 1998 on in-vitro diagnostic medical devices." *Official Journal of the European Communities* (C182).

US FDA. *Draft Guidance for Industry and Food and Drug Administration Staff—Applying Human Factors and Usability Engineering to Optimize Medical Device Design*. Rockville, MD.

Gehman HWJ. (2003). Columbia Accident Investigation Board Report. National Air and Space Administration. Washington, DC. Government Printing Office.

Guldenmund FW. "(Mis)understanding safety culture and its relationship to safety management." *Risk Analysis*. 2010, 30(10):1466–1480.

Hopkins A. "For whom does safety pay? The case of major accidents." *Safety Science*. 32:143–153.

Hopkins A. "Studying organizational cultures and their effects on safety." *Safety Science*. 2006, 44(10):875–889.

IEC 62366 *Application of Usability Engineering to Medical Devices*. International Electrotechnical Commission, Geneva, Switzerland.

Major changes in medical device regulations in China affecting market access. Cocir website. Accessed 15 January 2016. http://www.cocir.org/index.php?id=110&tx_ttnews%5Btt_news%5D=829&cHash=063fb2c037498f396b95dc52e8527f4a .

Mintzberg H. *Structures in five: Designing effective organizations*. 1983, Simon & Schuster, Englewood Cliffs, NJ.

Ostrom L, Wilhelmsen C, et al. "Assessing safety culture." *Nuclear Safety*. 1993, 34(2):163–173.

Reason JT. *Managing the risks of organizational accidents*. 1997, Aldershot, Hants, England; Brookfield, VT, USA, Ashgate.

Roberts KH, Bea R. *Must accidents happen? Lessons from high-reliability organizations*. 2001, Academy of Management Executive.

Stein MA, Christiansen L. *Successful Onboarding: A strategy to unlock hidden value within your organization*. 2010. Boston, McGraw-Hill.

Sullivan J, Beach R. "Improving project outcomes through operational reliability: A conceptual model." *International Journal of Project Management*. 2009, 27(8):765–775.

Columbia Accident Investigation Board. *Columbia Accident Investigation Board Report*. Washington, DC, 2003, National Aeronautics and Space Administration.

Weick KE. (2004). "Normal accident theory as frame, link, and provocation." *Organization & Environment*. 2004, 17(1):27–31.

Whittington R, Panny K. *Principles of auditing and other assurance services*. 2004, Boston, McGraw-Hill.

6 Global Medical Device Labeling Strategies

By Elisabeth George and Michael A. Siano

Introduction

Labeling is one of many key elements to consider in supporting a global marketing and regulatory strategy. A product's labeling serves to identify it throughout the supply chain, to the user and to authorities such as Customs and health regulators. It contributes to safe, effective and proper use by the intended user(s), promotes the device's intended performance, and is an important element in the manufacturer's risk management, in that residual risks are communicated to users and/or patients. Well-crafted, clear and concise labeling compliant with international standards serves all parties involved.

First, it is necessary to understand the scope of the term "labeling" as it is used in the context of medical device and in vitro diagnostic (IVD) device regulations. No strict definition can be applied globally, but the term "labeling" generally is regarded as information provided by the manufacturer with or on the product.[1] This often takes the form of physical labels attached to the device and/or the outer packaging, instructions for use (IFU), service documentation and promotional materials. It also can take more abstract forms, such as software interfaces, displayed messages, websites or voice prompts. This chapter focuses on device and package labels, with some discussion of IFU contents.

The impact of labeling is broad, from providing basic information to liability if a user is injured because of poor labeling or instructions. Regulatory approval may depend on product labeling review and acceptance. As in many aspects of global market expansion, undetected errors made early in the process often are amplified as market expansion proceeds. Likewise, a well thought-out labeling strategy can improve time-to-market and yield great savings when a manufacturer extends its global reach.

Requirements differ greatly from one device type to another (e.g., sterile/non-sterile, electrical, etc.); however, many basic principles and successful practices can be applied broadly. This chapter highlights various strategic aspects involved in labeling for global markets, references applicable standards and guidelines and offers some suggestions on practical approaches.

Although the goal is to develop a global labeling strategy, it covers some label design fundamentals simply because success in the global arena is determined largely by correct application of basic requirements that might be found in the manufacturer's home country or any well-developed system, such as that of the EU.[2]

Strategic Considerations

From a strategic point of view, the primary goal—or ideal—is to design a single label that can be used internationally with minimal or no customization for individual markets. A common approach is to design a label for a major market (such as the EU or US) and then modify it for other markets. Along the same lines, it is advantageous to limit the need for, and associated costs of, translations.

Practical approaches to apply to accomplish these basic goals are addressed later in the chapter. However, first, it is useful to have a general understanding of common label contents.

Figure 6-1. Example of Orthopedic Implant Label for US and EU

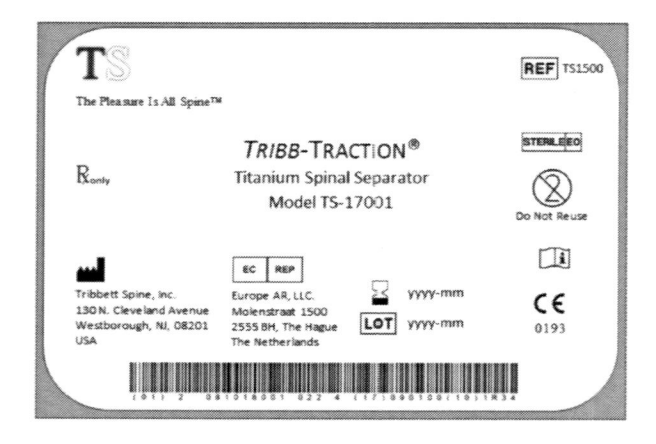

Label Contents

Basic labeling requirements overlap broadly across markets. While the entire set of information provided to the user varies with device type and intended use, some commonalities exist. Appendix C includes common label contents to consider.

General Requirements

Figure 6-1 illustrates common elements that might be included in a typical orthopedic package label for the US and EU and as a base for global labeling.

Figure 6-1 gives a brief description of the major elements (counterclockwise from the upper left).

1. Branding—although not required, branding generally is desirable for marketing and commercial reasons.
2. Prescription only—required by the US Food and Drug Administration (FDA) for prescription-only devices but not by EU standards. The symbol therefore is included in a common US/EU label but, as it is not included in the harmonized standard, would require explanation in the IFU.
3. UDI—Universal Device Identification code, human readable and barcode.
4. Manufacturer—the "manufacturer" symbol is included in ISO 15223-1 (and EN 980:2008) making it an acceptable EU manufacturer identification,[3] while FDA requires only the name and address, making the identification acceptable in both markets. All addresses used in international labeling should include the country; a reviewer in Saudi Arabia, Malaysia or Singapore cannot be expected to know where "Springfield, IL" or "Hartford, CT" is. See the section on Ensuring Consistency Across Documents."
5. EU Authorised Representative—foreign manufacturers selling in the EU are required to identify a EU Authorised Representative. The symbol is included to satisfy EU requirements only but can be included in US labeling (and other countries) as well.
6. Use-by date—the symbol is included in ISO 15223 and is acceptable in both the US and EU to identify the product's expiration date. It is not required for products without an expiration date, in which case the date of manufacture might be included instead.
7. Lot Number—the symbol is included in ISO 15223 and is acceptable in both the US and EU to identify the production lot number. Although the English word for "lot" is used, if it is included in symbolic form (all capital with outline), it does not require translation within the EU. Note, as required by the particular case, Batch or Serial number (or Control Number for IVDs) might have been included.
8. CE Mark—the CE Mark is required for medical devices sold in the EU (and some other countries). For devices requiring Notified Body assessment, the Notified Body number must be included under the symbol. The CE Mark is not required by FDA but may be included in labeling used in the US and other countries.
9. Consult Instructions for Use—the information symbol indicates additional instructions are included in the IFU. This is useful in meeting labeling requirements where product label space constraints do not permit the inclusion of all required labeling information.[4]
10. Do Not Reuse—although FDA recognizes ISO 15223, in practice, text often is requested in addition to symbols, whereas the symbol alone would suffice in the EU. This configuration allows the manufacturer to satisfy FDA (with text) and does not require translation within the EU, as the ISO 15223 symbol is used.
11. Sterile—the symbol is included in ISO 15223 and is acceptable in both the US and EU to indicate the product is sterile and the sterilization method (ethylene oxide, in this example). Because the symbol includes English text, it is acceptable in the US as well. Although the English word for "sterile" is used, if it is included in symbolic form (all capital with outline), it does not require translation within the EU.

12. Ref Number—the symbol is included in ISO 15223 and is acceptable in both the US and EU to identify the product's reference or catalog number.
13. Trade Name—a trade name is required in all markets.
14. Description—A brief product description is required in both the US and EU. This element would require translation within the EU and elsewhere.
15. Model Number—the word "model" may require translation in some markets.

Special Requirements

While a label designed to meet the EU and US requirements can serve "as is" in many international markets, some markets have local requirements in addition to translation. Often, the base global label can be used (translated where necessary) with an add-on label (commonly referred to as an "overlabel") applied in the form of a sticker to meet the local requirements. Local requirements often include information such as the local importer name and registration number. These generally are easy to include as an add-on label.

In some markets, however, local requirements make it more practical simply to create a market-specific label.

Appendix B includes a list of major markets with local requirements (other than translation).

Additional Considerations

This section calls attention to a few factors to be considered in the course of label design.

Country-of-Origin

Country-of-origin is an important and complex issue. As it pertains to labeling, several important aspects should be considered:
- what is meant by "country-of-origin"
- which countries require country-of-origin on the product label
- why country-of-origin is needed (e.g., Customs or regulatory purposes)

The country-of-origin definition in the particular market must be understood, as it is not consistent across all jurisdictions. In many countries—probably most—the country-of-origin is regarded as the country in which the legal manufacturer is based. The definition of "manufacturer" is not globally recognized but generally is regarded as the entity listed on the label as the manufacturer and maintains the device design files.[5]

Certain countries require the country-of-origin on the device labeling (e.g., Made in USA), while others do not. Thus, it is important for manufacturers to understand the specific requirements for their products' destination countries, and both Customs and regulatory requirements should be considered. It also is important to understand which labeling (e.g., shipping containers, packaging, device label, etc.) should include the information, if it is needed.

It may seem ideal simply to include both the legal manufacturer and the country in which the physical manufacturing is performed, but there are downsides to this. If a reviewer notes a manufacturer's address in Wisconsin, USA, and a "Made in Philippines" on the label together, this may prompt additional questions and requests for documentation. More text also means more translation.

Distributor/Importer Relationship

In some countries, the local distributor, importer or local representative's name and address must be included on the label. Different distributors and importers often are used in different markets, so it is common for this information to be included as an add-on label.

It is recommended manufacturers determine whether distributor information is required on the label in markets of interest and then confirm this information can be included in an add-on label.

Presentation

Product labeling presentation can take many different forms, depending on the product and its application. This section discusses several label presentation elements that may impact a global strategy.

Sizing Requirements

A label's size generally is dictated by the space available on the product and/or package and usability considerations, as well as the required label information. Few regulatory systems specifically establish size requirements but, in general, labels should be designed so a person with normal vision can read the label's contents easily. In the rare cases where regulation or standards stipulate size, these generally set extreme minimum limits (e.g., Australian Essential Principles specify a font height of 1 mm); thus, designing labels with font sizes legible to a person of normal vision in the environment in which the device is intended to be used will satisfy most specific requirements.

Device/Packaging versus IFU

Certain information is required on the device and/or packaging label, while other information is required in the IFU; some information can be included in either or both, and other information is required in both. Annex I of the *Medical Devices Directive* (Council Directive 93/42/EEC) addresses the different requirements: Sections 13.3–5 address information required on the label, and Sections 13.4 and 13.6 address information required in the IFU. This can serve as a general guideline for most systems.

Note the directive makes no distinction between the different tiers of labeling—that is, primary (attached to device), secondary (packaging) labeling, and so forth.[6] In practice, however, if constrained by space, the primary labeling must at least identify the device (make and trade name, model or REF number), while additional information can be included on the packaging.

Electronic Labeling

Electronic labeling is provided through a website, CD, videos, voice prompts, software help-system or other electronic media. This format has the potential to not only provide a greater variety of information to the user, but also avoid printing costs.

At the time of publication, regulatory authorities in major global markets recently have only begun to define their positions towards this alternative, and many have not formally addressed it at all. Thus, an exclusively electronic labeling approach may not, at the moment, be feasible for a global strategy. Nonetheless, ancillary materials, such as videos and instructional websites, generally are acceptable to authorities.

Although few authorities have addressed labeling for pure software medical devices specifically (e.g., image diagnostic software that might be delivered via internet download and never take physical form, such as a CD), in practice many authorities accept the application help-system in place of an IFU and the "About" screen as the label (i.e., providing information required on the primary product label or packaging). Many of the same considerations applicable to physical labeling should be applied to electronic labeling, with the major difference being cost of product and modes. Labeling included in pure software generally will be held to the same standards as physical labels.

Localization

The term "localization" refers to adapting product information to a specific region or country. This usually includes translation of text into the local language, converting units to the local system of measure and using appropriate date formats. A number of factors should be considered in localization, not covered in detail here; these include intended users, differences in practice of medicine and usability. For example, metric units might be appropriate internationally for a professional-use-only device; whereas, they may require conversion to the common units of the region for lay-use devices.

Language

Many countries require product labeling in the local language. The ultimate goal, of course, is to provide instructions in a language understood by the user to ensure safe and effective use of the device.

Language requirements often differ by the intended user. In many countries, the *lingua franca* of business, medicine and other professions is English, while it is not the country's official language. As a result, professional users in these countries are expected to be fluent in English, while lay users may not. For example, the official language in Saudi Arabia is Arabic, but English labeling is acceptable for professional-use-only devices.

It is important to understand the requirements based on the product's specific intended use and users. Local language labeling requirements generally are addressed in the medical device regulations or guidance. In some systems, language requirements are not addressed specifically but may be included in general consumer or import laws. If no exceptions are noted, requirements should be simply assumed based on the official national language.

Appendix A—Global Language Requirements includes a table of the world's largest markets' labeling language requirements.

Units-of-Measure

Units of measure in the labeling should be aligned with regional norms and regulatory requirements. Most of the world utilizes the International System (SI)—also referred to as "metric system." However, other systems also are used, including the Imperial system used in the UK and Canada, and the US Customary system. Even where non-SI systems are common, SI units may be appropriate for professional medical and scientific settings. Thus, it is necessary to understand both the country's official system and the system used for the product's specific application.

Date Format

Dates—such as the date of manufacture or expiration—often are required label elements. Date formats differ throughout the world for common use—for example, in the US, the date May 6, 2014, generally is written as "5/6/2014" (MDY); whereas, in the EU it would be "6/5/2014" (DMY).

The standard, ISO 8601, specifies a format of YYYY-MM-DD. This format is referenced by the EU Harmonized Standard EN1041:2008 and 21 CFR §801.18(a). While the format is not universally required, it generally is accepted throughout the world.

The use of written months (rather than numeric) might increase a label's usability but would not guarantee universal acceptance and would require translation. Ultimately, date format requirements must be identified on a per-market basis and clearly documented in the company's standard practices.

As a final note, the Gregorian calendar is commonly accepted, even in countries utilizing other calendars (e.g., the Islamic Hijri and Thai Solar calendars).

Practical Approaches

No single formula can be applied to all cases, but several practical approaches often are employed successfully in an international labeling scheme. Following is a brief discussion of some common tactics.

Base Global Label

When commercializing a device internationally, it is advisable to minimize the number of label versions to control costs and potential mix-ups. Thus, it is common to include US and EU requirements in a "base global label" and then apply an add-on label for market-specific requirements (e.g., Brazil registration number, Australian sponsor information). **Figure 6-1** is an example of common base global label elements.

The best representation of general international requirements comes from the EU, where labeling requirements are outlined in *Medical Devices Directive* Annex I, Section 13 and the relevant harmonized standard.

While it is ideal to have a base global label covering both EU and US requirements, space limitations and/or other factors may make it impractical. Where separate EU and US labels are maintained, the EU label usually would be most suitable as the base global label.

Where space permits, another common approach is to use a multi-lingual label including the major languages of the world.

Reducing Translation Costs

Two simple approaches to reducing translation costs center on minimizing text requiring translation.

First, avoid extraneous information, such as promotional tag lines. In some cases, these tag lines may have sufficient marketing value to justify their inclusion, but in others, they serve little purpose. A device description generally is necessary on the label; however, it can fulfill its purpose in very concise form, sometimes as part of the tradename.

Second, use symbols. Unlike text, a symbolic representation can serve in many markets without translation. While ISO 15223 is accepted throughout the EU and many other countries, it is not universal (e.g., currently not accepted in Australia). Thus, a common approach is to define the meaning of symbols used on the product and packaging labeling in the IFU. FDA recognized the standard in July 2014.

Additionally, to fulfill the product description requirement, device photos or illustrations sometimes are included on the package labeling. Incidentally, this also may reduce the likelihood of Customs opening a package for inspection.

Determining Language in the Absence of Guidance

In countries with poorly developed regulatory systems, language requirements may not be specified clearly and, in fact, there may be a lack of enforcement capabilities in addition to the lack of regulation. In the absence of specific regulation or guidance addressing language requirements, the best practice is to err on the side of caution and include labeling in a language commonly understood by the local population. This can reduce the chance of liability for any injuries that might result from the device's misuse due to a lack of comprehensible instructions and furthers the device's proper use; it also may support the product's market appeal.

Add-on Labeling

Many markets with specific local labeling requirements need only minor additions to a label designed to EU requirements. For example, a local registration number and/or the local importer's name and address may be required. Often these requirements can be met by add-on labeling, adding a sticker to the base global label. Generally, the add-on label is affixed to the package (or device) without obscuring the original label. This sometimes is referred to as "add-on labeling" or "overlabeling." However, in some cases, an add-on label is applied directly over part of an original label. This might be done, for example, if only a single line on a label requires translation.

Add-on labeling allows continued production with the standard label instead of creating a market-specific label and can reduce costs and maintenance. Add-on labeling is widely accepted, but manufacturers should confirm it is accepted on a per market basis.

Ensuring Consistency Across Documents

While FDA and EU Notified Bodies sometimes are lenient toward minor labeling inconsistencies (e.g., trade name, manufacturer's address, etc.), many other authorities are not. Issues as minor as including a nine-digit zip code in one document and a five-digit zip code in another, using a complete state name in one place and an abbreviation in another (e.g., Massachusetts vs. MA), or using "CT" in one document and "Computed Tomography" in another, may be enough to prompt a request for clarification or demand to correct the inconsistency from many authorities. These inconsistencies also may be flagged by Customs, looking for counterfeit products.

To address this, it is recommended manufacturers use a master list (including trade names, company name, site address, etc.) from which the information is propagated to all other documents. This ensures consistent use between documents within a department and across different company departments or branches.

Conclusions

Labeling is an important element in regulatory compliance, a device's safe use, user satisfaction and marketing. It identifies the product and conveys necessary information on proper product use and handling. Good labeling enhances a product's usability and reduces the chances of misuse that could result in an injury to the user and liability for the manufacturer.

Like all document management, labeling becomes more complicated as variations increase. As manufacturers expand into international markets with different requirements, languages and units of measure, it is important to minimize variation and, with it, cost. This can be achieved through thoughtful development of a single source (or base global label) from which other variants are derived, modifying the base label with sticker add-on labels where possible, and identifying countries in which the same labels can be shared.

A sound approach to an international labeling strategy begins with a thorough understanding and rigorous application of basic labeling requirements. Then, it is important to identify gaps between the base global label and target market requirements clearly and determine acceptable methods for filling those gaps.

Applying these principles can keep costs, effort and ongoing maintenance to a minimum.

References

1. See GHTF/SG1/N70:2011, *Label and Instructions for Use for Medical Devices.*
2. Note the EU is referenced frequently as a model system; this is because many systems around the world have been derived, to some extent, from the EU system.
3. Note that EN 980 is expected to be superseded by ISO 15223 in the near future, although it is, at the moment, the harmonized standard in the EU. For the remainder of this chapter, only ISO 15223 is mentioned, although EN 980 may be applicable in the EU.
4. Such a decision must be supported by the risk assessments and human factors evaluations.
5. A valuable reference is defined by GHTF/SG1/N055:2009, *Definitions of the Terms Manufacturer, Authorised Representative, Distributor and Importer.*
   "Any natural or legal person with responsibility for design and/or manufacture of a medical device with the intention of making the medical device available for use, under his name; whether or not such a medical device is designed and/or manufactured by that person himself or on his behalf by another person(s)."
6. Section 13.1 of the *Essential Requirements* states only, "As far as practicable and appropriate, the information needed to use the device safely must be set out on the device itself and/or on the packaging for each unit…"

Additional Reading

- *Regulation of the European Parliament and Of the Council on medical devices*, and amending Directive 2001/83/EC, Regulation (EC) No 178/2002 and Regulation (EC) No 1223/2009 (draft)
- Council Directive 93/42/EEC, *Concerning Medical Devices*
- *Federal Food, Drug, and Cosmetic Act (FD&C Act)*, FDA
- GHTF/SG1/N70:2011, *Label and Instructions for Use for Medical Devices*
- ISO 15223-1:2012 *Medical devices—Symbols to be used with medical device labels, labelling and information to be supplied—Part 1: General requirements*
- EN980 *Symbols for use in the labelling of medical devices*
- EN 1041:2008+A1:2013 *Information supplied by the manufacturer of medical devices*
- GHTF/SG1/N70:2011, *Label and Instructions for Use for Medical Devices*
- IEC 60601-1, *Medical electrical equipment - Part 1: General requirements for basic safety and essential performance*
- IEC 60878, *Graphical symbols for electrical equipment in medical practice*
- ISO 1000:1992, *SI units and recommendations for the use of their multiples and of certain other units* [revised by ISO 80000-1:2009]
- ISO 31-0:1992, *Quantities and units* (revised by ISO 80000-1:2009)
- ISO 8601, *Data elements and interchange formats—Information interchange—Representation of dates and times*
- ANSI/AAMI HE75, 2009/(R)2013 *Human factors engineering—Design of medical devices*
- IEC 62366-1:2014, *Medical devices—Part 1: Application of usability engineering to medical devices*

Appendix A—International Language Requirements[a]

The following table provides a rough guide to language requirements in the top 40 economies (in descending order of economic size, as of this writing).

Country	Professional Use[b]	Lay-Use[c]	Reference
US	English	English and Spanish (PR)	Code of Federal Regulations, Title 21, Sec. 801.15[d]
China	Chinese	Chinese (Simplified)	CFDA Order No. 6, *Medical Device Instruction and Labeling Regulations*[e]
Japan	Japanese	Japanese	General practice
Germany	German	German	*The Act on Medical Devices*, 2 August 1994, Section 11(2) (English translation)[f]
France	French	French	*Décret n° 95-292 du relatif aux despositifs médicaux définis à l'article L.665-3 du code de la santé publique et modifiant ce code Decree n° 95-292 of 03.16.1995 on medical devices* (Art. R. 665-11)[g]
UK	English	English	*The Medical Devices Regulations* 2002, 9(3)[h]
Brazil	Portuguese	Portuguese	RDC n° 185 (2001), Annex IIIB(1.1)[i]
Russia	Russia	Russia	Government Decree N 1037, 1997 *"On measures to ensure availability of information in Russian on non-food stuffs imported into the Russian Federation"*[j]
Italy	Italian	Italian	*Decreto legislativo del 24/02/1997n. 46, attuazione della direttiva 93/42/CEE concernente i dispositivi medici Legislative Decree of 24.02.1997 n. 46, implementing Directive 93/42/EEC* (Art 5(4))[k]
India	English	English	Section 6 of Schedule DII and Rule 96 of Drugs and Cosmetics Rules, 1945; GSR 703(E)[l]
Canada	English or French	English and French	*Guidance for the Labelling of Medical Devices*, Sections 21 to 23 of the *Medical Devices Regulations*, Section 23(1),(2),(3)[m]
Australia	English	English	ARGMD (2011), Version 1.1, p.192[n]
Spain	Spanish	Spanish	Royal Decree 1591/2009, Article 4(2)[o]
Mexico	Spanish	Spanish	*Regalamento de Insumos para la Salud*, Articulo 16[p]
Korea	Korean (Hangeul)	Korean (Hangeul)	*Enforcement Regulations of the Medical Device Act*, Article 28[q]
Indonesia	Indonesian	Indonesian	Regulation Number 1190/MENKES/PER/VII/2010 Article 26(5)[r]
Turkey	Turkish	Turkish	TITTUB About Updating Records (Part 3)[s]
Netherlands	Dutch	Dutch	Dutch Healthcare Inspectorate, Language requirement (English)[t]
Saudi Arabia	English	English and Arabic	MDS-IR6, Article 9[u]
Switzerland	German, French and Italian	German, French and Italian	Medical Devices Regulation (MepV), Article 7[v]
Iran	English	English and Persian	General practice
Sweden	Swedish	Swedish	LVFS 2003:11, 4§(3)[w]
Norway	Norwegian	Norwegian	*LOV 1995-01-12 nr 06: Lov om medisinsk utstyr* Law about medical devices (§7)[x]
Poland	English or Polish	Polish	*Act of 20 May 2010 on medical devices*, Article 14[y]

Chapter 6: Global Medical Device Labeling Strategies

Country	Professional Use[b]	Lay-Use[c]	Reference
Belgium	French, Dutch and German	French, Dutch and German	*Arrêté royal du 18/03/1999 relatif aux dispositifs médicaux*, Chapter VIII Royal Decree, 18/03/1999 relating to medical devices (Art 18)[z]
Argentina	Spanish	Spanish	Provision No. 2318/2002, Annex III.B[aa]
Nigeria	English	English	NAFDAC/RR/007/00 Part D(3)[bb]
Austria	German	German	*Bundesrecht konsolidiert: Gesamte Rechtsvorschrift für Medizinproduktegesetz* Federal law consolidates: Total legislation for *Medical Devices Act* §9(6)[cc]
South Africa	English and Afrikaans	English and Afrikaans	*Hazardous Substances Act 15* of 1973, Part 32[dd]
United Arab Emirates	Arabic or English	Arabic and English	*Medical Device Registration Guideline*, Part 9[ee]
Venezuela	Spanish	Spanish	Practice
Colombia	Spanish	Spanish	*Decreto Numero 4725 de 2005, Capitulo 8(57)*[ff]
Thailand	Thai	Thai	*Medical Device Act B.E. 2551* (2008), Clause 6. MDCD website[gg]
Denmark	Danish	Danish	*Bekendtgørelse om medicinsk udstyr* Executive Order No. 1263 concerning medical devices (§ 3)[hh]
Malaysia	English or Bahasa Malay	English and Bahasa Malay	Medical Device Guidance Document, 7.4.1[ii] Medical Device Regulations 2012, Part II, 5(1)
Singapore	English	English	GN-23: Guidance on Labelling for Medical Devices, 2.1[jj]
Chile	Spanish or English	Spanish or English	General practice
Hong Kong	English or Chinese (Traditional)	English and Chinese (Traditional)	GN-02 for Listing Class II/III/IV Medical Devices[kk]
Egypt	English or Arabic	Arabic	General practice
Israel	English	Hebrew, Arabic, and English (Russian preferred)	Labeling guidelines (in Hebrew)[ll]
Taiwan	Chinese (Traditional)	Chinese (Traditional)	*Regulations for Registration of Medical Device*, Chapter 5, Article 36

a. Note that where "and" is used, *both* languages must be included; where "or" is used, either language can be used.
b. The definition of "professional" varies from country to country, but for the purpose of this chapter and in general, the term is considered to include medically trained professionals such as doctors, nurses and medical technicians.
c. Lay-users would be regarded as patients or non-professional care provider using the product without the supervision of a professional.
d. www.accessdata.fda.gov/scripts/cdrh/cfdocs/cfCFR/CFRSearch.cfm?fr=801.15
e. http://www.cfda.gov.cn/WS01/CL0053/103758.html
f. www.bmg.bund.de/fileadmin/dateien/Downloads/Gesetze_und_Verordnungen/GuV/M/MPG_englisch.pdf
g. www.legifrance.gouv.fr/affichTexte.do?cidTexte=JORFTEXT000000350606&dateTexte=&categorieLien=id
h. www.legislation.gov.uk/uksi/2002/618/pdfs/uksi_20020618_en.pdf
i. www.anvisa.gov.br/anvisalegis/resol/2001/185_01rdc.htm
j. http://base.garant.ru/166145/
k. www.salute.gov.it/imgs/C_17_pagineAree_1636_listaFile_itemName_1_file.pdf
l. www.cdsco.nic.in/writereaddata/703(E)%20dated%2024_10_2013(12).pdf
m. www.hc-sc.gc.ca/dhp-mps/md-im/applic-demande/guide-ld/labl_etiq_dv10-eng.php#a13
n. https://www.tga.gov.au/publication/australian-regulatory-guidelines-medical-devices-argmd
o. www.boe.es/diario_boe/txt.php?id=BOE-A-2009-17606
p. www.salud.gob.mx/unidades/cdi/nom/compi/ris.html
q. www.mfds.go.kr/eng/eng/download.do;jsessionid=8yQabmYmgJdjzxhd7N7l6TpERodnvNTSvtviHbQWkzOGcKlMXdaF1CAWwOaTwl2C?boardCode=16771&boardSeq=66026&fileSeq=5
r. http://binfar.depkes.go.id/dat/05/Permenkes_Nomor_1190__5-12-11_-T-17.pdf
s. www.titubb.org/Lists/Duyuru%20%20SB/Announcement/displayifs.aspx?List=cfa0ac28-e217-4455-ab38-0f3cbcba43aa&ID=84&Web=d3530171-885f-44e3-9464-216a499aa4a4
t. www.igz.nl/english/medical_devices/language_requirement_and_labelling_of_medical_devices/

u. www.sfda.gov.sa/en/medicaldevices/regulations/DocLib1/MDS-IR6.pdf
v. www.admin.ch/opc/de/classified-compilation/19995459/index.html
w. www.lakemedelsverket.se/upload/lvfs/konsoliderade/LVFS_%202003_11_konsoliderad_tom_LVFS_2013_11.pdf
x. http://lovdata.no/dokument/NL/lov/1995-01-12-6
y. www.mz.gov.pl/__data/assets/pdf_file/0019/15346/ustawa_o_wyrobach_medycznych_en.pdf
z. www.ejustice.just.fgov.be/cgi_loi/loi_a.pl?language=fr&caller=list&cn=1999031834&la=f&fromtab=loi&sql=dt='arrete%20royal'&tri=dd+as+rank&rech=1&numero=1
aa. www.anmat.gov.ar/webanmat/normativa/Normativa/ProductosMedicos/Disposicion_ANMAT_2318-2002.pdf
bb. www.nafdac.gov.ng/images/GUIDELINES/MEDICAL%20DEVICES/IMPORTS/GUIDE39_GUIDELINES%20FOR%20REGISTRATION%20OF%20IMPORTED%20MEDICAL%20DEVICES%20IN.pdf
cc. www.ris.bka.gv.at/GeltendeFassung.wxe?Abfrage=Bundesnormen&Gesetzesnummer=10011003
dd. www.saflii.org/za/legis/consol_reg/hsa15o1973rangnr247681.pdf
ee. www.cpd-pharma.ae/downloads/4-Medical%20Device/MD%20guide%20line.pdf
ff. www.who.int/medical_devices/survey_resources/health_technology_national_policy_colombia.pdf
gg. www.fda.moph.go.th/eng/medical/pre.stm
hh. www.retsinformation.dk/Forms/R0710.aspx?id=122694#Kap2
ii. www.mdb.gov.my/mdb/documents/gd/gd_csdt_draft1.pdf
jj. http://wenku.baidu.com/view/879f47eb6294dd88d0d26b48.html
kk. www.mdco.gov.hk/english/mdacs/mdacs_gn/files/gn_02e_new.pdf
ll. www.health.gov.il/Services/ImportAndBusinessLicensing/AMR/regitration/Documents/AMR_marking.pdf

Appendix B—Local Labeling Requirements

The following table indicates whether specific labeling elements are required in the local market beyond those required for the base global label (based on EU/US requirements)—see **Figure 6-1**. This addresses both import and regulatory requirements. The requirements are not exhaustive, and special local requirements may be applicable to specific device types.

Country	Local Requirement
UAE	Base global label, Name and address of importer or distributor
European Union	Base global label
China	China Agent, site of actual manufacture and legal manufacture, CFDA registration number, CCC Mark for electronic devices; a sticker can be used for additions
Japan	Device class, local representative, MHLW Certification/Notification number; can be added as sticker
Brazil	Registration holder, Technically Responsible Person; can be added as sticker
Russia	GOST-R Mark (where applicable), Authorized Representative, importer, registration number; can be included as an over label
India	Importer name, address, DCG(I) license number; sticker can be added prior to entry into India
Canada	None
Australia	Australian Sponsor name and address; can be included as over label or leaflet[a]
Mexico	COFEORIS registration number and distributor information; can be added as sticker after importation.
Korea	MFDS registration number, importer; can be added as sticker after importation
Indonesia	Importer contact information
Turkey	Turkish importer and barcode; can be added as sticker in Turkey
Saudi Arabia	None
Argentina	Importer and Technical Director, ANMAT registration number; can be added as sticker
Nigeria	NAFDAC registration number
South Africa	None
Venezuela	None
Thailand	Local license number and importer name
Malaysia	Statement the device has been registered under the Act, and name and contact information for Malaysian Authorized Representative
Singapore	None
Chile	MINSAL registration number; can be added as sticker
Hong Kong	Special Listing Information (device listing number, name and contact information of LRP); can be included as package insert with each shipment
Egypt	Importer name, MoH registration number, country-of-origin
Israel	AMAR registration number, registration holder name and address; can be added as a sticker
Taiwan	TFDA registration number, Taiwan Agent name and address
New Zealand	None

a. Australian *Regulatory Guidelines for Medical Devices*, Section 12. Information about a medical device

Appendix C–Labeling Content

The following list is intended as a "tickler" for information to consider in a label; the list is not exhaustive, and not all information will be applicable to all devices.

Information	Label/Packaging	IFU
Trade name, make, model number	X	X
Manufacturer's full name and address	X	X
Size, quantity (if applicable)	X	
Intended use/purpose		X
Indications for use		X
Serial, lot or batch number	X	
Country-of-origin (where applicable)	X	
Expiration date (readable to user) or date of manufacture (may be encoded in serial number)	X	
Symbols per relevant standards	X	X
Definition of symbols		X
Latex/Natural Rubber indication	X	X
For US, "Manufactured for ___" or "Distributed by ___"	X	
For US, prescription device statement or "Rx only"	X	X
Storage, transport, handling and/or use conditions (e.g., temperature, humidity)	X	X
Installation, maintenance and calibration		X
Treatment (e.g., sterilization) needed before using device		X
Warnings and precautions		X
Performance and any undesirable side effects		X
Contraindications and precautions		X
Risks of electrical interference		X
Acceptable/unacceptable accessories, interfaces		X
Any detachable components		X
Processes to allow reuse (e.g., re-sterilization) and restrictions on reuse		X
Version/revision date	X	X
EN/IEC 60601 marking requirements	X	X
Individual country registration identifier (if applicable)	X	X
Sterility	X	X
Sterilization method	X	X

7 Manufacturing

By Melissa R. Gaynor, MS, RAC and Penny Northcutt, RAC, FRAPS

With the vast number and types of medical devices being developed and marketed today to address clinical needs with ever-changing technology and advancement, the regulatory professional faces many technical, legal and ethical challenges when supporting medical device manufacturing. Whether a small or large company, manufacturing may be conducted locally or at a separate site anywhere in the world. Many companies outsource all or specific manufacturing activities, most commonly terminal contact sterilization; however, other suppliers may be used for contract component or finished device manufacturing, depending on the company's capabilities. Regardless, controlling any supplier and the quality of its product(s) is the device manufacturer's responsibility. In all of these scenarios, the company's Quality Management System (QMS) must govern all manufacturing activities to ensure the quality and consistency of the finished device delivered to the user. This chapter discusses global regulations governing medical device manufacturing, critical QMS elements for successful device manufacturing, how devices transfer from the design phase into the manufacturing phase and strategies for managing changes to mature devices' design and/or manufacturing processes.

The Regulated Medical Device Manufacturing Environment

All medical devices manufactured and/or distributed in the US, regardless of classification, are subject to the US Food and Drug Administration's (FDA) general controls, which are tied closely to manufacturing practices, procedures and facilities. Regardless of device classification, manufacturers marketing devices in the EU must maintain a QMS compliant with the *Medical Devices Directive*'s requirements. Establishment and maintenance of a good QMS are key to operating a successful manufacturing operation, even for manufacturers that, in principle, are exempt from current Good Manufacturing Practice (CGMP), and are essential for regulatory compliance when no CGMP exemption has been granted based on device classification. Manufacturing process and quality control consistency are key across all regulatory considerations within a single facility, regardless of whether CGMP is "required."

Depending on device classification, risk and certification requirements, some manufacturers may be subject to periodic FDA, Notified Body or other regulatory body inspections and audits. These inspections can be announced or unannounced; therefore, the manufacturing facility should maintain a preparedness level for inspection or audit that will demonstrate compliance with applicable laws and regulations. Corrective and Preventive Action (CAPA) and internal audit processes are QMS elements that, when used correctly, will help prepare an organization for an unannounced audit or inspection.

For higher risk device classifications, facility certification or inspection may be required. For example, in the US, a Class III device manufacturer that proposes placing its device on the market for the first time must submit a Premarket Approval (PMA) application. One action FDA will take during a PMA review is a preapproval inspection (PAI) to assess the firm's compliance level with the

Quality System Regulation (QSR, 21 CFR 820; CGMP). During that time, FDA also may inspect significant firm subcontractors or suppliers if it deems that necessary. Class I and II device manufacturers in the US typically are not subject to PAIs; however, facility registration with FDA (required for manufacturers of all device classes) entitles the agency to inspect the facility at any time. These inspections may be conducted as part of routine surveillance or "for cause," due to a recall or high number of reportable adverse events. A manufacturer planning to market a Class I sterile or higher device in the EU must establish a quality system compliant with ISO 13485 and participate in an initial certification audit utilizing a Notified Body before it may place a CE mark on its product. The Notified Body will develop a surveillance program for continued facility certification depending on the facility's size (number of employees) and device type (sterile products will require separate audits from a microbiological expert in addition to QMS audits). The scope of QMS activities audited by the Notified Body is specified in the QMS certificate it issues (e.g., design and manufacture of X device). If the scope of activities in that location changes, a new QMS audit and certificate may be required. Similarly, if the manufacturer expands the QMS to include device categories not covered by the initial certificate, a new audit and certificate may be required. As of 2014, the Notified Body also must also conduct unannounced audits.

The QSR and Medical Device Manufacturing CGMPs

Whether a company is manufacturing and distributing in the US, EU or any other region where medical devices are regulated, compliance with CGMPs most likely will be required (some low-risk, non-sterile devices, such as a walking cane or tongue depressor not labeled as sterile, for example, are exempt from CGMP requirements, but CGMPs still should be followed as a matter of good business practice). For the purposes of this chapter, QSR, CGMP and QMS are used interchangeably. The regulatory professional, working with others, should develop a global regulatory strategy for the firm's manufacturing facilities to identify applicable laws, standards, regulations and certifications required to manufacture and distribute devices in selected or desired markets legally. If no QMS is in place, one must be designed, customized, implemented and maintained for compliance. If the QMS is missing or ineffective, the product may be declared adulterated by FDA through routine inspection, unannounced inspection, for cause inspection or review of marketing materials. The also firm may be refused permission to export to foreign markets or even denied access to the US market if there is risk of adverse events from product shipped in commercial distribution. In the US, an example of adulteration would be manufacturing a device not in compliance with the QSR or CGMPs. Adulteration could be placing a device on the market without a 510(k) clearance. In the EU and some other jurisdictions, failure to maintain an effective QMS fulfilling all requirements may result in withdrawal of the QMS certificate.

An effective (and compliant) QMS has numerous elements, but the regulatory professional responsible for keeping the manufacturing environment compliant should focus on the development and maintenance of the key subsystems discussed below, specific to manufacturing. Procedures, records and up-to-date training should be maintained to demonstrate compliance at all times.

- Management responsibility—manufacturing should participate in the procedures and programs put in place to help communicate the QMS' health effectively to senior management. The quality policy should be posted throughout the facility, and employees should be able to recite or locate the current policy. Management with executive responsibility not only has personal liability for noncompliance, but sets the tone for compliance throughout the organization.
- Design control—manufacturing's role in the design control process is related primarily to design transfer activities and product/process changes, which are discussed in detail later in this chapter.
- Document control—the QSR requires obsolete documents used in manufacturing to be removed from the production floor, so they cannot be mixed accidentally with current, approved procedures. QMSs require initiating documents to be controlled with approved signatures, revision history tracking and change control processes when updating any document, e.g. device master records (DMR) or design history file (DHF).
- Purchasing—the manufacturing facility must ensure it is receiving parts, raw materials, components, supplies, equipment, etc. only from approved suppliers reviewed by the quality unit for their ability to meet the firm's quality requirements. Incoming parts and materials should be inspected to a specification.
- Identification—manufacturing assigns control numbers (lot or serial) to establish a device's

traceability throughout its lifecycle and manufacture and movement through the facility prior to distribution.

- Production and process control—manufacturing processes should be controlled and validated if 100% inspection is not possible to confirm device specification and tolerances are met as established in the DMR. Validated processes should be revalidated when significant process changes occur that are documented in the procedures. Minor process changes may occur in manufacturing and are performed best with a variance within validated ranges and recorded during production runs in case a future device failure investigation is needed. If a process needs to be adjusted outside validated process settings, the firm must follow an established change control procedure to ensure the change will not have a negative impact on the resultant part or device's ability to meet end-user safety and effectiveness specifications. Equipment must be maintained, including performing and documenting preventive maintenance on regular schedules. Gauges or tools used for in-process quality inspection should be calibrated and maintained with the manufacturing equipment. The environment should be controlled to ensure devices are not adulterated; special environmental controls may be required depending on the device type, especially if it is designed to be delivered to the end user as a sterile product. Many manufacturers utilize cleanroom environments that must be monitored frequently for particulate and microbial contamination counts and require annual recertification. The production, warehouse and storage areas should be designed to prevent contamination or deterioration of critical raw materials, components and finished devices. All areas should be organized with parts clearly labeled to prevent mix-ups. Many firms implement strict line clearance and reconciliation procedures for the quality assurance unit to ensure work orders are set up correctly and manufacturing uses the correct materials. Cleaning procedures should be designed and validated to show their effectiveness and ensure cross-contamination does not occur between products or through interaction with cleaning solvents (cleaning activities should be documented).
- Acceptance activities—receiving operations should be designed so materials are inspected by the quality assurance unit before being released for manufacturing. Designated areas (such as incoming inspection, quarantine and released material) are helpful in demonstrating the firm takes steps to prevent mix-ups. Using color-coded labels helps identify materials' acceptance status as they move throughout the facility. The acceptance status of all manufacturing materials is followed by identification and traceability throughout the manufacturing process.
- Nonconforming product—each manufacturer must establish and maintain a procedure to control products that do not conform to specified requirements. Nonconforming product must be identified and segregated to prevent mix-ups with approved materials or devices.
- CAPA—when processes or products are found to be nonconforming, manufacturers are responsible for analyzing and investigating the problem and identifying existing or potential causes for the nonconformance. They also are responsible for correcting the predominant problem, implementing CAPAs to ensure such nonconformances do not recur and verifying and validating actions are effective and do not affect the finished device adversely.
- Labeling—within the manufacturing process, labeling must be controlled from time of receipt to time of placement on the device. Steps must be taken to ensure labels are legible and affixed to the correct product. The quality assurance unit is responsible for reviewing labeling for accuracy and disposing of unused labels during production runs to prevent mix-ups.
- DMR—the manufacturing team is the guardian of DMRs, which are the master "recipes" for how devices are built to specification. DMRs should not be changed without initiating change control. The DMR must include device specifications, production process specifications, quality assurance procedures, packaging and labeling specifications.
- DHR—also known as a "traveler" or "router," the DHR is the quality system record that proves each device or lot of devices was manufactured in accordance with the DMR. The DHR must contain the manufacturing date, quantity made and released, acceptance records from quality to demonstrate the devices met specifications, the primary device label and a unique device identifier and control number such as a lot or

serial number to ensure traceability throughout distribution to the end user.
- Training and qualified personnel—systems must ensure and document only appropriately qualified and trained individuals perform manufacturing and quality assurance tasks.
- Complaint files—records of customer dissatisfaction must be kept and investigated by a formally designated group within the company. If the complaints or dissatisfaction arise from a serious adverse event that caused permanent damage or death, the regulatory group must report it to regulatory authorities

Design Control, Verification, Validation and Design Transfer

The QSR and international standard ISO 13458 both require design and development activities to be performed and documented before placing a medical device on the market. Depending on the device's classification and risk level, a premarket submission to FDA or a Notified Body must be made to obtain approval or clearance prior to marketing. During this review period, FDA or the Notified Body shall review all design and development phases, including the development of design inputs from customer requirements and product specifications and design outputs, validation of test methods used to demonstrate performance, verification and validation protocols and reports, and the transfer of the design from R&D to operations ready for finished device manufacturing. For lower-risk class devices, premarket approval submission may not be required; however, the company's design control system must be followed for all devices it develops and markets, which also can help document design development for future reference in the case of design changes, postmarket investigations of issues such as complaints, and evaluating risk, based on postmarket surveillance and adverse event reporting. In addition, the system may be useful for internal audits and to demonstrate general compliance with regulatory requirements.

The device's specifications should be developed during the design and development phase and subsequently verified and validated through various methods, depending on the required performance criteria. Design verification activities demonstrate devices built during the verification and validation build (V&V build) meet the specifications developed and approved during design control activities. Through design validation testing, which may include simulated use or actual use testing (clinical trials), the device built for V&V (and subsequently shown to meet the specification through verification testing) is proven to meet users' needs, also known as design inputs. Appropriate statistical techniques should be used to determine appropriate sample sizes for verification and validation testing. The final device design must be proven to meet the design inputs, which may include customer requirements, product standards, marketing claims and competitive or substantially equivalent product performance. In some cases, simulated use testing may be inappropriate to fulfill design validation requirements adequately. Design validation testing in an actual use setting for a medical device that does not yet have premarket approval or clearance may be necessary (depending on the device's risk classification) to obtain an Investigational Device Exemption (IDE) from FDA and/or an Institutional Review Board (IRB) first to distribute the device into interstate commerce and second to use the device in a clinical setting without premarket approval or clearance (see Chapter 9 on clinical trials). When in doubt, the regulatory professional may consult with FDA or the Notified Body to help determine risk classification of a validation study involving clinical use and IDE and/or CE-marking requirements that may be prerequisites to initiate such a study.

Transferring a medical device design from the design and development phase to the finished device manufacturing phase is a critical component of medical device product development from both a compliance and practical perspective. Ideally, the actual device built during the design V&V build, sometimes referred to as the "pilot build," should be as similar as possible to the device to be produced and placed into commercial distribution following design transfer and approval. While this concept seems simple, in reality, it may be impractical to manufacture the V&V product using commercial equipment due to cost, scale and available resources. For example, procuring a commercial-scale, multi-cavity mold used to injection mold a plastic part may require significant investment. During design and development, in addition to the design activities, marketing decisions are being made that might drive design decisions prior to design transfer and could impact the final design. If a design modification is required after obtaining the design V&V results (based on a design V&V failure or change in stakeholder requirements), it is much more economical to modify a single cavity, prototype mold so the modified design can be evaluated. In the end, the business, with input from the regulatory professional, must make a sound decision on how to build the V&V product based on available resources and level of risk to the business, the patient and regulatory compliance.

Devices manufactured during the design V&V build may differ from the final device in labeling and record requirements. During design and development, the DMR, which serves as a centralized record locator or map to the location of approved component and finished device specifications, may not be complete. R&D should develop a preliminary DMR D, with input from quality assurance, quality control and operations, prior to the V&V build, to define as many DMR requirements as possible. A DHR for the design V&V build should be completed to document the V&V product's conformance with the preliminary DMR for traceability and history purposes. This DMR must be updated throughout the design phase if design modifications are made, followed by multiple design V&V testing iterations until design transfer. Packaging and labeling, as well as design usability, should be included in the design validation process to assess human factors implications and how product performance may be impacted in unexpected ways based on initial design interface, proposed labeling, instructions for use, warnings and precautions. The validation testing results can be used to update the risk analysis document, which may trigger changes to the labeling to mitigate risks associated with product misuse.

Once a final design has been determined, documented and fully vetted through the completion of design V&V testing, the R&D team is ready to transfer the device to manufacturing. Design transfer does not necessarily occur at a single point in time, as it takes place throughout the design process by engaging the operations team early in the process; the activity is formalized through the design transfer design review meeting, according to the company's design control procedures. Design transfer's objective is to ensure and demonstrate a device can be manufactured repeatedly and reliably on a commercial scale manufacturing line, using product specifications developed during the design phase. Therefore, full-scale equipment and process and test method validation activities are expected to demonstrate adequate process capability will be completed and documented. At the end of design transfer, the cross-functional team should review and address the following elements:

- assess product specification completeness and adequacy
- verify all action items noted in previous design reviews have been addressed and completed satisfactorily
- establish satisfactory completion of design verification and validation of all intended uses, user needs, design inputs and marketing claims using the final device design according to final design output specification
- update the risk management plan
- verify all specifications have been transferred correctly
- verify process and equipment validation have been completed, if required
- verify training materials are complete and implemented
- verify risk assessment has been completed and updated following the completion of V&V activities
- verify the DHF's completeness and adequacy
- verify final the DMR has been completed and implemented
- verify contract sterilizer (if employed) has current or updated establishment registration with FDA per 21 CFR 807.20(a)(2)
- verify supplier qualification
- verify completion of all global (if applicable) statutory and regulatory approval requirements, including PMA approval, 510(k) clearance, decision to file documentation, CE marking, declaration of conformity, satisfactorily filed technical updates, ISO 13485 certificate, FDA establishment registration, etc.

Following design transfer, the regulatory professional and/or a company quality representative should review the DHF for legibility, completeness and accuracy and to ensure the DHF's compliance with the applicable external requirements of 21 CFR 820.30 Design Controls and/or ISO 13485 (7.3) Design and Development. Design transfer activities are documented most often using a company-developed design transfer checklist, which becomes part of the DHF. The final product release may not occur until all incomplete, ambiguous or conflicting issues identified during the design transfer review meeting are resolved, and approval or clearance from regulatory bodies are in place, for countries in which the product will be distributed.

In some cases, actual medical device manufacture may take place at a contract supplier's location outside the company's control that designed the device. Regardless, the QMS requirements are the same for the supplier. From a regulatory perspective, the company that designed the device and gained regulatory approval or clearance owns the device technology and all its rights and, furthermore, ultimately is responsible for the distributed device's final quality, thus controlling the supplier's output. The key to successfully controlling a contract manufacturer is supplier management. The contact manufacturer's QMS should be assessed or audited to identify any potential compliance gaps that need to be overcome to ensure the finished device will comply with device design specifications. The regulatory professional may need to bridge the gap between the company and the contract manufacturer, especially if the contractor's raw materials and processes are protected by intellectual property rights. Many finished device manufacturers use contract sterilization facilities for terminal sterilization activities that also should be controlled through supplier management and considered during design transfer.

Changes to Mature Medical Devices and Manufacturing Processes

Design transfer activities may be repeated throughout the device's lifecycle when design modifications are made or manufacturing processes and/or locations change. These activities should be managed through the QMS change control process for a mature device. Extensive design changes may necessitate repeating design control activities. In addition, design changes, including labeling changes affecting the indications for use, technology or performance changes (e.g., adding another lumen opening above the inflatable cuff of an endotracheal tube to be used for suctioning), specification modifications (e.g., additional sizes), sterilization changes (e.g., gamma to EO) that may affect sterilization assurance level (SAL) and material changes (e.g., plastic to metal) that stimulate new risk questions may trigger the need for additional premarket notification from regulatory bodies. In all changes, the regulatory professional must determine whether the modifications do or do not trigger the need for new regulatory clearance in the countries in which the device is distributed. To do this successfully, the cross-functional team's design engineer or technical member must describe and document the proposed changes adequately and in sufficient detail for the regulatory professional to evaluate. For US distribution, the regulatory professional must use FDA's *Deciding When to Submit a 510(k) for a Change to an Existing Device (K97-1)*, published 10 January 1997, to evaluate the need for a new 510(k) clearance.[1] If changes are made to devices distributed outside the US, the regulatory professional must adhere to the requirements of those regulatory bodies. Notified Bodies that review devices distributed in the EU will review the device's technical files (similar to a premarket notification plus DMR). Regulatory agencies expect a company's QMS to be robust enough to evaluate and document all changes fully, and premarket review and approval are required in those cases where a risk to patient safety or the device's effectiveness may be introduced by the proposed change.

Other factors should be considered when the manufacturer wishes to make a change to the device. The regulatory approval timeline and cost should be communicated clearly to management with executive responsibility, so key stakeholders understand the required investment for the proposed change. Often, a series of small design or process modifications is made over time and documented internally without re-filing. The regulatory professional should be cognizant of multiple iterations and determine when it is necessary to re-file and document this recommendation to management. Monitoring competitors' (and substantially equivalent devices) filing activities can provide insight into the types of modifications the agency believes require a regulatory filing. Remember, the FDA inspector or Notified Body auditor always will have the benefit of hindsight, and perhaps data from actual field device use experience, when reviewing these determinations after the fact. Therefore, these decisions should be made using available guidance documents and other resources to make accurate determinations and document appropriately.

References
1. Food and Drug Administration. *Deciding When to Submit a 510(k) for a Change to an Existing Device (K97-1)*. 10 January 1997. FDA website. http://www.fda.gov/medicaldevices/deviceregulationandguidance/guidancedocuments/ucm080235.htm. Accessed 16 March 2016.

8 Nonclinical Laboratory Testing

By Dorota Grabowska, PhD, and Peter A. Takes, PhD, RAC, FRAPS

Introduction

Key to any global development strategy is nonclinical laboratory testing, since it provides the medical device's design foundation. Exhaustive device configuration evaluation is necessary throughout design evolution, not only to establish the medical device's technical and functional integrity, but also to infer its anticipated safety and efficacy before it is introduced into human subjects. This is achieved through systematic, controlled, bench and other "nonclinical" laboratory testing studies, appropriately broad in scope, but specific in detail, done with enough rigor to address most regulatory requirements. The essential nonclinical laboratory testing elements to be considered when planning medical device development and assessment strategies are discussed in this chapter.

Good Laboratory Practice

Good Laboratory Practice (GLP) is a quality system developed to ensure data integrity and quality from nonclinical studies, generated to support the approval of regulated products. GLP requires work to be done according to written protocols, standards and procedures, and the appropriate documentation of studies performed. GLP is followed to ensure data quality, traceability and integrity.

In 1979, the US Food and Drug Administration (FDA) published its first GLP regulation (21 CFR Part 58) in response to previous incorrectly documented and executed nonclinical tests performed by pharmaceutical companies and research organizations, and used to support regulatory submissions. GLP applies to *in vivo* and *in vitro* nonclinical studies done to ensure regulated products' safety and efficacy. Examples of studies subject to GLP regulations include *in vitro* and *in vivo* biocompatibility testing and animal studies.[1]

Incorporating GLP into regulatory strategy largely depends on the product type and subsequent preclinical testing to be executed. The GLP process does not apply to clinical, bench (i.e., research and development) and basic exploratory studies and is not intended to be used to evaluate scientific values.[2] Practical examples of investigations not within the scope of GLP include stability tests and device performance evaluations; such elements might be routinely within design controls.

In vitro diagnostics (IVDs) are classified as medical devices, but most studies done to establish their safety employ human specimens and directly involve human subjects. Thus, GLP generally does not apply to IVDs subjected to human subject research regulations (see below).

FDA requirements notwithstanding, GLP is an expected and accepted standard of practice globally for such evaluations. ISO 10993, an international standard for medical device biocompatibility testing, states any nonclinical test shall be done in compliance with GLP. FDA's regulations provided the basis for The Organization of Economic Cooperation and Development's (OECD), the international organization of North American, European and Asian countries, published Principles of Good Laboratory Practice.[3] Most developed countries have adopted the OECD Principles of Good Laboratory Practice, which have become universally *accepted standards*.

Table 8-1. The Universal Elements of GLP

Element	Description

Resources (organization, personnel and infrastructure)	The facility's structure must be defined clearly and includes:
	• Facility manager
	   - formal responsibility for the facility
	• Study director
	   - oversees results' interpretation, analysis, documentation and reporting
	• Appropriately documented competent, educated and trained personnel operating according to approved protocols
	• Organizational chart to illustrate relationships between the personnel
	• Controlled environmental factors such as temperature, humidity and light, with suitable separation between various distinct operations
	• Adequately maintained, tested, calibrated and standardized equipment

Quality Assurance	• Oversees all operations relevant to GLP standards and ensures conformance with regulations • Functions independently from the departments that conduct studies Quality Assurance must: • maintain copies of a master schedule sheet containing records of all studies conducted at the facility, study plans and SOPs • inspect the facilities to verify all established standards are met • determine no deviation from approved protocols and SOPs is made without proper authorization and documentation • verify study plans comply with GLP • inspect review reports to ensure data integrity
Characterization	• Test articles (items)—a medical device or any other article studied under GLP to determine its safety • Test system—"any biological, chemical or physical system or a combination thereof used in a study"
Rules	The facility should operate according to clearly defined rules described in the following documents: • study protocol—an approved written protocol covering the study's scientific and organizational aspects, describing the study's general plan and providing information on its experimental design • standard operating procedures (SOPs)—written protocols providing step-by-step directions on how to perform the activities described in the study protocol; SOPs should be established for all activities and processes specific to nonclinical laboratory studies
Results	Results include: • all raw data • documentation • protocols • final report GLP regulates how results are collected, reported and archived.

There are some noticeable differences in verbiage and certain requirements between the FDA and OECD GLP; however, the general principles and objectives remain the same.[4] A comparison of FDA and OECD GLP can be found on FDA's website.[5]

GLP was established to promote international data acceptance and facilitate universal exchange. OECD principles have become an integral part of the Council Decision on Mutual Acceptance of Data (MAD), which states, "data generated in the testing of chemicals in an OECD Member country in accordance with OECD Test Guidelines and OECD Principles of Good Laboratory Practice shall be accepted in other Member countries for purposes of assessment and other uses relating to the protection of man and the environment."[6] This avoids duplication of tests and reduces the cost of products approved in more than one country.

Regardless of the geographic intent for medical device distribution, the basic GLP elements to be incorporated in any regulatory strategy are universal, and are summarized in **Table 8-1**.[7]

Regulatory authorities inspect and audit testing facilities to determine their degree of GLP compliance. Facilities conducting GLP studies to support US regulatory approval are inspected by FDA. In the US, serious GLP regulation violations are cited in FDA Warning Letters.[8] **Table 8-2** presents examples of Warning Letters illustrating the most common GLP violations.

The consequences of noncompliance can be severe. For example, if the violations are significant and adversely affect nonclinical laboratory studies' integrity and quality, a regulatory agency may disqualify the testing facility. Also, a regulatory agency may refuse to review data due to a high level of noncompliance, which may result in a

Table 8-2. Examples of GLP violations from FDA Warning Letters

Quality Assurance	"Failure of the quality assurance unit to determine that no deviations from approved protocols or SOPs were made without proper authorization and documentation, and to review the final study report to assure that such report accurately describes the methods and SOPs. [21 CFR 58.35(b)(5) and (6)] The quality assurance unit (QAU) shall determine that no deviations from approved protocols or standard operating procedures were made without proper authorization and documentation. In addition, the QAU shall review the final study report to assure that it accurately describes the methods and standard operating procedures, and that the reported results accurately reflect the raw data of the nonclinical laboratory study."
Training	"Failure to ensure that each individual engaged in the conduct of or responsible for supervision of a nonclinical laboratory study has education, training, and experience, and failure to ensure that the testing facility maintains a current summary of training and experience. [21 CFR 58.29(a) and (b)] Each individual engaged in the conduct of, or responsible for, the supervision of a nonclinical laboratory study shall have education, training, and experience, or a combination thereof, to enable that individual to perform the assigned functions. Additionally, each testing facility shall maintain a current summary of training and experience and a job description for each individual engaged in or supervising the conduct of a nonclinical laboratory study."
Record retention	"Failure to retain final reports generated as a result of the nonclinical laboratory study. [21 CFR 58.190(a)] Final reports generated as a result of a nonclinical laboratory study must be retained. Your facility did not retain copies of final reports for ANS 1313, 1338, 1375, 1376, and 1393."
Equipment issues	"Failure to adequately inspect, maintain, test, calibrate, and standardize equipment. [21 CFR 58.63(a)] Equipment shall be adequately inspected, cleaned, and maintained. Equipment used for the generation, measurement, or assessment of data shall be adequately tested, calibrated, and/or standardized. Your staff could not provide documentation that the [instrument] used in study [study name] was ever calibrated. This study required that the room temperature and humidity for the test systems be controlled within [degrees] and [degrees], respectively."
Study protocol and standard operation procedures	"Failure to ensure that all deviations from standard operating procedures are authorized by the study director and documented in the raw data [21 CFR 58.81(a)] A testing facility shall have SOPs in writing, which set forth nonclinical laboratory study methods that management is satisfied are adequate to ensure the quality and integrity of the data generated in the course of a study. All deviations in a study from SOPs shall be authorized by the study director and shall be documented in the raw data. Deviations from the SOPs shall be properly authorized in writing by management. Studies [study names] appear to have deviated from your company's SOPs in ways that were neither authorized by the study director nor documented in the raw data for the applicable study."

delayed approval process and increased product development costs.[9]

Risk Management

Risk analysis (risk management) encompasses a broad range of elements requiring nonclinical laboratory testing before proceeding to either animal or human *in vivo* studies. Some risk analyses may involve animal studies as well, as this may be the most effective means to make a hazard determination. This type of evaluation addresses device-associated hazards or potential sources of harm from association with and/or application of the device. In any formal quality system linked to a medical device's evolution, risk management should be an integral part of design controls; such hazard assessment must be documented and any risks detected mitigated appropriately.

Other sections within this chapter discuss testing related to risk analysis. Elements like biocompatibility and stability testing all should be executed with the expectation of identifying and mitigating potential device hazards. Medical device risks can be considered to occur within three basic categories: normal device function (the treatment or diagnostic itself), device use (operation) and, most commonly considered first in hazard analysis, the device's failure or malfunction. Typical risks to be considered in any regulatory strategy (depending on device type and intended use) include those of an electrical (e.g., shock from a poor connection), mechanical (e.g., gear breakage), magnetic (e.g., excess magnetic field affects pacemaker), thermal (e.g., device gets too hot), chemical (e.g., leakage of a corrosive chemical), radiological (e.g., not shielded properly for excess radiation exposure) and/or biological (e.g., implantation of a device facilitates

Table 8-3. Sources of Device Risk

Category	Device Example	Hazard
Normal function (treatment use)	Ablation catheter	Physician pushes with continuous pressure and burns a hole through the tissue
Device use (normal operation)	Electrical bone saw	Saw vibrates extensively during use to cause neurological damage in the hand of a repeat operator
Device failure or malfunction	Heart defibrillator	Does not charge or delivers too much voltage to the patient

inflammation at the localization site) nature, or, as applied to all, a component of human factors (direct device use). Examples of the three basic categories are provided in **Table 8-3**.

Certainly, not all risk elements apply to every device. A comprehensive and complete determination must be made as to which categories apply to a specific device or device type. Hazard analysis strategy must be tailored to and a written risk management plan designed for the device type under development. This needs to occur early in the design planning (design controls) of a new device, at least by Phase II or III of the design strategy.

FDA's guidance, *Medical Device Use-Safety: Incorporating Human Factors Engineering Into Risk Management*[10] provides a detailed strategic approach to performing hazard analysis. Regardless of the device's type (e.g., IVD, surgical, implant, robotic) or application, some general principles apply to risk evaluation:

- the environment in which the device is to be used—the effects of light, noise, external vibration or motion
- the device operator's knowledge, ability, required training and limitations
- device design factors—operational requirements and procedures, as well as user interface characteristics

Globally, risk analysis is critical to meeting the requirements of every formal regulatory system. It is prudent to investigate regulatory expectations in the specific regions in which the device will be marketed.

Biocompatibility

Biocompatibility is the ability of medical devices or materials to coexist with a living system without having a toxic or injurious effect. Medical devices can come into direct contact (e.g., implants, gloves, stethoscopes) or indirect contact (e.g., dialyzers, blood administration sets) with a patient's tissue. A device-living tissue interaction may affect a living system's functions adversely by inducing undesirable processes such as injury, inflammation or irritation.[11] Biocompatibility testing is intended to assess the living system's response to the medical device and determine whether the device presents any potential harm to the user. Since biocompatibility testing generally involves nonclinical studies done to support approval of regulated products, such evaluations should be conducted according to GLP.

A device's biocompatibility depends on the physical and chemical properties of its materials, its intended use, the tissue with which it will come into contact and the duration of the contact. Thus, biocompatibility can be assessed only in the context of these parameters. *In vitro* analysis of materials and components is the first step to determine the device's biological safety. This covers evaluating the genotoxicity, cytotoxicity and hemotoxicity of leachable materials extracted from the device or its components. The second step includes *in vivo* animal tests such as implantation, sensitization, irritation, etc. Depending on the specific tests needed, device biocompatibility evaluation may take up to several months, and the regulatory strategy and plan should account for those time requirements. Standard biocompatibility tests are presented in **Table 8-4**.[12]

ISO 10993, the principal guideline for biocompatibility testing, provides a set of harmonized standards for evaluation of biological safety of medical devices.[13] While national regulatory authorities generally recognize ISO 10993 standards, there are some differences in specific testing protocols and requirements among countries.

Selecting appropriate biocompatibility tests is the most critical step in medical device biological safety evaluation. ISO 10993 classifies medical devices based on the nature of the body contact (surface devices, external communicating devices and implant devices) and duration of the contact (limited exposure <24 hours, prolonged and repeated exposure 24 hours to 30 days and permanent contact >30 days) (**Table 8-5**). This classification is used primarily to select the appropriate biocompatibility tests for a medical device. Once the device has been classified, manufacturers may refer to the ISO 10993 matrices that indicate required tests.[14]

Table 8-4. Biocompatibility Tests

Test	Description
Sensitization	Evaluates the potential allergic reaction associated with exposure to device materials or their leachable extracts. The test is performed on animal models or humans.
Irritation	Estimates a localized inflammatory response to the test materials or their extracts. The areas tested include the animal model or human's skin, mucous membranes and eyes.
Toxicity	Employs an animal model to evaluate the test sample's toxic effect. Depending on the exposure duration, the following tests are performed: • acute toxicity (single or multiple exposures, in less than 24h) • subchronic toxicity (multiple or long-term exposure, in one day, but not exceeding 10% of the lifespan of the test animal) • chronic toxicity (multiple or long-term exposure, in at least 10% of the lifespan of the test animal)
Cytotoxicity	*In vitro* assay to determine cell damage (cell lysis, growth inhibition and other toxic effects) caused by the test materials or their extracts.
Pyrogenicity	Evaluates the potential febrile reaction to device materials or their leachable extracts.
Genotoxicity	*In vitro* assay employing mammalian and non-mammalian cells to determine gene mutations, changes in chromosome structure and number and other DNA or gene toxicities caused by test materials or their extracts.
Implantation	Employs an animal model to assess implantable material's local effect on living tissue.
Hemocompatibility	Employs an animal model to evaluate an effect of blood-contacting devices or materials on blood components.
Carcinogenicity	*In vivo* animal test evaluating the carcinogenic effect of the test materials or their extracts.
Reproductive and Developmental Toxicity	Evaluates the potential effect of the test materials or their extracts on reproductive function and development.
Biodegradation	*In vivo* animal test to determine the potential effect of degradation products of test materials or their extracts.
Immune Response	Evaluates potential adverse immunological effects of test materials or their extracts.

Table 8-5. Medical Device Classification Based on the Nature of Body Contact and Contact Duration

Nature of Body Contact	Examples
Surface devices • skin • mucosal membranes • breached or compromised surfaces	adhesive bandages, stethoscopes, gloves, external prostheses, contact lenses, urinary catheters
External communication • blood path, indirect • tissue/bone/dentin communication • circulating blood	dialyzers, blood administration sets, laparoscopes, dental filling materials
Implant • tissue/bone • blood	heart valves, pacemakers, orthopedic implants
Contact Duration	
Limited exposure <24h	gloves, bandages
Prolonged and repeated exposure 24h to 30 days	catheters, skin closure devices, infusion cannulas
Permanent contact >30 days	heart valves, pacemakers, orthopedic implants

Table 8-6. Basic Animal Study Protocol Elements

- Study purpose
- Justification for the use of animals, describing the advantages of the animal model versus non-animal models
- Rationale for selecting a particular animal model
- Detailed description of the procedures performed on animals during the study and information on how the procedures will impact animals' well-being
- Justification of animal numbers required to achieve study objectives
- Appropriate humane endpoints
- Animal husbandry
- Training, qualification and experience of personnel who will work with animals
- Description of appropriate sedation, analgesia and anesthesia methods
- Potential occupational health and safety issues that may arise due to the use of hazardous materials

While ISO 10993 provides a framework for biocompatibility strategy, it is the manufacturers' responsibility to ensure selected tests evaluate biological safety adequately. Good scientific knowledge must be applied when planning a project. In some situations, additional tests, not included in ISO 10993, may be needed to estimate biocompatibility comprehensively. In other situations, specific assessments may be avoided if relevant data exist already and can be documented. For example, information about predicate biocompatibility may be submitted to FDA instead of performing certain biocompatibility testing, but only if the predicate is made from identical materials, and the nature of body contact and its duration are the same. To avoid any biocompatibility test pitfalls that could delay product launch, manufacturers are advised to discuss the test plan with the appropriate regulatory agency before initiating testing.

Manufacturers should consider biocompatibility tests early in product development, when device materials are being selected. This decision should be based primarily on scientific literature and *in vitro* tests. By choosing device materials that have been tested and characterized, if data already exist, manufacturers may avoid performing specific tests. This strategy could reduce product costs and promote rapid development.

While testing raw materials can minimize the risk of device biocompatibility test failures, it is insufficient to demonstrate the finished device's biocompatibility. Production processes, such as sterilization or material interaction, may affect the finished device's properties.

Table 8-7. Animal Models for In Vivo Medical Device Assessment

Device Classification	Animal
Cardiovascular	
Heart valves	Sheep
Vascular grafts	Dog, pig
Stents	Pig, rabbit, dog
Ventricular assist devices	Calf
Artificial hearts	Calf
Ex-vivo shunts	Baboon, dog
Orthopedic/bone	
Bone regeneration/substitutes	Rabbit, dog, pig, mouse, rat, goat, non-human primates
Total joints—hips, knees	Sheep, goat, baboon
Vertebral implants	Rabbit, pig, dog, non-human primates
Craniofacial implants	Rabbit, dog
Cartilage	Dog, sheep
Tendon and ligament substitutes	Goat
Neurological	
Peripheral nerve regeneration	Rat, cat, non-human primates
Electrical stimulation	Rat, cat, non-human primates
Ophthalmological	
Contact lens	Rabbit
Intraocular lens	Rabbit, monkey

(Source: Ratner BD, Hoffman AS, Schoen FJ, Lemons JE. *Biomaterials Science: An Introduction to Materials in Medicine*. Elsevier Science; 2004.)

Figure 8-1. Strategy for Performing Animal Studies

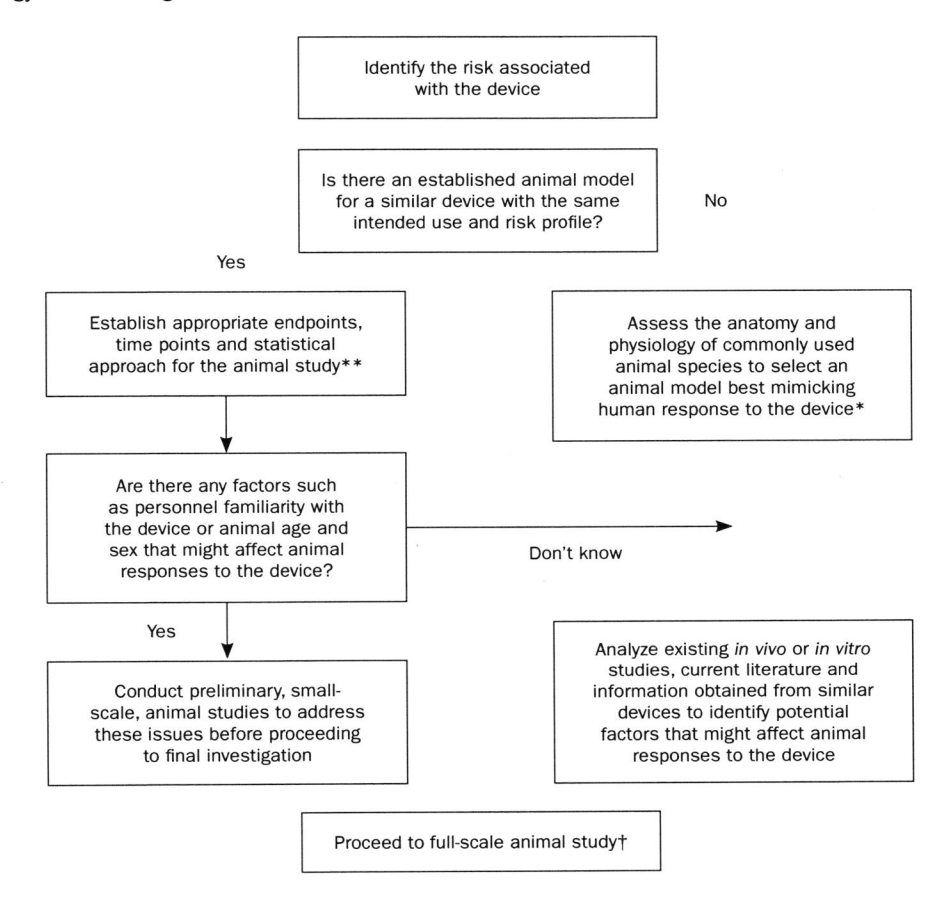

```
                    ┌─────────────────────────────┐
                    │ Identify the risk associated │
                    │      with the device         │
                    └──────────────┬──────────────┘
                                   ▼
                    ┌─────────────────────────────┐
                    │ Is there an established      │
                    │ animal model for a similar   │  No
                    │ device with the same         │─────────┐
                    │ intended use and risk profile?│        │
                    └──────────────┬──────────────┘         │
                         Yes       │                         ▼
                                   ▼              ┌──────────────────────┐
                    ┌─────────────────────────┐   │ Assess the anatomy   │
                    │ Establish appropriate    │   │ and physiology of    │
                    │ endpoints, time points   │   │ commonly used animal │
                    │ and statistical approach │   │ species to select an │
                    │ for the animal study**   │   │ animal model best    │
                    └──────────────┬──────────┘   │ mimicking human      │
                                   │              │ response to the      │
                                   ▼              │ device*              │
                    ┌─────────────────────────┐   └──────────────────────┘
                    │ Are there any factors    │
                    │ such as personnel        │
                    │ familiarity with the     │    Don't know
                    │ device or animal age     │─────────────────▶
                    │ and sex that might       │
                    │ affect animal responses  │
                    │ to the device?           │
                    └──────────────┬──────────┘
                         Yes       │
                                   ▼              ┌──────────────────────┐
                    ┌─────────────────────────┐   │ Analyze existing     │
                    │ Conduct preliminary,     │   │ in vivo or in vitro  │
                    │ small-scale, animal      │   │ studies, current     │
                    │ studies to address       │   │ literature and       │
                    │ these issues before      │   │ information obtained │
                    │ proceeding to final      │   │ from similar devices │
                    │ investigation            │   │ to identify potential│
                    └──────────────┬──────────┘   │ factors that might   │
                                   │              │ affect animal        │
                                   ▼              │ responses to the     │
                    ┌─────────────────────────┐   │ device               │
                    │ Proceed to full-scale    │   └──────────────────────┘
                    │ animal study†            │
                    └─────────────────────────┘
```

*If commonly used animal models are not suitable to evaluate safety and efficacy of the device, contact the appropriate regulatory agency to discuss alternative approaches.
**Identify humane endpoints and time points that meet study objectives. It is recommended to use endpoints and time points reported for a similar device that has the same indication for use.
†If, after completing the above process, there are still questions regarding the proposed animal study strategy, contact the appropriate regulatory agency to discuss these issues.

Thus, regulatory agencies typically require biocompatibility data to be completed on the finished device, not prototypes, interim design versions or pre-design transfer "final" product. Fulfilling this requirement requires advance planning and coordination with other functional areas, so necessary samples are available for testing when required to support submission plans.

Animal Studies

In nonclinical laboratory studies, biological specimens and/or live organisms (i.e., animals, microorganisms and cell lines) often are required to evaluate device safety and efficacy. Animal studies play a key role in this process, providing important information about a device's function in an *in vivo* system and the potential biological response to the device. Data obtained from these studies generally are evaluated in regulatory processes to assess potential device safety, performance and efficacy before it is used in human clinical studies.

Animal studies are performed according to written protocols and designed to address device risk analysis elements clearly. **Table 8-6** outlines the basic elements to be considered in designing an animal study protocol.[15] During the device development process, animal studies generally start after exploratory bench testing is completed, and resulting potential device risks are identified. The strategy for designing animal studies follows a simple, fundamental approach (**Figure 8-1**) determining the

Table 8-8. International Animal Research Laws, Policies and Guidelines

Country	Animal Research Laws, Policies and Guidelines
Australia	Australian Animal Welfare Strategy (AAWS)
Brazil	National Council for the Control of Animal Experimentation (CONCEA)
Canada	Canadian Council on Animal Care (CCAC)
European Union	European Directive 2010/63/EU
India	Committee for the Purpose of Control and Supervision of Experiments on Animals
Japan	Guidelines for Proper Conduct of Animal Experiments
Singapore	Agri-Food and Veterinary Authority of Singapore (the Guidelines on the Care and Use of Animals for Scientific Purposes)
Taiwan	Council of Agriculture (the Taiwan Animal Protection Act)
UK	Home Office webpage with information on requirements, licenses and regulation
US	Animal Welfare Regulations (USDA 1985; US Code, 42 USC § 289d) and the Public Health Service Policy on Humane Care and Use of Laboratory Animals (PHS 2002)

appropriate subject species model, endpoints and other factors that might influence results' integrity.

Selecting an appropriate animal model is a critical decision in medical device testing and should be made based on scientific evidence showing the model is suitable for the study. The advantages and limitations of using a particular animal model to mimic human responses to the device should be evaluated carefully when planning the study. For example, sheep have cardiac valve anatomy similar to that of humans, and their calcification process is clinically relevant to human physiology. Thus, sheep commonly are used as animal models for heart valve testing.[16] **Table 8-7** presents animal models customarily used for the *in vivo* assessment of medical devices.[17] Further, animal studies to support eventual safety and efficacy claims should be conducted under GLP.

Institutions and individuals conducting animal studies have a moral responsibility to ensure the animals' health and welfare are protected during all phases of the research. Animal care policies, standards and procedures are covered by a wide range of country-specific regulations (**Table 8-8**). These regulations must be taken into consideration when planning animal studies. However, regardless of geographic location, scientists are encouraged to follow the principles of the three Rs (Replacement, Reduction and Refinement), a set of internationally accepted standards for designing and conducting animal testing. "Replacement" refers to alternative methods, such as *in vitro* biological systems, mathematical modeling and computer simulations that can be used instead of live animals. "Reduction" promotes the use of a minimal number of animals to achieve project objectives. "Refinement" refers to husbandry and experimental procedures that should be performed to enhance animal well-being and minimize or eliminate pain or distress.[18] **Table 8-9** outlines useful resources for planning and conducting animal studies in accordance with the three Rs' principles.

Implementing the three Rs requires a testing facility to establish an appropriate animal care and use program that includes animal and veterinary care, policies and procedures, personnel and program management, occupational health and safety and adequately equipped animal facilities. To ensure the highest standards of animal well-being, the program needs to be managed and evaluated effectively. The Institutional Animal Care and Use Committee (IACUC) or international equivalent plays a key role in this process. An IACUC's functions include reviewing and approving animal use protocols, regularly inspecting facilities and animal use areas, assessing animal care and use and reporting and investigating animal welfare concerns at the institution.[19]

To show commitment to animal welfare and the highest standards, testing facilities are encouraged to become accredited by the Association for Assessment and Accreditation of Laboratory Animal Care (AAALCA), an international, private, nonprofit organization promoting the humane treatment of animals in science.[20]

Stability

Medical devices are susceptible to degradation that may change their physical, chemical, toxicological and microbiological properties significantly, potentially affecting a device's overall performance and safety. This susceptibility to degradation relates primarily to the device's nature, intended use, storage conditions (e.g., temperature,

Table 8-9. Useful Web Resources for Planning and Conducting Animal Studies in Accordance With the 3Rs Principles

The European Convention for the Protection of Vertebrate Animals used for Experimental and Other Scientific Purposes is a useful web resource for European regulations and standards relating to animal care and use in Member States (http://conventions.coe.int/treaty/Commun/QueVoulezVous.asp?NT=123&CM=0&CL=ENG). Accessed 16 March 2016.
The Interagency Coordinating Committee on the Validation of Alternative Methods (ICCVAM) provides many websites for decisions related to animal care and use, refinements, reductions and replacement of animal models and validated models (http://iccvam.niehs.nih.gov/home.htm). Accessed 16 March 2016.
The European Convention on the Validation of Alternative Methods is a useful web link to validated European alternative animal models (http://ihcp.jrc.ec.europa.eu/our_labs/eurl-ecvam). Accessed 16 March 2016.
The Japanese Convention on the Validation of Alternative Methods is a resource for those animal models and animal welfare items of interest from Japan (http://jacvam.jp/en/). Accessed 16 March 2016.
The Johns Hopkins Center for Alternatives (CAT) is a comprehensive web resource for all subjects related to global animal care and use, animal welfare and animal alternatives. (http://caat.jhsph.edu/). Accessed 16 March 2016.
The National Center for 3Rs is a comprehensive web link for animal care and use and animal refinement and replacement questions (http://www.nc3rs.org.uk/). Accessed 16 March 2016.

humidity, light, UV, etc.), storage time, packaging and manufacturing processes.

The United States Pharmacopeial Convention (USP) defines stability as "the extent to which a product, within specified limits, and throughout its period of storage and use, i.e., its shelf life, has the same properties and characteristics that it possessed at the time of manufacture."[21] Stability is a very important aspect of medical device development and manufacturing, since it demonstrates how long the product is safe for patients and performs according to its intended use. Thus, stability testing contributes substantially to medical devices' overall safety and reliability assessment.

Stability tests' main objective is to establish shelf life (i.e., the period during which the device maintains its original properties and performs according to its intended use) and expiration date (i.e., shelf-life termination). Additionally, stability testing provides information about product properties, such as degradation, mechanical resistance and durability and helps manufacturers establish appropriate storage, shipping and packaging conditions.

Commonly, two stability test types are applied: real-time stability testing and accelerated or stress stability testing. In real-time studies, a final product is stored at the recommended conditions and monitored over time until changes occur in its properties. Since this is a long-term process, manufacturers can use accelerated aging to estimate the product's stability. During this study, products are subjected to elevated stress storage conditions, such as temperature, pH, humidity, oxidation and repetitive freezing and thawing. Once the data are collected, the product's shelf life can be predicted based on the relationship between stress conditions and the degradation rate.

Regulatory agencies allow a tentative expiration date based on accelerating aging data for device clearance/approval, but those tests have to be followed and supported by real-time studies.[22] Planning stability evaluations, manufacturers need to define testing conditions and develop an adequate sampling plan, i.e., the number of products to be tested, frequency of sampling, sample collection criteria and lots to be sampled. Companies should begin with long-term stability testing on the first three production lots (or devices, as might be applicable), and thereafter, put at least one lot per year into real-time stability, or each lot if made less than once per year.[23]

The appropriate stability testing strategy is based on the estimation of whether the device degradation processes would lead to functional failure and how the failure impacts the patient. For example, some devices, e.g., tongue depressors, do not require stability testing, since there is a low probability product degradation adversely affects patients' safety. On the other hand, life-supporting devices, e.g., pacemakers, need comprehensive stability testing, since their degradation and failure may have serious patient consequences.

The ICH Q1A(R2) guideline adopted by the EU, US and Japan describes basic requirements for planning and conducting stability testing.[24] Although the guideline applies to drug substances and products, it can be used as a starting point in evaluating medical device stability.

In Vitro Diagnostics

IVDs (assays, reagents, equipment) require their own separate testing category, particularly the assays themselves. Such elements as biocompatibility generally do not

Table 8-10. Questions a Company Should Consider When Selecting a CRO

- Does the laboratory allow its laboratory facilities to be audited?
- What laboratory certifications, licenses and registrations does the laboratory hold? Do these meet the company's criteria for laboratory vendors?
- Has the laboratory been inspected recently by representatives of any state, federal or international organization(s) like FDA, the Environmental Protection Agency or Notified Bodies? Will the laboratory allow the company to see these audit or inspection results?
- Is the laboratory involved in any outside laboratory certification or performance testing, like Clinical Laboratory Improvement Amendments?
- What is the laboratory's business history?
- What are the laboratory staff's experience and capabilities?
- What is the average laboratory testing turn-around time?
- What are the laboratory's testing, research, experimentation development or analysis capabilities? What is the normal laboratory testing volume?
- Does the laboratory have a structured quality program in place with laboratory quality manual, quality procedures, quality policies and quality audits? Does the laboratory adhere to and maintain compliance with its laboratory quality program?
- How does the laboratory handle, maintain and store laboratory testing samples? Are these laboratory procedures adequate to avoid laboratory testing sample mix-up or contamination?
- How does the laboratory handle product, laboratory testing, laboratory test result and laboratory data confidentiality?
- Will the laboratory allow review of laboratory testing raw data?
- Is the laboratory financially sound and viable?
- What are laboratory personnel's education, experience and training? Are laboratory personnel experienced and knowledgeable in the laboratory testing areas the company needs? Do laboratory personnel receive adequate continuing education and training for their jobs? Are laboratory personnel up to date with current laboratory test methods, procedures, etc.?
- How are laboratory facilities, laboratory equipment, laboratory instruments and laboratory facility systems such as water systems and air systems maintained? Are these laboratory facilities, laboratory equipment and laboratory instruments adequate for the type of laboratory testing the company needs?
- How accessible and responsive is the contract laboratory to its clients?

(Adapted from ContractLaboratory.com)

apply, but considerations like basic risk analysis and stability testing are applicable universally. In addition, IVDs often require such nonclinical evaluations as method comparison, precision, reproducibility, analytical sensitivity, tissue sampling concerns and sample matrices (e.g., serum vs. plasma vs. whole blood samples). These types of analyses are critical to a successful regulatory outcome in IVD approval or clearance (refer to Chapter 10 for a more detailed discussion of IVD development strategy).

Outsourcing

Medical device preclinical research and development are expensive and time-consuming and require many resources (e.g., infrastructure, personnel and organization) and scientific expertise, particularly when the tests are conducted under GLP. For small, medium and even some large companies, setting up and running testing or manufacturing facilities may be costly and ineffective. Thus, a growing number of medical device companies turn to outsourcing as a way to reduce costs and increase efficiency.

There are three main steps in developing an outsourcing strategy: first, identifying which preclinical testing process needs to be outsourced and when; second, selecting an appropriate contract research organization (CRO); and third, managing the relationship with a CRO.

Companies usually decide to outsource when they lack the skills, expertise, facilities and equipment needed to complete the project. The decision requires careful evaluation of study goals and objectives, testing time, budget and handling intellectual property issues. CROs provide a wide range of services including biocompatibility testing, materials characterization, stability testing, chemical testing and device performance review.

When selecting an outsourcing partner, companies must review the CRO's accreditations, certifications, licenses, reputation and scientific expertise. Many companies perform a formal laboratory vendor qualification process using approved and documented requirements. For example, selecting a CRO may include completing a vendor quality survey or laboratory quality checklist, or it may be preceded by auditing a potential research partner. If the laboratory performs a critical product development function (e.g., product validation processes), a professional vendor audit should be conducted to evaluate the CRO's capabilities thoroughly. **Table 8-10** presents a list of questions the company should consider when assessing a potential partner's qualifications.[25]

After selecting a CRO, the company should implement a communication strategy to manage the relationship with the partner. Open and frequent communication between the sponsor and CRO can help identify and resolve potential issues early, thus increasing efficiency. It is good practice to conduct annual audits of CROs and/or manufacturing partners, which may be particularly necessary when the partner is involved in design validation, verification testing or performing studies under GLP.

Conclusion

Nonclinical laboratory testing takes significant time and effort and often requires prototype devices and/or finished device samples produced under Good Manufacturing Practices (GMPs). Thus, there is a clear need for advance nonclinical laboratory study planning, both for availability of appropriate samples and the duration and cost of the necessary tests. Such laboratory evaluations must be designed based upon the "system" being assessed to determine if and what form of bench, animal and/or human trials are appropriate and essential. The device's relative risk is also a determining factor.

An appropriate device development strategy must take laboratory testing requirements into account. It is the regulatory professional's responsibility to ensure good coordination between and among various functional areas. Synchronizing all relevant departments is critical to avoid surprises and subsequent project delays that may lead to potential compression or postponement of the time necessary to prepare a regulatory submission.

References

1. *The Applicability of Good Laboratory Practice in Premarket Device Submission: Questions and Answers; Draft Guidance for Industry and Food Administration Staff* (28 August 2013). FDA website. http://www.fda.gov/RegulatoryInformation/Guidances/ucm366338.htm. Accessed 16 March 2016.
2. Ibid.
3. Testing of chemicals. OECD website. http://www.oecd.org/chemicalsafety/testing/. Accessed 16 March 2016.
4. Huntsinger DW. OECD and USA GLP applications. NLM website. http://www.ncbi.nlm.nih.gov/pubmed/19352004. Accessed 16 March 2016.
5. Bioresearch Monitoring. Comparison Chart of FDA and EPA Good Laboratory Practice (GLP) Regulations and the OECD Principles of GLP. FDA website. http://www.fda.gov/ICECI/EnforcementActions/BioresearchMonitoring/ucm135197.htm. Accessed 16 March 2016.
6. Chemical safety and biosafety. OECD website. http://www.oecd.org/chemicalsafety/. Accessed 16 March 2016.
7. *Handbook: Good Laboratory Practice (GLP): Quality practices for non-clinical research and development*. 2009. WHO website. http://www.who.int/tdr/publications/documents/glp-handbook.pdf. Accessed 16 March 2016.
8. Warning Letters. FDA website. http://www.fda.gov/iceci/enforcementactions/WarningLetters/default.htm. Accessed 16 March 2016.
9. Op cit 1.
10. *Guidance for Industry and FDA Premarket and Design Control Reviewers: Medical Device Use Safety: Incorporating Human Factors Engineering into Risk Management* (18 July 2000). FDA website. http://www.fda.gov/downloads/MedicalDevices/.../ucm094461.pdf. Accessed 16 March 2016.
11. Anderson JM. "Biological Responses to Materials." *Annu. Rev. Mater. Res*. 2001;31(1):81–110. AR website. http://www.annualreviews.org/doi/abs/10.1146/annurev.matsci.31.1.81?journalCode=matsci. Accessed 16 March 2016.
12. Gad SC. *Safety Evaluation of Pharmaceuticals and Medical Devices: International Regulatory Guidelines*. Springer;2010.
13. *Use of International Standard ISO-10993, Biological Evaluation of Medical Devices Part 1: Evaluation and Testing. Draft Guidance for Industry and Food and Drug Administration Staff* (23 April 2013). FDA website. http://www.fda.gov/downloads/medicaldevices/deviceregulationandguidance/guidancedocuments/ucm348890.pdf. Accessed 16 March 2016.
14. Ibid.
15. *Guide for the Care and Use of Laboratory Animals: Eighth Edition*. The National Academics Press;2011.
16. Ali ML, Kumar SP, Bjornstad K, Duran CMG. "The sheep as an animal model for heart valve research." *Vascular*. 1996;4(4):543–549. NLM website. http://www.ncbi.nlm.nih.gov/pubmed/8866098. Accessed 16 March 2016.
17. Ratner BD, Hoffman AS, Schoen FG, Lemons JE. *Biomaterials Science: An Introduction to Materials in Medicine*. Elsevier Science. 2004.
18. Op cit 14.
19. Ibid.
20. Steps to Earning Accreditation. American Association for Accreditation of Laboratory Animal Care (AAALAC) website. http://aaalac.org/accreditation/steps.cfm. Accessed 17 March 2016.
21. Strength and Stability Testing for Compounded Preparations. United States Pharmacopeial Convention website. http://www.usp.org/sites/default/files/usp_pdf/EN/healthcareProfessionals/strength-stability-testing-compounded-preparations.pdf. Accessed 17 March 2016.
22. Clark GS. *FDA Guidance Document: Shelf Life of Medical Devices* (27 February 1977). FDA website. http://www.fda.gov/downloads/MedicalDevices/.../UCM081366.pdf. Accessed 16 March 2016.
23. Takes PA. "Stability, shelf life, and expiration dating." *Microsc. Today*. 1998;98(10):20–21.
24. *Guidance for Industry: Q1A(R2) Stability Testing of New Drug Substances and Products* (6 February 2003). FDA website. http://www.fda.gov/downloads/drugs/guidancecomplianceregulatoryinformation/guidances/ucm073369.pdf. Accessed 16 March 2016.
25. Selecting Contract Laboratories for Laboratory Testing, Contract Research, Studies, Development, Analysis, Experiments. Contract Laboratory website. https://www.contractlaboratory.com/labclass/lab_qualification.cfm. Accessed 17 March 2016

9 Global Medical Device Clinical Strategy

By Dawn Norman

Introduction

Depending on the source, "strategy" is defined as:
- a careful plan or method for achieving a particular goal usually over a long period of time[1]
- the art and science of planning and marshalling resources for their most efficient and effective use[2]
- a long-range plan for achieving something or reaching a goal, or the skill of making such plans[3]

Each definition acknowledges reaching goals over a lengthy period of time. When developing a clinical strategy for drug, biologic or medical device development, it is imperative to take multiple considerations into account for 'marshalling resources for their most efficient and effective use' to achieve a particular goal. These considerations are the focus of this chapter.

Clinical strategy, as a whole, is different than clinical study design and execution. While clinical study design and execution certainly are major strategy outputs, clinical strategy is what the quality system side would call the collection of design inputs to ensure outputs meet the requirements. These requirements span not only the medical or regulatory requirements of understanding the device's safety and effectiveness but also meeting the objectives needed for the business to market the device adequately and as aggressively as possible and achieve reimbursement when available.

Clinical strategy development also goes beyond the clinical trial's closure and inclusion of regulatory's premarket submission and postmarket requirements. This strategy also should look to the next step or future horizon of claims, additional indications for use, expansion of patient populations or additional international markets and next generation potential. If a clinical study can be designed to collect early baseline data that may be used for reference or future comparisons, it is an excellent opportunity. This may not be possible in all cases but certainly should be a consideration during strategic discussions.

It is important to note this chapter focuses on the considerations required to develop global clinical strategies and only touches on protocol design, site selection and study conduct but will not go in-depth into those topics.

Responsibility, Collaboration and Organization

A critical start to developing a global clinical strategy is determining who truly is responsible for driving, not only the clinical trial and its execution, but also bringing together the collaborators and collecting the information that will define the clinical study's objectives.

Most commonly, a project lead or clinical affairs department management would be in charge of defining clinical strategy. However, in smaller companies or start-ups, there may not be a clinical affairs department or management with true clinical affairs experience. Marketing or engineering leads or managers may be appointed this task if the company has decided to outsource its clinical activities, with the understanding they need to ignore the potential bias of their primary roles to ensure regulatory compliance.

Clearly, clinical consultants or contract research organizations (CROs) may be hired. Too often, CROs are hired only to execute the clinical study but not to develop the clinical strategy. The CRO may or may not have the opportunity to provide feedback on clinical study design or the overall clinical strategy. If a company is going to hire a CRO to conduct the study, it is suggested the CRO be given an opportunity to provide input into the strategic planning so it can understand the company's vision during the planning process. This will allow it to align its performance to ensure the company's satisfaction.

Whoever takes the lead, it is imperative the work be performed cross-functionally, with data gathered from respective stakeholders and their feedback organized accordingly.

Marketing/Clinical Claims

Premarket considerations generally are focused on how to complete the study as quickly as possible, while meeting regulatory requirements. The budget is scrutinized to allow enough funding to support the desired indications for use and basic desired claims, while complying with regulations. Yet, a poorly planned or rushed clinical strategy has the same negative bottom line impact as a poorly designed product.

As with the regulatory strategy, the clinical strategy should start considering the end goal and ask, "What do we want to say about this product to the customer?" One of the greatest conflicts between marketing and regulatory during product launches and post-clearance or approval is the lack of clinical evidence supporting the desired claims, competitive statistics, etc.

Clinical should be involved heavily with marketing, regulatory and reimbursement strategy groups in early brainstorming sessions, learning how the company wants to promote the product once cleared or approved. This will assist in fully assessing the market potential, competitive landscape, clinical trial requirements and anticipated efficacy or effectiveness to determine the product's commercial adoption.

The marketing, regulatory and clinical considerations listed below are the basis of the clinical strategy. All of these heavily contribute to initial product development planning:

- In which countries does the company want to market the technology?
- Do regulatory bodies in the desired country(ies) have clinical evaluation requirements, and what are they (e.g., EU, China, Russia, etc.)?
- Will the US Food and Drug Administration (FDA) accept data from outside the US? More importantly, will US data be accepted by other countries?
- What is the target patient population (age, race, sex, etc.)?
  - Patient populations can differ based on the indication; for example, sickle cell anemia is more prevalent in people from parts of the world where malaria is or was common[4,5]
- What are the published disease progress or procedure incidence rates in these countries?
- How well do the potential site locations match up to the enrollee target population geographic locations?
- Should patient development states be considered (e.g., birth–six months, seven months–two years, two years, one month–four years, etc., in pediatrics; stage I, II, III or IV for cancer)?
- In what setting(s) may the patient normally receive the treatment, procedure or device? Could it be multiple settings (hospital, clinic or at home or a Phase I/volunteer clinic, etc.)?
- Is this a nonsignificant risk device that could be studied with an IRB waiver?
- What is the competitive landscape?
- Must the product be compared to the gold standard or competitor for regulatory requirements, or can it be compared to literature?
- Must the product be compared to the gold standard, competitor or literature for marketing?
- What does the company believe the competitive advantages of its technology are over the predicate or current standard of practice, if any?
- What is the device's expected efficacy or effectiveness, and how is that estimated to compare to current standards?
- Could the product be reimbursable as a Category B (nonexperimental/investigation) IDE study with the US Centers for Medicare and Medicaid Services (CMS)?
- Is the product potentially reimbursable after clearance or approval? What type of data will CMS and the National Center for Health Statistics (NCHS) expect?
- What type of data does the customer review when purchasing the same type of products?

The number of requirements to consider is sizeable. However, review of these parameters will help establish the following for not only the clinical plan but also the business plan:

- the countries prioritized for market launches, thereby impacting sales projections
- patient populations to be included in the intended use
- data strength required for the regulatory submission
- data strength required for purchasing groups (group purchasing organizations (GPOs), government hospitals, etc.)
- peer-reviewed journal publications and podium presentations
- reimbursement strategies, based on peer-reviewed publications
- competitive marketing advantages, including claims
- understanding what competitors will say about the product

Prioritization

When the company's product marketing plans and expectations are understood, prioritization is the next step. What are the most critical needs and product attributes to gain marketing approval as soon as possible and achieve early adoption for stakeholders from marketing, regulatory, reimbursement and engineering? These decisions will drive the clinical study's patient population, sample size, overall design, site selection, enrollment strategies, timeline, budget, resource plan and the sequence of phased trials or postmarket studies. Often, after thorough review of the clinical strategy, the intended use is changed (typically limited or scaled back) to accommodate for a smaller study populations, which allows the product to reach the market sooner.

Small and large companies alike should evaluate how desired claims and markets could be phased in so relevant data can be collected to allow a "go to market" plan that will generate revenue to support longer-term studies or additional claims fiscally.

Regulatory Considerations

Throughout the regulatory process, the sponsor has sole responsibility for providing valid clinical evidence of product safety and performance. Depending on the product and classification, clinical evidence may be presented by clinical evaluation reports of published literature or clinical studies, or both. There is a greater expectation globally for more thorough clinical evaluations as part of the technical documentation, now more than ever.

It is important to note, while not all regulatory submissions require prospective clinical studies, all clinical claims should be able to be supported by clinical data and/or literature. FDA does not require clinical studies for Class I devices, and for many Class II medical devices. For these products, engineering performance data meeting the substantial equivalence threshold to the predicate's performance or clinical literature may be sufficient. However, it is important to note, no matter the product or its classification, appropriate clinical data must be collected to support any claims quoting safety and effectiveness parameters or comparative data to avoid false or misleading labeling.[6] Strategically, companies often submit only the basic engineering, safety and effectiveness information required for initial clearance or approval, thereby going to market earlier than if they wait for additional data for certain claims. Data can be collected for extended clinical postmarket claims (within their cleared or approved intended use) and then used in a future submission, all selling the product.

Determining the Regulatory Requirement

When clinical data are required for a regulatory submission, the baseline requirement is the product must be safe for both the patient and user, and the product's performance must meet its intended use. In the US, manufacturers must prove their Class II products are substantially equivalent to the predicate or, for unique *de novo* or Class III products, must prove the products' safety profiles and effectiveness provide a benefit to the patient while outweighing their risks. For CE marking, clinical evaluation entails assessing and analyzing clinical data pertaining to a medical device and similar devices to verify the device's clinical safety and performance.

"Safety," "performance" and "effectiveness" all are generic words used in regulations, as regulators rely on manufacturers to research and determine the current gold standard of practice and compare their devices to that standard. Fortunately, over the years, FDA has issued multiple guidance documents relaying the type of safety and performance data, and sometimes even the study design, it expects to review for certain device types per disease process (e.g., spinal systems, in vitro diagnostic devices for influenza, percutaneous catheter ablation for atrial fibrillation, root-form endosseous dental implants and abutments, etc.). However, there is no way regulators can provide guidance for every disease process or device. Therefore, it is critical that manufacturers interview key opinion leaders in the field to understand current thoughts and trends but, more importantly, an extensive, scientific literature review should be performed to understand the current clinical landscape.

Notified Bodies encourage a modular approach where they can review the clinical evaluation plan prior to execution to ensure the clinical evaluation's adequacy to support technical files and dossiers, since the European Medicines Agency (EMA) expects clinical data to be scrutinized more heavily.

FDA has been a proponent of "pre-meetings" or "presubmissions" since the institution of the programs for Pre-Investigational New Drug (IND) meetings (circa 1988)[7] and Pre-Investigational Device Exemptions (IDE) meetings in 1999.[8] In many product-specific guidances, FDA encourages sponsors or investigators to initiate contact with the agency early in the product development process, so the company will have the opportunity to consider FDA's recommendations in planning preclinical and clinical development programs.

A serious amount of time and resources should be set aside for any presubmissions meetings with FDA or Notified Bodies. The meeting request itself requires significant effort, similar to a formal IDE or 510(k) submission, due to requirements in the pre-meeting guidance(s). However, to address the company's questions adequately, it is imperative FDA or the Notified Body be given ample background information. The meeting request should be laid out as a plan, providing FDA or the Notified Body with a detailed product background and clinical planning. If available, drafts of protocols, literature reviews and case report forms should be provided. However, depending on the questions at hand, those may or may not be available. Questions should be specific to parts of the plan. Open-ended questions asking the regulators what they want to see is not adequate, as the response likely will refer you to the regulations or guidances and not provide the desired feedback. It is the manufacturer's responsibility to provide rationale as to why its clinical plan is appropriate and ask FDA for clarifications on what data type would be suitable for supporting claims, etc.

It also is important to schedule plenty of time in the overall internal clinical plan if pre-meetings are going to be requested. FDA has 60 days to reply and schedule the meeting. While the agency tries to have the meeting within that timeframe, it is not guaranteed. Pre-meetings often can occur between 60 and 90 days from the time of the meeting request. And, depending on the topic, FDA may recommend updates to the clinical plan or protocol be resubmitted for review prior to conducting the study. For more-complex, high-risk devices, this back and forth is reasonable and could save hundreds of thousands to millions of dollars on a clinical study collecting insufficient data. For low-risk devices, it may be just as advantageous to submit the IDE without a pre-meeting, as FDA either will approve the IDE or request clarification, generally within the 30-day time period (which is shorter than the time to schedule a requested meeting).

Collection and Acceptance of Foreign Clinical Study Data

FDA recognizes sponsors may choose to conduct multinational clinical studies under a variety of scenarios. Multinational studies may include domestic and foreign sites conducted under an IDE, and/or foreign sites not conducted under an IDE. FDA reports an estimated 40–65% of clinical trials investigating FDA-regulated drug and biologic products are conducted outside the US.[9] No matter a clinical trial's location, within or outside the US, if the data will be used to submit to the US, regulations require sponsors to conduct the clinical trials in accordance with Good Clinical Practice, which is defined as:

> "a standard for the design, conduct, performance, monitoring, auditing, recording, analysis, and reporting of clinical trials in a way that provides assurance that the data and reported results are credible and accurate and that the rights, safety, and well-being of trial subjects are protected" (21 CFR §312.120(a)(i)).

Jurisdictions outside the US may want data collected specifically within their own countries to ensure the product works appropriately for their patient population or clinical practice. For example, China often requires studies for more-complex devices to be conducted in its territory because of anatomical and physiological differences (e.g., stature, clinical chemistries, etc.). Russia has its own device evaluation and submission requirements, part of which is the agency conducting a clinical product evaluation on its own. Extensive resources likely will be needed for more-frequent clinical study project management and monitoring to ensure GCP compliance when working outside the US.

Determining Customer Requirements

Data from published literature define the standard to which a company's product will be compared, not only by regulators but by customers. Throughout the 1900s, companies and patients alike thought only physicians assessed clinical data and would be on the podium presenting early data results. For decades, physicians drove what hospitals purchased, whether the product was good or bad. However, in the last 20 years, academia has evolved, physician and nursing standards have improved and healthcare provider reimbursement transparency has driven the industry to its current state of "evidence-based purchasing" and "evidence-based health practice".

Evidence-based purchasing and practice make scientific evidence accessible to decision makers, research relevant to real-world problems and decision makers aware of the evidence and how to interpret it in the context of their own problems. Thus, when developing a clinical strategy, manufacturers should consider the type of evidence customers are reviewing when making purchasing decisions and how that data may influence their buying decisions. In many international regions, physicians still drive purchasing decisions, but an increasing number of nationalized healthcare entities now require purchases to be justified by comparative data evaluations, especially for newer technologies.

Investigational Reimbursement

In the US, the *Medicare Prescription Drug, Improvement, and Modernization Act* of 2003 (*MMA*) allowed payment of routine costs of care for Medicare beneficiaries in certain IDE study categories. Approval of a Category A (experimental) IDE study allows coverage of routine study care items and services but not for Category A devices, which statutorily are excluded from coverage. Approval of a Category B (nonexperimental or investigational) IDE study allows coverage of Category B devices and routine trial care items and services. This program is intended to cover the costs in these IDE studies to remove a financial barrier that otherwise could discourage beneficiaries from participating. Previously, a company would request IDE study coverage approval from CMS but also would have to gain approval from each local CMS region. Changes in January 2015 moved approval from local IDE study Medicare Administrative Contractor (MAC) review and approval to centralized review and approval. Seeking investigational device and routine services' reimbursement may be worthwhile in studies with longer follow-up times and extensive requirements for x-rays, blood work, CAT scans, etc., typical in the course of patient care. However, device reimbursement cannot be for the device's market value but only for product research and development. Depending on the study design, reimbursement requests may or may not be worth the required time and effort.

Site Selection and Enrollment

Poor site selection and enrollment plans can be the start of a failed or delayed study. As days pass after the initial site visit without enrollment, the likelihood of meeting subject enrollment targets on time or at all dwindle. The company adds a new site or two, then more, to replace the ones that failed. During the site selection process, actual data should be gathered from the site, focused specifically on the number of patients who have been treated at the site and meet the study profile. Many investigators and research coordinators can unintentionally overestimate the applicable population at their site. In today's world of electronic medical records, gathering patient population data is much easier and should be done while assessing sites. During the selection process, sites should be questioned about other studies' enrollment statistics. In the author's experience, only 5–10% of the patient population at a site that meet inclusion/exclusion criteria and are willing to participate in an investigational study.

When looking at overall site profiles, there often is the desire to have several key opinion leaders involved as investigators. It is critical to have other investigators who are not key opinion leaders to ensure the device's safety and success in every day practitioners' hands. There always will be times when a site is added because its investigator is an important part of the study program. The site may not have the most relevant population, which should be acknowledged by both sides before the study begins. While it is important to have key opinion leaders involved in the study, it also is important they have enough time and can share potential patients. Often, key opinion leaders already have several ongoing studies, so their involvement should be understood thoroughly and their leadership acknowledged, not only for subject enrollment but driving their co-investigators to enroll.

References
1. Merriam-Webster. www.merriam-webster.com. http://www.merriam-webster.com/dictionary/strategy. Accessed 16 March 2016.
2. Business Dictionary. http://www.businessdictionary.com/definition/strategy.html. Accessed 16 March 2016.
3. Cambridge Dictionaries Online. http://dictionary.cambridge.org/us/dictionary/english/strategy Accessed 16 March 2016.
4. Centers for Disease and Prevention. Sickle Cell Disease (SCD), Data & Statistics. CDC website. http://www.cdc.gov/ncbddd/sicklecell/data.html. Accessed 16 March 2016.
5. Elhami SR, et al. "A 20-year incidence trend (1989-2008) and point prevalence (March 20, 2009) of multiple sclerosis in Tehran, Iran: a population-based study." PubMed website. http://www.ncbi.nlm.nih.gov/pubmed/21508646. Accessed 16 March 2016.
6. Labeling Requirements–Misbranding. FDA website. http://www.fda.gov/medicaldevices/deviceregulationandguidance/overview/devicelabeling/generaldevicelabelingrequirements/ucm052190.htm. Accessed 16 March 2016.
7. Pre-IND Consultation Program. FDA website. http://www.fda.gov/Drugs/DevelopmentApprovalProcess/HowDrugsareDevelopedandApproved/ApprovalApplications/InvestigationalNewDrugINDApplication/Overview/default.htm). Accessed 16 March 2016.
8. *Requests for Feedback on Medical Device Submissions: The Pre-Submission Program and Meetings with Food and Drug Administration Staff Guidance for Industry and Food and Drug Administration Staff*. FDA website. http://www.fda.gov/downloads/MedicalDevices/DeviceRegulationandGuidance/GuidanceDocuments/UCM311176.pdf. Accessed 16 March 2016.

9. Levinson D. *Challenges to FDA's Ability to Monitor and Inspect Foreign Clinical Trials* (OEI-01-08-00510, June 2010) DHHS website. http://oig.hhs.gov/oei/reports/oei-01-08-00510.pdf. Accessed 16 March 2016.

10 IVDs

By Jocelyn Jennings, MS, RAC and Nobuko Nakajima, MS, RAC

Introduction

This chapter focuses on the items to be considered when formulating a global regulatory strategy for an in vitro diagnostic medical device (IVD). One of the first steps in determining an IVD's global regulatory strategy is ensuring the product meets the definition of an in vitro diagnostic medical device.

The US Food and Drug Administration (FDA) defines in vitro diagnostic medical devices as "products that are those reagents, instruments, and systems intended for use in diagnosis of disease or other conditions, including a determination of the state of health, in order to cure, mitigate, treat, or prevent disease or its sequelae. Such products are intended for use in the collection, preparation, and examination of specimens taken from the human body. These products are devices as defined in section 210(h) of the *Federal Food, Drug, and Cosmetic Act*, and may also be biological products subject to section 351 of the *Public Health Service Act*." (21CFR809.3)[1]

The EU's *In Vitro Diagnostic Medical Device Directive*[2] defines an in vitro diagnostic medical device as "any medical device which is a reagent, reagent product, calibrator, control material, kit, instrument, apparatus, equipment, or system, whether used alone or in combination, intended by the manufacturer to be used in vitro for the examination of specimens, including blood and tissue donations, derived from the human body, solely or principally for the purpose of providing information;

- concerning a physiological or pathological state, or
- concerning a congenital abnormality, or
- to determine the safety and compatibility with potential recipients, or
- to monitor therapeutic measures"

Other regions or countries have different definitions of IVDs. For example, the Japanese *Pharmaceutical Medical Device Act* (*PMD Act*) defines IVD reagent products as "drug" products. It is important for a regulatory professional to know how a region or country defines these products before deciding where to market them.

Intended Use and Indications for Use

Intended use or purpose and indications for use are key in determining an IVD's regulatory strategy. The regulatory marketing authorization or submission process for most regulated countries takes a product's intended use and indications for use into account when determining its classification and in what environment the IVD can be marketed and used.

According to FDA, the regulatory term, "intended use," refers to the legally responsible persons' objective intent for the device's labeling. Intent may be determined by written expressions or may be shown by the circumstances surrounding the device's distribution. The concept of intended use has particular relevance in determining whether a device can be cleared for marketing in the US through the premarket notification (510(k)) process or must be evaluated in a premarket approval application (PMA).[3]

The International Organization of Standardization (ISO) Standard 18113-1:2009[4] defines "intended use" or "intended purpose" as the IVD manufacturer's objective intent regarding the use of the product, process or service as reflecting in the specifications, instructions and information supplied by the IVD manufacturer.

Several intended use definitions can be considered when developing an IVD:

- Diagnosis: tests used to determine, verify or confirm a patient's clinical condition as a sole determinant. This type of testing also includes sole confirmatory assays (to verify results of previous testing) and sole exclusion assays to rule out a particular condition. These tests are designed to evaluate a patient's current state.
- Aid in diagnosis: tests used to provide additional information to assist in the determination or verification of a patent's clinical status. The tests are not sole determinants. They are designed to evaluate a patient's current state.
- Screening: tests used to determine the status of a disease, disorder or other physiological state in an asymptomatic individual. They include genetic screening assays, tests for physiological typing and tests used to reduce the risk of infectious disease transmission. Depending on the nature of the condition and the targeted population, screening tests may be used routinely or may be restricted to "at risk" patients. They are designed to evaluate an individual's current state.
- Monitoring: tests used for the measurement of analyte levels for the purpose of adjusting treatments or interventions as required. Monitoring tests include:
  o Assays used to ensure an analyte remains within physiological levels or within an established therapeutic drug range. These types of tests are designed to evaluate an individual's current state.
  o Assays used for serial measurement, whereby multiple determinations are taken over time. These types of monitoring tests typically are used for the detection or assessment of disease progression or regression, disease recurrence, minimum residual disease, response or resistance to therapy and/or adverse effects due to therapy. These types of tests are designed to evaluate changes in an individual's state.
- Predisposition: assays used to determine the likelihood of disease onset (i.e., assessing the risk of developing the disease in future) in presymptomatic patients. For patients at sufficient risk (as determined by test results), preventive interventions may be taken. These tests are designed to evaluate a patient's future state.
- Prognosis: tests used to measure factors linked to clinical outcome regardless of treatment. Such tests may be used to estimate a disease's natural progression (i.e., outcome in the absence of treatment), or to determine the likelihood of a clinical outcome regardless of therapeutic intervention. These tests are designed to evaluate a patient's future state.
- Prediction (of treatment response or reaction): tests used to measure factors that determine the likelihood of patient responses or adverse reactions to a specific therapy. Predictive tests designed specifically for use with a targeted therapy sometimes are called "companion diagnostics" or "personalized medicine." These tests are designed to evaluate a patient's future state.
- Determination of physiological status: used to evaluate an individual's physiological state for the purpose of identifying a human condition or characteristic. These tests are designed to evaluate a patient's current state.

Further IVD characteristics related to intended use are whether the test is qualitative, quantitative or semi-quantitative.

- qualitative: test producing a descriptive result rather than numeric
- quantitative: test that gives a numeric amount or level (concentration) of analyte in a specimen
- semi-quantitative: test with a dose-response gradient that may be included in the reported result, but for which no authoritative calibration scales exist to determine inaccuracy and imprecision; tests yielding results in an approximate range of values (e.g., trace, moderate)

Some IVD reagents may not have a clinical intended use statement if they are for laboratory use only, are analyte-specific reagents (ASRs) or general purpose reagents. ASRs are antibodies (both polyclonal and monoclonal), specific receptor proteins, ligands, nucleic acid sequences and similar reagents that, through specific binding or chemical reaction with substances in a specimen, are intended for use in a diagnostic application for the identification and quantification of an individual chemical substance or ligand in biological specimens.[5] General purpose reagents are chemical reagents with general laboratory applications, used to collect, prepare and examine specimens from the human body for diagnostic purposes and not labeled or otherwise intended for a specific diagnostic application.[6] Both these reagent types can be combined or used in conjunction with appropriate combinations to be developed as part of a diagnostic test procedure or system constituting a finished IVD test by certified laboratories or IVD manufactures to support "clinical intended uses." They are mostly Class 1 medical devices exempt from premarket submissions.

IVD products currently under development and not approved for clinical diagnostic use for a clinical intended use may be distributed as research use only (RUO) or investigational use only (IUO) products when certain criteria are met.[7] Because they are shipped for investigations pertaining to product development, not for clinical use, these products are exempt from most regulatory controls, including IDE regulations. RUO refers to devices in the laboratory phase of development. IUO refers to devices in the product testing phase of development..[8]

The registration process and burden of proof to show safety and effectiveness can be daunting for some intended uses.

The general "Indications for Use" identifies the target population in a substantial portion of which sufficient scientific evidence has demonstrated the device as labeled will provide clinically significant results and at the same time does not present an unreasonable risk of illness or injury.[9] Is the IVD for pediatric patients? Is the IVD targeted for the geriatric population? Is it for both adult and pediatric patients?

Target Market

Additionally, the IVD manufacturer must identify the likely customer for its product. Is it for a lay person? Is the test to be used by professionals only? Or, is it to be used near patient?

- lay person—individual without formal training in a relevant medical field or discipline
- near patient testing—an IVD used outside a clinical laboratory, but at any other point of care near or at the side of a patient, such as a pharmacy, a healthcare professional's office or at the bedside. Near patient testing (NPT) or point-of care testing (POCT) are used synonymously to describe clinical diagnostic performed for patients by healthcare professionals outside of the conventional laboratory.
- professional use—an IVD intended for personnel qualified to perform IVD examinations through special education and training[10]

If the IVD will be for professional use only, the customer could be a hospital, healthcare clinic, medical practice, reference laboratory, academic laboratory or industry (i.e., pharmaceutical, biotechnology, vaccine or food company). The marketing authorization or submission requirements differ for certain professional environments. The IVD product's business plan should include a thoroughly documented regulatory strategy. This will take the marketing authorization or submission requirements for the different market segments and the targeted geographical regions into account. The regulatory professional needs to consider the business plan's initial commercialization plan and ask some of the following questions to provide a comprehensive regulatory strategy:

- What markets does the manufacturer want to enter?
- Which geographic location offers the biggest return on investment?
- Which markets can be entered quickly?
- What are the costs (direct and indirect) of marketing authorization applications as compared to potential commercial revenues?

Not all geographic regions have IVD marketing authorization or submission requirements (e.g., most African countries do not have IVD registration requirements (excluding South Africa), Qatar, Haiti, Nicaragua, Bahamas, etc.), while others have strenuous registration requirements (e.g., China, US). The business plan and regulatory strategy also should take the registration process timeline into account. Some countries have registration fees and fees associated with preapproval inspections (i.e., inspection fees, traveling costs, etc). These costs can influence the IVD manufacturer's decision on where to market a product. It may be quicker to register in some markets than others. The registration time is dependent on the testing required for the registration dossier. Additionally, some countries recognize other countries' marketing authorizations, thereby shortening the path to market. For example, Country ABC has stringent marketing authorization or submission requirements but accepts the CE Mark (EU registration), which shortens its registration process and alleviates the need to perform additional testing; it may be prudent from a financial, business and time-to-market standpoint to CE-mark the product first and then follow the abbreviated marketing authorization or submission process for Country ABC. Leveraging marketing authorizations or submissions from different geographic regions to shorten time-to-market should be considered in strategic planning.

Identifying Regulatory Classifications and Regulatory Pathways

Once the product's intended use or indications for use and the target market are determined, the regulatory professional can determine the product's regulatory classification and associated regulatory pathways worldwide to further formulate the regulatory strategy. In general, IVD product classification is risk-based and is the same or similar to the classification of other medical devices. This section discusses IVD-specific points to be considered in detail.

In the US, medical devices are classified as Class I (General Controls), II (Special Controls) or III (Premarket Approval), based on their risk level. When the IVD product is a system composed of multiple products (instrumentation, software, reagent for main reaction system and control/calibrators, etc.), the associated product's highest classification will become the entire system's classification. For example, when a main reagent's intended use is a Class III medical device, associated instrument, software and control/calibrators also will be classified as Class III and will be reviewed in a PMA, even though the instrument product alone may be a Class II device requiring only a 510(k) premarket notification. In such a case, the entire system will be expected to follow Class III postapproval requirements.

When the IVD is a *de novo* product, requiring the agency to evaluate novel devices anew in accordance with the criteria at section 513(a)(1) of the *Federal Food, Drug, and Cosmetic Act* (*FD&C Act*), the product may qualify for the *de novo* process, allowing a manufacture to submit a *de novo* 510(k), instead of going through the PMA process.[11] Recently, FDA clarified the process in the draft guidance document *De Novo Classification Process (Evaluation of Automatic Class III Designation)* that IVD and medical device manufacturers are encouraged to utilize.[12]

When the IVD reagent is to be marketed as an ASR with no manufacturer-provided clinical intended use statement but will be used as a component of a laboratory developed test (LDT), the product may be designated as a Class I device and may have no premarket submission requirement.[13] An LDT is an IVD intended for clinical use and designed and manufactured to be used within a single laboratory. It is easier to achieve shorter time-to-market for these products; however, regulatory professionals should make the company aware there are distribution and labeling restrictions for these products. ASRs may be sold only to IVD manufacturers or *Clinical Laboratory Improvement Amendment* (*CLIA*)-qualified, high-complexity laboratories. ASRs may not be promoted with specific analytical or clinical performance claims or instructions for use in a particular test, or promote a single ASR with another product such as other ASRs, general purpose reagents, controls, designated laboratory instrument(s), software, etc.[14] Considering FDA's recent expressions of its intent to increase oversight of LDTs,[15,16] regulatory and business professionals should evaluate options for the paths that make most sense for their companies. They also should keep in mind ASRs in the US market may be classified as IVDs with a specific use statement in other countries (i.e., EU, China and Japan) due to the differences in IVD definitions and classifications in these countries. These countries may require product performance data and premarket regulatory submissions for the same (US ASR) product for market entry.

Outside the US, it also is true the product's intended use will determine its classification and the associated regulatory pathways. As mentioned earlier, IVD reagent products in Japan are regulated under the *PMD-Act* as drugs and, therefore, the product's classification is based on drug classifications, concerning risks to disease diagnosis. IVD instrument products are classified as general medical devices (Class I), and no preapproval is required prior to the market entry (notification to the local government only); however, it may require licenses for sales or distribution and service-related activities.[17] In China, IVD reagents are regulated as IVDs, separate from general medical devices. IVDs are considered a type of medical device, and higher level regulations (e.g., Order 650) cover both medical devices and IVDs. However, for product registration, labeling and GMP-related activities, IVD reagents must follow different regulations.[18]

In the EU, currently, IVD products are classified as Annex II List A or B or Annex III products. Annex II products require a Notified Body design dossier review; however, most products are classified as Annex III self-declared products. This will change with implementation of the new *IVD Regulation*. Product classification will be aligned with the International Medical Device Regulators Forum (IMDRF), successor to the Global Harmonization Task Force (GHTF) classification model, with Classes A, B, C and D, where A is low risk and D is high risk.[19] Companies must determine how their products will be impacted by the proposed new *IVD Regulation*, i.e., how would their products be classified under the new regulation? These are questions the regulatory professional should be able to answer.

When the product is intended for distribution through World Health Organization (WHO) and United Nations (UN) tenders, it also is important to take into consideration the product may be required to undergo WHO regulatory assessment, the pre-qualification process. This process[20] typically involves product dossier review, site inspection and product laboratory performance testing by WHO officials.

Regulatory Requirements

General

As is the case for other medical devices, identifying key general regulatory requirements associated with the IVD product's identified classification for each target geographic region is important to determine global regulatory strategies. The following are examples of questions to be asked and answered to develop an effective global regulatory and business strategy:

- What are the premarket requirements to enter the target market?
- Do they involve facility registrations and/or licenses and periodic renewals?
- What product registrations, licenses, listing and periodic renewals are required?
    - How much do those renewals cost?
- What are the postmarket requirements?
    - Change control/notifications, quality and/or vigilance system maintenance?
    - Complaint handling, medical device reporting and recalls or Field Corrective Actions (FCAs) reporting?
    - How much does it cost to sustain these requirements?

Region-Specific Requirements

Once key general regulatory requirements are identified, determining specific IVD product registration requirements for key markets is essential. Can the company leverage common requirements from multiple countries during product development? How can the company assemble registration dossiers to meet global needs most efficiently? Finding answers to these questions enables the regulatory professional to provide recommendations to the company to execute IVD product development activities effectively.

- *CLIA* categorization requirements are unique to the US market. US clinical laboratories are regulated under *CLIA*, and must be certified under appropriate laboratory complexity categorizations (high-complexity, moderate-complexity or waived).[21] Each IVD product intended to be sold to US clinical laboratories also must be evaluated for inclusion in these categories. This usually is done in parallel with the product's premarket application reviews. When the product is targeted to be marketed to *CLIA*-waived laboratories (i.e., home use or point-of-care products), a specific study is required for the *CLIA*-waiver application.[22] IVD manufacturers are encouraged to incorporate *CLIA* waiver testing requirements into the product registration study design to be more cost efficient.
- As described earlier in this chapter, system-based product review and approval also are unique to the US, and should be considered during the product development process for the most-efficient testing approach, along with other regional registration requirements.
- For EU CE-marked IVD medical devices (CE-IVDs), Annex II-List A products are required to integrate common technical specification requirements[23] into performance evaluation study designs. Clinical evidence of the product also is required by the current *IVD Directive* as well as the upcoming *IVD Regulation*. It is important to note the clinical evidence requirement for IVD medical devices comprises scientific validity, analytical performance and clinical performance, unlike that for medical devices.[24] GHTF/SG5/N7:2012 clarifies when the scientific validity is well established, and IVD analytical performance is thoroughly demonstrated to conform with the relevant Essential Principles (EP); clinical performance data may not be necessary. Also, assay migration of the same reagents between instruments that share the same basic analytical technology, but may for example, vary in instrument throughput, whereby the assay's formulation and intended use do not change, clinical performance data are not expected. Identifying whether a product is established and standardized would help refine the scope of performance evaluation tests to demonstrate the product's clinical evidence. Staying current with updated harmonized international standards applicable to the company's IVD products also is important for the regulatory professional; standards can be found on the International Harmonized Standard website (www.ihs.com).
- Japan has prescribed IVD performance study requirements.[25] In addition to specific study design and sample sizes (i.e., correlation and stability studies), there are prescribed acceptance criteria a product should meet for a Japanese correlation study.

- Canadian Class III and IV IVD medical devices may have device-specific performance study design requirements.[26] As for CE-IVDs, it also is important for the regulatory professional to stay current with the product study designs in Health Canada's recognized standards on its website.[27]
- Chinese IVD reagent registration has proven to be one of the most challenging and still is evolving. It requires in-country clinical trials and government quality control testing. Recent changes in the IVD regulation required these two steps (reference laboratory testing and clinical trials) to be done sequentially, not in parallel, which added more time to product approvals for foreign manufacturers.[28] There are minimum lot number requirements for IVD reagent analytical studies and IVD instrumentation registrations. Approvals from the country of legal manufacture's regulatory authority of the entity legally responsible for the finished product or of manufacturing origin also are essential to enable timely product approval in China.
- IVD reagent stability studies are critical to IVD clearance or approval globally. In the EU, accelerated stability study data can be utilized to support the product's initial launch as long as the study design is in accordance with a harmonized international standard.[29] However, in the US, FDA requires real-time data to support the claim.[30] Japan and Canada also require real-time stability data for product submissions. In general, real-time stability study requirements for IVD reagents are increasing in emerging regions, i.e., Korea, China, Taiwan, Thailand, India, Singapore, etc. Korea has a prescribed stability study design timepoint requirement. Some countries (i.e., Japan and Taiwan) may have a minimum shelf-life requirement for product submissions.
- When the product must go through the WHO pre-qualification process, the manufacturer should evaluate the product's regional risks and identified risks as appropriate for the resource-limited environments in which the IVD products will be used.[31]

Global regulatory environments are dynamic and regional requirements continue to evolve. It is essential for the regulatory professional to identify applicable regulatory requirements and keep up with changes in requirements to develop the most-effective and efficient regulatory strategies, advising the company on optimum product development activities to enable timely regulatory approvals for key global markets.

Even if the target market does not have a structured product registration process, identifying import and export requirements (including labeling requirements) for the country of origin and tender-related requirements also helps the company achieve timely market access.

Performance Testing

Most countries with IVD registration requirements require some type of performance testing. The performance testing needed depends on the type of IVD (e.g., instrument, reagent, software), the IVD's classification (this is geographic region-specific) and the product's intended use and indications for use. Clinical testing and analytical testing are the two primary types of performance testing required to provide objective evidence supporting the IVD's safety and effectiveness.

Clinical testing is performed in a healthcare setting such as a hospital, clinic, private medical practice or reference laboratory. Part of the regulatory strategy should be determining the clinical tests needed to support the registration dossier. A number of aspects should be considered when designing the IVD product's clinical study:
- What will the required sample size be?
- Can leftover specimens be used?
- Will informed consent be necessary?
- What is the clinical endpoint?
- Will the study need to include multiple populations (e.g., adults and pediatrics)?
- What is the predicate device?
- Will there be multiple predicate devices?
- What reference method will be used?
- Is ethnicity or gender a consideration?

Some countries such as China require in-country testing to ensure the IVD performs as intended in their specific populations. These considerations should be included in the IVD product's regulatory strategy, which should feed into the product development strategy. Not considering these aspects during the product development could complicate IVD product clearance or approval during regulatory reviews.

A leftover specimen is the remnant of a human specimen collected for routine clinical care or analysis that would have been discarded.[32] Leftover specimens used in a clinical study cannot be identifiable individually. A specimen is not identifiable individually if the subject's identity is not known to or may not be ascertained readily by the investigator or any other individual associated with the investigation, including the sponsor.[33]

Obtaining informed consent from sick patients to acquire specimens for IVD performance testing can be avoided if leftover specimens can be used. Leftover specimens can be obtained from various clinical facilities with the necessary storage to maintain specimens' viability. Some facilities store and sell various types of banked specimens (i.e., blood, urine, plasma, etc.) confirmed as positive for a variety of organisms. A manufacturer can either buy the specimens to use for testing, or sometimes the facility can do the testing for the manufacturer. A prospective clinical trial's cost and time can be diminished greatly by using leftover specimens. In the US, to use banked specimens, FDA requires a study be performed proving frozen specimens are viable and "equal" to fresh specimens. This type of analytical test usually is simple unless the matrix (i.e., sputum) is difficult to test. Other geographic regions (i.e., the EU) also allow the use of leftover specimens. This viable and affordable option should be considered carefully by an IVD manufacturer.

Analytical testing usually is performed at reference laboratories, clinical laboratories or, if feasible, internally at the manufacturing facility. The analytical test types needed for the IVD depend on the factors listed above for clinical testing. Some of the required analytical tests are:

- analytical specificity—describes the ability of a measurement procedure to detect or measure only the measurand in the presence of other quantities present in the sample
- analytical sensitivity—the smallest difference in concentration that can be detected with confidence; the ability of a measurement procedure to discriminate between two concentrations of a measurand
- detection limit—is used to describe the lowest value of measurand that an examination procedure can report as present with a specified level of confidence
- quantitation limit— the lowest value of measurand an examination procedure can measure with a specified measurement uncertainty
- linearity—describes the ability of either the measurement indications or the measurement results to fit a straight line with respect to the samples' assigned values
- interference—systematic effect on a measurement caused by an influence quantity, which does not by itself produce a signal in the measuring system, but which causes an enhancement or depression of the value
- carryover—introducing material into a reaction mixture to which it does not belong (e.g., part of a sample, reagent, diluent or wash solution transferred from one container or from one reaction mixture to another during an examination
- cross-reactivity—the degree to which a substance other than the analyte binds to a reagent in a competitive binding immunochemical measurement procedure
- cut-off value—the quantity used as a limit to identify samples indicating the presence or absence of a specific disease, condition or measurand
- diagnostic sensitivity—the ability of an IVD examination procedure to identify the presence of a target marker associated with a particular disease or condition
- diagnostic specificity—the ability to recognize the absence of a target marker associated with a particular disease or condition
- measurement repeatability—measurement precision under a set of measurement conditions that includes the same measurement procedure, operators, measuring system, operating conditions and location, and replicate measurements on the same or similar objects over a short period of time
- measurement reproducibility— measurement precision under measurement conditions including different locations, operators, measuring systems and replicate measurements on the same or similar objects[34]

The Clinical and Laboratory Standards Institute (CLSI) develops analytical testing standards. These standards are harmonized and used by most regulated countries. They provide detailed information on how to set up analytical tests (i.e., sample size and design) and interpret the data (i.e., statistical analysis). Following CLSI standards ensures the data generation method is valid scientifically and accepted by regulators. CLSI standards can provide a starting place for new IVD manufacturers when developing an analytical testing strategy. Additionally, if a manufacturer is contemplating marketing a new IVD, the CLSI standards can be used to determine what analytical testing might be needed for a particular IVD product.

Analytical testing can provide the bulk of the evidence needed to show an IVD is safe and effective. A well-thought-out analytical testing plan can make the difference in a successful registration process. Ensuring the analytical testing performed is relevant and conducted appropriately (the testing may need to be conducted in a Good Laboratory Practice facility) per a detailed protocol is paramount.

The regulatory professional should determine a performance testing strategy in collaboration with relevant departments (i.e., research and development, engineering, clinical affairs, etc.) by reviewing region-specific directives, guidance documents, regulations, harmonized standards and labeling or other documentation on your proposed predicate device. Documentation on a predicate device can provide a wealth of information and lead to an outline for the manufacturer's regulatory strategy.

In the US, a presubmission[35] can be sent to FDA to garner feedback on the proposed IVD performance testing strategy. There are two ways to receive feedback from FDA using the presubmission process: written review memo or meeting with FDA representatives. For the presubmission, the manufacturer or sponsor sends a packet of information detailing its testing strategy, including the individual analytical or clinical testing plans or protocols. A list of questions pertaining to the testing strategy and other potential concerns is provided to FDA for review. FDA has 90 days to review the presubmission. The manufacturer or sponsor will receive a written review memo from FDA providing feedback on the plans or protocols and responses to the specific questions posed. FDA also may request more information or clarification on points in the testing plans or protocols. If the manufacturer requests a meeting, FDA will provide its availability for a meeting with the review memo. While FDA's feedback is not binding, it will give the IVD manufacturer or sponsor an idea of FDA's current thinking concerning the required testing needed to provide objective evidence of IVD safety and effectiveness. The presubmission program is a good mechanism to use for negotiation with FDA prior to starting expensive analytical and clinical studies. The IVD manufacturer can use the presubmission process as an opportunity to open a dialogue with the review division. This is especially important if the IVD is a new product. The earlier the discussions start, the more advantageous for the IVD manufacturer. The presubmission gives the IVD manufacturer an opportunity to introduce its product to FDA in a benign environment.

For IVD instruments, additional performance testing may be applicable. Restriction of the use of hazardous substances (RoHS) for electrical and electronic equipment (Directive 2011/65/EU),[36] electrical safety (EN 61010-2-101),[37] low voltage (2006/95/EC)[38] and emission control (EMC) (2004/108/EC)[39] are additional EU directives and standards that could apply to an IVD instrument. The cost and timing for conducting these tests either internally or at an external facility must be factored into an IVD instrument's regulatory strategy.

IVDs containing software or standalone software have additional applicable harmonized standards and US guidance documents describing the testing needed. The specific expectations vary but, overall, software must follow the same rigorous process as any other IVD. Software must undergo verification testing, code reviews, risk analysis and validation testing. Other testing considerations are dependent on the software type (i.e., Off-the Shelf) and software controls. FDA has several software guidance documents, and there is a harmonized software standard (IEC 62304)[40] that provides more insight into software testing requirements throughout its lifecycle.

If a reagent comprises animal- or human-origin raw materials, additional testing may be needed prior to registration. Some countries require any animal raw materials to come from Bovine Spongiform Encephalopathy (BSE)-free countries and sources. When choosing raw materials for an IVD reagent, processes and checks should be in place to ensure the origin of all components is known. Obtaining the needed BSE certificates upfront can save time in the long run when registrations are filed.

Other IVD Trends

Personalized medicine is increasing in healthcare. Personalized medicine is defined as the tailoring of medical treatment to the individual characteristics of each patient. It does not necessarily mean the literal creation of drugs or medical devices unique to a patient, but rather the ability to classify individuals into subpopulations differing in their susceptibility to a particular disease or response to a specific treatment. From an IVD perspective, FDA released a comprehensive draft guidance document 14 July 2011 on in vitro companion diagnostic devices or companion diagnostics (CoDx). The final guidance document was issued 6 August 2014. FDA defines a CoDx as an in vitro diagnostic device that provides information essential for the safe and effective use of a corresponding therapeutic product.[41]

In recent years, FDA has approved several CoDx devices for the US market. FDA has been developing best practices for these products to ensure their review and performance testing requirements are not overly burdensome to either the drug or IVD manufacturer. The majority of CoDx are Class III; therefore the safety and effectiveness burden of proof is high. The process demands a tremendous amount of coordination among the various FDA centers. To be successful, the regulatory strategy must look at both the drug and the IVD product, and there must be active collaboration among the pharmaceutical and IVD manufacturers and regulatory bodies. Mapping out all of the presubmission and submission phase steps helps create a clear picture of what will be needed to commercialize both products. The regulatory environment for CoDx products outside the US still is evolving. The EU intends to regulate CoDx under its upcoming *IVD Regulation*, and Japanese and Chinese agencies have indicated their intention to structure the regulatory process specifically for CoDx; however, the development and implementation process still is underway.

Medical device cybersecurity is being scrutinized more heavily in this age of wireless, network and Internet-connected medical devices, including IVDs, and with the exchange of medical device- and IVD-related health information. A draft FDA guidance document was issued 14 June 2013, with the final document issued 2 October 2014. The burden is on the IVD manufacturer to look at possible cybersecurity measures to assist in preventing an intentional or unintentional breach of its IVD and risking patient safety.[42] Additionally, international standards exist addressing cybersecurity. Cybersecurity is a global regulatory issue and should be evaluated for IVD products with electronic transmission and/or access capabilities. Even non-networked products need some level of cybersecurity, such as individual user authentication (e.g., username, password). A thorough strategy for an IVD containing or connected to software, middleware or firmware will ensure cybersecurity is evaluated in the design and development stages.

FDA recently released a few draft guidance documents on social media. The documents focus on ensuring IVD advertising and promotion on social media relay all risks and benefits accurately to the public regardless of the social medium's character limitations. FDA views the posts on social media as an extension of labeling; therefore, the expectation is that truthful and non-leading information will be presented. Additionally, FDA is concerned about information on social media posted by a third party and that is not accurate. FDA's expectation is the IVD manufacturer will ensure the inaccurate information posted is corrected as soon as possible.

RECAST or reclassification is a trend occurring in several countries. The EU has released new IVD regulations, including an update to IVD classification. The classification scheme for IVDs now will follow a risk-based rule system modeled on the GHTF classification guidelines (see Identifying Regulatory Classifications and Regulatory Pathways above for information on IVD classification). Asian countries (i.e., Vietnam, Thailand, Philippines, etc.) setting up new regulations are expected to follow the Association of Southeast Asian Nations (ASEAN) *Medical Device Directive* and GHTF guidelines for classifying IVDs. These RECAST efforts will assist in ensuring IVD products follow the same classification scheme (harmonized) and are not country- or region-dependent. The efforts also could reduce instances of a single IVD product having multiple classifications in the future.

Authorities' Perspectives

Regulatory authorities usually welcome being informed of new products and consulted on key issues the manufacturers may identify as necessary. This provides authorities opportunities to become familiar with new products and technologies and allows them to plan the resources to assure timely product review. Manufacturers are advised to utilize available presubmission or consultation processes from regional regulatory authorities when planning a new product registration.

As noted previously, US FDA has a formal presubmission program,[43] Japan's Pharmaceuticals and Medical Devices Agency (PMDA) also accommodates consultations. Even if there is no formal consultation process (i.e., EU Notified Bodies and Health Canada), the authorities or regulatory review bodies usually are open to discussing specific presubmission questions.

Common Pitfalls

The common pitfalls into which global IVD manufacturers can fall are:
- too US- or EU-centric approach
- over-accommodation of requirements from markets other than the US or EU

When the IVD manufacture is too focused on the EU and/or US market(s) and does not consider regulatory requirements in other countries, it may impede product entry in growing, emerging markets or require repeating some key performance studies to meet regional registration requirements, which could result in significant, unplanned costs.

In contrast, if the IVD manufacturer is too accommodating of other registration requirements, without applying business priorities, it could prolong time-to-market to any market. Regulatory professionals should look at similarities and differences between each set of regional requirements to see whether any opportunities exist to leverage similar requirements for a study design. However, it also is important to balance the registration requirements for the target market and time-to-market based on business priorities. For example, some countries may have minimum shelf-life requirement of six months (or longer) with real-time data, while other countries may accept accelerated stability data. It may be more efficient for a company to achieve time-to-market when it plans to register the product as applicable data become available.

Identifying "key" target markets and balancing the time and cost to make the most impact are essential.

Conclusions

To develop an effective regulatory strategy, it is essential the business plans, priorities and product concepts first be understood and defined clearly. Regulatory implications based on the business plan then can be identified along with premarket requirements and time-to-approval, postmarket requirements and product maintenance costs. This regulatory assessment may change business priorities, and strategies may be solidified to enable the most effective and efficient product entry into the target market.

The global regulatory environment is dynamic. It is essential the regulatory professional identifies applicable regulatory requirements and keeps up with constantly changing regulatory requirements to develop the most effective and efficient regulatory strategy, and to advise the organization on optimum product development activities to enable timely regulatory approvals for key global markets.

References

1. Code of Federal Regulations, Title 21 Section 809.3. FDA website. http://www.accessdata.fda.gov/scripts/cdrh/cfdocs/cfcfr/cfrsearch.cfm?fr=809.3. Accessed 2 December 2015.
2. Directive 98/79/EC, *In Vitro Diagnostic Medical Device Directive*. EUR-Lex website. http://eur-lex.europa.eu/legal-content/EN/TXT/?uri=CELEX%3A31998L0079. Accessed 2 December 2015.
3. *Deciding When to Submit a 510(k) for a Change to an Existing Device (K97-1)*, 10 January 1997. FDA website. http://www.fda.gov/MedicalDevices/DeviceRegulationandGuidance/GuidanceDocuments/ucm080235.htm. Accessed 2 December 2015.
4. ISO 18113-1:2009, *Information supplied by the manufacturer (labelling), Part 1: General requirements, Appendix A*.
5. 21 CFR 864.4020 Analyte specific reagents. FDA website. http://www.accessdata.fda.gov/scripts/cdrh/cfdocs/cfcfr/cfrsearch.cfm?fr=864.4020. Accessed 2 December 2015.
6. 21 CFR 864.4010 General purpose reagent. FDA website. http://www.accessdata.fda.gov/scripts/cdrh/cfdocs/cfcfr/cfrsearch.cfm?fr=864.4010. Accessed 2 December 2015.
7. *Distribution of In Vitro Diagnostic Products Labeled for Research Use Only or Investigational Use Only: Guidance for Industry and Food and Drug Administration Staff*, 25 November 2013. FDA website. http://www.fda.gov/medicaldevices/deviceregulationandguidance/guidancedocuments/ucm253307.htm. Accessed 2 December 2015.
8. Ibid.
9. Ibid.
10. Op cit 4.
11. *De Novo Classification Process (Evaluation of Automatic Class III Designation), Draft Guidance for Industry and Food and Drug Administration Staff*, 14 August 2014. FDA website. http://www.fda.gov/medicaldevices/deviceregulationandguidance/guidancedocuments/ucm273902.htm. Accessed 2 December 2015.
12. US Food and Drug Administration, Product Classification. FDA website. http://www.accessdata.fda.gov/scripts/cdrh/cfdocs/cfpcd/classification.cfm?id=mvu. Accessed 2 December 2015.
13. Op cit 7.
14. *Guidance for Industry and FDA Staff: Commercially Distributed Analyte Specific Reagents (ASRs): Frequently Asked Questions*, 14 September 2007. FDA website. http://www.fda.gov/medicaldevices/deviceregulationandguidance/guidancedocuments/ucm078423.htm. Accessed 2 December 2015.
15. *Draft Guidance for Industry, Food and Drug Administration Staff, and Clinical Laboratories: Framework for Regulatory Oversight of Laboratory Developed Tests (LDTs)*, 3 October 2014. FDA website. http://www.fda.gov/downloads/MedicalDevices/DeviceRegulationandGuidance/GuidanceDocuments/UCM416685.pdf. Accessed 2 December 2015.
16. *Draft Guidance for Industry, Food and Drug Administration Staff, and Clinical Laboratories: FDA Notification and Medical Device Reporting for Laboratory Developed Tests (LDTs)*, 3 October 2014. FDA website. http://www.fda.gov/downloads/MedicalDevices/DeviceRegulationandGuidance/GuidanceDocuments/UCM416684.pdf. Accessed 2 December 2015.
17. *Fundamentals of Japanese Regulatory Affairs, First Edition*. Regulatory Affairs Professionals Society, Rockville, MD, USA, 2010.
18. Circular on the Printing and Distribution of the Measures on the Management of Registration of In Vitro Diagnosis Reagents, No.229 Document of the China State Food and Drug Administration (2007). http://www.mianfeiwendang.com/doc/a9986a968d29bf933d777aa8. Accessed 17 March 2016.
19. Spencer S. "Medical technology, The draft in vitro diagnostic regulation." Regulatory Rapporteur, 10(6)June 2013. The Organisation for Professionals in Regulatory Affairs. BSI website. http://medicaldevices.bsigroup.com/LocalFiles/en-GB/Whitepapers/BSI-md-ivd-regulations-whitepaper-UK-EN.pdf. Accessed 2 December 2015.
20. World Health Organization. Prequalification of in vitro diagnostics. WHO website. http://www.who.int/diagnostics_laboratory/evaluations/en/. Accessed 2 December 2015.
21. *Clinical Laboratory Improvement Amendments (CLIA)*. Centers for Medicare and Medicaid Services. http://www.cms.gov/Regulations-and-Guidance/Legislation/CLIA/index.html?redirect=/clia/. Accessed 2 December 2015.
22. CLIA waiver by application. FDA website. http://www.fda.gov/medicaldevices/deviceregulationandguidance/ivdregulatoryassistance/ucm393233.htm. Accessed 2 December 2015.
23. 2009/108/EC—Commission decision of 3 February 2009 amending Decision 2002/364/EC on common technical specifications for in vitro-diagnostic medical devices. EUR-Lex website. http://eur-lex.europa.eu/legal-content/EN/TXT/?uri=uriserv%3AOJ.L_.2009.039.01.0034.01.ENG. Accessed 2 December 2015.
24. GHTF/SG5/N7:2012, *Clinical Evidence for IVD medical devices—Scientific Validity Determination and Performance Evaluation*. IMDRF website. http://www.imdrf.org/docs/ghtf/final/sg5/technical-docs/ghtf-sg5-n7-2012-scientific-validity-determination-evaluation-121102.pdf. Accessed 2 December 2015.
25. Op cit 16.
26. *Guidance for Manufactures of Human Immunodeficiency Virus (HIV) Test Kits intended to be used in the Laboratory*, 7 December 2011. Health Canada website. http://www.hc-sc.gc.ca/dhp-mps/md-im/applic-demande/guide-ld/md_gd_hiv_im_ld_vih-eng.php. Accessed 2 December 2015.
27. List of Recognized Standards for Medical Devices. Health Canada website. http://www.hc-sc.gc.ca/dhp-mps/md-im/standards-normes/md_rec_stand_im_norm_lst-eng.php. Accessed 2 December 2015.
28. China Food and Drug Administration Administrative Order No. 5. CFDA website. http://www.sda.gov.cn/WS01/CL0053/103756.html. Accessed 2 December 2015.

29. ISO 23640:2011 *In vitro diagnostic medical devices—Evaluation of stability of in vitro diagnostic reagents*
30. Recognized Consensus Standards; CLSI EP25-A, *Evaluation of Stability of In Vitro Diagnostic Reagents; Approved Guideline*. FDA website. http://www.accessdata.fda.gov/scripts/cdrh/cfdocs/cfstandards/detail.cfm?standard__identification_no=30533. Accessed 3 December 2015.
31. Instructions for Compilation of a Product Dossier; Prequalification of In Vitro Diagnostics Programme. WHO website. http://www.who.int/diagnostics_laboratory/evaluations/140828_pqdx_018_dossier_instructions_v3.pdf?ua=1. Accessed 3 December 2015.
32. *Guidance on Informed Consent for In Vitro Diagnostic Device Studies Using Leftover Human Specimens that are not Individually Identifiable*, 25 April 2006. FDA website. http://www.fda.gov/RegulatoryInformation/Guidances/ucm078384.htm. Accessed 3 December 2015.
33. Op cit 4.
34. Op cit 26.
35. *Requests for Feedback on Medical Device Submissions: The Pre-Submission Program and Meetings with Food and Drug Administration Staff: Guidance for Industry and Food and Drug Administration Staff*, 18 February 2014. FDA website. http://www.google.com/url?sa=t&rct=j&q=&esrc=s&source=web&cd=1&cad=rja&uact=8&ved=0ahUKEwiRx_O3wcDJAhUP5WMKHRNVDDAQFggcMAA&url=http%3A%2F%2Fwww.fda.gov%2Fdownloads%2Fmedicaldevices%2Fdeviceregulationandguidance%2Fguidancedocuments%2Fucm311176.pdf&usg=AFQjCNFz7V0nXT5uHI1Yun5pKxWH4hTqaQ. Accessed 3 December 2015.
36. Directive 2011/65/EU of the European Parliament and of the Council of 8 June 2011 on the restriction of the use of certain hazardous substances in electrical and electronic equipment. EUR-Lex website. http://eur-lex.europa.eu/legal-content/EN/TXT/?uri=celex:32011L0065. Accessed 3 December 2015.
37. EN 61010-2-101 Safety requirements for electrical equipment for measurement, control and laboratory use. Particular requirements for in vitro diagnostic (IVD) medical equipment. BSI website. http://shop.bsigroup.com/ProductDetail/?pid=000000000030079607. Accessed 3 December 2015.
38. Directive 2006/95/EC of the European Parliament and of the Council of 12 December 2006 on the harmonisation of the laws of Member States relating to electrical equipment designed for use within certain voltage limits. EUR-Lex website. http://www.google.com/url?sa=t&rct=j&q=&esrc=s&source=web&cd=1&cad=rja&uact=8&ved=0ahUKEwjGl7H7u8DJAhVM-GMKHU_DCDAQFggoMAA&url=http%3A%2F%2Feur-lex.europa.eu%2FLexUriServ%2FLexUriServ.do%3Furi%3DOJ-%3AL%3A2006%3A374%3A0010%3A0019%3Aen%3APDF&usg=AFQjCNF4SIeInbJ62kuzfFAxV1OIsbwFBQ. Accessed 3 December 2015
39. Directive 2004/108/EC of the European Parliament and of the Council of 15 December 2004 on the approximation of the laws of the Member States relating to electromagnetic compatibility and repealing Directive 89/336/EE EUR-Lex website. http://eur-lex.europa.eu/legal-content/EN/TXT/?uri=celex:32004L0108. Accessed 3 December 2015.
40. IEC 62304 Medical device software—Software lifecycle processes. ISO website. http://www.iso.org/iso/catalogue_detail.htm?csnumber=38421. Accessed 3 December 2015.
41. *In Vitro Companion Diagnostic Devices Guidance for Industry and Food* (August 2014). FDA website. http://www.fda.gov/downloads/medicaldevices/deviceregulationandguidance/guidancedocuments/ucm262327.pdf. Accessed 17 March 2016.
42. "Content of Premarket Submissions for Management of Cybersecurity in Medical Devices—Final Guidance (Webinar)," 29 October 2014. FDA website. http://www.fda.gov/MedicalDevices/NewsEvents/WorkshopsConferences/ucm419118.htm. Accessed 3 December 2015.
43. Op cit 35.

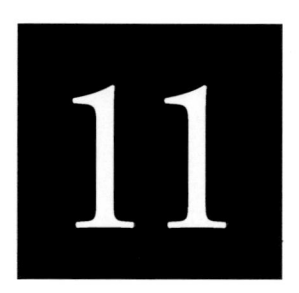

11 Combination Products

By Allyson B. Mullen and Jeffrey N. Gibbs

Building on technological advancements, companies are combining various types of drugs, devices and biologics to create novel products and better meet clinical needs. For example, stents now are coated in drugs, orthopedic implants are combined with growth factors, bandages are impregnated with antibacterial drugs to promote healing and monoclonal antibodies are combined with therapeutic drugs.

The statutory definitions of drugs, devices and biologics are broad and overlap, sometimes presenting uncertainty as to how a product will be regulated. Combining regulated product types has presented regulatory challenges for companies and the US Food and Drug Administration (FDA). To develop and commercialize combination products, it is important to understand how FDA regulates these products.

FDA has specifically defined the terms "combination products." This is the starting point in analyzing how a product will be classified. It is important to note, under FDA's regulations, a combination product can arise in several different ways. This chapter focuses on FDA's definition and regulation of combination products. Other countries' regulatory bodies regulate combination products differently.

What is a combination product?

A Combination Product is defined as:
> "1. A product comprised of two or more regulated components, i.e., drug/device, biologic/device, drug/biologic, or drug/device/biologic, that are physically, chemically, or otherwise combined or mixed and produced as a single entity;
> 2. Two or more separate products packaged together in a single package or as a unit and comprised of drug and device products, device and biological products, or biological and drug products;
> 3. A drug, device, or biological product packaged separately that according to its investigational plan or proposed labeling is intended for use only with an approved individually specified drug, device, or biological product where both are required to achieve the intended use, indication, or effect and where upon approval of the proposed product the labeling of the approved product would need to be changed, e.g., to reflect a change in intended use, dosage form, strength, route of administration, or significant change in dose; or
> 4. Any investigational drug, device, or biological product packaged separately that according to its proposed labeling is for use only with another individually specified investigational drug, device, or biological product where both are required to achieve the intended use, indication, or effect."[1]

In short, combination products can take one of three different forms: 1) single-entity combination product; 2) co-packaged combination products; and 3) cross-labeled combination products.

A single-entity combination product is a product that physically consists of a drug, device and/or biologic. For example, dental floss (device) coated with fluoride (drug), pre-filled syringe (drug in the syringe—device) and a bone void filler (device) containing an antibiotic (drug) all are examples of single-entity combination products.

A co-packaged combination product is two or more single-entity products packaged together. Common examples of co-packaged combination products are drug delivery systems (e.g., a drug packaged with a device delivery system) and kits (e.g., a bag containing surgical instruments and drugs or biologics).

A cross-labeled combination product is two or more regulated products required to achieve the products' intended use, but the products are not physically packaged together. Contrast media and an imaging system are one example of a cross-labeled combination product. Both elements are needed to perform the imaging. However, the two products generally are not packaged together for practical reasons: the imaging system is a piece of capital equipment used repeatedly, whereas the contrast media is a single-use product. Because combination products can occur in various ways, companies need to be alert to whether their products may constitute combination products.

Combination Product History and FDA's Office of Combination Products

While the examples discussed above may seem relatively straightforward, it is not always clear whether a product is a single entity (just a drug, device or biologic) or a combination product, and if it is a combination product, which FDA center has regulatory responsibility.

Prior to the *Safe Medical Devices Act* of 1990 (*SMDA*), FDA decided how combination products would be regulated on an ad hoc basis. This ad hoc review sometimes led to inconsistent and confusing outcomes regarding combination product regulation.

As part of the *SMDA*, Congress sought to bring some clarity to the combination product process. The *SMDA* included enactment of new Section 503(g) of the *Federal Food, Drug, and Cosmetic Act* (*FD&C Act*). This section requires FDA to decide which center has "primary jurisdiction" over a combination product. This decision is based on the combination product's "primary mode of action" (discussed further below). Corresponding regulations were published on 21 November 1991 (21 CFR Part 3).[2]

These new statutory and regulatory provisions, however, did not bring uniformity and clarity to the combination product process. Nor did they necessarily result in simplicity. In fact, in some cases, it made it more difficult for combination products to reach the market. For example, in the case of the drug ursodiol for use with lithotripters, FDA required two separate product approvals, one for the device and one for the product's drug element. This created difficulty and significant delay in getting the products approved.[3]

Subsequently, the Office of Combination Products (OCP) was created as required by the *Medical Device User Fee and Modernization Act* of 2002 (*MDUFMA*). OCP serves a number of roles, including acting as FDA's product jurisdiction officer.[4] In that role, OCP is responsible for assigning the center with primary jurisdiction over combination products and single-entity products where the center assignment is unclear.[5] In addition, OCP issues guidance documents regarding combination product issues, resolves disputes regarding the timeliness of combination product premarket review and submits annual reports to Congress regarding OCP's activities. These annual reports include metrics regarding the number and timing of requests for designation (RFDs) submitted to OCP, frequency of informal feedback provided to industry, the number and timing of combination product premarket review and other OCP activities.[6]

Primary Jurisdiction

Combination products are assigned for review to, and regulated by, one of FDA's centers: Center for Devices and Radiological Health (CDRH); Center for Drug Evaluation and Research (CDER); and Center for Biologics Evaluation and Research (CBER).[7] This assignment is intended to eliminate the need for approvals from more than one FDA center for the combination product, which previously was a problem for these products.

The center with primary jurisdiction is determined based on the combination product's primary mode of action. A mode of action is "is the means by which a product achieves an intended therapeutic effect or action."[8] A combination product can have more than one mode of action. Each mode of action is a drug mode of action, device mode of action or biologic mode of action.

A combination product or part thereof has a drug mode of action if it meets the drug definition in Section 201(g)(1) of the *FD&C Act* and does not have a biologic or device mode of action.[9] A combination product or part thereof has a device mode of action if it meets the device definition in *FD&C Act* Section 201(h), does not have a biologic mode of action and "it does not achieve its primary intended purposes through chemical action within or on the body of man or other animals and is not dependent upon being metabolized for the achievement of its primary intended purposes."[10]

The last clause was intended by Congress to distinguish devices from drugs. It still, however, can be difficult to distinguish between a drug and device because the definitions functionally overlap. The drug and device definitions are essentially the same, except for the clause stating a device "does not achieve its primary intended purposes through chemical action within or on the body of man or other animals and which is not dependent upon being metabolized for the achievement of its primary intended purposes."[11]

FDA had issued draft guidance regarding the meaning of "chemical action" with respect to devices.[12] A number of comments were submitted to FDA challenging aspects of this document. FDA subsequently stated it was evaluating this draft guidance in light of the Prevor decisions (discussed further below).[13]

A combination product or part thereof has a biologic mode of action if it acts by means of a virus, therapeutic serum, toxin, antitoxin, vaccine, blood, blood component or derivative, allergenic product or analogous product applicable to the prevention, treatment or cure of a disease or condition of human beings, as described in section 351(i) of the *Public Health Service Act*.[14]

In deciding which center has jurisdiction, OCP employs a three-step algorithm. The first step is determining the product's "primary mode of action." A combination product's primary mode of action is:

> "the single mode of action of a combination product that provides the most important therapeutic action of the combination product. The most important therapeutic action is the mode of action expected to make the greatest contribution to the overall intended therapeutic effects of the combination product."[15]

When a combination product has a drug primary mode of action, CDER will have primary jurisdiction. When a combination product has a device primary mode of action, CDRH will have primary jurisdiction. And when a combination product has a biologic primary mode of action, CBER will have primary jurisdiction.[16] Although one center will be given primary jurisdiction and regulatory authority for a combination product, it does not preclude another center from consulting with the primary center.[17] Indeed, consultations between centers are common.

In many instances, a combination product's primary mode of action is not obvious to the manufacturer or FDA. For some novel products, there may not be enough information to know the relative contributions of the different modes of action. When a combination product's primary mode of action cannot be determined, OCP uses the algorithm's second step, assigning primary jurisdiction to the center that regulates "other combination products that present similar questions of safety and effectiveness."[18] Finally, if there are no other such combination products, OCP will assign primary jurisdiction of the combination product to the center with "the most expertise related to the most significant safety and effectiveness questions presented by the combination product." Despite this seemingly clear algorithm for determining primary jurisdiction, OCP may apply it in unexpected ways. For example, CDER may be given jurisdiction over a product where the device component has been approved by CDRH many times and CDER has much less experience with the component, on the theory the novel questions are best addressed by CDER.

In 1991, the three FDA centers entered into nonbinding intercenter agreements among one another. These agreements allocated responsibility for various combination product categories among the three centers.[19] Although these intercenter agreements were entered into more than two decades ago, they can represent useful guidance for industry regarding which center will have primary jurisdiction for different combination product types. However, FDA is not bound by these intercenter agreements, and companies should confirm the jurisdictional allocation still applies to a particular product. OCP has indicated it welcomes informal inquiries.

In addition, in June 2011, FDA issued *Draft Guidance for Industry and FDA Staff: Classification of Products as Drugs and Devices & Additional Product Classification Issues*.[20] This draft guidance was intended to provide additional clarification on whether a product is a device or a drug, which can be helpful in determining a product's mode of action. This draft guidance, however, caused substantial controversy because it introduced the concept a product cannot be a device if it "depends, even in part, on chemical action within or on the body of man to achieve any one of its primary intended purposes."[21] This standard—which had not been publicly articulated previously—was rejected by a court after FDA applied it in determining the regulatory status of a product designed to protect workers against chemical burns. This case is discussed further below.

RFD Process

An RFD is a formal process by which a company can request a decision from OCP regarding a product's regulatory identity (drug, biologic or device) and/or the center that will regulate or have primary jurisdiction for single-entity products and combination products, respectively. The RFD process formally was established in 1997 pursuant to Section 563 of the *FD&C Act*, added as part of the *Food and Drug Administration Modernization Act* of 1997 (*FDAMA*).

An RFD jurisdictional determination is legally binding on FDA. In contrast, discussions with a center are not binding. For example, a company could have multiple contacts with CDRH, including review of a presubmission document for a 510(k) premarket notification, and be told later the product may not be a device, and an RFD should be submitted.

If a company plans to submit an RFD, it should be submitted once the company has sufficient information regarding the product's classification (including, if applicable, its primary mode of action), but before submitting a premarket submission for review (e.g., a marketing application or an investigational notice). An RFD must contain sufficient information for OCP to make an informed decision. Although companies often are eager to solidify their regulatory strategies at an early stage, submitting an RFD too early, before the product and its operation are understood fully, can have adverse long-lasting implications for a company. For example, without clear, persuasive and robust information about the proposed product, FDA could get the wrong impression about the product and regulate it differently than the company believes it should be regulated. Further, once FDA has made a decision regarding how a product will be regulated, it is very difficult to get the agency to change its decision.

RFDs are formal and definitive. A company can try an alternative: an informal communication with OCP. Companies can submit a Pre-RFD (or informal RFD) package to obtain early, nonbinding feedback before submitting the formal RFD. A Pre-RFD could focus on a single element that ultimately could be only one factor in the formal RFD, or could submit a document much like the projected RFD. There is no official process for submitting a Pre-RFD, and there is no requirement to submit a Pre-RFD. A Pre-RFD can help a manufacturer if there is a key question or aspect of its RFD on which it would like to get feedback. OCP's response to a pre-RFD is not legally binding, but it would give useful insights into the likely fate of the RFD.

In addition, OCP can facilitate meetings between industry and the applicable centers(s) to obtain informal feedback regarding regulatory strategy and jurisdictional questions. Companies can contact OCP informally for assistance in identifying the correct center staff to attend and set up these meetings.[22]

While it is important to include clear, persuasive and robust information about the proposed product, it is also important to be concise. RFDs cannot exceed 15 pages, including attachments. It is not clear why this 15-page limit originated. Other FDA submission types do not have page limits. Given OCP's increasing demand for more information, including more data on the relative contribution of the constituents, the 15-page limitation can create major practical problems.

According to FDA regulations, an RFD must include the following information:

"1. The identity of the sponsor, including company name and address, establishment registration number, company contact person and telephone number.
2. A description of the product, including:
    (i) Classification, name of the product and all component products, if applicable;
    (ii) Common, generic, or usual name of the product and all component products;
    (iii) Proprietary name of the product;
    (iv) Identification of any component of the product that already has received premarket approval, is marketed as not being subject to premarket approval, or has received an investigational exemption, the identity of the sponsors, and the status of any discussions or agreements between the sponsors regarding the use of this product as a component of a new combination product.
    (v) Chemical, physical, or biological composition;
    (vi) Status and brief reports of the results of developmental work, including animal testing;
    (vii) Description of the manufacturing processes, including the sources of all components;
    (viii) Proposed use or indications;
    (ix) Description of all known modes of action, the sponsor's identification of the single mode of action that provides the most important therapeutic action of the product, and the basis for that determination.
    (x) Schedule and duration of use;
    (xi) Dose and route of administration of drug or biologic;
    (xii) Description of related products, including the regulatory status of those related products; and
    (xiii) Any other relevant information.
3. The sponsor's recommendation as to which agency component should have primary jurisdiction based on the mode of action that provides the most important therapeutic action of the combination product. If the sponsor cannot determine with reasonable certainty which

mode of action provides the most important therapeutic action of the combination product, the sponsor's recommendation must be based on the assignment algorithm set forth in 3.4(b) and an assessment of the assignment of other combination products the sponsor wishes FDA to consider during the assignment of its combination product."[23]

Some of this information is of secondary importance in determining jurisdiction. Given the 15-page limit, companies will want to be judicious in deciding how to cover these multiple topics.

FDA recently estimated in a *Paperwork Reduction Act* filing it will take companies 24 hours to complete an RFD (and 84 RFDs will be submitted annually).[24] It is not clear how FDA derived this estimate. Based on past experience, and given the complexities of the RFD process, companies should anticipate spending substantially more than 24 hours in preparing, crafting and assembling their RFDs.

OCP also has issued guidance on writing an RFD and its content.[25] This guidance includes an RFD Screening Checklist, used to perform a completeness review of all RFDs within five working days after FDA receives the RFD.[26] OCP can and does refuse to file RFDs.

Within 60 days after FDA receives an RFD, OCP will respond formally in writing to the applicant, specifying the center with regulatory authority or primary jurisdiction for the product's premarket review and regulation, as well as any consulting agency components.[27] OCP may request a meeting with the applicant during the 60-day review period to discuss the RFD, although this is very rare given the short timeframe. Also, due to the short timeframe for RFD review, OCP generally does not accept requests for meetings when an RFD is submitted. The company should expect to hear from OCP by Day 60. If OCP does not respond within the 60-day review timeframe, the applicant's recommendation for regulatory jurisdiction becomes binding.

If an applicant disagrees with OCP's RFD decision, it may file a written request for reconsideration with OCP within 15 days of receiving OCP's initial determination.[28] A request for reconsideration may not exceed five pages and cannot include any new information. OCP must review and act on a request for reconsideration within 15 days of receiving same. Companies should not expect a request for reconsideration to succeed.

An adverse RFD can be appealed to the Office of Special Medical Programs (OSMP). There is no time limit for submitting the appeal, nor is there any deadline in which OSMP must decide.

RFDs should not be confused with §513(g) requests. Those apply only to devices. A §513(g) request is used to obtain "information respecting the class in which a device has been classified or the requirements applicable to a device under [the] Act."[29] Although the *FD&C Act* does say the response time for a §513(g) request should be within 60 days, unlike RFDs, a belated reply carries no consequences for FDA. Thus, unlike RFDs, responses to §513(g) requests can take much longer than 60 days. Also, unlike RFDs, §513(g) requests are nonbinding on FDA.

Labeling Claims and OCP Decisions

Historically, OCP posted redacted copies of its RFD decision letters on its website. Beginning in 2009 or 2010, however, OCP stopped posting these decision letters. OCP has reviewed and provided opinions on many RFDs since 2010 (when the last decision letter was posted). In fact, according to FDA's report to Congress, from Fiscal 2011 through 2014. FDA reviewed and issued RFD decision letters for 75 products, eight of which were in 2014. Now, however, to gain access to these decision letters, companies must submit a request under the *Freedom of Information Act*. Without transparency regarding OCP's rationale for center assignment, it often is difficult to understand how OCP reaches these jurisdictional decisions. Previously, OCP had indicated it posted the RFD summaries to promote transparency.[30] In practice, OCP appears to give little weight to precedents; prior jurisdictional decisions are readily deemed distinguishable by OCP unless they are essentially identical.

Those prior decisions were particularly helpful for companies in determining what labeling claims might cause them to end up in one center versus another. In determining center assignment, it is critical for companies to understand intended use can determine product jurisdiction. For example, products intended for wound management historically have been regulated by FDA as devices. On the other hand, products intended for wound treatment or wound healing generally have been regulated as drugs. Access to RFD summaries helped companies understand these finer distinctions.

One recent case sheds some light on OCP's decision-making process and the need to identify both a product's primary mode of action and the proposed product claims clearly. This case involves Prevor and its product, Diphoterine® Skin Wash (DSW).[31] To date, this is the only court case in which an RFD was challenged.

DSW is a liquid substance in a spray canister. DSW is intended as a "first response" product to help prevent and minimize chemical burn injuries occurring due to accidental exposure to chemicals. DSW achieves its intended purpose in two ways: 1) it is sprayed onto the skin to physically and mechanically remove or wash away the offensive chemical; and 2) it neutralizes those acids and bases. Like many skin and wound cleansers, which are regulated as devices, Prevor believed DSW had a device primary mode of action, and CDRH should have primary jurisdiction.

In August 2009, Prevor submitted an RFD for DSW. In October 2009, OCP issued a Letter of Designation concluding DSW is a drug-device combination in which the liquid is the "drug" constituent part, and the canister is the "device" constituent part. OCP assigned primary jurisdiction to CDER based on its finding DSW has a "drug" primary mode of action. In March 2010, Prevor requested reconsideration of this decision by FDA's Office of Special Medical Programs. On 25 April 2011, more than a year later, FDA's OSMP issued a letter affirming OCP's October 2009 decision.

Out of options with the agency, in June 2011, Prevor filed suit in the US District Court for the District of Columbia, challenging FDA's determination DSW was a drug-device combination product with a drug primary mode of action. In September 2012, the court found for Prevor, determining FDA acted arbitrarily and capriciously. Specifically, the court concluded FDA failed to provide a reasoned basis for its classification decision, in part, because FDA employed "extraordinarily expansive language" in making its classification decision. It did so, without offering "more than its say-so." Further, the court rejected FDA's assertion the standard it applied was not new, and the court noted the agency "fails to cite a single prior instance in which it has applied an 'even in part' standard." The court vacated FDA's decision to designate DSW as a drug-device combination product with a drug primary mode of action, and remanded the case to FDA to make a determination in compliance with the court's ruling.

Eight months later, FDA issued a new classification decision for DSW. FDA reached the same conclusion, to regulate DSW as a drug-device combination product with a drug primary mode of action. In this decision, FDA introduced another new standard for determining whether a combination product "achieves" its primary intended purpose through chemical action by assessing whether the chemical action "meaningfully contributes" to the product's intended effect. In response, on 31 July 2013, Prevor filed a lawsuit against FDA in the US District Court for the District of Columbia challenging, for a second time, FDA's determination DSW is a drug-device combination product with a "drug" primary mode of action. The complaint alleged FDA failed to follow the court's September 2012 ruling when, on remand, it arrived at the same conclusion it had reached in its earlier decisions.

On 9 September 2014, the court again found for Prevor and adopted Prevor's plain meaning of "achieves" and rejected FDA's contention that "meaningfully contributes" is synonymous with "achieves." The court also found "[t]he statute does not demand that FDA quantify the exact contribution of a product's ultimate goal [in order to classify it as a drug]. However, it does require more than simply finding that the product would not work as claimed without chemical action." The court rejected FDA's decision. The court denied Prevor's request that the court find the product a device, and again remanded the case to FDA "to determine a standard that complies with the statutory requirements and to classify DSW accordingly."

On 13 January 2015, FDA issued a new classification decision for DSW again finding DSW was a drug-device combination product. FDA relied heavily on statements made by Prevor outside the RFD. While companies are limited to 15 pages in support of an RFD, FDA apparently may go outside the record to look for information it considers relevant to jurisdiction.[32] Prevor did not challenge this decision in court.

This case is included as a cautionary tale about the importance of providing clear and specific information about the primary mode of action and the product claims in early interactions with FDA, as well as not relying heavily on existing precedents. During the litigation, FDA repeatedly distinguished all precedents or suggested they previously had been decided wrongly. This case further highlights how incredibly difficult (if not impossible) it can be to persuade FDA to change its mind, even when a court has (twice) instructed FDA that it is wrong. It also illustrates a tendency for OCP to set a high bar for a company seeking device designation.

Premarket Review of Combination Products

The center with primary jurisdiction for a combination product is responsible for performing the product's premarket review. Consequently, the combination product's premarket submission will be required to be submitted to the center to which it is assigned. This principle applies to both premarket clearance and approval submissions and submissions for investigational exemptions.

Even though one center is assigned primary jurisdiction for the combination product's premarket review, other centers may consult in the review. In addition, centers may review combination products collaboratively. For example, drug eluting stents are drug-device combination products with a device primary mode of action. Thus, CDRH was assigned primary jurisdiction. Drug eluting stent premarket applications, however, were reviewed collaboratively by CDRH and CDER. Industry has expressed concern that even after designation has occurred, there is not always clarity regarding the regulatory requirements. There also have been concerns about slow review times and disagreements among the centers. OCP has said it can help resolve disputes regarding the timeliness of a combination product's review.

FDA has issued draft guidance regarding postapproval changes to combination products.[33] The draft guidance aims to provide industry with information regarding the type of submission required prior to making changes to an approved product. The draft also supplies guidance regarding ways in which an applicant can discuss its options and questions regarding postapproval changes with FDA.

Combination Product Regulatory Strategy

For the reasons discussed above, a regulatory strategy for a combination product is different from a regulatory strategy for a single-entity product. In fact, a combination product regulatory strategy may contemplate various scenarios depending on how FDA could respond to an RFD or different labeling claims or dual-center review.

The regulatory strategy also should outline what presubmission interactions the company plans to have with FDA. Will the company submit an RFD? If so, on what data will it rely in the request? As discussed above, the advantage of an RFD is it is legally binding on FDA, unlike interactions with a center. Indeed, a center could process an application initially, e.g., grant an investigational device exemption, and then ask the sponsor to submit an RFD.

Companies must consider every word of an RFD carefully. Thus, before assuming the company wants to pursue the RFD route, it should outline (probably in the regulatory strategy) the information known about the product's primary mode of action (e.g., test data, published literature), intended product claims, what similar products currently are in the marketplace, how they are regulated and how the company's product and its claims differ from those products currently in the marketplace. In applying its algorithm, OCP may focus on how the product differs from current products, rather than its similarities.

Many companies focus solely on their test data in preparing or considering an RFD. FDA, however, may look at published materials even if the company has not included them in its RFD. Thus, companies should check to see what, if any, information has been published about the proposed product or similar product. The company should even consider OUS publications or publications by scientists that may be relevant to the jurisdictional determination.

Companies also should understand fully what claims they wish to make about the proposed product. Then the company should assess: 1) how products with similar technological characteristics are regulated and 2) how products with similar claims are regulated. These may not always be the same. The company may find similar technological products are regulated in one way, but products with similar claims are regulated in another. This can inform the company's thinking about claims it may want to avoid and alternative intended uses.

The regulatory strategy may contemplate using either of two submission types contingent upon the lead center assignment. For example, the strategy document may say a new drug application (NDA) may be needed if the lead center is CDER, and a 510(k) premarket notification may be available if the lead center is CDRH. While some may prefer the more cumbersome NDA premarket pathway to prevent future competitors from easily entering the marketplace or other commercial reasons and obtaining patent restoration, for most companies, the significantly greater level of effort, cost and time to market for an NDA or biologic license application (BLA) generally is outweighed by the ease of a device submission (e.g., 510(k) premarket notification or *de novo*, and to a lesser extent, a premarket approval (PMA)), if that device pathway is available to the company. OCP, however, based on the authors' experience, appears to be assigning CDER or CBER as the lead center for an increasingly large number of combination products, even when very similar products have been regulated as devices in the past.

Finally, the regulatory strategy should assess the types of data required to support the premarket application. NDAs, BLAs and PMAs all require clinical trial data. 510(k)s may include, but do not always, clinical data. Companies should determine whether submissions for similar products included clinical data and the type(s) of trial(s) performed. This information will provide the company with a starting point to estimate its future burden. In addition, companies will want to consider human factors issues.[34] To obtain additional feedback regarding proposed clinical trial design, once the lead center is known, the company can submit a request for feedback through the applicable mechanism, for example, a Presubmission (device) or Pre-IND (drug).

Good Manufacturing Practices

There are no specific Good Manufacturing Practices (GMPs) for combination products. Combination products, like their constituent parts, are required to comply with GMPs. The rule for combination product GMPs is set out in Part 4 of the regulations and, in short, states a combination product's constituent parts are required to comply with the applicable GMPs. For example, in a drug-device combination product, the drug component needs to comply with the requirements set forth in 21 CFR Parts 210 and 211, and the device component needs to comply with the requirements set forth in 21 CFR Part 820. Similarly, if the combination product contains a biologic component, the component needs to comply with 21 CFR Parts 600–680, and human cells, tissues and cellular and tissue-based product (HCT/P) components need to comply with 21 CFR Part 1271.

In theory, the combination product GMP rule seems straightforward, and it is for cross-labeled combination products packaged separately. It is less clear, however, how this rule works for single-entity combination products or co-packaged combination products, because the design and manufacturing processes for these combination products' component parts overlap. Thus, which part(s) of the regulations apply for those overlapping processes? In this case, the regulations specify certain elements of the component part GMPs with which a company must comply, if a company's quality system meets one of the specified GMP standards for a component of the combination product (the "Streamlined Approach").[35] For example, if a product is a drug-device combination, and the manufacturer's quality system meets the requirements of 21 CFR Parts 210 and 211 (drugs), the regulations specify which elements of 21 CFR Part 820 (devices) the manufacturer must implement. Notwithstanding the foregoing, if a component of the co-packaged or single entity combination product is manufactured in a facility separate from the other product component, the facility must comply with only those requirements applicable to the component being manufactured there.[36]

In January 2015, FDA issued draft guidance, with the goal of providing additional clarity regarding GMP requirements for combination products.[37] The guidance did not provide any novel information but did clarify the Streamlined Approach and provide helpful background for companies that do not have a full understanding of another center's GMP requirements.

Adverse Event Reporting

To date, there is no specific requirement for reporting combination product adverse events. OCP, however, has issued a proposed rule for reporting adverse events related to combination products.[38] The proposed adverse event rule would require companies to continue submitting reports under the applicable rules for the associated component part—specifically, 21 CFR Part 803 for device component parts, 21 CFR §§314.80 and 314.81 for drug component parts and 21 CFR §§600.80 and 606.170 for component parts licensed under the *Public Health Service Act* (biologics). In addition, combination product companies would need to submit additional reports, as applicable:

- "5-day Report" as required by 21 CFR §803.53(a) for device constituent parts of combination products
- "30-day Malfunction Report" as required by 21 CFR §803.20(b)(3)(ii) for device constituent parts of combination products
- "Postmarketing 15-day Alert Report" as required by 21 CFR §§314.80(c)(1) and (e), and 600.80(c)(1) and (e) for drug and biological constituent parts of combination products
- "3-day Field Alert Report" as required by 21 CFR §314.81(b)(1) for drug constituent parts of combination products
- "Blood Fatality Report" as required by 21 CFR §606.170 for biologic component parts of combination products

If a company is responsible for all of a combination product's constituent parts, it is required to report all adverse events for all constituent parts. On the other hand, if the company is responsible for only one combination product constituent part, under the proposed rule, the company is required to report only adverse events for the constituent part for which it is responsible. The reporting methods and recordkeeping requirements would remain unchanged under the proposed rule.

The proposed rule has its notable flaws, including not addressing how adverse events would be handled for convenience kits, risk of duplicate reporting and, in practice, may cause difficulty in identifying which component part is the cause of the adverse event.

In general, since there is no specific rule in place, adverse events are reported in accordance with the rules applicable to the center with primary jurisdiction for the product. Until a final rule is issued (and perhaps even afterward), there will continue to be inconsistency and uncertainty regarding adverse event reporting for combination products.

There have been legislative initiatives designed to address some of the issues that have arisen during the review of combination products. As of this writing, it is unclear whether congressional relief will be forthcoming.

Conclusion

Combination products are increasingly common. To avoid roadblocks to market, companies should understand how and by which center their products will be regulated. Companies should, however, be wary of submitting an RFD too early in the process before the product and its mechanisms of action are understood adequately, because incomplete information can lead to undesirable, binding decisions by OCP. The RFD should be written carefully because it will be scrutinized very closely by OCP. Once the product's regulatory jurisdiction is defined, it is essential to understand how the company will comply with the product's pre- and postmarket requirements.

References
1. 21 CFR §3.2(e). FDA website. https://www.accessdata.fda.gov/scripts/cdrh/cfdocs/cfCFR/CFRSearch.cfm?fr=3.2. Accessed 17 March 2016.
2. Assignment of Agency Component for Review of Premarket Applications, Final Rule, 56 *Fed. Reg.* 58,754 (21 November 1991).
3. M-D-D-I Rep. (*The Gray Sheet*), 8 January 1996, at 9-10; M-D-D-I Rep. (*The Gray Sheet*), 24 September 1990, at 4-5.
4. 21 CFR §3.6. Government Printing Office (GPO) website. http://www.gpo.gov/fdsys/granule/CFR-2010-title21-vol1/CFR-2010-title21-vol1-sec3-6. Accessed 17 March 2016.
5. 21 CFR §3.2(o). FDA website. https://www.accessdata.fda.gov/scripts/cdrh/cfdocs/cfCFR/CFRSearch.cfm?fr=3.2. Accessed 17 March 2017.
6. US Food and Drug Administration, Fiscal Year 2014 Performance Report to Congress for the Office of Combination Products as required by the *Medical Device User Fee and Modernization Act* of 2002, FY 2012. FDA website. http://www.fda.gov/downloads/AboutFDA/ReportsManualsForms/Reports/PerformanceReports/CombinationProducts/UCM460836.pdf. Accessed 17 March 2016.
7. 21 CFR §3.1. GPO website. http://www.gpo.gov/fdsys/pkg/CFR-2010-title21-vol1/xml/CFR-2010-title21-vol1-sec3-1.xml. Accessed 17 March 2016.
8. 21 CFR §3.2(k). FDA website. https://www.accessdata.fda.gov/scripts/cdrh/cfdocs/cfCFR/CFRSearch.cfm?fr=3.2. Accessed 17 March 2016.
9. 21 CFR §3.2(k)(3). FDA website. https://www.accessdata.fda.gov/scripts/cdrh/cfdocs/cfCFR/CFRSearch.cfm?fr=3.2. Accessed 17 March 2016.
10. 21 CFR §3.2(k)(2). FDA website. https://www.accessdata.fda.gov/scripts/cdrh/cfdocs/cfCFR/CFRSearch.cfm?fr=3.2. Accessed 17 March 2016.
11. 21 USC §321(h). GPO website. http://www.gpo.gov/fdsys/granule/USCODE-2010-title21/USCODE-2010-title21-chap9-subchapII-sec321/content-detail.html. Accessed 17 March 2016.
12. *Draft Guidance for Industry and FDA Staff: Interpretation of the Term "Chemical Action" in the Definition of Device under Section 201(h) of the Federal Food, Drug, and Cosmetic Act* (June 2011). FDA website. http://www.fda.gov/RegulatoryInformation/Guidances/ucm259059.htm. Accessed 17 March 2016.
13. Letter from Thomas A. Kraus, Associate Commissioner for Legislation, to The Honorable Joseph R. Pitts, Chairman, Subcommittee on Health, Committee on Energy and Commerce, House of Representatives (12 November 2014).
14. 21 CFR §3.2(k)(1). FDA website. https://www.accessdata.fda.gov/scripts/cdrh/cfdocs/cfCFR/CFRSearch.cfm?fr=3.2. Accessed 17 March 2016.
15. 21 CFR §3.2(m). FDA website. https://www.accessdata.fda.gov/scripts/cdrh/cfdocs/cfCFR/CFRSearch.cfm?fr=3.2. Accessed 17 March 2016.
16. 21 CFR §3.4(a). GPO website. http://www.gpo.gov/fdsys/pkg/CFR-2001-title21-vol1/xml/CFR-2001-title21-vol1-sec3-4.xml. Accessed 17 March 2016.
17. 21 CFR §3.4(c). GPO website. http://www.gpo.gov/fdsys/pkg/CFR-2001-title21-vol1/xml/CFR-2001-title21-vol1-sec3-4.xml. Accessed 17 March 2016.
18. 21 CFR §3.4(b). GPO website. http://www.gpo.gov/fdsys/pkg/CFR-2001-title21-vol1/xml/CFR-2001-title21-vol1-sec3-4.xml. Accessed 17 March 2016.
19. 21 CFR §3.5(a)(2). FDA website. http://www.gpo.gov/fdsys/pkg/CFR-2001-title21-vol1/xml/CFR-2001-title21-vol1-sec3-5.xml. Accessed 17 March 2016.
20. *Draft Guidance for Industry and FDA Staff: Classification of Products as Drugs and Devices & Additional Product Classification Issues*. FDA website. http://www.fda.gov/downloads/RegulatoryInformation/Guidances/UCM258957.pdf. Accessed 17 March 2016
21. Op cit 5.
22. "Frequently Asked Questions About Combination Products." FDA website. www.fda.gov/CombinationProducts/AboutCombinationProducts/ucm101496.htm. Accessed 17 March 2016.
23. 21 CFR §3.7(c). GPO website. http://www.gpo.gov/fdsys/pkg/CFR-2001-title21-vol1/xml/CFR-2001-title21-vol1-sec3-7.xml. Accessed 17 March 2016.
24. 81 Fed. Reg. 4923 (Jan. 28, 2016).
25. *Guidance for Industry: How to Write a Request for Designation (RFD)* (April 2011). FDA website. http://www.fda.gov/RegulatoryInformation/Guidances/ucm126053.htm. Accessed 17 March 2016.
26. 21 CFR §3.8(a). GPO website. http://www.gpo.gov/fdsys/pkg/CFR-2001-title21-vol1/xml/CFR-2001-title21-vol1-sec3-8.xml. Accessed 17 March 2016.
27. 21 CFR §3.8(b). GPO website. http://www.gpo.gov/fdsys/pkg/CFR-2001-title21-vol1/xml/CFR-2001-title21-vol1-sec3-8.xml. Accessed 17 March 2016.
28. 21 CFR §3.8(c). GPO website. http://www.gpo.gov/fdsys/pkg/CFR-2001-title21-vol1/xml/CFR-2001-title21-vol1-sec3-8.xml. Accessed 17 March 2016.
29. 21 USC §360c(g). GPO website. http://www.gpo.gov/fdsys/pkg/USCODE-2010-title21/html/USCODE-2010-title21-chap9-subchapV-partA-sec360c.htm. Accessed 17 March 2016.
30. RFD Jurisdictional Decisions. FDA website. http://www.fda.gov/CombinationProducts/JurisdictionalInformation/RFDJurisdictionalDecisions/default.htm. Accessed 17 March 2016.
31. Hyman, Phelps & McNamara, P.C. represented Prevor in this litigation.
32. Prevor v. U.S. Food and Drug Administration, No. 1:13-cv-01177-RMC, Status report by United States Food and Drug Administration, Attachment A, Prevor—Remand Decision (D.D.C. 13 January 2015).
33. *Draft Guidance for Industry and FDA Staff: Submission for Postapproval Modifications to a Combination Product Approved Under a BLA, NDA, or PMA* (January 2013). FDA website. http://www.fda.gov/downloads/RegulatoryInformation/Guidances/UCM336230.pdf. Accessed 17 March 2016.
34. *Human Factors Studies and Related Clinical Study Design Considerations in Combination Product Design and Development,*

Draft Guidance for Industry and FDA Staff (February 2016). FDA website. http://www.fda.gov/downloads/RegulatoryInformation/Guidances/UCM484345.pdf. Accessed 17 March 2016.

35. 21 CFR §4.4(b).
36. 21 CFR §4.4(c).
37. *Draft Guidance for Industry and FDA Staff: Current Good Manufacturing Practice Requirements for Combination Products* (January 2015). FDA website. http://www.fda.gov/downloads/RegulatoryInformation/Guidances/UCM429304.pdf. Accessed 17 March 2016.
38. Postmarketing Safety Reporting for Combination Products. *74 Fed. Reg. 50744* (1 October 2009). GPO website. http://www.gpo.gov/fdsys/granule/FR-2009-10-01/E9-23519. Accessed 17 March 2016.

12

Global Regulatory Processes

By Xianjun Chen, Manuel Urena and Brian Young

Introduction

The recent acceleration in understanding human physiology and tremendous growth in medical technology has increased the complexity of regulatory processes and classification decisions dramatically. More and more products incorporate elements of different regulated product categories, and companies increasingly are grappling with novel technologies containing device, drug and/or biologic elements, thereby introducing uncertainty for companies and regulators. Global regulatory processes begin with an initial classification determination in all intended markets. Product classification determines the product's fundamental regulatory requirements in each jurisdiction and impacts strategy and planning significantly.

A company's regulatory obligations extend throughout the product's life. Once a product is approved (or "cleared") and placed on the market, the key regulatory obligations include compliance with quality system requirements, adverse event analysis and reporting vigilance information to authorities and initiating and reporting product recalls. Some countries also require approvals for substantial product changes, and others require periodic product registration renewal.

The goal is to obtain and maintain needed regulatory registration approvals for the company's products in the most commercially viable, cost-effective, timely, efficient, compliant and predictable way possible. Achieving this goal requires well-thought-out processes and strong cross-functional and cross-geographical communication and collaboration. To be successful, regulatory professionals must understand the company's needs and be able to communicate and collaborate across functional and geographic boundaries effectively.

Global regulatory processes' scale and complexity vary significantly based on company size, location, product classification, product design and global marketing plans. However, these processes share common principles that, when applied properly, lead to a well-defined and efficient process for global product registrations and continued support throughout the product lifecycle. This chapter explores key elements of effective global regulatory processes, while allowing for essential variations in complexity based on product design, company size and the global footprint of the business. While no prescriptive approach will work for all companies and all products, this chapter provides a foundation that can be individualized to meet specific company needs.

Strategy and Planning

The global regulatory landscape is evolving and changing constantly with a clear trend toward more regulation and greater complexity. To be successful, regulatory professionals need to anticipate changes and provide clear guidance on how to meet requirements. A good regulatory strategy is actionable, measurable and supports the business strategy. A great regulatory approach anticipates and takes advantage of changes, thereby providing the company a competitive advantage.

Linking Regulatory Strategy with Commercial Strategy

Regulatory strategy should support and complement the company's commercial business strategy. Regulatory professionals must consider the ability to sell and defend the business against competition within the constraints of regulatory approval. Therefore, the easiest regulatory pathway is not necessarily the best. Although this is a fundamental regulatory concept, it often is difficult for management and business strategists to understand and grasp its strategic importance, especially when driven by financial commitments. It is important for the regulatory specialist to strive to impart this concept's importance.

In some instances, it may be preferable to pursue a more onerous regulatory pathway to obtain approval with additional claims and create a high regulatory barrier to competition. For example, taking advantage of a classification exempt from premarket requirements, or with minimal premarket requirements, may allow early market entry. However, the company will need to abide by the approval or exemption's limitations. This approach may severely restrict marketing claims about the product and may enable competitors to enter the market rapidly and easily with competitive product offerings having the same claims and indications. In some cases, being first to market outweighs potential downsides. However, in other cases, it may be preferable to pursue a more-complex regulatory pathway that affords the company greater ability to differentiate and protect its product.

Similarly, the company must consider the claims required to support the product's value proposition, obtain desired reimbursement and enable the product to be commercialized effectively. In some instances, it may be preferable to obtain initial approval with minimal claims, and then perform postmarket testing to support additional claims. A phased approach like this can take advantage of regional regulatory requirement differences. For example, approval could be obtained quickly in a jurisdiction with minimal requirements, followed by postmarket testing in that jurisdiction to support submissions with expanded claims in high-value markets with more rigorous regulatory requirements.

Managing Uncertainty and Risk

No one-size-fits-all approach exists for all companies and products. The regulatory professional should collaborate with marketing and the commercial side of the business to establish the best regulatory approach given the company's specific needs. In this context, the regulatory professional can be a valued partner guiding marketing through various options. In doing so, it is important to convey the uncertainty or risk level associated with each regulatory approach. For example, pursuing expanded claims relying on clinical data carries additional uncertainty related to the clinical study's outcome and whether regulatory authorities will grant the requested claims. Further, regulatory requirements are subject to change over time, which can have a major impact on the business. Therefore, regulatory professionals need to consider and anticipate the possibility of regulation changes. It is vitally important to communicate this information to the company early in the concept and development process, so it can be factored into the return on investment calculation and used as an aid in determining which projects and strategies to pursue.

Deciding on a Single Global Product or Multiple Versions for Local Markets

Any given product's market potential can vary significantly from one country to another based on local economics, competition, transportation, distribution, healthcare practices, patient population differences, infrastructure, etc. In some instances, it may be preferable to seek approval for the same claims and indications globally. However, companies need to be open to localizing the product, claims and indications to meet local needs. For example, the US Food and Drug Administration (FDA) often is reluctant to allow strong clinical or performance claims in the indications for use of Class II devices. However, the EU is open to strong clinical and performance claims for Class IIa and IIb devices where there is valid scientific evidence to support such claims. In such cases, the company must consider whether to introduce a single global version of the product adhering to the constraints of the most restrictive jurisdiction, or whether to introduce multiple versions of labeling based on local requirements. In grappling with this decision, the company should balance the marketing advantage of more expansive claims in one or more target markets against the additional costs of managing multiple product codes and associated labeling.

Balancing Regulatory Costs With Commercial Potential

Regulatory requirements can vary significantly between jurisdictions, and pursuing approvals in some markets can be very expensive and time consuming. Before investing time and resources in the registration process, it is important to establish the market opportunity and estimate the time and cost required to obtain registrations in each

Table 12-1. Global Submission Planning and Prioritization Process

Regulatory	Commercial Team
Establish classification for each market	Establish required product characteristics
Identify submission requirements	Establish desired claims and indications
Calculate regulatory costs	Determine business risks
Establish approval timeline	Establish sales forecast
Determine regulatory uncertainties	Identify strategic value to the business
Determine resource needs	Calculate return on investment (ROI)
Aggregate Plan	
Establish ROI and strategic value for the products	
Rank products and markets by ROI and strategic value	
Align prioritized list with available resources	
Establish and communicate global registration plan	

target country. This cost needs to be factored into the business case for each market.

A well-thought-out regulatory strategy takes these factors into account and should be incorporated into the return on investment calculation and used as an aid to determine which countries to pursue. This process leads to a systematic plan that identifies and prioritizes registrations around the world. The basic registration planning and prioritization process is shown in **Table 12-1**.

Planning and Prioritization

Because companies may lack sufficient resources to pursue all registrations at the same time, the ability to prioritize is essential to the registration planning process. The following basic information can be used to prioritize global regulatory submissions:[1]

- market potential (sales forecast)
- predicted regulatory review and approval timeline
- uncertainty regarding approval timeline and likelihood
- regulatory costs[2]
- whether another country's approval is a submission prerequisite
- other strategic considerations[3]

Companies should assess their planning processes' effectiveness periodically by measuring their past plans' accuracy in predicting actual approval times, costs and revenues. Likewise, regulatory groups should measure and analyze their performance. Such metrics as number of submissions filed over a given time period (throughput), rounds of questions from regulators, review time and approval percentage can be useful for this purpose. This sort of review of past plans and performance can lead to valuable planning and regulatory submission process improvements.

Classification

Product classification determines the regulatory approval pathway and may influence a device's reimbursement. Accordingly, determining product classification is an essential first step in establishing target nations' regulatory requirements. Most countries employ a risk-based classification approach that considers the product's design, intended use and proposed claims. Notwithstanding classification regulation similarities, there can be significant differences in a product's classification across geographies. The classification process should consider national differences and incorporate strategic decisions about the likelihood of success and reimbursement implications of pursuing various claims.

Confirming the Product Is Regulated as a Medical Device

When determining classification, the first question to consider is whether the product meets the definition of a medical device using each jurisdiction's established definition. Global strategy must acknowledge differences in medical device definitions among jurisdictions and the potential for the same product to be regulated as a device in one jurisdiction and as a drug or biologic in others. It also is important to recognize the profound importance of claims on this decision. For example, a variety of wound dressings contain silver as a means of controlling bacteria. The EU regulates the included silver as a pharmaceutical agent, whereas it is regulated as a device in the US if its purpose is to control bacteria within the wound dressing. However, if the company claims the included silver releases into the wound and controls bacteria in the wound, the silver component will be regulated in the US as a drug, and the product will be regulated as a combination device-drug product. In this instance, the company must decide whether the claims that render the product a drug in the US have sufficient value to outweigh the substantial additional investment required to obtain approval. Because data requirements and regulations differ profoundly for drugs, biologics and devices, it is imperative regulatory professionals invest the necessary time, effort and energy to ensure the company understands how its products will be regulated in each target market. It also is important to communicate and collaborate with marketing and the commercial side of the business to ensure the regulatory pathway selected is consistent with the company's business strategy.

Establishing Device Classification

After concluding a regulated product is a medical device within each jurisdiction, the next step is to classify the device. Classification rules differ across the various regulatory authorities, but there generally are three classes of devices: low risk, moderate risk and higher risk devices. The EU further differentiates moderate risk devices into two classes (Class 2a and 2b), and Canada has four device classes. Classification is defined further by medical specialty, technology and indication. For example, at this time, FDA has established classifications for approximately 1,700 different generic types of devices and grouped them into 16 medical specialties referred to as panels.

Several nations, e.g., the US, Brazil and China use similar classification criteria, there can be major differences between jurisdictions. For example, calcium sulfate bone void fillers containing human demineralized bone matrix (DBM) are regulated as Class II medical devices in the US. These same products currently are regulated as medicines in Germany due to the inclusion of human tissue. The UK currently regulates the same product as a human tissue if there are no active (medicinal) claims for the DBM. If there are active claims for the DBM, it will be regulated as a medicine in the UK. However, for now, manufacturers need to contend with different national requirements. These regional or national classification regulation differences can serve as barriers to entry for certain markets and have a profound effect on global strategy. Because of these differences, companies need to consider adapting their products and associated claims to meet local regulatory and clinical needs.

It also is important to understand some special cases exist in the global medical device classification scheme. For example, classifications typically do not differentiate between adult and pediatric patient populations. Accordingly, approved indications at times can be silent regarding adult and pediatric use. However, companies assuming they can promote their products for pediatric use because their approved indications are silent as to patient age do so at their own peril. Accordingly, it is important for regulatory professionals to research requirements within each jurisdiction thoroughly before rendering advice and committing the company to a course of action.

Regulatory professionals need to be aware medical device classifications evolve over time to keep pace with technology advancements and clinical experience in the field. For example, a device may be up-classified to a higher risk category based on adverse events in the field. Similarly, a device may be down-classified to a lower risk category based on years of favorable clinical experience in the field. Regulators also may separate a group of like products from an existing classification into a new classification group without affecting the risk category. Accordingly, classification changes may be favorable, neutral or unfavorable to the company's interests. Regulatory professionals need to monitor trends and engage proactively in reclassification discussions. In some instances, it may be in a company's best interest to advocate for stricter regulation, as it may help improve patient safety and weed out competition. However, in other cases, the company may have significant data supporting a particular technology and indication's relative safety that would be useful to regulators as they attempt to balance data requirements and compliance oversight with device risk.

Data Considerations

Once target markets are identified, and the product has been classified within each market, the process for establishing data requirements to support global registrations can begin. This should be done early in product development so all required data can be identified and included in the product development plan.

The data identification process should consider both national requirements and the aggregate data and information required to support all desired global approvals.

How much is enough?

One essential consideration is how much data are needed for submissions. It may be in the company's best interest to engage the regulatory authority early to determine what data will be required to obtain approval. This can be done through either informal correspondence or formal correspondence and meetings. For complex and costly submissions with lengthy review timelines, e.g., US Premarket Approval (PMA) submissions, it makes sense to clarify the requirements with the regulatory authority well in advance of the submission. However, the regulatory agency's feedback often is not binding, and scheduling meetings can take a long time. Therefore, for more routine submissions, companies may conduct their own analyses or correspond with independent experts to define requirements.

A baseline for how much data are required can be established from regulations, guidance, standards and prior submissions for similar products. However, submission requirements often change informally based on the individual reviewer, what the regulator has learned from other submissions, adverse event information and other field experience. Further, companies may want to pursue additional claims for their products to differentiate them from the competition. All of these factors raise uncertainty about precisely how much data will be required to support timely regulatory approvals. With this in mind, regulatory professionals need to develop data strategies to optimize approval likelihood and timeliness while minimizing risk.

Generally, companies opt to submit the minimum required data and perform additional testing or provide more documentation only at the reviewer's request. This approach shortens the time to submission but, ultimately, may extend the overall time to approval. Another option is to go beyond the minimum requirements and offer additional data upfront if it is likely to be requested during the review process. An alternative strategy is to file with the minimum requirements and perform additional testing in parallel with the review. All of these approaches are logical and reasonable. However, the regulatory professional must bear in mind a minimalist approach potentially can lead to lengthy reviews, as questions are asked and testing is designed and completed to address them. Therefore, regulatory professionals should research thoroughly what data and information will be necessary to obtain needed approvals.

As companies expand into other markets, regulatory professionals need to consider the risk of disclosing proprietary and confidential information to review authorities that could make its way into the hands of local competitors. This is rarely an issue but should be considered in markets with an unfavorable corruption index[4] or for products with very sensitive proprietary information. Providing detailed drawings and proprietary processes generally is not required for submissions in emerging markets, and it is inadvisable to volunteer such information in the absence of a requirement to do so.

Too much detail also can be problematic in mature markets, albeit for different reasons. Mature markets often have strict requirements for when new submissions are required in response to changes. If the item to be changed was not in the original submission, modifying it may not require a new submission. The logic is if the government did not require or consider it in the approval process, modifying it would be less likely to trigger the need for a new submission. While this certainly is not a universal rule, it is fair to say adding too much detail could tie the company's hands with regard to potential future changes.

Accuracy and Integrity

Most countries have requirements for regulatory submission accuracy and integrity, and there may be serious consequences for submitting inaccurate or misleading information. Further, some countries have onerous and lengthy device change review and approval processes. Submitting changes required to correct errors in the original application can be especially problematic. Therefore, submission accuracy and integrity are important to avoid compliance action and delays in product marketing. This has become an increasing concern, with the expanded data amount and complexity required for global submissions. With this in mind, companies should incorporate a systematic process for verifying data accuracy and integrity into the regulatory submission process.

The data integrity verification process involves confirming the premarket submission is supported adequately by the underlying data. At minimum, integrity review should confirm:

1. protocols were in place and acceptance criteria defined prior to initiating testing
2. test articles are representative of the final packaged, sterilized product
3. test articles pass acceptance criteria
4. test equipment was maintained and calibrated properly
5. raw data exist to support the final report's conclusions
6. documentation exists to justify any changed or excluded raw data
7. final report calculations and statistical analyses are accurate
8. protocol deviations are explained and justified
9. submission is supported fully by the underlying data

Figure 12-1. Data integrity verification process outline

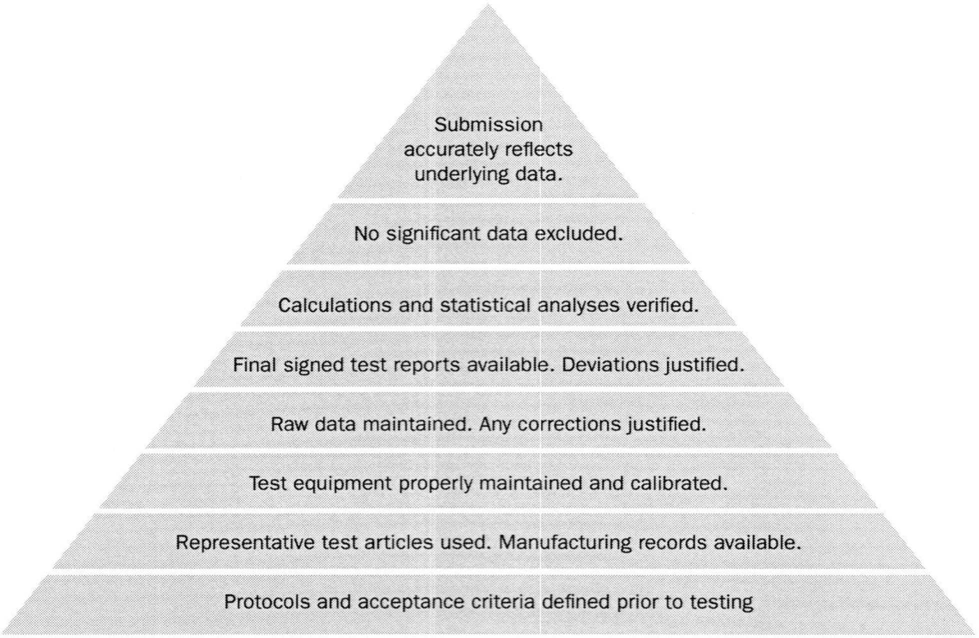

- Submission accurately reflects underlying data.
- No significant data excluded.
- Calculations and statistical analyses verified.
- Final signed test reports available. Deviations justified.
- Raw data maintained. Any corrections justified.
- Test equipment properly maintained and calibrated.
- Representative test articles used. Manufacturing records available.
- Protocols and acceptance criteria defined prior to testing

Figure 12-1 provides a basic process outline for confirming data integrity.

Data integrity should be assessed by an independent qualified person or entity. From a process perspective, it makes sense to incorporate the integrity assessment into the test report review and approval process. This approach reduces the risk of delays if test report problems go undetected until the final submission package is complete.

Clinical Data

Special consideration should be given to the need for clinical data due to the time, expense and uncertainty associated with data collection. For submissions requiring clinical data, the company must decide how, where and when to collect that data. When some target markets will require clinical data for approval and others will not, it may be possible to collect the data via postmarket studies in jurisdictions that do not require clinical data as a basis for approval. In such instances, the company must consider whether foreign clinical data will be representative of the target population and whether such data are acceptable for review.

Companies often are concerned with situations where clinical data are not required for regulatory approval but will be required to support commercial efforts. The question then becomes whether to collect the data before or after regulatory approvals are obtained. The commercial side of the business often will wish to accelerate the clinical study and run it prior to approval. This may be the best option, but it has several potential downsides. For example, initiating the study premarket will require additional time to obtain approvals necessary to begin the study. The regulatory authorities also may want to delay marketing approval pending the study's outcome. Additionally, the study's outcome may be unclear. It may support the proposed approval or raise new questions that could delay the approval process further. With this in mind, regulatory professionals must help guide the company toward the best approach given the situation's unique circumstances. In doing so, regulatory professionals should seek to determine the proposed study's purpose. Often, the commercial side of the business simply is looking to "prime the pump" with the personal experience of key opinion leaders. In such a case, a simple, limited launch user preference study, immediately following marketing approval, may be the best option.

Dossier Assembly

For the purpose of this discussion, "dossier" describes a regulatory authority or review agency's required information and documentation to grant approval to market a medical device in certain jurisdictions. Depending on the device classification and jurisdiction, that documentation may be subject to review before approval is granted, or may need to be available for review during periodic audits.

From a regulatory perspective, creating and collecting dossier documentation is one of the most critical activities for an efficient and successful regulatory approval. Reconvening the product development team to perform additional testing after product development is complete is very inefficient and time consuming. Therefore, careful planning of the required regulatory submission documentation and information should start at the product development project concept stage or beginning.

Establishing a Dossier Assembly Foundation

Assuming a product is developed with the intent of introduction on traditional medical device markets (like the US or EU), the bulk of the documentation will be developed following the standard approach and structure required by those jurisdictions' regulations. In most cases, a European Technical File and a US 510(k) or PMA[5] application form a suitable documentation foundation for regulatory approval in other countries.

Assembling data and coordinating global regulatory submissions is a complex task simplified by the fact various countries and regions have many common data requirements. This supports the development of a single global dossier, or Summary Technical Document (STED), containing the information required for most global submissions. The format and content structure of the STED are available as a guidance document developed by the Global Harmonization Task Force (GHTF) on the International Medical Device Regulators Forum's website. While not all countries accept the STED format, many do, and together with a European Technical File and a US 510(k) or PMA application, most of the documentation required for regulatory submissions globally will be in one or more of these documents.

A significant amount of the data required to support global registrations is developed during routine product design and development. For example, the documentation related to device description, design verification, manufacturing validation, risk management and labeling, if developed following recognized international standards and commonly accepted best practices from industry, can be used for submissions in any country. In countries where the regulatory review focus is not so technical or the regulatory scheme's maturity or capacity is not so extensive (e.g., Costa Rica, Indonesia, Colombia), summaries of some of those activities, e.g., design verification, normally are provided in lieu of actual reports.

Design validation and clinical information requirements may vary widely across jurisdictions. Some venues may accept analysis of equivalence to an existing device as with the US 510(k) process, but that approach may not be recognized or acceptable in other jurisdictions.

The need to conduct clinical investigations to support regulatory approval must be considered during the regulatory planning process. Countries such as Russia and China may require clinical investigations conducted locally, which can be costly when compared to the financial benefit of marketing the product in these countries. Consulting with regulatory authorities or local regulatory experts is recommended to decide the best approach in these situations. In contrast, some countries may forego the clinical evidence requirement if the product already is approved in certain mature reference markets such as the US, Europe, Australia, Canada or Japan. Other countries, e.g., Australia and New Zealand, may accept a medical device approved in Europe for market introduction.

Certificates of Free Sale

A key requirement in many countries, included as part of the dossier, is evidence of regulatory approval in the country where the product owner (manufacturer or legal manufacturer) is established. This regulatory approval is demonstrated by a Certificate of Free Sale (CFS) or equivalent (e.g., Certificate to Foreign Government in the US), issued by the country's regulatory authority. This document confirms the products within the scope of the certificate are marketed legally in the country issuing the certificate and comply with that country's regulatory requirements. Certain countries require the CFS to include a schedule of product codes, descriptions and information about the physical manufacturers and their locations. For large manufacturers, product configuration complexity and subcontracted manufacturing sites can make obtaining a CFS that satisfies regulatory authorities' expectations challenging.

Legalization

Regulatory agency documentation, such as a CFS, in many instances requires a degree of legalization before it can be used in another country's submission dossier. The legalization types normally required are:

- Notarization—performed by a public notary, justice of the peace or similar figure, this certifies a signature or document copy's authenticity.
- Apostille—provided by a dedicated government agency, typically a trade agency, state secretary or similar entity, confirming a document's authenticity. An apostille normally is accepted as the single certification required by countries

members of *The Hague Convention*. *The Hague Convention*'s aim is to simplify trade and official documentation recognition among its members.
- Consular certification—provided by the target country's local consular service, certifying a document's authenticity. It normally requires notarization first and is the common certification method for nonmembers of *The Hague Convention*.
- Chamber of Commerce certification—rare, this is required in some countries to certify the medical device company's legal status in documents such as manufacturing licenses or establishment registrations.

Translation and Localization

During the common dossier creation process, the manufacturer's regulatory professional gathers the required documentation and makes it available for the translation and localization stage. Depending on the geographical reach and capability, these last steps may be performed in the manufacturer's country or by a regional or local representative. Section filing provides more detail about local regulatory representation approaches.

Regardless of dossier completion responsibility, two final steps normally are conducted before filing. The first is translating the documentation. Many countries (Russia, China, US, Turkey, Mexico) require all dossier documentation to be in the local language. Sufficient time and budget should be allowed for this requirement. It is important a manufacturer's representative review and approve the translated documents. If the manufacturer's representative does not have capability in a particular language, it should use a certified translator to ensure no translation errors could affect the registration. However, manufacturers' use of certified translations is recommended highly.

The second step is to include local documentation in the dossier. Many countries require local documentation—forms to be completed and evidence of fee payment—to be included in the submission dossier. These activities normally are conducted by the manufacturer's Authorized Representative.

Specific Country Considerations

Most countries share common product registration principles. However, regulatory requirements can vary significantly across geographies, and seeking approvals in some markets can be very expensive and time-consuming. Therefore, before investing time and resources in the registration process, it is important to consider and understand particular markets' special requirements.

Basic Requirements in Established Markets

In the US, basic requirements include establishment registration, device listing, premarket notification or approval and postmarket compliance. Most Class I devices are exempt from premarket notification requirements and, therefore, do not undergo US review prior to commercialization. Most Class II devices require 510(k) clearance before they can be marketed, whereas most Class III devices require PMA applications. The vast majority of medical devices subject to FDA review are brought to market via the 510(k) notification process. The 510(k) process requires the applicant to demonstrate "substantial equivalence" to a legally marketed "predicate device" having similar technology and the same intended use.

In the EU, companies are required to meet the Essential Requirements of all relevant medical device directives and place a CE Mark on the product before it can be commercialized. The CE-marking process includes preparing a legally binding manufacturer statement attesting its product has met all of the medical devices' (Directive 90/385/EEC, active implantable medical devices; Directive 93/42/EEC, medical devices; and Directive 98/79/EEC, in vitro diagnostic medical devices) requirements. The company should compile a medical device technical file to demonstrate conformity to the directives' Essential Requirements. Manufacturers also must determine the appropriate conformity assessment route for their devices. Depending on the medical device type, a Notified Body must review manufacturers' quality systems and technical documentation before products are placed on the market. For example, devices subject to regulation under Directive 93/42/EEC require Notified Body review and issuance of an EC certificate for Class I sterile devices or Class I devices with a measuring function, Class IIa, IIb and III devices.

In Australia, the Therapeutic Goods Administration (TGA) oversees medical device regulation. Registering the device with TGA entails risk-based classification; compliance with quality, safety and performance principles; compliance with regulatory controls for manufacturing processes; listing in the Australian Register of Therapeutic Goods; and postmarket vigilance programs. Devices with a CE Mark from Notified Bodies can substantiate conformity to TGA requirements more easily. Manufacturers also must provide Declarations of Conformity to the Australian regulations to register their devices with TGA. If a device has a European CE Mark, the classification likely will be the same. A CE-marking certificate from a

Notified Body would be accepted as part of the registration in most cases for low- and moderate-risk devices. Medical device approvals in Australia do not expire as long as no changes are made to the product or its intended use and the annual ARTG listing fee is paid.

Health Canada issues two licenses. Class I medical device manufacturers must secure a Medical Device Establishment License (MDEL) if marketing in Canada. Instead of an MDEL, a Canadian Medical Device License (MDL) is required for Class II, III and IV medical devices manufacturers. The MDL is a product approval and a permit for the company, distributor or importer. The MDL is comparable to the US FDA 510(k) process, except the process of securing a MDL usually is faster for Class II devices, about the same for Class III devices and more complicated for Class IV devices.

In Japan, Class I device manufacturers must submit a Premarket Submission (*Todokede*) to the Pharmaceutical and Medical Devices Agency (PMDA), with no PMDA assessment. For Class II specified controlled devices, a Premarket Certification application (*Ninsho*) must be submitted to a Registered Certified Body (RCB) authorized to issue certifications. This procedure is quite similar to European CE-marking using a Notified Body. In fact, several European Notified Bodies also are authorized Japanese RCBs. Each specified controlled medical device must apply internationally harmonized standards as CE -arking. If no certification standards exist for a Class II device, it is subject to the same regulatory approval pathway as highly controlled devices. For Class III and IV highly controlled devices, a Premarket Approval application (*Shonin*) must be submitted, as well as a registration dossier in STED format. These documents are submitted to PMDA to obtain approval. All documents must be in Japanese.

Special Requirement: Type-Testing in China and South Korea

According to the China Food and Drug Administration (CFDA) and Korean Ministry of Food and Drug Safety (MFDS) regulations, product registration in China and Korea involves not only submitting a dossier but also type-testing in most instances. A manufacturer develops a product standard detailing it's product's specifications and how to test for those specifications. A testing house then will conduct those tests on company-provided samples based on the product standard.

Developing the product standard is one of the most important parts of registration. Product samples are tested for conformity to the company's product standard. If the testing result is deemed unsatisfactory, the regulatory agency may ask the company to revise the product standard and retest, resulting in potentially significant approval process delays. Also, CFDA will reference the product standard to determine whether different models can be registered under one import device license. Therefore, it is vitally important to provide sufficient information to support the Chinese product standard. It also is highly advisable for the company to test samples from the same lot or batch for product standard conformity before shipping product to the authorities.

In China, all Class II and III devices require type-testing. Type-testing normally takes six to nine months, depending on the device type. Test reports are valid for only one year, so timely registration application submission after type-testing is critical. If the test report expires before the regulatory approval application is submitted, it will need to be performed again. Also, it is important to ensure the testing house selected is experienced with similar medical device types. CFDA has certified testing centers with different technology expertise. The testing centers will use the product standard to determine what tests to conduct. The company also is required to submit a product standard according to China's "Product Regulation Standard" for CFDA's records. If a laboratory cannot test a device (due to the lack of a Chinese national standard or because the company's specific standard is beyond the laboratory's testing capability), CFDA will accept tests conducted in the product's country of origin.

In Korea, all Class II, III and IV medical devices must undergo type-testing by an independent laboratory, not MFDS. Type-testing takes one to three months, depending on the device type. When testing is completed, the laboratory will issue a certificate of compliance. To lower fees and reduce review time, it also is possible to submit equivalent test reports done abroad and have them validated. However, foreign testing must meet certain international standards.

Special Requirement: Testing-Based Product Registration in Russia

Medical device and equipment registration in Russia can be challenging, as the country still relies on a local product testing system as a tool to determine product safety and efficacy. Since Russia has its own national standards, such testing also is required for products already having CE marking, US FDA 510(k) clearance or other national approvals. Even products that have been for sale on the US and EU markets for many years require product testing to Russian standards as well. Prior to registration, medical devices must undergo toxicology, technical, electrical and electromagnetic compatibility (EMC) tests. For these tests, manufacturers are required to submit medical device samples to accredited Russian test laboratories. If these tests are completed successfully, the manufacturer submits the technical dossier to *Roszdravnadzor*,[6] including the product description and test results. The test results are reviewed by *Roszdravnadzor*-recognized experts. If the medical device is considered safe, the Russian authority issues a registration certificate and adds the device to the national medical device register.

After obtaining the product registration license, a medical device Declaration of Conformity must be obtained from an accredited Russian certification body. The Declaration of Conformity can be issued only to companies located in Russia, in either the manufacturer's or distributor's name. However, if the documents are issued in the distributor's name, and the manufacturer moves to another distributor, all certificates will have to be reissued. To avoid this costly and time-consuming process, it is advisable to have the documents issued in the medical device manufacturer's name. In this case, distributors will obtain a notarized copy of the registration certificate, permitting them to import and sell the devices in the Russian Federation. The Declaration of Conformity confirms the medical device complies with all applicable Russian technical requirements and standards. The registration certificate and Declaration of Conformity are mandatory export documents required by the Russian customs authorities.

Special Requirement: Compliance With Good Manufacturing Practices

Most medical device manufacturing facilities types are required to comply with Good Manufacturing Practices (GMPs) in most countries. In the US, 21 CFR Part 820 is the quality system regulation (QSR) codifying US medical device GMP requirements. Outside the US, ISO 13485 is the most commonly chosen path for medical device companies to meet quality system requirements in the EU, Canada, Japan, Australia and other countries. Although implementing ISO 13485 is voluntary for manufacturers selling in the EU, most companies opt to apply this standard to demonstrate compliance with the directives. In Canada, Canadian Medical Devices Conformity Assessment System (CMDCAS) ISO 13485:2003 is mandatory for Class II, III and IV medical device manufacturers, with additional requirements imposed under Canadian law. Compliance with Japan's Ministerial Ordinance #169 is quite similar to ISO 13485, with additional requirements imposed under Japanese law.

In Japan, some Class I devices may be subject to an RCB QMS audit. For specified controlled Class II devices, the RCB performs a QMS audit. For controlled Class II, Class III and Class IV devices, the PMDA or the prefectural regulator performs the QMS audit. On-site audits typically are required for "new" devices with no existing Japanese Medical Device Nomenclature (JMDN code), Class IV devices and those requiring clinical investigations.

In South Korea, Class I specially controlled, Class II, III and IV device manufacturers must implement a quality system compliant with Korean GMPs (KGMPs). These requirements are similar to ISO 13485 and the US QSR. On-site audits may be required for new manufacturers or any manufacturer with a quality problem reported within the past three years. The estimated KGMP certification timeline is three to four months (performed in parallel with product registration review). The KGMP Certificate is valid for three years. KGMP compliance audits are performed by MFDS and third-party inspectors. Both manufacturers and their Korea License Holders are subject to KGMP audits. Upon approval of the medical device registration application, MFDS will issue a Certificate of Product Approval and a KGMP Certificate.

The Taiwan Food and Drug Administration (TFDA) requires two sequential processes: manufacturing facility licensing and medical device permit licensing. Foreign manufacturer medical device GMP inspections are conducted through a quality system documentation review. The manufacturing facility license also is known as a QSD letter. At the time of publication, the QSD letter application fee was $750 (USD) and took about six months to process. Once issued, the QSD letter is valid for three years. Apart from the regular route, TFDA allows a simplified QSD application for US manufacturing facilities and EU facilities with ISO 13485:2003 certifications issued by qualified Notified Bodies, but the same fees and processing times apply. The simplified application requires an Establishment Inspection Report (EIR) for US manufacturers or Audit Report for EU manufacturers. The simplified application also requires Free Sales Certificate (FSC) or Certificate to Foreign Government (CFG) notarization by the Taiwan Representative Office in the country of origin (the regular route does not require this). The foreign manufacturer or its initial importer may apply for on-site inspections in accordance with GMP, ISO 13485:2003 or Chinese National Standard (CNS) 15013.

Special Requirement: Brazilian ABIMED Shortcut[7]

In Brazil, all Class III and IV device manufacturing facilities are required to fulfill Brazilian GMP requirements, based on the ISO 13485 norm and the Brazilian Health Surveillance Agency's (ANVISA) RDC 15/2014. The Brazilian GMP certificate must be included with the product registration application. This also applies to plants outside Brazil, and if a product is produced in more than one facility, they all must be inspected. The waiting time for such an inspection now is three years or more, creating a significant entry barrier for foreign companies wishing to enter the Brazilian market.

ABIMED is a Brazilian industry association representing importers' and foreign manufacturers' interests. ABIMED spoke to ANVISA in its members' interest, requesting GMP inspection process improvements, without success. Thus, ABIMED took legal action against ANVISA, requiring it to accept foreign GMP certificates (fulfilling the ISO 13485 norm) temporarily until ANVISA completes its own inspection. A judge granted the lawsuit injunction. It is important to note this ruling benefits only ABIMED and its member companies but not other companies with a similar problem. This is an important point for foreign companies; unless they or their partners in Brazil are members of ABIMED, they will not benefit from this ruling. This also refers to the "ABIMED shortcut."

When registering products in Brazil, many foreign companies use a so-called "hosting company" or in-country caretaker. Such companies are service providers in whose name the products can be registered. This is especially useful if the foreign company does not have a legal entity in Brazil and does not want to register the product in its distributor's name, since registration approvals are not transferrable. If the hosting company is an ABIMED member, its clients can use the ABIMED shortcut. If a company is not an ABIMED member and does not want to use a hosting company, an alternative is to take legal action against ANVISA on its own, which a judge may approve very quickly, but should be submitted only six months after requesting a GMP inspection. This legal action's result is not to oblige ANVISA to accept a foreign GMP certificate but to speed up the foreign plant's inspection.

Since this legal action has become standard practice, a new line has ensued for this "fast-track" inspection, with a corresponding three to four month waiting time. Even those companies taking the ABIMED shortcut take this legal action, knowing the shortcut is only a temporary solution, thus wanting to speed up the definitive approval.

The following points need to be taken into consideration when choosing the ABIMED shortcut:

1. The ABIMED shortcut with a foreign GMP certificate is a temporary, not a permanent, solution. Foreign companies have to be ready for the ANVISA inspection at any time.
2. Having an FDA or CE approval is not a guarantee ANVISA will grant a certificate, since ANVISA uses some of its GMP norm and method particularities in the inspection.
3. The foreign GMP certificate can be submitted only six months after requesting the ANVISA GMP inspection, the logic being ANVISA has six months to conduct the inspection.
4. The GMP certification is only one part of the ANVISA product registration process, and other parts still may incur long delays. As a rule of thumb, these other parts today take an average of one year. Adding the six-month waiting time for submitting the foreign GMP license, the total time required to register a product with ANVISA today is approximately 18 months (for products needing GMP inspection and only for ABIMED members).
5. ANVISA has appealed the ruling and, should it win, there is a risk ANVISA may suspend product registration granted using the ABIMED shortcut, at least until ANVISA has inspected the plant abroad.

Filing

Filing a submission may appear to be a simple regulatory process step, but certain considerations can define a regulatory approval's success during this stage.

Most, if not all, countries require a local representative to file the submission and, eventually, hold the license. The most common arrangement is the manufacturer's direct presence in the country through a subsidiary office or a local third-party Authorized Representative, which could be a distributor or independent registration holder (in-country caretaker).

It is advantageous, but costly, to have an in-country subsidiary, and a manufacturer's decision to opt for this model relies less on the convenience for regulatory submissions and more on the commercial, financial and strategic advantages of having a local presence. Normally, this is the preferred model for mid-size to large medical device organizations, especially in countries with important sales potential. However, in some countries, such as Saudi Arabia or Singapore, a commercial office is not authorized to file regulatory submissions or hold product licenses. In these cases, the local office needs to comply with certain requirements, such as having a responsible technical officer or holding a Good Distribution Practice (GDP) certificate.

Having an Authorized Representative probably is the most common option for smaller companies, particularly in emerging markets with limited commercial potential. Using a distributor as the Authorized Representative

Table 12-2. Considerations for Selecting In-Country Agents

	Pros	Cons
Distributor	Inexpensive	Possible contract-related submission delays
	Convenient	Typically not regulatory experts, which may result in submission errors and compliance problems
	Vested interest in the business	New submissions may be required to change distributors
		May delay or fail to file needed submissions in response to changes
In-country caretaker	Regulatory experts, who may be able to accelerate approval timelines and reduce the risk of submission-related compliance problems	Expensive
	Enable use of multiple distributors and the ability to change distributors without filing new licenses	

provides the convenience of working with a single entity and the advantage of the distributor having a vested interest in obtaining timely regulatory approval and maintaining compliance with local regulatory requirements to ensure market continuity. However, several potential disadvantages exist to having the distributor hold the license: distributor contracts are complex agreements addressing all distribution and sales activities, meaning the legal review and approval process potentially can be lengthy and delay submissions; distributors typically are not regulatory experts and often make errors in the submission process; and, in many countries, product registration is issued in the Authorized Representative's name, meaning changing distributors would trigger the need for new submissions.

Cost is another consideration in deciding whether to have the distributor hold the license. In-country caretakers can charge considerable amounts of money to obtain and hold the license, whereas distributors often do this for free. However, problems may arise when companies make changes to the product, triggering the need for new submissions. Distributors may delay or fail to make submissions in response to changes, thereby putting the manufacturer at risk.

A variant of the Authorized Representative is a local agency (in-country caretaker) that holds the product registration but is not engaged in distribution activities. Legal or regulatory consultancies in some countries can provide this service, which provides the flexibility to change local distributors without affecting product registration. Legal and regulatory consultancies offer a major advantage, since they often are regulatory experts, and their expertise may accelerate the approval timeline and reduce the risk of compliance problems related to the submission, e.g., classification errors. **Table 12-2** provides a list of pros and cons related to selecting a distributor or in-country caretaker.

The manufacturer should insist on receiving a copy of the final submission documents, regardless of the representative selected. This is necessary to ensure the manufacturer's information is incorporated correctly into the submission. Because of its importance, this requirement should be written into the contract as a condition for payment.

For both Authorized Representative variants, a legal document (normally a Letter of Authorization or Power of Attorney) is included in the submission dossier to confirm the manufacturer has an Authorized Representative to file and hold a product registration in its name.

In some countries, before a submission is filed, meeting or consulting with regulatory authorities to plan the submission and confirm requirements is required or advised. Some common discussion points in these meetings include confirming the device classification, the need for clinical investigation data and the application of special standards or requirements from local regulations. Also as part of this discussion, the regulatory submission strategy for that country can be finalized, considering approaches related to product grouping or extending an existing registration's product scope, to ease the regulatory approval process.

Regulatory authorities have different methods of receiving submission dossiers. The process may involve printing and delivering hard copies, submitting online applications, transferring files electronically or some combination thereof.

Review Correspondence, Communication and Approvals

After a dossier has been submitted, it is not uncommon for regulatory reviewers to request more information before completing the review and making a decision about a medical device's safety and effectiveness. These requests for additional information can be triggered because either the original dossier was not complete or reviewers require more detail to make a decision.

In those cases, the regulatory agency or reviewer communicates with the person submitting the dossier with a list of questions or additional required information. These communications normally define a time period for the manufacturer or its representative to provide the information. It is important to understand the query clearly and provide clear and comprehensive responses and documentation addressing all concerns. Failure to provide a satisfactory answer within the specified time can lead to submission disapproval.

It is good practice to track the submission's timeline, including the dates when additional information was requested and responses were provided. Some regulatory agencies have set timeframes for making a decision on a regulatory application; keeping track of those timelines helps the manufacturer plan product launch activities. Internal company communication is critical to keep management informed of any potential regulatory approval delay or risk. Also, sharing questions and concerns from a regulatory reviewer internally can enable the company to update its submission documents to prevent the same questions or concerns from arising in future reviews in other jurisdictions.

When a regulatory review is completed, and the device has been approved, certain activities take place. One is filing and storing the submission history, including the original dossier, any additional correspondence and documentation generated during the review and the final approval certificate or notification. Once approval is granted, any device shipping controls for that jurisdiction can be lifted, so distribution can begin. If the approval has conditions, such as specific postmarket surveillance or periodic reporting, these should be identified and systems implemented to ensure they are met. Finally, some jurisdictions grant regulatory approvals for a limited time period and the registration expiration date should be recorded. This way, registration renewal can be planned in advance, to ensure the product's market continuity throughout its lifetime.

Changes

Medical devices often are subject to changes, which can be related to manufacturing process and equipment, components, materials, design, packaging, sterilization, software, expiration dating, manufacturing location, intended use, indications for use, identification labels or instructions for use. Such changes can be major or minor. In general, regulatory authorities' position on changes is conservative, meaning many changes related to a medical device are required to be reported or approved by the regulatory authority before distributing the modified device. Failure to obtain needed approvals for significant changes can have a devastating impact on business, resulting in potential enforcement action, sale cessation and/or unapproved product recall. A number of jurisdictions have vague or unclear change requirements, creating an element of uncertainty for the regulatory professional.

Although it sometimes is impractical, a new medical device should be submitted for regulatory approval only when no changes are expected in the near future, i.e., when the design and manufacturing process have been completed and validated. In reality, given the different regulatory approval timelines, it is likely, when a device is ramping-up production and real-use experience is being gathered from the markets launching the product first, the need to make an improvement or change to the device will be identified. In such cases, it is the regulatory professional's role to assess these proposed changes' impact changes and provide advice on the best time to implement and submit them for regulatory approval.

Changes implemented during a regulatory submission typically are difficult to manage. However, several potential approaches exist depending on the proposed change's criticality. For example, the applicant could wait until regulatory approval is granted to amend the existing submission with the change. Alternatively, the applicant could introduce the change as part of a response to a request for additional information. This last approach is an amendment and should be disclosed fully and agreed with the regulatory reviewer, as some regulatory agencies do not accept amendments to submission documents.

Some jurisdictions do not recognize the concept of a minor change. For those regulatory agencies, e.g., Taiwan or Singapore, any change, regardless of its magnitude or criticality, at least should be reported and, in most cases, approved before implementation. For other jurisdictions, the criteria used to distinguish a minor change often are based on its impact on the device's safety or effectiveness and/or the need to conduct additional verification or validation (particularly clinical studies) to ensure the change has the desired effect and no unintended adverse effects.

Depending on the device classification and change assessment (minor or significant), regulatory authorities impose different manufacturer reporting requirements. For example, the US has no premarket reporting requirements for changes to Class I devices exempt from 510(k) clearance. However, a new 510(k) must be submitted and cleared before marketing a Class II device subject to

510(k) review if a manufacturer significantly modifies the device or changes its indications for use. Insignificant changes to 510(k)-cleared devices do not require reporting. Change reporting requirements for Class III devices subject to PMA review are much more onerous. For example, even very minor changes must be documented and submitted to the agency on an annual basis.

A common regulatory professional task is assessing the proposed change's impact and planning the regulatory strategy for implementing those changes. This high-stakes activity can have a major impact on the business. If the regulatory department is overly conservative, it can introduce unneeded and potentially significant delays in change implementation. Alternatively, if the regulatory department is too liberal, it can expose the company and employees to serious enforcement consequences. Therefore, it is advisable to document the company's analysis and decision making carefully and seek advice from independent experts for borderline decisions.

Renewals

In some countries, e.g., China and Brazil, product registrations are valid for a defined time period and may require renewal prior to license expiration. Certain countries, e.g., China, require the renewal to be approved before product manufactured after the license expiration date can continue accessing their markets. Therefore, planning to start the renewal process well in advance of expiration is critical to ensure the product's market continuity. Additionally, repeat sample testing and postmarket quality and safety surveillance information need to be taken into account when considering the renewal timeline. Sample testing is the most time-consuming part of the process in China and the testing standard may be different from that for initial registration. If the product's postmarket history includes serious adverse events and/or field safety corrective actions, questions could be raised and more testing or validation required demonstrating the product is still safe and effective. In reality, submission and renewal timelines can be very difficult to predict. A renewal application reviewer change can require new testing and additional information. Therefore, the need to file renewals prior to expiration cannot be overemphasized.

Some nations, e.g., Brazil, require renewal applications to be submitted six months before license expiration but allow the product to remain on the market while the application is under review. In addition to product license renewal, Brazilian GMPs need to be renewed every two years; ANVISA, alone, determines whether subsequent evaluations can be completed remotely through a paperwork audit or must involve onsite inspection.

Product registration approvals do not expire in some countries, e.g., South Korea, Russia and the US. However, the Korean GMP certificate has to be renewed every three years, and Russia's GOST-R certificate has a one-year (without expert assessment) or three-year term (with expert assessment). Canadian and US establishment registrations require annual renewal and payment of a fee.

Strategic renewal planning is critical for product supply continuity. Keeping up with the license and certificate renewal variation requirements around the world presents a major challenge. Therefore, manufacturers are advised to utilize a product licensing database to track license and certificate expirations globally to minimize the risk for market interruption.

Distribution Control

Understanding importing requirements and processes in different countries is critical to staying compliant with specific countries' importation regulations. More importantly, it helps ensure smooth product customs clearance. After obtaining the product registration license, import license application is the final required step for many nations to allow product to enter their markets.

For instance, devices can be imported into the Russian Federation upon presentation of a registration license, hygiene certificate (if needed, depending on the device type) and GOST-R Certificate,[8] plus other typical international commercial shipping documents (e.g., cargo customs declaration and declaration of conformity with Russian standards and regulations). As discussed above, these two certificates can be issued only after the registration license is obtained. The GOST-R certificate has a one-year term for a shipment or several shipments under one contract or three years if GSOT-R[9] experts visit and assess a foreign producer's manufacturing facility in the country of origin.

Controlling distribution to ensure product goes only to those countries in which it is approved becomes critical after the import license is obtained. Shipments to unapproved locations can be extremely costly to companies and subject them to substantial compliance risks. Establishing shipping restriction control through enterprise application software is the most common approach to preventing unregistered product shipments to global markets. However, small companies may use very simple systems such as product approval spreadsheets checked before each shipment. Regardless of the solution employed, inclusion and exclusion tables are needed to control product shipments. Inclusion rules allow shipment only to a specific country or group. Exclusion rules override any inclusions and block shipments to a specific country or group.

Medical device exports also require compliance with country of origin (COO) requirements. Companies often are vulnerable to COO errors due to differing requirements among jurisdictions. The applicability of multiple standards greatly increases the risk of error. Medical device manufacturers often get their components or parts from multiple sources in different countries, and switch such component suppliers frequently. That makes the correct COO (particularly for customs purposes) a moving target. It is essential companies update their COO determinations regularly to ensure their current determinations correctly reflect supply changes and labeling, packaging and marketing materials.

Controlling a product with two or more countries of origin by segregating the variants into special stock locations is a common shipping control used by many companies to prevent COO errors. Depending on business capacity, smaller companies may use physical restriction or control areas in their warehouses, combined with color codes or country flags to identify products and their associated COO. Automatic software-driven COO shipment controls typically are used by bigger companies to control products made in different COOs. In this case, product shipments are controlled by serial numbers (for capital equipment or reusable devices) and by batch numbers (for sterile or disposable devices). For example, products with serial numbers or batch numbers from 000001 to 000100 are made in country A, and 000101 to 000200 are made in country B. A physical restriction or controlled stock location is not necessary for products controlled by serial or batch numbers, provided the system is capable of restricting shipments of correct serial or batch numbers to specific markets.

Customs violations can have serious enforcement consequences, including significant fines and individual criminal liability. Therefore, compliance with import/export regulations should be considered equally important as product registration requirements.

Conclusion

This chapter addresses main points to consider when developing a regulatory plan and registration strategy, from the initial product development stages through approval and registration maintenance. Some country-specific examples were provided to illustrate the kind of requirements the regulatory plan must address. It is important to note not all country requirements are included, and those that are, are presented only in summary form. It is the regulatory professional's job to determine regulatory requirements and develop a comprehensive regulatory plan covering the specific product characteristics, timeline and resources required for success in all intended markets.

Regulatory planning is a key activity for medical device manufacturers and, if conducted properly, can save the business money and time and create a strong competitive advantage over medical device manufacturers with a less sophisticated regulatory function. Getting product into a market earlier or setting a high quality standard brings real business benefits and can be a competitive advantage. This is one of the main assets a competent regulatory strategist can provide to a company.

Finally, another important aspect of the global regulatory process is compliance with postmarket requirements.

References

1. Young BJ, Tran A. "A Practical Approach to Global Medical Device Registration." *Regulatory Affairs Focus*, April 2002, pp 16–21.
2. Regulatory costs should include expenses for product testing, translations, consulting fees, filing fees and recurring administrative fees if an in-country caretaker is used.
3. Other strategic considerations include the potential value of gaining an early foothold in a small but growing region. Companies also may consider de-prioritizing submissions if changes are anticipated in the near future, e.g., it måay be better to delay submissions in markets with rigorous change control requirements until planned changes are complete.
4. Transparency International produces an annual ranking of countries and territories by their perceived level of public sector corruption. More information can be obtained on www.transparency.org.
5. PMA stands for Premarket Approval and, in general terms, is the process FDA requires for the approval of high-risk devices. 510(k) is FDA's required process for market clearance of medical devices comparable to devices already on the market. European Technical File is the documentation used to demonstrate compliance to the medical device directives.
6. *Roszdravnadzor* is the Russian equivalent of FDA and stands for Federal Service on Surveillance in Healthcare and Social Development of the Russian Federation.
7. Büttner M. Swiss Business Hub Brazil, "A remarkable legal action in Brazil."
8. The GOST-R certificate of conformity signifies the imported products comply with Russian standards, quality and safety requirements. The certificate is mandatory for customs clearance in Russia and for sale and/or marketing within the country.
9. *Gosstandart* is a National Certification Body of the Russian Federation, in charge of maintaining and enforcing the certificate of conformity system.

13

Global Regulatory Process—Third-Party Point of View

By Gert Bos

Introduction

This chapter provides a third-party perspective on some of the key elements manufacturers need to put in place before being allowed to market their medical device in key regulated jurisdictions. It explores the benefits of implementing a quality management system (QMS) supporting multi-jurisdictional medical device marketing and considers the resources needed.

It explains how the medical device regulatory environment is changing constantly—in small and large ways—and the regulatory professional's role in anticipating those changes and developing strategies to prepare and respond. The changes encompass internal systems and processes, as well as possible product design and manufacture changes, clinical evaluation and technical file development. These changes will trigger changing relationships with regulators, conformity assessment bodies and Notified Bodies.

As an example, the chapter uses the coming changes in the EU medical device regulatory regime to illustrate how a manufacturer should be alert to, analyze and prepare for regulatory environment changes. Finally, it challenges the regulatory professional to be seen as an effective leader in preparing employers and customers for change.

This chapter's contents reflect the author's viewpoint.

Using MDSAP as Basis for an ISO 13485 and QSR-Based QMS

Chapter 4 discussed establishing an effective QMS from a practical perspective. What about the strategic level? Does a company build a small QMS sufficient for its first market of entry, or does it embrace the future and build a QMS to cover global requirements?

It is necessary to be realistic. A start-up company should focus on its core business: building a company from the business case that led to its initiation. Often, a first product is in development or, alternatively, selected products' sales of the own-brand labeler are beginning. In other cases, early sales of "me too" products will support independent product portfolio development funding. In the early phases, a company should attempt to achieve key processes that work properly. When developing new products, it is important for a company to follow Good Laboratory Practice (GLP) and adopt a controlled design and validation document system, so it can use early-stage development data later. Additionally, data integrity measures and configuration control systems should be put in place. After that, requirements will depend on the key market of first entry. If it is the US, Quality System Regulation (QSR) requirements will be a necessary. For Europe, minimum requirements from *Medical Device Directive* (*MDD*) Annex II or similar full quality assurance modules from other device directives are essential, together with some key requirements from the legislation's main text, e.g., quality objectives and a quality manual.

However, most products placed on the European market (intermediate- and high-risk devices) must satisfy the requirements of the Notified Body that will review its quality system, so it is easiest to apply harmonized standard EN ISO 13485:2012 from the start. Although Class I (low-risk) device manufacturer supervision is relatively limited, using the standard as guidance to prevent major failures commonly is seen as best practice. Knowing the quality system likely will be implemented, it might be useful for the company to consider having it certified. This would be another milestone in the company's development plan and business case. For a venture capital-funded start-up, this may be utilized as a first step to demonstrate good quality product and production facilities.

Companies with a rapid market launch scheduled for key markets such as the US and Europe should realize QSR and ISO 13485 concepts can be combined easily. On first reading, these appear to be focused on different perspectives: compliance-based QSR instructive requirements, focusing on design control and a control and preventive action (CAPA) system, versus ISO's conformity to less-detailed standard requirements. In reality, the key document control, management control, training and qualification, design and development, production and QC checks and traceability requirements, etc., are very similar. As both jurisdictions accept a double-focused QMS, creating a combined QMS structure is the best solution. In such cases, the company should ensure it uses the correct terminology to match regulatory expectations from both jurisdictions. Even if the intent is not to market to other markets quickly, Medical Device Single Audit Program (MDSAP) principles may be utilized. MDSAP is the officially accepted merger of requirements from member MDSAP jurisdictions, currently the US, Canada, Brazil, Australia, and Japan. Other International Medical Device Regulators Forum (IMDRF, www.imdrf.org) jurisdictions (such as the World Health Organization (WHO) and the European Union) are observers in the process, allowing them to ensure requirements match their jurisdictions' interpretation. Building a system with MDSAP concepts as the foundation should make the system "future proof," even if no MDSAP audits will be requested at first. Once the company starts placing devices on the market in various IMDRF jurisdictions, it is time to prepare for formal MDSAP inspections. When MDSAP is implementedfully, it is expected to reduce the need for individual regulators to verify the QMS with their own site audits, because one concise third-party audit will cover all jurisdictions.

In-House Versus External Resources

Developing a QMS is a time-consuming effort; therefore, a company may think hiring a consultant to do the work is a good solution. In many cases, a consultant will not deliver the system best suited for the company's purpose, and implementation of such a 'bought-in' system will be more difficult for staff to adopt in their daily work routine. The best route to compliance is to ensure sufficient resources from within the company to build a dedicated QMS.

On the other hand, consultants do have experience in building and maintaining QMS, so it would be a shame not to utilize it. Best practice could be to use external support to guide the company in building its own dedicated QMS. Contracts and internal communication should define the role, responsibility and authority of such external resources clearly.

Obviously, if the company has internal resources well-versed in building and maintaining a medical device QMS, it would make sense to utilize these unless extra resources are needed to meet timelines and objectives. Especially in a start-up, it also is helpful to have external resources assisting with some of the internal audits, to create sufficient independence from the work performed by the company's quality staff. These external resources must be qualified within the company's QMS.

Market Entry Strategy

In the past, creating a marketing strategy seemed simple: local market first, together with a selection of countries that did not have many medical device-related legislative requirements. But, with global harmonization in place and many countries developing their own requirements, deciding where to start is becoming more complex. It remains true, however, wherever in the world a company is located, its own country or region in many cases might be a first market of entry, unless getting its specific products on the home market means more years of development and data collection than other jurisdictions such as Europe or the US. Sometimes, the US Food and Drug Administration's (FDA) 510(k) route (substantial equivalence to products already on the market), for low- and intermediate-risk "me too" products is a relatively smooth path into the market. But, while this route did not require clinical studies in the past, the last few years have seen a steady rise in clinical data demand. Getting products cleared via the 510(k) route gradually is becoming more difficult. For higher-risk devices, Europe typically has been the preferred regulatory arena in which to apply first for marketing approval. Although the requirements are increasing in preparation for new regulations for high-risk and active implantable devices, it still is a very good entry market. However, meeting the requirements is becoming more challenging, as expectations are changing without proper advance notification or guidance being available. More on this subject and how to handle this coming 'quantum leap' best are found later in this chapter.

European market access has two key market entry hurdles. The first is CE marking; getting formal market access by obtaining a CE Mark for a medical device often is used as a first financial milestone in start-up companies or companies looking for first time European sales. The second hurdle (sometimes overlooked in early project planning) is reimbursement. Unlike CE marking, recognized in all EU Member States, reimbursement has to be negotiated in each country separately. Some countries might require clinical data. If the product is innovative, the company might be required to provide a comparison to current clinical treatment. For regular products, an assessment of comparability with already approved and reimbursed devices on the market might be needed. Realizing many countries in Europe are considering moving into the realm of comparative trials for "me-too" products entering the market under the new regulations, the company should contemplate the benefits of getting such data early in development, as they might be needed for reimbursement in the future. If that is the case, collecting them in such a way they can be used for both CE marking and reimbursement review might well mean both smoother acceptance in Europe and an evidence file more ready to withstand future review of essential performance and safety requirements during the transition to the new EU *Medical Device Regulation*.

Collecting Clinical Data

Regardless of the world market, all six continents tend to require a device's safety to be proven by independent tests rather than based on equivalence validation. Due to a recent change in Chinese regulations, many devices now will require (comparative) clinical trials, often with a specified minimum numbers of patients, performed in China, whether or not clinical data exist elsewhere or the product has a long marketing history in other jurisdictions.

This trend is pushing manufacturers to enhance their clinical strategies. Regulators, reimbursement and payment authorities have rising expectations for more clinical evidence, e.g., increasing percentage of FDA 510(k) files needing clinical data; the EU's focus on clinical evaluation in the Directive 2007/47/EC revision moving to demand (comparative) clinical trials; and China and other Asian countries demanding more locally generated clinical evidence. These seem to be driving manufacturers to increase the numbers of trials they perform, as well as change the study design and type they undertake. Multiregion trials rarely are approved any longer, perhaps due to perceived authorities' uneasiness about multinational design potentially leading to debates and disagreements among authorities, which transparency measures would place in the public domain. Therefore, it is worthwhile to try setting up trials in different regions, so primary and secondary endpoints are identical or largely similar, enhancing broader meta-analysis options across the company's own studies.

It now is time to think about future requirements. If more and more data are requested in comparative trials, the only way to generate sufficient data for "me-too" products may be through a collective approach, in which manufacturers jointly commission clinical trials. This obviously will not happen for innovative products, where the race to reach market first is an essential driver for return on investment. For well-known products, this might be the only way to obtain relevant data. For example, current market access for a patient-side infusion set typically is based on performance data and bench analysis, but in Europe this could fall under the special Notified Body regime with extra, government-controlled peer review (scrutiny) in the future because they relate to pharmaceutical product administration. While it will be hard to find clinical investigators willing to work on an individual product, large comparison trials might interest investigators. Reaching agreement among competitors, and selecting comparator mechanisms will be only the first problem. Independent coordination and funding by multiple companies of such trials might be key to achieving this goal. Independent monitoring and transparent external supervision will help build continued government and patient trust in the healthcare industry.

Defining Where to Source Expertise

Chapter 5 discusses creating technical files during development. The strategic question is, what resources will the company use? Does it have the necessary in-house knowledge and, if so, is it best for the company to utilize those resources to build these files? If the company does not have much experience, using external sources to support the in-house development team to build the dossier will help improve its quality from the start. Even if in-house expertise is available, external support can help overcome resource crunches. If any technical writing and compilation is outsourced, a process should be in place to ensure the responsible manufacturer is in charge of the content generated. As such, it is essential external resources are supported by sufficiently clear internal authorities while maintaining appropriate company input and control levels.

Another element is the file format. Currently, each jurisdiction requires or suggests its own format. While the Summary Technical Documentation (STED) and Common Submission Dossier (CSDT) templates are gaining momentum and could form a good basis to prevent recomposing files repeatedly, IMDRF has developed two table of contents instructions for electronic submissions encompassing member jurisdictions' content requirements. With classification matrices providing guidance on each jurisdiction's application, companies should consider using this IMDRF format in addition to or instead of previous styles. Since the IMDRF structure is the most detailed, a company simply could map back how to compile a STED or CSDT automatically by grouping contents together.

Timely Asian Regulatory System Focus

The time is past when a relatively small number of jurisdictions in Asia-Pacific had medical device legislation. Under the auspices of the Asian Harmonization Working Party (AHWP, www.AHWP.info), a growing number of countries have collaborated to learn from each other while developing their own rules. And, while harmonization is a key goal, all countries need to fit new requirements into their existing frameworks; consequently, all legislation is different. AHWP has developed a playbook for its members on implementing medical device regulatory frameworks, promoting international regulatory convergence. It suggests each economy must ensure it also devotes sufficient resources and appropriately qualified people to the establishment, conducting and continuing regulatory systems' evolution.

In addition, the Association of Southeast Asian Nations (ASEAN) countries have reached consensus on their directive, where member economies will be developing or adjusting their legislation over the next few years. Much work can be anticipated preparing file submissions for many jurisdictions, occasionally with short deadlines to get products reviewed and approved under a new regime. Having submissions prepared in the IMDRF table of contents, STED and CSDT formats will enhance the speed at which any new submission type can be compiled. An ideal model would include a mini-database for each file, where (semi-) automatic generation of any technical file structure is restricted to generating the protocol to pick and merge specific files based on their meta-tags.

Rapidly Changing Regulatory Outlook

It is true there is no boring day in the life of a regulatory professional. But, what if the regulatory world is being turned upside down? How does a professional prepare for a hurricane, knowing it will hit sometime, but not sure exactly when or where, and how much it will affect the individual, the company and its neighbors. This section reviews some of the essentials for preparing to withstand the challenging evolution called "regulatory improvement" and come out the better for it.

Regulatory is not the only part of the company that will experience this change; other departments will have to change and improve too. The regulatory professional can check what others are doing, but it is better if he or she takes control and starts preparing in advance of the crowd. How does the regulatory professional prepare and help the company get ready for the future, to be ready when the storm hits? The trick lies in continuous improvement, and that starts today. This section uses the current EU legislative reform as an example.

The EU Regulatory Hurricane

The EU is in greater flux than has been true for decades. This goes beyond the tension felt in the medical device industry when the original medical device directives took effect. At that time, much of the generic wording from the draft texts was quite open to interpretation and left industry in uncharted waters. It has taken a decade or more to come to a relatively consistent interpretation, shared by all stakeholders and applied consistently throughout industry. MEDDEV guidance documents were drafted and agreed by experts, and a settled system worked well for 15 years.

During that time, the EU doubled in size with new Member States. The new members brought additional languages and national legislation that, by default, deviated in some places from the instructions given to legislators in the central directives. Over time, the interpretations, business cultures and habits diverged. At the same time, medical technology continued to evolve rapidly. While in the first 15 years stakeholders had worked cooperatively to interpret the legislation and wrote guidance jointly, the next era introduced a split between stakeholders. Guidance documents no longer were initiated by debates between manufacturers and Notified Bodies, subsequently improved and endorsed by authorities. Instead, initiatives on new and changing documents shifted to the regulators. New pieces of implementing legislation appeared for devices with components derived from human blood and animal tissue, introducing more central regulatory involvement in the premarket review phase. The initial changes were minor and focused on selected high-risk and, typically, long-term invasive and implantable devices.

The onset of the coming storm was the drafting of what became Directive 2007/47/EC. Looking back, the directive appears to address only minor changes to clinical evaluation and postmarket surveillance (PMS). But its effects have been huge and still are not implemented fully. For the first time, changing legislation was applied to all medical device categories. Clinical evaluation became obligatory for all and forced more proactive postmarketing surveillance (PMS) into a continuous improvement mode of the original design dossier and technical file. The directive came into force 21 March 2010, and since then Notified Bodies have recertified all technical files and dossiers and completed first level evaluations on dossiers' completeness. By now, the initial effect of the *Medical Devices Directive* (*MDD*) and *Active Implantable Medical Device Directive* (*AIMDD*) should have abated, but, in reality, this is not the case. Understanding the reasons for this will help regulatory professionals prepare for the upcoming changes.

Changing Interpretation

EU regulators' intent with the changes in Directive 2007/47/EC was based on a long-term wish to see more clinical evidence in the premarket phase and continued gathering of clinical product information during the product lifecycle. Vigilance investigations have shown, in many cases, as soon as the products were allowed on the market, postmarket activities dropped down to compulsory complaint handling and vigilance reporting. Some active PMS might have been in place for innovative products, but largely due to the development of line extensions, not necessarily safety related. The two key changes implemented regulators' desires to have clearer premarket clinical data and an ongoing assessment of long-term safety data gathered in postmarket clinical follow-up (PMCF). This continuous improvement introduced the need to learn from market feedback to improve product safety levels over time. With these measures, Directive 2007/47/EC brought needed improvements to reinforce these elements, originally put forward in Notified Body recommendation NB-MED/2.12/Rec1.

During the early implementation phase of Directive 2007/47/EC, the European Commission began discussing a comprehensive recast of the overall medical device legislation system. At that point, the effects of Directive 2007/47/EC's changes were not evident yet. Initial key elements of the revision's changes included clinical evaluation and PMS. However, as the first revision attempt did not have a chance to be perceived as successful, events raised the stakes.

During the legislative process, a number of scandals involving different long-term implants confirmed clinical data were not gathered consistently or analyzed systematically. An example often cited was the continued tweaking of hip implants and other orthopedic implants; after many iterations, the products placed on the market hardly resembled the ones in the original clinical studies. The debate fed into the discussion on equivalence. This lead to the position that the clinical evidence for a new product equivalency claim should be based largely on clinical data from one equivalent product; minor deviations may be referenced from additional products. The matrix approach used historically to collect equivalence data has been replaced by a stricter interpretation frequently necessitating clinical trials for new generation devices prior to placing them on the market. In some cases, a balanced approach can be seen between partial equivalence, premarket clinical trials to fill the evidence gap and PMCF. PMCF studies will focus in depth on long-term safety and, secondly, might focus on confirming the results in a more closely controlled patient population used in premarket studies.

Meanwhile, as the legislative process and the debate continue, proposals have focused more on device effectiveness in premarket evaluation, similar to the clinical trials in Regulation No 536/2014 (the *Pharmaceutical Regulation*), and on other debates such as those in the reimbursement circuit. The benefit-risk interpretation has changed over the years, from not even needing a clinical claim in the *MDD* and *AIMD*, to the clinical claim being the heart of the evaluation. Doubtless, it will continue to the next level where innovative product manufacturers will need to prove noninferiority to current standards of care, and comparative evaluation in larger numbers of patients will be required for future products entering the market. In scheduling time-to-market for products in the early development pipeline, it would seem sensible to consider such high levels of evidence from the start and to plan for more time and resources.

In addition, no "grandfather" provision has been suggested yet by any of the legislative stakeholders drafting the legislation. Therefore, manufacturers may be required to collect sufficient clinical data for products currently on the market. Although these products may have long marketing histories, that history, lack of complaints, limited number of vigilance cases, etc., will be sufficient to demonstrate clinical performance, safety and potential effectiveness positively. Collecting more scientific evidence from currently marketed products and feeding that into improving product documentation will help smooth the transition. Resources should focus on collecting data for all products intended to remain on the market after the transition.

Consequently, it would make sense to evaluate the product portfolio to confirm which product versions are worth elevating evidence to the next level. Older product versions currently sold in small quantities, or for which the CE Mark is held only for the purpose of marketing outside the EU, might be removed from the market. However, some older products will remain on the market; following efforts to raise clinical evaluation levels under

Directive2007/47/EC, manufacturers should begin collecting more substantial clinical data as soon as possible.

Removing Notified Bodies From the Equation

As a follow-up to the PIP breast implant scandal, the European Commission and EU Member States initiated an action plan with some key measures to improve oversight of the medical device regulatory system quickly, before the new legislation would enter into force. This joint action plan included raising the bar for Notified Bodies. One of the four key planned future legislation changes was brought forward: joint audits by Notified Bodies' designating authorities and reassessing Notified Bodies' existing designations, especially those with designations covering high-risk medical devices. Joint audits follow a two-tier approach, with voluntary and mandatory phases. In the voluntary phase, all countries with Notified Bodies organized at least one such audit, focusing on observing, learning and setting expectations for future designation reviews. The next step was to use that as a baseline for initial designations, renewals and scope extensions. Meanwhile, the voluntary phase continues at some level for audits not covered by the mandatory phase.

For various reasons, including the joint audits, fear of not passing such audits, code of conduct audits by the association of Notified Bodies (TEAM-NB) and general business decisions, the number of Notified Bodies is dropping significantly, and a continued decrease in Notified Bodies is anticipated for the next few years. Others likely will drop out when it is time to re-apply for Notified Body designation under the new regulations. Nonetheless, Notified Bodies under the old directive may remain in place for quite a while, during transition and, as long as some older certificates are in place, even after the transition period ends.

Market thought leaders among device manufacturers have started to reassess and rationalize Notified Bodies' numbers and strengths, in many cases looking for corporately approved Notified Bodies from which subsidiaries may select. Also, companies have started looking for Notified Bodies more likely to remain active under new system requirements, for the scope of products relevant to them. However, it is hard to predict where to go, as future requirements are not yet fully visible. At this point, looking at the restructured Notified Body designation scopes following authority joint audits gives a good first impression. It certainly is a topic companies should discuss with their Notified Bodies. What is likely to happen? What are Notified Bodies doing to ensure their future status? Do they intend to apply for Notified Body status under the new system and with what designation? How many qualified reviewers and auditors do they have under the essential scope for the company's product and how many certificate holders do they serve in that area?

Unsure Where and When It Wil Take Effect, but Surely Coming

Once the proposed legislation is adopted, there probably will be two main implementation stages. The first wave is Notified Bodies re-applying for evaluation in their roles, where their status will be reassessed to meet the new requirements. Depending on designated authorities' available resources and the level of individual Notified Bodies' needed improvements, this process may take from six months to a few years. If a company's Notified Body is not in the first approved group under the new legislation, pressure will build for a potential transfer to another provider. That will continue until the second wave, which is when the transition deadline is nearing, and Notified Bodies will have to answer no, as their staffs will be booked fully until the transition period ends.

Moving forward, a smaller group of current Notified Bodies will have to review whether all products on the EU market meet the new requirements for about 30 months; the normal reassessment cycle for these products would be 60 months. The number of reviews will be doubled for fewer available Notified Bodies. This will result in a Notified Body review "crunch."

To avoid this, companies' should have their files reviewed as early as possible during the transition period. This can be achieved only when most further evidence collection and dossier improvements are begun before legislation finalization. Many topics are no longer contentious and will be included in the legislation. Having Notified Bodies review revised clinical evidence files before this stage, for example, might smooth the review process and transition to the new system. For IVDs, where many files will need a first Notified Body review, a first-level voluntary review might be contemplated, by either Notified Bodies or consultants with experience as Notified Body reviewers.

Now and Future—Continuous Improvement

Another element of change that can be embraced already is a further enhancement of a manufacturer's continuous improvement systems and processes. These will consist of continuous feedback on postmarket phase product improvement information, risk management dossier updates, clinical experience and more. Fully embedding such improvement loops into the current QMS once again will help companies be prepared better for the future requirements and allow more time to collect more-comprehensive PMS data. Such market feedback also will help prioritize dossiers that need to be reviewed under the new system and place some selected products on the back burner.

How to Deal With a Moving Target

Reviewing the upcoming clinical evidence requirement changes illustrates how a company can start contemplating meeting a moving target in interpreting the Essential Requirements. The Commission proposal includes the proposed amendments from the European Parliament, reflections on these from the Commission and draft amendments from the European Council, indicates many requirements will change. The clinical evaluation scenario illustrates it is likely by the time the drafts are adopted, the current interpretation of requirements will shift on all fronts. It is in manufacturers' interests to establish early improvement elements well before the legislation is fully in force.

Determine What Is Likely to Occur and Develop a Plan

Companies need to determine a way forward and start drawing up their own plans. They should take control by analyzing what is likely to change for their product(s) or portfolio and start building a priority list of those elements requiring the most data collection and dossier revision or, in some cases, even product redesign. With the likelihood of future legislation, efforts to comply with the revised requirements and prioritizing products essential to marketing can start now.

Such analysis can be conducted by each company, but it might be worth sharing views and interpretations with other manufacturers, Notified Bodies and other stakeholders. Such content-related discussions with the company's Notified Body or, for example, with Notified Body panels at conferences, also will help the regulatory professional evaluate the company's Notified Body(ies) and rationalize the decision to work with one or a few in the future. Working with multiple Notified Bodies also helps the regulatory professional reduce the risks of not having access to Notified Bodies during the transition period. That and more should feed into the company's business continuity plan. If that element is not detailed in the company's quality system, the regulatory professional should start working on business continuity, contingency planning, etc., using, for example, ISO 22301:2012 as guidance. To engage the company in discussion on this level now, it could be helpful for the regulatory professional to set a goal to certify the company for business continuity, where a first-line requirement is to work through the upcoming regulatory storm, but the concepts will have much wider application.

Risk Assessment—ALAP Versus ALARP

A key change in interpretation of the current directive's regulatory requirements goes further than the evolving expectations in the clinical evaluation field into the risk management field. European Commission Recommendation 2013/473/EU (September 2013) started challenging the long-used as low as reasonably practicable (ALARP) risk management concept. The challenge is to not stop once a risk is within an acceptable range, but further mitigating individual risks where possible. This should go further than balancing work with economic factors. The directives' recitals often cited in debates on the matter are identified for the legislator's purpose and do not necessarily identify formal requirements for regulated industry. On the other hand, it clearly is possible to go further in risk mitigation, largely by expanding the number of patients in premarket clinical trials until no further risk reduction is possible. A new, balanced interpretation of this, as low as possible (ALAP), will need to be adopted. Basically, ALAP confirms each individual risk needs to be mitigated as far as possible, regardless of costs or difficulty, as it ultimately helps improve the benefit-risk ratio. Ideally, this change should be made before the new legislation is in place, so all dossiers may be revised to this new risk principle during reassessment. But, companies should be cautious and realize some things are impossible and, ultimately, there always will be risks remaining.

Annex Z to the Next Level

This is a key element in the continuing debate about the use of annex Z on EN ISO 14971:2012. Therefore, it will be crucial for all stakeholders to attempt to complete the revision process for all harmonized standards' Z annexes, assuming the new regulations will retain the current presumption of conformity. However, it also means, once the legislation is in place, all annex Zs in the relevant harmonized European norms will need to be revised on very short timelines. Since the current work already takes several years, this will be a difficult challenge, as manufacturers, experts and other stakeholders will be focusing their resources on implementing the revised QMS and product file requirements. Yet, spending time early to interpret the new legislation jointly and noting the revised annex Zs' interpretation will speed up the review. Forward thinking by involved parties will be required to finalize the annex Z revisions according to the current directives before moving directly on to draft and prepare future regulations' new annex Zs. In the meantime, regulatory professionals can only justify any deviations found in these annexes and support their improvement over time. Also, when transitioning to the new legislation, the regulatory professional will need to justify why the applied solutions are deemed sufficient to fulfill the Essential Requirements, while the standards' annex Zs have not been adjusted to the new legislation.

IVD—New Risk Classification

The current IVD classification system is a static list based on risk assessment and product and technology available two decades ago and will be modified drastically into the Global Harmonization Task Force's (GHTF) risk-based classification model. This change is not being contested, but it implies a large number of dossiers will need to be reviewed in future by a small group of IVD Notified Bodies with limited resources. Knowing time and resources will be tight in the second half of the transition period, it is essential to start preparing now.

The regulatory professional's first step is to start reviewing and improving existing technical documentation to a level acceptable to a Notified Body. Anticipated elements of future legislation should be taken into consideration in improving the documentation. The regulatory professional might consider having one or a selection of different technologies be prereviewed by a Notified Body or, alternatively, by a consultant previously employed as a Notified Body reviewer in the IVD field. It also is essential to start selecting IVD Notified Body(ies) to work with in the future at this stage, realizing there likely will be fewer of them. ThedNotified Body should convince the regulatory professional it has a clear vision and plan for the future. Getting into the Notified Body's client base now, e.g., by attaining ISO 13485 certification, will make it easier when the legislation enters into force and the company needs a Notified Body for the first time.

Unannounced Visits

Since mid-2014, Notified Bodies have been conducting unannounced production audits of manufacturing sites at least once every three years, more often for high-risk devices, frequently noncompliant devices or suspected nonconformities. Such unannounced audits can involve checking a sufficient quantity of recently manufactured products to assess technical documentation and legal requirement conformity and a file review. This includes verifying all critical component and material traceability and the manufacturer's traceability system.

Not only must manufacturers be able to accommodate such unannounced audits, so must their critical subcontractors and crucial suppliers; good preparation is indispensable. Obviously, in many cases, subcontractor and supplier contracts will need to be amended; regulatory sometimes must work hard to persuade suppliers to cope with these changes. It further may be foreseen some suppliers and subcontractors will choose to decline future business because of the new requirements' diversion and risks. The medical device sector return on investment might be too low for suppliers to accept these new rules of engagement. In more-positive cases, where a revised contract is in place, it does not stop: since the manufacturer normally is not present during such audits, essential preparation includes having procedures and processes in place and performing mock audits. The same is true for in-house production elements, e.g., when the next internal audit series might be utilized to build experience with unannounced auditing. Alternatively, external auditors may be used for mock audits.

Since the Notified Body will base its decision to visit a specific subcontractor on whether control can be exerted more efficiently there, it is important to provide accurate data on what happens where. In addition, the auditor will base its decision on a risk assessment. This risk assessment might be influenced by whether the subcontractor is under a high level of finished device legal manufacturer control. Therefore, it is good practice for the regulatory professional to revisit the actual supplier and subcontractor audit practices and reevaluate the assessment methodologies, potentially moving to unannounced supplier visits as well.

Role, Responsibilities, Authorities

At the ISO 13485 audit stage, many nonconformities are related to unclear roles, responsibilities and authorities. Since there will be a number of changes in this area, the regulatory professional should start making up the current balance as a first step. Following current legislation and harmonized standards' definitions and requirements, the regulatory professional should go through the organization's processes to verify whether current documentation matches authorities sufficiently to assigned responsibilities. A second step is to verify what is documented also is current company practice.

When that step is in place, and current representation is correct, the regulatory professional can begin studying the likely changes. Most will be related to the "Qualified Person." The regulatory professional should note the fact the draft regulations' responsibilities and authorities deviate significantly from the current Qualified Person role in European pharmaceutical legislation. In addition, the draft wording seems to allow the responsibilities to be divided among several people, as long as the knowledge and experience are available. Such knowledge should be available largely in-house; if that is not the case, human resources should be looking for such a regulatory expert. The bare minimum seems to be having access to such resources at all times. In addition, the new legislation aims at reinforcing QMS and compliance management responsibility.

Budget for Quality

This chapter makes it clear the legislative reforms will bring about many challenges. The regulatory professional needs to prepare for the unknown, as the transition time usually is short. Enough resources must be hired and trained in advance, and workload brought forward as much as possible. For that to happen, companies should budget for quality and regulatory well in advance of these changes.

14 Regulator's View on Global Device Strategy Trends

By Raymond Chua, MD, MSc and Rama Sethuraman PhD, RAC

Introduction

As a regulator, the primary mandate always is protecting public health and ensuring medical devices marketed in their jurisdictions are safe and continue to be of good quality and efficacy. While acting as gatekeepers to prevent the entry of poor quality, unsafe or non-efficacious medical devices, regulators should be mindful it also is within their mandate to promote and advance public health by facilitating timely access to safe but new innovative devices to meet patients' medical needs.

To do so effectively and ensure timely medical device product realization in various jurisdictions, it is important for industry to develop a comprehensive, effective and robust regulatory strategy. Typically, this regulatory strategy should cover the device's entire lifecycle from conception, research and development through product realization and postmarket follow-up. An ideal device development strategy should take into account the various regulatory risks associated with the design and manufacturing process at the premarket stage and extend to developing appropriate labeling strategies and postmarket marketing claims. A well-strategized regulatory approach could be the key to successful, timely medical device access for patients.

As the medical device market becomes more globalized, it is imperative device developers and regulatory professionals develop regulatory strategies from a global perspective as well. While medical device regulations are more established in some jurisdictions, the regulations still largely are in their infancy in many parts of the world, including Asia. Considering the nascent status of device regulations, it is critical for regulatory professionals to keep abreast of new and existing global developments and duly consider them when developing and refining regulatory strategy for marketing existing and new devices.

From a regulator's perspective, it is critical to collaborate and leverage strengths, capabilities and information of other agencies' to regulate new generation devices more efficiently. Where possible, duplication of work (e.g., multiple agency audits of the same facility) should be minimized, unless necessary. Thus, a convergence of medical device regulatory requirements among the various agencies globally is needed.

It is common for agencies' legislative provisions and administrative procedures to differ, as they could be influenced by political, social, historic and geographic considerations. However, recommending and applying similar technical and validation standards for medical devices globally to device development processes could be a huge step toward convergence. Global device verification and validation plans and guidelines could be developed as part of convergence activities, making regulatory requirements predictable globally for most devices. This would make regulatory compliance less burdensome for industry stakeholders and enable faster patient access to safe and novel technologies around the globe.

On the other hand, clinical evidence for medical device authorization in various jurisdictions still is largely unaligned. Unlike drugs, medical device clinical evaluation requirements cannot be standardized. Clinical evidence, typically comprising literature search, clinical experience and clinical evaluation, works well for established medical devices. However, for innovative devices, available scientific data and clinical experience to support these devices' marketing authorization likely will be limited. Some jurisdictions require randomized controlled trials, especially for novel and innovative devices, while they may not be mandatory in others. This requirement is determined largely by the agency's device risk tolerance and conformity assessment procedures. In addition, regulatory agencies do not have an aligned approach for novel and innovative technologies as to whether demonstrating device efficacy and superiority is necessary, or equivalence to previously marketed devices is acceptable.

Medical devices come in a wide variety: noninvasive, implantable active diagnostic and therapeutic. These devices' differing designs, technologies, modes of action and intended uses generate a wide range of clinical questions. They also make the development of consistent and standardized clinical evidence requirements for all medical devices challenging. Further, unlike drug studies in which placebo (e.g., inert sugar pill) use is quite common, controlled studies may not be appropriate for surgically invasive and implantable devices. Sham surgery in a control population to remove any bias or placebo effect from the intervention clouding the device's efficacy outcomes, in reality, may not be practicable in all circumstances. Sham surgeries carry inherent risks—such as the effect of anesthesia, incisional trauma and pre- and postoperative care—that may conflict with ethical principles. Since device clinical evidence requirements are clouded by many questions and imbalanced expectations, it would be a huge step forward to develop global medical device clinical evaluation strategies. This will help address some imbalances in regulatory requirements and also can help promote consolidated global clinical trials to avoid duplication in various jurisdictions to address similar device safety and efficacy questions.

ASEAN Medical Device Directive (AMDD)

As part of the Association of Southeast Asian Nation's (ASEAN) mandate to enhance economic integration among ASEAN Member States (AMS) and move toward the ASEAN Economic Community (AEC) in 2015, healthcare was identified as a high priority sector for integration across the region. The need for healthcare regulation harmonization and efficiency is recognized as vital for successful ASEAN integration. To this end, the Medical Devices Product Working Group (MDPWG) under the ASEAN Consultative Committee for Standards and Quality (ACCSQ)[1] has been working to develop a standardized medical device regulatory framework among all ASEAN nations—the *ASEAN Medical Devices Directive* (*AMDD*).

The *AMDD* was developed with the objective of harmonizing key medical device regulatory control components[2] among ASEAN countries to reduce technical barriers and facilitate medical device trade across the region, without compromising public health and safety. The key *AMDD* elements are:

a. regulatory technical requirements for medical device regulatory controls within ASEAN member economies, including:
  i. medical device definition
  ii. Essential Principles (EP) for medical device safety and performance
  iii. medical device risk classification
  iv. medical device postmarket controls for importation, distribution and complaint handling records, adverse event and fields safety corrective action reporting requirements
b. marketing authorization approval submission format, i.e., ASEAN Common Submission Dossier Template (CSDT)
c. regulatory convergence within ASEAN on internationally recognized medical device standards

The *AMDD* establishes medical device safety, quality and performance standards across ASEAN countries and is intended as an ASEAN framework. Depending on the regulatory framework's development stage and the individual AMS industry's maturity, the framework can be complemented further by country-specific requirements. The *AMDD*'s regulatory controls and principles are based on Global Harmonization Task Force (GHTF) recommendations as set out in its medical device regulatory control guidance documents, including risk classification and definitions. These documents now can be accessed on the International Medical Device Regulators Forum (IMDRF) GHTF archive webpage.[3]

AMDD Elements and Regulatory Convergence

Medical Device Definition and Risk Classification

The medical device definition in the *AMDD* is aligned largely with the globally adopted definition. This is the first step toward convergence in defining the scope of medical products subject to medical device regulatory controls in the region. Medical devices include a wide range of products, from simple devices such as bandages and wound dressings to long-term implantable devices like heart valves, pacemakers and diagnostic imaging equipment such as x-ray and MRI machines. Classifying these various devices into four risk classes forms the regulatory framework's backbone and enables regulatory oversight based on device risk. The device classification determines premarket registration requirements (e.g., level of clinical evidence), registration costs and processing timelines. The *AMDD* lays out a risk classification system for medical devices largely based on GHTF's medical device risk classification system. Any member state's differences in medical device risk classification or reclassification must be notified to the ASEAN medical device committee (AMDC), established to coordinate and monitor *AMDD* implementation.

Medical Device Registration

Under the *AMDD*, a medical device is required to be assessed by either the member state's regulatory authority or any appointed bodies recognized by the member state. Such a medical device assessment system is to be based on *AMDD* requirements. The regulatory authority is allowed to modify the registration requirement for certain medical devices (e.g., exception from registration) as it deems appropriate, and the modification is deemed to be in the interest of public health protection. Additionally, the person(s) responsible for placing the medical devices on the member states' markets is required to be licensed by the respective member state's regulatory authority.

Member states are required to adopt and implement the following harmonized medical device technical documents as specified in the *AMDD*:

- submission format for medical device registration—ASEAN Common Submission Dossier Template (CSDT)
- Postmarketing Alerts System (PMAS) requirements
- elements for the Declaration of Conformity (DoC) from the product owner or manufacturer

The CSDT, which is the submission format for medical device registration, is the most significant part of the *AMDD*, as it potentially would eliminate the need to prepare multiple dossiers in different formats for each ASEAN country. The CSDT dossier elements are very similar to those in the GHTF Summary Technical Documentation (STED)[4] for medical devices. The key CSDT elements include:

- executive summary (which covers the medical device's commercial marketing history and a list of regulatory approval or marketing clearances obtained previously)
- device description, including intended use and indications, instructions for use, warnings and precautions, potential adverse effects, alternative therapy and materials and relevant specifications
- Essential Principles conformity checklist
- design verification and validation documents (which cover the results of preclinical studies, such as biocompatibility, mechanical testing, software validation, etc. and clinical evidence)
- risk analysis and risk management report
- manufacturer information (including relevant information on the manufacturing process)

Medical devices are required to meet the Essential Principles of safety and performance in the directive. The *AMDD* also states medical devices placed on member states' markets must conform to relevant technical standards. Such standards could be those recognized by the ASEAN committee overseeing *AMDD* implementation or as accepted by the member state's regulatory authority for the device to comply with the applicable Essential Principles of safety and performance. A DoC for the essential requirements, as applicable for the medical device, also is required.

In addition to premarket requirements, the *AMDD* requires member states to establish a system to record and evaluate medical device adverse events brought to their attention systematically. The directive includes these requirements in a Postmarket Alert System and sets forth reportable adverse event criteria and requirements for handling adverse events, recalls and field safety corrective actions related to medical devices' safety and performance. Manufacturers, Authorized Representatives and distributors are required to maintain distribution and complaint records. They also are required to investigate reported events in a timely and effective manner. Member states, in coordination with the product owner, may notify other ASEAN countries of the event and any corrective actions taken.

AMDD development, which is largely aligned with global medical device regulatory principles and GHTF recommendations, is indeed a huge step toward regional regulatory convergence. This will minimize trade barriers for global device companies looking to enter the ASEAN market and promote economic development in ASEAN countries. This potentially would make regulatory compliance more achievable. For instance, a manufacturer may be able to use the same dossier for medical device registration or marketing authorization in all member states.

ASEAN member states are required to transpose these requirements into their national legislation and take

Figure 14-1. Rollout of the Medical Device Regulations in Singapore

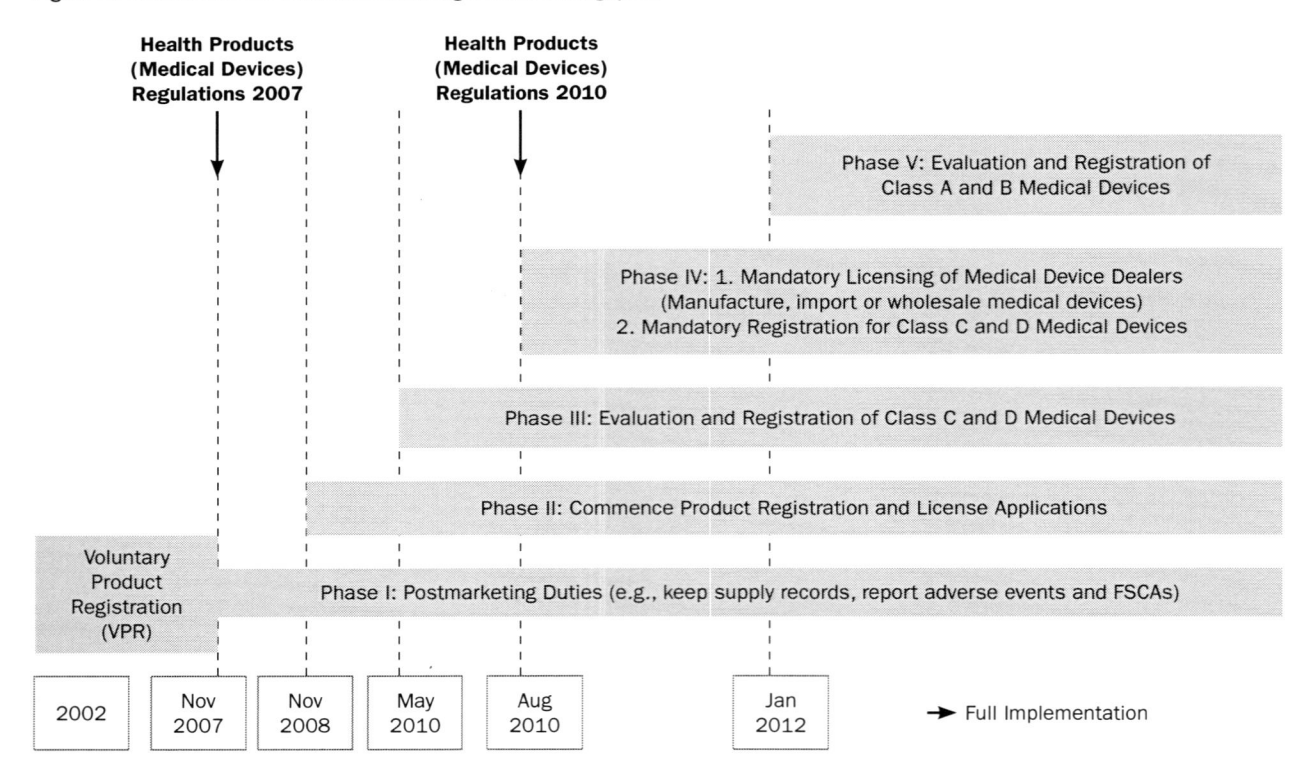

- Health Products (Medical Devices) Regulations 2007 — Nov 2007
- Health Products (Medical Devices) Regulations 2010 — Aug 2010
- Phase V: Evaluation and Registration of Class A and B Medical Devices
- Phase IV: 1. Mandatory Licensing of Medical Device Dealers (Manufacture, import or wholesale medical devices) 2. Mandatory Registration for Class C and D Medical Devices
- Phase III: Evaluation and Registration of Class C and D Medical Devices
- Phase II: Commence Product Registration and License Applications
- Voluntary Product Registration (VPR) — 2002
- Phase I: Postmarketing Duties (e.g., keep supply records, report adverse events and FSCAs)
- Timeline: 2002, Nov 2007, Nov 2008, May 2010, Aug 2010, Jan 2012 → Full Implementation

AMDD and the EU Medical Devices Directive (MDD)

In the EU, regulations relating to medical device safety and performance were harmonized in the 1990s. Their core legal framework[5] consists of three directives: 1) Directive 90/385/EEC regarding active implantable medical devices (*AIMDD*), 2) Directive 93/42/EEC regarding medical devices (*MDD*) and 3) Directive 98/79/EC regarding in vitro diagnostic medical devices (*IVDD*). The *AMDD* is similar to the EU *MDD* in that both directives aim to harmonize the medical device regulatory framework in their respective regions. The *AMDD* is not legally binding, but member states are required to comply with the directive's provisions. Both directives require medical device design and manufacture to meet their essential safety and performance requirements. One key method of demonstrating essential requirement compliance is conformity to international or harmonized standards relevant to the devices. Both directives cover labeling requirements for key information required to accompany the medical device, and both allow for flexibility in terms of including country-specific language on device labels.

Both directives include requirements for device conformity assessment procedures but differ in their approaches. The EU *MDD* is more prescriptive, while the *AMDD* provides more flexibility for conformity assessment procedures. The EU *MDD* stipulates the member states shall designate independent bodies (Notified Bodies) to contribute to applying these procedures to devices, except those representing a minimal risk. The EU *MDD* also covers various conformity assessment routes (i.e., medical device CE marking) the manufacturer may adopt in consultation with its Notified Body, depending on the medical device's risk classification. The *AMDD* requires a medical device to be assessed by either the member state's regulatory authority or an approved appointed body. It only emphasizes such a medical device assessment system be based on *AMDD* requirements.

Singapore Perspective—Embracing Best Practices and Understanding Gaps

In Singapore, the medical device regulatory framework was rolled out in phases over a period of five years,

Table 14-1. Risk Classification of Medical Devices in Singapore

Singapore Risk Classification	Risk Level	Device Examples
Class D	High Risk	Implantable cardiac pacemakers, heart valves, cardiovascular stents, neurological stents, IUDs **IVDs:** HIV diagnostic assays, ABO blood grouping tests
Class C	Medium-high Risk	Lung ventilators, orthopedic implants, IOLs, x-ray devices, blood bags **IVDs:** Blood glucose meters for self-testing, prenatal Down's syndrome assays
Class B	Medium-low Risk	Hypodermic needles, single-use catheters, contact lenses, digital blood pressure monitors, hearing aids **IVDs:** Pregnancy tests, ovulation kits, clinical chemistry assays (e.g., liver function tests)
Class A	Low Risk	Wheelchairs, tongue depressors, bandages, walking aids **IVDs:** Noninvasive sample collection kits, general microbiology media

2007–12 (**Figure 14-1**). Previously, a voluntary product registration scheme was implemented in 2002 to invite companies already supplying medical devices in Singapore to submit medical device registration applications to the regulatory authority voluntarily. These voluntary applications were intended to serve as a capacity-building exercise for local industry and regulators alike to have first-hand experience in preparing and reviewing device registration dossiers. This also allowed regulators to check the pulse of medical devices already on the local market. No fees were applicable for these voluntary registrations, and more than 4,500 medical devices were registered during this voluntary phase.

The regulatory authority responsible for medical device regulation in Singapore is the Health Sciences Authority (HSA). The phased implementation approach was intended to reduce any potential burden and facilitate stakeholder regulatory compliance. It also allowed regulators time to stabilize the various systems and processes being put into place to implement the framework. A medical device definition on the scope of products subject to medical device regulatory controls and a risk classification system to stratify devices into four classes were developed. Medical device risk classification principles from GHTF recommendations were embraced. Medical devices were classified into GHTF's four risk classes (**Table 14-1**).

The first medical device control phase in Singapore was implemented in November 2007,[6] and the following mandatory duties and obligations for all medical device dealers were implemented first:
1. duty to maintain import and supply records
2. duty to maintain complaint records
3. reporting defects and adverse effects to the authority
4. notifying the authority about field safety corrective actions, e.g. recalls
5. prohibiting false and misleading advertisements

The first phase largely encompassed postmarket regulatory control aspects. After a regulatory agency first considers implementing a regulatory framework, there always will be numerous devices on the market that have been used for many years. Establishing a postmarket surveillance system is practical, since it allows the regulator to review devices already on the market and monitor and support their continued safe and effective use without impeding their existing use.

In parallel, premarket registration systems were developed simultaneously, which included regulatory guidance on medical device registration submission, an online platform for product registration application submission and a register for listing medical devices with marketing authorization. The authority has accepted medical device registration applications since November 2008.

The second implementation phase was in August 2010, when mandatory high- and medium-high-risk medical device (Class C and Class D) registration requirements were implemented. Mandatory licensing of all medical device dealers (i.e., manufacturers, importers and wholesalers) in Singapore was implemented at the same time.

The final regulatory framework implementation phase was in January 2012, when mandatory registration requirements for all low- and low-medium-risk medical devices (Class A and Class B) were implemented. This staggered regulatory control implementation is similar to the progressive medical device regulatory model published by GHTF's ad hoc working group later in 2011,[7] laying out various building blocks—components of a new regulatory framework and their suggested progressive implementation.

Singapore's medical device regulatory framework is based largely on GHTF guidance documents. It was a conscious decision not to reinvent the wheel but to adapt the available GHTF guidelines. The GHTF documents are based on the best practices from various regulatory agencies (e.g., European Medicines Agency (EMA), Health Canada, Japan's Ministry of Health, Labour and Welfare (MHLW), Australia's Therapeutic Goods Administration (TGA) and the US Food and Drug Administration (FDA)) with established and relatively mature medical device regulatory frameworks. This provided a unique opportunity not only to learn from best practices but also to understand the pitfalls and challenges.

Some of the best practices HSA has embraced or aligned with various global regulatory agencies include but are not limited to:
1. medical device definition
2. Essential Requirements for medical device safety and performance
3. risk classification of general medical devices and in vitro diagnostic medical devices
4. postmarket reporting system
5. regulatory controls, including classification of medical devices containing drugs (combination products)
6. ISO 13485 as the quality system requirement for medical device manufacturers
7. registered medical device change management system

When implementing a new medical device framework, many regulatory agencies tend to extrapolate their existing regulatory systems, such as applying those designed for drugs to medical devices. Although this may be a practical choice in terms of the jurisdiction's available resources and experience, it has created huge hurdles for medical device innovators, manufacturers and regulators alike.

Medical devices are a distinct group of products with their own specific challenges and regulatory considerations, such as a short product lifecycle with continuous iterative improvements; huge diversity in design, form and functions; maintenance and service considerations; and high distribution cost warranting a lifecycle approach to device regulations. Extrapolating drug regulatory models clearly could be a misfit.

On the contrary, a more device-specific system based on available resources, such as the experiences of mature regulatory agencies and guidance documents from international bodies or forums (e.g., the International Medical Device Regulators Forum (IMDRF)), makes regulatory compliance less burdensome. A strong device framework potentially enables safe innovations and advanced patient care, especially in today's global society where interstate and intercontinental boundaries have become less conspicuous in medical device trade and commerce.

Singapore Perspective

Leveraging Existing Medical Device Premarket Assessments or Marketing Authorizations and Experience

Since a large percentage of medical devices in Singapore are imported, and a majority of those are from GHTF founding member countries (Australia, Canada, Europe, Japan and the US) with established medical device regulations, most of these devices have prior marketing authorization in one or more of these jurisdictions. As a country just embarking on medical device regulations, the premarket review processes in place for medical devices in these jurisdictions were studied. Significant overlaps in terms of medical device premarket review scope exist in various jurisdictions. Therefore, in designing its premarket evaluation system, Singapore adopted two guiding principles:
1. A risk-based regulatory approach to ensure the regulatory requirements put in place are appropriate and commensurate with the device's risk profile
2. A confidence-based approach relying on the device's marketing authorization assessments of safety, quality and efficacy from a recognized list of reference regulatory agencies overseas (in this case, GHTF founding countries with well-established device regulatory frameworks) as well as the safety profile of devices marketed overseas

Hence, Singapore implemented several medical device registration routes, from "Full route," for totally new or "first in the world" devices (no marketing authorization from reference regulatory agencies) to "Abridged" and "Expedite and Immediate" registration routes for devices already approved by other reference regulatory authorities.[8] The abridged, expedited and immediate routes leverage the marketing authorization review and outcome in one or more of these reference agencies and these devices' safe marketing history in those jurisdictions (for at least three years at the point of submission of the device registration application to HSA).

The GHTF founding members (Australia, Canada, the EU, Japan and the US) had well-established device regulatory frameworks when Singapore began to implement its framework. The process began with an overall review of these countries' medical device marketing authorization procedures. It was noted some of these countries have multiple medical device marketing authorization routes, tied to the device risk classification in those jurisdictions. For example, type-examination, full quality assurance, design dossier review, product verification and product quality system are some of the routes available to obtain the EU medical device CE Mark.[9] Understanding the reference regulatory agencies' various marketing authorization routes, a closed list of marketing authorization or approval types was created. Medical devices with marketing authorizations from the reference agencies on the closed approval list qualify for abridged evaluation in Singapore. Medical devices with marketing authorizations from the reference agencies through routes not included on the closed list, for example, devices with a self-declared EU CE Mark, do not qualify for abridged evaluation in Singapore.

For premarket submissions qualifying for abridged evaluation, summary reports of various device verification and validation studies are acceptable in lieu of complete reports. Other submission requirements such as the Essential Requirements for safety and performance checklist and DoC, evidence of ongoing sterilization validation and ISO 13485 certificates for all manufacturing and sterilization sites still are applicable. These devices also go through the local evaluation process to ensure they continue to be safe and effective since being authorized in other jurisdictions. However, the abridged evaluation process allows more-focused premarket review for these medical devices, resulting in faster marketing authorization. These primarily are devices with established safe marketing histories.

The abridged evaluation allows regulators to use resources effectively by avoiding duplicate reviews. Available resources can be deployed efficiently in high priority areas such as: medical devices with no prior marketing authorization from reference regulatory agencies; reviewing other critical safety or performance considerations unique to local context (e.g., an IVD intended to test for a biomarker the prevalence of which is distinctly different in the local population than in the reference agency countries and most likely was not covered by their review); registered device change management systems to ensure they continue to be safe and effective postmarketing; or postmarket surveillance and vigilance activities.

From industry and other stakeholders' perspectives, this approach reduces time-to-market for devices, especially for products that have been marketed safely in other jurisdictions while maintaining their safety and efficacy for patients and users. With the experience gathered in premarket device review and understanding iterative changes occurring with various devices, continuous enhancements to the medical device regulatory framework have been implemented in Singapore over recent years.

Further, the advent of novel technology and devices including mobile applications, telehealth, combination products and 3-D printing are challenging regulatory framework boundaries continuously. Therefore, it is essential for a robust device regulatory framework also to be accommodative and practical.

User Proficiency and Competency

It is important for regulatory professionals to understand and acknowledge the safe use of medical devices goes beyond design and manufacturing standards and verification and validation efforts performed during device development. No matter how well the device may be designed, manufactured and validated for its proposed intended purpose, its safe and effective use also is dependent on user proficiency. User proficiency could vary depending on the individual user's educational background, knowledge and experience. Clinical investigations and trials, no matter how well-designed, cannot address device safety- and performance-related variability adequately in terms of actual users once marketed. Standardized and tailored user training programs could help reduce, although not remove completely, the user-related variable in the equation of safe medical device use.

Rapid advancements in technology at large and the increasing sophistication in medical equipment make training users of state-of-the-art devices of paramount importance. Device users include doctors, nurses and other healthcare professionals who diagnose and/or deliver therapeutic care. Medical devices are not always used in isolation. They typically are used with other medical equipment (e.g., in a hospital ICU, a patient may be on ventilator support, under IV infusion of fluids or drugs and simultaneously may be connected to a patient monitor). A device's safe use in such circumstances could be dependent on the effective functioning of other device(s) in the environment. Similarly, the user's skills and experience operating the device also determine the device's safe and effective use. For example, a life support machine for a critically ill patient may be deemed highly complex for staff in a step-down or community care center, while it is routine for intensive care staff. Appropriate and individually targeted user training can enable some of these complex medical devices for long-term or palliative care to be used safely, even in step-down care centers or home settings.

Since a user is a significant component of the medical device ecosystem, it is important the user is trained adequately on the devices to enable informed choices when procuring and using them. Further, training device users on device operations and their management throughout the lifecycle goes a long way toward ensuring device safety and performance. When choosing a medical device for use in a facility, careful consideration must be paid to the physical environment in which the device will be used, the device's targeted user or operator, available training on monitoring and maintaining the equipment during its lifecycle, previous experience using this or similar devices and expected outcomes.[10]

Some key aspects of which the device user should be aware or receive training prior to use include device operation and control, monitoring the device while in use, recognizing a device failure or fault and knowing appropriate action to take in the event of a device failure or fault. A significant percentage of reported medical device adverse events are errors in their use[11] from, e.g.:

- device use by improperly or inadequately trained users
- device use for a purpose beyond the one for which it was designed
- device use by users with inadequate technical expertise or professional knowledge
- local device modification to address a clinical need beyond the manufacturer's intent

Taking the variety of settings where medical devices are used into consideration, users, device manufacturers and distributors should take appropriate steps to ensure access to appropriate service and maintenance programs for the device's safe and effective functioning. Timely device maintenance, service and repair and prompt implementation of a manufacturer's recalls and corrective actions are critical to ensure device safety and efficacy throughout its projected useful life.

Other Local Considerations

Medical devices are prone to continuous innovation in not only device design and technology but also indications for use. A single device technology may be engineered, modified and validated for use continuously in various novel medical applications. For instance, extracorporeal shockwave therapy has evolved constantly, and these devices now are being developed by various manufactures for different indications, including pain relief, plantar fasciitis, lithotripsy and erectile dysfunction. Since the technology is similar, such devices' quality and safety still can be deemed comparable if they are manufactured under the same or similar quality systems. However, these devices' efficacy is tied primarily to the manufacturer's intended indication for use. Some of these indications likely have more scientific and clinical evidence to support their use and clinical benefit than others.

For medical devices based on established technology and intended for standard and clinically accepted indications, adequate clinical evidence generally is available in the form of published scientific literature and clinical experience. However, for novel indications for use, further clinical evidence in the form of clinical investigation or trials will be required to substantiate the device's efficacy for the indication. With such clinical evidence, it is likely the device's regulatory approval or marketing authorization may be granted, but the bigger challenge might be winning the acceptance of local clinical practitioners for such novel applications. Typically, clinical practice globally is tied to the concept of evidence-based medicine or healthcare.[12] Acceptance of new therapeutic or diagnostic devices by clinical practitioners is determined primarily by the strength of scientific evidence available to support such use.

The level of scientific evidence clinical practitioners' require often is not aligned with what is required to gain medical device marketing authorization. This difference between regulatory approval and clinical practice acceptance in a jurisdiction is unique to medical devices and more common for low- and medium-risk devices (Class II or equivalent). For such medical devices, the level of evidence required to support the marketing authorization globally generally is lower and sometimes limited to substantiating device performance. This evidence is not always equivalent to the scientific and clinical data needed to substantiate the devices' evidence-based therapeutic or clinical use in clinical practice in a jurisdiction.

Device manufacturers and regulatory professionals need to understand the typical validation data applicable to a medical device from the start, even when designing the device and conceiving its intended use. This is important to ensure the device's timely marketing during the product realization phase. Manufacturers must understand the device's safe use may be subject to multiple regulatory requirements in another jurisdiction. For example, an x-ray machine likely will be subject to the regulatory requirements applicable to medical devices and radiation protection, in many cases administered by more than one agency. It sometimes may be prudent initially to start small when developing a medical device by designing the device for standard, clinically accepted indications and validating it appropriately to enable initial marketing authorization. Subsequently, the manufacturer may choose to expand the device's use to novel indications during its lifecycle by building on the experience gathered on the device's effectiveness, safe use and technology after initial marketing. Regulatory professionals should have a good understanding of the legal framework and applicable regulations in the jurisdiction(s) where the medical device is intended to be marketed to enable timely patient access to safe and effective therapies.

Medical Device Change Management

Compared to drugs and other healthcare products, medical devices have a much shorter lifecycle and undergo continuous iterative improvements or modifications known as "changes." Changes could be related to device technology, design, manufacturing, specifications or performance. Such changes could be continuous improvement initiatives to extend or improve the device's capability and/or functions or could be part the manufacturer's efforts to fix device-related issues identified in postmarketing. Regardless of the purpose, such changes to marketed device are required to be managed efficiently within the scope of quality management system (QMS) requirements.

Medical device design and manufacture could include a wide range of technologies and applications, from simple tools to complex robotic or computer-controlled machines, depending on the device type. Further, the medical device manufacturer could be large or small with different management methods. Implementing appropriate quality controls into the medical device design and manufacturing process is the backbone of QMS compliance and remains relevant to all changes, including those occurring postmarket. From a manufacturing perspective, QMS requirements adequately cover device design and development change control. Such changes are required to be identified, recorded, reviewed, verified and validated as appropriate, with approval prior to implementation. Changes resulting from corrective and/or preventive actions under the QMS also will require validation of their appropriateness and effectiveness. However, from the product (i.e., medical device) perspective, the change's impact on safety, quality and efficacy needs to be reviewed and revalidated if necessary.

Changes to medical devices can involve design, functionality, specifications, manufacturing, packaging and labeling. It is important for a regulatory professional to understand the change and assess its impact on the device's quality, safety and effectiveness rationally. Many jurisdictions have premarket registration or listing systems in place for medical devices with guidelines and stipulated submission requirements (e.g., Summary Technical Documentation, Common Submission Dossier Template).

Whether the medical device continues to be safe and efficacious post-registration is a question that daunts regulators globally, especially in countries with developing regulatory systems. This concern on the part of regulators has resulted in medical device re-registration requirements every three to five years in some jurisdictions. This translates into a huge resource burden for both industry and regulators and also involves duplication of work.

The solution lies in developing a pragmatic and holistic approach to managing registered medical device changes. Just as medical device premarket regulatory requirements are stratified based on device risk classification, changes should be classified by their impact on device quality, safety and/or efficacy. Such stratification allows regulators to ensure appropriate oversight is placed on critical, impactful changes not burdening industry with noncritical change requirements. Some global regulatory agencies[13] have published guidelines on their websites for medical device change management, stratifying changes into significant or otherwise, based on the change type and impact. Similarly, in Singapore, changes to registered medical devices are required to be notified to the authority. This includes changes to the registered device affecting device quality, safety and efficacy.

Changes affecting the registered device's safety, quality and efficacy (e.g., sterilization method or process changes) are deemed "technical changes," subject to authority review. Such changes would warrant appropriate and adequate verification and validation of relevant parameters, depending on the change's impact on the device.

On the other hand, administrative changes or those not affecting registered device safety, quality and efficacy are classified as nontechnical changes (e.g., aesthetic or ergonomic changes, such as color or shape with no impact on the device's performance characteristics).

Transparent change stratification criteria in the form of flow charts or decision trees could enable clearer regulatory compliance understanding from the manufacturer's perspective. This also would facilitate adequate validation of all significant registered device changes and regulatory agency review and approval where necessary to ensure the device's continued safety and effectiveness, without affecting market and patient access to the "changed" devices. This confidence allows regulatory agencies to move from mandating periodic re-registration of older marketed devices toward a lifecycle monitoring approach, enabling efficient regulatory resource utilization.

Developing a Diverse Regulatory Tool Kit

With ever-increasing medical device complexity and diversity, driven by the development of combination products (e.g., device-drug products), personalized medicine, companion diagnostics and application of highly automated and wireless technology, the device regulatory framework's focus inevitably has to move

Figure 14-2. Medical Device Lifecycle

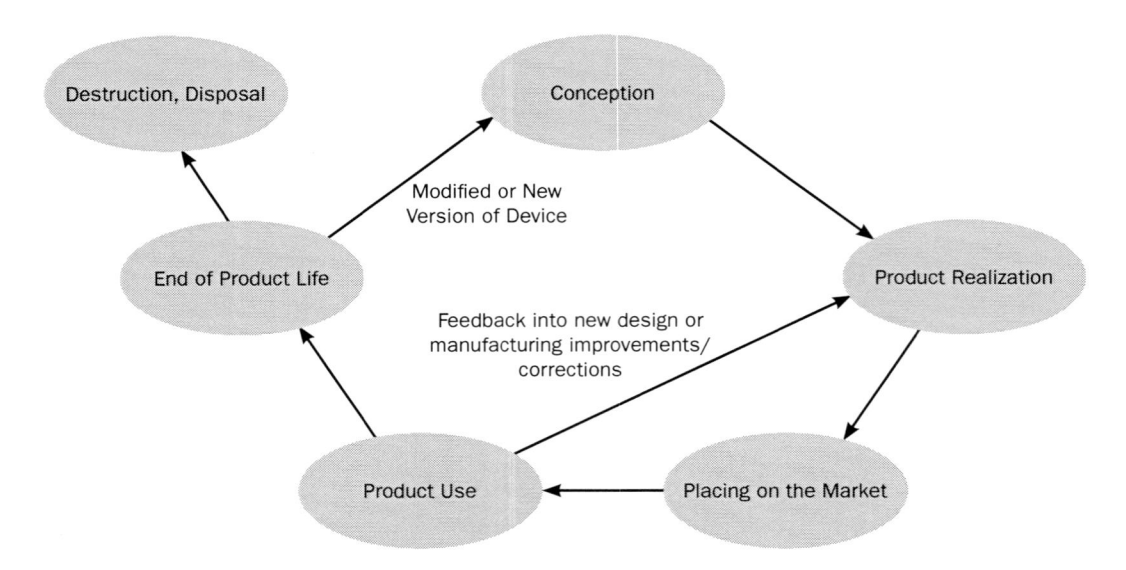

Source: The GHTF Regulatory Model, 2011

beyond traditional premarket controls. The medical device distribution and supply chain is becoming more complex, as more manufacturing activities are outsourced, especially components and subcomponents for complex device systems that potentially could impact final product quality and performance.

Considering medical devices' diversity in design, technology and applications, the reasons these devices fail also are disparate. An FDA report[14] including an analysis of medical device adverse event report and recall trends attributes the majority of catheter product recalls to manufacturing issues and process defects. Pump products, e.g., infusion pumps, largely suffer from design-related issues. Hence, a lifecycle-oriented approach to medical device regulations is essential.

The medical device lifecycle defined in ISO 14971:2007 refers to all phases in a medical device's life, from initial conception to final decommissioning and disposal (**Figure 14-2**). It covers various processes along the way, such as product realization; placing the device on the market; marketing the product through distribution, promotion, advertising, servicing, product modifications and upgrades; and monitoring the device's postmarket effectiveness. The various lifecycle phases actually are linked and feed back into one another.[15] For example, user complaints or preferences gathered in the marketing phase actually feed back into new or modified product design and testing to enhance safety and performance. Where applicable, some modifications also could be corrective actions implemented for existing or marketed versions of the medical device.

With due consideration of the device's lifecycle, the medical device regulatory framework should cover various lifecycle stages and processes. The entire lifecycle typically should be subject to QMS regulatory processes, risk management and regulatory auditing. Premarket regulatory controls, such as device registration, marketing authorization by a Competent Authority or conformity assessment body review of summary technical files, may apply during product realization. The product then is placed on the market subject to regulatory controls, such as registration of the manufacturer, importer and/or distributors. Postmarket surveillance, vigilance controls and adverse event reporting apply during the device marketing phase (**Figure 14-3**).

Medical device product realization typically is based on the concept of meeting device design and manufacturing process quality system requirements together with adequate and appropriate validation (preclinical studies and clinical evidence) to ensure the device meets the manufacturer's quality, safety and efficacy requirements for the intended purpose. This is supported further by appropriate medical device labeling and presentation to ensure the user is well-informed and equipped to use the device safely and effectively for its intended and validated use. Clinical investigations' (controlled trials')

Figure 14-3. Lifecycle Approach to Medical Device Regulatory Framework

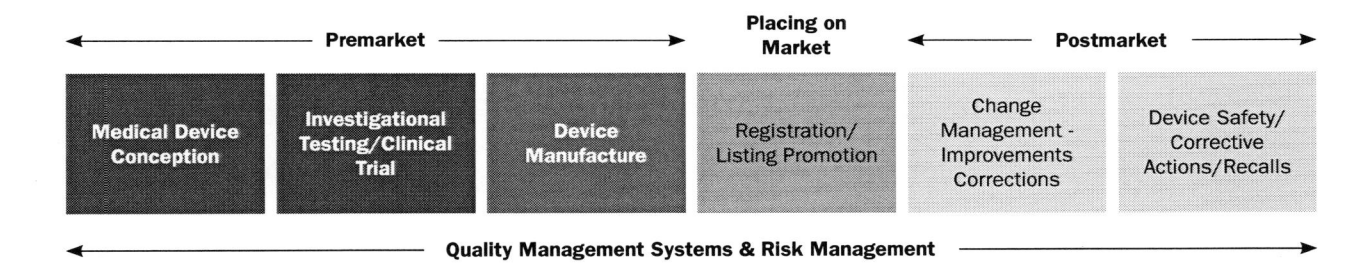

Premarket			Placing on Market	Postmarket	
Medical Device Conception	Investigational Testing/Clinical Trial	Device Manufacture	Registration/ Listing Promotion	Change Management - Improvements Corrections	Device Safety/ Corrective Actions/Recalls

Quality Management Systems & Risk Management

inherent limitations, such as subject number and relative heterogeneity, especially for rare conditions, investigator and care-giver heterogeneity and clinical conditions encountered in actual medical practice compared to those in controlled clinical settings, must be considered. The extent of the data gathered in the premarket phase typically does not cover rare complications or problems that become apparent only after the device's widespread or long-term use. Hence, to enable timely novel medical device access while ensuring safety, regulatory tools beyond premarket evaluation should be considered.

A novel medical device should be considered favorably for marketing authorization, leveraging the best possible and available clinical evidence, including clinical trial data, to support its safety and efficacy for the proposed intended use. In some circumstances, it may not be feasible to address all questions related to medical device safety, quality and/or efficacy by traditional premarket requirements. This is especially true for a novel medical device such as software. For such devices, certain process-based controls beyond traditional premarket requirements should be explored. The manufacturer must mitigate and all foreseeable risks associated with the medical device's use adequately and appropriately. The device must conform to the Essential Requirements for safety and performance or equivalent as laid out in the various jurisdictions' device regulatory frameworks where it is to be marketed. Beyond this, any residual questions surrounding the device's actual effectiveness during real-time use could be managed by activating other regulatory tools and mechanisms.

One such tool, especially for medium- and high-risk medical devices (Class III or IV), is setting up postmarket registries. These registries facilitate recording various key safety and efficacy outcomes related to the device's use on individual patients. Registries, especially if established globally, allow not only monitoring individual patient outcomes but also trending data to monitor the device's overall safety and effectiveness. This increases the possibility of early device failure detection, e.g., the Australian Orthopaedic Association National Joint Replacement Registry (AOANJRR), an initiative of the Australian Orthopaedic Association (AOA). Another valuable tool is postmarket clinical follow-up studies that enable device clinical evaluation throughout its lifecycle, thus ensuring devices' long-term safety and efficacy. These tools, i.e., postmarket studies or registries, are not intended to replace premarket device validation studies but rather to support, reinforce and cover device safety and efficacy aspects not reasonably possible to address holistically during the premarket phase in controlled settings. When exploring such tools, it is important to be mindful of the challenges and opportunities they bring and deploy them pragmatically in regulating the medical device's lifecycle. Other key components of a medical device regulatory tool kit include risk management processes and quality management systems to enable effective risk management.

Risk-free medical devices are more a myth than reality. No level of verification and validation can ensure 100% medical device safety. In general, risks can be introduced throughout the device lifecycle, not just during the development and premarket phases. As set out in ISO 14971:2007, risks that become apparent at any one point in a medical device's lifecycle can be managed by action taken at a completely different point in the lifecycle.

After a systematic risk analysis and risk evaluation process, the following risk control options typically have to be considered carefully:
- where practicable, the medical device design should be inherently safe
- if this is not practicable, such protective measures as alarms or barriers could be incorporated as appropriate for the risk identified
- the least recommended or preferred risk control option is including a written warning or contraindication in device labels

For example, there may be no practicable way to reduce all life-supporting or life-sustaining device risks to acceptable levels. In such circumstances, the risk management process hinges on benefit:risk assessment. This determines whether all identified, foreseeable risks associated with the medical devices (including design, manufacturing, performance and use) have been reduced as much as reasonably possible. The benefit from the medical device's use for its intended purpose must outweigh any remaining residual risks after all possible risk mitigation measures have been considered and implemented.

Beyond the risks associated with medical devices conceived and developed for a specific intended purpose, other risks inherent to specific devices may be related to:
- device technology (e.g., risks associated with radiofrequency or lasers used in a medical device)
- intended use (e.g., risk associated with self-testing IVD use for blood glucose)
- actual use (e.g., risk associated with inappropriate contact lens maintenance and care); and disposal (e.g., inappropriate disposal of used needles)

The manufacturer may be unable to mitigate certain inherent risks at the device design or manufacturing level. Some of these risks might be included in device labels to inform users of the risks and any possible mitigation or precautionary measures.

From a regulator's perspective, not all risks can be addressed at the product level, especially those introduced in the device post-product realization lifecycle or arising from inappropriate use. For such risks, active communication and public education on the device's appropriate use should be considered. Regulators worldwide have acknowledged the importance of communication and are working actively on various social media and communication platforms to enhance consumer education efforts.

A successful medical device regulatory framework is one able to ensure patient safety and facilitate timely access to meet patients' clinical needs. This will require a lifecycle approach to regulations with a diverse and inclusive toolkit. The toolkit covers activities from device conception, through understanding regulatory authorities' requirements and developing clear postmarketing surveillance and vigilance initiatives to ensure the device's continued favorable benefit-risk profile. Besides industry and healthcare professionals, training users on the device's appropriate use and its associated risks or hazards goes a long way toward ensuring the device's safe and effective use. Continual review and refinement of the regulatory framework also are critical to maintain effective and sustainable regulations to support a quality healthcare system for the global patients.

References

1. Association of South East Asian Nations—ACCSQ Structure. ASEAN website. http://www.asean.org/?static_post=accsq-structure. Accessed 8 February 2016.
2. Improving ASEAN Healthcare Through Medical Device Regulation Harmonization. ASEAN website. http://www.asean.org/improving-asean-healthcare-through-medical-device-regulation-harmonization/. Accessed 8 February 2016.
3. GHTF Archived Documents, IMDRF website. http://www.imdrf.org/ghtf/ghtf-archived-docs.asp. Accessed 8 February 2016.
4. Asian Harmonization Working Party (AHWP) Technical Committee. AHWP website. http://www.ahwp.info/index.php?q=node/287. Accessed 8 February 2016.
5. European Union—Medical Devices Regulatory Framework—Legislation. European Commission website. http://ec.europa.eu/health/medical-devices/regulatory-framework/index_en.htm. Accessed 8 February 2016.
6. Singapore Health Sciences Authority. Medical Device Regulatory Framework. HSA website. http://www.hsa.gov.sg/content/hsa/en/Health_Products_Regulation/Medical_Devices/Overview/Regulatory_Framework.html. Accessed 8 February 2016.
7. *The GHTF Regulatory Model*. Ad Hoc GHTF SC Regulatory Model Working Group, 13 April 2011. IMDRF website. http://www.imdrf.org/docs/ghtf/final/steering-committee/technical-docs/ghtf-sc-n1r13-2011-ad-hoc-regulatory-model-110413.pdf. Accessed 8 February 2016.
8. HSA SMaRT E-Guide. HSA website. http://www.hsa.gov.sg/content/hsa/en/Health_Products_Regulation/Medical_Devices/Application_Registration/HSA-SMaRT_E-Guide.html. Accessed 8 February 2016.
9. Medical Devices. European Commission website. http://ec.europa.eu/health/medical-devices/documents/guidelines/index_en.htm. Accessed 8 February 2016.
10. NIAIC Device Bulletin – Equipped to Care: The Safe Use of Medical Devices in the 21st Century – DB/2000/06 https://www.dhsspsni.gov.uk/sites/default/files/publications/dhssps/DB-2000-06.pdf
11. Ibid.
12. "Barriers and bridges to evidence based clinical practice." *BMJ* 1998; 317: 273.
13. Guidance for the Interpretation of Significant Change of a Medical Device. Health Canada website. http://www.hc-sc.gc.ca/dhp-mps/md-im/applic-demande/guide-ld/signchng_modimportante-eng.php. Accessed 8 February 2016.
14. *Understanding Barriers to Medical Device Quality*. FDA website. http://www.fda.gov/downloads/AboutFDA/CentersOffices/OfficeofMedicalProductsandTobacco/CDRH/CDRHReports/UCM277323.pdf. Accessed 8 February 2016.
15. Ibid.

15

Use of Standards in Medical Device Global Regulatory Strategy

By Prithul Bom RAC, Michelle Wu and Michael Morton

Introduction

At the most basic level, standards are documents providing requirements, specifications, guidelines and characteristics that can be used to ensure materials, products, processes and services consistently are fit for their purpose.[1] The International Electrotechnical Commission (IEC) defines "standard" as a:

"Document, established by consensus and approved by a recognized body, that provides for common and repeated use, guidelines or characteristics for activities or their results, aimed at the achievement of the optimum degree of order in a given context." (ISO/IEC Directives, Part 2:2011-04, definition 3.1.1)

Within the context of medical device development, using standards helps provide consistency in both how a medical device is developed and the performance and expected results for certain, typically established, medical device types. Standards' compliance may lead to faster regulatory approval and, for some countries, compliance with certain standards is required. Thus, there is a strategic advantage to understanding standards and their role in the medical device development and regulatory approval process.

Navigating standards' complexity can be confusing to both medical device development and approval process newcomers and veterans. First, there are different types of standards: process standards and product standards. The former provide guidance on medical device development and numerous manufacturing and assessment processes. The latter generally provide desired results and testing and assessment means, specific to such factors as the medical device type, i.e., implantable, and the materials from which the device is made.

Second, there is no one centralized listing, database or decision tree to determine the standards to which a manufacturer needs to conform for a particular medical device's development and regulatory approval. Relevant standards can vary among regulatory authorities. Many relevant standards are written specifically for the medical device industry, while others are written generically to apply across industries, e.g., ship testing standards. Such standards are relevant to both medical device manufacturers and regulators because they provide requirements that can be used consistently to ensure the device is fit for its intended use. More frequently used standards are discussed in this chapter.

Standards are not maintained by one organization. Many organizations issue standards used in medical device development and regulatory approval. This chapter provides an overview of the largest standards development and maintenance participants. Standards change over time; some are revised, while others become obsolete and are replaced. Further, since there is no centralized body issuing standards, it can be difficult to keep up with the various revisions, especially in the middle of the product development or regulatory submission process.

Another difficulty, in most instances, is these standards organizations are separate from regulatory agencies. While regulatory agencies, such as the US Food and Drug Administration (FDA), recognize certain standards and standards' clauses, this recognition often lags behind the effective date of new revisions for certain device classes.

Each regulatory agency may recognize different standards or different standards' revisions, thus the list of standards to which a manufacturer must adhere varies among jurisdictions. If a product is intended for multiple jurisdictions, regulatory professionals should start by researching common and similar requirements simultaneously applicable to each.

To meet regulatory expectations, standards are not standalone documents, may be referenced or accepted by various regulatory authorities around the world and must be viewed in parallel with local regulations. An entity dedicated to creating standards is called a standards development organization (SDO). Standards developed by an SDO are intended to be voluntary and, as such, do not aim to replace local regulations. This is the reason certain regulatory authorities may determine standards will be mandatory in their jurisdictions; this type of determination, however, is uncommon. On certain occasions, for certain jurisdictions, even a widely used standard may not address a medical device's safety and performance concerns adequately. An example of this is FDA's *Guidance on Radio Frequency Wireless Technology in Medical Devices*.[2] This guidance states the IEC 60601-1-2 consensus standard did not address wireless technology electromagnetic compatibility (EMC) adequately at the time the final guidance was issued in August 2013. A manufacturer intending to seek market approval in multiple jurisdictions should consult international standards and local regulations in parallel.

In the US, a 'consensus standard' is one developed by an SDO using the consensus process, while a 'recognized consensus standard' is a standard FDA has evaluated and recognized for use and published in the *Federal Register*. The consensus process is described later in this chapter. If a manufacturer chooses not to comply with certain sections of a recognized consensus standard when compliance with the standard is expected (i.e., if the standard is referenced within an FDA guidance document), the regulatory submission should justify the deviation and provide the alternative used. A manufacturer must understand the risks it takes by not complying with applicable standards. If a manufacturer wishes to use a national standard of a country other than the US for US market clearance or approval, it may discuss the plans with FDA in the presubmission process. In contrast, the EU *Medical Devices Directive* (*MDD*), and directives in other industrial sectors, rely on "harmonized" European Norms (EN) or standards. Those standards are prepared in response to a mandate from the European Commission (EC). They are intended to be used to demonstrate conformity to the Essential Requirements in one or more directives and are developed by the European standardization bodies,

the European Committee for Standardization (CEN), European Committee for Electrotechnical Standardization (CENELEC) or European Telecommunications Standards Institute (ETSI). Notices on the standards are published in the EU *Official Journal*. Use of these voluntary standards confers a presumption of conformity with the directives' mandatory regulatory requirements.

In Australia and some countries in Asia and South America, the extent to which a standard is accepted or recognized may vary by local law. For example, in China, foreign manufacturers may submit a notarized quality system certificate of compliance to a standard, such as ISO 13485 or FDA's Quality System Regulation (QSR), to the China Food and Drug Administration (CFDA). It is possible the Chinese version lags behind the international version. In this case, the manufacturer has to demonstrate compliance with the Chinese standard and provide the necessary test reports. IEC 60601-1 second and third editions may serve as another example; a manufacturer would need to meet second edition test report requirements in China, while in much of the rest of the world, it would in fact meet third edition test reports. The Brazil Good Manufacturing Practice (BGMP) is similar to ISO 13485 per Brazilian Resolution RDC 185/2001 and, therefore, a certificate of compliance to ISO 13485 may be acceptable. It is important for regulatory professionals to consult with local regulatory agencies to understand which international standards and editions currently are accepted and whether backward compatibility is accepted.

To summarize, the use of standards to demonstrate medical device regulation conformity differs among countries. These differences pose a challenge to the medical device regulatory professional in developing a global medical device regulatory strategy. Fortunately for the medical device industry, multiple SDOs create standards deemed to offer the presumption of conformity to specific regulatory safety and performance requirements, and these documents, as mentioned earlier, usually are the recognized standards.[3] Manufacturers may rely on documents published by the International Medical Device Regulators Forum (IMDRF), which make multiple normative references to numerous medical device standards. A later section in this chapter discusses IMDRF's work in more detail.

Understanding Standards Numbering

Many regulatory professionals find standards' versioning or numbering confounding and, when dealing with standards, the numbering system indeed can be so. For example, one of the most well-known standards in the medical device industry is ISO 13485 Medical

Devices—Quality Management Systems—Requirements for Regulatory Purposes. An Internet search of "ISO 13485" could yield the following results:
- ISO 13485:2003
- EN ISO 13485:2012
- CAN/CSA-ISO 13485:03
- DS EN ISO 13485:2012

Now, the question is what are the differences?

To answer this question, start with the base document: ISO 13485:2003. In general, the structure followed is:
- ISO 13485:2003
    - the preceding letters indicate the issuing organization; in this case, the International Organization for Standardization (ISO)
    - 13485 is the standard number
    - 2003 is the revision year, sometimes using only the last two numbers

Then, the numbering changes as various regulatory bodies in different jurisdictions adopt the standard, to meet their specific requirements. EN ISO 13485:2012 is the version of ISO 13485:2003 adopted by one of the pan-European standard bodies, CEN, CENELEC or ETSI. CEN, CENELEC and ETSI are recognized officially by the EU. Official EU recognition means these organizations may adopt European Norms (EN) that can become candidates for harmonization (recognition) in Europe under the directives. Appendices were added to indicate the aspects of the EU *MDD* the standards satisfy. CAN/CSA-ISO 13485:03 is the ISO 13485:2003 version adopted by the Canada National Standard/Canadian Standards for use in Canada. DS/EN ISO 13485:2012 is the version adopted by Denmark's Dansk Standards Association,[4] the same version approved by the European Committee for Standardization as EN ISO 13485:2012 without any modifications.

While some regulatory jurisdictions include the year of adoption, some jurisdictions do not, such as CAN/CSA-ISO 13485:03. Reviewing the adopted version's scope is necessary to understand which standard version was adopted. For example, ISO 13485 was revised in February 2016 and its adoption by various standard bodies is ongoing. There is a three-year transition period for ISO 13485:2016, thus it is necessary to understand the revision to which manufacturing organizations will comply.

SDOs

As defined earlier, an SDO is an organization dedicated to developing standards. Several SDOs support the medical device industry and it, therefore, is important for a regulatory professional to know who they are and understand why they exist.

An SDO provides consumers, industries and governments a platform to discuss and develop international standards. Each SDO, when appropriate, cooperates with another and its stakeholders to produce joint publications, help promote the importance of standardization globally, coordinate any potential overlaps in work and ensure international standards are seamless and complementary with each other. Some significant SDOs are profiled in this chapter.

ISO develops and publishes international standards.[5] Created in 1947, ISO is an independent, nongovernmental organization with 162 member countries. Each member has a national committee representing ISO in its country. For example, the American National Standards Institute (ANSI) represents ISO in the US. Through ANSI, the US participates heavily in ISO technical committees (TC), such as ISO/TC 194—Biological and Clinical Evaluation of Medical Devices. ISO/TC 194 is responsible for publications such as ISO 10993—Biological Evaluation of Medical Devices and ISO 14155:2011—Clinical Investigation of Medical Devices for Human Subjects—Good Clinical Practice series. The British Standards Institute (BSI) represents ISO in the UK. ISO representatives in specific jurisdictions can be found on the ISO members' web page.[6]

The International Electrotechnical Commission (IEC) prepares and publishes international standards for electrical, electronic and related technologies, known collectively as electrotechnology.[7] IEC members are called National Committees (NCs) who represent all electrotechnical standardization concerns and conformity assessments in their countries. IEC's objective is to promote international cooperation on all questions concerning standardization in the electrical and electronic fields. IEC publishes international standards, technical specifications, technical reports, publicly available specifications (PAS) and guides, and collaborates closely with ISO. The US participates through ANSI in the medical device standards development subcommittees (SCs).

ANSI is a private, nonprofit entity coordinating and administering the US voluntary standards and conformity assessment systems. ANSI, itself, is not an SDO but accredits SDOs that adhere consistently to the ANSI Essential Requirements for openness, balance, consensus and due process, a set of procedures governing the consensus standards development process. ANSI is a founding member of ISO, and the ANSI Essential Requirements embrace ISO and IEC's globally accepted standardization principles. As the US member body of ISO, ANSI accredits US Technical Advisory Groups (TAGs). US TAGs, through ANSI, promote the use of US standards, policies and technical positions internationally and advocate the adoption of international standards as US national standards when they meet the healthcare community's needs. Because ANSI is a leader in ISO's governing body and an IEC participant, via the US National Committee, the US has immediate access to both the ISO and IEC standards development processes. As the accreditor of US voluntary consensus SDOs, ANSI ensures SDOs maintain integrity in developing American national standards.

The Clinical and Laboratory Standards Institute (CLSI), successor to the National Committee for Clinical Laboratory Standards, exists to develop applicable clinical and laboratory consensus standards and guidelines for clinical laboratories and promote their use globally.[8] CLSI is accredited by ANSI and actively promotes global harmonization of clinical laboratory testing standards through its participation as the Secretariat of ISO TC 212, Clinical Laboratory Testing and In Vitro Diagnostic (IVD) Test Systems. CLSI also serves as the administrator for the US TAG for ISO TC 212. The CLSI consensus process includes stakeholder experts from industry, government and healthcare professions, gathering to develop standards for improved clinical laboratory testing quality, safety and efficiency. An example of a CLSI published guideline is *Point-of-Care IVD Testing*, providing guidance to IVD device users outside a clinical laboratory setting on how to ensure results are comparable to those obtained in laboratories.

In addition to these organizations, other SDOs exist that either publish technical standards in a wide range of industries or collaborate with ISO and IEC in standards development and publications. The Underwriters Laboratories (UL) develops a wide variety of standards to measure and validate performance, environmental health and sustainability.[9] Standard UL 60601-1 Medical Electrical Equipment, Part 1: General Requirements for Safety references 36 additional UL standards that may be used in lieu of IEC 60601-1 if the differences in the two documents' particular requirements are recognized and understood for effective implementation in a global regulatory strategy. It is important to note, however, many UL standards are not recognized by regulatory authorities outside the US.

Other professional organizations' work includes coordinating and publishing technical standards or models the medical device industry may utilize. The Institute of Electrical and Electronics Engineers (IEEE) is a professional association dedicated to advancing technological innovation. IEEE, among other services, publishes engineering technical standards and models. Medical device software engineering professionals and software medical device and mobile medical app (MMA) manufacturers continue to draw from well-established IEEE standards, such as IEEE 1012-2012 Standard for System and Software Verification and Validation.

The Association for the Advancement of Medical Instrumentation (AAMI) is a nonprofit organization founded in 1967 supporting the healthcare community in developing, managing and using safe and effective medical technology. AAMI's standards program consists of more than 100 technical committees and working groups that produce standards, recommended practices and technical information reports for medical devices. Standards and recommended practices represent a national consensus and many have been approved by ANSI as American National Standards. AAMI also administers a number of international ISO and IEC technical committees as well as US TAGs.[10] An example of an AAMI standard is AAMI ANSI HE75:2009(2013) Human Factors Engineering—Design of Medical Devices.

Formally known as the American Society for Testing and Materials, ASTM International currently has more than 7,000 standards that have been adopted as the basis of national standards or referenced in regulations around the world in a wide variety of industries. These technical standards are used in product development, product testing and quality systems.[11] Examples of standards include ASTM F2516-07 Standard Test Method for Tension Testing of Nickel-Titanium Superelastic Materials and ASTM F1980-07(2011) Standard Guide for Accelerated Aging of Sterile Barrier Systems for Medical Devices.

Additional Related Organization

As noted earlier, IMDRF is the successor to the Global Harmonization Task Force (GHTF). IMDRF is not an SDO but is an international group of volunteers representing medical device regulatory authorities from Europe, the US, Canada, Japan and Australia who develop medical device and IVD guidance documents. The Asian Harmonization Working Party (AHWP),[12] ISO and IEC joined IMDRF as liaison members in 2012. AHWP represents 26 member economies.[13]

IMDRF's purpose is to continue GHTF's work, producing a series of guidance documents describing a risk-based regulatory model to ensure medical device safety, effectiveness, performance and quality. These guidance documents are intended to harmonize documentation and procedures on basic regulatory practices used to assess whether a medical device conforms to applicable regulations in each jurisdiction. These harmonized documents and procedures are aimed at reducing, if not eliminating, differences among jurisdictions, thereby decreasing the regulatory compliance costs and allowing patients earlier access to new technologies or treatments. IMDRF guidance documents reference standards,[14] such as those developed and disseminated by ISO and IEC, a regulatory professional can implement both within a global regulatory strategy and throughout the medical device's lifecycle.

Following is an example of how a global regulatory professional may benefit from understanding IMDRF's work. A manufacturer has identified Australia as a potential target market for its medical device and asked its global regulatory executive to determine market access requirements. Since Australia was a founding IMDRF member and contributed to the guidance document, many standards referenced in IMDRF documents are accepted, even if certain versions are not recognized, by Australia's Therapeutic Goods Administration[15] (TGA). By examining IMDRF documentation, a regulatory professional will be able to determine the list of applicable standards for premarket evaluation, assessment and implementation.

The same principle applies for market access in the other IMDRF founding economies of the US, Japan, Canada and AHWP. Guidance documents published by IMDRF may help a medical device global regulatory professional determine reference standards to be used as part of the conformity assessment process to meet different countries' regulatory requirements.

Using Standards to Demonstrate Conformity With Regulatory Requirements

While differences in medical device regulations exist across jurisdictions, a regulatory professional may apply international standards to demonstrate conformity to essential regulatory elements to help get the manufacturer's technologies and treatments to patients faster. In the US, international standards often are referenced in FDA guidance documents. When developing a strategy, the regulatory professional is advised to reference and implement these standards in parallel with guidance documents to meet FDA requirements, specifications and guidelines to ensure the medical device is fit for its intended use. For example, by utilizing the internationally recognized ISO 14971 risk management standard, a manufacturer can demonstrate conformity with medical device risk management requirements. ISO 14971 is referenced in numerous FDA guidance documents, including *Guidance for Industry and Food and Drug Administration Staff: Content of Premarket Submissions for Management of Cybersecurity in Medical Devices* and *Factors to Consider When Making Benefit-Risk*

Figure 15-1. Document Hierarchy

Determinations in Medical Device Premarket Approval and De Novo Classifications, which addresses the intersection of the guidance with ISO 14971 in great detail.

As mentioned earlier, the IMDRF guidance documents also reference standards, such as ISO 14971. A regulatory professional developing a medical device global regulatory strategy, must apply local guidance document recommendations, reference standards and regulations to increase chances of getting medical technology to patients faster.

A standard is not a regulatory agency's recommendation or guideline presented in a guidance document. A guidance document, such as the FDA's *General Principles of Software Validation; Final Guidance for Industry and FDA Staff*, contains suggested regulatory guidelines and reflects the agency's current thinking and recommended best practices for the medical device regulatory process. Like IMDRF documents, FDA guidance documents may reference numerous process, safety and performance standards, such as those developed and disseminated by ISO and IEC.

A standard is a not a regulation. A regulation is a national rule implementing a law, which, if violated, can result in a penalty. A national regulatory body develops a regulation. **Figure 15-1** presents a graphic representation of the hierarchical relationship between regulations, guidance documents, standards and technical reports. It is important to remember regulatory agencies issue regulations and guidance documents, while SDOs, which are nongovernmental entities, issue standards and technical reports.

Product Standards and Process Standards

Standards can be grouped into three major categories: compatibility, process and safety and performance. Universal serial bus (USB) and blue-ray disc standards are specific examples of compatibility standards. Process standards cover a medical device product's lifecycle. Process standards dictate a process or overall system's requirements but do not dictate how a medical device manufacturer should meet these requirements. Standards also can be categorized as vertical or horizontal. For medical devices, horizontal standards would be "general" standards applicable to almost all medical devices. For example, ISO 13485 quality systems, ISO 14971 risk management and ISO 15223 symbols for labelling would apply to most regulated medical devices. In contrast, vertical standards apply to specific devices or device categories, such as the IEC 60601 family of standards that apply to electromechanical medical devices.

SDOs and professional associations have developed and published numerous compatibility, process and safety and performance standards. Only standards relevant to the medical device lifecycle, from concept to market, are within this chapter's scope. While more than 1,000 standards are used in the medical device industry, a few are worth profiling in this chapter due to their broad usage and recognition.

These profiled standards, recognized and referenced by multiple regulatory authorities and generally applicable to all medium- to high-risk medical devices, include ISO 13485, ISO 14971 and IEC 62366 Medical Devices—Application of Usability Engineering to Medical Devices. IEC 62304 Medical Device Software—Software Life Cycle Processes will be profiled and, as the title indicates, is applicable to medical devices containing software, standalone software or mobile medical applications. Last but not least, ISO 14155:2011 Clinical Investigation of Medical Devices for Human Subjects—Good Clinical Practice, also will be profiled in this chapter, since clinical investigation is a critical process by which a manufacturer collects safety and performance data to support medical device market approval.

ISO 13485—Medical Devices—Quality Management Systems—Requirements for Regulatory Purposes

ISO 13485 gives available quality management system (QMS) requirements an organization can use for medical device design and development, production, installation and servicing, and designing, developing and providing related services.[16]

ISO 13485 is derived from historic versions of ISO 9001 (versions prior to 2015), a standard containing QMS requirements used around the world for various manufacturing and service industries. ISO 13485 and ISO 9001 are moving farther apart, however, as ISO 9001 evolves into a true 'quality system.' In the past, most of the ISO 9001 clauses, subclauses and format, were identical to those in ISO 13485; this will change since the next edition of ISO 13485 no longer will be comparable to ISO 9001:2015. Currently, differences and reasons for differences between these two standards are contained in an Annex to ISO 13485.

For most jurisdictions, including the EU, Australia and Canada, the preferred method to prove conformity with regulatory requirements is certification of the manufacturer's QMS to ISO 13485. One notable exception is the US. Manufacturers wishing to distribute their devices in the US are required to establish and maintain a quality system that meets FDA's QSR (21 CFR Part 820), that includes current Good Manufacturing Practices (CGMP) for medical devices.[17] Part 820 is broadly consistent with the current 2003 edition of ISO 13485:1996; thus, many elements are similar.[18] However, some requirements differ and are more specific; therefore, care must be taken to ensure a manufacturer's quality system addresses all aspects of both the QSR and ISO 13485 if the product is to be distributed in multiple countries.

As described previously, process standards largely are nonprescriptive: the requirements are presented, but how to meet those requirements is not specified. The standard recognizes a wide variety of medical devices (from simple and low-risk to complex and high-risk) are developed by a multitude of organizations (from small start-ups with small staffs to large, multi-national corporations with thousands of employees); thus, processes successful for one organization will not be the same as those for another.

ISO 13485 includes general QMS requirements; management's overall QMS responsibility; resource management (both human and physical resources); product realization; and measurement, analysis and improvement.

In the US, FDA stipulates a manufacturer (domestic or importer) must have a QSR-compliant QMS. The QMS standard, ISO 13485, was adopted in the US as ANSI/AAMI/ISO 13485:2003. Although ISO 13485 and QSR elements are similar, they are not identical. A manufacturer may need to fulfill certain obligations to comply with the QSR that are not part of ISO 13485. One example is the QSR requirement to use statistical techniques not specified in ISO 13485.

It should be noted EN ISO 13485:2012 outlines the gaps between ISO 13485 and the *MDD*'s QMS requirements. ISO 13485, by itself, does not address all *MDD* requirements, and the manufacturer must review the directive carefully to ensure compliance.

Despite these differences, using ISO 13485 still can streamline QMS establishment to meet the majority of regulatory agency requirements around the world. It is worth noting here links exist between other standards and ISO 13485. How ISO 13485 outlines the basic manufacturer QMS framework was described earlier. However, other process standards less overarching than ISO 13485 exist that help frame QMS subprocesses or subsections. Examples include ISO 14001 Environmental Management Systems and ISO 14971 Risk Management.

ISO 14971 Medical Devices—Application of Risk Management to Medical Devices

ISO 14971 specifies the process to identify hazards associated with medical devices, to estimate and evaluate and control those risks and monitor the controls' effectiveness throughout the product lifecycle.[19] It is referenced in ISO 13485 and numerous other standards, as the one in which guidance related to risk management during product realization may be found.

To emphasize, this standard outlines the risk management process but does not prescribe the specific hazards and risks to be mitigated and controlled for each medical device type. Given the wide range of medical devices, from thermometers to surgical tools, and the technologies in use, an encyclopedia of hazards and risk mitigation measures would be large, unwieldy and out-of-date as soon as it was published. The range of risks varies from device to device depending on the technology used, its intended use and its method of use. For example, dental hygienists use tools such as scalers and hand instruments to scrape bacterial deposits from teeth. Micro-ultrasonic scalers also are available for the same purpose—removing bacterial deposits—but use vibration and a pressurized stream of water. The risks of the simple hand tool scaler are much different than those of the micro-ultrasonic scaler.

As technologies evolve, new hazards will be introduced that may not be foreseen; thus, there is a need for a standardized risk identification, mitigation and control process.

The general process outlined by ISO 14971 creates a risk management plan to document how risk management activities will be performed. The next step is risk assessment to identify potential hazards and estimate the risk for each situation associated with the potential hazards. In the example of the scaler hand tool, the sharp tip presents a potential hazard.

IEC 62366-1 Usability in Medical Devices

As healthcare and technology have progressed over time, more-complicated medical devices and device use by less-skilled users, including patients themselves, have followed suit.[20]

IEC 62366 was published in 2007 and amended in 2014, expanding the standard's scope to include all medical devices, non-active implantable medical devices and active implantable medical devices. More recently, IEC 62366 was revised in 2015 to IEC 62366-1. The updated standard divides IEC 62366 into two parts: IEC 62366-1 and IEC/TR 62366-2. The first part discusses usability engineering principles and provides an overview of how usability is incorporated into medical device development. The second part has not been published yet and will be a technical report including guidance on compliance with IEC 62366-1.

This standard addresses the need for usability engineering to minimize use errors and use-associated risks. Similar to other standards discussed previously, and for similar reasons, IEC 62366 does not prescribe the specifics of a medical device user interface, but does describe the analysis, specification, design, verification and validation usability processes related to device safety. The standard has close ties and many references to ISO 14971. If designed well, a manufacturer's risk management and usability processes will dovetail efficiently into each other. One IEC 62366 appendix includes a diagram mapping the inputs and outputs between risk management and usability processes.

IEC 62304 Edition 1.1 2015-06 Medical Device Software—Software Lifecycle Processes

Software is incorporated into many medical devices. Just as it is necessary to ensure safe and effective mechanical and electromechanical devices, devices incorporating software also must be safe and effective. This standard was created in the belief software testing alone is insufficient to ensure safe operation. Thus, IEC 62304 provides a framework for safe software design and maintenance processes throughout the product lifecycle. It assumes software activities occur within a QMS and risk management system, specifically ISO 14971. This standard includes general requirements for software development, maintenance, risk management, configuration management and problem resolution processes. Similar in nature to the standards cited above, this standard does not prescribe what software code should look like but focuses on the processes to create safe and effective software.

ISO 14971 is referenced in several of the standards mentioned above. Sometimes, an SDO publishes a TR to guide a manufacturer or regulatory professional in applying a certain standard. IEC TR 80002-1—Medical device software—Part 1: Guidance on the Application of ISO 14971 to Medical Device Software is one example. This TR is the result of collaborative work by joint working groups IEC SC 62A: Common Aspects of Electrical Equipment Used in Medical Practice, IEC 62 Electrical Equipment in Medical Practice and ISO TC 210: Quality

Management and Corresponding General Aspects for Medical Devices. IEC TR 80002-1 is extremely helpful in understanding how to apply risk management principles in ISO 14971 to medical device software.

ISO 14155:2011 Clinical Investigation of Medical Devices for Human Subjects—Good Clinical Practice

ISO 14155 is intended to ensure Good Clinical Practice (GCP) is followed during a medical device clinical investigation to ensure subject safety.

ISO 14155 details the baseline clinical investigation requirements for market approval safely. Key stakeholders, e.g., the sponsor and principal investigators, are required to follow the standard's requirements. Recognized by FDA, ISO 14155 can be applied in parallel with FDA's GCP and guidance on an investigational device exemption (IDE); however, it should be noted, while consistent with FDA's GCP requirements, conformity with ISO 14155 alone is insufficient for US clinical investigations. Further, conformity with ISO 14155 may not be sufficient for FDA to accept data from clinical investigations conducted outside the US. A medical device global regulatory professional must understand the common principles in all these documents are pertinent when a medical device is investigational, i.e., undergoing safety and performance evaluations, under applicable laws and GCP.

Some of the additional normative standards referenced in ISO 14155 are ISO 13485; ISO 10993; ISO 15223: Symbols to be Used With Medical Device Labels, Labeling and Information to be Supplied, Part 1—General Requirements; and EN 1041: Information Supplied by the Manufacturer of the Medical Device. A regulatory professional must not assume, however, that normative references in a standard are recognized automatically.

Benefits of Using Standards

The Standards Program[21]

A key reason for complying with standards and integrating them into product development is to enable an easier approval process with regulatory bodies. Standards are voluntary but, in some jurisdictions, have a particular regulatory status and are recognized as a (the) preferred means by which the manufacturer may demonstrate conformity with the mandatory regulatory requirements. Thus, it generally is easier to conform to the standard instead of providing justification for not using it.

Standards play an important role throughout the medical device lifecycle. Various standard types exist to support all involved medical device products and processes, such as risk management and quality systems. Multiple medical device industry stakeholders are involved in developing standards and stay involved in updating them as necessary. Standards help harmonize regulatory processes to ensure medical devices' safety and performance are not compromised at any point during their lifecycle, playing an important role during medical device and diagnostic product conformity assessments.

As mentioned above, various standards exist to support medical device processes and can help manufacturers streamline their risk management processes. Standards generally are established to promote consistency and best practices leading to devices meeting current safety and effectiveness state-of-the-art expectations. Designing to a standard can mitigate potential application (use) and design risks. For example, a device's electrical power results in risks associated with shock hazards. UL 60601-1 Medical Electrical Equipment, Part 1: General Requirements for Safety, outlines standards for electrical safety protection methods; designing a device to comply with this standard can be documented as mitigation measures taken for shock hazard risks. This documentation also can support ISO 14971 requirements, the medical device risk management standard.

In the US, FDA's guidance, *Center for Devices and Radiological Health (CDRH) Standard Operating Procedures for Identification of Candidate Consensus Standards for Recognition,* provides an established process for standards' recognition.[22] A Standards Task Group (STG), reporting to the Standard Management Staff (SMS), is responsible for coordinating all CDRH consensus standards' activities within its assigned technical area with relevant SDOs. The recognition process begins when an STG identifies an existing and needed standard within its technical area and prioritizes required activities per common criteria. Then, the STG coordinates an assessment of whether the standard can be used to meet a particular premarket or statutory requirement. Upon completing the assessment, it then recommends the standard be recognized through publication in the *Federal Register*. The *Federal Register* notice includes not only the newly recognized standards; it also includes modification to the previously recognized standard and identifies any previously recognized standard(s) that no longer will be recognized.

Any medical device industry stakeholder may propose a standard for recognition. The process includes submitting the standard title, reference number, date and SDO. In addition, the stakeholder must list device types to which the standard would apply and a brief identification of device testing, performance and/or other characteristics a declaration of conformity to that standard would address.

Outside the US, several regulatory authorities have processes in place to recognize standards within their jurisdictions. Globally, SDOs have established standards development processes, described in the following section.

Standards Development Process

A 'consensus standard' is designated as such because it takes all stakeholders' interests into consideration and defines what they have agreed.

Consensus is considered a general agreement, characterized by the absence of sustained opposition to substantial issues by any important stakeholders, through a process that takes all concerned parties interests into account and reconciles conflicting arguments. However, it is important to remember consensus need not imply unanimity but rather agreement to most of the proposed requirements or guidelines by the majority of the stakeholders. Care also is taken to ensure a standard does not confer a competitive advantage on individual operators.

The standardization process encompasses standards' development, promulgation, implementation and compliance. While some governmental bodies develop standards, most are written by nongovernmental entities, several of which were profiled earlier in this chapter. Those organizations follow a transparent process open to public scrutiny, where participation is balanced, and an appeals process is included. Behind each medical device standard is a comprehensive process including extensive data gathering, analysis and discussion from all stakeholders' perspectives and agreement on critical factors. Stakeholders, such as regulatory agencies and IMDRF, support standards' use by referencing them in guidance documents and publications. In some cases, national regulatory authority experts participate in standards development.

Finally, medical device SDOs rely on standards' sales to support their programs' and services' continuous improvement. By charging for standards, an SDO also can ensure it is not influenced unduly by a single party's interests.

How to Choose Medical Device Standards

A regulatory professional needs to consider standards from design and development through the medical device's lifecycle. This is an integral part of global regulatory and clinical strategy, since standards help demonstrate a device's safety, performance and efficacy to meet regulatory requirements.

Case study: Standards' Use in Developing a Hypothetical Artificial Pancreas Device System (APDS)

This case study assumes the manufacturer is responsible for developing an APDS and its clinical investigation approval in the US and EU. An APDS is a complex, connected IVD device system comprising several components, and is an excellent example of the use of vertical and horizontal standards. An APDS device includes a glucose meter, an insulin pump, an insulin reservoir, a sensor, a display for acquired glucose values and a transmitter. The device also contains some complex software. This device is an improvement on the traditional continuous glucose monitoring system design because the sensor monitors cell glucose values continuously and transmits these values to the insulin pump. The device's software allows it to be programmed to carry out one of three specific tasks: deliver insulin automatically should glucose level fall below a predefined threshold; control insulin delivery based on predefined low and high thresholds; or control insulin delivery to a predefined glucose target level.

The meter component is designed to measure and display glucose values continuously, so basal insulin may be calculated and delivered. A reporting feature reports glucose trending information in real time. The device can be programmed to stop or suspend insulin delivery automatically for two hours when the sensor detects the glucose level has fallen below a preset value. The glucose sensor is inserted through the patient's abdomen and senses or measures glucose values. These values are transmitted to the insulin pump and displayed for the patient to see. The insulin is delivered by the pump through the infusion set.

Since an APDS is a complex system, the device's failure can cause death or serious injury and, therefore, falls under the highest risk classification, Class III in both the US the EU.

How are standards chosen for this device? Fortunately, for this case study, several guidance documents exist, including *Final Guidance for Industry and the Food and Drug Administration Staff: The Content of Investigational Device Exemption (IDE) and Premarket Approval (PMA) Applications for Artificial Pancreas Device Systems*. Horizontal and vertical standards comprise the body of knowledge to help a regulatory professional choose the correct standards. In addition, FDA has compiled a guidance entitled, *Frequently Asked Questions on Recognition of Consensus Standards*, as a primary guide to understanding the agency's current thinking on how to identify standards applicable to a certain medical device and why to apply standards to US and EU submissions.[23]

The device development team can reference this guidance to demonstrate the device is safe and works as intended, as can the regulatory and clinical teams, to ensure the device is investigated to conform to local regulations and international standards.

A regulatory professional should start by identifying US Code of Federal Regulations notice(s) on Essential Requirements for medical device safety and efficacy or performance based on functionality and mode of action, intended use, site of action and mode of operation. A search for a relevant FDA guidance document would be conducted. Standards referenced in the relevant guidance document then can be selected. Using standards will help the manufacturer identify the device's preclinical and clinical testing and critical postmarket requirements. Fortunately, there is an FDA APDS guidance document. The guidance references several horizontal and vertical standards. In addition, a summary of safety and effectiveness data (SSED) for a similar device or precedent, if one exists, may be examined. From these documents and the referenced standards, a fairly comprehensive list of standards can be obtained that might cover the majority of, if not all, preclinical testing requirements and bench performance objective performance criteria, EMC, biocompatibility, sterility assurance, packaging, shelf life, shipping, software and human factors.

The various research and development, engineering, quality and clinical cross-functional groups within the organization will need to ensure all regulatory requirements are met. In addition, a discussion about standards should occur, since standards play a significant role in helping establish and communicate baseline expectations at each APDS product lifecycle stage. A few examples of the applicable numerous horizontal and vertical standards for disparate APDS components are discussed below.

Since the APDS insulin set component is inserted under the patient's skin, regulators would be interested in the set materials' biocompatibility. Certain Parts of the ISO 10993 series may be examined to understand and meet APDS biocompatibility requirements within a risk management process. An FDA blue book memo, entitled *Use of International Standard ISO 10993, Biological Evaluation of Medical Devices Part 1: Evaluation and Testing*, can be consulted in parallel.[24] A manufacturer will need to provide biocompatibility testing result summaries, since the standard, itself, does not include pass/fail criteria. ISO 11137—Sterilization of Health Care Products—Radiation helps in understanding sterility testing and validation requirements. The device system's sensor component, which is a single-use disposable device, is intended to be inserted under the patient's skin and remain there for up to six days. In addition to the sensor, the pump, transmitter, reservoir and infusion set also are sterile components. ISO 11137 provides baseline requirements for the electron beam sterilization process and validation used to sterilize all components provided as sterile, regardless of whether they are for single or multiple use. ISO 11607—Packaging for Terminally Sterilized Devices, ASTM D4169—Standard Practice for Performance Testing of Shipping Containers and Systems and ASTM D642-00—Standard Test Method for Determining Compressive Resultant of Shipping Containers, Components and Unit Loads were applied to sensor packaging. For the manufacturer to ensure baseline packaging and shipping requirements are met for this sterile, single-use device, these three standards were applied to validate the sensor is packaged for device sterilization and protection adequately. Packaging standards for device components provided sterile, as opposed to those provided non-sterile differ. IEC 62366:2014, discussed previously, helps analyze, specify, design, verify and validate the device's usability for safety. Finally, ISO 14155:2011 is applied in global APDS clinical investigation. ISO 13485 for quality systems and ISO 14971 for risk management also would apply.

Standards cited in the discussion above are not intended to be comprehensive. This case study is intended to demonstrate the breadth of standards applicable to a typical, complex, highest-risk IVD device system. Identifying, understanding and applying relevant standards may help the manufacturer's cross-functional team develop a device that eventually will meet regulatory requirements in the US and other countries.

Case Study: Use of Standards in Developing a Hypothetical Replacement Heart Valve

The replacement heart valve provides another case study of the application of both vertical and horizontal standards in developing a medical device. Heart valves are high-risk devices, Class III in the US and under the EU *MDD*.[25] Heart valves are in constant contact with the patient's blood and can cause death or serious injury if they fail. The widely publicized failures of the Shiley Heart Valve in the 1980s led to heightened awareness of valves by all stakeholders, including doctors and patients, regulators and manufacturers.[26] Concerns about the Shiley Heart Valve and other devices were factors in enacting the *Safe Medical Devices Amendment* of 1990.[27]

Replacement heart valves can be made of various materials. Mechanical heart valves usually consist of one or two tilting discs or "leaflets" operating inside a ring or housing. The discs often are made of ceramic, such as pyrolytic carbon; the housings also can be made of ceramic or a metal, such as titanium. Tissue heart valves use animal-derived tissue, such as bovine pericardium or an intact porcine valve. The tissue is treated during the manufacturing process, often with glutaraldahyde or a similar fixative. Most surgically-implanted valves also have a "sewing ring," often of polyester, to enable the surgeon to suture the prosthetic valve into the patient's native tissue annulus.

For this case study, however, assume the device manufacturer wants to incorporate the latest technological innovations. To treat patients at a high risk of complications in traditional open-heart surgery, the valve will be delivered via a catheter. The catheter will be introduced into the patient's groin, will pass through the femoral artery and up through the aorta. The valve then will be released from the catheter and fixed in place of the patient's native aortic valve. The valve itself will need to be flexible and compressible to be loaded onto a catheter. To avoid potential risks associated with tissues of animal origin, the manufacturer has decided to manufacture the valve housing and leaflets from a polymer material.

The manufacturer intends to offer this valve to patients worldwide and has developed a regulatory strategy to begin clinical studies in the US and then use those data to submit marketing applications in other regulated countries.[28]

The manufacturer will adhere to a rigid design control process that will include adequate periods of time to define user needs and develop design input leading to design output. Further, the manufacturer will schedule a series of design reviews to act as gating mechanisms throughout the development process. As certain milestones are reached during design and testing, these reviews will either confirm the design is meeting expectations and move activities into the next phase, or direct the design and development team to return to the previous phase for retesting or design revision. The development team will be expected to establish an overall protocol for verifying and validating the design, relying on state-of-the-art thinking about valves and the most appropriate available standards and guidance.

Because the manufacturer intends to study and market the valve first in the US, the development team should be knowledgeable about FDA expectations. FDA first published *Draft Guidance for Industry and FDA Staff, Heart Valves—Investigational Device Exemption (IDE) and Premarket Approval (PMA) Applications* in 1994. The guidance was revised and reissued in 2010. ISO first published ISO 5840 Cardiovascular implants—Cardiac valve prostheses in 1996.[29] The standard was revised in 2005 and reaffirmed in 2010. This standard has since been revised by ISO 5830-2:2015 Cardiovascular Implants—Cardiac Valve Prostheses—Part 2: Surgically Implanted Heart Valve Substitutes.

The manufacturer, then, would use guidance documents and standards in parallel in the development process. ISO 5840 provides an excellent outline of general requirements, even specifying design input, output and transfer, and risk management. The standard goes on to identify further general requirements, such as material property assessment, hydrodynamic performance assessment, structural performance assessment, etc., with some specific requirements defined in the annexes.

The FDA guidance provides more detail in some areas and is intended to be complimentary to ISO 5840. Specific requirements are identified for *in vitro* testing, including durability, fatigue, dynamic failure mode and cavitation. Similar levels of detail are provided for preclinical animal testing, along with specific recommendations on how to submit the data in IDE and PMA applications. As expected, the guidance provides a great deal of information about clinical testing, including objective performance criteria. Finally, there is a section on labeling. The appendices also provide a wealth of detail regarding shelf life, cavitation, verification of Bernoulli's principle and a protocol for echocardiographic assessment.

The sponsor would develop an overall testing protocol for the valve carefully, following the ISO standard and paying particular attention to the FDA guidance. Sponsors may elect to develop the protocols themselves or contract with third-party experts to develop the protocols or conduct testing. The manufacturer probably would want to consult with FDA prior to commencing lengthy and expensive testing to ensure the agency's expectations would be met. Note, FDA guidance even calls out the presubmission process to make sponsors aware of these options.[30]

The manufacturer would use not only the international standard and FDA's heart valve guidance but also look to a number of applicable horizontal standards. Because the heart valve is implantable and, further, because the manufacturer has elected to use a polymer, a material with limited usage in this application, the materials' biocompatibility will be of particular interest to the manufacturer and regulators. ISO 10993 provides biocompatibility testing requirements. The manufacturer also should consult FDA's draft guidance on the use of ISO 10993.[31]

Other horizontal standards would be necessary in the development process to help define requirements common to all implantable medical devices, e.g., symbols and labeling, packaging and sterilization. Other broad horizontal standards critical to any development process include ISO 14971 for risk management and the ISO 13485 or QSR for QMS.

Finally, because this hypothetical heart valve will be delivered by catheter, a specific part of the vertical standard, ISO 5840-3:2013 Cardiovascular Implants—Cardiac Valve Prostheses—Part 3: Heart Valve Substitutes Implanted by Transcatheter Techniques, defining operational conditions and performance requirements for the catheter delivery system must be applied.[32]

This case study illustrates, even though the device design output is innovative and incorporates features uncommon or even unavailable in some markets, the manufacturer and the development team have an available body of knowledge based on years of experience with replacement heart valves. Through the available horizontal standards, and especially the vertical standards and guidance, the manufacturer is able to identify FDA and other regulators' expectations. The manufacturer can develop an overall test protocol and even vet that protocol with FDA through the presubmission process. The sponsor can test the device and challenge the results through the manufacturer's own design assurance process. Through the appropriate and rigorous application of international standards and regulatory guidance, the manufacturer can establish the device's safety and effectiveness and provide valid scientific evidence to support PMA approval in the US and marketing approval in other countries.

How to Find Standards for a Medical Device

Several SDOs provide search engines to locate standards. Most standards must be purchased in electronic or paper form from the SDO's website. Many standards developers collaborate with re-sellers authorized to market the documents on their behalf.

In addition to visiting SDO websites, regulatory professionals may utilize one of many standards search engines. These search engines interface with specialized databases that aggregate all major developers' standards. One such search engines is the ANSI-based NSSN http://www.nssn.org/. When the key search term 'medical device' is entered, a list of device-relevant standard documents with associated titles and SDOs' names appears. Other search terms to be considered include the device's primary function and application, i.e., drug delivery, therapy, ablation.

Some regulatory authorities like FDA and bodies like the EC medical devices unit also have databases a manufacturer can search for recognized consensus standards applicable to the device being developed. For FDA, one helpful method is determining potential predicate(s) for the device under development and the corresponding FDA product code classification (e.g., DTC is the Pacemaker Generator Function Analyzer product code). FDA's database for recognized consensus standards can be searched to locate those associated with the same DTC product code. In this example, two recognized consensus standards appear: ISO 27185:2012 Cardiac Rhythm Management Devices—Symbols To Be Used With Cardiac Rhythm Management Device Labels and Information To Be Supplied—General Requirements; and ISO 27185 First Edition 2012-02-15 Cardiac Rhythm Management Devices—Symbols to be Used With Cardiac Rhythm Management Device Labels, and Information to be Supplied—General Requirements.

Note, this example also illustrates the importance of regulatory strategy. For many new technologies and potential medical devices, no clear predicate is on the market, but options exist for combining and choosing predicates. Because the associated consensus standards vary with each predicate, this search can determine the necessary effort to bring the product to market under various regulatory strategies.

Since clear product or process standards for a particular medical device may not exist, a regulatory professional may be unable to find specific relevant standards for a device. Typically, this situation would occur if the device utilizes a particularly novel technology and/or claims an especially innovative intended use. In such a case, standards may not be able to cover all aspects of the device under development. The earliest endovascular grafts utilized standards for surgically implanted grafts, intravascular catheters[33] and vascular stents.[34,35] Applicable sections of each of the separate standards were incorporated into design input for the new endovascular grafts. Similarly, some of the early catheter-delivered heart valves drew from standards established for surgically implanted valves and catheter delivery systems. Design teams need to be current on standards for all of their devices' design characteristics and draw broadly from standards that may even target a different device type.

For the EU (IMDRF for Australia, Japan, Singapore and Canada), the device's claimed intended use, purpose and primary intended mode of action must be identified first. MDD Essential Requirements (IMDRF Essential Principles) of safety and performance must be reviewed to identify those relevant to the particular device, the technologies it embodies and the processes by which it is to be manufactured.

A list of key words then can be generated to serve as key search terms for relevant standards using an SDO or service's (e.g., TechStreet or IHS Standards Store) standards search engine. The resulting standards' lists then can be examined for specific applicability and narrowed further per search terms.

A similar approach could be followed for the US, although FDA does not use the Essential Requirements model. For the US, the regulatory professional would begin by reviewing the US CFR to identify relevant regulations for the device. This review can be conducted using the database at http://www.ecfr.gov. FDA also encourages manufacturers to discuss plans to use standards or any specific issues relating to use of standards during a presubmission meeting.

Case Study: A Hypothetical Magnetic Needle and Suturing Thread Device

In this case, a regulatory professional is unable to locate relevant standards for a medical device easily. The manufacturer is developing a novel magnetic needle and suturing thread with a magnetic tip.[36] The search terms based on the claimed intended use, device's purpose, primary mode of action, Essential Requirements, technology and manufacturing processes could yield the following list:
- suture
- suturing
- surgical needle
- magnet
- magnetized instruments
- suture thread

Using these search terms, a list of standards is created:
- GME B 040 0367 Magnet Powder Paste
- BS 7507 Malleable Wires for Use as Sutures and Other Surgical Applications
- A-A-51410 Suture, Nonabsorbable, Surgical, Polypropylene, Monofilament, Single Armed

A review of these abstracts may eliminate certain nonapplicable standards. In this example, the Magnet Powder Paste standard would be eliminated because the magnet will not be in powder paste form. The remaining standards would be reviewed next. Reviewing the standards' texts is recommended to determine whether all or only certain clauses would apply to device development, evaluation and manufacturing, all critical global regulatory strategy elements.

It is important to remember a standard search is an iterative process dependent on the device development stage. A device in the conceptual or early development phase may change as new features, technologies, intended uses and/or purpose evolve. These changes, in turn, would affect the key search term list and resulting list of potential, applicable standards.

Case Study: A Hypothetical APDS With a Design Change

In this case, the manufacturer is developing a new and improved infusion pump for the hypothetical APDS device presented earlier in the chapter. The improvement is the introduction of a Bluetooth wireless communication device utilizing artificial intelligence in an MMA, allowing caretakers and healthcare providers to monitor basal insulin dosage delivery remotely. Key search terms now could include Bluetooth, wireless communication, software medical device and mobile medical device. Once a list of standards is generated, the manufacturer would examine the standards for relevance and select those matching its search criteria.

In this example, if the manufacturer intends to distribute the device in the US, FDA's presubmission process may be utilized to discuss a standard selection plan, any specific issues regarding the standards used relating to the specific design change, etc.

Finding Standards

This section examines a few additional scenarios where a regulatory professional may not find medical device standards easily. Examples include: a keyword search yielding an unreasonably long list of relevant standards; an existing standard no longer reflecting a particular medical device's state of the art; a standard currently being used changing in the middle of medical device development or regulatory review; subsequent revisions to existing standards used in the original device design process being incorporated retroactively in devices already in commercial distribution; and the standard used previously being revised and resulting in a device design change.

It is possible, even after examining the list of standards for specific applicability and narrowing it further, numerous standards appear relevant. One approach is to determine whether any of these standards overlap in any way or each addresses a set of unique topics. If one addresses performance requirements and another test methodologies, both would apply. If one addresses a set of topics (EN ISO 13485:2012) and another an adoption of the same topics for a different jurisdiction (CAN/CSA-ISO 13485:03), the one most-aligned with the target jurisdiction should be selected. Any standard on the list that is a recognized standard in any target jurisdiction should be identified. It is important the regulatory professional look for common and similar requirements applicable in various target jurisdictions. A gap analysis is recommended. The extent of commonality or differences would impact the overall regulatory strategy greatly.

If compliance with a standard's differences in any target jurisdiction leads to significant design and development changes and, therefore, increased time-to-market, the regulatory professional may recommend dropping the target jurisdiction.

A regulatory professional may find an existing standard no longer reflects a particular technology's state of the art. Typically, there is a lag between a new technology's introduction and its general acceptance as state of the art. It takes the user community and stakeholders several years to gain comprehensive knowledge of the technology, assess it and accept it until it can be formalized in a standard. If technology utilized in a device surpasses the standard, the manufacturer should assess the risk of incorporating it in a device under development. Factors to consider in this assessment include whether the perceived state of the art truly can become the new state of the art and benefits and downsides of using the state of the art compared to the existing standard's recommendations. If the existing standard also is a recognized standard in a certain jurisdiction, the manufacturer should be ready to explain why the device does not comply with that standard. Presumably, the justification explains how the new technology meets or exceeds the standard's intent.

A regulatory professional also may find a standard has changed while a device is under development or regulatory review. Before considering approaches, the regulatory professional should review the standards development process. SDOs release drafts for a comment period, address those comments and release the final version. Upcoming revisions to widely used standards generally are publicized by the SDO and industry through publications to make stakeholders aware of proposed upcoming changes. Since standards are subject to periodic review and revision, it is possible for a standard to evolve into a newer version in the middle of medical device development or regulatory review. If this occurs, the manufacturer should gather as much information as available on pending changes and determine whether there is a transition period for adopting the new revision and whether this is a recognized standard. This information can be used to determine the impact on the manufacturer's device development timeline and process. The manufacturer may choose from a few options:

1. Design to both the current standard and what the manufacturer understands will be the new revision, assuming provisional changes do not conflict and add significant, additional development time.
2. Design to the current standard if the manufacturer believes by doing so it can achieve quicker market access with the current device. The manufacturer then will modify its next-generation device to meet the new revision's changes. This option is recommended in instances when: a) there is uncertainty about the revision's release date; b) there is doubt the revision will become a recognized standard; or c) the adoption transition period is known and the adoption deadline falls after the next generation device's planned launch.
3. Design to the revised standard if the revision has been released already, the adoption transition period is known and occurs prior to the manufacturer's planned market approval and launch target dates.

It is important to note the adoption transition period for revised standards can vary from jurisdiction to jurisdiction, however, generally it is published by the SDO. One example is the known and expected transition period of 0 days between ISO 14971 and EN ISO 14971 in 2012. One caveat to revisions in the US is the revised version no longer may be recognized by a regulatory authority even if the previous version was an FDA-recognized standard.

A regulatory professional may learn a newer version of a previously utilized standard has been released after devices already are in production or commercial use. Whether subsequent revisions to existing standards used in the original device design process must be incorporated retroactively largely depends on the jurisdiction where the device currently is commercialized. In the US, FDA's Frequently Asked Questions on Recognition of Consensus Standards state changes in a recognized standard do not affect a product's clearance or approval status retroactively, so a revision is not required.

Finally, it also is possible a manufacturer that declared conformance to a previous standard needs to modify a device. For this scenario, the regulatory professional may assume the current revision is recognized by FDA. In determining whether to comply with all parts of the revised standard, consider FDA's current thinking:

"This depends on the effect that the modification has on the device's safety and effectiveness. If the device modification doesn't significantly affect safety and effectiveness, then the manufacturer should maintain records of the modifications and testing, in accordance with the Quality System regulation, and make them available to FDA investigators upon request during inspections… If the modifications significantly affect safety and effectiveness, then a new premarket submission is usually needed, as well as a new declaration of conformity, if the manufacturer decides to submit one. The new declaration of conformity would be for the revision recognized by FDA. As with the original declaration of conformity, it may not be necessary to comply with all parts of the revised standard(s), but the declaration of conformity should specify what parts of the revised standard(s) the device does not meet and explain any deviations."

This section addressed approaches to handling a few atypical situations where the regulatory professional cannot locate a set of relevant standards easily. In many situations, the regulatory professional may want to follow or become involved directly in the standards review or development process. In addition to being able to tackle atypical situations, there are several benefits to getting involved, which are discussed in the next section.

How to Get Involved

A medical device regulatory professional can become involved in the standards development or revision process by joining the working group in which he or she is most interested. The professional may start by exploring an SDO's website to understand various subcommittees', technical committees' or working groups' objectives and contacting the appropriate group. Generally, the group secretariat (lead) and local jurisdictional member organizations or members are posted on the SDO's website.

For example:
1. Enter "Medical Device" and other relevant terms in the search box online, e.g., http://www.iso.org/iso/home.htm.
2. Numerous standards supporting medical device products and processes will appear as search results. Select ISO 10993-1:2009 Biological Evaluation of Medical Devices—Part 1: Evaluation and Testing Within a Risk Management Process.
3. The next step is to select the link to TC/SC: ISO/TC 194.
4. Finally, select 'Contact details' to locate information for the TC/SC Secretariat and 'Participating Countries' for local country contact/s.

Even without being a member of a national standard committee or SDO technical committee, interested regulatory professionals may monitor developments and submit comments on draft standards, either directly or through industry associations. It is possible to join SDO email list services at no charge. As an example, steps for joining the ISO newsletter are:
1. Access http://www.iso.org/iso/home.html
2. Scroll down to "Keep up to date with ISO."
3. Select the subscribe button to enter contact information.

There are business advantages for manufacturers that invest resources in standards' development work. Having early access to information that could shape the market in the future and impact device development programs provides awareness of standards' development trends. Manufacturers can become involved by sharing experiences and expertise, and their interests potentially can be addressed by a standard under development or revision. Participation in voluntary working groups provides not only a way to add technical contributions to standards' development but also learn other contributors' concerns and discuss approaches to addressing those concerns.

Finally, if a US manufacturer believes it may benefit from submitting a standard for FDA recognition, it may review *Federal Register* Notice 63 FR 9531 of 25 February 1998 for specifications. A medical device manufacturer interested in proposing a standard for recognition would follow an established process, including submitting: the standard title, reference number, date and SDO; list of device types to which the standard would apply; and brief identification of the devices' testing, performance and/or any other characteristics that would be addressed by a declaration of conformity to that standard.

Summary

Standards, by definition, are documents established by consensus and approved by a recognized body. Medical device standards provide for common and repeated use, guidelines or characteristics for activities or their results, aimed at achieving the optimal degree of order. In the medical device global regulatory strategy context, standards are considered "norms" in some countries that must be followed during the conformity assessment process to meet regulatory Essential Requirements. Using standards confers a presumption of conformity with mandatory regulatory requirements of these countries. In other countries, standards, in the context of meeting regulatory requirements, are not standalone documents and must be applied in parallel with local regulations. Generally, standards developed by SDOs are voluntary and should be utilized in consultation with local laws and IMDRF guidelines.

References
1. IEC website. http://www.iec.ch/members_experts/refdocs/iec/isoiec-dir2%7Bed6.0%7Den.pdf. Accessed 23 March 2016.
2. *Radio Frequency Wireless Technology in Medical Devices—Guidance for Industry and Food and Drug Administration Staff.* FDA website. http://www.fda.gov/MedicalDevices/

DeviceRegulationandGuidance/GuidanceDocuments/ucm077210.htm. Accessed 23 March 2016.
3. *Principles of Conformity Assessment for Medical Devices, GHTF/SG1/N78:2012.* Global Harmonization Task Force. IMDRF website. http://www.imdrf.org/docs/ghtf/final/sg1/technical-docs/ghtf-sg1-n78-2012-conformity-assessment-medical-devices-121102.pdf. Accessed 23 March 2016.
4. Danish Standards Foundation website. http://www.ds.dk/da. Accessed 23 March 2016.
5. ISO Homepage. ISO website. http://www.iso.org/iso/home.html. Accessed 23 March 2016.
6. ISO Members. ISO website. http://www.iso.org/iso/home/about/iso_members.htm. Accessed 23 March 2016.
7. International Electrotechnical Commission website. http://www.iec.ch/. Accessed 23 March 2016.
8. CLSI Homepage. CLSI website. http://clsi.org/about-clsi/. Accessed 23 March 2016.
9. Ibid.
10. AHWP Homepage. AHWP website. http://www.ahwp.info/. Accessed 23 March 2016.
11. Representatives of Member Economies. AHWP website. http://www.ahwp.info/index.php?q=node/80. Accessed 23 March 2016.
12. Op cit 10.
13. Op cit 11.
14. GHTF Final Documents. IMDRF website. http://imdrf.org/documents/documents.asp#ghtf. Accessed 23 March 2016.
15. TGA Homepage. TGA website. http://www.tga.gov.au/. Accessed 23 March 2016.
16. Medical Devices—Quality Management Systems—Requirements for Regulatory Purposes, ISO 13485:2003, Section 0.1 General. ISO website. http://www.iso.org/iso/catalogue_detail?csnumber=36786. Accessed 23 March 2016.
17. *Quality System (QS) Regulation/Medical Device Good Manufacturing Practices.* FDA website. http://www.fda.gov/MedicalDevices/DeviceRegulationandGuidance/PostmarketRequirements/QualitySystemsRegulations/. Accessed 23 March 2016.
18. "What is the relationship between FDA's Quality System Regulation for Devices, Part 820 and ISO 9001: 2000?" FDA website. http://www.fda.gov/downloads/Medica...itySystemsRegulations/UCM134625.pdf. Accessed 23 March 2016.
19. Medical devices—Quality Management Systems—Requirements for Regulatory Purposes. EN ISO 14971:2012.
20. Medical Devices—Application of Usability Engineering to Medical Devices, IEC 62366:2014. ANSI website. http://webstore.ansi.org/RecordDetail.aspx?sku=IEC%2062366%20Ed.%201.1%20b:2014&source=google&adgroup=iec&gclid=CJi7n6Tv-MoCFdAWHwodh3QDVA. Accessed 23 March 2016.
21. Standards (Medical Devices). FDA website. http://www.fda.gov/MedicalDevices/DeviceRegulationandGuidance/Standards/default.htm. Accessed 23 March 2016.
22. CDRH Standard Operating Procedures for Identification of Candidate Consensus Standards for Recognition. FDA website. http://www.fda.gov/MedicalDevices/DeviceRegulationandGuidance/GuidanceDocuments/ucm077307.htm. Accessed 23 March 2016.
23. *Guidance for Industry and Food and Drug Administration Staff. Frequently Asked Questions on Recognition of Consensus Standards.* FDA website. http://www.fda.gov/MedicalDevices/DeviceRegulationandGuidance/GuidanceDocuments/ucm074973.htm. Accessed 23 March 2016.
24. *Use of International Standard ISO-10993, "Biological Evaluation of Medical Devices Part 1: Evaluation and Testing" (Replaces #G87-1 #8294) (blue book memo)(Text Only).* FDA website. http://www.fda.gov/MedicalDevices/DeviceRegulationandGuidance/GuidanceDocuments/ucm080735.htm. Accessed 23 March 2016.
25. Code of Federal Regulations, Title 21, Part 870, Subpart D, Sec. 870.3925, Replacement heart valve. FDA website. https://www.accessdata.fda.gov/scripts/cdrh/cfdocs/cfcfr/cfrsearch.cfm?fr=870.3925. Accessed 23 March 2016.
26. The Bjork-Shiley Convexo-Concave Heart Valve was removed from the US market in November 1986. See also Bjork-Shiley Heart Valve Recall. *Major Recalls of Organ Replacement Devices.* Brown University website. http://biomed.brown.edu/Courses/BI108/BI108_2007_Groups/group05/pages/bjork_shiley.html. Accessed 23 March 2016.
27. Samuel FE Jr. *Safe Medical Devices Act of 1990. Health Affairs*, 10, no.1 (1991):192–195. Health Affairs website. http://content.healthaffairs.org/content/10/1/192.short. Accessed 23 March 2016.
28. *Investigational Device Exemptions (IDE's) for Early Feasibility Medical Device Clinical Studies, Including First in Human (FIH) Studies, Guidance for Industry and Food and Drug Administration Staff,* Document issued 1 October 2013. FDA website. http://www.fda.gov/downloads/medicaldevices/deviceregulationandguidance/guidancedocuments/ucm279103.pdf. Accessed 23 March 2016.
29. Cardiovascular implants—Cardiac Valve Prostheses. ANSI/AAMI/ISO 5840:2005/(R)2010. ANSI website. http://webstore.ansi.org/RecordDetail.aspx?sku=ANSI%2FAAMI%2FISO+5840%3A2005+(R2010). Accessed 23 March 2016.
30. Requests for Feedback on Medical Device Submissions: The Pre-Submission Program and Meetings with Food and Drug Administration Staff: Guidance for Industry and Food and Drug Administration Staff. FDA Website. http://www.fda.gov/downloads/MedicalDevices/DeviceRegulationandGuidance/GuidanceDocuments/UCM311176.pdf. Accessed 23 March 2016.
31. *Use of International Standard ISO-10993, "Biological Evaluation of Medical Devices Part 1: Evaluation and Testing."* Draft document issued 23 April 2013. FDA website. http://www.fda.gov/downloads/medicaldevices/deviceregulationandguidance/guidancedocuments/ucm348890.pdf. Accessed 23 March 2016.
32. ISO 5840-3:2013—Cardiac valve prostheses—Part 3: Heart valve substitutes implanted by transcatheter techniques. ISO website. http://www.iso.org/iso/catalogue_detail.htm?csnumber=51313. Accessed 14 February 2016.
33. ISO 10555-4:1996—Sterile, single-use intravascular catheters—Part 4: Balloon dilatation catheters. ISO website. http://www.iso.org/iso/catalogue_detail.htm?csnumber=19056. Accessed 23 March 2016.
34. ISO 25539-2:2008—Cardiovascular implants—Endovascular devices—Part 2: Vascular stents. ISO website. http://www.iso.org/iso/iso_catalogue/catalogue_ics/catalogue_detail_ics.htm?csnumber=35887. Accessed 23 March 2016.
35. "FDA Insights: The ISO Standard for Endovascular Grafts." EndoVascular Today website. http://evtoday.com/2003/08/0703_131.html/. Accessed 23 March 2016.
36. "Magnetic Needle Tackles Suturing in Challenging Surgical Fields." Boston Children's Hospital website. http://vector.childrenshospital.org/2014/10/magnetic-needle-tackles-suturing-in-challenging-surgical-fields/. Accessed 23 March 2016.

16 Global Medical Device Marketing Strategy

By Maria Shepherd, MBA

Introduction

It is critical for a company selling medical devices to have an executive business strategy updated on an annual basis. From the onset of all projects, it is essential to ensure close integration between the marketing and regulatory strategies. Failure to understand the impact of regulatory requirements supporting the executive strategy places the entire plan at risk and can result in unnecessary expense, costly delays or failure to obtain approval.

Global Executive Strategy Development for Medical Device Companies

A medical device company's executive team selects its global strategy based on the company's target disease state and medical condition, focus and technological competency. For example, cardiovascular (CV) disease is a very broad disease state and CV medtech companies may specialize in one or more selected areas of CV treatment or therapy segments. For example, interventional cardiology is focused on the treatment of coronary vascular obstructions (stents, balloons). Electrophysiology devices are used to treat another CV disease state, conductive aberrations in the heart (ablations, pacemakers, etc.) or body; these devices may be diagnostic or interventional. Structural heart disease includes congenital cardiac defects or those caused by abnormalities of the valves and vessels (aortic valve implants, PFO closure devices). Each of these medical conditions is strategically different and requires a different medical device executive team planning process. This results from the difference in call points, technologies and treatments, service expectations from physicians and hospitals, and even the general personality of the medical specialty's physicians. Although making broad generalizations about physician personalities risks stereotyping, some truisms emerge. For example, electrophysiologists, in general, are considered highly scientific doctors who are slow to adopt new technologies. Interventional cardiologists, in general, are perceived as risk takers who are faster to adopt new technologies in treating CV disease than their other medical specialty peers.

A large medical device company could have a broad CV disease state base to address, while smaller CV companies may have only one or two. Once the disease state and corresponding technologies are selected, the executive team defines strategy further based on company shareholder and stakeholder returns. There are four basic categories of products from which to select—existing product portfolio, new products, products or services for adjacent markets or whitespace research (advanced technologies very early in the planning stage)—each requiring a different strategy. In some cases, the executive team will select a mix of product types to support the company's growth and profitability goals (**Table 16-1**). This chapter examines regulatory and business strategies for the two most common categories: the existing product portfolio and new products.

Table 16-1. Example of a CV Medical Device Company Product Development Matrix

Product Category	Examples of Products in the CV Space	Comments
Existing Product Portfolio	Angioplasty Balloons, Drug-Eluting Stents	Currently commercialized products
New Products	Bioresorbable stents	Product development complete or close to completion. When product is ready for commercialization, an additional investment in market development may be required to support the product launch.
Products for Adjacent Markets	Wireless monitoring of patients post-procedure	Adjacent markets are a distinct market or set of customers similar to the medical device firm's currently served markets sharing similar needs or business processes.
Whitespace (Advanced Technologies)	Coronary Artery Regeneration Technologies	Product development is in the early planning or concept development process. Expected to be commercialized in the next five to 20 years.

Global Marketing Support and Analysis for Executive Strategy Decision Making

The executive management team needs the marketing department to provide a global market assessment to identify which global regions have the disease state and are commercially viable sales targets. This allows the executive team to select geographic regions offering the best opportunity. Opportunity is assessed by analyzing:

- total opportunity (global market size by country/region, segmentation)
- addressable opportunity
  o In which market segments does the continuum of care fit well with the selected products?
  o Does reimbursement exist for selected products?
    - How large is the estimated population segment that can afford to use the selected product, if it is not reimbursed?
    - If required, what is the required reimbursement timeline/process?
  o What percentage of the population has geographic access to healthcare centers with the selected products and technology?
  o Do infrastructure, procedure rates and physician counts all support the selected product's use?
- What are the five-year financial projections by market, return on investment (ROI) and forecast?
- What competition is there (direct and indirect), and what are competitors' strengths and weaknesses?
- What is the product purchasing infrastructure, e.g., Group Purchasing Organizations (GPOs) and tenders?
- Does the political, economic, social and technological factor (PEST) analysis show any red flags?
- What are the market drivers? Have market barriers been identified and are there recommended mitigation strategies?
- What pricing will the market bear?

Critically important is a market segment analysis where delivery of care is different from US and European markets. In the planning process, these markets can be assessed to understand healthcare infrastructure, clinical workflow and unmet needs by region and/or county. Market research and human factors usability testing can inform these analyses to highlight continuum of care differences. Will existing products fit with the country's care delivery, or are new products and technologies required to enter this market?

Regional Strategy Development

Once the executive team has narrowed the target region and countries with the best product fit and overall company opportunity, each target region or country's market drivers and barriers to entry should be analyzed. The marketing team works with other company departments to develop function-specific information. Because the regulatory process typically is one of the largest barriers to entry in any given country, it is critical to involve the regulatory team at this point. As a team, the group determines the device's claimed intended use(s). This is critical in determining whether the product or product line is regulated as a "medical device," its regulatory classification, clinical evidence required for regulatory approval, device labelling and the regulatory pathway. The regulatory team informs this strategic process by ensuring the team complies with all regulations and laws and advises on the regulatory aspects and climate that will affect commercialization activities.

From a regulatory perspective, the regional strategy identifies:

- How does the regulatory environment in specific target regions or countries impact ROI?
    - What is the overall regulatory timeline?
    - What is the product's age?
        - Have regulatory requirements at time of initial approval in the targeted country changed compared to current requirements?
        - Do technical files need to be updated and at what cost?
    - Do favorable regulatory timelines for local medical device companies versus those for multinational companies create a competitive disadvantage?
    - Is there or will there be increased demand for clinical and safety data?
        - Will the regulatory authority accept data from clinical trials conducted in other countries, or will local clinical trials be required?
        - If acceptable, are the foreign clinical data consistent with existing clinical practices in target countries?
        - Are existing clinical data applicable to the target country population?
        - Are there any ethnic or continuum of care differences to consider?
    - What is the cost of sustaining registrations and required updates to technical files?
    - What resources are required to support new product registrations?
    - What is the device classification in the market?
    - How do claims and indications and the ability to differentiate the product vary by market?
    - Should the company outsource the regulatory process to local agents to enhance expertise and provide focus?
    - Are there local market regulatory representation requirements?
    - Does the team understand the scope and number of documents required for a device registration application submissions?
    - What are device labeling and translation requirements?
    - Is the product launch roadmap aligned with the target country or region's regulatory compliance steps?
    - What are the market's postmarket surveillance and vigilance requirements?

Segmentation and Classification of Regional High-to-Low Regulatory Barriers

Once all these questions have been answered, the next step is to segment and classify regulatory barriers to entry by selected target countries. The goal is to understand the high-to-low regulatory cost per market estimates to calculate true ROI. At this stage, collaboration between regulatory and the marketing team is essential to support a comprehensive and viable global executive strategy.

- Are in-country clinical trials required?
- What government and political hurdles exist?
    - What are possible regulatory mitigation strategies and their associated costs?
    - Are in-country manufacturing sites or offices required?
    - What type of patient safety data are required?
    - What are the estimated clearance timelines for product launch?
    - What resources are required to bring technical files up to date to meet local market standards?
- Are products existing, new, adjacent? (**See Table 16-1**)
    - What regulatory requirements must be met for each product type?

Prioritizing Segmented Targets for New and Existing Products

When a medical device company's executive management decides a new product meets the needs of the continuum of care in the selected countries, launch plans can be prioritized by selecting the countries with the lowest regulatory hurdles for new products. Selecting countries with the highest level of opportunity and the lowest barriers to entry is one of the most important business decisions the executive team can make.

Figure 16-1. Estimated Cost of Medical Device Regulatory Approval by Country

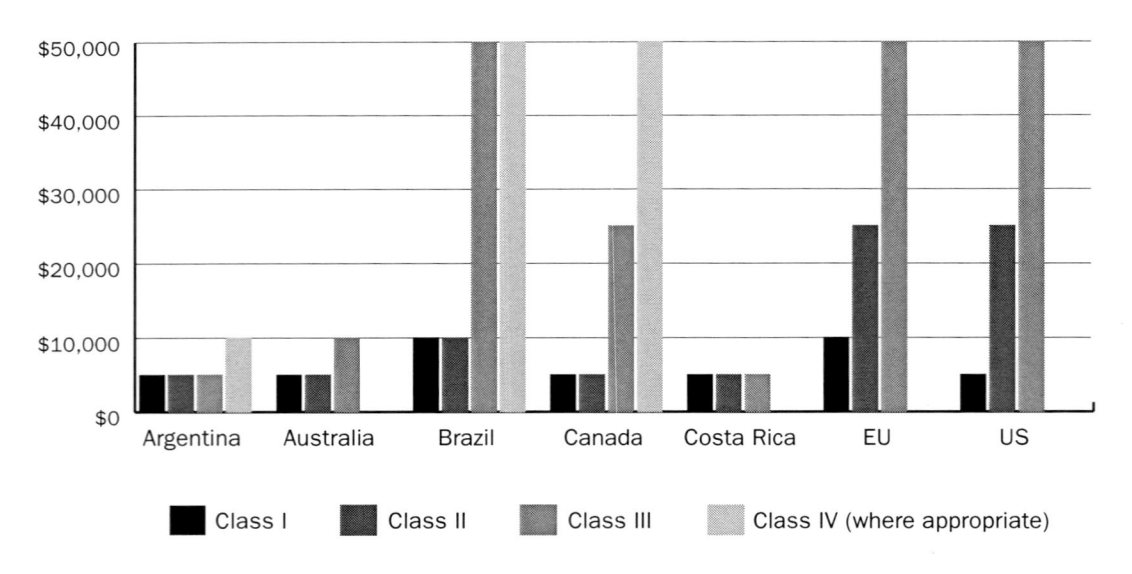

■ Class I   ■ Class II   ■ Class III   ■ Class IV (where appropriate)

Overall Cost of Gaining Regulatory Approval[1]

Calculating the cost of obtaining regulatory approval is a critical factor in estimating a medical device's ROI when gaining approval on a country-by-country basis. One company, Emergo Group,[2] has assessed the cost of gaining approval in selected countries. In this assessment, summarized in **Figure 16-1**, regulatory costs by country include registration application fees, product testing, in-country representation, submission preparation, consulting and registration document translation (not including IFU). This does not include the cost of implementing, auditing or updating a quality management system compliant with US 21 CFR Part 820 and/or international standard ISO 13485. Local clinical trials, if required to gain regulatory approval, will add to this cost. Emergo estimated the cost of gaining regulatory approval as:

- Low=Less than $5,000 (US)
- Midpoint=$15,000-$30,000
- High=More than $50,000

To summarize the data and to plot the costs in **Figure 16-1**, the midpoint costs have been defined further as:

- Low—$5,000
- Low to midpoint—$10,000
- Midpoint—$25,000
- High—$50,000 or more

The cost for EU in vitro diagnostic kits[3] is estimated to be:

- General—$5,000
- Self-testing—$25,000
- List A or B[4] (Annex ll)—$50,000 or more

Countries With Low Regulatory Barriers

Countries with low regulatory barriers today include, among others, Israel, Chile and Paraguay. According to Emergo,[5] Chile's medical device regulatory system is evolving to develop regulations closer to those found in the US, Canada and Europe. In a recent global report, *Medical Technology Score Card*,[6] medical device executive respondents ranked Israel a global first in overall ease of regulatory approval. Israel has a population of almost 8 million people[7] and a recognized commitment to GCP, making it an important clinical trial destination. Patient enrollment rates are good, with few participants lost to follow-up. In 2014, 6,772 clinical trials (20.2%) were registered in Israel, of a total of 33,430[8] clinical trials registered around the world. Clinical studies in Israel can be fast-tracked so final device approval is under the authorization of the medical institution's director,[9] saving time and money in the clinical trials process.

Countries With High Regulatory Barriers

Countries with high regulatory barriers include, among others, the US, China, India and Brazil. For example, in China, the China Food and Drug Administration (CFDA) review of Class III devices can take 12–18 months, and the entire registration process can take as long as 36 months (not including clinical trials).[10] By

Table 16-2. Country-Specific Information from the Handbook of Pharma and MedTech Compliance

Asia-Pacific	Europe & Eastern Europe	Latin & South America	North America
Australia	Austria	Argentina	Canada
China	Belgium	Brazil	US
Hong Kong	Czech Republic	Chile	
India	France	Colombia	
Japan	Germany	Mexico	
Malaysia	Hungary	Venezuela	
Philippines	Italy		
Singapore	Spain		
Russia	United Kingdom		
Taiwan			
Thailand			
Ukraine			
Vietnam			

comparison, European medical device review times are estimated to be 3.4 months,[11] a much shorter regulatory review time than China's.

Pending Changes in EU Approval Requirements and Times

EU review times may change based on pending legislation.[12] In 2012, the European Commission issued a draft of the new European medical device regulations. This change is based, in part, on such abuses of the EU system as the French Poly Implant Prothèse breast implant scandal,[13] where the manufacturer switched from medical-grade to industrial-grade silicone, causing implant rupture and numerous significant adverse events. The new regulations are designed to prevent these abuses from recurring in the future. Medical device experts warn the new EU regulations could increase costs and diminish the more-rapid European access to medical device technology innovation patients currently receive compared to the US and other high regulatory barrier countries.[14] After three years of intense deliberation on the modernization of EU medical devices and IVD rules, the Council of Ministers of the EU countries approved a full General Approach on the review of the medical devices and IVD frameworks.[15,16] The new EU regulations are the most comprehensive changes to medical device regulations in Europe in more than 20 years.

Global Advertising and Promotion Regulations

When planning international medical device marketing campaigns, medtech companies must observe all applicable laws in each individual country. Legal and regulatory requirements for the interaction of healthcare providers and the medtech industry differ substantially in various regions and by country within those regions. One major dissimilarity: in some countries, governing authorities require medical device and diagnostic kit regulatory approval before specific marketing and advertising programs can begin. In others, regulatory assessments are applied after marketing and advertising campaigns have been launched.

Country-by-country regulatory and compliance evaluation of advertising and promotion practices can be complex for transnational medtech companies. A routine part of compliance in the US is the open payments database, also known at the *Sunshine Act*. The *Sunshine Act* requires medical device manufacturers to report payments given to physicians and hospitals, and any investments physicians or their immediate family members have in the company. Reports are annual and are posted on a public website. Information posted includes physician:

- speaker engagements or other promotional activities
- travel expenses, meals
- entertainment
- gifts

Table 16-3. High-Level Marketing and Advertising Information for Countries in Asia-Pacific

	Advertising DTC	Advertising HCP	Samples	Value of Gifts	Entertainment (events)	Hospitality	MedEd	Grants	Conferences	Consulting
Australia	Yes	Yes	Sample Packs (Medtech)	<AUD 100	No	Educational context	Must have Educational Value	Credible Organizations	Credible Venue	Credible Value
China	Requires Approval	Requires Approval	Modest value	<RMB 200	In Business Context	Reasonable	No	NI	Credible Venue	Credible Value
Hong Kong	NI	NI	Sample Packs with labeling	Officers only <HLD 250	No	B, L < HKD 400, D <HLD 700	Need permission: employer	Credible Value	Credible Venue	Credible Value
India	Mostly prohibited	Ni	Limited in number	No	No	No	Conditional if training is in India	Publically approved facilities, may require publishing	Reasonable fees for speakers	Requires disclosure
Japan	Conditional[a]	Allowed, but not to general public	Limited in number	<JPY 3000-5000	In business context	<JPY 20000	Must have Educational Value	Credible Value	Seminars cannot be product specific	Credible Value
Malaysia	Disease-specific prohibitions	Current information preferred	< MYR 500	<MYR 100	Allowed as "Kind Discounts" but limited	Educational context	< MYR 1000 Educational Materials	Credible Value, transparent	Honoraria MYR 1000 – 2000/day	Credible Value, must be a written contract
Philippines	Prohibited	Allowed, but not to general public	Donated to medical institution, not to MDs	<PHP 1000 - 1500	Prohibited for public officials	Educational context	Must have Educational Value	Credible Value	Credible Venue Speaker travel/housing	Credible Venue
Singapore	Cannot state intended use without HSA submission	May require permit fees SGD 100-300 – not allowed to public	Allowed	<SGD 20-200, depending upon occasion	In business context – strictly regulated	<SGD 20-100 in an educational context	Must have Educational Value	Credible Value	Credible Venue Speaker- reasonable expenses/ honoraria	Credible value, requires disclosure
Russia	Unclear	Allowed but not to general public	Not allowed	Not allowed	Not allowed	Not allowed	Credible Venue, highly regulated	Credible Value	Not allowed	Credible Venue, highly regulated
Taiwan	Not allowed	PAL approval	Sample Packs (Medtech)	<TWD 500-3000, based on social norms	In business context	Not approved unless meets social norms	<TWD 5000/hour	Credible Value with disclosure	Credible Venue	Credible value, requires disclosure
Thailand	Unclear	Require approval from Thai FDA	Unclear							Credible Value
Vietnam	Generally not allowed	Unclear	< VND 500,000	Unclear		Reasonable		Unclear		Written pre-approval from manager, written contract

a. The Japan Federation of Medical Devices Associations. The Promotion Code of the Medical Devices Industry. JFMDA website. http://www.jfmda.gr.jp/e/promotioncode/03_en.html. Accessed 19 March 2016.

- educational materials: books, journal subscriptions or reprints
- medical advisory board compensation

There are significant consequences and legal actions in response to inappropriate marketing and advertising campaigns. Many countries employ healthcare providers through a public system, and anti-bribery laws, both in-country and in a company's home country, must be considered seriously. Almost all countries have strict rules to ban unethical behavior in the medical products industry and in-country healthcare providers. **Tables 16-2–5** reflect regulatory information on ethical business interactions between medical companies and healthcare providers worldwide. Every effort has been made to find information for all 196 countries in the world,[16] but in many cases, the data were difficult to find, interpret or collate. It is important to note the information in **Tables 16-2–5** on

Table 16-4. High-Level Marketing and Advertising Information for Countries in Europe

	Advertising DTC	Advertising HCP	Samples	Value of Gifts	Entertainment (events)	Hospitality	MedEd	Grants	Conferences	Consulting
Austria[a]	Prohibited	NI	Sample pack, labeling required	<€70	NI	<€70	Need institution approval, credible value	Credible Value, written contract	Credible Venue/ Value	Credible Value, disclosure, written contract
Belgium	Prohibited	NI	Requires written request by HCP	Low value	Credible Value	Authorized by MDEON[b]	Credible Value	Credible Value, written contract	Credible Venue/ Value, Need institution approval	Credible Value, disclosure, written contract MDEON filing
Czech Republic	Allowed, standards apply	Allowed, standards apply	Sample pack, labeling required	<CZK1500	Credible Value	Allowed, standards apply	Credible Value	Need institution approval, credible value, written contract	Credible Venue/ Value	Credible Value
France	Low-risk products only[c]	Allowed, high-risk products require approval: Medicines Agency	As per the Bertrand Law[d]						
Germany	Prohibited	Allowed, requires approval	Sample pack, labeling required	<€1	Prohibited	Credible Value	Credible Value	Need institution approval, credible value, written contract	Credible Value, standards apply	Credible Value, standards apply, written contract
Hungary	Prohibited	Allowed, standards apply	Sample pack, Maximum units=2	<HUF 4650	Unclear	<HUF 4650	Need institution approval, credible value	Need institution approval, credible value, written contract	Credible Value, standards apply	Credible Value, standards apply, written contract
Italy	Prohibited	Allowed, standards apply	Requires written request by HCP	Prohibited	Allowed if balanced	Allowed, standards apply	Encouraged	With institutions only	Credible Value	Credible Value, standards apply, written contract
Spain	Prohibited	Allowed, standards apply	Limited, labeled, authorized, written request	<€10-30	Unclear	Moderate, balanced	Need institution approval, credible value	Need institution approval, credible value	Credible Value, standards apply	Credible Value, written contract
UK	Unclear	Allowed, standards apply	Limited standards apply	<£6-25, standards apply	Credible Value, balanced	Credible Value	Credible Value	Need institution approval, credible value	Credible Value, standards apply, disclosure	Credible Value, institution approval

a. AustroMed website. www.austromed.org/. Accessed 19 March 2016.
b. Mdeon website. www.mdeon.be; Fédération belge de l'industrie des technologies médicales website. www.unamec.be//. Accessed 19 March 2016.
c. "France—A Revolution for the Medical Devices Industry." Covington and Burling website. New Advertising Rules http://www.cov.com/files/Publication/ef0a84c7-e9a0-4fc9-b35d-082d49629c97/Presentation/PublicationAttachment/0b887bd1-083f-4275-94ab-0c2c7da30047/France-A_Revolution_for_the_Medical_Devices_Industry.pdf. Accessed 19 March 2016.
d. "Physician Payment Sunshine: French Sunshine Act and Disclosure Rules for European Countries." Policy and Medicine website. http://www.policymed.com/2012/05/physician-payment-sunshine-french-sunshine-act-and-disclosure-rules-for-european-countries.html/. Accessed 19 March 2016.

global advertising and promotion regulations should be used for reference purposes only. The regulations in many countries are changing rapidly, and medtech professionals are strongly advised to seek specific and current information before engaging in marketing activities.

The US and EU[17]

The presentation, *Legal Implications & Compliance in the Sales & Marketing of Medical Devices in Europe*,[18] discusses a fragmented EU legal framework with low medical device advertising and promotion harmonization. The medical

Table 16-5. High-Level Marketing and Advertising Information for Countries in Latin America and South America

	Advertising DTC	Advertising HCP	Samples	Value of Gifts	Entertainment (events)	Hospitality	MedEd	Grants	Conferences	Consulting
Argentina	Prohibited	Allowed, standards apply	Allowed	Not permitted to public officials	Not allowed	Not permitted to public officials	Requires public invitation and selection criteria	Unclear	Credible value	Credible value, not permitted to public officials
Brazil	Prohibited	Allowed, standards apply	Sample pack	Low value, traceability	Unclear	Credible value, disclosure	Credible value credible venue	Credible value, written contract	Credible value, disclosure	Credible value, written contract
Chile	Unclear	Allowed, standards apply	Unclear	Low value	Unclear	Unclear	Unclear	Unclear	Credible value, recognized academic organization	Unclear
Colombia	Allowed, standards apply	Allowed, standards apply (scientific publications)	Unclear							
Mexico	Unclear	Allowed, standards apply (appropriate media)	Low value, traceability	Credible value—public officials <GBP30	Credible value—public officials <GBP30	Credible value	Credible value	Unclear	Credible value	Credible value—public officials <GBP30
Venezuela	Unclear	Allowed, standards apply	Unclear	Low value	Unclear	Credible value	Credible value	Unclear	Credible value	Credible value, standards apply

device organization, Eucomed, promotes self-regulation to its membership, and the *Eucomed Code of Business Practice*[19] notes "Members should ensure that all promotional presentations, including product claims and comparisons, are accurate, balanced, fair, objective and unambiguous. They should be justified by appropriate evidence."

Another resource, *Comparison of the AdvaMed Code of Ethics and the Eucomed Code of Business Practice*,[20] compares specific practices in the EU and the US and covers:
- company-conducted product training and education
- supporting third-party educational conferences
- sales, promotional and other business meetings
- consulting arrangements with healthcare professionals
- provisions on royalty payments
- entertainment and recreation
- modest meals associated with healthcare professional business interactions
- educational items, gifts
- provision of coverage, reimbursement and health economics information
- research and educational grants and charitable donations
- evaluation products and demo products

The *Handbook of Pharma and MedTech Compliance*[21] has useful information on promoting medical device products in various EU countries (**see Table 16-2**). **Tables 16-3–5** include continent-specific information with high-level medical device advertising and promotion regulation summaries by country.

The remainder of this chapter gives extensive and detailed information many regulatory professionals need to know. While in some cases regulatory personnel may not be responsible for compliance in these areas, regulatory vice presidents or directors often are responsible for monitoring compliance. This is especially true in small companies, where regulatory personnel are becoming more responsible for compliance.

Abbreviations and Disclaimers

All information presented below is referenced to its origin and has been taken from websites considered credible. When data are available, the information has been cross-checked to a second source.
- DTC—direct-to-consumer
- sample packs—generally smaller than retail packages, compliant labeling includes "not for resale," traceability required
- NI—no information

- standards apply—used when specific criteria too lengthy to note in a table are referenced; this detail is available online[22]
- balanced—when industry supplies travel, accommodations or registration fees, they must be moderate and subordinate to the meeting's main purpose, i.e., the ratio of entertainment to work-related activities must be low

DTC Advertising—Pharmaceutical Trends in Europe

DTC advertising best practices are important for regulatory vice presidents, directors or personnel in small companies responsible for compliance.

Medtech manufacturers can learn many DTC advertising best practices from pharmaceutical companies. Proponents believe DTC advertising provides valuable information to patients and makes them aware of new medical products' advantages and disadvantages. In addition, advocates believe DTC advertising can increase patient compliance with physician-based treatment programs.

DTC advertising scrutiny is growing, as demonstrated in the EU guidance published 10 December 2008.[23] In this guidance, the EU Commission stated its goal to provide a report on the benefits and risks of allowing information to be distributed via the Internet to the general public. European regulations place rigorous restrictions on using medical product names in patient awareness programs. DTC advertising is limited to educational and nonpromotional disease awareness campaigns that do not refer to the product or therapeutic class. If approved, European DTC advertising is not expected to adopt the highly branded US approach.[24] For example, in France, DTC advertising of nonprescription medical products is permissible only if purchasers are not reimbursed by the social security system. In Spain, DTC advertising is allowed only for products that treat minor symptoms.

The Future of DTC Advertising in Europe

European medical companies are realizing DTC advertising, in addition to increasing patient awareness, can demonstrate credibility and gain branding recognition to increase market share. This is important for regulatory vice presidents, directors or personnel in small companies responsible for compliance. European DTC advertising is expected to move from a short-term emphasis on advertising to strategic marketing programs focused on improving patient outcomes and creating high-level value to balance commercial benefit and social obligations. The most recent data available on European pharmaceutical DTC advertising spending is from 2004, when the total European pharmaceutical company nonbranded DTC advertising expenditure was estimated to be $85 million (US), and was projected to grow at a compound annual growth rate of 42%, to reach $345.5 million by 2008.[25] A relatively high percentage of European pharmaceutical advertising is targeted to the UK and German segments, where many global pharmaceutical manufacturing centers are located. In 2004, about 35% of the total European pharmaceutical DTC advertising expenditure was in the UK, with 25% in Germany and about 20% in France. Spain and Italy had much lower levels of DTC advertising expenditures, accounting for 6% and 4%, respectively.[26]

This is a controversial topic in Europe. Since 2009, there have been initiatives by the European Parliament to improve patient access to information on prescription medications, in the face of opposition concerned this will lead to DTC advertising. Opponents state DTC bypasses the healthcare professional in Europe and is an inappropriate method for pharmaceutical companies to communicate with patients.

KOL Development and Regulatory Compliance

It is vital to a medical device company's health to develop relationships with important medical thought leaders. In-country key opinion leaders (KOLs) provide critical support to medical device company executive management and marketing in building business strategy. Ideally, KOLs selected in the target country should include those with expertise to inform on marketing, regulatory, reimbursement and clinical trial strategies and help mitigate barriers to entry in the approval and commercialization process. This is important for regulatory vice presidents, directors and personnel in small companies responsible for compliance. Over the past few years, KOL relationships have faced increased scrutiny. New regulations like the *Sunshine Act*[27] call for more transparency around physician payments. These regulations create the need for new approaches to thought leader management through metrics to balance legitimate KOL business expenses and mandates like the *Sunshine Act*, the International Medical Device Manufacturers Association Code of Ethical Conduct (IMEDA) guidelines[28] and the *Eucomed Medical Technology Guidelines on Interactions with Healthcare Professionals.*[29]

Human Factors Usability Testing

Medical device human factors engineering is a scientific discipline informing global product commercialization and regulatory strategy by assessing how a selected medical device fits with global user segments. Human factors engineering studies how clinicians and patients interact with medical products and systems and focuses on ensuring medical devices, products and systems are safe, effective and usable. Superior usability can be a competitive advantage and ease-of-use is a top priority for most clinicians.[30] Usability testing is the human factors engineering arm that assesses a medical device design's usability and risk and mitigations applied by the design team. FDA has guidance on human factors assessments in medical device design validation.[31] Human factors engineering also should be considered in pre- and post-marketing risk assessments.

Marketing can assist the commercialization team by identifying medical device user segments and these segments' needs and fit with the company strategy. They can advise the regulatory or quality team on how to create a usability testing end user profile, the number of users (in the cases where there is more than one product user) and use environments. When considering the use environment, the marketing team can provide valuable information on competitor and legacy systems in terms of the targeted country's established gold performance standards. Understanding the use environment is critical to choosing products with the best overall potential to be commercialized in the target country. This will help create a baseline of questions and assumptions to be validated with in-country experts and KOLs and assist the regulatory team in assessing the future regulatory approval cost and its impact on ROI by country.

Market Research, Regulatory Compliance and Cost Assessment

Market research, using such tools as observational research, focus groups and user interviews, is a critical step in understanding workflow and target countries' continuum of care. This is important for regulatory vice presidents, directors and personnel in small companies responsible for compliance, to ensure the company is meeting the legitimate market research guidelines to support the company's commercial goals. In addition, the regulatory team can participate proactively in early-stage market research and usability testing to understand whether there is good fit between the product and the target country's gold standard of use. This helps create a baseline of questions and assumptions that can be validated with in-country experts and KOLs, to assist the regulatory team in assessing regulatory approval's cost and its impact on ROI by country.

Distribution and In-Country Partner Search and Selection

In some areas of the world, medical device distributors also provide access to regulatory services. Proper evaluation and due diligence of new distributors and their competencies is an essential first step for global commercialization. Choosing the wrong distributor can lead to sales loss, poor relationships with KOLs and other healthcare decision makers and delays in regulatory approval that may be expensive and overwhelm the company regulatory team's capacity.

The first step in profiling distribution partners is to ensure they meet the medical device company's partnership needs. Most important, does the distribution partner have product category experience? If they promise regulatory services, what prior experience can they disclose to assist in product approval? Do they understand the device's complexity and, if appropriate, what is their experience with new or advanced technology? References should be checked and distribution partners interviewed to learn details on how they intend to launch the product and get it approved and on the market as quickly and profitably as possible. Medical device regulations and general commercial law should be reviewed to determine which party—the manufacturer or distributor—"owns" any required device registrations or marketing authorizations. Failure to do so may complicate future changes in a manufacturer's direct in-country affiliate or subsidiary's distribution partners and/or establishment significantly.

When conducting due diligence, and the distribution partner choice has been narrowed to a few, the distributor and medical device company should identify a strategy framework together. The strategy framework should include a target market overview, new technology adoption rates, competitor assessments, KOL profiles and relationships and regulatory pathways. Advance regulatory requirement knowledge will help identify the amount of regulatory support each country and distributor requires. Unfortunately, no consistent template exists for marketing to provide to regulatory colleagues that identifies product approval requirements in different parts of the world and specifies the amount of paperwork and resources needed. Without a proactive approach to gaining advance knowledge, the workload for launching in a new country may exceed the regulatory team's capacity, putting the strategy at risk. In start-up companies, where there may be few resources to support the regulatory team, it is especially important to target a specific number of countries the team can support.

Social Media

A recent survey[32] shows the average physician's use of the Internet for professional reasons has increased to more than eight hours per week, a significant increase from the average of 2.5 hours estimated in 2002. In addition, the survey estimated more than 60 million US adults utilize health-related social media, and that 10 million consumers use mobile devices for health and medical purposes. As medical device companies grapple with the challenges their sales representatives have in reaching target physicians, social media programs offer an attractive strategic opportunity to reach the digitally proficient clinician or patient, provide product information and build and fortify relationships.

The challenge is leveraging the rapid pace of change in social media while meeting regulatory compliance in the vacuum of clear guidelines for social media use from FDA and other regulatory bodies. During the current period of uncertainty where few countries have established guidelines, medical device companies still can create policies based on the principles set forward in countries that have taken the initiative in shaping regional social media promotion policies. In many cases, the medical device community can look to its sister industry, pharmaceuticals, and its regulatory bodies for valuable information on strategy and policy creation. For example, the UK's Prescription Medicines Code of Practice Authority[33] (PMCPA) was established by the Association of the British Pharmaceutical Industry (ABPI) to operate the APBI *Code of Practice*.

Called *The Code*, this document sets standards for medical product promotion to UK health professionals and health administrators to ensure medical products' companies work with British healthcare providers in a responsible, ethical and professional manner. *The Code* is similar to the voluntary codes developed by AdvaMed to guide medical device companies on how to serve patients best through ethical collaborations with healthcare professionals. The goal is to improve medical technologies, ensure medical technologies' safety and efficacy, support research and education and meet the highest ethical standards. The *AdvaMed Code of Ethics on Interactions with Health Care Professionals*[34] and *The Code* both provide direction on:

- advertising (journal, direct mail and digital)
- industry representative activities and interactions, including sales and promotional materials
- samples
- gifts, hospitality, promotional meetings
- scientific and other meeting sponsorship; payment of travel and accommodation expenses
- exhibitions and digital communications
- information for patients or for patient organizations.

FDA Draft Guidance on Using Internet/Social Media Platforms

In 2014, FDA published two draft guidance documents for medical device companies on using social media. The first draft guidance reviewed the use of social media platforms with character space limitations.[35] The second draft guidance provides detail on how medical device companies can address misinformation delivered on third-party social media platforms.[36] Both guidance documents provide valuable direction to medical device companies.[37]

FDA's draft guidance on messaging platforms such as Twitter, entitled *Internet/Social Media Platforms with Character Space Limitations—Presenting Risk and Benefit Information for Prescription Drugs and Medical Devices*, is intended only for social media limited to 140 character spaces. The guidance states any medical device company using Twitter or a similar limited character social media platform to make product benefit claims also must incorporate risk information, regardless of character space constraints. If the medical device company cannot meet these guidelines, it should use another social media platform. When using Twitter or other character-constrained social media platforms, FDA encourages medical device companies to direct readers to their company websites for more information. The guidance specifies the URL in the communication should be a dedicated landing page specific to the content shared in the message, and the URL name should not imply a benefit.

FDA's social media guidance, *Internet/Social Media Platforms: Correcting Independent Third-Party Misinformation About Prescription Drugs and Medical Devices*, details how medical device companies should respond to misinformation about FDA-cleared products. These are communications uploaded or commented on by independent third parties through social media, such as a blog or other third-party site not related to the named medical device company. The medical device company is not required to correct misinformation, but the draft guidance advises the information can be corrected, as long as the information is true, not promotional, is appropriate and responds only to the misinformation. The draft guidance also advises approved labeling be included or be made readily available. Several approaches to correcting misinformation are provided.

Two other FDA guidance documents are *Fulfilling Regulatory Requirements for Postmarketing Submissions* of Interactive Promotional Media for Prescription Human and Animal Drugs and Biologics,[38] published January, 2014 and Responding to Unsolicited Requests for Off-Label Information About Prescription Drugs and Medical Devices,[39] published in December, 2011. Both are important documents to guide the marketing, sales and regulatory departments of medical device companies.

Conclusion

Regulatory strategy is one of the cornerstones of medical device commercialization and can have a significant impact on ROI. Companies should expect change and investigate markets thoroughly from both a marketing and regulatory point of view to ensure the right decisions are made.

References

1. Resource Library for Medical Device Professionals. Emergo Group website. http://www.emergogroup.com/resources/download-regulatory-process-charts. Accessed 19 March 2016.
2. Ibid.
3. Op cit 1.
4. Directive 98/79/EC of the European Parliament and of the Council of 27 October 1998 on in vitro diagnostic medical devices Annex II List of Devices Referred to in Article 9(2) and (3). Emergo Group website. http://www.emergogroup.com/resources/regulations-europe/98-79-ec#annexII. Accessed 19 March 2016.
5. Customized Regulatory Pathway Reports for Smaller International Markets. Emergo Group website. http://www.emergogroup.com/services/chile-regulatory-strategy. Accessed 19 March 2016.
6. Medical Technology Score Card, PWC, January 2011.
7. "Israeli Population Nearly 8 Million; 20% Are Arab, Government Says." Al Monitor website. http://www.al-monitor.com/pulse/culture/2012/09/as-jewish-new-year-nears-number.html#ixzz40YXfr9wE. Accessed 10 February 2016.
8. ClinicalTrials.com website. https://www.clinicaltrials.gov/. Accessed 19 March 2016.
9. Koren A. "Successful Start of Clinical Trials in Israel A Roadmap for Pharmaceutical and Medical Device Trials." GCP Clinical Studies Ltd. website. http://www.gcp.co.il/images/Successful%20Start%20of%20Clinical%20Trials%20In%20Israel.pdf. Accessed 19 March 2016.
10. Resource Library for Medical Device Professionals, China. Emergo Group website. http://www.emergogroup.com/files/china-webinar-slides-emergo-group.pdf. Accessed 19 March 2016.
11. The Boston Consulting Group. Regulation and Access to Innovative Medical Technologies A comparison of the FDA and EU Approval Processes and their Impact on Patients and Industry (June 2012). MedTech Europe website. http://www.medtecheurope.org/sites/default/files/resource_items/files/01062012_BCG_Regulation%20and%20Access%20to%20Innovative%20Medical%20Technologies_Backgrounder.pdf. Accessed 19 March 2016.
12. Hartford J. "What to Expect from New EU Medical Device Regulations." MDDI website. http://www.mddionline.com/article/what-expect-new-eu-medical-device-regulations/. Accessed 19 March 2016.
13. Poly Implants Prothèses (French Breast Implant Scandal). The New York Times website. http://topics.nytimes.com/top/news/business/companies/poly_implants_prothese/index.html. Accessed 19 March 2016.
14. Op cit 12.
15. Proposal for a Regulation of the European Parliament and of the Council on medical devices, and amending Directive 2001/83/EC, Regulation (EC) No 178/2002 and Regulation (EC) No 1223/2009. EC website. http://data.consilium.europa.eu/doc/document/ST-12040-2015-REV-1/en/pdf. Accessed 19 March 2016.
16. Proposal for a Regulation of the European Parliament and of the Council on in vitro diagnostic medical devices. EC website. http://data.consilium.europa.eu/doc/document/ST-12042-2015-INIT/en/pdf. Accessed 19 March 2016.
17. Op cit 12.
18. Dekoninck C and Valluet S. "Legal Implications & Compliance in the Sales & Marketing of Medical Devices in Europe" (January 2012). CrowellMoring website. https://www.crowell.com/files/2012-Legal-Implications-and-compliance-in-the-sales-and-marketing-of-medical-devices.pdf. Accessed 19 March 2016.
19. Eucomed Code of Ethical Business Practice. MedTech Europe website. http://www.medtecheurope.org/sites/default/files/resource_items/files/14042014_MTE_Code%20of%20Ethical%20Business%20Practice%20-%20%20Procedural%20Framework.pdf. Accessed 19 March 2016.
20. Comparison of the AdvaMed Code of Ethics and the Eucomed Code of Business Practice. Advamed website. http://advamed.org/res.download/133/. Accessed 19 March 2016.
21. Handbook of Pharma and MedTech Compliance. Baker & McKenzie website. http://www.bakermckenzie.com/promotingmedicalproductsglobally/. Accessed 19 March 2016.
22. Ibid.
23. Public Health. European Commission website. http://ec.europa.eu/health/index_en.htm. Accessed 19 March 2016.
24. "Pharmaceutical direct-to-consumer advertising in Europe." Pharmaceutical Field website. www.pharmafield.co.uk/features/2005/12/Pharmaceutical-direct-to-consumer-advertising-in-Europe/. Accessed 19 March 2016.
25. Ibid.
26. Op cit 21.
27. Physician Financial Transparency Reports (Sunshine Act). American Medical Association website. http://www.ama-assn.org/ama/pub/advocacy/topics/sunshine-act-and-physician-financial-transparency-reports.page? Accessed 19 March 2016.
28. International Medical Device Manufacturers Association Code of Ethical Conduct for Interactions with Healthcare Professionals. European Coordination Committee of the Radiological, Electromedical and Healthcare IT Industry website. http://www.cocir.org/site/fileadmin/4.1_Business_and_Innovation/Code_of_Conduct/IMEDA_Code_of_Ethics_NEW_01_09_2013.pdf. Accessed 19 March 2016.
29. Code of Ethical Business Practice Eucomed Guidelines on Interactions with Healthcare Professionals (September 2008). Eucomed website. http://www.medtecheurope.org/sites/default/files/resource_items/files/11092008_MTE_Eucomed%20Guidelines%20on%20Interactions%20with%20Healthcare%20Professionals.pdf. Accessed 19 March 2016.
30. Data on file at Medi-Vantage Data Decision Group
31. Premarket Information—Device Design and Documentation Processes. FDA website. http://www.fda.gov/MedicalDevices/DeviceRegulationandGuidance/HumanFactors/ucm119190.htm. Accessed 19 March 2016.
32. von Muhlen M, Ohno-Machado L. "Reviewing social media use by clinicians." Oxford Journal website. http://jamia.oxfordjournals.org/content/jaminfo/19/5/777.full.pdf. Accessed 19 March 2016.

33. Welcome to the Interactive Code - Second 2012 Edition. Prescription Medicines Code or Practice Authority website. http://www.pmcpa.org.uk/thecode/interactivecode/Pages/Default.aspx/. Accessed 19 March 2016.
34. AdvaMed Code of Ethics on Interactions with Health Care Professionals. AdvaMed website. http://advamed.org/res/112/advamed-code-of-ethics-on-interactions-with-health-care-professionals. Accessed 19 March 2016.
35. *Draft Guidance for Industry Internet/Social Media Platforms with Character Space Limitations—Presenting Risk and Benefit Information for Prescription Drugs and Medical Devices* (June 2014). FDA website. http://www.fda.gov/downloads/Drugs/GuidanceComplianceRegulatoryInformation/Guidances/UCM401087.pdf. Accessed 19 March 2016.
36. *Draft Guidance for Industry Internet/Social Media Platforms: Correcting Independent Third-Party Misinformation About Prescription Drugs and Medical Devices*. FDA website. http://www.fda.gov/downloads/Drugs/GuidanceComplianceRegulatoryInformation/Guidances/UCM401079.pdf. Accessed 19 March 2016.
37. Op cit 35.
38. *Draft Guidance for Industry Fulfilling Regulatory Requirements for Postmarketing Submissions of Interactive Promotional Media for Prescription Human and Animal Drugs and Biologics* (January 2014). FDA website. http://www.fda.gov/downloads/Drugs/GuidanceComplianceRegulatoryInformation/Guidances/UCM381352.pdf. Accessed 19 March 2016.
39. *Draft Guidance for Industry Responding to Unsolicited Requests for Off-Label Information About Prescription Drugs and Medical Devices* (December 2011). FDA website. http://www.fda.gov/downloads/Drugs/GuidanceComplianceRegulatoryInformation/Guidances/UCM285145.pdf. Accessed 19 March 2016.

Acknowledgement
Many thanks to Rob Miragliuolo, Vice President Regulatory Affairs, Regina McIntosh, VP of Marketing and Doug Ferguson, VP of Regulatory and Quality, who all shared their expertise on regulatory strategy, marketing and business decision-making at medical device companies.

Case Study—Assessing Business Opportunity for Global Targets Part 1

Situation: A gastrointestinal (GI) endoscope company is considering launching an Endoscopic Retrograde Cholangiopancreatography (ERCP) endoscope in China.

Strategic Questions: Is the Chinese market a judicious choice for the launch of a GI biliary endoscope? What is the size of the ERCP endoscope market in China? What marketing and sales investment will be necessary to launch a biliary endoscope to the Chinese market? Is the market established, nascent or mature? Assuming it is established or nascent, what level of market development investment is required?

Supportive Data: In 2006, a total of 63,787 ERCP procedures were performed in mainland China, with an estimated annual rate of 4.87 per 100,000 inhabitants. This rate is much lower than in developed countries,[a] indicating the GI ERCP endoscope market in China is not well-established. Further investigation is needed.

Challenge: A low ERCP procedure rate indicates launching the ERCP endoscope would require a market development strategy in addition to typical product launch costs. Market development is a business strategy used to develop new groups of buyers with high growth potential to expand the market for existing products and services. Is a market development strategic investment feasible and viable for the GI endoscope company? In other words, is the market nascent (with high opportunity for growth with the right level of market development investment) or mature (with no real growth potential projected and not warranting the expense of market development)?

Supportive Data and Assumptions: Most global strategies are assumption-based. In the global strategy analysis, the endoscope marketing team could present the following data: If the company has the financial resources, and the executive team feels the Chinese ERCP opportunity is better than other regions/countries, one possible option could be to plan a market development strategy to support ERCP endoscope launch in China. The following data can be used to build assumptions to validate the Chinese market opportunity:

Data and Assumptions for the ERCP Scope Opportunity in China

Supportive Data	Assumptions from Data
China's large population of 1.4 billion people[b]	Very large market
95.5% of Chinese hospitals provide ERCP service[c]	Large existing infrastructure
2013 gross domestic product (GDP) growth rate[d] in China estimated at 7.7%	Rapidly growing economy
Statistically significant correlation between the Chinese ERCP rate and GDP per capita ($r = 0.871$, $p < .001$)[e]	Demonstrates market growth potential

Conclusion: China's current under-utilization of ERCP and the data in this table demonstrate a good business opportunity could exist in China. The ERCP endoscope market is nascent and reasonably can be expected to grow with an appropriate investment in market development and product launch, as long as no other significant barriers to entry exist.

Next Steps: What is the return on investment (ROI) and how is it affected by the costs of doing business in China, such as regulatory costs and the cost of overcoming market barriers to entry?

a. "ERCP service in China: results from a national survey." PubMed website. Gastrointest Endosc. 2013 Jan;77(1):39-46.e1. doi: 10.1016/j.gie.2012.08.035. Accessed 18 February 2016.
b. China Population 2016. World Population Review website. http://worldpopulationreview.com/countries/china-population/. Accessed 19 March 2016.
c. Op cit a.
d. GDP growth (annual %). World Bank website. http://data.worldbank.org/indicator/NY.GDP.MKTP.KD.ZG. Accessed 19 March 2016.
e. Ibid.

Case Study—Assessing Business Opportunity for Global Targets Part 2

Situation: A gastrointestinal (GI) endoscope company is considering launching an Endoscopic Retrograde Cholangiopancreatography (ERCP) endoscope in China.

Strategic Questions: Part 1 reviewed the choice of the Chinese market for the launch of a GI biliary endoscope. In Part 2, the effect on ROI by the regulatory cost of doing business in China and cost of clinical trials are assessed. Could regulatory considerations potentially alter the marketing case presented in Part 1?

Supportive Data: US FDA classifies the biliary endoscope as a Class II device.[a] A device considered Class II in the US or Class IIa/IIb in the EU could be considered Class III in China, meaning a longer and costlier registration.[b]

Supportive Data and Assumptions: The following data can be used to build assumptions to validate Chinese regulatory approval and clinical trial costs:

Data and Assumptions for the ERCP Biliary Endoscope Regulatory and Clinical Trial Costs in China

Supportive Data	Assumptions from Data
The cost of gaining regulatory approval in China is high.[c]	Greater than $50,000 (US)
A medical device clinical trial can cost between $5 and $10 million in the US or EU.[d]	Average is $7.5 million
The cost of clinical trials conducted in China is estimated at 30–50% of what a comparable trial would cost in the US.[e]	At a range of 10-25%, the estimated cost of conducting a clinical trial in China could be between $750,000 and $1,875,000

Conclusion: China's current under-utilization of ERCP and the data in this table demonstrate a good business opportunity could exist in China. The ERCP endoscope market is nascent and reasonably can be expected to grow with an appropriate investment in market development and product launch. All products have different profit margins, so the ROI formula will be different for every product line. Because costs are high in China, regulatory approval and clinical trial cost is critical in determining ROI. China's market presents a major opportunity, so future profit margins may outweigh regulatory and clinical trial costs.

a. 21 CFR Part 876—Gastroenterology-Urology Devices, Subpart B—Diagnostic Devices. FDA website. http://www.accessdata.fda.gov/scripts/cdrh/cfdocs/cfcfr/cfrsearch.cfm?fr=876.1500 Accessed 19 March 2016.
b. "China CFDA Regulatory Approval Process for Medical Devices." Emergo Group, 2014. https://www.emergogroup.com/resources/china-process-chart. Accessed 19 March 2016.
c. Regulatory Process Charts. Emergo Group website. http://www.emergogroup.com/resources/download-regulatory-process-charts. Accessed 19 March 2016.
d. Good Clinical Practice for Medical Device Trials http://www.standardslearn.org/documents/good_clinical_practice_for_medical_device_trials_rev_1.pdf. Accessed 19 March 2016.
e. Bio 2012: Development cost comparison, China vs. US. Nature.com website. http://blogs.nature.com/tradesecrets/2012/07/02/bio-2012-development-cost-comparison-china-vs-us. Accessed 19 March 2016.

17 Global Postmarketing Regulatory Strategy

By Scott D. Dickerhoff

Introduction

An often overlooked and sometimes underappreciated facet in a medical device's lifecycle is postmarket regulatory strategy. If successful, it can yield the manufacturer and, ultimately, shareholders, a larger contribution to the bottom line and maintain a solid reputation with the customer and regulators. No manufacturer considers cost avoidance of a field action or recall into product development. The ultimate goal, beyond company revenue, should be to focus on the customer. The manufacturer has a duty and responsibility to ensure the medical device's overall quality and safety.

An overall medical device regulatory strategy (including devices, in vitro diagnostic devices and combination products regulated primarily as devices) should be global in nature and address both pre- and postmarket considerations. There should be a direct link between pre- and postmarket strategy. The primary emphasis of most medical device companies is on premarket strategy and getting the product to market. But, device manufacturers are responsible throughout the product's lifecycle. Companies should be concerned about not only obtaining marketing authorization, but doing everything in their power to keep the device on the market once cleared or approved. That presumes the device, in fact, is safe for use and performs as intended. That is why equal emphasis should be applied to postmarket regulatory strategy. The US Food and Drug Administration (FDA) has discovered product safety issues not found during development often surface following market release, when the device is in users' hands. Crafting a successful regulatory strategy is critical and ensures potentially dangerous products do not reach the market; if they do, it ensures product issues are addressed expeditiously. Ideally, if it is demonstrated a product is not operating as designed, problems may be caught early enough to prevent patient injury or death. In the unlikely event a product is removed from the market, whether voluntarily or at a regulatory agency's request, it is imperative the affected product is identified and dealt with quickly. A successful postmarket regulatory strategy can contribute to commercial success through customer satisfaction and positive customer relations.

Medical devices' global nature brings a different set of challenges. Medical device manufacturers operate under different Quality Management System (QMS) regulations, depending on where the product is manufactured and distributed. Europe, for instance, has postmarket regulatory requirements: postmarket surveillance, generally, and more specifically, postmarket clinical follow-up and vigilance reporting. Annual surveillance audits and re-certifications (generally every five years) ensure this activity is maintained. Each QMS is intended to ensure the medical device is safe and effective for use and its overall quality is maintained. Complying with all of these requirements requires knowledge of state-of-the-art principles and current standards. As new standards are introduced and old ones modified, existing products need to be checked for compliance, and design modifications or product obsolescence managed accordingly.

Device changes are made for a variety of reasons. Sometimes they are necessitated by product surveillance data and/or driven by marketing input to add new claims or adjust performance expectations. Manufacturing facilities are under constant pressure to reduce manufacturing costs, and changes to processes or materials must be monitored closely. Other potential changes include components no longer being available, obsolete manufacturing processes and new test methods. Medical device manufacturers must oversee all changes to ensure the device's safety and efficacy or performance. Implementing these changes should be covered in the global postmarket regulatory strategy and governed by the manufacturer's QMS.

It is clear developing and maintaining a successful postmarket regulatory strategy is compelled by more than just regulations but, more importantly, is a solid business practice. Responsibility for the device does not end at market release. Postmarket surveillance feedback is critical to understanding customers' minds and how products are being used. Maintaining a high quality standard and ensuring customer loyalty will pay dividends in the long term. Further benefits include developing a solid relationship with regulators and building a positive reputation based on compliance principles.

What Is Postmarket Regulatory Strategy?

Postmarket regulatory is the overall regulatory strategy element dealing with the device manufacturer's obligations following market release. Postmarket regulatory responsibilities begin as soon as the device has been cleared or approved in a specific country or region. Post- and premarket regulatory strategies must be linked and coordinated.

To understand how they are linked, the premarket phase deals with product control, while the postmarket phase deals with use control. Product control designs the product based on user input and develops a finished product validated to be safe and effective for use. This also includes making sure product labelling and advertising represent the product and what was cleared/approved by regulators correctly. Use control takes the finished device and measures its effectiveness or performance through postmarket surveillance activities to ensure the product was built correctly and confirms its safety and effectiveness. A medical device regulatory strategy includes the activities a manufacturer must complete to maintain a safe and effective product to the consumer, from inception to market release and throughout the device's life.

An effective postmarket regulatory strategy is linked to the premarket strategy, and the two are developed together in the initial stages of development. Postmarket regulatory strategy takes into account the pertinent sections of the device manufacturer's QMS. Postmarket activities can be divided into the following three categories:

Proactive Postmarket Surveillance

This was defined by the Global Harmonization Task Force (GHTF) as the proactive collection of information on medical devices' quality, safety or performance after they have been placed on the market. GHTF also developed guidance for manufacturers and Notified Bodies on postmarket clinical follow-up (PMCF) studies. The purpose of the guidance is to help fulfill the *Active Implantable Medical Devices Directive* (90/385/EEC) (*AIMDD*) and *Medical Devices Directive*'s (93/42/EEC) (*MDD*) postmarket surveillance (PMS) obligations.[1]

PMS is a shared responsibility between the manufacturer and regulatory authorities to monitor medical devices' safety and effectiveness once they are on the market. Manufacturers implement PMS not only to comply with regulatory requirements, but also because it is good business practice. These activities are designed to generate information to identify poorly performing devices and other safety problems quickly, accurately characterize real-world device performance and clinical outcomes and facilitate the development of new devices or new uses for existing devices.[2] The data collected provide information about device performance through continuous feedback. This allows manufacturers to maintain high product quality and customer satisfaction. Information can come from a variety of sources and methods. Procedures should provide guidance to determine whether reported issues are considered complaints or, perhaps, warranty or maintenance concerns. Issues deemed to be complaints then must be analyzed to determine whether they are reportable under one or more authorities' regulatory requirements. Including such tools as decision trees is useful for consistency in determining whether the issue is a reportable adverse event. Thorough investigations are required, and obtaining suspect product for evaluation often can present a challenge. Adverse events must be reported in a timely manner, and failure to do so could create risks of noncompliance. Ongoing reports to regulators documenting progress and agreed-upon actions should be provided expeditiously and routinely until the issue is closed. Complaint trending should be reviewed frequently and at least during quality management meetings. Corrective and preventive actions (CAPAs) may be required when trends are detected to handle any changes properly through the change management system. The postmarket regulatory plan should reference the systems mentioned above as required PMS resources. Regulator and internal QMS audits should ensure processes and procedures are both compliant and executed properly.

PMS data include a clinical follow-up as part of the PMS report. An adequate rationale is necessary if the manufacturer deems a postmarket clinical study unnecessary. For EU markets, manufacturers must demonstrate conformity to the .[3] The European Commission recently revised its guideline, MEDDEV 2.12/2 on PMCF. This document is intended as a guide for manufacturers and Notified Bodies on how to carry out PMCF studies to fulfill PMS obligations according to the *MDD* and *AIMDD*.[4]

Reactive Postmarket Vigilance

These are incidents that could occur with medical devices and in vitro diagnostic devices (IVDs) when they do not perform as intended, thereby leading, in the worst case, to injury or death. Manufactures must have systems in place to capture and analyze data to react quickly when problems arise, thus avoiding public relations exposure from recalls and other regulatory actions such as Warning Letters. Implementing effective product monitoring procedures, including field actions and recalls, is essential.

Each year, FDA receives several hundred thousand medical device reports of suspected device-associated deaths, serious injuries and malfunctions. Medical device reporting (MDR) is one of FDA's postmarket surveillance tools to monitor device performance, detect potential device-related safety issues and contribute to these products' benefit-risk assessments.[5] FDA uses the Manufacturer and User Facility Device Experience (MAUDE) database[6] to maintain information regarding MDRs submitted by mandatory reporters (manufacturers, importers and device user facilities) as well as voluntary reporters such as healthcare professionals, patients and consumers. In 2012, FDA announced MAUDE would be replaced by Pharmacovigilance Report Intake and Managed Output (PRIMO). The agency says it eventually will be able to "Quickly identify poorly performing devices, accurately characterize and disseminate information about real-world device performance and efficiently generate data to support premarket clearance or approval of new devices and new uses of currently marketed devices."[7]

The medical device vigilance system's principal purpose is to improve health and safety protection of patients, users and others by reducing the likelihood of incidents recurring related to a medical device's use. Under the EU medical devices directives, adverse incidents are evaluated and, where appropriate, information is disseminated via a National Competent Authority Report (NCAR) aimed at preventing repetition of such incidents through the adoption of appropriate field safety corrective actions (FSCAs).[8]

Eudamed[9] is the European databank for medical devices. Its purpose is to strengthen market surveillance and transparency in the medical device field by providing Member State Competent Authorities with rapid access to information and to contribute to uniform application of the directives, particularly related to registration requirements.

The medical device vigilance system is intended to facilitate direct, early and harmonized implementation of FSCAs across those Member States in which the device is in use, in contrast to action taken on a country-by-country basis. Corrective action includes but may not be confined to: device recall; field safety notice issuance; additional surveillance and modification of devices in use; modifying future device design, components or manufacturing process; modifying labelling or instructions for use.[10]

The European Commission makes many guidance documents available aimed at promoting a common approach by manufacturers and Notified Bodies involved in the conformity assessment procedures according to the relevant directives' annexes, and by the Competent Authorities charged with safeguarding public health.[11]

Postmarket Maintenance and Sustaining Activities

This category covers those manufacturer activities not driven by either product surveillance or vigilance. Manufacturers receive feedback from consumers in many ways not related to complaints or not posing safety and efficacy issues. To remain competitive in the market, manufacturers look to gain advantages in marketing claims, performance expectations and manufacturing costs. Existing products need to be checked for compliance to new requirements, design modifications or product obsolescence. These adjustments are coordinated by change control processes and managed by the overall regulatory strategy plan.

New or updated standards also must also be considered. EU Notified Bodies will verify compliance during annual surveillance audits and certificate renewals. Under the EU legislation, manufacturers must keep abreast of new or updated standards and implement changes expeditiously. Being proactive in postmarket maintenance will ensure compliance and continue to provide a safe and effective product for consumers.

Postmarket Regulatory Requirements

The medical device regulator's goal is to ensure products are safe and effective for consumer use. There still is global inconsistency in how manufacturers meet those goals. One consistent requirement is a manufacturer QMS to support compliance with standards and applicable regional requirements. Manufacturers have postmarketing responsibilities, regardless of the country or region in which products are marketed, and there are various methods to meet those commitments. Many PMS elements, including adverse event data collection, are common requirements by most regulators. The differences mainly are in the assigned responsibilities and mechanisms for collecting and analyzing data related to device safety and efficacy.

Medical device manufacturers, distributors and importers are required to develop and follow specific QMS requirements, as well as specified regulations, to manufacture and market a medical device.

Postmarket requirements for a medical device include:
- PMS, postapproval studies or postmarketing clinical trials
- safety reporting
- establishment registration and product listing
- inspections
- product license renewal
- managing changes or modifications to cleared or approved products

Regional QMS Requirements

QMS requirements by region differ slightly and are summarized below:

US

Manufacturers must establish and follow a QMS to help ensure their products meet applicable requirements and specifications consistently. FDA's Quality System Regulation (QSR) (21 CFR Part 820) requires manufacturers of medical devices marketed in the US to follow current Good Manufacturing Practices (CGMPs). Domestic and foreign medical device manufacturers are required to establish a QMS that addresses medical device design, manufacture, packaging, labeling, storage, installation and finished device servicing of products marketed in the US.[12]

PMS studies also are required under Section 522 of the *Federal Food, Drug and Cosmetic Act* (*FD&C Act*), as are postapproval studies at the time of Premarket Approval (PMA), humanitarian device exemption (HDE) or product development protocol (PDP) application.[13] The Postmarket Surveillance Studies Program encompasses design, tracking, oversight and review responsibilities for studies mandated under *FD&C Act* Section 522. The program helps ensure well-designed PMS studies are conducted effectively, efficiently and in the least burdensome manner.

EU

ISO 13485:2003, Medical Devices—Quality Management System requirements for regulatory purposes specifies QMS requirements for an organization that needs to demonstrate its ability to provide medical devices and related services to meet customer requirements and regulatory requirements applicable to medical devices and related services consistently.

ISO 13485:2003's primary objective is to establish medical device QMS requirements for regulatory purposes. All ISO 13485:2003 requirements are specific to organizations providing medical devices, regardless of the organization's type or size.[14]

ISO 13485:2003 is recognized by the EU, Japan, Australia and many other countries. Compliance with the standard is required by Health Canada.[15] ISO 13485 is modeled on ISO 9000:2000, with additional requirements for documentation and provisions specific to medical devices. The standard is compatible with FDA's QSR requirements. Those requirements include establishing and following quality systems to help ensure products meet applicable requirements and specifications consistently. FDA's device CGMP requirements were authorized under *FD&C Act* Section 520(f).[16] ISO 13485 also specifically requires risk management throughout the product lifecycle, usually addressed through implementation of ISO 14971:2012.

The manufacturer's QMS certification to ISO 13485 requirements is part of the most common route to an EC Declaration of Conformity. The relevant sections of the European directives on postmarket surveillance are:[17]
- *AIMDD* Article 8 and Annexes II, IV, V
- *MDD* Article 10 and Annexes II, IV, V, VI, VII
- *In Vitro Diagnostics Devices Directive 98/79/EC* (*IVDD*) Article 11 and Annexes III, IV, VI

Japan

Japan's Pharmaceuticals and Medical Devices Agency (PMDA) collects safety information related to medical device adverse events. That information is stored in a database for scientific analysis and investigation. Investigation findings are reported to the Ministry of Health, Labour and Welfare (MHLW), which may result in administrative actions to ensure safe product use.[18]

Further information can be found on either the PMDA (http://www.pmda.go.jp/english/index.html) or MHLW website (http://www.mhlw.go.jp/english/).

China

The central government's Ministry of Health (MOH) is responsible for drafting basic device oversight regulations and overseeing their implementation through the China Food and Drug Administration (CFDA).[19] Information on medical devices marketed in China can be found on CFDA's website (http://eng.sfda.gov.cn/WS03/CL0755/).

Australia and New Zealand

Australia's Therapeutic Goods Administration (TGA) is the country's primary regulatory authority. It conducts a range of assessment and monitoring activities to ensure available therapeutic goods are acceptable to ensure Australians have access, within a reasonable time, to therapeutic advances. Medical devices are entered in the Australian Register of Therapeutic Goods (ARTG) and tracked and monitored for safety. The TGA website, http://www.tga.gov.au/, contains links for such safety information as recalls and alerts.

The New Zealand Medicines and Medical Devices Safety Authority (MEDSAFE, http://www.medsafe.govt.nz/index.asp) is the regulatory authority governing medical devices' safe and effective use in New Zealand. MEDSAFE's role is ensuring medicines and medical devices have acceptable efficacy, quality and safety. For medical devices to be supplied legally in New Zealand, they must be notified to the Web Assisted Notification of Devices (WAND) database. MEDSAFE manages medical device adverse event reports and processes corrective actions and product recalls. It also provides early warning information on medical device safety concerns.[20]

Latin America

Latin America is a rapidly growing medical device market. Many countries' regulations still are evolving. Many countries with regulations in place are tightening requirements, some previously without regulations now regulate to some degree and some remain unregulated. Many countries' ministries of health control all health-related products (Brazil and Colombia). It is especially important to stay current on country-specific requirements. Manufacturers are urged to work with a reputable distributor that can assist in interpreting local laws and regulations. Eventually, many, if not all, Latin American countries probably will adopt harmonized regulations. However, there is no schedule for when this may occur. Until it does, manufacturers should expect frequent changes.

The Brazilian Health Surveillance Agency (ANVISA, http://portal.anvisa.gov.br/wps/portal/anvisa-ingles) has launched a new program to monitor medical device quality, the Monitoring Project on Health Products Marketed in Brazil. The agency also launched the Center for Management of Emergency Health Surveillance Information (EVISA). This new ANVISA unit will organize the process of capturing and monitoring information and responding to health emergencies. EVISA was inspired by the Global Alert and Response (GAR) public health emergency network, consisting of centers in various countries and the World Health Organization (WHO) in Geneva, gaining momentum from implementation of the *International Health Regulation*.[21]

Canada

Health Canada's (http://www.hc-sc.gc.ca/index-eng.php) Canada Vigilance Program is a postmarket surveillance program to collect and assess reports of suspected health product adverse reactions. PMS enables Health Canada, to monitor safety profiles of health products once they are marketed to ensure the products' benefits continue to outweigh their risks.[22]

GHTF/IMDRF

GHTF has been replaced by the International Medical Device Regulators Forum (IMDRF), conceived in February 2011 as a voluntary group of medical device regulations from around the work, to discuss future medical device regulatory harmonization. IMDRF is building on GHTF's strong foundational work to accelerate international medical device regulatory harmonization and convergence.[23] Final GHTF guidance documents, including those on PMS and vigilance, remain available on IMDRF's website. They form the basis for several national and regional medical device regulatory systems, e.g., Singapore and the Association of Southeast Asian Nations (ASEAN).

Manufacturer, Distributor and Importer Responsibilities

The European medical devices directives impose significant responsibilities on manufacturers, Member States and NBs. However, the directives define far fewer responsibilities for importers and distributors. As a result, manufacturers and distributors do not always have a clear concept of these responsibilities or those specified by national laws and regulations.[24]

A medical device manufacturer exporting products to the US must be aware of US importer and distributor requirements. Non-US manufacturers must meet the following requirements and regulations.[25]

- corrections and removals
- registration and listing
- adverse event reporting
- MDR event files
- distributor event records

Factors Influencing Postmarket Regulatory Strategy

Balance Between Regulatory Compliance and Commercial Imperatives

There is a delicate balance of priorities between keeping shareholders happy and the complying with regulatory requirements. The regulatory professional's job is to find that balancing point. Not all regulatory decisions are black and white.

All regulatory decisions have compliance implications. Very little latitude exists in regulatory strategy regarding compliance to standards and regulations. Generally, the grey area in a compliance decision revolves around the path to achieve compliance. The regulatory professional is responsible for determining the least burdensome path to device clearance or approval-. Interpreting standards and regulations while keeping abreast of changes can be very challenging. Many resources are available to assist in making the best regulatory strategy decision and remaining compliant. Guidance documents can be very helpful, not only in providing options but also providing useful tips. The regulatory professional is responsible for presenting the regulatory options and their risks. Ultimately, the manufacturer is responsible for considering the inherent business risks and least burdensome regulatory strategy to a compliant solution.

The regulatory professional also provides advice on regulatory matters not necessarily compliance-related but more strategic in nature. For instance, a manufacturer may decide to manufacture a product at risk, pending verification and validation testing, while holding finished product in quarantine until testing results are known. Being too aggressive and taking unnecessary business risks can delay product launch and possibly upset regulators. Manufacturers' decisions reflect not only on the company but also the regulatory professional in the regulator's eyes. Building a good reputation and providing solid submissions is very beneficial in maintaining a solid relationship.

Situations that could prompt business risk decisions may include:

- file change versus submission
- submission options
- supporting evidence to substantiate proposed claims (clinical versus verification testing)
- evidence quality to substantiate proposed claims
- sample or subject quantity (statistical significance)
- submission timing

For example, a medical device manufacturer may be considering a change to a currently marketed device requiring a regulatory assessment of the change to determine the proper regulatory pathway. The manufacturer may choose to introduce a revised product to market sooner and obtain regulatory clearance or approval by limiting indications or intended use claims to beat competitors to market. Another option, which would take more time, may be providing the necessary clinical evidence or verification testing results to get regulatory clearance or approval for more-specific performance claims. The regulatory professional may recommend more than one regulatory pathway and present the risks inherent with each option. It then is up to management to decide how much business risk to take. Business decision-makers should consider possible quality or efficacy risks and others. Manufacturers are under tremendous pressure to get new or updated product to market as quickly as possible. It is the regulatory professional's job to balance the company's business needs with delivering a safe product that meets customer requirements.[26]

Managing the Risk

Medical devices often are defined in terms of safety, performance, efficacy and effectiveness. They are developed for a designed purpose, generally captured through user needs and defined requirements' documents. Translating those requirements to be clinically effective requires managing risks efficiently. A clinically effective medical device produces the manufacturer's intended effect for the intended use situation. Clinical effectiveness is one factor in determining device performance.

The regulatory professional is responsible for ensuring the manufacturer has implemented QMS requirements effectively, including risk management. It also is the regulatory professional's responsibility to ensure compliance with relevant standards and regulations.[27] Risk analysis can be achieved through various methods to identify failure modes, risks and critical device/user interactions. A few of the more popular risk analysis methods include:

- Fault Tree Analysis (FTA)
- Failure Mode and Effect Analysis (FMEA)
- Failure Mode Effect and Criticality Analysis (FMECA)
- Hazard Analysis Critical Control Points (HACCP)
- Hazard and Operability Study (HAZOP)

Early detection of PMS problems can provide valuable data for medical device improvements. PMS information can come from many different sources, including customer complaints, CAPA, field servicing, customer focus panels' marketing feedback on customer concerns, Medical Device Reporting (FDA) and Medical Device Vigilance Reporting (EU), to name a few. Monitoring this information frequently and reviewing possible trends are essential in reacting quickly to problems in the field when necessary. These data can be used to review and update risk management documents, possibly leading to design and/or process changes. Using the risk analysis methods mentioned above, coupled with PMS field experience, adjustments not identified during premarket approval can be made. Even the most benign design or process changes can yield major problems if not implemented properly. Every change to a device should include revisiting risk management documents to identify any new risks and implementing mitigation steps to minimize patient risk to an acceptable level. Manufacturers always should document proof PMS is being conducted, and the information is being fed back into the system for review. Risk management is conducted throughout the device's lifecycle, and PMS is a critical tool.

A manufacturer has many ways to manage a medical device's risk both during development and after it has been placed on the market. A solid foundation for a safe and effective device starts with a product development process that incorporates design controls. Design controls are intended to ensure products can be manufactured consistently to meet applicable requirements and regulations. FDA provides guidance for medical device manufacturers to assist them in understanding regulations' intent but does not prescribe how the manufacturer should implement them.[28] Specific requirements can be found in the QSR, 21 CFR 820.30 and ISO 13485 Section 4.4.9. Design controls are applicable throughout the device lifecycle, not just in initial development. All design control aspects apply equally when a device change occurs after the device is on the market. This is to ensure the device will continue to be safe and effective for consumer use. The QMS defines how a device manufacturer applies design controls in product development and to changes occurring during the product's life.

FDA strongly encourages device manufacturers to implement a risk-based verification and validation approach for initial device development and postmarket changes. Manufacturers must identify high risks and mitigate those appropriately to an acceptable level so the benefit exceeds the risk. Regulators are taking a risk-based approach by mandating what changes must be submitted for approval prior to implementation. Developing a master validation plan incorporating the elements of ISO 14971, hazard analysis and risk management are essential and should be considered good business practice. Regulators have focused on this approach due to recent high-profile field problems where it was concluded manufacturers had not performed proper verification and validation to their marketed devices. Suitable up-front risk management planning and execution can avoid most product safety and efficacy concerns.

Complying With State-of-the-Art Principles and Current Standards

Manufacturers are required to ensure devices meet the "state-of-the-art." Summarizing an article in *Quality Digest*, June 2014, Annex 1 of the "Medical Device Directive 93/42/EEC—Essential Requirements—Section 2," states, "The solutions adopted by the manufacturer for the design and construction of the devices must conform to safety principles, taking account of the generally acknowledged state of the art." European Notified Bodies recognize standards such as IEC 60601-1 are voluntary for CE-marking, but the standards' criteria were conveyed to industry as legal qualifications. Although retesting medical devices never was required by law for CE-marking, many Notified Bodies indicated receiving a CE Mark depended on a costly reassessment to IEC 60601-1 criteria. Unless such an effort had been taken, the manufacturer could be denied a CE certificate. According to the European Commission, state of the art does not mean "ensuring use of latest standards." Compliance to state-of-the-art principles and current standards, as explained in EN ISO 14971:2012 Medical devices—Application of risk management to medical devices, is application of "best practices as used in other devices of the same or similar type." This also includes "standards used for the same or similar devices." A product's proven safety record generally results from following safety and performance standards or solutions. Current clinical use and safety records should be collected routinely by the manufacturer and can be used to validate many solutions adopted to achieve high safety and performance.

Compliance with current standards is an ongoing challenge. As new standards are being developed and current standards updated, manufacturers are expected to implement them in their master verification and validation plans and/or product specifications.

Manufacturers can be proactive in staying abreast of standards' changes and influence a particular standard. Although not related directly to regulatory strategy development, manufacturers should take the following suggestions into consideration to increase chances for success. Becoming an active standards committee participant can help shape the direction of requirements being considered for a particular standard. This also provides the manufacturer insight into the particular standard to help comply with specific requirements. Subscribing to services specializing in maintaining the most current version of a standard or specification can be very useful. These services can provide notices of when a standard is changing and the change's specifics. Becoming active in organizations such as the Regulatory Affairs Professionals Society (RAPS) and the Advanced Medical Technology Association (AdvaMed) benefits both the regulatory professional and the manufacturer. RAPS is the largest global organization of and for those involved with the regulation of healthcare and related products, including medical devices, pharmaceuticals, biologics and nutritional products.[29] AdvaMed is a trade association that leads the effort to advance medical technology to achieve healthier lives and healthier economies around the world.[30]

Subscribing to FDA's updates also is very useful. Daily news articles and relevant FDA subjects are discussed. Regulatory professionals can subscribe and search for helpful guidance documents by visiting FDA's website.[31]

Effects of Changes After Initial Market Release

Changes are made to medical devices after initial market release for many reasons. PMS allows a manufacturer to discover issues not found during development. Once in a consumer's hands, a device may not operate as intended, and inherent flaws could begin to surface. Sometimes, these changes are defined as user inconveniences and assessed as nonsignificant changes or ones requiring technical file amendments but no submission. Other times, changes may pose potential safety or efficacy concerns. The device also may be used in unintended ways requiring the manufacturer to modify labelling. Risk management plans do not catch everything, and adjustments may need to be made. Improvements can be made based on actual user field experience with the device. New generations of the device containing updated software or new features may be introduced. New standards and regulations must be considered and implemented.

Effectively implementing and controlling a change for a globally marketed device can be very complicated. What may appear to be a minor and inconsequential change ultimately could lead to a catastrophic failure and possible patient injury or death. Regulatory professionals are responsible for ensuring all changes are evaluated fully and assessed accurately to determine whether they are significant or require document clarifications rather than regulatory action. A significant change, as defined by Health Canada,[32] is a change that reasonably could be expected to affect the device's safety or effectiveness. It includes a change to:

- the manufacturing process, facility or equipment
- manufacturing quality control procedures, including the methods, tests or procedures used to control the device or manufacturing material's quality, purity and sterility
- device design, including any new or extended use, device contraindication addition or deletion or any change to the expiry date period

An individual change could seem insignificant in nature and may not affect device safety or efficacy. However, individual changes, when combined, could tip the balance and become significant. Every change from the start of the last submission must be considered and factored into the regulatory plan. Does the sum of the changes require a submission or notification of change? Is this truly a filing change? Perhaps the most important decision a regulatory professional makes is how to manage a device change and that decision's inherent risk(s). FDA offers guidance to help manufacturers make these decisions. For devices cleared under a 510(k) submission, FDA published *Deciding When to Submit a 510(k) for a Change to an Existing Device (K97-1)*; for devices approved through the PMA process, FDA provides guidance on PMA supplements and amendments.[34] These documents provide useful information to assist manufacturers before making any change that potentially could affect the device's safety or effectiveness.

In Europe, MEDDEV guidance documents also provide helpful guidance. They are developed through a consultation process with Competent Authorities and European Commission representatives, Notified Bodies, industry and other parties interested in the medical devices sector. As an example, the Co-ordination of Notified Bodies Medical Devices (NB-MED) made a recommendation regarding the reporting of design changes and changes of the QMS under Council Directives 90/385/EEC, 93/42/EEC and 98/79/EC.[35] This document assists manufacturers in categorizing and documenting any device design or type changes (including software) and/or QMS as either substantial or not substantial.

Developing and Executing a Successful Global Postmarket Regulatory Strategy

Regulatory professionals develop strategy and provide advice on regulations and requirements. They can present various regulatory strategies' inherent risks but, ultimately, management makes the final-decisions and is responsible for how its products are represented in the marketplace. Executive management demonstrates support through critical risk-based decisions that could impact patient safety. A successful regulatory strategy starts with the regulatory professional's recommendation, followed by upper management approval, subsequently supported by the entire organization.

Building good relationships with regulators through early collaboration is useful in many regards. First, it demonstrates the desire for openness and early understanding of proposed regulatory strategies. Second, a meeting with the regulator early in a project can be used to provide a thorough understanding of the manufacturer's device and its operating principles. This can add benefit later when the regulator is reviewing the manufacturer's submission. Third, timely communication with regulators to gain consensus for regulatory strategy can help the manufacturer avoid doing either too much or too little to gain device clearance or approval. While regulators typically will not provide advice on what a manufacturer should do, they can say what a manufacturer cannot do and provide valuable guidance. For instance, there may be an opportunity to negotiate and explain a particular regulatory or clinical strategy. Establishing the right balance between premarket clinical investigations and PMS in advance allows the manufacturer to focus specifically on what the regulator wants to see in the submission. PMS information could complement the knowledge and experience gained in a project's premarket stages. It removes guessing what the regulator may expect in the submission. If a manufacturer has established credibility and a good reputation with the regulator for PMS, it could negotiate, for instance, at a project's onset for less burdensome premarket requirements instead of greater postmarketing controls.

After a product is on the market, the regulatory professional continues to be responsible in the product lifecycle's postmarket phase, including sustaining activities and product maintenance. Change control after market release and postmarket surveillance comprise postmarket regulatory planning and strategy activities.

Medical device development and changes are iterative processes. Skipping any design control process steps could result in a less than desirable outcome. Proper advance planning will ensure fewer retraced steps in the development cycle, ultimately leading to a shorter overall development schedule.

The regulatory professional must develop a successful regulatory strategy at product conception. Ensuring a device is developed properly following the product development process and premarket stage design control limits problems after market release.

Executing a successful regulatory strategy requires a great deal of planning and coordination. Manufacturers must communicate effectively and invest in quality. Developing and maintaining a medical device requires a commitment that starts at the top and permeates the organization.

Recognizing and Overcoming Obstacles

There are many obstacles for medical device manufacturers. Recognizing those obstacles before they become real problems is critical. Overcoming these obstacles is relevant to having a successful postmarket strategy with a lasting and compounding postmarket affect. In other words, if ignored, premarket issues and concerns can and usually do morph into bigger problems later in the product's postmarket lifecycle.

Postmarket problems can result from one or more of the following:

- rushing through development and submitting too quickly
- late regulatory professional involvement
- making significant changes before device clearance or approval
- poorly written verification and validation reports
- working to outdated standards and guidance documents
- poorly managed CAPA system

In theory, completing the above correctly means building a better product with improved customer satisfaction and placing a safer product in users' hands. This translates into fewer complaints and adverse reactions and, ultimately, fewer manufacturer changes to the product.

Product complaint and adverse event monitoring provide real-world information on a medical device's use. Tracking and trending specific issues can pinpoint problems needing attention. Ignoring this information will not make problems disappear. Adverse events must be reported properly and, if necessary, field actions or recalls initiated.

Proactive companies that invest in robust compliance programs in advance will reap benefits later in the product lifecycle. Planning to avoid obstacles before they happen is much easier than dealing with them after they occur.

Contracting an independent source to audit the QMS can identify both pre- and postmarket product lifecycle gaps. Identifying those gaps is beneficial only if the manufacturer actually uses the information for improvement. Companies that are not prepared and have reactive strategies are destined to experience regulatory violations. These could result in product seizures, civil monetary penalties and criminal penalties for manufacturers (including corporate officers). In cases where noncompliance does not rise to the level of such a serious penalty, the effect still can be detrimental for an organization. Future interactions with regulators can be tense and combative. Once a reputation has been tarnished, it is difficult to restore. The negative public relations resulting from regulatory actions also can impact shareholder investments significantly. While it is difficult to place an actual value on compliance and goodwill with regulators, it certainly will pay dividends in the future. To be successful, establishing and keeping a good reputation with regulators should be a part of every manufacturer's regulatory strategy.

Postmarket Reporting

Medical device adverse event reporting is a critical component of PMS activities. It helps ensure medical devices are being used properly and patient safety is protected.

For certain high-risk devices, PMS is a critical activity. Manufacturers must follow certain requirements and regulations, including conducting postclinical studies to collect safety and efficacy data following market release. FDA also could order the medical device manufacturer to implement a tracking system. FDA recently put regulations into effect establishing a Unique Device Identification (UDI) system that requires medical devices to be labeled with a unique identifier, permitting identification of the device through distribution and use and, when required by FDA, including the lot or serial number.[36] The UDI is much more than just a bar code to identify the lot or serial number. Having a unique identifier benefits people around the world by providing access to the information (metadata) via FDA's UDI database. It also can provide information about the device, e.g., whether it contains latex or is MRI compatible, much of which is stored in an accessible database. This information then can be used for many purposes, including postmarket reporting. FDA also established the Sentinel Initiative, an active surveillance system for monitoring and tracking the safety of marketed drugs, biologics and medical devices. The Sentinel Initiative is in development and pilot testing, and it is not clear yet what medical device manufacturers' obligations will be or how data collection might affect them.[37]

The US and Europe have differing data requirements for high-risk (PMA) devices but have more similar requirements for low- to moderate-risk devices (510(k) in the US). Generally, low-risk 510(k) devices do not require clinical trials and can be cleared using clinical evidence such as literature searches instead of clinical trials. Most moderate-risk devices require some type of clinical use data, however small the trial. A "Summary of Safety and Effectiveness Data" and discussion of reported adverse events help provide the rationale for high-risk device approval. The US publishes summaries of safety and effectiveness to quantify risks for certain medical devices. However, in Europe, Notified Bodies are not obliged to publish evidence provided by sponsors or about their decision-making processes. The US and Europe face unique difficulties with their individual systems; both are challenged by time-to-approval and perceived regulatory barriers. In Europe, public availability of pre- and postmarket surveillance data is limited compared to the US. More transparency by European countries could improve information-sharing about device safety and performance. This increased information-sharing would assist regions in making more timely decisions and coordinating responses to adverse events. The challenge then is not only device introduction, but keeping it on the market while still generating business revenue.[38]

Medical device manufacturers and distributors must adhere to certain requirements and regulations once devices are on the market. These include such things as tracking systems; reporting device malfunctions, serious injuries or deaths; and registering the manufacturing and distribution establishments.

Postmarket requirements also include PMS studies required under *FD&C Act* Section 522 as well as postapproval studies required as conditions of approval for a PMA, HDE or PDP application.[39] Health Canada provides guidance on reported medical device problem investigations. It outlines the underlying risk management principles and the roles and responsibilities of manufacturers, importers and distributors. It describes what a company's procedures should contain and what kinds of records should be kept to comply with the *regulations.*[40]

Desired Outcomes of a Successful Strategy

A successful medical device regulatory strategy must have a coordinated pre- and postmarket approach. With an appropriately developed regulatory strategy, manufacturers can benefit from regulations' built-in flexibility to minimize the regulatory burden and ultimately reduce the time to market. If the device is not developed correctly using design controls and transferred to manufacturing, the likelihood of postmarket problems can increase significantly. Capturing and translating customer needs and wants in advance is crucial to answering key questions before market launch. Properly designing and developing products to meet user requirements and industry standards helps answer the question, was the right product built? Using a risk-based approach to mitigate risk to its lowest level will reduce the chance for complaints and adverse events when used by customers. Implementing a solid manufacturing plan to ensure the process is robust and repeatable gives the product the best chance for market success in providing a quality product. Successfully passing verification and validation testing will confirm the product was built correctly. Doing all of these things correctly in the premarket phase will make the postmarket phase much easier and, through avoiding unexpected costs, add revenue for investors. An additional benefit is the initial submission may undergo less reviewer scrutiny. All the monitoring activity following market release also provides the data to help answer the question, was the product built correctly?

Receiving device clearance or approval with fewer obstacles likely will get product to market sooner and add value for shareholders. Establishing a good reputation with regulators for providing solid submissions is extremely useful and builds a level of trust. Goodwill between manufacturers and regulators is difficult to measure but assuredly provides benefits in the form of cost avoidance. Consistently submitting incomplete or poorly written submissions reflects poorly on both the regulatory professional and the manufacturer. Repeating the same mistakes can trigger negative attention on an organization.

Once the product obtains marketing authorization, the manufacturer is responsible for ensuring safety and efficacy are maintained. Taking a proactive approach to monitoring the product and trending results allows the manufacturer to take quick action if product problems occur.

The regulatory environment is fluid and changes occur routinely. Keeping current with new and changing standards will keep the product at state-of-the-art. When changes are required, whether due to performance enhancements or because customer feedback demands them, proper verification and validation must be performed. CAPA procedures, if followed correctly, will identify the root cause and help pinpoint a sustainable corrective action. Regulators frequently list product monitoring and CAPA deficiencies as areas for manufacturer improvement. As noted previously, if the premarket work is done correctly, feedback after release to market should be positive. Fewer device adjustments and corrections

will be required. A cascade of positive outcomes occur for the manufacturer. The business costs are lower, and customers respond to better quality by continuing to buy the product. It is difficult to quantify cost avoidance, but it is certain high complaint rates, CAPAs, design changes resulting from poor quality or performance, product recalls and negative inspections will impact the bottom line significantly. A Warning Letter, for instance, reallocates valuable resources to fix a problem instead of focusing on innovative new products. Manufacturers receive negative publicity when this happens and investors are notified. Doing the right thing in the pre- and postmarket phases can avoid these problems. By planning proper pre- and postmarket regulatory strategies, a manufacturer can minimize introduction of a poor design and handle issues promptly when they occur.

Upper management's attitude and support determine overall QMS and regulatory strategy plan implementation success. Posting the quality policy statement at the building's entrance is insufficient. Attitude is reflected in action, and management must be willing to make tough decisions where product quality is concerned. The balance between pleasing investors and marketing a safe and effective product cannot be blurred. Deciding to manufacture good products and increasing revenue need not conflict. In fact, when done correctly, these will complement one another and lead to a very successful product lifecycle.

A company establishes a good reputation with customers and regulators over time based on how it conducts its business. Unfortunately, a bad decision can have an immediate impact, and recovery can take a long time. A very popular case study is the Johnson & Johnson (J&J) Tylenol recall in 1982.[41] Even though it was determined not to be the company's fault, J&J took quick and decisive action to pull the product from the market, reintroduced it with tamper-proof packaging and offered replacement product in the safer tablet form free of charge. The cost to perform these actions was astounding but far less than it could have been had J&J not acted quickly and responsibly. J&J took what could have been a catastrophic event and salvaged its reputation while also restoring customer confidence. It took only a few months for J&J's stock to rebound to pre-recall levels.

The bar an organization sets for itself must be high enough to maintain compliance and provide a safe and effective product, yet low enough to keep investors satisfied. Manufacturers must operate within those parameters or face extinction. The core question's response must be, what is best for the end user? Asking whether a regulatory professional would use this device on his or her child or spouse and not be concerned is where the bar ultimately should be set. The challenge is quantifying that decision.

Standards and regulations are quantitative measures a manufacturer should use when establishing where the bar should be set for its products. A successful company will do its homework, plan for contingencies and react quickly when the unexpected occurs.

References

1. GHTF/SG5/N4:2010. *Postmarket Clinical Follow-Up Studies* (18 February 2010. IMDRF website. http://www.imdrf.org/search.asp?zoom_query=postmarket%20clinica. Accessed 21 March 2016.
2. Device Postmarket Surveillance. FDA website. http://www.fda.gov/MedicalDevices/Safety/CDRHPostmarketSurveillance/default.htm. Accessed 21 March 2016.
3. *The Postmarket Priority: Understanding and Meeting Demand for Effective Postmarket Clinical Follow-Up*. BSI Group website. http://medicaldevices.bsigroup.com/LocalFiles/en-GB/Whitepapers/BSI-md-the-postmarket-priority-whitepaper-UK-EN.pdf. Accessed 21 March 2016.
4. *MEDDEV 2.12/2 rev2, Guidelines on Medical Devices, Guidelines on Medical Devices Postmarket Clinical Follow-up Studies: A Guide for Manufacturers and Notified Bodies*. European Commission website. http://ec.europa.eu/health/medical-devices/files/meddev/2_12_2_ol_en.pdf. Accessed 21 March 2016.
5. Medical Device Reporting (MDR). FDA website. http://www.fda.gov/MedicalDevices/Safety/ReportaProblem/default.htm. Accessed 21 March 2016.
6. MAUDE—Manufacturer and User Facility Device Experience. FDA website. http://www.accessdata.fda.gov/scripts/cdrh/cfdocs/cfmaude/search.cfm. Accessed 21 March 2016.
7. "FDA Lays out Plan for National Medical Device Surveillance System" (September 2012). RAPS website. http://www.raps.org/focus-online/news/news-article-view/article/2216/. Accessed 21 March 2016.
8. Market surveillance and vigilance. EC website. http://ec.europa.eu/growth/sectors/medical-devices/market-surveillance/index_en.htm. Accessed 21 March 2016.
9. EUDAMED—European Database on Medical Devices. EC website. http://ec.europa.eu/idabc/en/document/2256/5637.html. Accessed 21 March 2016.
10. Guidelines on a Medical Devices Vigilance System. EC website. http://ec.europa.eu/growth/sectors/medical-devices/guidance/index_en.htm. Accessed 21 March 2016.
11. Guidance MEDDEVs. EC website. http://ec.europa.eu/growth/sectors/medical-devices/guidance/index_en.htm. Accessed 21 March 2016.
12. *Quality System (QS) Regulation/Medical Device Good Manufacturing Practices*. FDA website. http://www.fda.gov/medicaldevices/deviceregulationandguidance/postmarketrequirements/qualitysystemsregulations/. Accessed 21 March 2016.
13. Postmarket Requirements (Devices). FDA website. http://www.fda.gov/MedicalDevices/DeviceRegulationandGuidance/PostmarketRequirements/default.htm. Accessed 21 March 2016.
14. ISO 13485:2003 Medical devices—Quality management systems—Requirements for regulatory purposes. ISO website. http://www.iso.org/iso/catalogue_detail?csnumber=36786. Accessed 21 March 2016.
15. Medical Devices. Health Canada website. http://www.hc-sc.gc.ca/dhp-mps/md-im/index-eng.php. Accessed 21 March 2016.
16. Op cit 12.
17. Medical Devices. EC website. http://ec.europa.eu/health/medical-devices/index_en.htm. Accessed 21 March 2016.
18. Post-marketing Safety Measures. PMDA website. http://www.pmda.go.jp/english/safety/index.html. Accessed 21 March 2016.
19. Regulations for the Supervision and Administration of Medical Devices. China Food and Drug Administration website. http://eng.sfda.gov.cn/WS03/CL0767/61641.html. Accessed 21 March 2016.
20. MEDSAFE—New Zealand Medicines and Medical Devices Safety Authority website. http://www.medsafe.govt.nz/index.asp. Accessed 21 March 2016.
21. ANVISA Brazilian Health Surveillance Agency website. http://portal.anvisa.gov.br/wps/portal/anvisa-ingles. Accessed 21 March 2016.
22. Canada Vigilance Program. Health Canada website. http://www.hc-sc.gc.ca/dhp-mps/medeff/vigilance-eng.php. Accessed 21 March 2016.
23. International Medical Device Regulators Forum (IMDRF) website. http://www.imdrf.org/. Accessed 21 March 2016.
24. Donawa ME. "The Responsibilities of Importers and Distributors." *Med Device Technol*. 1998 Sep;9(7):12-4, 16-8. NCBI website. http://www.ncbi.nlm.nih.gov/pubmed/10186979. Accessed 21 March 2016.
25. Donawa M. "US Importer and Exporter Requirements." Med Device Technol. 2005 June, 23–25. Donawa Consulting website. http://www.donawa.com/donawa/files/5%20US%20Importer%20&%20Distributors%20June2005%20MDT%20issue.pdf. Accessed 21 March 2016.
26. Lincoln JE. "Medical Device Product Verification and Validation." *Journal of Validation Technology* (Spring 2010). Institute of Validation Technology website. http://www.ivtnetwork.com/sites/default/files/MedicalDeviceProduct.pdf. Accessed 21 March 2016.
27. *Medical Device Regulations, Global overview and guiding principles*. World Health Organization website. http://www.who.int/medical_devices/publications/en/MD_Regulations.pdf. Accessed 21 March 2016.
28. *Design Control Guidance for Medical Device Manufacturers*. FDA website. http://www.fda.gov/MedicalDevices/DeviceRegulationandGuidance/GuidanceDocuments/ucm070627.htm. Accessed 21 March 2016.
29. Regulatory Affairs Professionals Society (RAPS) website. http://www.raps.org/. Accessed 21 March 2016.
30. Advanced Medical Technology Association (AdvaMed) website. http://advamed.org/page/56/about-advamed. Accessed 21 March 2016.
31. Medical Devices. FDA website. http://www.fda.gov/MedicalDevices/default.htm. Accessed 21 March 2016.
32. *Guidance for the Interpretation of Significant Change of a Medical Device*. Health Canada website. http://www.hc-sc.gc.ca/dhp-mps/md-im/applic-demande/guide-ld/signchng_modimportante-eng.php. Accessed 21 March 2016.
33. Deciding When to Submit a 510(k) for a Change to an Existing Device (K97-1). FDA website. http://www.fda.gov/MedicalDevices/DeviceRegulationandGuidance/GuidanceDocuments/ucm080235.htm. Accessed 21 March 2016.
34. PMA Supplements and Amendments. FDA website. http://www.fda.gov/MedicalDevices/DeviceRegulationandGuidance/HowtoMarketYourDevice/PremarketSubmissions/PremarketApprovalPMA/ucm050467.htm. Accessed 21 March 2016.
35. Reporting of design changes and changes of the quality management system—MEDDEV 2.5.2. MEDDEV website. http://www.meddev.info/_documents/R2_5_2-2_rev7.pdf. Accessed 21 March 2016.
36. FDA, Unique Device Identification—UDI. FDA website. http://www.fda.gov/MedicalDevices/DeviceRegulationandGuidance/UniqueDeviceIdentification/. Accessed 21 March 2016.

37. FDA's Sentinel Initiative. FDA website. http://www.fda.gov/Safety/FDAsSentinelInitiative/default.htm. Accessed 21 March 2016.
38. Kramer DB, Xu S and Kesselheim AS. "Regulation of Medical Devices in the United States and European Union." *N Engl J Med* 2012; 366:848-855. *NEJM* website. http://www.nejm.org/doi/full/10.1056/NEJMhle1113918. Accessed 21 March 2016.
39. Postmarket Requirements (Devices). FDA website. http://www.fda.gov/MedicalDevices/DeviceRegulationandGuidance/PostmarketRequirements/. Accessed 21 March 2016.
40. *Guidance on Investigation of Reported Medical Device Problems (GUI-0065)*. Health Canada website. http://www.hc-sc.gc.ca/dhp-mps/compli-conform/prob-report-rapport/gui-0065_md-im_problem_doc-eng.php#a21. Accessed 21 March 2016.
41. Rehak J. "Tylenol made a hero of Johnson & Johnson: The recall that started them all." *The New York Times,* 23 March 2002. *The NY Times* website. http://www.nytimes.com/2002/03/23/your-money/23iht-mjj_ed3_.html. Accessed 21 March 2016.

18   Regulatory Resources for Strategy Development

By Gretchen Parker, PhD, RAC, CIP and Philip E. Sax

Personnel Resources

Regulatory professionals are a diverse and committed group of highly motivated and trained experts. In a recent survey of regulatory professionals at every level, there was one overwhelming fact linking them—most stated their careers were "accidents" and few stated regulatory was their initial career goal. Their undergraduate degrees included political science, social science, biology, chemistry, mechanical engineering, and quality engineering. In the survey, more than half had graduate degrees including masters, PhDs and law degrees. Almost all had special certifications in quality, regulatory and/or auditing.

A growing trend is pursuing graduate degrees in regulatory and quality designed for individuals working in the field (Temple University has offered a program since 1968; other schools, like George Washington and Johns Hopkins, are offering professional graduate degrees). Others seek professional certifications to demonstrate sufficient knowledge and experience.

Certainly, successful regulatory professionals appreciate detail and are patient, yet driven, to achieve results. Often, a key question for these professionals is "What does it take to get a medical device to market?" While the question is straightforward, the answer is not—devices vary from ventilators to skin creams and MRI equipment to bandages. As such, some new products may require clinical studies to demonstrate safety and efficacy. Other "me too" products may require a 510(k) to prove "substantial equivalence"— similar to "biological equivalence" for generic drugs. Class I products require documentation but not submissions. Given the wide range of requirements, what actions are needed to accomplish a submission correctly, effectively and efficiently?

Regulatory professionals need specific knowledge of the regulations, quality processes and products they are supporting. The US Food and Drug Administration (FDA) is very proficient but is working with many new challenges. With that in mind, the regulatory professional must be able to communicate with regulators, coworkers, executive and middle management, research and development (R&D), engineers, marketing, sales, finance and quality, and incorporate both US and international regulatory requirements. The regulatory professional also must be able to understand the product concept, yet be free to question both concept and design.

Regulatory professionals' responsibilities may be limited to regulatory issues or they may be responsible for quality processes and systems as well. The regulatory professional's primary job is to protect: the patient and product users; the company; and those who make and support the products. Successful submissions require strategy based on a thorough understanding of both the product and the relevant regulatory and quality requirements.

Regulatory professionals must have:
- detailed knowledge and understanding of regulations
- the ability to interpret regulations and guidance documents
- freedom and confidence to say what is contrary to good practices, illegal, unethical, etc.
- the ability to research regulations (No one can know everything. The skilled regulatory

professional knows where to look for the answers and is not afraid to say "I do not know, but I will find out." As a professor once said, "An educated person is not someone who knows everything, but who knows where to find the answers.")
- the ability to develop a submission plan and ask appropriate questions:
  o Is this a new and unique product (requiring Premarket Approval (PMA)), 510(k) or *de novo* submission?
  o Is this Class I, II or III?
  o What are the patient and business risks?

Business realities are critical, and the regulatory professional must understand both time and cost constraints. However, at no time can safety and efficacy be compromised. The regulatory professional must be aware of new complex technologies but cannot overlook safety and regulatory requirements because the product is new and exciting.

A successful regulatory professional is a good communicator. In today's business environment, communication may be complicated by the use of emails, digital messaging, etc. Communication is not the product of technology. Communication strategy must be developed. It includes conversations, written reports, phone calls, meetings, letters, notices, emails and more. The selected tools must meet the need. Often communication spans distances, but developing trust is critical. Face-to-face meetings can provide the ability to assess nonverbal communication. All decisions and disagreements must be documented so there is no disagreement about status.

Ethics, above all, is a fundamental issue as the healthcare product industry self-regulates. FDA has more than 100,000 registered sites to inspect. These inspections would take more than 1,900 years to accomplish, assuming an inspection time of one week per site visit, making this an impossible task. Two investigators spending a week at a major or even small firm cannot find everything. As good as the investigators are, and they are very good, compliance remains self-motivated: a product of the company and team's established philosophy and practices. The regulatory officer is the compliance point person but not the only one who needs to be committed and focused.

In addition to these issues, the regulatory professional must be aware of the following:

Testing

The regulatory professional must know the type of testing required for varied products and processes. This might include software testing, cytotoxicity and biocompatibility. Sterilization verification and quality testing for incoming, in-process and finished product also may be included. Testing is complex and clearly very important.

Documentation

"If it is not in writing, it did not happen." The regulatory team must define documentation, verification, change control, validation and retention methods to ensure compliance and effectiveness. Retention rules and procedures must be developed. This often is complicated by the fact the US and other countries have different documentation requirements and methods.

Risk Management

Risk management and hazard assessment are critical to today's regulatory professional because most decisions are based on risks to users, both regulatory and business risks. Tools like fault tree and failure mode effect analyses, hazard analysis and critical control points and ISO 14971 help qualify the risks but, ultimately, a decision must be made on acceptable risk and how is it verified (identified issues and values).

Regulatory Requirements

Certainly, regulatory professionals are familiar with relevant regulations. Device teams need knowledge of not only 21 CFR 820, but also 21 CFR 54 and 58, Parts 11 and 211, etc. Knowledge of ISO 13485, 14971, 10993 and 9001 also are important and often required.

Manufacturing Process

Understanding the manufacturing process system, methods validation and sterilization all are necessary. No product can be better than its production process. The regulatory professional participates in process and change planning. Regulatory inspections and reporting require manufacturing and related requirements' knowledge.

Process and Computer System Validation

Installation, operational, performance and design qualification, along with software validation, all are key regulatory tools. Quality "cannot be inspected in;" it must be part of the process. This concept recognizes no product can be better than its manufacturing process and materials.

Quality System

Quality system requirements (21 CFR 820, Good Manufacturing Practices (GMPs), ISO

13485:2003—Quality management systems—Requirements for regulatory purposes, quality agreements and ongoing support including documentation, training, testing and auditing) must be incorporated.

Prepare Staff

Staff must have the appropriate skills and be trained and prepared for each project. Regulatory management must be engaged actively in all communications with regulatory agencies.

Communicate Truthfully With Regulators

It is important to recognize regulators share industry's goal to protect the patient through the development and approval of safe products. Once that is understood, mutual respect is more likely and communication more effective. Regulatory professionals should not hesitate to talk to agency staff. They are not industry consultants but their insight can be helpful and is important.

Communicate With Technical Staff

Engineers, technicians, and software developers usually find regulations cumbersome and time-consuming. Regulatory professionals must train and meet regularly with the technical staff. It must be understood the same goals are shared by all—safe, effective, high-quality and compliant products. Resources must be planned, trained and available, as required.

Project Staff

Project staff must be trained and motivated. Regulatory understanding is critical. Product development is time- and sequence-dependent. Requirements must be defined in advance; compliance must be designed in, and processes must be defined to conform to the quality system and relevant regulations. Retrospective design and requirements are not effective.

Cooperate With Regulators

Patient or product user well-being is the first priority. The regulatory professional must be involved early to ensure compliance and keep the focus on safety and compliance. Regulations require Design History Files (DHFs), Device Master Files (DMFs) and all living documents to be updated as the project continues.

Regulatory Strategy

The regulatory professional must be able to develop a strategy to meet regulatory, ethical and business requirements. This requires knowledge of the regulations, personal motivation and clear understanding of business goals. Decisions must be made for the path to submission and clearance—510(k), PMA or *de novo*.

Intended Use and Indications

The regulatory professional must understand the product's intended use and indication. These must be clear, and all product claims must conform to these statements.

Time and Cost Constraints

Every product and project has time and cost limitations. The regulatory professional must be able to identify regulatory requirements related to time and cost to allow effective planning. Regulatory requirements cannot be compromised.

Manage Expectations

The regulatory professional must manage expectations. For example, marketing teams must know a 510(k), on average, takes 167 days to clear. The regulatory professional must know how much time comparable products required for clearance and understand FDA inspection processes and duration times.

Clinical Process

Clinical processes and studies are vital to new products. The regulatory professional must know when a study is required and when it is not. The regulatory professional should be able to work with Institutional Review Boards (IRBs) and Principal Investigators (PIs), and must be able to understand a study's statistics and develop effective data reporting and summarization to know what is important.

Clearly, regulatory's role is complex, challenging, important, sometimes exhausting, frustrating and very rewarding. Rarely do individuals have an opportunity to impact so many people's well-being without knowing them or directly communicating with them.

The consensus among regulatory professionals is this is a great career; one that is not easy, but is important, challenging and very satisfying. Numerous resources are available to help professionals along the way.

Table 18-1. African and Middle Eastern Regulatory Agencies

Country	Agency	Additional Information/Website
Algeria	Ministry of Health, Population and Hospital Reform (Ministère de la Santé, de la Population et de la Réforme Hospitalière)	Obtain authorization from the Ministry of Health and Population before the device can be imported. To commercialize a product, proof of market authorization in country of origin is required as well as quality certificates. All documentation must be translated into either French or Arabic. (www.ands.dz)
Bahrain	Ministry of Health	www.moh.gov.bh
Botswana	Ministry of Health	www.moh.gov.bw/
Egypt	Ministry of Health and Population (MOHP) and the Committee on Registration of Medical Devices	Standardization in Egypt is coordinated by the Ministry of Health and Population (MOHP) through the Drug Policy and Planning Center (DPPC) and the Central Administration of Pharmaceutical Affairs (CAPA). (www.mohp.gov.eg/default.aspx)
Ghana	Ministry of Health	www.moh-ghana.org
Iran	Ministry of Health and Medical Education	www.imed.ir/Uploads/Forms/Documents/73a82691-3330-4eef-a1d1-36c769376672.pdf
Iraq	Ministry of Health, Kimadia	http://kimadia-iraq.net/ar/ www.izdihar-iraq.com/resources/papers_pdfs/pharmaceutical_and_medical_products_in_Iraq_0appx_rev_web2.pdf
Israel	Israel Institute for Biological Research	P.O.B 19, 74100, Ness-Ziona, Israel www.iibr.gov.il/
Israel	AMAR, Israel's Ministry of Health	2 Ben Tabai St., Jerusalem, Israel 91010 www.health.gov.il/
Jordan	Ministry of Health	http://www.moh.gov.jo/en/Pages/default.aspx
Kenya	Ministry of Health	http://www.health.go.ke/
Lebanon	Ministry of Health	Hussein Mansour Bldg., Museum St, Beirut, Lebanon http://www.moph.gov.lb/Pages/Home.aspx
Maldives	Ministry of Health	Ameenee Magu, Malé 20379 www.health.gov.mv/
Mauritius	Ministry of Health and Quality of Life	5th floor, Emmanuel Anquetil Building, Port Louis, Mauritius http://health.govmu.org/English/Pages/default.aspx
Morocco	Ministry of Public Health	335, Avenue Mohammed V www.sante.gov.ma/
Namibia	Medicines Regulatory Council	www.nmrc.com.na/
Nigeria	National Agency for Food and Drug Administration and Control (NAFDAC)	Plot 2032, Olusegun Obasanjo Way Wuse Zone 7, Abuja www.nafdac.gov.ng/
Oman	Ministry of Health	Manufacturers selling devices through public tenders must register with Oman's Directorate General of Medical Supplies and obtain Qualification Certificates. A Qualification Certificate is issued to a manufacturing facility rather than a device and can be used to cover all products manufactured at an approved facility. https://www.moh.gov.om/en
Qatar	Registration: Ministry of Economy and Commerce (MEC)	http://www.mec.gov.qa/en/departments/administration_Trade/registration-and-license-business
Qatar	Request for inspections: Ministry of Municipal Affairs and Agriculture (MMAA)	http://portal.www.gov.qa/wps/portal/homepage
Saudi Arabia	Saudi Food and Drug Authority (SFDA)	http://old.sfda.gov.sa/En/Home
Senegal	Ministry of Health, Hygiene, and Prevention	Fann Résidence, Rue Aimé Césaire, 2ème étage www.sante.gouv.sn

Country	Agency	Additional Information/Website
South Africa	Medicines Control Council	www.mccza.com/
	South African Bureau of Standards (SABS)	Provides wide range of services to the medical device industry. Private Bag X191, Pretoria, 0001 www.govpage.co.za/south-african-bureau-of-standards-sabs.html
	Department of Health	Requires registration and CE Marking for electromagnetic and radiation-emitting devices. Electromedical devices fall under the scope of the Hazardous Substances Act, No. 15 of 1973. www.health.gov.za/
Tanzania	Ministry of Health, Community Development, Gender, Elderly and Children	Samora Avenue, P.O. Box 9083, Dar es Salaam http://www.moh.go.tz/
	Tanzanian Food and Drugs Authority (TFDA)	TFDA regulations are based on Global Harmonization Task Force (GHTF) recommendations and require all device manufacturers to have certificates of registration prior to market entry. Off-Mandela Road, Mabibo-External P.O. Box 77150, Dar es Salaam, Tanzania www.tfda.or.tz
Tunisia	Ministry of Health	Bab Saadoun-1006 Tunis
Uganda	Ministry of Health	Plot 6 Lourdel Rd, Wandegeya P.O. Box 7272 Kampala Uganda www.health.go.ug/
United Arab Emirates	Ministry of Health Drug Control Department	Based on GHTF guidelines and EU requirements. Market authorization requires registration with the Drug Control Department and obtaining an Accreditation of Company certificate. UAE, Abu Dhabi, P.O. Box 848 Abu Dhabi, Hamdan Street www.moh.gov.ae/en/Pages/default.aspx
Zimbabwe	Ministry of Health and Child Care	http://www.mohcc.gov.zw/

Strategic Resources

Strategies and Resources for Successful Product Submissions

Where can global regulatory information be found? What electronic databases are available, and how might they be employed? What are the key online resources of country-to-country regulatory agencies? What drives a successful product submission?

Unfortunately, a regulatory formula to guarantee success in medical device product submissions has not been established. However, regulatory professionals who either possess or can hire and retain individuals with the knowledge appropriate to a task will succeed. Honing this skill is not as easy as it sounds. Professionals not only must be able to recognize they need help, but must know where to find appropriate and competent assistance. Further complicating matters, individuals possessing the skills mentioned earlier are highly prized.

Global regulatory experts might be found by leveraging contacts made through business associates, at symposiums or over the Internet. However, while foreign markets often boast tempting cost savings, companies must spend enormous amounts of money and effort to develop suitable business connections overseas. Device manufacturers must consider a number of issues during their products' lifecycles, including:

- finding appropriate Competent Authority or regulatory organizations
- interpreting laws, regulations and guidances
- business licensing and registration
- device marketing clearance classification and requirements
- quality management system and Good Manufacturing Practice requirements
- adverse incident or event reporting
- medical device recalls and removals

Table 18-2. Asia/Pacific Regulatory Agencies

Country	Agency	Website
Australia	Therapeutic Goods Administration	www.tga.gov.au
China	China Food and Drug Administration	http://eng.sfda.gov.cn/WS03/CL0755
China	General Administration of Quality Supervision, Inspection and Quarantine—Certification and Accreditation Administration	www.cnca.gov.cn
China	Ministry of Health	www.moh.gov.cn
Hong Kong	Medical Device Administrative Control System (MDACS) Medical Device Control Office (MDCO)	www.mdco.gov.hk
India	Ministry of Health and Family Welfare Department of Health	http://mohfw.nic.in
India	Central Drugs Standard Control Organization	www.cdsco.nic.in
India	Indian Radiological and Imaging Association	www.iria.in
Indonesia	Ministry of Health Republic of Indonesia	www.depkes.go.id
Japan	Ministry of Health, Labour and Welfare	http://www.mhlw.go.jp/english/
Japan	Pharmaceuticals and Medical Devices Agency	http://www.pmda.go.jp/english/
Kazakhstan	Ministry of Healthcare and Social Development of the Republic of Kazakhstan (KKMFD)	http://www.mzsr.gov.kz/en
Malaysia	Malaysian Ministry of Health	www.moh.gov.my
New Zealand	New Zealand Ministry of Health	www.moh.govt.nz/moh.nsf
Philippines	Bureau of Health Devices and Technology (BHDT)	www.doh.gov.ph/bhdt
Philippines	Bureau of Food And Drugs	http://www.fda.gov.ph/
Singapore	Singapore Health Sciences Authority (HSA), Health Product Regulation Group (HPRG)	www.hsa.gov.sg
South Korea	Korean Testing Laboratory (KTL)	http://www.ktc.re.kr/u_eng/guide/guide_05_01.asp
South Korea	Korean Food and Drug Administration, Medical Devices & Radiation Health Department	http://eng.kfda.go.kr/index.html
Taiwan	Ministry of Health and Welfare	http://www.mohw.gov.tw/EN/Ministry/Index.aspx
Thailand	Food & Drug Administration of Thailand—Medical Device Control Division	www.fda.moph.go.th/eng/index.stm
Vietnam	Ministry of Health	http://moh.gov.vn/sites/en-us/pages/home.aspx

Table 18-3. European Commission Competent Authorities

Country	Name of Agency	Contact Information/Website
Austria	Federal Ministry of Health	Radetzkystrasse 2, 1030 Wien/Vienna www.bmgf.gv.at
Belgium	MDD AIMDD Federal Agency for Medicines and Health Products Health Products Division	Place Victor Horta 40, boîte 40 B - 1060 Brussels www.health.belgium.be/eportal
Belgium	IVDMD Scientific Institute Public Health, Department Quality Medical Laboratories	J. Wytsmanstraat, 14 B-1050 Brussels www.wiv-isp.be/Pages/FR-Home.aspx
Bulgaria	Bulgarian Drug Agency Department Medical Devices	8 Damyan Gruev Str. BG - 1303 Sofia www.bda.bg
Cyprus	Cyprus Medical Devices Competent Authority	Prodromou 1 & Chilonos 17 Corner CY - 1449 Nicosia www.moh.gov.cy

Country	Name of Agency	Contact Information/Website
Czech Republic	Ministry of Health Department of Pharmacy, Medical Devices Unit	Palackého náměstí 4, CZ - 12801 Prague 2 www.mzcr.cz
Croatia	Agency for Medicinal Products and Medical Devices	Ksaverska cesta 4, 10 000 Zagreb www.almp.hr/?ln=en&w=zurno_obavjescivanje
Denmark	Danish Health and Medicines Authority	Axel Heides Gade 1 DK - 2300 - Kobenhavn http://sundhedsstyrelsen.dk/da/medicin/medicinsk-udstyr
Estonia	Health Board, Medical Devices Department	1a Põllu st., EE - Tartu 50303 www.terviseamet.ee
Finland	Valvira - National Supervisory Authority for Welfare and Health	Lintulahdenkuja 4, P.O.Box 210 FIN - 00531 Helsinki www.valvira.fi
France	Agence nationale de sécurité du médicament et des produits de santé (ANSM)	143-147 boulevard Anatole France FR - 93285 Saint Denis Cedex http://ansm.sante.fr/
Germany	AIMDD, MDD, IVDMD Legislation Federal Ministry of Health	Rochusstrasse 1, D - 53123 Bonn www.bmg.bund.de/ministerium/presse/english-version.html
Germany	AIMDD, MDD, IVDMD Designating Zentralstelle der Länder für Gesundheitsschutz bei Arzneimitteln und Medizinprodukten (ZLG)	www.zlg.de/
Germany	AIMDD CA Federal Institute for Drugs and Medical Devices	Kurt Georg Kiesinger Allee 3, D - 53175 Bonn www.bfarm.de/cln_103/DE/Home/home_node.html
Germany	IVDMD CA Paul Ehrlich Institute	Paul-Ehrlich-Strasse 51-59, D - 63225 Langen www.pei.de/DE/home/de-node.html
Greece	National Organization for Medicines	284 Mesogion Ave GR- 15562 Holargos, Athens www.eof.gr
Hungary	Health Registration and Training Centre, Department of Medical Devices	1051, Budapest, Zrínyi street 3, Hungary http://ogyei.gov.hu/presidency2011/about_department_for_medical_deviceseekh
Iceland (EFTA)	Icelandic Medicines Agency	Vínlandsleið 14, IS-113 Reykjavík www.lyfjastofnun.is/
Ireland	Health Products Regulatory Authority	Kevin O'Malley House, Medical Devices Department Earlsfort Centre, Earlsfort Terrace, IE - Dublin 2 https://www.hpra.ie/
Italy	Ministry of Health, Department of Planning and Organisation of the National Health Service - Directorate General of Medical Devices, pharmaceutical services and safety in healthcare	Via Giorgio Ribotta 5, IT- 00144 Roma http://www.salute.gov.it/
Latvia	State Agency of Medicines	15 Jersikas street, LV- 1003 Riga https://www.zva.gov.lv/?setlang=en
Liechtenstein (EFTA)	Amt für Gesundheit	Äulestrasse 51, Postfach 684 FL- 9490 Vaduz www.llv.li/#/1908/amt-fur-gesundheit
Lithuania	The State Health Care Accreditation Agency under the Ministry of Health of the Republic of Lithuania	Jeruzales str. 21, LT-08420 Vilnius www.vaspvt.gov.lt
Luxembourg	Ministère de la Santé Direction de la Santé	Villa Louvigny - allée Marconi L- 2120 Luxembourg www.etat.lu/MS/
Malta	Malta Competition and Consumer Affairs Authority	Mizzi House, National Road, Blata l-Bajda, HMR 9010, Malta http://mccaa.org.mt/

Country	Name of Agency	Contact Information/Website
Netherlands	Law Enforcement (a.o. vigilance and market surveillance)	Dutch Healthcare Inspectorate, IGZ information office (Meldpunt)
	Notification/Registration CIBG Farmatec-BMC	PO box 16114, NL - 2500 BC The Hague www.farmatec.nl
	Dutch Healthcare Inspectorate	P.O. Box 2680 NL- 3500 BS Utrecht www.igz.nl
Norway (EFTA)	Helsedirektoratet Norwegian Directorate for Health	P.O. Box 7000 ST. Olavplass N- 0130 Oslo https://helsedirektoratet.no/english
Poland	Competent Authority Office for Registration of Medicinal Products	Al. Jerozolimskie 181C, 02-222 Warsaw http://www.urpl.gov.pl/
	Legislation - Designation of NBs Ministry of Health	Miodowa 15, PL - 00-952 Warsaw http://en.urpl.gov.pl/en-information-about-the-office
Portugal	Infarmed - National Authority of Medicines and Health Products, IP	Parque da Saúde de Lisboa Av. do Brasil, n° 53 PT - 1749-004 Lisboa www.infarmed.pt
Romania	National Agency for Medicnes and Medical Devices	58, Sos. Nicolae Titulescu, sector 1, Bucharest www.ms.ro
Slovenia	Agency for Medicinal Products and Medical Devices of the Republic of Slovenia	Ptujska ulica 21, SI-1000 Ljubljana http://www.sukl.sk/en?page_id=256
Spain	Agencia Española de Medicamentos y Productos Sanitarios	Edificio 8. C/ Campezo 1 ES - 28022 Madrid http://www.aemps.gob.es/
Sweden	Medical Products Agency 'Läkemedelsverket' Medical Devices	Box 26, SE-751 03 Uppsala www.lakemedelsverket.se/
Switzerland (EFTA)	Swissmedic Swiss Agency for Therapeutic Products	Hallerstrasse 7, CH -3012 Bern 7, https://www.swissmedic.ch/medizinprodukte/02636/index.html?lang=en
Turkey	Ministry of Health DG for Pharmaceuticals and Pharmacy	Department of Medical Device Services, Market Surveillance Section Mithatpasa Cad. No:3, Sihhiye 06434, Ankara/TÜRKIYE http://www.saglik.gov.tr/TR/ana-sayfa/1-0/20160303.html
United Kingdom (UK)	Medicines & Healthcare products Regulatory Agency (MHRA)	Floor 4-O, Buckingham Palace Road - London SW1W 9SZ www.mhra.gov.uk

European Free Trade Association (EFTA); Active Implantable Medical Devices Directive (); (); Directive ()
http://ec.europa.eu/health/medical-devices/links/contact_points_en.htm

Table 18-4. Eastern European Agencies

Country	Agency	Website
Russia	Roszdravnadzor	4 Slavyanskaya Square, Building 1, Moscow, 109074 Russia http://www.roszdravnadzor.ru/
Slovakia	State Institute for Drug Control, Medical Devices Section	Kvetna 11, SK - 825 08 Bratislava 26 www.sukl.sk/en?page_id=256
Ukraine*	Ministry of Public Health State Inspectorate for Quality Control.	http://www.moz.gov.ua/ua/portal/

*Registration with the Ukrainian Ministry of Health, obtaining a National Mark of Conformity and listing in the State Registrar of Medical Equipment and Products are all required.

Table 18-5. Latin American Regulatory Agencies

Country	Agency	Website
Argentina	National Administration of Drugs, Foodstuffs and Medical Technology (ANMAT) under the Ministry of Health	www.anmat.gov.ar
Bolivia	Bolivian Ministry of Health Unit of Drugs and Health Technology (UNIMED)	http://www.unimed.coop.br/pct/index.jsp?cd_canal=49146
Brazil	Ministry of Health	www.saude.gov.br
Chile	Health Ministry	www.minsal.cl
Chile	Institute of Public Health	www.ispch.cl
Colombia	Ministry of Health and Social Protection	https://www.minsalud.gov.co/sites/english/Pages/default.aspx
Colombia	Instituto Nacional de Vigilancia de Medicamentos y Alimentos (INVIMA)	https://www.invima.gov.co/
Costa Rica	Ministry of Health	www.ministeriodesalud.go.cr
Cuba	Centro para el Control Estatal de Medicamentos, Equipos y Dispositivos Médicos (CECMED)	www.cecmed.sld.cu/
Ecuador	Ministry of Public Health	http://www.salud.gob.ec/
Guatemala	Ministry of Health	www.mspas.gob.gt
Honduras	Secretariat of Health	www.salud.gob.hn/
Jamaica	Ministry of Health	http://moh.gov.jm/
Mexico	Ministry of Health	http://www.gob.mx/salud
Nicaragua	Ministry of Health	www.minsa.gob.ni/
Panama	Ministry of Health	www.minsa.gob.pa
Paraguay	Office of Professional Monitoring and Health Facilities, Division of the Ministry of Public Health and Social Welfare	www.mspbs.gov.py
Peru	Ministry of Health	www.minsa.gob.pe
Puerto Rico	Department of Health	http://www.salud.gov.pr/Pages/Home.aspx
Uruguay	Ministry of Public Health	www.msp.gub.uy
Venezuela	Ministerio del Poder Popular para la Salud (MPPS)	www.mpps.gob.ve/

Source: Morroney R, Arrieta J, Belza A, Biere M, Castaneda G, Funari L, Gilbert S, Marinaro B, Obando Y. 2010. "Medical Device Regulation in Latin America." *Regulatory Affairs Focus*. February 2010.

Table 18-6. North American Regulatory Agencies

Country	Agency	Website
Canada	Health Canada	www.hc-sc.gc.ca/dhp-mps/md-im/index-eng.php
US	US Food and Drug Administration (FDA)	www.fda.gov/MedicalDevices/default.htm

These issues are compounded when working in a global market. Therefore, it is important to have the right tools and resources to find both assistance and information regarding medical device regulations. Using some standard means and philosophies will enable the regulatory professional to assess and manage staff and complete the product clearance and/or approval process successfully. In addition to the general rules discussed throughout this book, specific instruments and strategies may be employed to increase the likelihood of a successful device submission. The tables in this chapter present global regulatory resource sites by region and include web addresses a regulatory professional needs to find medical device information and assemble regulatory intelligence and strategy.

General Strategies and Resources for a Successful Product Submission

While preparing a medical or diagnostic device marketing submission, a regulatory professional will encounter

Table 18-7. Global Regulatory Professional Trade Organizations

Organization	Website
Africa: South Africa	
Medical Device Manufacturers Association of South Africa (MDM)	www.mdmsa.co.za/
Southern African Laboratory Diagnostic Association (SALDA)	http://salda.org.za/
South African Medical Device Industry Association (SAMED)	www.samed.org.za/
Asia/Pacific: Australia	
AusBiotech	www.ausbiotech.org/
Australian Dental Industry Association	www.adia.org.au/
Australian Medical Association (AMA)	https://ama.com.au/
IVD Australia	www.ivd.org.au/
Medical Technology Association of Australia (MTAA)	http://mtaa.org.au/
Science Industry Australia (SIA)	http://scienceindustry.com.au/#axzz34flZw5GD
Asia/Pacific: China	
China Medical Device Information Network (CMDI)	www.cmdi.gov.cn/english/publish/default/
Asia/Pacific: India	
Association of Diagnostics Manufacturers of India	www.admi-india.org/
Association of Indian Medical Device Industry (AIMED)	www.aimedindia.com/
Asia/Pacific: Japan	
American Medical Devices and Diagnostics Manufacturers' Association (AMDD)	http://amdd.jp/en/index.html
Association for Promotion of Health Care Services (APHCS)	http://ikss.net/index.html
Japan Association for the Advancement of Medical Equipment (JAAME)	www.jaame.or.jp/index.php
Japan Association of Clinical Reagents Industries (JACRI)	www.jacr.or.jp/
Japan Contact Lens Association (JCLA)	www.jcla.gr.jp/
Japan Dental Materials Association (JDMA)	www.jdma.jp/archives/2525
Japan Electronics and Information Technology Industries Association (JEITA)	www.jeita.or.jp/english/
Japan Federation of Medical Devices Associations (JFMDA)	www.jfmda.gr.jp/e/
Japan Hearing Instruments Dispensers Association (JHIDA)	www.jhida.org/
Japan Industries Association of Physical Therapy Device (JIAPTD)	http://nichirikiko.gr.jp/
Japan Medical Imaging and Radiological Systems Industries Association (JIRA)	www.jira-net.or.jp/e/index.htm
Japan Medical Devices Manufacturers Association (JMED)	www.jmed.jp
Japan Ophthalmic Instruments Association (JOIA)	www.joia.or.jp/
Asia/Pacific: Malaysia	
Association of Malaysian Medical Industries (AMMI)	www.ammi.com.my/content/home/index/site:ammi-link:6191
Eastern Europe: Russia	
International Medical Device Manufacturers Association (IMEDA)	www.imeda.ru/
European Commission	
European Coordination Committee of the Radiological, Electromedical and Healthcare IT Industry (COCIR)	www.cocir.org/site/
European Disposables & Nonwovens Association (EDANA)	www.edana.org/
Medtech Europe—currently has two members: European Diagnostic Manufacturers Association (EDMA), representing the European in vitro diagnostic industry; and European Confederation of Medical Devices Associations (EUCOMED), representing the European medical devices industry.	http://www.medtecheurope.org/
EuropaBio—European Association for Bioindustries	www.europabio.org/
European Health Industry Business Communications Council (EHIBCC)	www.ehibcc.com/

Organization	Website
Medical Device and Diagnostic Industry	http://www.mddionline.com/
Health First Europe	www.healthfirsteurope.org/
The Organisation for Professionals in Regulatory Affairs	http://www.topra.org /
European Free Trade Association: Switzerland	
FASMED	www.fasmed.ch/
European Union: Austria	
Austromed	www.austromed.org/
European Union: Belgium	
Agoria-Hospibel	www.agoria.be/
Bio.be	www.essenscia.be/en/bio.be
pharma.be.diagnostics	www.pharma.be/
Belgian Federation of the Medical Technology Industry (UNAMEC)	www.unamec.be/
European Union: Denmark	
Association of Biotechnology Industries in Denmark	www.danskbiotek.dk/
Danish Diagnostic & Laboratory Association (DADIF)	www.dadif.dk/
MedicoIndustrien	www.medicoindustrien.dk/
European Union: France	
Appamed	www.appamed.org/
Comident	www.comident.asso.fr/
Comité Interprofessionnel des Fournisseurs du Laboratorie (CIFL)	www.cifl.com/cifl/UK/index.php
French National Association for Medical Technology Industries (SNITEM) and Syndicat des Fabricants et Fournisseurs d'Optique de Contact (SYFFOC)	www.snitem.fr/index.php?glang=EN
European Union: Germany	
Bundesverband Medizintechnologie (BVMed)	www.bvmed.de/?language=2
Bundeszahnarztekammer Arbeitsgemeinschaft der Deutschen Zahnarztekammern eV	www.bzaek.de/
Deutsche Gesellschaft für Telemedizin	www.dgtelemed.de/index.php?lang=de
Deutsche Krankenhausgesellschaft	www.dkgev.de/
Fachverband Biomedizinische Technik e.V	http://fbmt.eu/
GKV Spitzenverband	www.gkv-spitzenverband.de/
Kassenärztliche Bundesvereinigung (KBV)	www.kbv.de/html/
Spectaris eV	www.spectaris.de/english.html
VDGH Verband der Diagnostica-Industrie eV	www.vdgh.de/
Zentralvereinigung medizin-technischer Fachhändler, Hersteller, Dienstleister und Berater e.V	www.zmt.de/
Zentralverband Elektrotechnik- und Elektronikindustrie e.V. (ZVEI)	www.zvei.org/Seiten/Startseite.aspx
European Union: Greece	
Hellenic Dental Association	www.eoo.gr/
Institute of Biomedical Technology (INBIT)	www.inbit.gr/index.php?lang=en
European Union: Ireland	
Irish Medical Device Association (IMDA)	www.ibec.ie/imda
European Union: Italy	
Assobiomedica	www.assobiomedica.it/it/index.html
European Union: Portugal	
Apormed	www.apormed.pt/
European Union: Spain	
Federacion Española de Empresas de Technologia Sanitarial (FENIN)	http://www.fenin.es/
Sociedad Española de Implantes (SEI)	http://sociedadsei.com/

Organization	Website
European Union: Sweden	
Swecare Foundation	www.swecare.se/
Swedish Medtech	www.swedishmedtech.se/
European Union: The Netherlands	
Diagnostica Associatie Nederland (DIAGNED)	www.diagned.nl/
European Federation of the Contact Lens Industry (EFCLIN)	www.diagned.nl/
INDENT	www.indent.nl
NEFEMED	www.nefemed.nl/
European Union: United Kingdom	
Association for Clinical Biochemistry	www.acb.org.uk/
Association of British Healthcare Industries Limited (ABHI)	www.abhi.org.uk/
Association of X-Ray Equipment Manufacturers (AXrEM)	www.axrem.org.uk/
BAREMA	www.barema.org.uk/
BioIndustry Association (BIA)	www.bioindustry.org/home/
British Healthcare Trades Association (BHTA)	www.bhta.net/
British In Vitro Diagnostics Association (BIVDA)	www.bivda.co.uk/
British Medical Association (BMA)	http://bma.org.uk/
Dental Laboratories Association	www.dla.org.uk/
GAMBICA	www.gambica.org.uk/
Medilink	www.medilink.co.uk/
Multidisciplinary Assessment of Technology Centre for Healthcare (MATCH)	www.match.ac.uk/
National Institute for Health and Care Excellence	www.nice.org.uk/
The Association of Contact Lens Manufacturers (ACLM)	www.aclm.org.uk/
International	
International Society for Pharmacoeconomics and Outcomes Research (ISPOR)	http://www.ispor.org/
International Organization for Standardization (ISO)	www.iso.org/iso/home.html
World Health Organization (WHO)	www.who.int/en/
World Trade Organization (WTO)	www.wto.org/
Latin America: Brazil	
Associação Brasileira dos Importadores de Equipamentos, Produtos e Suprimentos Médico-Hospitalares (ABIMED)	www.abimed.org.br/
Sociedade Brasileira de Biotecnologia (SBBiotec)	www.sbbiotec.org.br/v2/
Brazilian Association of Medical Devices Manufacturers (ABIMO) & Union of the Industry of Dental, Medical and Hospital Articles and Equipment (SINAEMO)	www.abimo.org.br/
Latin America: Mexico	
Cámara Nacional de la Industria Farmacéutica (CANIFARMA)	www.canifarma.org.mx/
Cámara Nacionalde la Industria de Transformación (CANACINTRA)	www.canacintra.org.mx/principal/
North America: Canada	
BioAlberta	www.bioalberta.com/
Canadian Association of Professional Regulatory Affairs (CAPRA)	www.capra.ca/
LifeSciences British Columbia	www.lifesciencesbc.ca/
Canada Medical Technology Companies (MEDEC)	http://www.medec.org/
North America: US	
Advanced Medical Technology Association (AdvaMed)	http://advamed.org/
American Association for Clinical Chemistry (AACC)	www.aacc.org/Pages/default.aspx
American Institute of Ultrasound in Medicine (AIUM)	www.aium.org/

Organization	Website
American Society for Quality (ASQ)	http://asq.org/index.aspx
Analytical & Life Science Systems Association (ALSSA)	http://thealda.org/
Association for the Advancement of Medical Instrumentation (AAMI)	www.aami.org/
Association of Clinical Research Professionals (ACRP)	www.acrpnet.org/
Association of Medical Device Reprocessors (AMDR)	www.amdr.org/
Association of Medical Diagnostics Manufacturers (AMDM)	www.amdm.org/
BIOCOM	https://www.biocom.org/s/Home
BioForward	www.bioforward.org/
Clinical and Laboratory Standards Institute (CLSI)	http://clsi.org/
Diagnostic Marketing Association (DxMA)	www.dxma.org/
Emergency Care Research Institute (ECRI)	www.ecri.org/Pages/default.aspx
Indiana Medical Devices Manufacturers Council, Inc. (IMDMC)	http://www.imdmc.org/
LifeScience Alley (LSA)	https://www.medicalalley.org/
Massachusetts Medical Device Industry Council (MassMEDIC)	www.massmedic.com/
Medical Device Innovation, Safety and Security Consortium (MDISS)	http://mdiss.org/Home/MedicalDevices
Medical Device Manufacturers Association (MDMA)	www.medicaldevices.org/
MichBio	www.michbio.org/
Regulatory Affairs Professionals Society (RAPS)	www.raps.org/
Southern California Biomedical Council (SoCalBio)	http://www.socalbio.org/

Adapted from www.emergogroup.com/resources/medical-device-associations

country and/or regional requirements that vary from the sophisticated and comprehensive to the rudimentary. In many cases, medical device requirements are the same as, or derived from, requirements for medicinal products. Although these requirements often are inappropriate or problematic, the regulatory professional must be prepared to manage them.

While working on a global strategy, the regulatory professional must strive to ensure regulatory intelligence quality is not compromised. Numerous resources available to assist a professional with this process are included in this chapter. Regulatory requirements and sources change frequently, so it is necessary to reverify information periodically.

Cross-Cultural Negotiation Skills and Translation Services

When preparing to market a medical or diagnostic device, it is increasingly likely a regulatory professional will work with an individual in another country. From governmental agencies and local consultants to local dealers or distributors, regulatory professionals may come into contact with a wide array of experts. Rigorous due diligence is crucial to understanding international regulatory requirements, legal systems and cultural differences. Regulatory professionals have a number of general issues to remember and resources they can use in the effort to cross cultural barriers. Respecting other cultures and making an effort to manage language issues will enhance the cross-cultural working experience greatly. Managing virtual meetings conducted via email or Internet also is necessary. A search engine such as Google can be used for language translations, culturally specific holiday schedules, time-difference calculators and web conferencing (e.g., WebEx, GoTo Meeting) to facilitate negotiations. Many global sites are not in English, but many translation sites are available to regulatory professionals. Although professional translation services are necessary for medical device submissions, many free services found via the web are appropriate for general information.

Meeting With Regulatory Agencies

Exceptional science and long-term regulatory planning are essential for effective product submission, and getting started in an international market requires general knowledge of medical device registrations and regulations. Often, a key roadblock to product approval and clearance is the absence of agreement between the medical device manufacturer and the applicable regulatory agency regarding scientific and regulatory requirements, or how agency

Table 18-8. Miscellaneous Resources

Information Source	Name	Website
Blogs/Discussion Groups	BioPharm Devices—Infinata	www.infinata.com/biopharma-solution/by-product/biopharm-devices.html
	Drug and Device Law	druganddevicelaw.blogspot.com/
	Eye on FDA	www.eyeonfda.com/
	FDA Voice	blogs.fda.gov/fdavoice/
	International Association of Medical Equipment Remarketers/Servicers (IAMERS)	www.iamers.org/
	LinkedIn Groups	www.linkedin.com/groups/
	Medical Device Daily	www.mdd.blogs.medicaldevicedaily.com/
	Patent Baristas	www.patentbaristas.com/
	The Regulatory Intelligence Blog	www.regulatory-intelligence.eu/
Journals/Newsletters	Clinica	www.clinica.co.uk/
	Emergo Group	www.emergogroup.com/newsletters
	FDA Info.com	www.fdainfo.com/
	FDA News Website	http://www.fdanews.com/
	Guide to Good Clinical Practice	www.thompson.com/public/offerpage.jsp?prod=clin
	Inside Health Policy	http://insidehealthpolicy.com/
	Journal for Medical Device Regulatory Affairs	www.globalregulatorypress.com/about_journal/description.shtml
	MassDevice	www.massdevice.com/
	Medgadget	www.medgadget.com/
	Medical Device & Diagnostic Industry (MDDI)	www.mddionline.com/mddi-index-ad.html?gotourl=http://www.mddionline.com/
	Medical Device Asia	http://medicaldeviceasia.in/
	Medical Device Daily	http://medicaldevicedaily.com/
	Medical Product Outsourcing	www.mpo-mag.com/
	Qmed	www.qmed.com/newsletters
	Regulatory Focus	www.raps.org
	Regulatory Rapporteur	http://www.topra.org/TOPRA/TOPRA_Member/Regulatory_Rapporteur.aspx
	Warning Letter Bulletin	www.fdainfo.com/index.php?id=wlb
Software	Clinivation Worldview	www.clinivation.com/worldview/
	Cortellis	http://lifesciences.thomsonreuters.com/products/cortellis
	Medtrack	http://medtrack.com/
	Tarius	www.tarius.com/

concerns should be handled. Global regulatory inconsistencies and misunderstandings may occur regarding documentation, quality management, device classification, adverse event reporting or any other process aspect.

Meeting with the proper agency at an early product development stage allows a regulatory professional to inform the company more completely on whether individual device design features or labeling claims will lead to substantial regulatory hurdles. Regulatory professionals should encourage device manufacturers to pursue thorough, truthful and accurate communication with the appropriate regulatory agency at the earliest possible point in the process. Regulatory agencies are listed by region in **Tables 18-1–6**. Regulatory professionals must consider the following when working with regulatory agencies:

- write succinctly and clearly in all communications; avoid use of slang terms
- understand the agency's rules, regulations and guidances
- meet with the agency early in the development process to establish a healthy relationship with the appropriate department and reviewer
- track emergent agency interests and product concerns

Information Source	Name	Website
Educational Resources	Association for Medical Research Professionals	www.acrpnet.org/
	Association for the Advancement of Medical Instrumentation	http://www.aami.org/
	Barnett International	www.barnettinternational.com/Live-Seminars/
	Center for Professional Advancement	www.cfpa.com/
	Centers for Medicare and Medicaid Services	www.cms.gov/Outreach-and-Education/Outreach-and-Education.html
	Emergo Group	www.emergogroup.com/resources/whitepapers
	FOI Services, Inc.	www.foiservices.com/
	Global Compliance Panel	www.globalcompliancepanel.com/
	Medical Technology Learning Institute (MTLI)	www.advamedmtli.org/
	Organisation for Professionals in Regulatory Affairs	www.topra.org/
	Regulatory Affairs Professionals Society	www.raps.org
	FDA	www.fda.gov/MedicalDevices/default.htm
	FDA News	www.fdanews.com
	FDA WebView	http://fdaweb.com/
	Health Reform KnowlEDGE Center	healthreformknowledge.com/
	Inside Health Policy	http://insidehealthpolicy.com/
	Regulatory Affairs Professionals Society	www.raps.org
	Tarius	www.tarius.com/
Regulatory Information Providers	Datamonitor	www.datamonitor.com/
	FDA	www.fda.gov
	Graematter	www.graematter.com/
	Regulatorium	www.regulatorium.com/
	Regulatory Affairs Professionals Society	www.raps.org
Clinical Trial Registries	AIDS Clinical Trials Information Service (ACTIS)	www.actis.org/
	National Institutes of Health (NIH)	www.ClinicalTrials.gov
	National Cancer Institute Cancer Clinical Trials Listing (Physician Data Query [PDQ])	www.cancer.gov/cancertopics/pdq

- depending on the submission type, a regulatory professional may need to ensure appropriate safety and efficacy data or develop a strong predicate relationship
- outline appropriate endpoints and generate a protocol to validate the study hypothesis statistically

A proactive communication pattern should continue throughout the product application process.

Industry Associations and Trade Organizations

Questions will arise while a regulatory professional is preparing a medical or diagnostic device marketing submission. Early regulatory research and analysis are crucial. When issues arise, medical device trade associations provide exceptional networking opportunities for regulatory professionals to find information, tools, seminars, and resource materials. **Table 18-7** gives some examples.

Clinical Trial Databases

Clinical trial registries publish the results of global publicly and privately funded human clinical studies. For example, the US National Institutes of Health (NIH) ClinicalTrials.gov website is a web-based resource providing public access to information on ongoing and completed clinical studies on an array of diseases and conditions. Studies are posted on the website when the trial begins, and information is updated continuously by the study sponsor or PI. This database also is known as a "results database." Currently, the results from studies conducted in 188 different countries are listed on ClinicalTrials.gov.

Table 18-9. African/Middle Eastern Intelligence Resources

Source	Website
African Medicines Regulatory Harmonization (AMRH) Programme	http://amrh.org/
East African Community (EAC)	http://eac.int/
Harmonization for Health in Africa (HHA, registration required)	http://hha-online.org/hso/
Pan African Harmonization Working Party on Medical Devices and Diagnostics	http://pahwp.org/
World Trade Organization (WTO)	www.wto.org/

Other clinical trial listing service examples include the NIH National Cancer Institute's cancer clinical trials listing (Physician Data Query (PDQ)) and the US-government-sponsored AIDS Clinical Trials Information Service (ACTIS, **Table 18-8**).

Professional Literature and Notification Services

Regulatory service providers and professional and trade organizations distribute medical device publications and information to help regulatory professionals assemble medical device development intelligence and strategy. This information often comes from discussion groups, blogs, journals, newsletters and regulatory information databases. **Table 18-8** includes other miscellaneous resources for this information.

Software

Most regulatory professionals find it difficult to track and understand existing global regulations, manage regulatory changes effectively across geographies and keep current on pending regulatory legislation. Subscription-based software packages exist to provide access to global medical device regulatory information supporting regulatory intelligence and compliance activities. **Table 18-8** lists some of these software providers.

Conferences

Conferences focus on supporting regulatory experts' professional growth and advancement through education, discussions and peer-to-peer meetings. Internet searches and websites are available to help regulatory professionals locate current professional conference information.

Education, Training and Certification Programs

Various educational and certification programs are available for regulatory professionals. Designations like the Regulatory Affairs Certification (RAC) confirm the regulatory professional is proficient in key regulations and requirements. Numerous incentives exist for obtaining and maintaining professional certification, including:

- certification affords the regulatory professional a positive reputation in the industry
- enabling regulatory professionals to hone their knowledge
- certification often translates into better compensation and improves career advancement opportunities
- recertifying establishes a professional's continuing proficiency in a chosen field and enhances networking opportunities

International Medical Device Resources

To be successful internationally, a regulatory professional must have access to appropriate guidances, regulations, standards and consultants. General information about regional device and diagnostic markets is listed in **Tables 18-9–13**, with links to helpful organizations and intelligence resources. Again, international regulatory requirements vary, so regulatory professionals must seek out and receive qualified assistance to ensure compliance with global medical device guidelines. As a general rule, the following themes are consistent globally:

- device registration is required
- countries utilize risk-based device classification
- approval times, registration requirements and regulatory legislation are variable
- many follow ISO standard 13485 requirements (or a system based on or similar to ISO 13485) for a comprehensive quality management system

Africa

The African and Middle Eastern medical device markets have grown and made substantial progress. The demand for medical products is rising in all these countries, often driven by population growth, urbanization and increasing government investment in healthcare. African and Middle

Table 18-10. Asia/Pacific Intelligence Resources

Source	Website
Asian Harmonization Working Party (AHWP)	www.ahwp.info/
Asia-Pacific Economic Cooperation (APEC)	www.apec.org
Association of Southeast Asian Nations (ASEAN)	http://www.asean.org/
Australian Advisory Committee on Medical Devices (ACMD)	www.directory.gov.au/directory?ea0_lfz99_120.&&14d8be5c-1610-405c-8ebb-7d6929e48e3b
CCC Mark - China Compulsory Certification Mark	www.ccc-mark.com/ www.ccc-us.com/
Crimson Life Sciences, a division of TransPerfect	http://lifesciences.transperfect.com/solutions/meddev
International Society for Pharmacoeconomics and Outcomes Research Global Health Care Systems Road Map (ISPOR Road Map)	http://www.ispor.org/HTARoadMaps/
Medical Device Registrations Applications	www.microsofttranslator.com/bv.aspx?ref=SERP&br=ro&mkt=en-US&dl=en&lp=ZH-CHS_EN&a=http%3a%2f%2fwww.cmdr.cn%2f
Medical Device Regulatory Requirements (Export.gov)	www.trade.gov/td/health/regulations.html

Eastern countries with formal medical device regulatory program and policies are listed in **Table 18-1**.[1]

In Africa, device regulatory requirements range from the rudimentary to the complex.[2] For example, in Tanzania, a business must obtain marketing authorization from the Tanzanian Food and Drugs Authority (TFDA) to commercialize a device. TFDA regulations are based on Global Harmonization Task Force (GHTF) recommendations and require all device manufacturers to have certificates of registration prior to market entry. In other countries, individual ministries of health oversee product approvals. Oman is an example. Manufacturers selling devices must register with Oman's Directorate General of Medical Supplies and obtain Qualification Certificates. Certificates are issued to manufacturing facilities, not devices, and can be used to cover all products manufactured at a certified facility. By contrast, the South African Department of Health requires registration and CE marking for electromagnetic and radiation-emitting devices. Generally, device manufacturers can bring their products to market in South Africa rapidly if they have obtained a CE Mark elsewhere already. African trade organizations are listed in **Table 18-7**, and regulatory information resources are listed in **Table 18-9**.

Asia

Asia's medical device and diagnostic market also is expanding rapidly. China's medical device market now is the sixth largest in the world and is expected to be worth more than $28 billion by 2020; this market is bigger than every other medical device market except the US and EU.[3]

To meet the stringent requirements of the international market, many Asian countries (**Table 18-10**) are adopting additional regulations for the registration, production and control of medical devices manufactured in the region.

China's medical device market is overseen by the China Food and Drug Administration (CFDA, formerly the State Food and Drug Administration (SFDA)). CFDA is the sole entity authorized to approve device applications and issue registration certificates required for all medical devices sold in China. Market clearance in China requires a manufacturer to have prior approval in the device's country of origin. The approval process requires CFDA approval of all devices except those in the lowest-risk category; third-party device reviews by accredited persons are not allowed. In August 2007, CFDA issued standardized medical device product registration procedures.

The Thai Food and Drug Administration's Medical Device Control Division (MDCD) oversees Thailand's medical device market and requires all device manufacturers to obtain premarket authorization before importing or selling their products in the country. Thai medical device regulations currently are being modified (i.e., regulations regarding the inspection of foreign manufacturers) but, in the meantime, manufacturers are expected to comply with existing laws and requirements. In general, many Asian countries have issued guidances regarding medical device development.

It can be very challenging for a foreign manufacturer to satisfy Japan's 2005 *Pharmaceutical Affairs Law* (*PAL*).[4] Limited English language documents have been issued by the Ministry of Health, Labour and Welfare (MHLW) and its review body, the Pharmaceuticals and Medical

Table 18-11. European Commission Intelligence Resources

Source	Website
European Commission Medical Device Overview	http://ec.europa.eu/health/medical-devices/index_en.htm
European Free Trade Association (EFTA)	www.efta.int/
European Medical Technology Industry (Eurom VI)	www.eurom.org/index.php?option=com_content&task=view&id=10&Itemid=10
European standards; Medical devices	http://ec.europa.eu/growth/single-market/european-standards/harmonised-standards/medical-devices/index_en.htm
Global Medical Device Nomenclature (GMDN) System	https://www.gmdnagency.org/
International Society for Pharmacoeconomics and Outcomes Research Global Health Care Systems Road Map (ISPOR Road Map)	http://www.ispor.org/HTARoadMaps/
List of Contact Points within the National Competent Authorities	http://www.meddev.info/_documents/ca_vig.htm
MEDDEV Guidances	http://www.meddev.info/
MEDEC	http://www.medec.org/
Medicines & Healthcare products Regulatory Agency (MHRA)	www.mhra.gov.uk/
New Approach Notified and Designated Organisations (Nando) Information System – List of Notified Bodies	http://ec.europa.eu/enterprise/newapproach/nando/
Treaty of Lisbon, full text	http://europa.eu/lisbon_treaty/full_text/index_en.htm

Devices Agency (PMDA, **Table 18-2**). The lack of appropriate guidance in a language understandable to many and a complicated registration process make Japan one of the most problematic medical device and diagnostic markets for manufacturers to enter.

A business license, or "Kyoka," is required for Marketing Authorization Holders (MAHs), manufacturers, repairers and distributors. An MAH must be based in Japan, be formally licensed by MHLW and employ specific individuals tasked to develop and market the medical device.[5] If manufacturing facilities are located outside Japan, foreign manufacturer accreditation is required instead of a manufacturer license.[6] Japan also employs a risk-based medical device classification system. Class I devices require premarket submission; Class II specified controlled devices require premarket certification; and other Class II, III and IV medical devices require premarket approval.

Progress has been made harmonizing medical device regulations in Asia with other regions. The Asian Harmonization Working Party (AHWP) is comprised of 23 member countries from Asia, the Middle East, Africa and South America. The harmonization efforts are coordinated by numerous groups including AHWP, the International Medical Device Regulators Forum (IMDRF), the Association of Southeast Asian Nations (ASEAN) and the Asia-Pacific Economic Cooperation (APEC). Harmonization's overall goal is to eliminate trade and investment obstacles within the region and fully integrate Asia into the global economy. These resources are listed in **Table 18-10**, and Asian trade organizations are listed in **Table 18-7**.

Europe

Significant harmonization also has been developed between the EU and the European Free Trade Association (EFTA). EFTA members include Iceland, Liechtenstein, Norway and Switzerland, listed with EU Members States in **Table 18-3**.[7] The UK also oversees several territories in Latin America (**Table 18-5**). These include Anguilla, British Virgin Islands, Cayman Islands, Falkland Islands and Turks and Caicos Islands. These territories, along with the Netherlands Antilles and Aruba, were invited to develop association agreements with the EU. EU law applies to these countries to the extent necessary to execute association agreements. French Guiana, Guadeloupe and Martinique are part of France and considered EU Outermost Regions (OMR). Lastly, per the *Treaty of Lisbon*,[8] Saint Barthélemy and Saint Martin are considered French territories and also are part of the EU.

EU legislation consists of three principal medical devices directives that have been modified over time. These include the *Medical Devices Directive 93/42/EEC* (*MDD*); the *Active Implantable Medical Devices Directive 90/385/EEC* (*AIMDD*); and the *In Vitro Diagnostic Devices Directive 98/79/EC* (*IVDD*) (**Table 18-3**). The European Commission (EC) is responsible

Table 18-12. Latin American Intelligence Resources

Source	Website
Brazilian Health Devices	http://brazilianhealthdevices.com/en
Central and South American Health Ministries	http://www.msssi.gob.es/en/home.htm
International Society for Pharmacoeconomics and Outcomes Research Global Health Care Systems Road Map (ISPOR Road Map)	http://www.ispor.org/HTARoadMaps/
Medical Device Regulatory Requirements (Export.gov)	www.trade.gov/td/health/regulations.html
Mercado Común del Sur (MERCOSUR)	www.mercosur.int/
Pan American Health Organization (PAHO)	www.paho.org/hq/

for proposing legislation and implementing decisions in the EU and has adopted several measures based on the medical device directives. These include consensus statements and guidance documents (Guidance MEDDEVs). Guidance MEDDEVs, adopted by the Commission's Medical Device Expert Group, are not legally binding but present directive requirements to Notified Bodies and manufacturers. A Notified Body is able to issue a CE Mark (conformité européenne), after reviewing a medical device's technical file, the Essential Requirements checklists (as applicable) and ensuring a manufacturer is ISO 13485-certified and compliant.[9] A manufacturer then is able to prepare a "Declaration of Conformity," designating a medical device conforms with *MDD*, *AIMDD* or *IVDD* requirements. With this declaration, the manufacturer may label its product with the CE Mark. If a product is not a non-sterile Class I device, a CE Mark is required for its distribution and sale in the EU and certifies it has met EU health, safety and environmental requirements. Medium- and high-risk devices, sterile Class I medical devices and medical devices with a measuring function all require Notified Body assessment. Links to intelligence resources within the EU are listed in **Table 18-11**.

Latin America

Central and South American countries also represent an evolving medical device and diagnostic market. Those countries having a formal medical device regulatory program for medical device manufacture and importation are listed in **Table 18-5**.

Only 19 Latin American countries (not including the French Collectivities and EU Outermost Regions mentioned above) have implemented medical device regulatory systems. These programs are in various development stages, with the principal attribute being premarket controls.[10] In some countries, medical device regulations are advancing rapidly, while in others, the regulations are unchanging and rather unclear. These regulations are driven in part by trade agreements seeking to create a common market comparable to that of the EU, where goods and services move easily between Member States. For example, Mercado Común del Sur (MERCOSUR) is intended to promote free trade and the fluid movement of goods, people and currency throughout Latin America.[11] MERCOSUR members include Argentina, Brazil, Paraguay, Uruguay, Venezuela, Chile, Bolivia, Colombia, Ecuador and Peru.[12]

As the largest medical device market in the South and Central American region, Brazil has established medical device regulations; Mexico closely follows many US FDA regulations; and Aruba, Curacao, Haiti and Trinidad and Tobago all require ministry of health notification to place a device on the market. Other general themes in Latin America are:

- foreign manufacturer inspections are not mandatory or enforced if a GMP equivalence certificate is obtained from the country of origin
- some countries require a foreign company to have a local distributor or an office in a Latin American country to register a device[13]

Numerous countries in this region also are modernizing their regulations. Useful Latin American resources are listed in **Table 18-12**.

North America

Canada has an established and profitable medical device market. The Medical Devices Bureau of Health Canada's Therapeutic Products Directorate (TPD) monitors and assesses diagnostic and therapeutic medical devices' safety, effectiveness and quality in Canada. Canadian medical device classes closely correspond to the EU *MDD* classifications. Under Canada's *Medical Devices Regulations*, SOR/98-282, manufacturers of Class II, III and IV devices must obtain a Medical Device License prior to selling a device in Canada and be certified to ISO 13485. Although Class I devices do not require a license, they are

Table 18-13. North American and Other Critical Intelligence Resources

Source	Website	Crucial Information
Canada Justice Laws Website	http://laws-lois.justice.gc.ca/eng/acts/F-27/	Medical Devices Regulations, SOR/98-282
Export.gov	http://search.export.gov/search?affiliate=47593d2fa&query=Doing+Business+In&submit.x=0&submit.y=0	"Doing Business In" guides
FDA Advisory Committees	www.fda.gov/AdvisoryCommittees/default.htm	FDA Advisory Committee updates
FDA CDRH Foreign Liaison List	www.fda.gov/medicaldevices/deviceregulationandguidance/importingandexportingdevices/ucm050356.htm	Foreign Liaison list, import/export information
FDA International Program List	www.fda.gov/InternationalPrograms/default.htm	Geographic Program list
FDA Device Guidance Documents	www.fda.gov/MedicalDevices/DeviceRegulationandGuidance/GuidanceDocuments/default.htm	Guidance
Global Medical Device Nomenclature (GMDN) System	https://www.gmdnagency.org/	List of internationally agreed terms used to identify medical devices
Health Canada	http://hc-sc.gc.ca/dhp-mps/md-im/applic-demande/guide-ld/index-eng.php	Canadian guidance
International Society For Pharmacoeconomics and Outcomes Research Global Health Care Systems Road Map (ISPOR Road Map)	http://www.ispor.org/HTARoadMaps/	International updates and links
MEDEC	http://www.medec.org/	Quick, international links
Office of Health and Consumer Goods; Export.Gov	http://trade.gov/td/health/regulations.html	Global country regulatory profiles, regulations for pre-owned medical devices
Qmed	www.qmed.com	Directory of pre-qualified suppliers to the medical device and in vitro diagnostics industry

monitored through Establishment Licenses. The Canadian Special Access Programme (SAP) permits doctors emergency access to medical devices not already licensed.

FDA's Center for Devices and Radiological Health (CDRH) regulates the firms that manufacture, repackage, re-label and/or import medical devices sold in the US.[14] CDRH also regulates radiation-emitting electronic devices such as lasers, x-ray systems and ultrasound equipment. The US utilizes a risk-based device classification method as described in 21 CFR 860. Chapter 12 discusses other regulatory requirements manufacturers of medical devices circulated in the US must consider.

Several regional regulatory guidelines and guidances have been established for device development. In North America, Health Canada has provided more than 30 applicant guidances. Similarly, FDA has issued numerous guidances outlining its recommendations for medical device development and approval and determining animal and/or clinical testing requirements on a per-product basis following comparative analytical data assessment. **Table 18-13** lists links to appropriate sites where these guidances and other information may be found.

Conclusion

Internationally, a familiar theme arises: collaborating in global regulatory markets can be challenging because various countries within a geographic region might have very different regulations. Regulatory professionals need appropriate resources to assemble successful regulatory intelligence and strategy. This chapter supplies an essential listing of noteworthy tools and resources for information about medical device regulations.

References
1. Fisher I, Dowling L. "Africa and the Middle East: Two regions united by their diversity." *Regulatory Rapporteur*, Vol 11, No 2, February 2014. TOPRA website. https://embed.topra.org/node/5563. Accessed 24 March 2016.
2. Ibid.
3. Gross A. "Pitfalls in China's Medical Device Market." *Medical Device Daily*. 22 April 2013. Pacific Bridge Medical website. http://www.pacificbridgemedical.com/publications/pitfalls-in-chinas-medical-device-market/. Accessed 24 March 2016.
4. Nozawa S, Adachi H, Shouji K. 2010. *Fundamentals of Japanese Regulatory Affairs, First Edition*. Regulatory Affairs Professionals Society.
5. Ibid.
6. Ibid.

7. Patel Bhoomi B, Patel PM, Patel NM. "An Overview on Drug Regulatory Agencies: Europe and India." *International Journal of Pharmaceutical & Biological Archives* 2011; 2(3):819-821. IJPBA website. http://www.ijpba.info/ijpba/index.php/ijpba/article/view/270. Accessed 24 March 2016.
8. *Treaty of Lisbon*. EUR-Lex website. http://eur-lex.europa.eu/legal-content/EN/ALL/;ELX_SESSIONID=lln2JgNJTXjR74KqT2mSlHgHShs8Npgvy1TxtTJXFXySp2Y25fJL!-364680198?uri=OJ:C:2007:306:TOC. Accessed 24 March 2016.
9. Opt cit 7.
10. Klonsky J, Hanson S, Lee B. "Mercosur: South America's Fractious Trade Bloc." 31 Jul 2012. Council on Foreign Relations website. http://www.cfr.org/trade/mercosur-south-americas-fractious-trade-bloc/p12762. Accessed 24 March 2016.
11. Ibid.
12. Ibid.
13. The Outlook for Medical Devices in Latin America." Sep 2014. Espicom Business Intelligence. The Street website. http://www.thestreet.com/story/11548639/3/the-outlook-for-medical-devices-in-latin-america.html?startIndex=0. Accessed 24 March 2016.
14. George B. Registration of Medical Devices. Perspect Clin Res. 2010 Jul-Sep; 1(3): 90–93. NCBI website. http://www.ncbi.nlm.nih.gov/pmc/articles/PMC3146078/. Accessed 24 March 2016.

19 Borderline Regulation of Stem Cell Technologies: Therapies, Devices and Combination Products

By James A. Smith, Sue Dopson, Benjamin M. Davies, Karolina Wartolowska, Andrew J. Carr and David A. Brindley

Introduction

Stem cell technology is an emerging technology in the healthcare industry with the potential to transform dramatically the way many diseases that do not have current adequate standards of care are treated.[1] Indeed, many products relying on stem cell technology now are being marketed and used around the world for a wide range of indications (**Table 19-1**). However, the development of a fundamentally new and different medicinal product category brings many challenges and uncertainties, including, of course, regulation.[2]

Cell and medical device combination products are becoming increasingly prevalent, and the regulation of stem cell-containing combination products is an even greater challenge than stem cell products alone. Medical device regulation has enjoyed a much longer history and, like other medical regulation areas, for the most part, is more established and clear.[3] Cellular products, on the other hand, are a relatively recent development posing unique regulatory questions.[4] linked to an increasingly aging population, necessitates new approaches to therapeutic intervention. One potential class of health care innovation that may offer an alternative approach to addressing current shortfalls is stem cell therapies. With such an explosive rate of research and innovation, it has been difficult for regulators to keep pace. As a result, the regulatory path for cellular products has not always been completely clear and often is perceived as a central challenge facing stem cell products.[5,6] However, attempts have been made to simplify and clarify the complex worldwide regulatory landscape for cellular products, and clearer regulatory pathways for stem cell products and stem cell-device combinations are emerging. This chapter reviews the current state of affairs and improves understanding of the regulations applicable to stem cell technology devices.

A single chapter cannot provide a comprehensive treatment of worldwide stem cell technology and device regulation; therefore, this chapter introduces general ideas and considerations for stem cell product regulation, and outlines regulatory requirements and possible regulatory strategies to address them. Further, the text highlights sources of more detailed information. Discussion is restricted largely to US and EU regulation, as these are the most active areas in terms of stem-cell based therapy human trials.[7]

Regulatory Route for Cell and Device Combination Products

The use of cells and tissues as therapeutics generally is highly regulated worldwide. Stem cells usually are regulated the same way as other cell or tissue types; for example, the US Food and Drug Administration (FDA) does not consider stem cell-based products to require a distinct regulatory approach from other cellular therapies.[8] Most cell-based products are considered to be medicinal/biologics products or devices, meaning they typically are subject to up to three regulatory regimes: public health legislation, pharmaceutical legislation and medical device legislation.[9] However, in certain cases, only public health legislation will be applicable. The following US and EU

Table 19-1. Summary of Select Revenue-Generating Cell Therapy Products Currently on the Market

Company	Lead Product(s)	Indication	Current Markets
Dendreon (Seattle, WA)	Provenge	Prostate cancer	US, EU
Organogenesis (Canton, MA)	Apligraf	Diabetic foot ulcers	US, Canada
	Dermagraft	Venous leg ulcers/ diabetic foot ulcers	US, Saudi Arabia
NuVasive (San Deigo, CA)	Osteocel Plus	Skeletal defects	US
Orthofix (Curaçao, Netherlands Antilles)	Trinity Evolution	Musculoskeletal defects	US
Genzyme (Cambridge, MA)	Carticel	Articular cartilage repair	US, EU
	Epicel	Severe burns	US, EU
Anterogen (Seoul)	Cupistem	Crohn's disease	South Korea
Avita Medical (Perth, Australia)	ReCell	Burns, scars	EU, Australia, Canada
Pharmicell (Seoul)	Hearticellgram	Acute myocardial infarction	South Korea
Japan Tissue Engineering (Gamagori)	J-TEC Epidermis/ Cartilage/ Corneal Epithelium	Burns, cartilage repair, ocular repair	Japan
Medipost (Seoul)	Cartistem	Cartilage injury or osteoarthritis	South Korea
TiGenix (Leuven, Belgium)	ChondroCelect	Articular cartilage repair	EU
Osiris Therapeutics (Columbia, MD)	Prochymal	Refractory paediatric graft-versus-host disease	Canada

Adapted and updated from French A, Buckler RL, Brindley DA. Commercialization of regenerative medicine: learning from spin-outs. Rejuvenation Res. 2013 Apr;16(2):164–70.

examples illustrate the differences in opinions on product classifications and regulatory routes existing worldwide.

In the EU and US, there is substantial overlap in the criteria for determining whether cellular products will be regulated as medicinal products, although clear differences exist for regulation as a device. If a product meets the following criteria, it is regulated only under public health legislation.

- It is minimally manipulated (US) or not substantially manipulated (EU) (**Table 19-2**).
- It is intended for homologous use, meaning the cells are used for essentially the same function in the donor and host.
- It is not combined with another product or article:
  o EU: a medical device or an active implantable medical device under Regulation (EC) No 1394/2007 (*ATMP Regulation*)
  o US: as determined in 21 CFR 1271.10: "The manufacture of the [Human Cells, Tissues and Cellular and Tissue-Based Products (HCT/P)] does not involve the combination of the cells or tissues with another article, except for water, crystalloids, or a sterilizing, preserving, or storage agent, provided that the addition of water, crystalloids, or the sterilizing, preserving, or storage agent does not raise new clinical safety concerns with respect to the HCT/P; and"
- US only: "Either:
  i. The HCT/P does not have a systemic effect and is not dependent upon the metabolic activity of living cells for its primary function; or
  ii. The HCT/P has a systemic effect or is dependent upon the metabolic activity of living cells for its primary function, and:
      a. Is for autologous[10] use;
      b. Is for allogeneic use in a first-degree or second-degree blood relative; or
      c. Is for reproductive use."

This is a significant distinction because, in these cases, no premarket approval is required. In the EU, such products are regulated under the *EU Tissue and Cells Directives* (*EUTCD*), including Directive 2004/23/EC. In the US, products must conform to Good Tissue Practices and are regulated under Section 361 of the *Public Health Service Act* (*PHS Act*; 42 USC 264), referred to as '361 products.'[11]

In the US, if one of the above criteria is not met, the product is regulated under *PHS Act* Section 351 as a biologic, drug or device, and, therefore, requires FDA approval. Products regulated under Section 351 are designated as '351 products.'

In the EU, if one of the above criteria is not met, the product is regulated as an advanced therapy medicinal product (ATMP) under the *ATMP Regulation* and Directive 2001/83/EC (*Medicinal Products Directive*). Importantly, Directive 93/42/EEC (the *Medical Devices Directive*) explicitly does not apply to "transplants or tissues or cells of human origin nor to products incorporating or derived from tissues or cells of human origin," with the exception of devices incorporating medicinal products derived from human blood or plasma but not including blood cells (as noted in *Medicinal Products Directive* Article 3). Thus, in the EU, an ATMP-device combination cannot be regulated primarily as a device, regardless of whether it otherwise can be argued to satisfy the definition of a device[12] (regulatory routes and relevant documents are summarized in **Table 19-3**).

ATMPs and 351 products require premarket approval, including demonstration of safety and efficacy.

US Regulation of Stem Cell Technology Devices

In the US, devices incorporating HCT/Ps will be regulated as combination products, with the lead center for regulation determined by the product's primary mode of action (PMOA). The PMOA is defined as "the single mode of action of a combination product that provides the most important therapeutic action of the combination product. The most important therapeutic action is the mode of action expected to make the greatest contribution to the overall intended therapeutic effects of the combination product" in 21 CFR Part 3, which details regulations for combination products' assignment to FDA centers.

A Request for Designation (RFD) must be submitted, following the process described in 21 CFR 3, to determine the center with primary jurisdiction, or lead center. The Office of Combination Products (OCP) also can be approached to discuss product classification, which may be useful in early product development stages to inform the likely regulatory route. However, any informal designations from OCP are not legally binding.[13]

In the case of stem cell devices, the designated office will be either the Center for Biologics Evaluation and Research (CBER), if the cell component provides the PMOA, or the Center for Devices and Radiological Health (CDRH), if the device component provides the PMOA. In 'borderline' cases, where the PMOA cannot be determined, FDA looks first at previous products that may have posed similar safety and efficacy questions as the combination product as a whole, and assigns the product to the same lead center to which those previous products were assigned. In the absence of a previous, comparable product, FDA assigns the product to the center considered to have the most expertise with products presenting similar perceived risks.[14]

Therefore, as with other combination products, there is no steadfast, certain route for stem cell technology device regulation in the US. Each particular product requires individual assessment, with the decision depending largely on the PMOA. However, once a lead center is assigned, the secondary center remains involved in the review process, particularly with matters concerning the second component.

In the majority of cases, a single Investigational New Drug (IND) or Investigational Device Exemption (IDE) is required to begin clinical studies for products with a biologic or device PMOA, respectively. Regulations regarding IND applications are detailed in 21 CFR 312, and those for IDE applications are in 21 CFR 812. However, there are some cases where two marketing applications, i.e., a Biological License Application (BLA) and a Premarket Approval (PMA), may be necessary from a regulatory perspective to ensure safety, efficacy or adequate postmarket regulation. FDA released a paper for comment entitled, "Number of Marketing Applications for a Combination Product," which discusses the number of marketing applications required for combination products.[15] Of particular relevance, two marketing applications might be required:

> "when a "BLA for Further Manufacture"… is appropriate to ensure the identity, safety, purity and potency of certain biological products (e.g., cell and gene therapy, therapeutic proteins, monoclonal antibodies, blood products) when the combination product as a whole is being regulated under the device or drug provisions."

Further manufacture could necessitate a BLA because the *PHS Act* requires an intermediate product used in manufacturing specifically identified biological products to be licensed; thus, if a biologic and device are combined

Table 19-2. Definitions of Manipulations Considered Minimal (US) or Not Substantial (EU)

US	EU
(1) For structural tissue, processing that does not alter the tissue's original relevant characteristics of relating to the tissue's utility for reconstruction, repair or replacement; and (2) For cells or nonstructural tissues, processing that does not alter the cells or tissues' relevant biological characteristics (21 CFR 1271.3) Specific manipulations considered to be minimal (66 FR 5447 at 5457): • cutting • grinding • shaping • centrifugation • soaking in antibiotic solution • ethylene oxide treatment or irradiation sterilization • cell separation • density gradient separation • lyophilization • freezing • cryopreservation • selective removal of B-cells, T-cells, malignant cells, red blood cells, or platelets	The cells or tissues have not been subject to substantial manipulation, so biological characteristics, physiological functions or structural properties relevant for the intended regeneration, repair or replacement are achieved (Regulation (EC) No 1394/2007). Specific manipulations not considered substantial according to Annex I of the same regulation: • cutting • grinding • shaping • centrifugation • soaking in antibiotic or antimicrobial solutions • sterilization • irradiation • cell separation, concentration or purification • filtering • lyophilization • freezing • cryopreservation • vitrification

Adapted from PAS 83: 2012 Developing human cells for clinical applications in the European Union and the United States. 2012.

during manufacture, a second marketing application may be required, in addition to the application for the product as a whole.[16] For such potentially complex regulatory routes, it is recommended to engage the relevant authority at an early stage.

Point-of-Care Autologous Therapies and Devices in the US

A particularly complex regulatory scenario occurs with devices intended for processing autologous cells intraoperatively,[17] also called 'point-of-care' processing.[18] 21 CFR, Section 1271.15 states compliance with Part 1271 is not required "if you are an establishment that removes HCT/Ps from an individual and implants such HCT/Ps into the same individual during the same surgical procedure." In draft guidance entitled, *Cell selection devices for point of care production of minimally manipulated autologous peripheral blood stem cells (PBSCs)*, FDA outlines five specific criteria supporting the removal and subsequent implantation of PBSCs in the same surgical procedure. It is assumed these will apply to other stem cell types:

1. "The cells are autologous and are intended for use for a specific clinical indication;
2. The cells are minimally manipulated;
   a. The device is solely responsible for the production of the autologous cells (i.e., no other manufacturing steps take place outside of the device other than the recovery of the source cells);
3. The cells are used within a short period of time (i.e., they are not stored or shipped); and
4. The device and selected cells are only used at the point of care (i.e., cell processing is performed at and by the clinical site where cells are directly administered)."

When these five conditions are met, FDA does not require compliance with 21 CFR 1271 and no IND or BLA is warranted for the cellular product. The product is regulated as a device, not a combination product.

Device regulation, in such cases, can be assigned to either CDRH or CBER. FDA has released specific guidance on what devices will be regulated by which center in a jurisdictional update, *Guidance for Industry and FDA Staff—Devices Used to Process Human Cells, Tissues, and Cellular and Tissue-Based Products (HCT/Ps)*.[20] The assignment depends on the device output's intended use: if the therapeutic effect is mediated by the device's biologic output, the device most likely will be regulated by CBER. In contrast, if the device simply is intended to isolate or

Table 19-3. Summary of Regulatory Routes and Documents Applicable to Stem Cell and/or Device Products

Product Type	US	EU
Public Health Legislation for Cell Containing Products	(1) Good Tissue Practices (2) *PHS Act* Section 361 (42 USC 264)	(1) *EU Tissue and Cell Directive (EUTCD)* (2) Directive 2004/23/EC
Combination Cell-Device Products	(1) *PHS Act* Section 351 (42 USC 262) (2) 21 CFR 1271 (3) The primary mode of action dictates the regulatory route: ☐ Biologics: regulated primarily by the Center for Biologics Evaluation and Research (CBER) and 21 CFR 312 applies OR ☐ Devices: regulated primarily by the Center for Devices and Radiological Health (CDRH) and 21 CFR 812 applies *Note: although one center is designated the lead center, the other still has some involvement in regulation*	(1) Directive 2001/83/EC (2) Regulation (EC) No 1394/2007 (*the ATMP regulation*) *Note: Directive 93/42/EEC, the medical device directive, explicitly does not apply to ATMPs*
Point-of-Care Autologous Therapies and Devices	(1) 21 CFR 1271 does not apply if cell processing occurs within the same surgical procedure (2) Information on what constitutes the same surgical procedure can be found in *Draft Guidance for Industry: Cell Selection Devices for Point of Care Production of Minimally Manipulated Autologous Peripheral Blood Stem Cells*	(1) Same regulations apply as to cellular or device products that are not point-of-care
Borderline Classifications	(1) 21 CFR 3 describes submission of a Request for Designation (RFD) (2) "Number of Marketing Applications for a Combination Product," an FDA paper for comment, has information	(1) Regulation (EC) No 1394/2007 (*ATMP Regulation*) gives recommendations
Additional Comments	N/A	(1) Member States can impose additional requirements and are responsible for clinical trial authorization, rather than the central EMA

concentrate cells used for in vitro diagnostics (i.e., they are not re-implanted into the patient), the device likely will be regulated by CDRH.

EU Regulation of Stem Cell Technology Devices

Unlike the US, the EU regulates all cell-containing devices, including stem cells, as ATMPs, regardless of the PMOA. With regard to designation, the EU situation, therefore, can be considered simpler. ATMPs, according to the *ATMP Regulation*, belong to one of the following product classifications:

- gene therapy medicinal product (GTMP; defined in *Medicinal Products Directive*, Annex 1, Part IV)
- somatic cell therapy medicinal product (CTMP; defined in *Medicinal Products Directive*, Annex 1, Part IV)
- tissue-engineered product (TEP; defined in *ATMP Regulation*, Article 2)

These classifications are organized into a hierarchy that allows an ATMP falling within the definition of both a TEP and a CTMP to be considered a TEP, and a product falling within the definition of CTMP or TEP and GTMP to be considered a GTMP.

All ATMP Marketing Authorisation Applications (MAAs) must utilize the European Medicines Agency's (EMA) Centralised Procedure, and are reviewed by the Committee for Advanced Therapies (CAT), established under the *ATMP Regulation*. CAT reviews the dossier and prepares a draft opinion for the Committee for Medicinal Products for Human Use (CHMP), which is responsible for final approval. Products must comply with the *ATMP Regulation*'s requirements and the *Medicinal Products Directive*.[21]

In addition to the Centralised Procedure, ATMPs also are regulated at the national level under the *EUTCD* regarding donation, procurement and testing of human cells and/or tissues. Besides an EMA license, a national Competent Authority also is required (e.g., Human Tissue Authority in the UK). EMA provides general authorization via the CAT and CHMP, but product transfer among Member States may require additional testing or evidence to comply with the local Competent Authority.[22] Requirements generally are similar among Member States, with most implementing the minimum *EUTCD* recommendations into national law. However, there are differences, resulting in a patchwork of EU regulations, posing a challenge to industry professionals and needing to be taken into consideration.[23]

ATMPs incorporating devices still are regulated as ATMPs, although they must conform to additional requirements, as detailed in *ATMP Regulation* Article 6:
1. "A medical device which forms part of a combined advanced therapy medicinal product shall meet the essential requirements laid down in Annex I to Directive 93/42/EEC.
2. An active implantable medical device which forms part of a combined advanced therapy medicinal product shall meet the essential requirements laid down in Annex 1 to Directive 90/385/EEC."

The two directives referenced are for medical devices and active implantable medical devices, respectively. These criteria are assessed by a Notified Body and taken into account by EMA in evaluating the combination product but will require only a single MAA containing all relevant information.

Each Member State in which a trial will be conducted requires a clinical trial authorization (CTA), because trials are governed by national procedures.[24] An investigational medicinal product dossier (IMPD) and clinical protocol must be submitted. IMPD information can be found in EC Communication 2010/C82/01 Section 2.[25]

Regulating the device and medicinal components together is appropriate only for products that will be placed on the market as a single, integral product; if the device is intended only to deliver a medicinal product and clearly is a separate entity from the medicinal product, it instead will be subject to the *MDD*.

The Hospital Exemption

The *ATMP Regulation* includes a special provision that, in some cases, does not require products meeting the definition of an ATMP to have market authorization: the hospital exemption. It states:

"Advanced therapy medicinal products which are prepared on a non-routine basis according to specific quality standards, and used within the same Member State in a hospital under the exclusive professional responsibility of a medical practitioner, in order to comply with an individual medical prescription for a custom-made product for an individual patient, should be excluded from the scope of this Regulation whilst at the same time ensuring that relevant Community rules related to quality and safety are not undermined."

This exclusion allows small-scale, developmental treatments to continue in certain hospitals, as some were already making ATMPs occasionally, before the *ATMP Regulation* came into force. This is intended for rare, custom-made treatments, and such products cannot be marketed or advertised openly.[26]

Point-of-Care Autologous Therapies and Devices in the EU

There is little explicit EU guidance on the regulation of devices intended for autologous point-of-care cell processing. However, if such a device's cellular output still meets all the criteria precluding ATMP classification, the cellular component likely will be regulated only by the *EUTCD* and not be considered an ATMP and, therefore, not require premarket approval. Notably, minimal manipulation alone is not sufficient to avoid classification as an ATMP; if cells are manipulated minimally but used non-homologously, they still are classified as an ATMP. A recent reflection paper noted, "some products initially considered as non-ATMP because of an essentially minimal manipulation or maintenance of the initial biological properties and autologous origin have been classified by the CAT as ATMP due to their intended heterologous use."[27] This is in contrast to the criteria for the surgical exemption detailed above in the US, which does not mention intended use of the cell or tissue.

Borderline Classifications in the EU

The *ATMP Regulation* provides explicit information on borderline classifications:

"The Agency [EMA] should be empowered to give scientific recommendations on whether a given product based on genes, cells or tissues meets the scientific criteria which define advanced therapy medicinal products, in order to address, as early as possible, questions of borderline with other areas such as cosmetics or medical devices, which may arise as science develops. The Committee for Advanced Therapies, with its unique expertise, should have a prominent role in the provision of such advice."

The recently released draft guidelines[28] and their predecessor[29] also are useful sources of information on ATMP regulation and borderline issues. As in the US, when the regulatory route likely will be complex, approaching the authorities at an early stage is recommended.

Comment on Regulatory Routes in Other Jurisdictions

As between the US and EU, the exact classification of cell-based technologies and devices worldwide varies depending on the jurisdiction's particular regulations. In this case, general recommendations are difficult to make. While the particulars vary by jurisdiction, similar criteria are used to determine whether products require premarket authorization (like ATMPs and HCT/P 351 products); however, certain jurisdictions, e.g., Japan and South Korea, have introduced conditional approval laws for regenerative medicine, including stem cell, technologies that allow faster market authorization for promising therapies.[30] Regardless of the particular route, in both the US and the EU, a combination product as a whole ultimately is evaluated for safety and efficacy (even if some constituent parts are evaluated individually); this is true for most combination products worldwide. Notable divergence occurs in autologous point-of-care regulation, and as that field evolves, regulation, too, will adapt and, hopefully, converge. When determining the regulatory route at present, developers need to look specifically at the relevant legislation in the region in which they want to market the product.

Safety and Efficacy in Cellular Products

Like biologics, drugs and devices, stem cell products must demonstrate quality, safety and efficacy in both the product and process to gain market approval, and must maintain them following marketing approval. However, cellular products present additional challenges and considerations that, in some cases, lead to additional regulatory requirements. This section focuses on those issues specific to stem cell technologies, as the counterparts for devices are covered elsewhere in this book. Internationally, cell product safety requirements are similar; however, there are marked differences in the evidence required to gain market authorization as a result of new regulatory paradigms for regenerative medicine products in certain areas. Unless specified, this discussion is applicable specifically to US and EU regulation, although it generally is more broadly applicable.

Cellular Material

Typically, similar principles apply to donating, procuring and testing starting cell materials for stem cell technologies. In donation, Good Clinical Practice (GCP), including ethical considerations, full protocols detailing acceptable donor criteria and donor history and screening, must be followed. With stem cells, ethics are especially important, because a single person's cells theoretically could be used to treat many people for many different conditions; donor consent, therefore, must be explicit, and possible future uses of the cells explained. For autologous therapies, however, these requirements typically are not applicable. Post-donation or harvest, a number of procedures must be in place to ensure adequate safety and traceability. These include cell material handling methodologies, storage facilities, labeling, transportation, tracking systems and waste tissue protocols. Cell material must be tested for the presence of a variety of potentially transmissible diseases, such as HIV and syphilis.[31] The exact requirements for each of these procedures vary by geography; for example, even within the EU, Member States may impose additional requirements to those set out in the *EUTCD*.

Clinical Manufacture and Distribution

To manufacture a product for use in a clinical setting, Good Manufacturing Practice (GMP) guidelines should be followed. Facilities may be required to conform to specific regulations; for example, in the US, both Current Good Tissue Practice (CGTP) requirements in 21 CFR 1271.150 and GMP requirements in 21 CFR 210 and 21 CFR 211 must be met. Notably, in January 2015, FDA established the Office of Pharmaceutical Quality, responsible for overseeing all aspects of pharmaceutical product quality throughout the lifecycle, which also may apply to cell therapies. In the EU, guidance on GMP requirements can be found in Annex 2 to Volume 4 of *EU guidelines for good manufacturing practice for medicinal products for human and veterinary use*.[32] As with other products, establishing standard operating procedures is essential.

A fundamental difference in device and cell product manufacture is the inherent variability in cellular products. Unlike traditional biologics (e.g., monoclonal antibodies) that are separated from their cellular expression systems during the manufacturing process, in cell therapies, cells are the product.[33] Since many cell product manufacturing processes are manual, the same level of process consistency is not possible, and procedures for evaluating cell-based product production processes must allow some flexibility. To address this, quality risk management approaches have been suggested[34] and regulatory guidelines have emphasized their importance.[35] Manufacturing processes require validation; however, validating cell manufacturing processes is more complex than other product types, and reference materials, with which the method can be validated, are difficult to establish.[36,37] Process limits should be set and in-house process control operational parameters defined, all based on and supported by appropriate data.[38]

Again, unlike other products, in the stem cell product manufacturing process, it is not possible to deplete or eliminate adventitious and contaminating agents, e.g., by sterilization or ultrafiltration. As such, risk assessment of the starting materials and any materials that come into contact with cells during manufacture is required, and all materials should be manufactured under GMP standards when possible. The following criteria should be considered for each material to ensure adequate quality:[39]

- identity: a unique product identifier
- purity: desired cell population concentration
- impurities: including product related (e.g., dead cells), process related (e.g., antibiotics) and contaminants (e.g., bacteria, viruses)
- biological activity (if applicable)
- general quality attributes

These same characteristics also are required to define product release specifications and an indication of a particular dosage unit of the product.

Finally, if any changes are made to the process, a comparability protocol must be in place to demonstrate the final product is equivalent to that in the original protocol. If the protocol was changed to enhance product quality, e.g., by removing impurities, achieving this also must be demonstrated. Importantly, significant process changes may require clinical or nonclinical product evaluation.[40]

Compliance with practices relating to finished products also is required. Finished product distribution, holding and packaging are particularly challenging for cellular products, which can be especially susceptible to environmental changes. The EU has issued guidelines on *Good Distribution Practice*[41] based on Directive 2001/83/EC, although they are not specific to cellular products. FDA has not adopted the same terminology, instead using *Good Manufacturing Practice for Finished Pharmaceuticals*, detailed in 21 CFR 211.

Clinical Trials With Stem Cell Products

Clinical trial requirements for stem cell products are similar to those for drugs and devices. As with other products, GCP is necessary, and clear endpoints and success criteria must be defined. However, particularly in Phase 1 trials, there is divergence between cell therapy and conventional pharmaceuticals. Usually, healthy volunteers are recruited for Phase 1 trials, and the primary endpoint is safety; however, healthy volunteers usually are not used in cell therapy trials, primarily due to the ethical issues of administering a potentially permanent, irreversible treatment to a healthy individual. Therefore, patients from the intended target population are used, and some efficacy may be demonstrated in Phase 1 trials.[42]

As some cellular products will be administered in surgical procedures, it may be necessary to control trials with placebo surgery. The benefit-risk ratio for placebo surgical procedures is particularly complex because there always is some intraoperative risk. However, in general, the placebo arm is safer than the surgical arm, and this type of randomized clinical trial is an effective means to demonstrate surgical procedures' efficacy.[43] Blinding the investigator and/or subject can be challenging, although it has been successful for many surgical procedures,[44] including trials of cell-based therapies.[45] Thus, cell therapy trials may be required to demonstrate efficacy in a placebo-controlled manner. Given the high cost frequently associated with cell-containing products, there also may be a need to use control treatments with the current 'gold standard' treatment and a placebo arm. This is to show the cell-containing treatment is more effective than current treatments that likely are less expensive.

Additionally, special attention should be given to:
- clear protocols for storing and manipulating cell products in the operating room
- adequate operating room staff training, if the product is complex
- ethical considerations

- patient understanding that demonstrating safety in Phase 1 trials does not necessarily equate to efficacy
- cell donor anonymity
- long-term patient tracking, given the field's relative infancy[46]

Postmarketing Surveillance

Given the nascent state of stem cell technology, specific postmarketing requirements are limited and still developing. A critical post-product launch consideration at present, therefore, is maintaining and storing data pertaining to patient, product and starting materials' traceability. Further, quality assurance and quality control must continue. Pharmacovigilance reporting is required, including adverse event recordings, periodic safety update reports (PSURs) and, in some cases, post-authorization safety studies. Over time, these data will allow more specific strategies to be developed to regulate stem cell technologies post-authorization.

Efforts Toward International Harmonization

The EU *ATMP Regulation*'s success has demonstrated the possibility of at least partial regulatory harmonization for stem cell technology (although national Competent Authorities retain some licensing authority under the *EUTCD*, as discussed). The International Convention on Harmonisation (ICH) has not published guidelines specific to cellular products, but it has published extensive guidelines covering quality, safety and efficacy, including guidelines on biotechnology products.[47,48] For ICH regions, market authorization requirements, therefore, should be similar.

Other nonbinding guidelines have been published, such as the International Society for Stem Cell Research's (ISSCR) *Guidelines for the Clinical Translation of Stem Cells*,[49] which recommends "general principles for scientific, clinical, and ethical conduct that should be followed by all translational stem cell researchers, clinician-scientists, and regulators in the international community." In general, fundamental market authorization requirements appear to be similar. Further, initiatives such as FDA's Advancing Regulatory Science Initiative, which aims to accelerate delivery of healthcare advances to patients safely, may generate data and regulatory strategies that can inform regulators worldwide. This could improve the chances of international consensus on optimal regulatory routes, and perhaps facilitate greater agreement on how to classify and regulate borderline products best.

Summary

- Regulatory routes for stem cell technology devices vary by jurisdiction and depend on the specific nature of the product in question.
- In the EU and US, similar criteria dictate whether a cell-containing product requires pre-market authorization.
- Combination stem cell technology devices are correlated somewhat in their regulatory pathways, with the US regulating as 351 products and the EU as ATMPs. However, in the EU, combination ATMPs cannot be regulated primarily as devices, while combination 351 products incorporating cell material can be regulated primarily as devices, depending on the PMOA.
- Point-of-care autologous therapy devices represent a complex regulatory scenario and an area of divergence between the EU and US.
- Stem cell products' safety and efficacy requirements are similar to those of other product types; however, there are additional considerations.
- Cell starting materials must meet donation, procurement and testing criteria, including traceability, methodology documentation and tests for transmissible diseases.
- Manufacturing processes must conform to GMP guidelines (or equivalent) and sometimes additional requirements, as well. Quality risk management is recommended due to the biological processes' inherently variable nature during manufacture. Starting materials' quality and final product release specifications must be defined.
- Stem cell product clinical trials are similar to those for other products, although some issues require special attention.
- While some attempts to harmonize the regulatory landscape worldwide are underway, general market authorization criteria are similar.

References

1. Mason C, Brindley DA, Culme-Seymour EJ, Davie NL. "Cell therapy industry: billion dollar global business with unlimited potential." *Regen Med.* 2011 May;6(3):265–72.
2. Davies BM, Rikabi S, French A, Pinedo-Villanueva R, Morrey ME, Wartolowska K, et al. "Quantitative assessment of barriers to the clinical development and adoption of cellular therapies: A pilot study." *J Tissue Eng.* 2014 Jan 1;5:2041731414551764.
3. French A, Buckler RL, Brindley DA. "Commercialization of regenerative medicine: learning from spin-outs." *Rejuvenation Res.* 2013 Apr;16(2):164–70.

4. French A, Bure K, Brindley DA. "CASMI TSCC Launch Event, Paris, France, July 2013: An Assessment of the Key Barriers to the Commercialization and Clinical Adoption of Pluripotent Stem Cell Therapies." *Rejuvenation Res.* 2014 Feb 1;17(1):84–8.
5. French A, Suh JY, Suh CY, Rubin L, Barker R, Bure K, et al. "Global strategic partnerships in regenerative medicine." *Trends Biotechnol.* 2014 Sep;32(9):436–40.
6. Brindley DA, French A, Suh J, Roberts M, Davies B, Pinedo-Villanueva R, et al. "The Implementation of Novel Collaborative Structures for the Identification and Resolution of Barriers to Pluripotent Stem Cell Translation." *Stem Cells Dev.* 2013 Dec 1;22 (Suppl 1):63–72.
7. Daley GQ. "The promise and perils of stem cell therapeutics." *Cell Stem Cell.* 2012 Jun 14;10(6):740–9.
8. Fink D W. "FDA Regulation of Stem Cell Therapeutics." *Science.* 2009 Jun 26;324:1662.
9. PAS 83: 2012 Developing human cells for clinical applications in the European Union and the United States. 2012.
10. Autologous products use a patient's own cells for treatment, while allogeneic products use a single donor to generate cells used in other patients. For every new patient requiring an autologous treatment, a new manufacturing process will be required. For allogeneic products, a single manufacturing process can produce products to be used on many patients, more like traditional pharmaceuticals.
11. Op cit 9.
12. Ibid.
13. Frequently Asked Questions About Combination Products. FDA website. http://www.fda.gov/CombinationProducts/AboutCombinationProducts/ucm101496.htm. Accessed 2 March 2016.
14. Jennings J. "Combination Products." *Fundamentals of US Regulatory Affairs, Eighth Ed.* Regulatory Affairs Professionals Society; 2013. p. 311–8.
15. Number of Marketing Applications for a Combination Product. FDA website. http://www.fda.gov/downloads/CombinationProducts/RequestsforComment/UCM108197.pdf. Accessed 2 March 2016.
16. Siegel EB. "Detailed Regulatory Approaches to development, Review and Approval." *Development and Approval of Combination Products: A Regulatory Perspective.* John Wiley & Sons; 2008.
17. Intra-operative means that cells are harvested, processed and used for their purpose within the same surgical procedure. Processing might include concentrating a particular cell-type from a tissue sample, with the aim of implanting the concentrated cells in another location. Such approaches have been used to heal bone defects by concentrating certain cells from bone marrow, for example.
18. Coelho MB, Cabral JMS, Karp JM. "Intraoperative Stem Cell Therapy." *Annu Rev Biomed Eng.* 2012;14:325–49.
19. *Draft Guidance for Industry: Cell Selection Devices for Point of care Production of Minimally Manipulated Autologous Peripheral Blood Stem Cells (PBSCs).* FDA website. http://www.fda.gov/OHRMS/DOCKETS/98fr/07d-0290-gdl0001.pdf. Accessed 2 March 2016.
20. Guidance *for Industry and FDA Staff—Devices Used to Process Human Cells, Tissues, and Cellular and Tissue-Based Products (HCT/Ps).* FDA website. http://www.fda.gov/RegulatoryInformation/Guidances/ucm126052.htm. Accessed 2 March 2016.
21. Zwart I. "Human Tissue Regulation." *Fundamentals of US Regulatory Affairs, Sixth Ed.* Regulatory Affairs Professionals Society; 2012. p. 255–67.
22. Op cit 9.
23. Op cit 21.
24. Op cit 9.
25. *Detailed guidance on the request to the competent authorities for authorisation of a clinical trial on a medicinal product for human use, the notification of substantial amendments and the declaration of the end of the trial (CT-1).* EC website. http://eur-lex.europa.eu/legal-content/EN/TXT/?uri=uriserv:OJ.C_.2010.082.01.0001.01.ENG. Accessed 2 March 2016.
26. Bravery C. "A CATalyst for Change: Regulating Regenerative Medicines in Europe. The Delivery of Regenerative Medicines and their Impact on Healthcare." CRC Press; 2010. p. 285–312.
27. "Reflection paper on classification of advanced therapy medicinal products." EMA website . http://www.ema.europa.eu/docs/en_GB/document_library/Scientific_guideline/2012/12/WC500136422.pdf. Accessed 2 March 2015.
28. "Draft: Reflection paper on classification of advanced therapy medicinal products." EMA website. http://www.ema.europa.eu/docs/en_GB/document_library/Scientific_guideline/2012/12/WC500136422.pdf. Accessed 2 March 2016.
29. Op cit 27.
30. Cyranoski D. "Japan to offer fast-track approval path for stem cell therapies." *Nat Med.* 2013 May;19(5):510–510.
31. Op cit 9.
32. *EudraLex, The Rules Governing Medicinal Products in the European Union, Volume 4, EU guidelines for Good Manufacturing Practice for Medicinal Products for Human and Veterinary Use.* EC website. http://ec.europa.eu/health/files/eudralex/vol-4/vol4-an2__2012-06_en.pdf. Accessed 2 March 2016.
33. Brindley DA, French A, Baptista R, Timmins N, Adams T, Wall I, et al. "Cell Therapy Bioprocessing Technologies and Indicators of Technological Convergence." *BioProcess Int.* 2014.
34. Lopez F, Bartolo CD, Piazza T, Passannanti A, Gerlach JC, Gridelli B, et al. "A Quality Risk Management Model Approach for Cell Therapy Manufacturing." *Risk Anal.* 2010;30(12):1857–71.
35. Op cit 32.
36. C, Wall IB, Chandra A, Archibald P, Gold J, et al. "Enabling Consistency in Pluripotent Stem Cell-Derived Products for R&D and Clinical Applications Through Material Standards." *Stem Cells Transl Med.* In press.
37. Bravery CA, French A. "Reference materials for cellular therapeutics." *Cytotherapy.* 2014 Sep 1;16(9):1187–96.
38. Op cit 9.
39. Ibid.
40. Ibid.
41. *Guidelines of 5 November 2013 on Good Distribution Practice of medicinal products for human use.* EUR-Lex website. http://eur-lex.europa.eu/LexUriServ/LexUriServ.do?uri=OJ:C:2013:343:0001:0014:EN:PDF. Accessed 2 March 2016.
42. Op cit 3.
43. Wartolowska K, Judge A, Hopewell S, Collins GS, Dean BJF, Rombach I, et al. "Use of placebo controls in the evaluation of surgery: systematic review." *BMJ.* 2014 May 21;348(may21 2):g3253–g3253.
44. Ibid.
45. Gross RE, Watts RL, Hauser RA, Bakay RA, Reichmann H, von Kummer R, et al. "Intrastriatal transplantation of microcarrier-bound human retinal pigment epithelial cells versus sham surgery in patients with advanced Parkinson's disease: a double-blind, randomised, controlled trial." *Lancet Neurol.* 2011 Jun;10(6):509–19.
46. Op cit 9.
47. Op cit 26.
48. George B. "Regulations and guidelines governing stem cell based products: Clinical considerations." *Perspect Clin Res.* 2011;2(3):94–9.
49. *Guidelines for the Clinical Translation of Stem Cells.* ISSCR website. http://www.isscr.org/docs/default-source/clin-trans-guidelines/isscrglclinicaltrans.pdf. Accessed 2 March 2016.

Recommended Reading

British Standards Institute. PAS 83: 2012 Developing human cells for clinical applications in the European Union and the United States. 2012.

Daley GQ. The promise and perils of stem cell therapeutics. Cell Stem Cell. 2012 Jun 14;10(6):740–9.

George B. "Regulations and guidelines governing stem cell based products: Clinical considerations." *Perspect Clin Res*. 2011;2(3):94–9.

Silva M, Daheron L, Hurley H, Bure K, Barker R, Carr AJ et al. (2015). "Generating iPSCs: Translating Cell Reprogramming Science into Scalable and Robust Biomanufacturing Strategies." *Cell Stem Cell*, 16(1), 13-17.

Acknowledgements

The authors express sincere thanks to the following organizations that have contributed to the CASMI Translational Stem Cell Consortium (CTSCC) as funding and events partners, without whom the consortium and the benefits it will bring to stem cell translation would be constrained: GE Healthcare, the Center for Commercialization of Regenerative Medicine (CCRM), Sartorius Stedim Biotech (formerly TAP Biosystems), Lonza, the California Institute for Regenerative Medicine (CIRM), the Strategies for Engineered Negligible Senescence (SENS) Research Foundation, UK Cell Therapy Catapult, NIH Centre for Regenerative Medicine, the New York Stem Cell Foundation (NYSCF), ThermoFisher Scientific, Eisai, Medipost (US), Medipost (Korea), Celgene, Roche and Oxford BioMedica. Author Brindley gratefully acknowledges personal funding from the Oxford Musculoskeletal National Institute for Health Research (NIHR) the Saïd Foundation, and the SENS Research Foundation. Smith gratefully acknowledges support from the CASMI Translational Stem Cell Consortium (CTSCC) and from the UK Medical Research Council.

Disclosure and Conflicts of Interest

This article represents the authors' individual opinions and may not necessarily represent the viewpoints of their employers. Brindley is a stockholder in Translation Ventures Ltd. (Charlbury, Oxfordshire, UK) and IP Asset Ventures Ltd. (Oxford, Oxfordshire, UK), companies that, among other services, provide cell therapy biomanufacturing, regulatory and financial advice to pharmaceutical clients. Smith is a consultant with IP Asset Ventures Ltd. Brindley also is subject to the CFA Institute's codes, standards and guidelines, so he must stress this piece is provided for academic interest only and must not be construed in any way as an investment recommendation. Additionally, at time of publication, Brindley and the organizations with which he is affiliated may or may not have agreed and/or pending funding commitments from the organizations named herein.

20 Patents and Intellectual Property

By Joanna T. Brougher, Stanley F. Chalvire, Sean D. Detweiler, David A. Fazzolare and Lisa M. Warren

Introduction

The US is the largest medical device market in the world, projected to reach $133 billion in 2016.[1] Medical devices are increasingly as varied and complex technologically as the diseases and conditions they are used to treat, diagnose or prevent. Moreover, medical devices often feature multiple technologies, which in many instances function or are presented in combination with one another to address an unmet medical need or solve a technical problem. They may include, for example, mechanical devices used in combination with software or with therapeutic drugs or biologics. Due in part to their varied nature, medical devices frequently may comprise or rely on multiple intellectual property (IP) categories. As a result, the strategies employed to protect such medical devices and their underlying IP need to be considered carefully and thoughtfully to afford maximum protection. A "one size fits all" approach to protecting such IP may not be appropriate for all medical devices. Rather, the most effective IP strategies are considered early in a particular medical device's development and periodically reassessed and refined, giving particular consideration to the medical device's features or properties that may distinguish it from other competing or commercially available products.

The term "intellectual property" refers to creations of the mind, such as inventions, literary works, artistic works and names and images used in commerce. For medical devices, IP generally comprises trademarks, copyrights, patents and trade secrets, each of which affords the subject IP owner distinct rights and protections. For example, and as discussed in greater detail below, patents in the US represent one federally recognized form of IP protection available to protect "any new and useful process, machine, manufacture, or composition of matter, or any new and useful improvement thereof," and afford the patentee the right to exclude others from practicing the claimed invention for a limited period of time. This exclusionary right afforded to a patentee is distinct from the rights afforded to the owner of, for example, a trademark or copyright. A basic appreciation of the distinctions in both the scope of rights afforded and the subject matter such rights may protect remains key to recognizing the IP and then taking the critical steps necessary to protect it.

Securing protection for a medical device's associated IP also remains critically important to establishing and preserving the device's value. In particular, identifying and strategically considering how to protect the medical device's valuable IP aspects best may be used effectively to limit or preclude competitors' ability to copy or replicate the IP in their own competing devices, thereby placing such competitors at a disadvantage. Likewise, a clear and early understanding of third-party IP rights and how they may restrict a sponsor's ability to commercialize a medical device also may provide valuable insights that may be useful to inform a medical device's development and limit potential issues, and could frustrate a sponsor's plans to commercialize the device.

This chapter explores the various types of available IP protections and discusses relevant considerations during a medical device's development. Similarly, the importance of aligning a medical device regulatory strategy with a global IP strategy to maximize afforded protections and, thus, extend the exclusivity to which the medical device may be subject, also is examined in the context of illustrative medical devices. Armed with a well-defined IP strategy, a device sponsor is poised to maximize the value of its development efforts and the resulting medical device.

Types of Medical Device IP

Four basic IP types can be used to protect different medical device aspects, including copyrights, trademarks, trade secrets and patents.

Copyrights

A copyright is a right granted to an original work's creator or author upon the work being fixed in a tangible medium of expression.[2] A copyright gives its owner the exclusive right to, and to authorize others to, reproduce the work, prepare derivative works, distribute copies, publicly perform the work and/or publicly display the work. Examples of such works of authorship include, but are not limited to, literary works, musical works, dramatic works, pictorial or graphic works and software.[3] For medical devices, a copyright can be used to protect against copying of software code, as well as published works, including websites, collateral, designs, product specifications, instructions for use, data sheets and product photographs. It is important to emphasize, however, the copyright protects only the expression of ideas within the works and not the information or ideas presented in those works.

Copyright protection is automatic once the created work is fixed in a tangible form perceptible by others; however, copyright registration entitles the registrant to certain benefits and, therefore, is recommended. Registration in most countries, including the US, can be accomplished easily by submitting a completed form with the requisite fee and depositing a copy of the work with the national Copyright Office. There is no international copyright; protection against unlicensed use in any particular country depends on the that country's copyright laws, including whether the country is a party to one of two major international copyright conventions governing how the rights of authors in one country are dealt with in another, namely the Berne Union for the Protection of Literary and Artistic Property and the Universal Copyright Convention (UCC).[4] For example, under the UCC, any formality in national law can be met by using a copyright notice © accompanied by the year of first publication and the name of the copyright proprietor. The copyright notice must be placed in a way to provide reasonable notice of the copyright claim. Before registering for copyright protection in a country, a medical device company first should determine whether copyright protection in that country extends to foreign authors' works. Preferably, this determination should be made before the work is published anywhere by consulting with local experts in countries where copyright protection is desired.

Trademark

Trademarks are indicia, e.g., a word, name, symbol, slogan, color or product shape, identifying and distinguishing one producer's goods from another's. Trademark rights can be used to stop others from using a confusingly similar mark in commerce, but they cannot be used to stop others from making or selling the same goods or services under a different mark. Trademarks used in interstate commerce can be registered federally by filing trademark applications at a national trademark office, such as the US Patent and Trademark Office (USPTO). Anyone who uses a mark in US commerce is permitted to use the trademark symbol ™ or service mark symbol ℠ to give public notice of the mark owner's rights. However, the ® symbol can be used only after USPTO approves the mark for registration after a trademark application is filed. In addition, the federal registration symbol may be used only with the mark for the classes of goods and/or services identified in the federal trademark registration.

For medical devices, trademarks can be used for brand development to protect the goodwill attributed to a medical device but not to prevent others from using the device. Medical device companies can obtain trademark protection in foreign countries using the Madrid system for international trademark registration,[5] which enables a medical device company to register for trademarks in as many as 92 contracting countries, including the US, EU, China, India, Russia and Japan, by filing one trademark application in a single trademark office in any one of the 92 contracting countries.

Trade Secret

A trade secret is any information deriving independent economic value from not being generally known or readily ascertainable. In some jurisdictions, reasonable steps must be taken to protect the information's secrecy. A trade secret can protect a wide array of subject matter, including, without limitation, a formula, pattern, compilation, program, device, method, technique or process, as well as a customer list. Trade secret law is governed by various national legal systems. In addition, Article 39 of *The Agreement on Trade Related Aspects of Intellectual Property* provides international standards for protecting undisclosed information (i.e., trade secrets) against unauthorized use in member states.[6]

Trade secret protection for medical devices can be used to protect company information from being used by former employees and to protect underlying source code for medical devices relying on proprietary software. Trade secret protection, however, might not be effective for protecting information or designs that enter the public domain because, in contrast to patents, trade secrets do not protect against reverse engineering. Medical device companies should consult an IP attorney to determine whether certain medical device aspects can and should be protected by trade secret.

Patents

A patent provides its owner with an exclusionary right, for a limited period of time known as the patent term, which prevents others from making, using, selling or offering for sale, a patented invention in the country in which the patent is granted.[7] A patent comprises a specification describing the invention, one or more drawings illustrating the invention and a set of claims defining the exclusionary rights the patent affords. While conferring an exclusionary right, patents do not grant their owners the right to practice the claimed invention; such freedom to operate is dependent on the rights of third parties, including patent rights. Generally, the patent term begins on the date on which a patent is granted and continues for 20 years from the earliest claimed priority date. It should be noted, however, the actual patent term can vary depending on whether the term has been adjusted or extended, as discussed in more detail below.[8]

Patent Types and Applications

Two patent types can be used to protect medical devices: utility patents and design patents. A utility patent can protect a device's functional aspects, including the device structure itself and processes for making and using the device. A design patent can be used to protect a device's ornamental features. Because most devices' commercial value lies in their function rather than their appearance, design patents generally are of limited value in protecting medical devices, while utility patents are crucial. Since patents typically are the most useful type of IP protection for medical devices, the remainder of this chapter focuses on patents, particularly utility patents.

Patents are territorial, meaning applicants must file for protection in each country where protection is desired because there is no international patent granting protection worldwide. Nonetheless, the *Patent Cooperation Treaty* (*PCT*)[9] provides a mechanism simplifying the process of obtaining patents worldwide by permitting an applicant to file a patent application in a single member country in one language that serves as a placeholder application, preserving the applicant's ability to file patent applications later with national patent offices in other member countries.

Some countries, including the US, allow provisional applications to be filed as placeholder patent applications, eliminating many formal regulatory utility patent application requirements and costing less to file because they are not examined. However, a provisional application expires if a regular utility application claiming priority to the provisional application is not filed within one year. A provisional application, therefore, can be filed to preserve a medical device company's rights to file a utility application covering an invention later, while the medical device company assesses the device's commercial feasibility.

Numerous strategies can be implemented to protect medical devices throughout their lifecycles using provisional, utility and *PCT* applications. A common approach during medical device development is filing a first provisional application followed by one or more additional provisional applications during the subsequent 12 months to cover medical device aspects as the device is developed or improved. Before the first provisional application's one-year expiration date, a utility or *PCT* application, or both, claiming priority to all provisional applications, is filed. Approximately 18 months later, as the *PCT* application expires, a final decision can be made on the countries in which to file national phase patent applications. Even though foreign filing decisions can be delayed for up to about 30 months from filing the earliest provisional application, the patent attorney should have a general sense of the countries in which protection is desired, because patentable subject matter and patentability requirements can differ greatly from country to country.

Patentability Requirements

A patent application typically is examined by the national patent office in the country in which it is filed. During examination, the national patent office reviews the application to determine whether it is drawn to patentable subject matter and satisfies that nation's patentability criteria (e.g., is described adequately for persons skilled in a particular field to make and use the invention without undue experimentation). Basic patentability requirements principally are the same in each country; however, the manner in which each country applies those requirements can differ.

Generally, an invention is patentable in most countries if it is useful (has utility),[10] novel,[11] not obvious in view of prior art[12] and directed to patentable subject matter.[13] An invention satisfies the utility requirement if it has any practical use—a certainty for virtually every medical device invention. An invention is novel if the device has not been disclosed previously to the public. An invention is obvious if it is so close to the prior art it would have been obvious to a person having ordinary skill in the relevant field. Lastly, an invention is patentable if it falls within a statutorily defined category of inventions and does not fall within a statutorily or judicially defined exception.

In the context of medical devices, an invention deemed useful, novel and nonobvious in one country generally will satisfy these criteria in others. In this regard, patent prosecution highways established between certain countries to expedite prosecution greatly increase the likelihood an invention considered useful, novel and nonobvious in one participating country will be deemed the same in other participating countries. In contrast, certain patentability requirements, such as whether an invention is directed to patent-eligible subject matter, can differ significantly from country to country.

A claimed invention is considered patent eligible in the US if it is directed to one of four statutory subject matter categories: a process, machine, article of manufacture or composition of matter; or an improvement of any of those categories.[14] US courts have interpreted statutory subject matter as excluding inventions directed to abstract ideas, physical phenomena, natural principles, natural correlations and natural products from patent eligibility.[15] In contrast, European Patent Convention (EPC) Article 53(c) excludes methods for treating the human or animal body by surgery or therapy from patent eligibility,[16] whereas medical devices generally are eligible for EU patent protection.

Patents Foster Medical Device Development and Commercialization

The complexity associated with pursuing and obtaining valid and valuable patent rights might raise the question whether the resource expenditure is worth the return on investment. The benefit associated most commonly with patent rights is exclusivity, as mentioned above: the right to exclude others from practicing the claimed invention. However, there are numerous other reasons to pursue IP rights. First, a well-planned IP strategy and at least some initial filings generally are critical for medical device companies to obtain funding, whether from angel investors, venture capitalists or private equity investors. Attention to IP demonstrates a medical device company management team's sophistication and provides a tangible asset with which to secure the investment. Depending on the company's business strategy, a solid patent foundation also can be a pivotal factor in attracting strategic partners for partnerships or collaborations. Moreover, patent infringement allegations almost inevitably follow medical device commercialization; a strong and varied patent portfolio provides negotiation leverage to minimize the company's exposure to infringement claims by third parties, sometimes turning the negative of potential litigation into a positive strategic partnership. Finally, companies recognizing and rewarding their employees' creative efforts in patent filings and corresponding royalty streams, among other things, create continued innovation incentives.

Developing a Comprehensive Global Patent Portfolio

Patents can be used to help fund medical device development and commercialization and protect against competition and copying; therefore, developing a comprehensive global patent portfolio including device patents, its components, device ancillary or companion products and patents protecting against reverse engineering or design-arounds of any of these is important. Ideally, patent protection covering these features should be sought in each country in which the device is expected to be developed, manufactured or commercialized by a medical device company or its competitors. Such strategic foreign filing decisions (and associated costs) can be delayed by filing international *PCT* applications to protect those features; however, decisions must be made early in product development as to what medical device aspects should be protected and how to protect them best throughout the device's lifecycle because medical device development is an iterative process. Strategic planning for a comprehensive patent portfolio, therefore, must begin early in the development process and should continue throughout the entire product lifecycle.

A plethora of potentially patentable inventions that could give rise to a comprehensive patent portfolio may arise throughout a medical device's lifecycle. It can be cost-prohibitive, however, to file patents on every one of those potentially patentable inventions; therefore, deciding the subject matter for which to pursue patent protection must be driven by business considerations. Three primary business considerations should inform patent filing decisions: 1) whether obtaining a patent will serve to protect a company's product from a competitor copying that product; 2) whether the patent will serve as a potential source of revenue for the company; and 3) whether the patent can be used as leverage to negotiate a settlement if the company is sued for patent infringement. If an invention fails to meet one or more of these criteria, it might not be worth pursuing patent protection for it. Patent searching from both a patentability and freedom-to-operate perspective can be useful in informing these business decisions and should be performed for each potentially patentable invention arising throughout the development cycle. Such search results also can be useful to guide development as a device concept advances through its lifecycle.

Following are example scenarios that can arise in each medical device development cycle stage that can give rise to potentially patentable inventions.

Conception

The conception stage is fertile ground for patentable inventions. For example, a company may be contemplating multiple medical device designs at this stage. A patentability and freedom-to-operate search for each of these different designs can help inform which design is worth pursuing. In particular, a device design with less prior art for patentability purposes and no blocking patents uncovered that could give rise to a patent infringement suit would be preferable to one in which the art is crowded, and patents are uncovered protecting certain proposed device design components or aspects. If a patent search for a proposed medical device concept uncovers blocking patents, the development team has more freedom in conception to consider ways to design around the discovered patents in a way that could lead to new potentially patentable devices free and clear of blocking patents. This is one way the patent search process can inform a medical device's conception, giving rise to patentable inventions that otherwise would not have been conceived.

Prototype

The prototyping stage also can also give rise to patentable inventions in some circumstances. For example, as a concept is implemented in a prototype, technological or manufacturing issues may surface that were not considered or recognizable when the invention was merely a concept. Such hurdles may provide an opportunity to redesign and reengineer the product in a manner that could generate new or different IP in the form of new patentable inventions.

Preclinical

During the preclinical phase, testing sometimes can reveal additional prototype shortcomings. Again, such hurdles present an opportunity for further patentable innovation. These situations are referred to as hurdles rather than roadblocks because they can be overcome with enough thought and innovation.

Clinical

In the clinical development phase, safety and efficacy become the focus. With a different focus, and potentially a different cross-section of scientists and engineers, new ideas and innovations also can be generated and create further opportunity for patent protection.

Manufacturing

In the manufacturing phase, yet another group of scientists and engineers become involved in product development, and there is another opportunity for new ideas and innovation.

Marketing

After a product enters the market, companies often follow up with customers to obtain product feedback. While a company cannot pursue new ideas generated by a customer, there may be an opportunity if a customer points out a previously undiscovered problem or issue, and the solution lends itself to further innovation and patentability. When working on solutions based on customer feedback, the company should be careful to understand and identify the solution's proper and correct inventors. If a customer is involved in inventorship, the potential for a joint venture or, at minimum, joint ownership with that customer inventor should be explored. It is important to note, if an individual should have been identified in a patent application and patent as an inventor but was not, and the inventorship later is challenged, the patent may be rendered unenforceable. As such, it is important to identify complex inventorships as early as possible and involve a patent attorney to review or perform the proper inventorship analysis.

Commercial Use

If a product performs poorly, design updates to improve performance can generate new possibilities for patentable invention.

Obsolescence

After products have been on the market for extended time periods, they may become obsolete. A system can be created to search and monitor competitor activity constantly for new patent applications for products attempting to innovate beyond aging products. Likewise, the company making and selling aging products should review new patents in the space regularly to motivate new ideas that iterate beyond competitor patents.

What to Protect

Developing a comprehensive patent portfolio also requires understanding what medical device aspects should be protected, as potentially patentable inventions arise throughout a device's development cycle.

Protect Device, Device Components, etc.

Often, a product under development will contain multiple patentable inventions. It is important to look at the product with the idea it may be patentable as a whole and/or may contain a number of innovative advancements that could be patented separately. For example, a medical device may have a unique structural design, novel and nonobvious in comparison with other devices; it also may be made of a different composite material, novel and nonobvious; and/or the device may include a new coating material for carrying a therapeutic substance to a patient in a novel and non-obvious manner. Each of these areas may be worthy of a patentability assessment. Addressing these issues with a patent attorney will enable a strategy to be created to protect all of a new product's important inventions.

Protect Ancillary or Companion Products

When assessing patentability and how the eventual patent will fit a company's business strategy, it is worth considering how separately patentable inventions may relate to ancillary or companion products. Taking the above medical device example with three different possible patent protection areas (device structure, device composition material and coating for the device to deliver a therapeutic substance), each separately patentable invention may be used on ancillary or companion products. As such, when these inventions are developed for a first product (e.g., a stent), and the patent application(s) is drafted, thought should be given to whether the invention also should be described and claimed for use with other medical devices.

Protect Improvements

One mistake inventors and companies often make is assuming incorrectly improvements to an existing product are not patentable. In reality, the vast majority of patent applications filed are for existing product or invention improvements, rather than groundbreaking, revolutionary ideas. Whenever a problem relating to an existing company product is given to an engineer or scientist, its solution should be assessed for patentability and fit with business strategy to determine whether a patent application should be pursued. This decision should not be made by the inventor, who may be unaware of other company areas that could benefit from the improvement or actually may be patentable in its original context.

Product improvements should be tracked and documented with each product specification change throughout the development cycle. Device or product developments are iterative processes, and designs may change during commercialization. Further, as the engineers and scientist iterate product improvements, regular meetings with regulatory, legal and engineering teams to review the work being done should occur. Otherwise, product development and invention cycles may be wasted pursuing an improvement that may require more additional testing or regulatory work than financially worthwhile. Appreciating such limitations early in the development cycle can help avoid lost time and resources.

Protect Against Reverse Engineering

Reverse engineering is the process by which a product is reviewed, dismantled and assessed to determine how it was made to enable creation of a competing product. In contrast to trade secrets, patents can provide protection against such activity. Patents should protect inventions if they either can be reverse-engineered readily or are likely to be evaluated and copied by competitors. Because patents ultimately require the idea's full public disclosure, if trade secret protection can apply, pursuing a patent may be less preferable than the trade secret route. Trade secrets may be preferable for protecting anything not easily reverse-engineered that can be kept secret by enforcing confidentiality restrictions for all individuals with access to the information. One difficulty with trade secrets is if a third party figures out the secret independently, without illegal activity or breach of a nondisclosure agreement, or independently develops the idea, there typically is no recourse. To preserve trade secret protection, it is important to ensure adequate systems for maintaining that information's secrecy are in place. Consulting a patent attorney is advisable to decide whether patent protection or trade secret protection is appropriate in any given circumstance, particularly when there is a risk of reverse engineering, as well as to ensure systems for maintaining trade secret confidentiality are adequate.

Protect Against Design-Arounds

A commercially valuable patent should protect not only the core invention, but also protect against competitors' attempts to design around patent claims. Those involved in medical device development, therefore, should collaborate with the attorney drafting the core invention patent application to determine various ways to implement the invention differing from the core invention and disclose and claim those alternatives in the patent application. Protecting the core invention and as many conceivable alternative implementations as possible can provide the broadest invention protection possible and maximize the likelihood competing products will infringe patent claims.

Third-Party Patents' Impact on Medical Device Development and Commercialization

Much of this chapter's discussion has focused on protecting innovations and developing a comprehensive IP strategy, particularly patent protection. However, no IP medical device strategy discussion would be complete without reviewing the impact of third-party rights on development and commercialization. Even the most innovative medical device combined with the most elegantly designed protection strategy can be of no avail if proper attention is not given to whether the device can be made and used without infringing the rights of others (so-called "freedom-to-operate"). This is particularly relevant in the medical device industry, which is one of the most litigious with respect to patent enforcement.

Generally, a medical device company becomes aware of third-party patents in one of two ways: direct communication from the third party or its own proactive search. As mentioned above, companies typically search for third-party patents during development (prior to filing a patent application) and/or at commercialization. While early searching can aid in determining patentability and guide preliminary design efforts, a search just prior to commercialization is equally critical. First, the final commercial design allows a more definitive analysis of third-party patent claims to be conducted. Second, patent filings typically are not published until 18 months after the earliest filing date, so there is a rolling 18-month blackout period for identifying potential third-party rights. Thus, a later search will reveal additional patents that may be relevant to the commercial device. Continuing to search and monitor third-party patent publications throughout the device's lifecycle also is a sound practice, as situations may arise where the company may intervene in the prosecution of problematic filings by providing relevant prior art to the national patent office or applicant. Some countries have mechanisms for opposing recently granted patents as well. These strategies may narrow patent claims or even prevent such claims from being included in a patent.

Identifying potentially problematic patents early provides the device company greater flexibility in addressing issues and more time to assess its options. If such patents are identified, the device company can consider whether modifications are needed to design around patent claims, possibly prior to regulatory clearance or commercial launch. In making such a determination, the company should consider whether the patent holder has the ability to pursue alternate claims in subsequent patent filings. If so, a design-around strategy simply may postpone the need to engage with the patent holder.

Alternatively or additionally, the company might consider contacting the patent holder to discuss obtaining a license to the patent. This, of course, is a risky option if the medical device has not come to the patent holder's attention, and the company may choose to take a "wait-and-see" approach to allow the patent holder to contact the company when and if it chooses. Unfortunately, the patent holder's first contact could be notice of a patent infringement suit, so a wait-and-see strategy is not without its own risks.

With any of the above approaches, the company should assess the desirability of obtaining a patent counsel's opinion on the validity or enforceability of problematic claims based on prior art or other considerations. While such an opinion will not shield the company from ultimate infringement liability, it generally will immunize the company from a finding of willful infringement and potential treble damages. It also may provide a starting point to negotiate a license and/or establish such a transaction's economic value, because a patent holder may be less inclined to pursue an infringement suit when facing a strong noninfringement, invalidity or unenforceability position. Identifying third-party rights early permits the medical device company to consider its options on its own terms rather than being forced to evaluate the third-party position and develop a strategy to address it under time pressure of an invitation to take a license, a cease-and-desist letter or an infringement suit.

Patents and Regulatory Considerations

Medical devices promise to advance medical technology and healthcare delivery and will experience continued market growth. The regulatory process, however, continues to present hurdles delaying market entry. To navigate the regulatory process successfully and maximize a product's lifecycle, it is important to align a product's patent strategy with its regulatory strategy. Those handling the product's patent strategy must collaborate with the professionals in charge of the regulatory strategy and understand the potential tensions between patents and medical device regulation. Together, these professionals can ensure patent filings adequately support the arguments, data and/or information required for the regulatory authority.

Patent Applications Can Provide PMOA Support

To ensure medical products made or sold in the US are safe and effective, FDA assigns each product to one of three centers for review based on whether the product is a device, biologic or drug.[17] Products used for drug delivery are sent to the Center for Drug Evaluation and Research (CDER); products used as devices are sent to the Center for Devices and Radiological Health (CDRH); and biologics are sent to the Center for Biological Evaluation and Research (CBER).

While each center is responsible for evaluating product safety and efficacy, they vary in regulatory approval time and cost. To demonstrate efficacy, for instance, both CDER and CBER require at least one randomized, placebo-controlled study, while CDRH is more flexible and allows other study designs. Moreover, application fees vary significantly among the different classifications, with the fees for drugs and biologics approximately double those for devices.

Therefore, it is important for manufacturers to ensure their products go to the appropriate center for approval to minimize time and cost. Products are assigned to a center based on their "primary mode of action" (PMOA). PMOA is the mode of action expected to make the greatest contribution to the product's overall intended therapeutic effects (e.g., combination product). For example, if a product's PMOA is the biologics component, CBER should have jurisdiction over its premarket and postmarket review.

Problems arise, however, because PMOA is not defined clearly by either statute or FDA and, accordingly, incorrectly classified products may end up at the wrong center. The court, in *Bracco Diagnostics, Inc. v. Shalala*,[18] examined the implications of different FDA classifications. In that case, most manufacturers of ultrasound contrast agents, device-drug combination products, received drug classifications for their products. However, one manufacturer's product was classified as a device. Manufacturers whose products were classified as drugs incurred about $3.5 million more in regulatory approval costs than if their products had been classified as devices. Premarket review process differences between the classifications were highlighted before the court: "The usual development of a device takes less time than development as a drug. It requires fewer patients and less safety and efficacy data. This results in development cost savings and increased development speed."[19] The court ultimately held FDA had discretion in how to approve a product but could not treat two similar products dissimilarly on two different regulatory tracks without having legitimate justification.[20]

Since an unfavorable FDA designation can present significant time and financial hurdles to reaching the market, companies should be prepared to make a case for why their combination products should be assigned to a particular center. One way to accomplish this is to highlight the product's PMOA or "primary" feature in the patent application itself. Highlighting the primary feature can be done, for example, by discussing it first in the application. For a device and drug combination product the company wants classified as a device, the patent application should discuss the product's device feature before addressing its drug feature. Patent application claims also should be directed first to the device rather than the drug. By drafting a patent application highlighting the product's primary feature, companies may increase their likelihood of receiving a favorable classification from FDA.

Patent Applications Can Support Substantial Equivalence

Once the product is assigned to the desired center, the patent application can help support a 510(k) application finding of substantial equivalence. Demonstrating a product is substantially equivalent to an existing product can be accomplished by highlighting the product's similarities in the patent application. For example, the applicant's written description can show the new product has the same intended use, technological characteristics and safety and efficacy profile as the existing product.

While it is important to describe the new product's similarities to the existing one, it is important the applicant not do so at the expense of showcasing the differences. A finding of patentability by USPTO requires novelty and nonobviousness. If the applicant focuses too much on the two products' similarities, it may demonstrate substantial equivalence but may not satisfy patentability requirements. To achieve the right balance, the patent application should be drafted with input from both regulatory and patent professionals.

Maximizing Product Lifecycle

Maximizing a product's value is critical to any company's success, including medical device companies. A product's value, in part, is related to its patent's lifetime. In general, the longer a product is protected by patents, the greater the revenue and profit it can generate.

In many other industries, companies can begin selling their products before a patent has been issued and, thus, are able to benefit from most of the 20-year patent term. This is not the case with medical devices, which require regulatory approval before they can be marketed. With medical devices, a patent application usually is filed early in the development process, often before a prototype has been developed. By the time the device is approved by a national regulatory authority and ready for marketing, the device likely will have fewer than 20 years remaining on its patent term.

To encourage medical device innovation, various governments have passed incentive programs to provide additional patent exclusivity. Certain countries, for instance, allow recovery of patent term to account for delays in patent application examination and regulatory approval time. Some countries in which medical device patent applications are filed and their respective patent term extension policies are outlined below. Regulatory professionals should understand how regulatory delays regarding patent term are treated in countries where a product will be protected and should work with the patent attorneys to ensure any deadlines for filing for patent term extension are met. Without such coordination, important patent term can be lost.

US

Patent Term Adjustments for Delays Due to USPTO Approval

One mechanism for extending the patent term is to adjust for delays occurring during the patent prosecution process. These extension types are calculated under 35 USC §154.[21] According to Section 154, USPTO provides a one-day extension for each day it fails to meet certain deadlines, such as issuing a first Office Action within 14 months or responding to a reply within four months, as well as for each day the patent application is pending beyond three years from the filing date. The first extensions are known as "A delays," and the second are known as "B delays." To the extent the A and B delay periods overlap, Section 154 provides "the period of any adjustment granted under this subsection shall not exceed the actual number of days the issuance of the patent was delayed."

Patent Term Extensions for Regulatory Approval Delays

In the US, the *Hatch-Waxman Act*, codified at 35 USC §156,[22] grants patent term extensions to offset patent term eroded during the regulatory review process. In particular, term extensions are available for patents claiming "a product, a method of using a product, or a method of manufacturing a product subject to regulatory delays caused by FDA's premarket approval process."[23] The US Supreme Court has interpreted Section 156 as applicable to medical devices.[24] The extension, however, is available only for patents on products undergoing a "regulatory review period," which means devices subject to review under Section 515 (i.e., PMAs), not devices reviewed under Section 510(k).[25]

Under Section 156, a Class III medical device developer can recapture lost patent term for all delays resulting from regulatory approval and half of the time lost during preclinical studies, except the overall extension may neither exceed five years nor extend the remaining patent life beyond 14 years from the FDA approval date. In addition, only one patent may be extended for every approved product, and that patent must be valid and not expired. Moreover, the patent may be extended only to the point the patent claims cover the approved product or its usage method.

To obtain the benefit of a patent term extension under 35 USC §156, certain deadlines must be met. For instance, a patent term extension application must be submitted within the 60-day period beginning on the date the product received commercial marketing or use permission. If the extension application is not submitted during that timeframe, the product may not receive the extension to which it may be entitled. To ensure these important deadlines are met, regulatory professionals should keep patent attorneys informed of delays during regulatory review and actual approval dates.

EU

The EU offers a similar mechanism for extending patent term based on regulatory process delays. EU regulations specify original medicinal products will benefit from an eight-year data protection period, a further two-year marketing protection period and a possible one-year extension if the originator company can show a new therapeutic indication for the product. Thus, a new chemical entity may achieve 11 years of exclusivity. In the EU, patent term extensions may be obtained through Supplementary Protection Certificates (SPCs). SPCs are available to extend patent terms for various regulated, biologically active agents, namely human or veterinary medicinal and plant protection products (e.g., insecticides and herbicides). SPCs also are available in certain EU countries to extend certain medical devices' patent terms.[26] To qualify, the products must be protected by a patent, subject to an administrative authorization procedure and not have been placed on the market anywhere in the European Economic Area (EEA) as a medicinal product before being subject to safety and efficacy testing and a regulatory review.[27] The SPC usually can extend the patent term by a maximum of five years. However, it can be extended by six additional months when the SPC relates to a human medicinal product for which data from an agreed Pediatric Investigation Plan's (PIP) clinical trial have been submitted.[28]

Japan

In Japan, regulatory delay patent term extensions are available. The patent term can be extended by a maximum of five years. Unlike the US, more than one patent can be extended. In addition, a product is eligible for patent extension even if its patent life after approval has 14 or more years.

China

In China, patent term extensions for regulatory delays are not available.

Brazil

In Brazil, patent term extensions for regulatory delays are not available.

Canada

In Canada, no patent term restoration or extension is available, in contrast to other industrialized nations.

Patent Infringement Safe Harbor for Medical Device Regulatory Review

The *Hatch-Waxman Act* also codified 35 USC §271(e)(1), providing a safe harbor exempting medical device developers from patent infringement for conducting activities pursuing regulatory marketing approval.[29] In particular, the safe harbor permits medical device developers to undertake activities to enable approved or cleared medical devices to enter the market immediately upon patent expiration.

The Supreme Court held, in *Eli Lilly & Co. v. Medtronic, Inc.*, making and using a patented device to satisfy PMA requirements was sufficiently "reasonably related" to regulatory approval to warrant protection under the safe harbor.[30] The Court, however, did not address whether §271(e)(1) applies equally to devices not subject to PMA, such as those cleared under 510(k) or exempted from premarket review. The Federal Circuit, nevertheless, eventually addressed that issue and held the safe harbor exemption under §271(e)(1) applies to devices cleared under 510(k)[31] but does not extend to devices entirely exempt from premarket review.[32] Thus, medical device developers should consult with both regulatory professionals and patent attorneys to determine whether a particular device being developed is subject to premarket review and eligible for protection under the safe harbor before engaging in otherwise infringing activity using patented devices.

510(k) as Prior Art

Medical device developers must be careful not to disclose too much information in their 510(k)s because such documents are publicly accessible through the *Freedom of Information Act* or FDA and, therefore, may be available as prior art against a later filed patent application. This risk may be significant because a 510(k) asserts a device is substantially equivalent to a predicate device, and this could be construed as an admission of the existence of prior art, anticipating or rendering obvious the device claimed in the patent application. Medical device developers can avoid this situation by filing patent applications in advance of 510(k) submissions. However, delaying patent filing until after submitting a 510(k) may extend the patent term covering the device advantageously. To that end, the regulatory professional can collaborate with the patent attorney to ensure the 510(k) application discloses enough product technical aspects to claim substantial equivalence in a way unrelated to patentability and without disclosing all elements of the invention the patent application discloses and claims. The regulatory professional also may consider including a disclaimer in the 510(k) submission defining "substantial equivalence" according to the *Food, Drug, and Cosmetic Act* while disclaiming its definition under the *Patent Act* (i.e., the term "substantial equivalence" is used herein as defined in 21 CFR §807.87, and not as defined in Title 35 of the US Code). Thus, collaboration between the regulatory professional and patent attorney in preparing a 510(k) submission can mitigate the risks of having a 510(k) serve as invalidating prior art against a later filed patent application.

510(k) as an Admission of Patent Infringement

Medical device manufacturers have argued a 510(k) ought to be acceptable proof of patent infringement.[33] The Federal Circuit has held that asserting substantial equivalence in a 510(k) submission does not constitute an admission of infringement[34] because alleging a later device exhibits the same safety and efficacy as an existing device is not tantamount to admission the latter device infringes a patent covering the former device. Nevertheless, the courts have not addressed definitively whether a 510(k) could be used to establish patent infringement under the doctrine of equivalence, which could render a product literally not infringing a patent claim to infringe it nonetheless if it performs "substantially the same function in substantially the same way to obtain the same result" as the product claimed in the patent.[35] The Supreme Court, however, has held the doctrine of equivalence analysis can be applied by comparing each element of an accused product to that of a patent claim to see whether each is identical or equivalent to the element claimed.[36] Because a 510(k) submission's assertion of substantial equivalence generally is considered to be equivalence to an existing device as a whole, rather than asserting each 510(k) device element is substantially equivalent to each predicate device element, courts are unlikely to consider a 510(k) substantial equivalence claim as supportive of infringement under the doctrine of equivalence. Nevertheless, no court has ruled definitively that a 510(k) is inadmissible *per se* for establishing infringement under the doctrine of equivalence. Thus, the regulatory professional should consult with a patent attorney to ensure no statements made in the 510(k) submission reasonably can be relied on to support an allegation of patent infringement under the doctrine of equivalence.

Conclusion

As the medical device field and its underlying technologies continue to evolve, the importance of developing and executing a thoughtful and comprehensive IP strategy will continue to increase. The foundation for a successful IP strategy is the fundamental premise the medical device company owns and controls its IP rights; the most successful intellectual property strategies can be derailed if this is not the case. To that end, personnel employed, contracted or otherwise engaged by the medical device company to render services should agree in writing to assign their rights in and to any developments, inventions or works they may develop, invent, conceive, and reduce to practice or author on the company's behalf. A medical device company's failure to secure these exclusive rights to IP developed on its behalf may limit such IP's value materially, for example, by compromising company's afforded exclusivity, thereby rendering a well-planned IP strategy ineffective.

Considerable time, effort and resources are expended in successfully developing a commercial medical device, and a cohesive IP strategy remains a vital aspect of preserving the value these resources create. By developing an IP strategy, integrating it into the business plan and revisiting that strategy periodically as business objectives evolve, a medical device company positions itself to both create and preserve its business value. Moreover, the more a medical device's IP and regulatory strategy are integrated and informed by one another, the more likely the corresponding medical device's exclusivity may be prolonged and its value enhanced.

References

1. US Department of Commerce, SELECT USA website, http://selectusa.commerce.gov/industry-snapshots/medical-device-industry-united-states.html. Accessed 27 March 2016.
2. 17 USC §102.
3. Ibid; 17 USC §106.
4. Berne Union for the Protection of Literary and Artistic Property; Universal Copyright Convention.
5. *Madrid Agreement Concerning the International Registration of Marks* (1891); *Protocol Relating to the Madrid Agreement* (1989).
6. Article 39, *The Agreement on Trade Related Aspects of Intellectual Property* (1994).
7. 35 USC §154(a)(1).
8. 35 USC §154(a)(2).
9. *Patent Cooperation Treaty*, 19 June 1970, 28 UST 7645, 1160 UNTS 231 reprinted in 9 I.L.M. 978 (1970).
10. 35 USC §101.
11. 35 USC §102.
12. 35 USC §103.
13. Op cit 10.
14. Ibid.
15. *Association for Molecular Pathology v. Myriad Genetics, Inc.*, 689 F.3d 1303, 1333-35 (Fed. Cir. 2012), aff'd in part and rev'd in part on other grounds, 133 S. Ct. 2107, 2116 (2013); *Mayo Collaborative Services v. Prometheus Laboratories, Inc.*, 132 S. Ct. 1289, 101 USPQ2d 1961 (2012).
16. *Convention on the Grant of European Patents of 5 October 1973*, Article 53(c).
17. *Federal Food, Drug, and Cosmetic Act*, 21 U.S.C. § 393(b)(2)(B)-(C) (2000).
18. *Bracco Diagnostics, Inc. v. Shalala*, 963 F. Supp. 20 (D.D.C. 1997).
19. Ibid. at 29.
20. Ibid. at 29 note 9.
21. 35 USC §154(b).
22. 35 USC §156.
23. 35 USC 156(d)(1).
24. See *Eli Lilly & Co. v. Medtronic, Inc.*, 496 US 661, 661 (1990).
25. 35 USC 156(g)(3)(A).
26. FPC, Decision 14W (pat) 12/07 of 26 January 2010.
27. ECJ cases C-195/09 and C-427/09.
28. Article 36 of Regulation (EC) No 1901/2006.
29. 35 USC §271(e)(1).
30. See *Eli Lilly & Co. v. Medtronic, Inc.*, 496 US 661, 665–66 (1990).31. See *Abtox, Inc. v. Exitron Corp.*, 122 F.3d 1019, 1029 (Fed. Cir. 1997).
32. See *Proveris Scientific Corp. v. Innovasystems, Inc.*, 536 F.3d 1256, 1265 (Fed. Cir. 2008).
33. *See, e.g., CardioVention, Inc. v. Medtronic, Inc.*, 483 F. Supp. 2d 830, 840 (D. Minn. 2007).
34. See *Innovative Therapies, Inc. v. Kinetic Concepts, Inc.*, 599 F.3d 1377, 1382 (Fed. Cir. 2010).
35. *Graver Tank & Mfg. Co. v. Linde Air Prods. Co.*, 339 US 605, 608 (1950).
36. *Warner-Jenkinson Company, Inc. v. Hilton Davis Chemical Co.*, 520 US 17 (1997).

21 Software

By Taranjit Samra, DRSc, MSEE and Stewart Crumpler, MSPH, CSQE

Introduction

Today, medical devices rely extensively on software for a wide variety of functions not feasible previously without integrated software solutions. As a result of complex hardware and software integration into a working device to design next-generation products, the medical device industry has become highly interdisciplinary.[1] Numerous device applications are being implemented through software, including higher-risk functions. For example, software controls an infusion pump's prescribed drug infusion rate, user interface and safety functions in making the device easier and safer to use. In radiation therapy, various embedded and standalone software systems are used for such critical functions as control systems, treatment planning, image review, patient positioning and patient records, involving a variety of hardware and computer platforms as well as capital equipment. In robotic surgery, the delicate movements of laparoscopic surgical instruments are controlled by software. Medical device software is being changed constantly, so strict integration of risk management and comprehensive risk-based regression testing in the software change process are essential for patient safety.

As software solutions have replaced hardware functions like switches and other electromechanical control systems, many additional risks have emerged.[2] Additionally, inherent differences exist in how engineers handle hardware and software components, as though they were separate, freestanding functions rather than interdependent systems. Medical devices are safety-critical systems requiring risks associated with hardware, software, human (e.g., patient, operator) and environmental (e.g., physician's office, surgical suite) interactions to be mitigated to ensure safety and efficacy.[3]

Software integration has enhanced medical devices' ability greatly and brought new technologies, not previously feasible, to life; but, many challenges have emerged as well. Researchers at the US Food and Drug Administration (FDA) found software design failures were the most common recall cause, comprising about 15% of all device recalls between 2008 and 2012.[4] FDA noted increasingly complex medical device use environments, with increased connectivity and interoperability, may lead to software anomalies, often requiring correction or removal if software design controls are not implemented effectively. The emerging view seems to be the medical device industry has not yet incorporated a sufficiently robust and systematic framework to ensure medical device safety, functionality and clinical performance, particularly with growing reliance on the software.

The medical device industry requires focused software-specific development and global regulatory strategies in addition to traditional approaches, especially as innovation in this sector accelerates. A major challenge to industry professionals is the absence of a comprehensive framework for pursuing this objective systematically. It is the manufacturer's responsibility to establish the most applicable, practicable and comprehensive strategies based on software engineering and medical device industry best practices, along with internationally harmonized and recognized standards, and provide adequate training and tooling to developers to design safe and effective software devices.

A disciplined, well-defined software development and maintenance process must be applied throughout the product lifecycle, from early development through product retirement. Such an effort ultimately may reduce risks engendered by medical device software and improve the confidence of both the regulators and manufacturers, so such unpleasant surprises as patient or operator injury, device malfunctions and recalls can be avoided.

There also has been a massive increase in automated tools' availability and use for product design and development, production processes, quality system workflows, document and records management and product management. When FDA implemented 21 CFR Part 11 for electronic records and electronic signatures, very few compliant software solutions were available but, today, a wide variety of software with electronic audit trails, electronic signatures and other technical features meet regulatory requirements. More recently, numerous tools have become available to automate the software development process and regulatory information management (RIM), to name a few.

While automated tools can be extremely useful and effective, their validation and maintenance can be very costly. As many medical device manufacturers have grown through multiple mergers and acquisitions, they have inherited a wide variety of automated tools at multiple sites (or even within the same site) serving much the same purpose, or incompatible with one another. Each tool has security controls, data backup and recovery, user support, change management or other undesirable overhead. As a result, most global companies' information technology (IT) departments are searching for a global strategy to rationalize their automated tool selection, simplify tool management, and reduce tool validation, maintenance cost and complexity.

Most legacy tools usually are embedded deeply into the organization and its personnel's culture, so upgrading or totally replacing a tool can be traumatic. Some companies have retained their legacy tools too long because they are reluctant to address a change's negative impact. However, after a cost-benefit analysis of a change, many companies are pursuing system replacements, integration and global IT strategies systematically.

An organization's global tool strategy enables and encourages greater information sharing and collaboration across multiple worksites. Home-based or remote worksite arrangements and virtual work teams are direct results of today's automated tools.

Evolving Healthcare Environment

While there seemingly are endless debates regarding the economics of healthcare delivery, a fairly broad global consensus exists that software plays a key role in making healthcare more effective, efficient and accessible. The rapidly increasing cost of healthcare delivery is one of the most important factors driving adoption of health information technology (HIT) and software-automated healthcare delivery tools. For example, national governments have played a central role in incentivizing and mandating electronic medical record (EMR) system adoption and key initiatives such as "meaningful use," accountable care organizations (ACOs) and hospital readmission reduction programs. The increasing use of HIT is tied to its demonstrated success in improving healthcare delivery efficiencies and effectiveness while lowering costs. Implemented correctly, HIT prevents medical errors and improves healthcare accuracy and procedural correctness while extending real-time health informatics communications among healthcare professionals and expanding access to affordable healthcare.

At the same time healthcare facilities are implementing hospital information systems (HIS) and EMRs, they also are demanding greater integration with their medical imaging and other automated medical devices. Medical devices are required to be more interoperable, standardized, accurate and complete to improve clinical outcomes and patient safety and to enable remote patient monitoring. While there is a general consensus to not regulate EMR systems as medical devices, the increasingly complex integration of EMR systems and HIS with medical devices tends to blur the line between what is and is not regulated. This can be especially challenging when assessing a networking or systems problem.

Telemedicine and mobile medical applications (apps) also are having a profound effect on healthcare delivery and patient access. There are daily reports of numerous new software applications implemented on tablet computers, smart phones, watches, eyewear and other mobile platforms. Viewing patient data and medical images remotely, and remote patient monitoring systems for diabetes, cardiology and home healthcare have become commonplace. Disabled and elderly patients no longer are required to make difficult visits to their doctors or to clinics for routine monitoring. Software controlled pen injectors to allow the patient to self-administer drugs safely, and numerous software-enhanced diagnostic tests, are becoming available. Mobile technology offers ways to help with the challenges of healthcare access, affordability and quality by addressing potential disparities based on income and geography, and providing patients and providers access to reference materials, laboratory tests and medical records.

Bioinformatics and new "big data" computer capabilities provide the possibility to collect, screen and manage massive volumes of patient information. The mapping of the human genome and the use of high-throughput genome sequencing, or Next Generation Sequencing (NGS), have opened new doors for personalized preventive medicine based on screening large populations for specific risks, such as cancer. Mass economics make the cost-benefit argument for such large-scale screening more palatable. Integrating NGS technology into the clinical laboratory is in its infancy but holds immense promise for patient care, enabling personalized intervention to prevent and treat disease. While NGS' full clinical and economic value is only beginning to be understood, the technology likely will alter the economics of medicine and disrupt established stakeholder business models. With these new opportunities come associated issues regarding patient privacy protection and ethical concerns regarding what to do with the newly available diagnostic information.

Emerging Technologies—Opportunities and Challenges

Medical devices increasingly are becoming part of a larger ecosystem combining medical device systems and HIT. Healthcare systems are embedded partially in medical devices, and partially in information systems running on enterprise IT infrastructures. Interoperability, global networks, wireless, mobile platforms, cloud computing, apps and big data are enabling a healthcare evolution.

Interoperability

Various healthcare initiatives are pushing to integrate medical device data with HIT systems. Medical device interoperability is the ability of medical devices, clinical systems or their components to communicate with each other to fulfill an intended purpose safely.[5] Interoperability is becoming vital to healthcare providers because one of the US government's meaningful use program's core goals is to create a nationwide exchange of electronic health information.[6]

> "In healthcare, interoperability is the ability of different information technology systems and software applications to communicate, exchange data, and use the information that has been exchanged. Data exchange schema and standards should permit data to be shared across clinicians, lab, hospital, pharmacy, and patient regardless of the application or application vendor. Interoperability means the ability of health information systems to work together within and across organizational boundaries in order to advance the effective delivery of healthcare for individuals and communities."[7]

Interoperability encourages innovation and quality by allowing start-ups to enter the competitive and specialized healthcare environment, as different products can be combined without complicated and expensive interfaces, and healthcare providers are not forced to seek solutions only from large vendors dominating the market.

Networks—Wired and Wireless

Medical device systems consist of conventional software devices connected via networks, wireless or wired, to applications operating on general purpose computing platforms. Networks enable medical devices' functionality and automate workflows such as EHR clinical documentation, alarm notification, remote surveillance and therapy delivery.

Since many healthcare delivery activities inherently are mobile—as patients, personnel and equipment are constantly moved to meet changing needs at the point of care involving diagnostics, surgery and other therapies—a growing number of medical device systems are being deployed with wireless rather than wired connectivity. On the other hand, wired networks are fast, stable, readily available and allow connectivity in a closed environment. Wired networks' initial installation and subsequent maintenance may be more expensive than wireless networks. Similarly, wireless devices such as radios face many challenging requirements including power consumption and management, authentication, encryption, antenna design and radio frequency (RF) performance.

Mobile—Platforms and Applications

Traditionally, the medical device industry has concentrated on manufacturing medical equipment and devices with embedded software for healthcare providers. The advent of handheld smartphones with touch screens, smart Bluetooth technologies and Internet connectivity are changing the healthcare landscape, and device companies increasingly are switching to mobile apps as their mainstream offering. As a result, a wide variety of medical apps are available for such purposes as monitoring body temperature, measuring heart rate, medical references, baby care, vision care and medical sensors, as well as specialized apps for patients with psoriasis and cardiovascular conditions, and those needing cancer support; these apps are becoming increasingly smarter, multi-functional and patient-centric.[8]

Mobile medical apps are bringing a paradigm shift in healthcare by being more accessible to patients, as the majority of these apps are intended for direct consumer and patient use rather than doctors and caregivers. This technology puts healthcare decisions into patients' hands through its patient-centric approach. Because mobile apps are designed so easily and distributed so widely, they no longer are novelties. This accessibility and ease of use allows patients with chronic conditions such as diabetes and asthma to monitor their health conveniently from their own homes, while allowing caregivers to make informed decisions faster with better outcomes.

Cloud Computing

Cloud computing or "cloud" is a model for enabling ubiquitous, convenient, on-demand network access to a shared pool of configurable computing resources such as networks, servers, storage and applications, hence providing delivery of computing as a service rather than a product.[9] It maximizes the effectiveness of resources shared not only by multiple users but also reallocated dynamically per demand, with minimal management effort or service provider interaction. Cloud can be classified as public, private or hybrid, and has three service models: Software as a Service (SaaS), Platform as a Service (PaaS) and Infrastructure as a Service (IaaS). In healthcare, cloud provides an infrastructure allowing healthcare providers more computing and data storage (e.g., for EHR, radiology images, genomic data) resources for less capital and IT expenditure while potentially lowering innovation and modernization barriers for HIT systems and applications.[10]

Cloud computing brings new challenges to data integrity primarily due to third-party management models, for example, loss of control and governance due to third-party dependence, unclear roles and responsibilities and multi-tenancy. Since healthcare data have stringent confidentiality, integrity and data availability requirements, cloud vendors must account for these needs while conforming to government regulations and industry requirements. When moving to the cloud, healthcare providers and industry must select and monitor cloud vendors carefully, and consider a risk-based approach in deciding the applications being moved to the cloud, e.g., clinical (EHR, physician order entry and software for imaging and pharmacy use) and nonclinical (revenue cycle management, automatic patient billing, cost accounting, payroll management and claims management). Maintaining vendor control is important, including strong emphasis on contracts, usage policies, certifications, quality systems, security, auditing and inspections to ensure compliance in the cloud at all times until decommission.

Cybersecurity and Data Privacy

Medical device system security concerns range from mundane patient care unavailability issues depriving patients of the care they deserve, to hacked implanted pacemakers and patient-worn insulin pumps, making them vulnerable to critical risks. Along with their many advantages, networked medical devices, including mobile and cloud applications, present serious challenges because they inherently are less secure and more vulnerable to support and maintain.

Beyond those challenges lies another data security and privacy issue, resulting from device security breaches due to loss, theft or attack. Data maintained in a cloud or transmitted over networks may contain personal, private or confidential healthcare-related information requiring proper safeguards to prevent disclosure, compromise or misuse.

Most recently, some technologically savvy patients and their relatives have begun to use mobile apps and RF technology to "hack" their own home-use medical devices to gain greater access to their own medical data. A recent *Wall Street Journal* article highlighted this new trend and provided several examples, including the parent of a child with Type-1 diabetes who developed a device interface and app to intercept and transmit the child's glucose monitor data to the parent's cell phone to track the child's glucose levels remotely. Users are sharing such software with one another and making changes and "improvements," much the same as with "open source" software. Similar tinkering incidents involving devices such as insulin pumps, defibrillators and devices used to measure esophagus acidity levels also have been reported. Other patients are converting their hearing aids to play music or using 3-D printers to make their own prosthetics. By developing functionality other than that available through the manufacturer, patients are engaging in off-label use of their device, frequently without their physicians' knowledge or oversight. Such device modifications are raising concerns among regulators, device manufacturers and clinicians because they are unauthorized changes to the device's intended use and raise both liability and regulatory concerns. For now, regulatory authorities have taken a risk-based approach and are meeting with representatives of such citizen hackers to discuss concerns, including how hacking impacts patient safety, how users can get technical support, how software updates are distributed and whether there are steps to prevent unauthorized access to the data.[11]

Bioinformatics and Genomic Sequencing

Bioinformatics is an interdisciplinary field involving computer science, statistics, mathematics and engineering to develop methods and software tools for understanding biological data. Computer programming is used in identifying candidate genes and nucleotides, to develop a better understanding of a disease's genetic basis, and unique adaptations or differences among populations. Since the human genome comprises about 3 billion building blocks called nucleic acids, research typically involves analyzing a large amount of data by "sequencing" (determining the order in which the nucleic acids occur) either in the entire genome or a specific part of it. Identifying nucleic acid sequence changes that might be mutations causing specific diseases could allow researchers to determine the basis of various diagnostic tests, new treatments or ways to track certain products' quality, such as vaccines made from viruses.

The high demand for low-cost sequencing has driven the next generation sequencing (NGS) revolution. NGS produces a dataset (big data) so large and complex it can overwhelm most computer systems' ability to store, search and analyze it or transfer it to other computer systems. Using a complicated technique, NGS cuts the genome into millions of small pieces, then ignores "junk" pieces via sophisticated chemical tricks and technologies, and makes as many as hundreds of copies of each piece selected for the study. NGS enables scientists to fast-track this process by analyzing millions of pieces of the genome at the same time and identifying changes in the nucleic acid sequences that might be mutations.[12]

Regulatory Framework

Medical Device Software Regulation

Regulating software is not easy. Software can put regulators in difficult positions because developing comprehensive regulation has been problematic. Regulators appreciate the importance of streamlining regulations to avoid unnecessary fractionation and overregulation that might impede important new technologies' development unnecessarily, yet they must ensure sufficient guidance and oversight to recognize problems and minimize failures as part of their responsibility for public health. While there still are some slight differences among regulatory jurisdictions regarding the medical device definition, there is a growing consensus certain higher-risk medical software should be regulated, and many current medical device definitions in regulations and laws specifically include software. FDA regulates software through 21 CFR Part 820 Quality System Regulation, Subpart C—Design Controls,[13] which requires medical devices to have a controlled design process including several activities and deliverables throughout the design lifecycle. In the EU, software is regulated under the *Medical Devices Directive (MDD)*[14] or *In Vitro Medical Devices Directive (IVDD)*,[15] as determined by a decision tree provided in EU MEDDEV 2.1/6 on qualification and classification of standalone software used in healthcare.[16]

Internationally, ISO 13485[17] is a quality management system (QMS) standard for medical device manufacturers, certification to which global medical device companies seek because several international regulatory agencies, including those in the EU and Canada, require compliance to this standard before a product can be commercialized in their jurisdictions. Harmonized with FDA's quality system regulation (QSR) design controls requirements, ISO 13485 Part 7.3, Design and development, also requires various design lifecycle activities applicable to software. Software is regulated by these overarching regulations and standards, in conjunction with ISO 14971[18] for risk management, one of the most harmonized standards across various global regions, including the US. Otherwise, specific medical device software regulations are hard to find.

Various information sources exist to assist medical device manufacturers in their efforts to implement software best practices. First are guidance documents and other types of advice authored by FDA, or comparable bodies in other constituencies, in which the regulatory agencies illustrate what they see as appropriate practices. Second is a growing number of voluntary standards promulgated by international standards-setting bodies and task forces with both private and public sector representation. The first and possibly most influential document was issued in June 1997 and updated in September 1999 to its current form: *Guidance for Industry, FDA Reviewers and Compliance on Off-The-Shelf Software Use in Medical Devices*.[19] This guidance outlined the documentation type and level expected to justify the safe use of commercial off-the-shelf (COTS) products and introduced the very important concept of lifecycle management. At about the same time, FDA published a detailed guidance to help medical device manufacturers with the design control process, *Design Control Guidance for Medical Device Manufacturers*.[20]

Another important guidance document, *General Principles of Software Validation; Final Guidance for Industry and FDA Staff*,[21] drew attention to Good Software Engineering Practices. In addition, *Guidance for the Content of Premarket Submissions for Software Contained in Medical Devices* discussed software classification according to level of concern, with greater scrutiny directed at higher-risk software with major or moderate levels of concern.

Note: The level of concern is "major" if a software failure or a latent defect could result directly in death or serious injury to the patient or operator; it is "moderate" if a failure or defect could result in a minor injury; and it is "minor" if a failure or defect is unlikely to cause any injury.

Internationally, the Association for the Advancement of Medical Instrumentation (AAMI) has been an important body in developing standards related to medical product software. Its next-generation standard, IEC 62304, *Medical device software—Software lifecycle processes*, has been harmonized across other organizations (ANSI/AAMI/IEC 62304:2006).[23] It assists manufacturers in implementing a risk-based approach to software development and maintenance.

For medical device software developers, a collection of standards and FDA guidance on human factors and usability engineering are available, to apply ergonomic methods proactively and avoid confusing buttons, ambiguous icons and other design flaws that ultimately can lead to use and user errors.[24-27] Similarly, IEC TR 80002-1[28] provides guidance on the application of risk management to medical device software per ISO 14971. Other FDA guidance documents address various software applications in different environments.[29-31]

Regulation of Automated Tools and Enterprise Systems

Regulations concerning electronic record and electronic signature computer systems have been in place in the US for more than 15 years,[32] and related regulatory guidance has been stable for the past decade.[33] Except for emerging labeling regulations for unique device identification (UDI), the regulatory framework for automated tools and enterprise systems is well established and unlikely to have many significant changes in the near future. Historically, the regulatory framework for automated tool validation and management was highly dependent on guidelines issued for the pharmaceutical industry. For example, there is an overall *Good Automated Manufacturing Practice (GAMP 5)* guide, a specific *Good Practice Guide for Global Information Systems* and multiple *Good Practice Guides* dealing with specific automated tools used for process control, laboratory, calibration, IT infrastructure and electronic recordkeeping, as well as a very detailed guide on testing GxP systems.[34-41] Similarly, the Pharmaceutical Inspection Convention and Pharmaceutical Inspection Co-operation Scheme (jointly referred to as PIC/S) is a consortium of 44 global health authorities that develop guidelines for use in their regulatory inspections. Annex 11 of the PIC/S *Guide to Good Manufacturing Practice for Medicinal Products*[42] establishes the basic requirements for computerized systems, while the PIC/S guidance on *Good Practices for Computerised Systems in Regulated "GXP" Environments*[43] provides detailed information for regulatory inspections of those systems. More recently, the medical device industry has developed its own guidance in *AAMI TIR 36, Validation of Software for Regulated Processes.*[44]

Evolving Regulatory Landscape

The software regulatory landscape is very much in flux, as advances in information technology are driving changes to the regulatory frameworks in numerous jurisdictions. Those frameworks are tied closely to harmonized, internationally recognized standards and guidance that, themselves, are evolving quickly to try to keep pace with changes in the healthcare environment. Many governments have imperatives for both technology promotion and technology controls in the healthcare arena. The emergence of mobile technology platforms, wireless technology and cloud computing are changing the face of healthcare and the regulatory landscape around the world, as their use introduces new challenges involving multiple governmental agencies. Regulatory changes are somewhat unpredictable and certainly are not consistent across multiple jurisdictions. However, there is a growing consensus among many regulatory authorities regarding which healthcare software is (and is not) to be strictly regulated.

In recent years, there has been increased cooperation, policy coordination and data sharing among regulatory authorities (including health authorities and other regulators). For example, the International Medical Device Regulators Forum (IMDRF) was created to foster regulatory alignment among member countries including Australia, Brazil, Canada, China, Europe, Japan, Russia and the US. The IMDRF is a voluntary organization, and implementation of IMDRF recommendations varies from one regulatory jurisdiction to another. In December 2013, IMDRF issued two important software-related documents:

- *Software as a Medical Device (SaMD)* is the first of several documents dealing with the medical device aspects of standalone software. The document provides a consensus decision by IMDRF member countries, defining standalone medical software as a medical device and also stating a mobile medical app is a medical device.
- *Unique Device Identification (UDI) System for Medical Devices* clarifies an earlier document and establishes a framework for implementing global UDI systems.

In the past year in the US, FDA has issued its final unique device identification regulation and multiple guidance documents on its implementation, while China, Japan, Canada and the EU have announced their intent to take similar actions. The extensive data system changes necessary to comply with US UDI requirements, and the pending emergence of similar UDI regulations in other jurisdictions, provide an important opportunity for device manufacturers to rethink their strategies for automated tools and their integration. UDI compliance will dictate much greater interaction and information-sharing across computer systems used for ERP, device distribution, adverse event reporting, recall reporting, device tracking, postmarket surveillance and premarket submissions. The mandate for UDI compliance has created the impetus to make long-needed computer system changes for greater interoperability.

In the EU, work is progressing rapidly on a new medical device regulation that will regulate more strictly how devices (including software devices) are cleared for marketing. The regulation is intended to remove much of the variability among different EU Member States and is expected to be less favorable to device manufacturers compared to the current EU regulatory review timeframes.

At the same time, some regulatory jurisdictions have initiatives to relax regulatory requirements for certain software types. For example, on 9 July 2012, the *Food and Drug Administration Safety and Innovation Act* (*FDASIA*) became law in the US and included several significant changes that impact medical device software. In response to the new law, FDA, the Office of the National Coordinator (ONC) for Healthcare Technology and the Federal Communications Commission (FCC) jointly issued their *FDASIA Health IT Report* in April 2014. The report describes a risk-based HIT regulatory framework intended to promote innovation while maintaining patient safety. It focuses on the HIT functionality rather than the platform or technology. The report specifically identifies three HIT functionality categories (i.e., administrative functionalities, health management functionalities and medical device functionalities). Under the proposed voluntary approach, an HIT safety center would:
- promote use of quality management principles
- identify, develop and adopt standards and best practices
- leverage conformity assessment tools such as product testing, certification and accreditation
- create an environment of learning and continual improvement

Based on those voluntary initiatives, administrative and health management information systems (including most clinical decision support systems) would not be regulated by FDA, even if they meet the statutory definition of a "device." Some significant examples include software systems for most drug dosing calculations, for drug interaction/contraindication alerts, for preventive care reminders and for suggestions of possible diagnoses. However, FDA still would regulate higher-risk clinical decision support systems, such as computer-aided diagnosis, radiation treatment planning and electrocardiography analysis actively, and would continue to regulate software implementing medical device functionalities.

Another key aspect of the *FDASIA Health IT Report* is its discussion of the importance of interoperability among multiple devices and data systems to promote greater clinical information sharing. The basis for that data sharing is adherence to a common set of internationally recognized standards. One of the earliest and most successful interoperability standards is NEMA/ISO 12052, Digital Imaging and Communications in Medicine (DICOM), first developed more than 20 years ago and the foundation for transmitting and viewing medical images among multiple data systems. More recently, a series of IEEE/ISO 11073 health informatics standards defined the design features needed for interoperability among various device types. The *FDASIA Health IT Report* recommends conformance assessment entities be identified to develop tests to validate interoperability, test product conformance with standards and transparently share product performance results to promote broader adoption of interoperable solutions.

Interoperability is linked closely to software security, which itself is a growing global concern. There are extensive and rapidly increasing numbers of international hacking attacks, data piracy and personal privacy breaches, both in the marketplace at large and in the medical device industry. When these occur, they bring increased regulatory authority scrutiny and expectations device manufacturers will provide additional safeguards to protect their healthcare databases, patient records and medical device software. Note, from a business perspective, medical device manufacturers have the same kinds of concerns regarding protecting their intellectual property and proprietary trade secret information, much of which is held on computer systems.

Regarding cybersecurity, FDA issued a guidance[45] in 2005 regarding medical devices' vulnerabilities to such cybersecurity threats as viruses and worms as well as threats posed by unauthorized access to the network or the medical device connected to it. In addition, FDA recently issued a safety communication[46] recommending medical device manufacturers and healthcare facilities take steps to ensure appropriate safeguards are in place to reduce the risk of failure due to cyberattack, which could be initiated by introducing malware into the medical equipment or unauthorized access to medical devices and hospital networks' configuration settings. In an effort to reduce cybersecurity risks before devices even arrive on the market, FDA also has issued a proactive draft guidance[47] requiring device manufacturers to include their plans to address cybersecurity in their premarket submission, allowing FDA to block a device's clearance or approval if the plans are inadequate.

Internationally, several widely recognized standards address IT and network security risks[48-53] device manufacturers should use to enhance their device software and IT networks' robustness and security. In 2013, FDA recognized 25 voluntary standards pertaining to interoperability and cybersecurity to help medical device manufacturers create secure devices that work well together and with other HIT products and systems.[54] Similarly, FDA issued a guidance[55] to assist industry on RF wireless technology in medical devices.

Concerns related to data jurisdiction, security, privacy and compliance are impacting healthcare organizations' adoption of state-of-the-art technologies around the world. In the US, a federal law—the *Health Insurance Portability and Accountability Act* (*HIPAA*)—requires healthcare organizations to protect patients' health information, while mandating and enforcing strict security and privacy rules for how medical information is collected, handled, used, disclosed and protected. Failure to do so results in reputation damage and stiff penalties per the *Health Information Technology for Economic and Clinical Health Act* (*HITECH Act*) of 2009. Likewise, the EU has implemented data privacy requirements in Directive 95/46/EC, which provides protection for individuals with regard to the processing of personal data and on the free movement of such data.[56]

Additionally, as another part of its response to *FDASIA*, FDA recently proposed guidance to exempt medical device data systems, medical image storage devices and medical image communication devices from having to comply with the QSR. All three of these software-intensive products are lower-risk, Class I devices. However, of particular interest is the fact this proposed action is through guidance rather than a classification regulation, and FDA is proposing exempting the products from design controls.

As noted previously, one key aspect of *FDASIA* and the *FDASIA Health IT Report* is the focus on promoting technological innovation, such as use of mobile computing platforms (e.g., touchscreen tablet computers and cell phones) and mobile medical apps. FDA has published mobile medical apps guidance[57] and adopted a risk-based approach to regulate only the small subset of mobile medical apps that could present risks to patients if the app does not work as intended. The agency guidance defines mobile platforms as handheld COTS computing platforms, with or without wireless connectivity. FDA has stated clearly it does not consider mobile platform manufacturers (e.g., cell phone makers) to be medical device manufacturers solely because their mobile platforms can be used to run a mobile medical app. The agency intends to focus on the mobile app software's functionality—not the platform on which it runs. FDA also has reiterated it does not intend to focus on EMRs and will exercise enforcement discretion for most medical apps even if they technically meet the definition of a medical device. For example, FDA generally would not enforce regulatory requirements for mobile apps promoting health by encouraging lifestyle changes or providing information to help manage diseases or health conditions. Rather, FDA is regulating higher-risk medical device functions (e.g., apps transforming a mobile platform into an ultrasound device to monitor an unborn fetus' health). Additionally, FDA has stated clearly in the guidance it does not intend to regulate the use of software app distribution channels such as the iTunes App Store or the Android Market.

Further, cloud computing's popularity is prompting regulators around the world to develop "cloud initiatives" regarding compliance with their regulations. For example, FDA formed a cross-center workgroup in January 2013 involving the Center for Drug Evaluation and Research (CDER), Center for Biologics Evaluation and Research (CBER), Center for Devices and Radiological Health (CDRH), Center for Veterinary Medicine (CVM) and Office of Regulatory Affairs (ORA) in its cloud initiative.[58] It has interacted with large, mid- and small-size pharmaceutical and biotechnology firms to understand their deployment models, cloud strategies and challenges, and reviewed input from large and small IT consulting firms and consultants, IT experts, auditors and quality and regulatory professionals. Today, a device manufacturer's cloud compliance strategy may include:

- FDA QSR or ISO 13485—for quality system purchasing controls including cloud supplier audits
- 21 CFR Part 11—for records and recordkeeping in the cloud[59]
- ISO/IEC 27001— providing specification and certification, for information security management system including the cloud[60]
- National Institute of Standards and Technology—NIST SP 800-144, providing an overview of cloud security and privacy challenges and insights on its threats, technology risks and

safeguards, and presenting recommendations for organizations to consider when outsourcing data, applications and infrastructure to a public cloud environment[61]

Making changes to medical device software poses a difficult business and regulatory dilemma for a medical device manufacturer. There are strong customer and business imperatives for frequent software changes and pressure to fix known software problems, and business pressure to add desirable new software features to prompt the customer to want the new software. Multiple software changes (including new features, enhancement and bug fixes) frequently are bundled into a single product release. Software changes can be implemented much more rapidly if they do not require a regulatory submission and prior regulatory clearance. Internally, there is business pressure to make as few regulatory submissions as possible because they slow the product release process so significantly. However, some significant regulatory penalties exist for making a wrong decision regarding whether a new regulatory submission is needed and in which regulatory jurisdictions. Regulatory agency criteria are nebulous on determining which software changes do or do not require a regulatory submission and vary dramatically from one jurisdiction to another. Therefore, it is imperative to review every software change robustly vis-à-vis regulatory reporting requirements in all jurisdictions. Most changes in a new release do not trigger a regulatory submission, but some may. During design validation, each software change needs to be assessed individually versus the last software version that received regulatory clearance to decide whether a new 510(k) is required. Current FDA guidance from 1997 does not address specifically when to submit a new 510(k) for software changes but states the decision is to be based on whether design validation results raise new safety or effectiveness issues. In 2011, FDA issued draft guidance providing additional clarity on when to file a new 510(k) for a software change, but the agency withdrew that draft guidance in 2012 as required by *FDASIA*. In its subsequent Report to Congress on 7 January 2014, FDA stated its intent to develop a separate 510(k) guidance specifically for software changes.[62]

CBER has enabled the development of the High-Performance Integrated Virtual Environment (HIVE)—a powerful computer technology that can consume, digest, analyze, manage and share extensive NGS data—for genomic sequencing. This will facilitate FDA's review and understanding of NGS data interpretation and significance in regulatory submissions. HIVE is a private cloud-based environment containing a storage library of data and a powerful computing capacity. HIVE already has helped CBER scientists in a number of ways, e.g., helping Office of Vaccines Research and Review scientists study influenza A viruses' genetic stability used to make vaccines. Following up on HIVE's success, CBER now is collaborating with CDRH to provide a second installation with greater capacity and computer power, to develop an inter-center resource to handle regulatory submissions including NGS.[63] Additionally, FDA's Genomic Working Group is working with the National Institutes of Health (NIH), Center for Disease Control and Prevention (CDC), National Institute of Standards and Technology (NIST), academia and industry to develop IT infrastructure, material and data standards and analytic approaches required to support NGS technology use and application to solve scientific questions and support regulatory decision making. It also aims to ensure the resources and expertise required are identified, implemented and developed in a coordinated fashion, both internally at FDA and, where feasible, with other government agencies.[64]

Global Software Strategies for Medical Device Manufacturers

Strategies for Medical Device Software

Software regulation has been of particular concern due to the number of failures seen to date. Reviewing FDA records 1999–2005 shows one in every three medical devices using software has been recalled for software failure, and 11.3% of all FDA recalls are attributable to software failures. As more and more products have incorporated software in medical devices, a troubling trend is an increasing number of software failure recalls.[65-68] More recently, in 2008–12, software design failures accounted for approximately 15% of all device recalls.[69]

Regulators around the world obviously are concerned about device failures. Medical devices are meant to be safe and effective, to save lives and improve individuals' health. Regulators like FDA are responsible for protecting public health while avoiding over-regulation and unnecessary duplication. This can be achieved by streamlining regulations globally within a single cohesive framework, which requires relying on internationally harmonized standards for specific guidance relevant to software's unique challenges. FDA expressed this requirement in the QSR preamble: "FDA believes that sufficient domestic and international guidelines are available to provide assistance to manufacturers for the validation of software and risk analysis."[70]

IEC 62304[71] assists the manufacturer in applying a risk-based approach to software development and maintenance throughout the product lifecycle. It assigns a software safety "class" to the software "system," and software "items" based on possible hazards their malfunction can cause to patients, operators or other people: Class A if no injury or damage to health is possible, Class B if non-serious injury is possible, or Class C if death or serious injury is possible. IEC 62304 may be the most widely referenced and useful risk-based software lifecycle standard in the medical device industry today, and also is recognized by FDA.

Industry uses various software development methodologies or lifecycle models, providing a structured approach to developing and maintaining medical device software as it matures throughout the lifecycle. These often are characterized by a sequence of phases from the time the product is conceived until its obsolescence. IEC 62304 does not require a particular method; it implies logical dependencies between various processes' inputs and outputs that can be applied to any methodology:

- Waterfall: The "once-through" strategy consists of performing the development process a single time. Simplistically: determine customer needs, define requirements, design the system, implement the system, test, fix and deliver.
- Incremental: This determines customer needs and defines the system requirements, then performs the rest of the development in a sequence of builds. The first build incorporates part of the planned capabilities, the next build adds more capabilities, and so on, until the system is complete.
- Evolutionary: This strategy also develops a system in builds, but differs from the incremental strategy in acknowledging the user need is not fully understood, and all requirements cannot be defined upfront. In this strategy, customer needs and system requirements are defined partially up front, then refined in each succeeding build.

Waterfall Methodology

A linear or Waterfall model (or its variant V-model) traditionally has been employed by the medical device industry and remains the most commonly used method.[72] Reasons for this preference include years of experience with this method and its recognition and acceptance by regulators, who appreciate its structure allows it to be integrated quite easily into design controls and other regulatory requirements. The Waterfall model has several strengths. It is easy to use and understand even for inexperienced members of software and other cross-functional teams. Resource planning and management are intuitive. It provides an orderly tracking system by mimicking the design control process and, thus, can be mapped readily to ensure quality, reliability, maintainability and compliance objectives are met through objective evidence, documentation and reviews. However, it is easy to fall into the trap of relying on gated reviews to catch major issues and leaving critical system integration and testing toward the end of projects, when serious design defects are more difficult to correct. Other Waterfall method weaknesses include its lack of flexibility, slowness, relatively high costs and significant structural overhead requirements restricting opportunities to iterate or respond to requirement or design changes. It also provides few customer or internal stakeholder participation opportunities in the process before the project ends.[73]

The V-model is a variant of Waterfall methodology. It is popular among medical device companies because it helps build traceability between requirements and design elements, with related verification and validation steps, in addition to providing structure and ensuring transparent compliance with the development process. Different testing levels, e.g., unit, integration and system, are carried out at the corresponding levels of system requirements and design specification.

Agile/Scrum Methodology

A software development methodology that has sparked widespread interest among software development professionals in recent years is the Agile methodology, a collection of methods based on iterative and incremental methodologies. Agile Alliance,[74] a nonprofit organization to promote Agile development, described the evolution of this methodology:

"In the late 1990s several methodologies began to get increasing public attention. Each had a different combination of old ideas, new ideas, and transmuted old ideas. But they all emphasized close collaboration between the programmer team and business experts; face-to-face communication (as more efficient than written documentation); frequent delivery of new deployable business value; tight, self-organizing teams; and ways to craft the code and the team such that the inevitable requirements churn was not a crisis."

To understand the inherent difference between Agile and traditional methods, it is important to appreciate the background and philosophy behind Agile. Agile Alliance launched the Agile movement and wrote the Agile Manifesto.[75] The Agile Manifesto was developed to value certain items more than the others, for example: individuals and interactions over processes and tools; working software over comprehensive documentation; customer

Figure 21-1. Details of Scrum Methodology (Agile for All, 2011)*

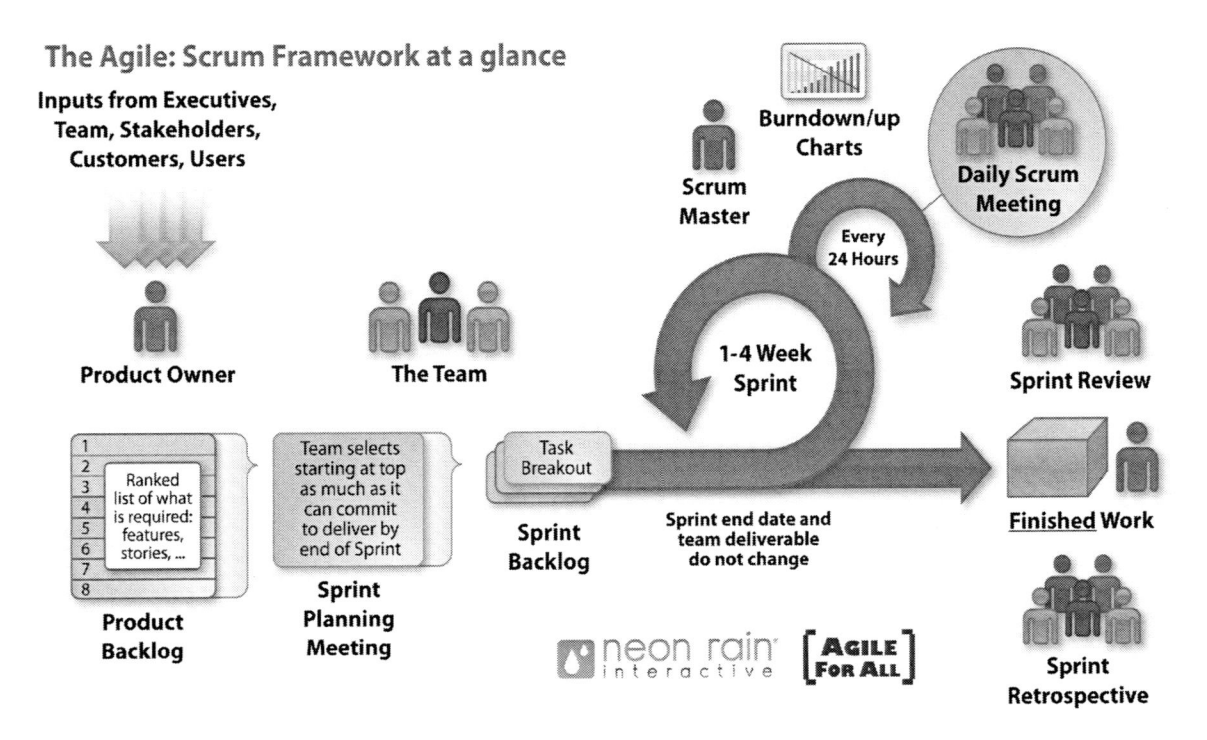

The Agile: Scrum Framework at a glance

Inputs from Executives, Team, Stakeholders, Customers, Users

- Product Owner
- The Team
- Scrum Master
- Burndown/up Charts
- Daily Scrum Meeting (Every 24 Hours)
- 1-4 Week Sprint
- Sprint Review
- Finished Work
- Sprint Retrospective

Product Backlog: Ranked list of what is required: features, stories, …

Sprint Planning Meeting: Team selects starting at top as much as it can commit to deliver by end of Sprint

Sprint Backlog → Task Breakout

Sprint end date and team deliverable do not change

neon rain interactive [AGILE FOR ALL]

*Source: *Intro to Agile*. Agile for All website. http://www.agileforall.com/intro-to-agile/. Accessed 13 March 2016.

collaboration over contract negotiation; and responding to change over following a plan.

There are several Agile methods, but one, called Scrum, seems most popular. Scrum Alliance,[76] a not-for-profit professional membership organization dedicated to increasing awareness and understanding of Scrum, describes Scrum methodology (**Figure 21-1**):

> "A product owner creates a prioritized wish list called a product backlog. During sprint planning, the team pulls a small chunk from the top of that wish list, a sprint backlog, and decides how to implement those pieces. The team has a certain amount of time, a sprint, to complete its work—usually two to four weeks—but meets each day to assess its progress (daily scrum). Along the way, the Scrum Master keeps the team focused on its goal. At the end of the sprint, the work should be potentially shippable, as in ready to hand to a customer, put on a store shelf, or show to a stakeholder."

The sprint ends with a sprint review and retrospective. As the next sprint begins, the team chooses another chunk of the product backlog and begins working again. The cycle repeats until enough items in the product backlog have been completed, the budget is depleted or a deadline arrives. Which of these milestones marks the end of the work is entirely project-specific. No matter which impetus stops work, Scrum ensures the most valuable work has been completed when the project ends.[77]

Numerous medical device companies have reported using the Agile/Scrum method to a varying degree, but the hybrid of Agile and Waterfall seems to be the most popular approach.[78] A hybrid model fulfills the challenges of working in a highly regulated environment to ensure all applicable regulatory requirements are fulfilled, while at the same time realizing the Agile development method's potential benefits. These companies started small with a pilot project and later expanded to other teams as the practice matured and confidence grew. The end-to-end product development process uses Waterfall as before, but the development phase employs the Agile method. In this intermediate phase employing Agile, each sprint behaves like a "mini-Waterfall," with iterations of requirements, design, implementation, verification and validation. At the end of each sprint, various documents are baselined and reviewed comprehensively to ensure compliance with regulatory requirements. After the various iterations, the developers could interact actively with and demonstrate working software to marketing, which serves as a customer representation and provides feedback to developers to be incorporated in the next Agile iteration. Agile practitioners in the medical device industry report several benefits of this method, e.g., eliminating risks associated with the traditional Waterfall methods in situations where processes did not respond well to changing business needs, or the software abstraction progress was insufficiently visible. Other benefits included Agile's focus on quality by ensuring: product correctness using prioritized feature sets; customer collaboration to address needs and effectiveness; productivity through improved efficiency, speed and lower costs; and predictability through improved estimation and planning.

Emerging trends show Agile practices enhance patient safety compared to Waterfall methods, since the latter was built on the false premise that requirements gathered before the development phase never change. The long Waterfall project cycle times (12–24 months) encourage feature creep beyond initial requirements, delaying product release even further. Agile, on the other hand, uses the philosophy changes should be expected and encouraged, as learning takes place during the product development lifecycle. Further, Waterfall customer feedback is sought late in the project, after requirements, design and coding are completed, at which time complete changes to the design might be needed to incorporate customer requests. The Agile methodology addresses this problem by delivering working code to the intended recipient at frequent intervals to obtain feedback for the next iteration. The Agile method tends to increase interactions and reduce barriers existing among various stakeholders, both internal and external.

Although Agile is less common than Waterfall in the medical device industry, its use is growing rapidly among software teams preferring to remain in sync with the software industry at large, where Agile is the most popular method.[79]

AAMI TIR 45

AAMI recently released AAMI TIR 45:2012[80] *Guidance on the use of AGILE practices in the development of medical device software*, to help clarify how Agile methodology could be tailored for the medical device industry's regulated environment of the medical device industry. This guidance introduces perspectives from regulatory agencies and the Agile user community, including the medical device industry, and provides alignment on goals, values, principles and practices. For example, it relates Agile practices with FDA's QSR, ISO 13485, ISO 14971, IEC 62304 and FDA guidance on general principles of software validation and content of premarket submissions for software contained in medical devices. It includes such topics as planning, documentation, design reviews, product definition and requirements, software architecture, detailed design, implementation and unit verification. Earlier, differing nomenclatures in the two environments previously presented communication challenges for communication. Examples also are given where Agile terms, such as pair-programming, test driven development (TDD) and user stories, could be matched with medical device industry terms, such as design review, verification and product definition, respectively. This work emphasizes ways to apply the Agile methodology within the context of a QMS to manage business and safety risks and produce documentation with business value.

FDA also encourages Agile's use in the medical device industry as long as companies comply with the regulations. FDA representatives worked on the AAMI TIR task group that developed this publication. FDA's guidance on general principles of software validation and its recommendation on integrating software lifecycle management and risk management activities, show that using Agile can facilitate risk management throughout the lifecycle, and validation can be spread throughout the lifecycle instead of occurring as an activity at the end of the process. The Agile method's testing, reviewing and sprinting activities can be tailored to fulfill regulatory requirements and address specific FDA QSR and ISO 13485 elements that impact Agile's use directly, for example, 21 CFR 820.30 Subpart C and ISO 13485 Clause 7.3 (Design Controls) and 21 CFR 820.100 Subpart J and ISO 13485 Clause 8.5 (Corrective and Preventive Action). AAMI TIR 45 provides details about FDA and international regulatory expectations regarding Agile's use in the medical device industry and a list of important regulatory requirements with which companies must comply.

Software of Unknown Provenance or Pedigree (SOUP)

A growing medical device industry trend is the use of "open source" software as both software tools and components within medical device software. An identifiable entity is responsible for COTS software. However, sometimes the software code developer or provider cannot be identified and the product is referred to as SOUP. IEC 62304 defines SOUP as software "already developed and generally available and that has not been developed for the purpose of being incorporated into the medical device (also known as 'off-the-shelf software') or software previously developed for which adequate records of the development processes are not available." Because there is no identifiable supplier, such traditional purchasing controls as supplier qualification or assessment are not possible. Unlike COTS, the medical device manufacturer cannot examine or depend on the developer's systems development lifecycle (SDLC) because the SOUP was not developed using any known and documented software development process or methodology.[81] The medical device manufacturer has the SOUP source code but does not have most of the artifacts resulting from a robust and well-documented SDLC process. The most significant SOUP issue is establishing a clearly defined relationship between the software and hazards associated with the device being developed or managed. Incorporating SOUP may be appropriate for certain devices using a risk-based approach as outlined in IEC 62304 and supplemented by additional controls applied by the medical device manufacturer. For example, SOUP should be challenged and evaluated using such tools as code reviews, static analysis and extensive testing. SOUP is not appropriate for higher-risk applications unless it can be fully evaluated for safety.

Strategies for Design History File Documentation

Software documentation practices are fairly consistent among global software teams in any organization, owing to the harmonized design controls requirements of FDA's QSR and ISO 13485 and risk management requirements of ISO 14971. Software team members require no further explanation of the deliverables to support various software lifecycle activities including software requirements, architecture diagram, design description or specification, design and code reviews, verification and validation (or unit, integration and system tests), risk management and traceability matrix. Many of these deliverables are included in premarket submissions across various regions, such as US 510(k)s and PMAs and EU Tech Files and Design Dossiers. Additionally, standard software development methodologies, e.g., Waterfall, Agile and software-specific harmonized standards such as IEC 62304, further align global teams in using a common lifecycle framework, terminology, practices and deliverables. It is not a question of which software documentation global teams are required to submit demonstrating compliance to various regulators around the globe. Instead, the manner in which industry today generates this documentation and maintains it throughout product lifecycle can be improved considerably.

The traditional software document production methods are increasingly inefficient, ineffective and impractical, in an iterative environment where cross-functional stakeholder reviews and approvals are mandatory throughout the SDLC (see **Figure 21-2**). Rather than generating software documentation as a standalone activity during development and maintenance, software engineers should be able to publish and update documents with each software iteration easily and frequently, in the same ecosystem in which their design and coding tools live. There must be a better way to capture useful content in design documents in real-time, as a byproduct of various SDLC activities throughout the product lifecycle. This also would allow software engineers to use their creativity to do what they do best, i.e., coding, while spending less time on documentation.

A number of SDLC tools are available in today's marketplace, allowing software teams to collaborate actively during development and maintenance and publish requirements, design, tests, code and design reviews, traceability and other deliverables in real-time. Using end-to-end SDLC tools and built-in electronic templates, design documentation can be captured semi-automatically throughout the SDLC. While these tools may not be 21 CFR Part 11-compliant, they either can be integrated into traditional document control systems, or be customized to handle formal review and approval workflows within an electronic Design History File (eDHF) system. SDLC tool vendors also must be vigilant in addressing such medical device software industry needs. As the development environment becomes more powerful and regulatory implications more profound, e.g., software teams adopting Agile/Scrum methodology, the concept of traditional documentation evolves significantly, and there is a need for next generation of SDLC tools that are integrating fully into the QMS.

Furthermore, as more and more controls are demonstrated through SDLC tools, they also may reduce the documentation burden for regulators and regulatory professionals. For example, these tools can execute software configuration effectively and build management in a continuous integration system. They also support visual dashboards with real-time key risk and safety metrics that may predict the software's health (e.g., number, type and severity of outstanding defects) before it is released to the customer. It could facilitate increased productivity and spare software engineers from generating manual deliverables with no perceived value in making products safe and effective. End-to-end automation using SDLC tools may help strike a balance between the commercial imperatives and compliance with regulatory requirements.

Figure 21-2. Software Development Lifecycle Tools for DHF Documentation and Other Artifacts*

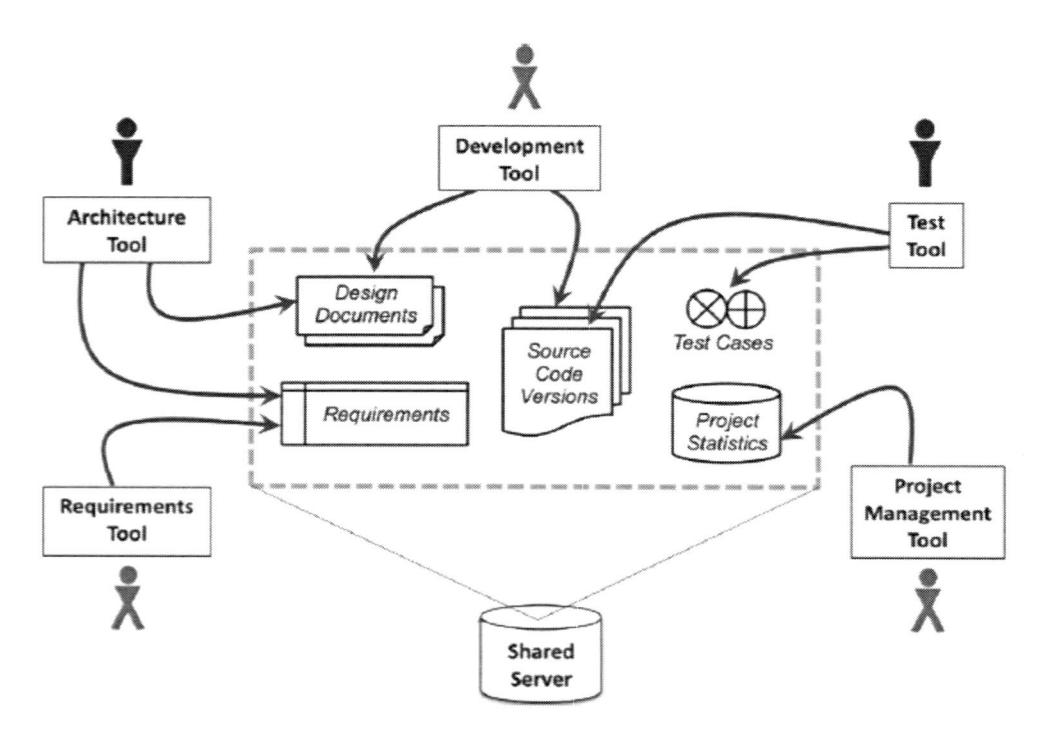

*Source: AAMI TIR45:2012 Guidance on the use of AGILE practices in the development of medical device software. AAMI website. http://my.aami.org/aamiresources/previewfiles/TIR45_1208_PREVIEW.PDF. Accessed 13 March 2016.

Regulatory and quality professionals often are at odds with software developers and IT about regulatory and business risk, and misinformation is circulated about how much documentation really is required, and what is acceptable to regulatory agencies. Out of fear and uncertainty, many medical device companies default to the most cumbersome documentation approach, which, itself, can cause certain unintended consequences. In any case, adequate, high-quality software documentation clearly has legitimate business value in the medical device software industry, for both internal stakeholders, such as software development teams and project management, and external stakeholders, such as customers and regulators, and is an essential deliverable for every software development project.[82]

Strategies for Automated Tools

Widespread access to the Internet and global broadband networking have enabled and empowered a revolutionary change in the way automated tools are being used, and those innovations are expanding at an exponential rate. As a result, there are more and more opportunities to link multiple medical device company locations for global product development, quality system implementation and regulatory management. Global collaboration tools and shared data systems also enable global product development teams, staffed with team members around the world.

Automated tools and data systems are implemented most effectively under a global enterprise-wide computer systems strategy, including:
- a global inventory of all computerized systems and software applications
- oversight and controls for procuring new automated tools, applications and databases
- identifying the responsible "system owner" (for the business) for each global system
- global system conformance assessments for each system
- global validation master planning, based on risk-based system classification
- global contingency planning and disaster recovery strategies

There are several business case aspects to this global enterprise-wide approach. First, using the same tool and database across multiple sites allows substantial cost savings from more-efficient workflows and data capture, ready access to shared data when needed for decision making, and up-to-date metrics and data for tracking regulated activities' progress and status. It also is costly to purchase, implement, validate and maintain redundant computerized systems. Therefore, from an overall overhead perspective, it usually is much more cost effective to use the same system for the same purpose at all sites. Global data sharing also provides greatly increased flexibility to match the right human resources with the right tasks. For example, global data systems enable using virtual multi-site teams for truly global product development.

Global automated tool strategies can be grouped into the following categories based on the tool types and purposes:
- IT infrastructure support tools
- production and quality system tools
- software development and application management tools
- regulatory information management tools

Available commercial and open-source automated tools address most functions medical device manufacturers need, and the use of open source tools is growing steadily as they demonstrate their usefulness and reliability.

Global IT Infrastructure Support Tool Strategies

Underpinning an effective global software strategy is an effective and comprehensive IT infrastructure. Examples of IT infrastructure support tools include:
- email, phone, facsimile
- collaboration tools (video conferencing, desktop sharing)
- global data warehouse
- website management
- social media management
- data center
- networks
- servers
- individual computing platforms (desktop, laptop, tablet, smart phone)

Regulated computer applications that must be validated require underlying IT infrastructure support tools to be qualified.[83] In most cases, the same IT infrastructure can support both nonregulated business applications and regulated applications, and the IT strategy needs to consider one of two options carefully:

- either document and qualify all IT infrastructure with the assumption it will need to support regulated activities

or

- segregate regulated from nonregulated infrastructure, so regulated activities are not carried out on nonregulated (unqualified) infrastructure tools

In addition, in most companies, the IT department is responsible for implementing and administering global IT security policy and procedures, such as issuing and revoking user accounts, password change practices and system backup and recovery.

Many companies also separate IT and manufacturing tools, and the IT department is responsible for neither the manufacturing system infrastructure on the shop floor nor individual automated laboratory instruments. However, of necessity, IT is very involved in implementing and validating global multi-site systems. In all cases, for every automated system, a clearly defined owner should be identified who is responsible for ensuring all business and regulatory obligations (including validation and regulatory compliance) are met.

New software delivery and data management tools, such as SaaS and cloud computing, present new and unusual supplier qualification and management challenges. A vendor's willingness to provide transparency in its own quality systems is a key factor in deciding whether these tools can be used in a regulated environment. Nondocumented assurances by the SaaS or cloud vendor are inadequate to meet the medical device manufacturer's regulatory obligations. The techniques for qualifying these tools are similar to the approach for outsourcing data center functions. Cloud capability must be specified and controlled adequately to ensure regulated data and applications will not be compromised.

When IT infrastructure and systems are implemented properly to meet user needs, the result usually is very positive and well received by users. However, failure to fully address user needs, e.g., adequate broadband network access at remote sites, can undermine a global strategy and encourage problematic local workarounds. For example, a dental instrument subsidiary routinely used high-resolution digital images to document its complaint failure investigations of returned broken dental instruments. However, the network bandwidth did not support uploading very large images to the global complaint handling data system. The remote site was forced to store partial investigation results on two separate computer systems, one of which was not secured adequately. The global IT group responsible for networking did not have adequate knowledge of the serious response time issues at the remote site and was unaware of the local workaround that was adopted.

Production and Quality System Tool Strategies

Automated tools and enterprise-wide systems enable global quality management system implementation. Some production and quality system tool examples include:
- enterprise resource planning (ERP)
- incoming component acceptance
- warehouse management and distribution control
- process control, data acquisition and analysis
- automated manufacturing
- complaint tracking
- adverse event/vigilance reporting
- nonconformance tracking
- corrective and preventive action (CAPA) tracking
- document management
- learning management system (LMS)
- laboratory information management system (LIMS)
- environmental/building management
- calibration management
- label printing

At most medical device manufacturers, automated manufacturing tools frequently are localized to an individual manufacturing site and not shared across multiple sites. Production operations and the quality organization frequently are responsible for managing and validating production, environmental and laboratory systems.

Most global medical device companies have realized the business imperative for global ERP, supplier management, warehousing and distribution, document management and change control, and complaint management and CAPA tracking. On the other hand, lack of global automated quality system tools results in extra work and long delays in investigating and closing complaints and CAPAs. Some regulatory authorities are using powerful automated tools to screen regulatory data, and their responsiveness expectations require such capabilities from global device manufacturers. In one example, because there was no global complaint handling system, the complaint information initially collected by the service organization in one country was keyed into a local data system, then transferred by email to the responsible manufacturing site in a different country. The manufacturing site had to re-key the information into its own data system for subsequent failure investigation management and required maintenance of a copy of the complaint.

Tool vendors and IT departments need to work toward providing more global interoperability among automated quality system tools to simplify historically complex quality system processes. However, unless there is customer demand, there is very little vendor incentive to provide interoperability with competitors' tools. Instead, each vendor tries to expand its own tool capabilities. As a result, medical device companies face a choice of either buying an integrated suite of tools from a single vendor or having to create their own custom interfaces for interoperability among their individual "best of breed" tools from multiple vendors.

Risk management is one quality system aspect for which additional integrated tools would be welcomed. Most device manufacturers still are using spreadsheets developed in-house to record and track risk management decision making and risk mitigations. However, spreadsheets do not provide the same flexibility and power as a risk management database to link device requirements, design features, production processes, risks and risk mitigations. There are a few such comprehensive risk management tools in the marketplace, but they are not in widespread use yet in the medical device industry.

Strategies for Software Lifecycle Management Tools

In the software development process, many labor-intensive tasks historically performed by the developer now can be accomplished better by a computerized program. For example, daily software code builds now are commonplace, and static code analysis and automated nightly tests can be "delegated" to the computer, freeing up time for the developer to focus creativity on writing smart code. This approach also provides more extensive regression testing to confirm daily software changes will not impact the product negatively. For very complex software, some medical device companies now have hundreds of thousands of test cases that can be repeated as often as necessary for comprehensive regression testing.

FDA often attributes major issues in the field to medical device software, and puts strong emphasis on the manufacturer ensuring "100%" code coverage through manual code reviews, supplemented by static analysis. Static code analysis techniques use computer programs (instead of humans) to trace all possible execution paths through the software. This powerful analytical technique examines the source code for potential design defects during code construction, when such issues can be addressed most efficiently and effectively. The amount of time required to process this labor-intensive activity can be reduced to acceptable levels by using a number of commercially available static analysis tools. Static code analysis typically is more invasive and exhaustive than manual code reviews and seeks subtle errors manual reviews may not detect. It does not require the software to run in a real or simulated environment, which typically can be provided only near the end of the development phase after most software has been validated. FDA views static code analysis tool use to be important. It reportedly is planning to process all medical device manufacturer's code through its own static analysis tools unless there is documented evidence the manufacturer already has used such a tool and provided the output to FDA. A manufacturer will be asked to explain every finding if FDA runs the static code analysis itself. However, if a manufacturer runs the static analysis and overrides certain exceptions, justifying these overrides appropriately in configuration documentation would be accepted by FDA.

Automated software tools also can help regulatory compliance by facilitating generation of requirements specifications, design documentation and test scripts, and their electronic review and approval. Tools also can help create and maintain traceability among requirements, design features, risk mitigations and verification and validation tests, and can provide effective project management through visual dashboards and metrics. When used appropriately, tools can facilitate the consistent and efficient delivery of high-quality, compliant, safe and effective software. Tool usage can make software code less prone to errors by individual developers, and can help set and enforce uniform expectations for repeatable, predictable and properly documented outcomes.

Automated tools used in software development and their usage have evolved dramatically over the last few decades.[84] Some examples of software development tools include:
- requirements management
- risk management
- automated design documentation
- software build management
- configuration/change management
- issue/bug tracking
- static code analysis
- test case management
- automated software testing
- integrated development environments
- automated test/trace/defect tracking/document management tool suites[85]

Tools were developed initially for such specific functions as writing and editing code; or compiling, building, testing or managing different code versions. Over time, these tools have been consolidated and combined into tool suites to allow software developers to perform a series of related activities more efficiently. These new tool suites have been accepted widely and are highly successful because developers can find and fix errors interactively in real time, as code is written and compiled. As global team-based software development has become popular, integrating tools to build, test and control source code has provided capabilities and efficiencies not possible when the individual tools were used in isolation.

While tool suites have provided important advances, further software development process optimization requires cradle-to-grave tooling for a much broader range of activities throughout the software development lifecycle, including such administrative functions as program and project management, requirements management, risk management and configuration management, as well as more traditional areas such as build management, test management, traceability management and defect management. While cradle-to-grave automation is desirable, it requires gradual maturation of the software development organization and availability of fully integrated tools not yet widely available for use. Such tooling integration is described in literature as application lifecycle management (ALM) and includes software product governance, development and retirement or obsolescence.[86]

Strategies for Regulatory Information Management Tools

Regulatory information management is among medical device manufacturers' most complex tasks, and integrating automated tools in this area has lagged well behind progress in other areas. Numerous obstacles exist for regulatory submissions and regulatory inspections. Different countries' and regions' regulatory requirements vary significantly in what is regulated versus what is not regulated, facility and product registration needs, premarket submission requirements, labeling language and data privacy protection. Regulatory sanctions are quite significant for unauthorized product claims and failure to pay fees, submit required reports on time and respond to regulatory agency inquiries. Likewise, failure to make regulatory submissions as planned or launch a product on time can have a devastatingly negative business impact. Being able to locate all devices quickly during a recall is a challenge for most device companies.

The issue for the regulatory professional is not a lack of information, but too much, frequently conflicting, information. Key questions are:
- Where is the information I can trust?
- How can everyone in the company (both in headquarters and in individual countries) have ready access to a reliable "single source of truth?"

Numerous individual tools are available to manage specific regulatory tasks. Some examples include:
- global registration tracking
- regulatory submission tracking
- labeling content management
- UDI labeling implementation
- clinical trials management
- content search and tracking
- content authoring and publishing
- regulatory commitment tracking
- health authority inquiry tracking
- correspondence management
- translation services
- artwork management
- regulatory resource planning and tracking

However, very few commercial interfaces are available among these tools. Device manufacturers currently are faced with the cumbersome task of transferring data manually from one tool to another, or having to build their own data-sharing interfaces. All too frequently, no high-level dashboard exists for tracking all related regulatory activities, and data sources cannot be searched easily for relevant information.

Again, the new UDI implementation offers device manufacturers a valuable opportunity to re-examine their regulatory information management needs. RIM tool users should demand vendors provide commercial interoperability solutions just as IT departments and software developers already have demanded of their tool vendors.

Global Policies and Procedure Strategies

Globally shared policies and procedures are the foundation of global medical device quality system and regulatory strategies. Those strategies are possible only with global document control computer applications empowering and implementing global document-sharing and change controls. Delays in accessing document changes not only impede business processes, but also create avoidable regulatory vulnerabilities. For example, a medical device software design facility was supposed to use global quality system procedures, but the response time for accessing the document system was so poor the site downloaded its procedures onto a local shared drive. However, inadequate manual controls existed to ensure the local shared drive always was updated when the corresponding global procedure was changed on the global document control system.

In a medical device company, it is critical for the IT department to understand its important role as a regulated entity in a highly regulated environment. Important information management policies and procedures, such as personal privacy, computer security, anti-corruption, business system integrity and disaster recovery usually are implemented, administered and enforced through the global IT department. Globally shared software tools and IT services' outsourcing decisions (e.g., cloud services and SaaS applications) usually are implemented and administered by the IT department. In addition, the IT department generally has its own separate IT policies and procedures, which frequently are isolated from, and not considered to be part of, the company's medical device quality system. Some legitimate IT procedural issues should be addressed, e.g., how to cover regulated activities in detail without being overly burdensome for nonregulated business activities. However, in an ever-changing environment, it often is difficult to segregate what is regulated from what is not, and it is crucial to identify clearly which IT policies and procedures are part of the medical device quality management system.

Conclusions

Regulatory professionals, in both the medical device industry and regulatory agencies, are faced with a wide variety of new software-based technologies and a diverse and rapidly changing regulatory landscape. Software presents regulatory challenges and solutions to some of the most difficult quality and regulatory problems. It also brings promising prospects to the current healthcare revolution. Globally, a general consensus on best practice approaches for medical device software development, as reflected in numerous harmonized international standards, guidelines and other available resources exists, but many device companies have not fully embraced and implemented those best practices yet. The Internet and automated tools have enabled far greater information sharing and global development strategies for quality systems, regulatory management and product development, but a need for greater software interoperability and integration exists. While regulatory personnel cannot become expert on emerging software technologies, it is essential they understand the basic concepts and techniques used, as well as the challenges software professionals face. It also is important for regulatory professionals to collaborate with software developers and IT personnel, to serve as terminology translators, explain and promote the regulatory requirement applications and develop mutual understanding of what is feasible, what is required and why.

References

1. Feldmann RL, Shull F, Denger C, Host M and Lindholm C. *A survey of software engineering techniques in medical device development.* Joint Workshop on High Confidence Medical Devices, Software, and Systems and Medical Devices Plug-and-Play Interoperability, Boston, MA. 2007; 46-54.
2. Hartkopf S. *From a single discipline risk management approach to an interdisciplinary one: adaptation of FMEA to software needs.* Software Technology and Engineering Practice, Eleventh Annual International Workshop. 2003; 204-213.
3. Jones PL, Jorgens III J, Taylor Jr AR, Weber M. "Risk management in the design of medical software systems." *Biomedical Instrumentation & Technology.* 2002; 36(4): 237-266.
4. *Medical Device Recall Report FY2003 to FY2012.* FDA website. http://www.fda.gov/downloads/AboutFDA/CentersOffices/OfficeofMedicalProductsandTobacco/CDRH/CDRHTransparency/UCM388442.pdf. Accessed 12 March 2016.
5. *Medical Device Interoperability (AAMI White Paper).* 30 March 2012, AAMI website. http://www.aami.org/interoperability/Materials/MDI_1203.pdf. Accessed 12 March 2016.
6. *EHR Buyers Guide.* Technology Advice Website. http://technologyadvice.com/medical/ehr-emr/smart-advisor/#guide. Accessed 13 March 2016.
7. *Become a Champion for Interoperability.* Healthcare Information and Management Systems Society. Amazon website. http://s3.amazonaws.com/rdcms-himss/files/production/public/FileDownloads/2014-02-11-InteroperabilityChampionDocument FINAL.pdf. Accessed 13 March 2016.
8. *The Evolving Landscape of Medical Apps in Healthcare.* HIT Consultant website. http://hitconsultant.net/2014/06/23/the-evolving-landscape-of-medical-apps-in-healthcare/. Accessed 13 March 2016.
9. *NIST SP 800-145 The NIST Definition of Cloud Computing.* NIST website. http://csrc.nist.gov/publications/nistpubs/800-145/SP800-145.pdf. Accessed 13 March 2016.
10. *Impact of Cloud Computing on Healthcare.* Cloud Standards Customer Council website. http://www.cloudstandardscustomer-council.org/cscchealthcare110512.pdf. Accessed 13 March 2016.
11. "Citizen Hackers Tinker With Medical Devices. *Wall Street Journal* website. http://online.wsj.com/articles/citizen-hackers-concoct-upgrades-for-medical-devices-1411762843. Accessed 13 March 2016.
12. *Developing new tools to support regulatory use of 'Next Gen Sequencing' data.* FDA website. http://blogs.fda.gov/fdavoice/index.php/2014/07/developing-new-tools-to-support-regulatory-use-of-next-gen-sequencing-data/?source=govdelivery&utm_medium=email&utm_source=govdelivery. Accessed 13 March 2016.
13. *Medical Devices; Current Good Manufacturing Practice (CGMP) Final Rule; Quality System.* FDA website. http://www.fda.gov/medicaldevices/deviceregulationandguidance/postmarketrequirements/qualitysystemsregulations/ucm230127.htm. Accessed 13 March 2016.
14. Council Directive 93/42/EEC of 14 June 1993 concerning medical devices, Article 1(2)(a). EUR-Lex website. http://eur-lex.europa.eu/LexUriServ/LexUriServ.do?uri=CELEX:31993L0042:en:HTML. Accessed 13 March 2016.
15. Directive 98/79/EC of the European Parliament and of the Council of 27 October 1998 on in vitro diagnostic medical devices. EUR-Lex website. http://eur-lex.europa.eu/LexUriServ/LexUriServ.do?uri=CONSLEG:1998L0079:20031120:en:PDF. Accessed 13 March 2016.
16. *MEDDEV 2.1/6. Guidelines on the Qualification and Classification of Stand Alone Software Used in Healthcare Within the Regulatory Framework of Medical Devices.* European Commission website. http://ec.europa.eu/health/medical-devices/files/meddev/2_1_6_ol_en.pdf. Accessed 13 March 2016.
17. *EN ISO 13485:2012 Medical devices—Quality management systems—Requirements for regulatory purposes.* BSI website. http://shop.bsigroup.com/ProductDetail/?pid=000000000030268037. Accessed 13 March 2016.
18. *EN ISO 14971:2012 Medical devices—Application of risk management to medical devices.* ISO website. http://shop.bsigroup.com/ProductDetail/?pid=000000000030268035. Accessed 13 March 2016.
19. *Guidance for Industry, FDA Reviewers and Compliance on Off-The-Shelf Software Use in Medical Devices,* 9 September 1999. FDA website. http://www.fda.gov/downloads/MedicalDevices/.../ucm073779.pdf. Accessed 13 March 2016.
20. *Design Control Guidance for Medical Device Manufacturers,* 11 March 1997. FDA website. http://www.fda.gov/downloads/MedicalDevices/DeviceRegulationandGuidance/GuidanceDocuments/ucm070642.pdf. Accessed 13 March 2016.
21. *General Principles of Software Validation; Final Guidance for Industry and FDA Staff,* 11 January 2002. FDA website. http://www.fda.gov/medicaldevices/deviceregulationandguidance/guidancedocuments/ucm085281.htm. Accessed 13 March 2016.
22. *Guidance for the Content of Premarket Submissions for Software Contained in Medical Devices,* 11 May 2005. FDA website. http://www.fda.gov/MedicalDevices/DeviceRegulationandGuidance/GuidanceDocuments/ucm089543.htm. Accessed 13 March 2016.
23. *ANSI/AAMI/IEC 62304:2006 Medical device software—Software lifecycle processes.* AAMI website. http://my.aami.org/aamiresources/previewfiles/623040606preview.pdf. Accessed 13 March 2016.
24. *Guidance for Industry and FDA Premarket and Design Control Reviewers; Medical Device Use-Safety: Incorporating Human Factors Engineering into Risk Management,* 18 July 2000. FDA website. http://www.fda.gov/downloads/MedicalDevices/.../ucm094461.pdf. Accessed 13 March 2016.
25. *Guidance for Industry and Food and Drug Administration Staff; Applying Human Factors and Usability Engineering to Medical Devices,* 3 February 2016. FDA website. http://www.fda.gov/downloads/MedicalDevices/DeviceRegulationandGuidance/GuidanceDocuments/UCM259760.pdf. Accessed 13 March 2016.
26. *ANSI/AAMI HE 75: 2009 Human factors engineering—Design of medical devices.* AAMI website. http://www.aami.org/publications/standards/he75.html. Accessed 13 March 2016.
27. *IEC 62366:2007, Medical devices—Application of usability engineering to medical devices.* ISO website. http://www.iso.org/iso/catalogue_detail.htm?csnumber=38594. Accessed 13 March 2016.
28. *IEC/TR 80002-1:2009 Medical device software—Part 1: Guidance on the application of ISO 14971 to medical device software.* ISO website. http://www.iso.org/iso/home/store/catalogue_tc/catalogue_detail.htm?csnumber=54146. Accessed 13 March 2016.
29. *Reviewer Guidance for a Premarket Notification Submission for Blood Establishment Computer Software,* 13 January 1997. FDA website. http://www.fda.gov/downloads/BiologicsBloodVaccines/GuidanceComplianceRegulatoryInformation/OtherRecommendationsforManufacturers/MemorandumtoBloodEstablishments/UCM062208.pdf. Accessed 13 March 2016.

30. *Guidance for Industry: Blood Establishment Computer System Validation in the User's Facility*, April, 2013. FDA website. http://www.fda.gov/BiologicsBloodVaccines/GuidanceComplianceRegulatoryInformation/Guidances/Blood/ucm072560.htm. Accessed 13 March 2016.
31. *Guidance for Industry—Computerized Systems Used in Clinical Investigations*, May 2007. FDA website. http://www.fda.gov/OHRMS/DOCKETS/98fr/04d-0440-gdl0002.PDF. Accessed 13 March 2016.
32. *21 CFR Part 11, Electronic Records; Electronic Signatures*. FDA website. http://www.accessdata.fda.gov/scripts/cdrh/cfdocs/cfcfr/CFRSearch.cfm?CFRPart=11&showFR=1. Accessed 13 March 2016.
33. *Guidance for Industry: Part 11, Electronic Records; Electronic Signatures—Scope and Application*, August 2003. FDA website. http://www.fda.gov/RegulatoryInformation/Guidances/ucm125067.htm. Accessed 13 March 2016.
34. *GAMP 5: A Risk-Based Approach to Compliant GxP Computerized Systems*. February 2008. ISPE website. http://www.ispe.org/gamp-5. Accessed 23 September 2014.
35. *GAMP Good Practice Guide: A Risk-Based Approach to Compliant Electronic Records and Signatures*. February 2005. ISPE website. http://www.ispe.org/gamp-good-practice-guide/electronic-records-signatures. Accessed 13 March 2016.
36. *GAMP Good Practice Guide: A Risk-Based Approach to GxP Process Control Systems*. February 2011. ISPE website. http://www.ispe.org/gamp-good-practice-guide/risk-based-gxp-process-control-systems. Accessed 13 March 2016.
37. *GAMP Good Practice Guide: A Risk-Based Approach to GxP Compliant Laboratory Computerized Systems*. October 2012. ISPE website. http://www.ispe.org/gamp-good-practice-guide/gxp-compliant-laboratory-computerized-systems. Accessed 13 March 2016.
38. *GAMP Good Practice Guide: A Risk-Based Approach to Calibration Management*. November 2010. ISPE website. http://www.ispe.org/gamp-good-practice-guide/calibration-management. Accessed 13 March 2016.
39. *GAMP Good Practice Guide: IT Infrastructure Control and Compliance*. September 2005. ISPE website. http://www.ispe.org/gamp-good-practice-guide/it-infrastructure. Accessed 13 March 2016.
40. *GAMP Good Practice Guide: Global Information Systems Control and Compliance*. November 2005. ISPE website. http://www.ispe.org/gamp-good-practice-guide/global-information-systems. Accessed 13 March 2016.
41. *GAMP Good Practice Guide: A Risk-Based Approach to Testing of GxP Systems*. December 2010. ISPE website. http://www.ispe.org/gamp-good-practice-guide/testing-gxp-systems. Accessed 13 March 2016.
42. *Guide to Good Manufacturing Practice for Medicinal Products (Annex 11 Computerized Systems)*. March 2014. (Ref: PE 009-11 (Annexes). PIC/S website. http://www.picscheme.org/publication.php?id=4. Accessed 13 March 2016.
43. *Good Practices for Computerised Systems in Regulated "GXP" Environments*. 25 September 2007. (Ref: PI 011-3). PIC/S website. http://www.picscheme.org/publication.php?id=8. Accessed 13 March 2016.
44. *AAMI TIR36:2007/Ed.1, Validation of Software for Regulated Processes*. AAMI website. https://standards.aami.org/kws/public/projects/project/details?project_id=327. Accessed 13 March 2016.
45. *Guidance for Industry—Cybersecurity for Networked Medical Devices Containing Off-the-Shelf (OTS) Software*, 14 January 2005. FDA website. http://www.fda.gov/MedicalDevices/DeviceRegulationandGuidance/GuidanceDocuments/ucm077812.htm. Accessed 13 March 2016.
46. *Cybersecurity for Medical Devices and Hospital Networks; FDA Safety Communication*, 13 June 2013. FDA website. http://www.fda.gov/medicaldevices/safety/alertsandnotices/ucm356423.htm. Accessed 13 March 2016.
47. *Content of Premarket Submissions for Management of Cybersecurity in Medical Devices; Guidance for Industry and Food and Drug Administration Staff*, 2 October 2014. FDA website. http://www.fda.gov/downloads/medicaldevices/deviceregulationandguidance/guidancedocuments/ucm356190.pdf. Accessed 13 March 2016.
48. *AAMI TIR57/Ed. 1 Principles for medical device information security risk management*. AAMI website. https://standards.aami.org/kws/public/projects/project/details?project_id=876. Accessed 13 March 2016.
49. *NIST SP 800-39 Managing Information Security Risk: Organization, Mission, and Information System View*. NIST website. http://csrc.nist.gov/publications/nistpubs/800-39/SP800-39-final.pdf. Accessed 13 March 2016.
50. *NIST SP 800-30 Revision 1 Guide for Conducting Risk Assessments*. NIST website. http://csrc.nist.gov/publications/nistpubs/800-30-rev1/sp800_30_r1.pdf. Accessed 13 March 2016.
51. *ISO/IEC 27001:2013 Information technology—Security techniques—Information security management systems—Requirements*. ISO website. http://www.iso.org/iso/home/store/catalogue_tc/catalogue_detail.htm?csnumber=54534. Accessed 13 March 2016.
52. *ISO/IEC 27005:2011 Information technology—Security techniques—Information security risk management*. ISO website. http://www.iso.org/iso/catalogue_detail?csnumber=56742. Accessed 13 March 2016.
53. *ANSI/AAMI/IEC TIR 80001-2-1:2012 Application of risk management for IT-networks incorporating medical devices—Part 2-1: Step by step risk management of medical IT-networks; Practical applications and examples*. AAMI website. http://my.aami.org/Zaamiresources/previewfiles/800010201_1209_preview.pdf. Accessed 13 March 2016.
54. *Federal Register Notice—Software and Informatics Standards Recognized by FDA*. US Government Printing Office (GPO) website. http://www.gpo.gov/fdsys/pkg/FR-2013-08-06/pdf/2013-19020.pdf. Accessed 13 March 2016.
55. *Radio Frequency Wireless Technology in Medical Devices; Guidance for Industry and Food and Drug Administration Staff*, 14 August 2013. FDA website. http://www.fda.gov/MedicalDevices/DeviceRegulationandGuidance/GuidanceDocuments/ucm077210.htm. Accessed 13 March 2016.
56. *Directive 95/46/EC of the European Parliament and of the Council of 24 October 1995 on the protection of individuals with regard to the processing of personal data and on the free movement of such data*. EUR-Lex website. http://eur-lex.europa.eu/LexUriServ/LexUriServ.do?uri=CELEX:31995L0046:en:HTML. Accessed 13 March 2016.
57. *Mobile Medical Applications; Guidance for Industry and Food and Drug Administration Staff*, 9 February 2015. FDA website. http://www.fda.gov/downloads/MedicalDevices/.../UCM263366.pdf. Accessed 13 March 2016.
58. Ghosh, K. *Cloud Computing and Data Security: A Regulatory Perspective*. IVT's 15th Annual Computer and Software Validation, San Diego, CA. 2014.
59. Op cit. 32.
60. Op cit. 51.
61. *NIST SP 800-144 Guidelines on Security and Privacy in Public Cloud Computing*. NIST website. http://nvlpubs.nist.gov/nistpubs/Legacy/SP/nistspecialpublication800-144.pdf. Accessed 13 March 2016.
62. *Federal Register Notice: Report to Congress, Report on FDA's Policy to be Proposed Regarding Premarket Notification Requirements for Modifications to Legally Marketed Devices*.

63. Op cit. 12.
64. Wilson CA. *FDA Genomics Working Group: Update to the FDA Science Board.* FDA website. http://www.fda.gov/downloads/AdvisoryCommittees/CommitteesMeetingMaterials/ScienceBoardtotheFoodandDrugAdministration/UCM341042.pdf. Accessed 13 March 2016.
65. Bliznakov Z. *Analysis and classification of medical device recalls.* World Congress on Medical Physics and Biomedical Engineering. 2006; 14: 3782-3785.
66. Baker T. "2002 Medical device recalls and field corrections—Year in review." *Journal of Clinical Engineering.* 2003; 28(4): 218-232.
67. Baker T. "2003 Medical device recalls and field corrections—Year in review." *Journal of Clinical Engineering.* 2004; 29(2): 90-105.
68. Thomas R. "2005 Medical device recalls and field corrections—Year in review." *Journal of Clinical Engineering.* 2006; 31(3): 177-201.
69. Op cit. 4.
70. Op cit. 13.
71. Op cit. 23.
72. Samra T. *Medical Device Software: Development LifeCycle Methodologies, Tools and Risk Management.* Saarbrücken, Germany: Scholar›s Press; 2013.
73. *Selecting a development approach.* CMS website. http://www.cms.gov/Research-Statistics-Data-and-Systems/CMS-Information-Technology/XLC/Downloads/SelectingDevelopmentApproach.pdf. Accessed 13 March 2016.
74. *What is Agile Software Development?* Agile Alliance website. http://www.agilealliance.org/the-alliance/what-is-agile/. Accessed 13 March 2016.
75. *Manifesto for Agile Software Development.* Agile Manifesto website. http://agilemanifesto.org/. Accessed 13 March 2016.
76. *Why Scrum?* Scrum Alliance website. https://www.scrumalliance.org/why-scrum. Accessed 13 March 2016.
77. Ibid.
78. Op cit. 72.
79. *Agile development: Mainstream adoption has changed agility.* Forrester website. https://www.forrester.com/Agile+Development+Mainstream+Adoption+Has+Changed+Agility/fulltext/-/E-RES56100?objectid=RES56100. Accessed 13 March 2016.
80. *AAMI TIR45:2012 Guidance on the use of AGILE practices in the development of medical device software.* AAMI website. http://my.aami.org/aamiresources/previewfiles/TIR45_1208_PREVIEW.PDF. Accessed 13 March 2016.
81. Hobbs C. *Industry Viewpoint: Device makers can take COTS, but only with clear SOUP.* Medical Design website. http://medicaldesign.com/prototyping/industry-viewpoint-device-makers-can-take-cots-only-clear-soup. Accessed 13 March 2016.
82. Chappell D. *Tools for team development: Why vendors are finally getting it right.* December 2008. David Chappell & Associates website. http://www.davidchappell.com/ALMToolEvolution--Chappell.pdf. Accessed 13 March 2016.
83. Op cit. 39.
84. Op cit. 80.
85. Op cit. 72.
86. Chappell D. *"What is application lifecycle management?"* David Chappell & Associates website. http://www.davidchappell.com/writing/white_papers/What_is_ALM_v2.0--Chappell.pdf. Accessed 13 March 2016.

22 Reimbursement

By Amit Kukreja, MBA

Introduction

The good old days of assured reimbursement are over. In the past, when a new medical device received market approval (such as a CE Mark or FDA approval), it was normal to expect the healthcare system automatically would ensure the product was covered for patients insured under public health systems. In today's world, reimbursement is not guaranteed and poses a huge hurdle to innovative medical device market entry and commercial success. Many innovative products do not reach intended patients because payers do not reimburse them due to lack of rigorous well-designed clinical and health economic evidence. This new hurdle has become a life-threatening challenge to the medical device industry surviving on innovation and products with relatively short lifecycles.

Many factors have led to significant changes in the medical device industry reimbursement environment, including:
1. healthcare costs increases
2. stagnant economic growth
3. aging population
4. changing lifestyle
5. higher healthcare needs
6. lack of long term investors
7. increasing role of nonclinical stakeholders in the reimbursement decision-making process
8. rising clinical and economic evidence assessments in reimbursement decision making
9. real-world evidence requirements to demonstrate effectiveness beyond safety and efficacy

Therefore, when planning a new device's development or expanding current product to new indications, a company must analyze critically and understand implications from not only the patient and provider's perspective but also the payer's perspective, since the latter has growing influence on what should or should not be reimbursed by a publicly funded healthcare system. The days when convincing physicians could be the decisive factor in a product's market success are gone. Today, a company must incorporate a targeted value proposition for a broad set of stakeholders, including physicians, patients, payers, policy advisors and policymakers. Each stakeholder group must be addressed and convinced a new medical product deserves true reimbursement approval and wider level adoption.

Innovative medical device manufacturers need to be strategic early in the process. Reimbursement implications' importance for a new medical device's long-term commercial success cannot be overvalued. It is essential to consider reimbursement input in the business planning phase when key decisions are made about product development, clinical evidence generation, product pricing and commercialization strategy. Failure to address key reimbursement issues while designing clinical trial and business strategies could lead to millions of dollars in futile investments or even complete market failure. Typically, medical device clinical trials are small and may have limited clinical (and economic) data when a product receives market approval. Therefore, unlike previously, payers today usually prefer to grant an initial temporary conditional reimbursement for new medical devices and monitor them for further clinical and economic

Figure 22-1. Market Access Key Stakeholders

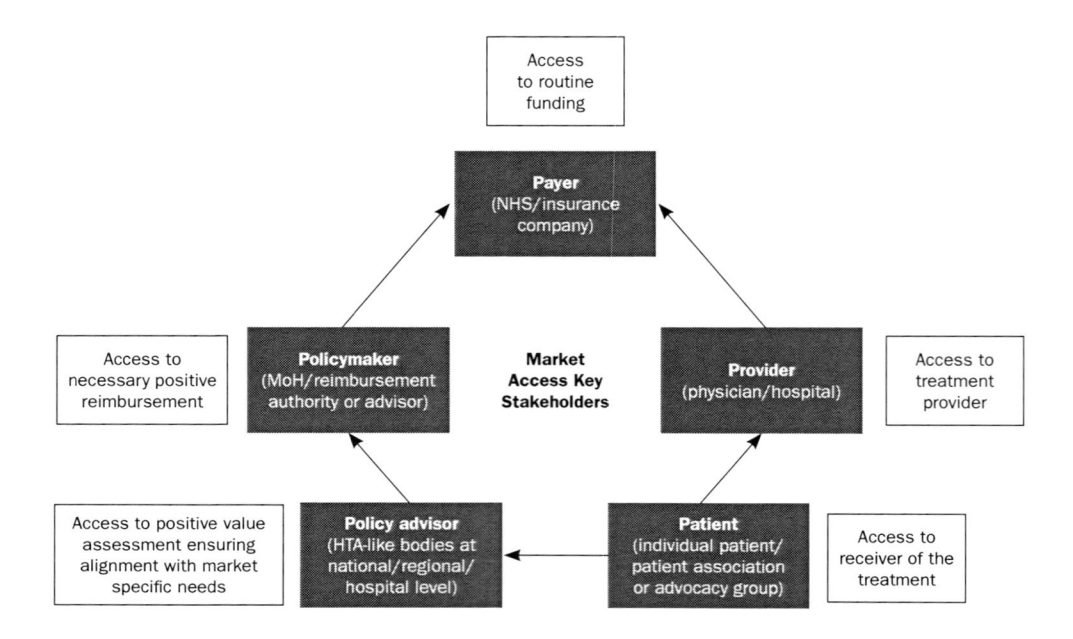

```
                            Access
                          to routine
                           funding

                            Payer
                         (NHS/insurance
                            company)

  Access to        Policymaker      Market      Provider         Access to
necessary positive (MoH/reimbursement Access Key (physician/hospital) treatment
reimbursement    authority or advisor) Stakeholders                provider

Access to positive value  Policy advisor      Patient          Access to
assessment ensuring   (HTA-like bodies at  (individual patient/  receiver of the
alignment with market  national/regional/  patient association    treatment
  specific needs        hospital level)    or advocacy group)
```

evidence-generated pathways. As new evidence becomes available, decisions are made either to prolong temporary reimbursement while requiring further evidence, grant a regular full reimbursement or reject it for further reimbursement due to undesirable evidence results. Even after being approved for standard reimbursement, positive decisions can be reversed if payers find it appropriate due to undesirable results from new evidence, poor patient outcomes, availability of a better competitive product, regulation changes, budget pressures, etc.

Increasingly, a number of stakeholders (e.g., policymakers, reimbursement authorities, payers, key opinion leaders (KOLs), hospital coding and billing staff, clinical and patient organizations) formally or informally play key roles in the reimbursement process at different levels. Therefore, reimbursement or related teams generally involve people from multidisciplinary specialties ranging from reimbursement, health economics, pricing, government policy, public affairs, outcomes research and business management. The reimbursement function's key objective is to bring together a broad set of stakeholders (**Figure 22-1**) to establish successful sustainable reimbursement and coverage for new medical devices. Depending on the business type and innovation level, reimbursement issues can range from a global, regional or national, to a local level. As most medical device companies increasingly rely on public healthcare funding as a major income source, the reimbursement function is at the core of the business. Consequently, it is imperative to maintain a close understanding of how changing regulations, economic conditions, healthcare needs, clinical practices and the competitive landscape affect a product's reimbursement conditions, to keep the business strategy resilient and adapt regularly to current needs.

Reimbursement of Public Health Services

Healthcare services are delivered primarily in inpatient, outpatient, rehabilitative care or home-based settings. In recent decades, significant changes have occurred in funding allocation and payment methods for healthcare services. While funding models for each setting have undergone some changes, a significant shift in inpatient hospital service funding has occurred, where new innovative medical technologies commonly are used. Inpatient hospital services also account for the vast majority of public healthcare expenditures in most developed countries. Today, many developed countries have moved away from the traditional annual budget hospital funding model to prospective payment systems. This means a physician no longer is allowed simply to procure a new medical device through the hospital budget and provide it to patients. Increasingly, the patient classification system's (PCS) role in managing quality, building transparency and improving healthcare system efficiency is acknowledged across the world. PCS classifies each patient based

Table 22-1. Original Purposes and Principal Purposes of DRG Systems in Europe

\multicolumn{4}{c	}{Purpose of DRG Systems in 12 Countries}
Country	Year of DRG Introduction	Original Purpose(s)	Principal Purpose(s) in 2010
Austria	1997	Budgetary allocation	Budgetary allocation, planning
England	1992	Patient Classification	Payment
Estonia	2003	Payment	Payment
Finland	1995	Description of hospital activity, benchmarking	Planning and management, benchmarking, hospital billing
France	1991	Description of hospital activity	Payment
Germany	2003	Payment	Payment
Ireland	1992	Budgetary allocation	Budgetary allocation
Netherlands	2005	Payment	Payment
Poland	2008	Payment	Payment
Portugal	1984	Hospital output measurement	Budgetary allocation
Spain (Catalonia)	1996	Payment	Payment, benchmarking
Sweden	1995	Payment	Benchmarking, performance measurement, hospital payment
US	1983	Monitor the utilization of resources and quality of service	Payment

Source: Geissler A, Quentin W, Scheller-Kreinsen D, Busse R. Introduction to DRGs in Europe: Common objectives across different hospital systems.(Available from website: http://eurodrg.projects.tu-berlin.de/publications/DRGbook/Ch2_Geissler.pdf, *accessed on 31 Oct 2014); Bushnell B. The Evolution of DRGs:* http://www.aaos.org/news/aaosnow/dec13/advocacy2.asp *Accessed October 31, 2014*

on such basic information as age, gender, diagnoses and the treatment provided. Over the years, PCS has grown in sophistication and use in reimbursement systems, such as Diagnosis Related Groups (DRGs). DRGs were adopted out of necessity, due to rapid medical advancements and increasing healthcare costs, requiring a payment management system to help map treatment, the number of patients receiving it and associated costs of care that could play a vital role in managing healthcare services' quality and costs.[1] Many countries already have adopted or are in the process of adopting a DRG or similar reimbursement system to pay for hospital services, while traditional reimbursement models still commonly are used to pay for ambulatory or home-care services. **Table 22-1** represents the shift of the DRG system's purpose over the years in several countries.[2]

Activity-Based Hospital (DRG) Reimbursement

The Yale School of Medicine devised the original DRG system, first introduced for the US Medicare program in 1983.[3] DRG was developed to assist decision makers (payers and policymakers) in managing healthcare services' quality and costs better.

In those countries that switched to DRG to finance hospital services, those services now are reimbursed according to DRG tariffs. DRG tariffs generally are based on the average national cost of treating a patient with a particular diagnosis. Thus, hospitals need to make their services "DRG-efficient." This means any hospital's average service costs must fall within the DRG rates to avoid incurring losses. On the other hand, to generate surplus, any hospital's average treatment costs should be lower than the respective DRG rate.

Similarly, if a treatment's actual cost is lower than some hospitals' DRG tariff, the hospital can continue to generate surplus until significantly more hospitals can provide the treatment below the prevailing DRG payment amount. This is because the DRG system is designed to adapt a treatment's reimbursement tariff by recalculating its average hospital cost regularly at a national or regional level. To adjust the difference between a treatment's actual average cost and the existing DRG payment, the DRG tariff will be reduced to match the true average treatment

Table 22-2. Names of Selected DRG Coding Systems and Numbers of Codes

Country/Region	Name of DRG or Similar Coding System	Numbers of Codes
US	MS-DRG	999
Germany	G-DRG	1,200
France	GHM	2,297
UK (England and Wales)	HRG	1,389
Austria	LKF	979
Switzerland	AP-DRG	679
Netherlands	DBC	30,000
Poland	JGP	518
Scandinavia	NordDRG	794
Australia	AR-DRG	665

Source: Quentin W. DRG-based hospital payment - Experiences from 12 European countries. Available from: http://www.thl.fi/documents/10531/120652/ Chess_seminar_DRG-based-payment_WQ2.pdf. Accessed October 31, 2014; Bushnell B. The Evolution of DRGs: http://www.aaos.org/news/aaosnow/dec13/ advocacy2.asp. Accessed October 31, 2014

cost. As a result, the succeeding year's DRG calculation will be lower for all hospitals in the region.[4]

Most DRG systems classify hospital cases into 500–1,500 groups (**Table 22-2** lists DRG coding systems and their respective numbers).[5] Such a patient classification system clearly correlates patients treated for a disease group with the respective treatment resources. Hence, DRGs have given a broader perspective to reimbursement systems' shifting hospital payment process line-item budgets to global budgets.

Despite the advances in hospital healthcare funding, many countries have no clarity on updating DRG methodology and frequency. The DRG tariff updating process becomes important when a new device enters the market without an existing DRG code and appropriate reimbursement tariff. For instance, when a device is introduced at a higher price compared to that of any existing technology, the current DRG code and tariff probably will not cover the new treatment's description appropriately and may not provide its necessary reimbursement. Therefore, reimbursement system discrepancies could delay the adoption of a novel, more expensive technology significantly.[6]

The DRG system's role also can vary depending on how the overall health system executes it. While the DRG payment method includes the majority of inpatient hospital care services, it is important to note it is just one part of a country's overall healthcare reimbursement system. Various other coding system types catering to reimbursement of ambulatory, outpatient, home-care or other settings also can be a part of a reimbursement structure. The US reimbursement system, the first to adopt the DRG approach, has an intricate coding structure (**Table 22-3** briefly summarizes the main code, application and system codes to be applied in the US reimbursement coding system). Even if reimbursement coding systems have existed for some years, proper industry understanding of complex coding systems, their necessity and different approval routes is difficult to achieve. The process of obtaining a new code can require extensive work, including application submission and multiple follow-up interactions with reimbursement coding authorities such as the US Centers for Medicare and Medicaid Services (CMS) or others, depending on the type of code needed. Such a process sometimes can take many years, exceeding the amount of time needed to get FDA approval.

New technologies or procedures conforming to reimbursement and coverage criteria significantly affect clinical practice and, in turn, support innovation by creating either incentives or disincentives for manufacturers to propose novel innovations. Reimbursement practices' adaptation to more-sophisticated technological advancements allows these innovations to be implemented in clinical practice as soon as supportive evidence is available. Data scarcity to support a new, more-expensive technology's benefits and cost-effectiveness poses problems in implementation when compared to currently used technology. If the additional costs will not be reimbursed, due to a void in technology assessment, the lack of any incentives will lead hospitals to not adopt the new technology. Thus, unadopted DRG systems would slow technological innovation. Additionally, other options exist with separate funding innovation budgets, but these systems have their own limitations.[7]

Table 22-3. Main Types of US Reimbursement Coding Systems

Coding System	Definition	Comment
DRG	Diagnosis Resource Groups	Diagnosis and procedure codes determine DRG for inpatient services
ICD-9-CM	International Classification of Diseases, 9th edition, Clinical Modification	Reporting diagnoses, disorders, conditions and symptoms
ICD-10-CM (Diagnoses)	International Classification of Diseases, 10th edition, Clinical Modification	When the code set is implemented, it will replace ICD-9-CM to report medical diagnoses
ICD-10-PCS (Procedures)	International Classification of Diseases, 10th edition, Procedure Coding System	When the code set is implemented, providers will use it to report procedures performed only in US hospital inpatient healthcare settings
CPT (HCPCS - Level I)	Current Procedural Terminology	Reporting healthcare procedures or services
HCPCS - Level II	Healthcare Common Procedure Coding System (Level II)	Reporting supplies, equipment, devices and some procedures
IPPS	Inpatient Prospective Payment System	Each case is categorized into a DRG, with a payment assigned to each DRG
OPPS	Outpatient Prospective Payment System	Payment for each case is determined by CPT and HCPCS

Source: Definitions and Payment Information, http://www.cms.gov/Outreach-and-Education/Medicare-Learning-Network-MLN/MLNProducts/Downloads/ICD9-10CM-ICD10PCS-CPT-HCPCS-Code-Sets-Educational-Tool-ICN900943.pdf. Accessed 1 November 2014; http://www.cms.gov/ Accessed 1 November 2014

A DRG payment system institutes novel financial incentives for hospital behavior differing from those found under both cost-based reimbursement and other prospective hospital payment plans. DRG payment gives rise to two basic incentives: reducing hospital costs for each inpatient hospital stay, and increasing the number of inpatient admissions.[8] The DRG payment method was designed to stop remuneration of hospitals admitting everyone, extorting huge amounts from patients, keeping patients too long and providing unnecessary services to obtain maximum payments.[9] It should be noted the DRG payment system's complexity has increased considerably, while DRGs also have evolved over time to adjust diagnosis severity or other co-morbidities.[10]

DRG tariffs cover all hospital operating costs, including administrative costs and overheads, but most exclude capital costs. Great variability exists in national and regional funding arrangements in some countries, e.g., Italy. Additionally, wide variations occur across regions regarding the DRG classification version adopted, the methodology employed to calculate tariffs, update frequency and criteria to differentiate tariffs across providers.[11] Hence, it is extremely important to understand whether payment target market systems are updated in a timely manner to maintain optimal reimbursement levels over time. Failure to do so leads to inadequate reimbursement, particularly for more innovative and/or expensive interventions. To keep this under control, many countries offer temporary additional reimbursement arrangements until payment systems are adjusted accordingly.[12]

DRG error chances prevail at various points in the pathway from patient admission to the paid account. Inappropriate reporting may affect hospital finances for years. A comprehensive revenue cycle monitoring process always must include regular sample case reviews to ensure the integrity of involved systems and entities is maintained.[13] Due to such implications, this payment structure encourages caregivers to use the most economically efficient patient treatment and reduce unnecessary services.

Alternative Reimbursement Routes

Providers may incur high costs for novel innovative medical devices before DRGs are adapted to reflect the new technologies' costs. This delays the adoption of new technologies and devices. As these technologies' use leads to increased expenditures, resources are utilized from other healthcare system components, where they might have led to greater benefits.

Today, many countries handle new technologies using standardized approaches to maintain balance. Under this approach, DRG systems pay supplementary reimbursement, which covers a considerable part of the overall expenditure. As a new technology is adopted, it first is covered by supplementary reimbursement, followed by embracing a separate DRG.[14] Supplementary reimbursement pathways, such as "new diagnostic and therapeutic procedures," NUB(*Neue Untersuchungs- und Behandlungsmethoden*) and ZE (*Zusatzentgelt*) funding in Germany, New Technology Add-on Payment & Outlier Payment (USA), *Forfait Innovation* funding in France, and many similar bridging pathways, stimulate faster patient access to innovative technologies.

From a coding and payment perspective, obtaining a DRG for the new treatment using a target medical device and providing appropriate payment is the ideal reimbursement situation, but could take many years. However, coding and payment without a payer treatment coverage or acceptance promise is of no real use. Increasingly, payers are limiting or denying coverage to new or existing approved medical device treatments due to higher costs or a lack of clinical and economic evidence. Evidence-based healthcare decision making is gaining attention from policymakers and payers working to control rising healthcare costs and provide high-quality healthcare services. Therefore, it is imperative to understand the new reimbursement and coverage decision-making criteria, methods and tools policymakers and payers use to assess new products' value.

Health Technology Assessments

To improve patient care quality and ensure healthcare services' cost-effectiveness, reimbursement decision making utilizes an evidence-based approach. These activities commonly are known as evidence-based medicine (EBM) or, more broadly, Health Technology Assessment (HTA).[15]

Generally speaking, EBM refers to an evidence synthesis and decision process intended to assist patients' and/or physicians' decisions. EBM evaluates the evidence regarding interventions' effectiveness and patients' values and looks at individual patients' decisions. The process also assists in developing clinical guidelines. HTA is a broader evidence synthesis system to analyze evidence pertaining to health technologies' clinical effectiveness, safety and cost-effectiveness, and also may include social, ethical and legal aspects of the health technologies' use. HTA is used principally to assist reimbursement and coverage decisions.[16] HTA principles are the base through which payers can balance competing access and affordability objectives.[17]

The US Congress first used the term "Health Technology Assessment" during the late 1960s. HTA then was defined as "a comprehensive form of policy research that evaluates the short- and long-term social consequences of the application or use of novel technology." Today, HTA's goal is to create a bridge between this information's researchers and consumers, i.e., decision makers. HTA transcribes both technical and scientific information encompassing an array of economic, social, ethical and other relevant factors into language understood by policy makers. HTA is based on patient health outcome assessment and/or costs involved compared to currently available treatment options. Policymakers then can use such outcome assessments to decide whether to pay for a certain healthcare product or service. HTA agencies, therefore, are playing an increasingly crucial role in the broader healthcare system function.

The Organization for Economic Co-operation and Development (OECD) defines HTA as a tool to:[18]

- determine evidence or lack thereof on health interventions' benefits and costs
- synthesize health research findings regarding health interventions' effectiveness
- assess economic implications and ascertain cost and cost-effectiveness
- audit social and ethical implications of health technologies' diffusion and use

Today, HTA-like approaches also are being used in a variety of situations, such as amending clinical practice guidelines; classifying new technologies' stage of development; restricting early use of developing technologies; avoiding the purchase of new technologies that might not be adopted due to a lack of human or financial resources; and identifying obsolete technologies or making disinvestments. HTA reports typically assist decision makers at the federal, provincial and local levels.[19]

Generally, an HTA takes about a year to complete. However, the duration may be extended for more-detailed reports.[20] While decision makers require quick advice, HTA agencies are not in a position to deliver it due to the resource-intensive, time-consuming nature of the process. Medical devices requiring an HTA could face a long wait before reimbursement is approved, creating a significant commercial barrier to public healthcare systems. While critics argue HTA has been used to limit access to new healthcare technology, process advocates state HTA is intended to promote efficient resource allocation and achieve population-based health.[21]

While HTA certainly provides key input in the reimbursement coverage decision-making process, economic, regulatory, cultural, professional and institutional factors also affect policy making. All these factors influence health technology adoption and dispersal decision making. Information and evidence from other significant sources also play roles in decision making. Of note, in many cases, technologies may be adopted on a political, informal or *ad hoc* basis. Sometimes, pressures from product champions, patient groups or health authorities also may guide decisions.[22] This reemphasizes the reimbursement process must deal with a continuously changing social, economic and political landscape; hence, it must include and serve the needs of a broad set of stakeholders such as payers, health authorities, regulators, physicians and patient groups.

Innovation is undeniably an ongoing process, especially for medical devices, but HTAs with long turnaround times cannot be repeated throughout the lifecycle of medical devices that typically have quite short market lives. Ideally, the HTA process should be able to update information whenever a product undergoes meaningful technological or other relevant changes, so decision makers can optimize their decisions continuously as a product evolves. However, in today's environment, resource limitations do not allow HTA bodies to update reports frequently at optimal levels, which impacts not only the reimbursement and coverage decision making but also product adoption and dispersal continuously.[23]

While HTA may encompass a health technology's clinical, social, ethical, legal and policy aspects, one of the most significant HTA focuses is on the new technology's economic aspect when evaluating outcome differences compared to the existing technology option.[24] Health economics plays a crucial role during various product lifecycle stages and provides a basic foundation for identifying and forming a product's core value.

Medical Device Health Economics

Health economics play a vital role and provide a solid basis for receiving appropriate reimbursement by ensuring a new healthcare intervention's clinical and cost effectiveness. Hence, designing a clinical trial to achieve both market approval and reimbursement approval cannot be overemphasized.

Even if medical device manufacturers have little experience with health economics, this topic is gaining importance among top medical device companies due to stricter reimbursement requirements.[25] While health economics usually are not assessed until sufficient clinical evidence has been accumulated, this often is conducted as a part of clinical trials to gain preliminary understanding of a new product's economic impact. Frequently, integrating health economics into the clinical trial requires an increased sample size to get reliable health economics results. This higher bar can pose a challenge for many medical device companies (typically, small and medium firms) that barely can make ends meet with piecemeal funding from investors and quicker returns on investment.

Developing evidence is an integral part of the reimbursement strategy, and a randomized controlled clinical trial (RCT), preferably double-blinded, would be ideal in convincing payers. Unfortunately, this is not always feasible or appropriate for novel medical devices due to product nature, financial, ethical or other issues. Therefore, other types of nonrandomized clinical data such as prospective registries, case control studies, etc., commonly are used to gain market and reimbursement approval, with declining success rates. Most clinical trials generally follow a strict regime, and such controlled conditions make it difficult to generalize results for the long term, thereby creating a need for postmarketing studies to collect additional clinical and health economic evidence in real-life conditions.[26]

To guarantee a technology's success, it is becoming essential to develop value propositions carrying information beyond traditional safety and efficacy data. One way of addressing the growing need of real-world evidence is to include the patient's treatment perspective. This can be done through patient-reported outcome (PRO) measures to evaluate patient views on a product's effectiveness. PRO is a broad term, often used to describe outcomes accumulated from patients without any clinician evaluation and explanation. Such data often are aggregated on the basis of standardized questionnaires designed to measure symptoms, function (activity limitations), health-related quality of life (HRQL) or quality of life (QoL). Despite being used in limited medical device clinical trials, PRO data use is gaining significance rapidly and playing a crucial role in health-economics evaluations.[27]

Types of Health-Economics Evaluations

Different approaches to assess health economics from prospective or retrospective clinical and economic data used most commonly are:[28,29]

- Cost-minimization analysis: a method of calculating costs to project the least expensive therapeutic modality. The competing therapies' outcomes are equivalent, so the less-expensive therapy is preferred.
- Cost-benefit analysis: used to value both incremental costs and outcomes in monetary terms, allowing a direct calculation of the net monetary cost to achieve a health outcome. A gain in life-years (survival) may be regarded as the productive value's cost to society of that life-year using, for example, the average wage. Methods for QoL valuation gains include such techniques as willingness-to-pay, assessing the amount individuals would be willing to pay for a QoL benefit. If the monetary outcome value (benefit)

Table 22-4. Types of Economic Evaluations

Types	Number of Health Outcomes	Unit of Health Outcome
Cost-minimization analysis	None	None
Cost-benefit analysis	Many	Dollars
Cost-effectiveness analysis	One	Clinical
Cost-utility analysis	One	QALYs

Source: Cape JD, Beca JM, Hoch JS. Introduction to Cost-Effectiveness Analysis for Clinicians. UTMJ 2013;90(3):103-5.

exceeds its monetary value, the new therapy is preferred.

- Cost-utility analysis: used to determine utility cost, especially quantity and quality of life. However, it is difficult to put a value on health status or an improvement in health status as perceived by different individuals or societies. Unlike cost-benefit analysis, cost-utility analysis is used to compare two different procedures whose benefits may differ. Cost-utility analysis expresses a single healthcare outcome type's monetary value. The incremental cost-effectiveness ratio (ICER) in this case usually is expressed as the incremental cost to gain an extra quality-adjusted life-year (QALY). This allows for easy comparison across different health outcomes but still requires value judgments about QoL (utility) increases associated with different health outcomes.
- Cost-effectiveness analysis: involves a more-comprehensive look at costs. While cost is measured in monetary terms, effectiveness is determined independently and may be measured in terms of a clinical outcome such as number of lives saved, complications prevented or diseases cured. Cost-effectiveness analysis measures the cost of achieving an incremental health benefit expressed as a particular health outcome. Examples of ICERs using this approach are:
  o cost per extra patient achieving a 10 mmHg drop in blood pressure
  o cost per extra acute rejection episode avoided in patients with kidney transplants
- Budget impact analysis: typically used to determine the financial impact (cost saving or incurring potential) of introducing a new product into the healthcare system under current circumstances over a specific period of time, typically one to 10 years, depending on the product, treatment and health system nature.

Table 22-4 shows the number and units of health outcomes used in different approaches.

In some regions, such as Australia and parts of Canada, it is mandatory for sponsors to present health economic data to gain approval for a new medical technology's public reimbursement. Information regarding the impact of covering a particular technology is warranted in terms of the healthcare budget. If a positive reimbursement decision is made, payers still can restrict the diffusion by regulating product volume, provider certification or reimbursement levels.[30]

The fact new technology possibly can reduce healthcare costs, e.g., by preventing hospital visits and labor hours lost, is another reason health economics should play a central role in HTA assessments of new health technologies. Governments in several countries around the world now are acknowledging the value of health economics and beginning to provide support and funding to help develop novel testing methods, with the objective of establishing a more efficient and cost-effective healthcare system.[31]

Harmonization of Evidence Assessment Approach

Today, there are more than 100 national, regional and local HTA agencies globally, and evaluation methods are upgraded constantly as technology advances. Some competent HTA systems functioning in different countries include: UK (National Institute for Health and Care Excellence, NICE), Germany (*Institut für Qualität und Wirtschaftlichkeit im Gesundheitswesen*, IQWiG), France (*Haute Autorité de Santé*, HAS), Italy (*Agenzia nazionale per i servizi sanitari regionali*, AGENAS), Sweden (*Tandvårds- och läkemedelsförmånsverket*, TLV), Netherlands (*Zorginstituut Nederland*, ZIN), US (Agency for Healthcare Research and Quality, AHRQ) and Canada (Canadian Agency for Drugs and Technologies in Health, CADTH). Also, new HTA bodies are emerging in Brazil, Chile, Taiwan, Korea, and others. While such initiatives have been growing in Europe, North America and other parts of the world, in the past few years several efforts have been made to standardize the HTA process. However, based on each country's healthcare needs, priorities and legal frameworks, HTA organizations are bound to use different evaluation methodologies and criteria to assess new innovations. Nevertheless, several initiatives aimed at harmonizing HTAs are in progress. Some of the more prominent are the International Network of Agencies for Health Technology Assessment (INAHTA), the European network for Health Technology Assessment (EUnetHTA) and Health Technology Assessment international (HTAi). An outcome of several efforts of these international societies is significant progress in bringing together many leading HTA bodies to collaborate, share and exchange information. However, the idea of a fully harmonized evaluation and decision-making HTA body is quite distant and still a dream to be realized.

Therefore, medical device manufacturers have to consider the growing need for understanding different criteria, evaluation methodologies and individual HTA agencies' roles in the decision-making process, so they can develop an appropriate business strategy and ensure selecting and prioritizing target markets (and their HTA processes) whose healthcare priorities are aligned best for the product's clinical and economic value proposition.

While HTA remains far from harmonization in terms of final decision making, getting positive HTA recommendations from one leading agency could speed up and influence other HTAs with similar requirements that follow similar evaluation methodologies, while the same may be true for negative HTA recommendations.

Coverage With Evidence Development

Temporary or conditional reimbursement based on evidence development, commonly known as Coverage with Evidence Development (CED), increasingly is being adopted by payers globally.

When new medical devices are placed on the market, they generally lack strong and convincing clinical and economic evidence to be approved fully for reimbursement coverage. To manage the uncertainty around a lack of solid evidence for highly promising medical devices, policymakers worldwide are exploring solutions to ensure timely access for valuable and necessary medical interventions. With the CED approach, policymakers can avoid the binary decision-making dilemma for either fully accepting or rejecting access to new medical products. Instead, CED schemes offer a platform for policymakers to avoid rejecting life-changing and essential innovations that can help solve ongoing healthcare problems. While CED may not be the answer to all policymaking problems, it does address some very important ones, but not without costs. Setting up and operating a well-designed CED program could be an expensive venture and also may pose a political problem by withdrawing access to temporarily funded new treatments. Withdrawing access to new, innovative treatments that may be the only treatment for a target patient group could be quite challenging for policymakers especially if it is due to economic reasons. This also could imply policymakers are extremely cautious about choosing technologies for a CED program; therefore, the bar to qualify for a CED program tends to be higher.[32-34]

CED schemes certainly offer device manufacturers hope for placing their products on the market; however, they do not allow manufacturers to fully leverage the market. This is because CED schemes are designed to control new product diffusion through limited, time-bound funding, fixed patient numbers, limited provider numbers, etc.[35]

Several CED or similar approaches have been adopted and implemented in many parts of the world. Some of the more prominent ones are in the UK, US, Germany, Australia, France, New Zealand and Canada.[36,37] However, in spite of the CED's great potential, it still is new in most countries and lacks clearly detailed criteria for eligibility, technology selection, evaluation timelines and costs. The CED approach still will have to pass the test of time to prove its value in many countries and demonstrate its effective contribution to address short-term reimbursement challenges for new healthcare technologies. A clear need exists for a more transparent CED approach to make this process more meaningful for medical device manufacturers. On the other hand, manufacturers must seek advice proactively from responsible CED agencies and take appropriate, timely actions to avoid missing valuable reimbursement opportunities.

Conclusion and Recommendations

Over the last decade, many countries have controlled their rising healthcare expenses better and established affordable spending levels by applying new cost-containment mechanisms such as national coverage policies, reimbursement coding systems, value-based pricing policies, efficiency and affordability. These traditional approaches included reference pricing, price volume discounts, price cuts and centralized purchasing.[38] However, as more and more treatment solutions become available, providing a wide range of patient benefits such as improving patient outcomes, increasing patient life span, enhancing patient QoL and addressing unmet needs, budget pressure is building. Payers under current immediate budget pressures are moving from simple cost control to a maximum value-for-money approach "What is absolutely necessary and affordable for health system?" Clearly, under tremendous budget pressure, an evidence-based reimbursement approach is gaining importance globally, particularly among developed countries where healthcare costs are at an all-time high.[39] In the absence of reimbursement, most medical products will not find a market; policymakers have a vital responsibility to construct a favorable market environment for the most needed and valuable medical devices.[40]

The medical device industry undoubtedly is facing an unprecedented challenge and must be prepared to present the most credible and compelling clinical, social and economic evidence to justify a new product's value to a healthcare system. Formally or informally, in several countries, cost-effectiveness data also are required as part of the reimbursement approval process. HTAs, thus, are gaining significance in many countries.[41] A number of innovative instruments are being developed to bridge the reimbursement gap. While still in the early stage, one of the more promising and emerging mechanisms is a "Coverage with Evidence" approach that offers a great opportunity for innovative medical devices. As the policymaking environment is changing rapidly, a new approach to demonstrate medical devices' true value is needed urgently.

No empirical analyses can pave the way for off-the-shelf policy decisions; therefore, reimbursement strategy must not be limited to gaining reimbursement coding and payment.[42] The reimbursement process must include all relevant stakeholders and address individual needs when a new medical device is brought to the market. To ensure successful reimbursement approval, proving clinical effectiveness, economic value and real-life patient benefit to the target audience has become as important as proving safety. Consequently, integrating reimbursement and health economics parameters early in the evidence generation planning phase is key to gaining optimal reimbursement. The reimbursement process is a continuum, beginning with a medical device's conceptualization phase and running throughout the product lifecycle. Each product development stage must include reimbursement and health economics questions to predict business success when a product is approved for commercialization.

An in-depth reimbursement and health economics landscape analysis specific to the target therapeutic area for each market should be conducted to gain solid understanding of current existing reimbursement mechanisms. This is central to early business planning to understand the feasible available coding configurations relevant to a product, payment levels, treatment settings allowed for current system use, the minimum and maximum length of stay periods, clinical and health economics data requirements and clinical guidelines. This provides a fundamental basis for revenue forecasting, market adoption rate and profitability assessment.

To ensure every dollar of a company's investment serves the ultimate purpose, key reimbursement and health economics issues should be covered well when designing the clinical trial. This not only will help avoid another clinical trial to demonstrate the new technology's effectiveness and socio-economic impact but also save significant time to market and the company to stay ahead of competition.

Engaging payers from key target countries to understand their needs and vision and get feedback early in the process is warranted to integrate key reimbursement aspects into product planning. Reimbursement planning should be used as a key instrument to shape most important strategic business decisions such as product development, evidence planning, trial design, market selection, product pricing, positioning and commercial launch, to post-launch data collection process.

Upon reaching market launch, reimbursement roadmaps should be ready for each target market, and all relevant functions, e.g., sales and marketing, clinical support and product development, should be educated about emerging reimbursement, health economics and payer issues. Key business professionals responsible for commercialization should understand fully the crucial role reimbursement plays in business routines and guaranteeing the product's overall, long-term success. This helps avoid any fatal mistakes and prevents short-term, profit-oriented practices from jeopardizing long-term sustainable reimbursement strategy.

References

1. Dolenc DA, Dougherty CJ. "DRGs: The Counterrevolution in Financing Health Care." *Hastings Center Report* 1985;15(3):19-29.
2. Quentin W. "DRG-based hospital payment and medical innovation in Europe—Results of the EuroDRG project." Berlin University of Technology website. https://www.mig.tu-berlin.de/fileadmin/a38331600/2012.lectures/Brussels_2011.01.23.WQ_DRGs_innovation.pdf. Accessed 14 March 2016.
3. Op cit 1.
4. Ibid.
5. Quentin W. "DRG-based hospital payment—Experiences from 12 European countries." Berlin University of Technology website.: http://www.thl.fi/documents/10531/120652/Chess_seminar_DRG-based-payment_WQ2.pdf. Accessed 14 March 2016.
6. Boriani G, Burri H, Mantovani LG, et al. "Device therapy and hospital reimbursement practices across European countries: a heterogeneous scenario." *Europace* 2011; 13:ii59–ii65.
7. Ibid.
8. *DRG Payment and the Use of Medical Technology. In: Diagnosis Related Groups (DRGs) and the Medicare Program: Implications for Medical Technology—A Technical Memorandum.* Washington, DC: US Congress, Office of Technology Assessment, OTA-TM-H-17, July 1983.

9. Sturgeon J. "DRGs: Still Frustrating After All These Years." *For The Record* 2009;21(11):14.
10. Op cit 6.
11. Cappellaro G, Fattore G, Torbica A. "Funding health technologies in decentralized systems: A comparison between Italy and Spain." *Health Policy* 2009;92:313–21.
12. Sorenson C, Drummond M, Burns LR. "Evolving Reimbursement And Pricing Policies For Devices In Europe And The United States Should Encourage Greater Value." *Health Affairs* 2013;32(4):788-96.
13. Op cit 9.
14. Schreyögg J, Bäumler M, Busse R. "Balancing adoption and affordability of medical devices in Europe." *Health Policy* 2009;92:218-24.
15. Luce BR, Drummond M, Jönsson B, et al. "EBM, HTA, and CER: Clearing the Confusion." *Milbank Quarterly* 2010; 88(2):256–76.
16. Ibid.
17. Sullivan SD, Watkins J, Sweet B, Ramsey SD. "Health Technology Assessment in Health-Care Decisions in the United States." *Value in Health* 2009;12(Suppl. 2):S39-S44.
18. Roehrig C, Kargus K. "Health Technology Assessment in Canada and the G-7 Countries: A Comparative Analysis of the Role of HTA Agencies in the Decision Making Process." McGill University website. http://www.med.mcgill.ca/epidemiology/courses/EPIB654/Summer2010/Policy/HTA%20Paper%20Canada.pdf. Accessed 14 March 2016.
19. Ibid.
20. Ibid.
21. O'Donnell JC, Pham SV, Pashos CL, et al. "Health Technology Assessment: Lessons Learned from Around the World—An Overview." *Value in Health* 2009;12(Suppl. 2):S1-S5.
22. Op cit 18.
23. Ibid.
24. Kearney P, Stokoe G, Breithardt G. "Improving patient access to novel medical technologies in Europe." *Eur Heart J.* 2006;27:882-5.
25. "Highlights in Early Health Technology Assessment, Department Health Technology & Services Research." MIRA Institute for Biomedical Technology & Technical Medicine, July 2011.
26. Gelijns AC, Brown LD, Magnell C, et al. "Evidence, Politics, And Technological Change." *Health Affairs* 2005;24(1):29-40.
27. Doward LC, Gnanasakthy A, Baker MG. "Patient reported outcomes: looking beyond the label claim." *Health and Quality of Life Outcomes* 2010;8:89.
28. "Economic aspects of drug use (pharmacoeconomy)." In: *Introduction to Drug Utilization Research*. WHO website. http://apps.who.int/medicinedocs/en/d/Js4876e/. Accessed 14 March 2016.
29. Cape JD, Beca JM, Hoch JS. "Introduction to Cost-Effectiveness Analysis for Clinicians." *UTMJ* 2013;90(3):103-5.
30. Op cit 26.
31. Fatzinger G. "Beyond reimbursement: Health economics as a clinical and regulatory strategy." *Foresight* 2011;4(4).
32. Martelli N, van den Brink H. "Special funding schemes for innovative medical devices in French hospitals: The pros and cons of two different approaches." *Health Policy* 2014;117:1-5.
33. Donoghue E. *Non-Established, New or Experimental Treatments (NENET) Evidence Summary 2010*. TAC website. http://www.tac.vic.gov.au/providers/fees-and-policies/policy/non-established,-new-or-experimental-treatment/nenet20er.pdf. Accessed 14 March 2016.
34. Hutton J, Trueman P, Henshall C. "Coverage with Evidence Development: An examination of conceptual and policy issues." *Int J Technol Assess Health Care* 2007;23(4): 425–35.
35. Ibid.
36. Op cit 32.
37. Op cit 33.
38. Op cit 12.
39. Ibid.
40. Op cit 14.
41. Op cit 12.
42. Op cit 26.

Index

Throughout the index tables and figures are noted by "t" or "f" appended to the page numbers. Countries mentioned only in tables are not included in the index.

A

AAMI TIR 45:2012, guidance on Agile practices, 272
accountable care organizations (ACOs), 262
accreditation body, ISO compliance assessment, 40
Active Implantable Medical Devices Directive (90/385/ EEC, AIMDD)
    comparison with AMDD, 160
    established market requirements, 138
    EU effects of, 150–151
    FDA alignment process, 1
    PMS and, 202
    postmarket changes to, 208
    QMS conformity, 38
Active Implantable Medical Devices Directive (AIMDD, 90/385/ EEC)
    ATMPs and, 242
    EFTA harmonization, 232
activity-based hospital (DRG) reimbursement, 285
add-on labeling, 77–78
Advanced Medical Technology Association (AdvaMed), 60, 208
advanced therapy medicinal product (ATMP), 241–242
adverse event reporting
    automated tool use in, 276
    for combination products, 128
    MAUDE replacement for, 203
    non-US manufacturers and, 206
    PMS and, 40, 166, 210
    postmarket regulatory strategy and, 201–213
    software QSM tools for, 276
    stem cell technologies, 245
    stem cell technologies reporting and, 245
    technological change and, 3, 7
    UDI and, 266–267
    in verification and validation, 24t, 88
advertising and promotion
    country-specific regulations, 190t–192t
    DTC, 192–193
    KOLs, 193
    regulations, 189–191
    social media and, 117
    Sunshine Act, 189–190
    See also marketing strategy
Africa
    intelligence resources, 230t
    medical device markets, 230–231
    regulatory agencies in, 218, 218t
    See also South Africa
African/Middle Eastern intelligence resources, 230t
Agency for Healthcare Research and Quality (AHRQ), 29, 290
Agile/Scrum software development methodology, 270–272, 271f
ALAP (as low as possible), 153
ALARP (as low as reasonably practicable)), 153
AMBIMED, 205

AMDD
    CSDT elements, 159
    CSDT for, 158
    Declaration of Conformity (DoC) and, 159
    Essential Principles (EP), 158
    GHTF recommendations and, 158
    harmonization of regulation, 158
    key elements of, 158
    PMAS, 159
    PMAS and, 159
analyte-specific reagents (ASRs), 110–111
analytical performance of IVDs, 113, 115
analytical testing standards, 115
animal- or human-origin raw materials, 116
animal studies
    international guidelines for, 98t
    model selection for, 98
    models for in vivo assessment, 96t
    moral responsibility in, 98
    in nonclinical testing, 97–98
    planning resources for, 99t
    strategy for, 97f
    three Rs principles in, 99, 99t
Annex Z for harmonized standards, 153–154
ANSI/ AAMI/IEC 62304:2006, 266
ANVISA
    postmarket requirements in, 205
    registration requirements in, 140–141, 205
Argentina
    advertising and promotion for, 189t, 192t
    labeling requirements, 82t
    language requirements for, 80t
    MERCOSUR harmonization and, 233
    regulatory agencies in, 233t
    regulatory approval costs in, 188f
ASEAN Medical Devices Directive (AMDD). See AMDD
Asia, medical device markets, 231
Asia/Pacific
    intelligence resources, 231t
    regulatory agencies, 220t
Asian Harmonization Working Party (AHWP), 149–150
Associação Brasileira dos Importadores de Equipamentos, Produtos e Suprimentos Médico-Hospitalares (ABIMED). See AMBIMED
Association for Assessment and Accreditation of Laboratory Animal Care (AAALCA), 98
Association for Strategic Planning, 62
Association for the Advancement of Medical Instrumentation (AAMI), 266
association of Notified Bodies (TEAM-NB), 152

Association of Southeast Asian Nations (ASEAN)
    AMDC and PMAS, 159
    AMDD and regulatory convergence, 158–159
    Consultative Committee for Standards and Quality (ACCSQ), 158
    Economic Community (AEC), 158
    format consensus in, 150
    GHTF, 1–2
    medical device committee (AMDC), 158–159
    Member States (AMS), 158
    postmarket requirements, 205
    reclassification of IVDs in, 117
ATMP Regulation
    borderline cell/device classifications in, 243
    hospital exemption, 242
Audit Report (EU manufacturers), 140
audits
    duration of, 49t
    external audits, 46–47
    global product launch, 68–69
    internal, 54
    ISO 13485 audits, 47
    for Japanese registration, 140
    joint audits with Notified Bodies, 152
    in manufacturing process, 85–88
    on-site for Korean registration, 140
    of suppliers, 54
    TEAM-NB code of conduct, 152
    third-party supplier audits, 54
    unannounced Notified Body production audits, 154
Australia
    animal research in, 98t
    animal research regulation in, 98t
    ARTG postmarket requirements, 205
    CED implementation, 291
    choosing medical device standards, 180
    GHTF, 1–2
    ISO 13485 applicability in, 40t
    labeling requirements, 82t
    language requirements for, 79t
    MDSAP, 148
    postmarket requirements, 205
    regulatory submission requirements, 34t
    target market approval timelines, 33t
    TGA regulation of devices, 138–139
    trade/professional organizations, 224t
Australian Register of Therapeutic Goods (ARTG), 138–139
Authorized Representative. *See* in-country caretaker/agent
autologous intraoperative cell processing. *See* point-of care testing (POCT)

automated tool strategies
    infrastructure support, 275–276
    lifecycle management, 276–277
    production and quality system, 276
    regulatory information management, 277–278
    tool functions, 274–275
automated tools and RIM, 277
Axendia Medical Technology Globalization Report, 62

B

basic components of, 27–36
Belgium
    advertising and promotion in, 189t, 191t
    cell therapy products from, 238t
    language requirements for, 80t
    professional trade organizations, 225t
    regulatory agencies, 220t
bench testing
    and animal studies, 97, 101
    design and development process and, 20t
    GLP and, 91
    performance criteria, 178
    for well-known products, 149
biocompatibility
    defined, 94
    ISO 10993, 94–96
    standard test for, 95t
bioinformatics, 263, 265
Biological License Application (BLA), 127, 239–240
Blood Fatality Report, 128
Bovine Spongiform Encephalopathy (BSE), 116
Bracco Diagnostics, Inc. v. Shalala, 256
branding
    common label contents, 74–75
    in DTC advertising, 193
Brazil
    ABIMED shortcut, 140–141
    animal research in, 98t
    animal research regulation in, 98t
    ANVISA, 141, 205
    emerging HTA system in, 290
    IMDRF membership, 1–2
    labeling requirements, 82t
    language requirements for, 79t
    MDSAP, 148
    postmarket requirements, 205
    registration renewals, 144
    regulatory risk summary, 35t
    regulatory submission requirements, 34t
    target market approval timelines, 33t
    trade/professional organizations, 226t

British Standards Institution (BSI) BS 5750, 37
business development, 15

C

calendars, 77
Canada
    animal research in, 98t
    animal research regulation in, 98t
    Canadian Medical Device License (MDL), 139
    CED implementation, 291
    choosing medical device standards, 180
    CMDCAS ISO 1345:2003, 140
    establishment registration renewals, 144
    GHTF, 1–2
    HTA systems in, 290
    ISO 13485 applicability in, 40t
    ISO compliance assessment, 40
    IVD requirements in, 114
    labeling requirements, 82t
    language requirements for, 79t
    MDSAP, 148
    Medical Device Establishment License (MDEL), 139
    medical device markets in, 233–234
    postmarket requirements, 205
    real-time stability studies for IVD reagents, 114
    regulatory risk summary, 35t
    regulatory submission requirements, 34t
    target market approval timelines, 33t
    trade/professional organizations, 227t
Canadian Medical Devices Conformity Assessment System (CMDCAS), 140
case study examples
    business strategy, 198–199
    Johnson & Johnson Tylenol recall, 211
    patentable inventions in device development, 253–254
    standards in regulatory strategy, 177–179, 181
CE Mark
    EU requirements for, 113
    expedited approval and, 36
    geographic regional marketing and, 111
    global regulatory processes and, 138–139
    labeling, 74
    in manufacturing process, 85–86
    NB assessment of, 40
    in vitro diagnostic device (IVD), 48, 113
cell therapy products on market, 238t
Center for Biologics Evaluation and Research (CBER)
    combination products, 122
    stem cell technology devices, 239

Center for Devices and Radiological Health (CDRH)
    combination products, 122
    consensus standard recognition, 176
    stem cell technology devices, 239, 241
Center for Drug Evaluation and Research (CDER)
    cloud computing workgroup, 268
    combination product jurisdiction, 122–123, 126–127
    PMOA and patent application, 256
Center for Management of Emergency Health Surveillance Information (EVISA), 205
Centers for Medicare & Medicaid Services (CMS)
    clinical practice summaries, 29
    DRG reimbursement, 285–286
    regulatory resources, 229
    reimbursement by, 104, 107
Certificate of Free Sale (CFS), 137–138
Certificate of Product Approval (South Korea), 140
Certificate to Foreign Government (CFG)
    FDA shutdown and, 68
    for global registration, 137
    TFDA requirement of, 140
Chile
    advertising and promotion in, 189t, 192t
    evidence assessment approach, 290
    intelligence resources for, 233
    labeling requirements, 82t
    language requirements for, 80t
    regulatory agencies, 223t
    regulatory barrier in, 188
China
    in-country clinical testing of IVDs, 114
    emerging HTA system in, 290
    IMDRF membership, 1–2
    IVD reagent registration, 114
    IVD regulation in, 112
    labeling requirements, 82t
    language requirements for, 79t
    patent term extension in, 258
    postmarket requirements, 205
    registration renewals, 144
    regulatory risk summary, 35t
    regulatory submission requirements, 34t
    target market approval timelines, 33t
    trade/professional organizations, 224t
China Food and Drug Administration (CFDA)
    clinical trial exemptions, 2
    postmarket requirements, 205
    type-testing for device registration, 139
Class I (General Controls) devices
    in established markets, 138–139, 232–234
    FDASIA and, 268
    manufacturing, 86

marketing strategy for, 215–216
MDSAP and, 147–148
postmarket changes to, 143–144
premarket submission exemption of, 111
regulatory approval costs, 188t
regulatory processes and, 105, 112
Class II (Special Controls) devices
    Canada, 233
    China, 139
    clinical data requirements for, 13, 105
    established market requirements, 138
    Japan, 232
    manufacturing, 86
    market assessment, 199
    pathways for, 112
    postmarket changes to, 143–144
    postmarket registries for, 167
    regulatory approval costs of, 188f
    regulatory requirements for, 105
    scientific evidence requirements, 164
    strategy planning for, 132, 134
Class III (Premarket Approval) devices
    ABIMED shortcut, 140
    advertising and promotion, 188
    APDS system and, 177
    business opportunity and, 199
    Canada, 233
    clinical data requirements for, 13
    CoDx control, 116
    de novo classification, 112
    Japan, 140
    Korea, 139
    patents and, 257
    pathways for, 112
    PMA application and, 85, 138–139
    postmarket changes to, 143–144
    postmarket registries for, 167
    registration requirements for, 139–140
    regulatory approval costs of, 188f
    regulatory requirement determination, 105
    regulatory requirements for, 112
Class IV devices
    Canada, 139, 232–233
    GMP and, 140
    Japan, 139–140, 232
    regulatory approval costs of, 188f
classification of devices
    in global strategy, 133–134
    nature and duration of body contact, 95t
Clinical and Laboratory Standards Institute (CLSI), 115

clinical data
    Directive 2007/47/EC, 150–151
    global regulatory processes and, 137
    in global regulatory strategy, 136
    IVD performance, 113
    support for intended use, 164–165
Clinical Research Organization (CRO)
    in clinical strategy, 64f
    nonclinical laboratory testing, 100–101
    selection of, 100t
clinical strategy, 103–108
    basic components of, 104–105
    clinical testing of IVDs, 114–115
    clinical trial anticipation, 31
    customer requirements in, 106–107
    definition and scope of, 103
    foreign clinical study data use, 106
    human use studies in validation, 10
    investigational reimbursement and, 107
    modular approach by NBs, 106
    presubmission in, 106
    prioritization, 105
    regulatory considerations, 105
    regulatory requirement determination, 105
    scope of, 103–104
    site selection and enrollment, 107
    with stem cell technologies, 244–245
    study design in, 103
    study jurisdictions for studies, 106
clinical trial applications (CTAs), 24t
clinical trials
    application for, 24t, 230
    in business opportunity assessment, 199
    database updates by sponsor, 229
    for device marketing authorization, 2, 103–104
    GRS and, 33–34
    health economics and, 289
    health economics and HTA, 289
    listing services, 230
    marketing authorization and, 167
    PIP and, 258
    registries for, 229t
    and regulatory barriers, 188
    reimbursement issues and, 283, 292
    requirements for data from, 127
    stem cell devices, 241t, 242, 244
    stem cell products and, 244–245
cloud compliance strategy, NIST and, 268–269
cloud computing service models, 264
co-packaged combination products, 122
Code of Ethical Conduct guidelines (IMEDA), 193

Code of Federal Regulations (CFR), Title 21
    21 CFR §§210-211, 128, 243–244
    21 CFR §§600-680, 128
    21 CFR §3, 122, 239
    21 CFR §58, 91
    21 CFR §312, 106, 239
    21 CFR §314, 128
    21 CFR §801, 77, 79
    21 CFR §803, 128
    21 CFR §806, 51
    21 CFR §812, 239
    21 CFR §820, 1–2, 48–49, 85–86, 128, 140, 207, 265, 268–269, 272
    21 CFR §821, 51
    21 CFR §1271, 128, 240–241, 243
Colombia
    advertising and promotion in, 189t, 192t
    language requirements for, 80t
    MERCOSUR harmonization and, 233
    postmarket requirements, 205
    registration requirements for, 137
    regulatory agencies in, 205, 223
combination products, 120–130
    appropriate time for RFD submission, 129
    challenges of, 59
    clinical trial data for, 127
    co-packaged, 122
    collaboration for, 60
    collaborative review by FDA centers, 126–127
    cross-labeled, 122
    device adverse event reporting, 128
    drug mode of action, 122
    FDA definition of, 121–122
    GMPs and, 127–128
    labeling claims and OCP decisions, 125
    life science industry and, 62–63
    OSMP jurisdiction appeal, 125
    OUS publications and, 127
    postmarket review of, 126
    Pre-IND (drug), 127
    Presubmission (device), 127
    primary mode of action and jurisdiction, 122
    regulatory strategy for, 127
    RFD process and, 127
    risk assessment and documentation impact, 62
    single-entity, 122
    submission types for, 127
commercial off-the-shelf (COTS) software, 265, 272–273

commercial strategy
   design and development process, 10
   health economics integration in strategy, 291–292
   linked to regulatory strategy, 132
   marketing, 185–199
   patents, 249–259
   postmarket, 201–213
   reimbursement, 283–293
   single or multiple product versions, 132
   third-party patents and device development, 255
Commission's Framework for Environmental Health Risk Management, The, 66, 66f
Committee for Advanced Therapies (CAT), 242
Committee for Medicinal Products for Human Use (CHMP), 242
Committee of Sponsoring Organizations of the Treadway Commission COSO, 67
Common Submission Dossier Template (CSDT)
   development of, 149–150
   in risk management, 69
communication
   in CDT, 15–16
   international partners, 16–17
   with management and company organization, 16
companion diagnostics (CoDx), FDA definition and guidance, 116
Competent Authorities
   of EC, 220–221t
   intelligence resources, 231t
   licensing authority, 245
   market surveillance, 203
   MEDDEV development, 208
   NBs and ISO compliance, 40, 51–52
complaint files
   AMDD elements of, 158–159, 161
   CAPA and trends for, 57, 202, 209–211
   data system for, 275–276
   FCAs and, 113
   handling of, 50–51, 88, 151
   QMS and, 39–40
   requirements for, 53, 57
compliance, international labeling standards, 73
consensus standard, 170
copyrights, 250
core development team (CDT), 4–25
   activity ebb and flow, 23–24t
   ad hoc participants, 15
   business development, 15
   clinical affairs team member, 13
   communication in, 15–16
   composition of, 7–8
   cross-functional experts, 5

   development phases, 8t, 9–10
   fundamentals, 5–6
   harmonization of strategy and submissions, 7
   manufacturing team members, 12–13
   marketing, 12
   project milestones, 7
   quality and regulatory team members, 13–14
   quality assurance and risk management, 13–14
   R&D and, 11
   regulatory authority notification, 10–11
   regulatory interactions of members, 17
   regulatory pathway assessment, 16t
   risk management in combination products, 62
   roles and responsibilities, 6
   suitable projects for, 6
   supply chain, 15
   system and process feasibility, 6–7
core regulatory components, 27–36
Corrective and Preventive Action (CAPA)
   Agile/Scrum software development methodology, 272
   feedback process requirement, 57
   ISO compliance, 40
   in manufacturing process, 85
   within manufacturing process, 87
   postmarket regulatory strategy, 211
   postmarket regulatory strategy and, 202
   in QMS, 50–51
   risk management integration into, 61
   software QSM tools for, 276
COSO Enterprise Risk Management-Integrated Framework, 67
Council Decision on Mutual Acceptance of Data (MAD), OECD publication, 92
country of origin (COO)
   distribution control and, 145
   labeling requirements, 145
Coverage with Evidence Development (CED), 291
cross-functional expertise
   in clinical strategy, 104
   roles and responsibilities of CDT, 5–7
cross-labeled combination product, 122
culture and languages
   determination in absence of guidance, 77
   device design and, 63
   in labeling, 76
   units-of-measure in labeling, 76
current clinical practice summaries
   AHRQ, 29
   CMS, 29
current Good Manufacturing Practice (CGMP), 85–88. *See also* Good Manufacturing Practices (GMP), Good Clinical Practice (GCP)

cybersecurity, 59
  in medical devices, 117
cybersecurity and data privacy, 267–268

D

data integrity
  cloud computing challenges to, 264
  GLP and, 91, 92t
  with MDDS and EHR, 59
  personalized medicine and, 3
  processes for assessment of, 135–136
  QMS development and, 147
  in verification and validation, 63
  verification of, 136f
date format, EN1041:2008, 77
de novo products
  combination products, 127
  processes for, 112, 215, 217
  regulatory requirements for, 105, 112
decision-making process, CDT, 5
Declaration of Conformity (DoC), 159, 163
design and development process, 51f
  automated tool use in software development, 277
  combination product market risks, 59–60
  design transfer for global product, 68
  expiration date and protection in, 251
  global strategy planning, 61–62
  human factors in, 67–68
  mechanical engineering approach to, 2–3
  models/methodology for software, 269–270
  phases of, 8t, 9–10
  process standards, 169
  product technical file, 68
  regulatory convergence, 60
  requirements of design, 61–63
  risk analysis in, 65–68
  risk management, 59–72
  risk management failure, 69–71
  risk management in, 59–72
  steps in, 253–254
  total lifecycle approach in, 60
  total lifecycle risk management in, 60
  verification and validation, 63–65
  See also Unique Device Identification (UDI)
design control procedures
  Agile/Scrum software development methodology, 272
  approaches to, 51–52
  DHF in, 51
  manufacturing role in, 86
  materials and services purchase, 52–53
  mature device process change, 88–90
  in PMS, 207
  process validation, 53
  production and process control, 52
  traceability and identification, 52–53
  See also Quality System Regulations (QSR)
Design History File (DHF)
  manufacturing QSR and, 86
  in QRS, 51
  software documentation, 273
  See also device master records (DMR
design patent, 251
design requirements
  design specification determination, 63
  documentation of design history, 63
  intended use articulation, 63
  user need comprehension, 63
design transfer for global product, 88–90
development phases, 8t, 9–11
"Development Sequence in Small Groups," 15–16
device classification, Class I (General Controls), 112
device classifications
  Canada, 139–140
  Class III (Premarket Approval), 112
  EU, 30
  ISO 13485 and, 40t
  Japan, 139
  market assessment, 199
  US, 30, 112
  variations in regions or countries, 29
device design and development process
  Agile use in, 272
  FOI and, 258
  new product justification, 291–292
  open-source software use in, 272–273
device history record (DHR)
  design V&V, 89
  labeling records in, 53
  in QSR, 90
  traceability and identification, 52
device-living tissue interaction. *See* biocompatibility
device master records (DMR)
  core team activities, 23–24t
  in design V&V, 89
  in development phases, 8t
  in manufacturing process, 12–13
  manufacturing QSR and, 86
  mature device process change, 90
  product maintenance and, 10
  production and process control, 87
  QSR and CGMPs, 86–87
device strategy trends, 157–168

Index   301

Digital Imaging and Communications in Medicine (DICOM), 267
Diphoterine® Skin Wash (DSW, RFD process challenge, 125–126
direct reporting relationship, CDT and, 7
direct-to-consumer (DTC), 192–193
Directive 90/385/EEC. *See* Active Implantable Medical Devices Directive (AIMDD, 90/385/ EEC)
Directive 95/46/EC (data privacy), 268
Directive 98/79/EC. *See* In Vitro Diagnostics Directive (98/79/ EC, *IVDD*)
Directive 2001/83/EC (*Medicinal Products* Directive), 239, 241t, 244
Directive 2004/23/EC, 239
Directive 2004/23/EC (EUTCD), 239
Directive 2004/108/EC, emission control, 116
Directive 2006/95/EC, low voltage directive, 116
Directive 2007/47/EC, clinical evaluation, 150–152
Directive 2011/65/EU, RoHS in IVDs, 171
Directive ECC 2013/473/EU, ALARP challenge by, 153
Directive EN/ISO 13485. *See* ISO 13485
Directive EN/ISO 14971, 61, 153. *See also* Quality System Regulations (QSR)
Do Not Reuse labeling, 74
document management
　in GLP, 93t
　in labeling strategy, 78
　management in labeling strategy, 78
　in manufacturing process, 87–88
　manufacturing QSR and, 86
　software and, 78
　software for, 277
dossier assembly, 137–138
DRG (activity-based hospital) reimbursement, 285–287
Drug Information Association (DIA), 59

E

Eastern European Agencies, 222t, 225–226t
EC Declaration of Conformity, 204
ECC 2013/473/EU, risk management, 153
EDMA, 60
educational resources, 229t
Egypt
　label requirements for, 82t
　labeling requirements, 82t
　language requirements, 80t
　regulatory agencies, 218t
electrical/electronic safety
　EN 61010-2- 101, 116
　for IVDs, 116

electromagnetic compatibility (EMC), 96, 139–140, 170, 178
electronic health record (EHR), 59, 263–264
electronic medical record (EMR), 59, 262–264
elements of, 18–22t
Eli Lilly & Co. v. Medtronic, Inc., 258
emission control, 116
EN 61010-2- 101, electrical/electronic safety, 116
enterprise resource planning (ERP), 276
enterprise systems
　automated tool and system regulation, 266
　automated tool implementation, 274–275
　computer systems strategy, 274
　distribution control, 144–145
　IT infrastructures, 263
　production and QMS tools, 276
　risk management framework, 70
　shipping restriction control, 44
environmental health risk management, 66f
environmental influences
　device design and, 63
　software QSM tools for, 276
error potential of device, cultural effects, 67
Essential Principles (EP)
　AMDD and, 158
　IVD conformity in EU, 113
Essential Requirements of CFR, 177–178
Establishment Inspection Report (EIR), 140
ethical guidelines, 191–192, 195
EU Harmonized Standard EN1041:2008, date format, 77
EU *Medical Devices Directive (MDD). See Medical Devices Directive (MDD)*
EU *Tissue and Cells Directives (EUTCD)*, Directive 2004/23/EC and, 239
EU-US industry trade groups, 60
Eucomed, marketing ethical guidelines, 191–193
Eudamed
　database, 2
　medical device databank, 203
　principles for medical technology, 60
Europe, harmonization of devices in, 232–233
European Commission (EC)
　approval time changes, 189
　Competent Authorities, 220–222t
　Directive 2007/47/EC implementation, 151–152
　intelligence resources, 232t
　intelligence resources from, 232t
　MEDDEVs from, 203, 208, 232–233
　Recommendation 2013/473/EU, 153
　state-of-the-art meaning, 207
　trade/professional organizations, 224–225t

European Coordination Committee of the Radiological, Electromedical and Healthcare IT Industry (COCIR), 60
European Diagnostic Manufacturers Association (EDMA), 60
European Economic Area (EEA), 257–258
European Free Trade Association (EFTA), 232
European Medical Technology Industry Association (Eucomed), 60
European Medicines Agency (EMA)
   ATMP device application procedure, 242
   clinical evaluation data and, 106
   combination products, 59
European network for Health Technology Assessment (EUnetHTA), 291
European Technical File, dossier documentation, 137
European Tissue and Cells Directive (EUTCD)
   harmonization efforts, 245
   POC/autologous therapy devices, 242–243
   stem cell product regulation, 239, 241t, 242
European Union (EU)
   animal research in, 98t
   animal research regulation in, 98t
   borderline cell/device classifications in, 243
   CE Mark and approval, 36
   CE Mark and geographic regional marketing, 111
   CE-marked IVDs, 113
   changes for software control, 267
   CoDx regulation, 116–117
   date format in labeling, 76–77
   EFTA harmonization, 232
   Essential Principles (EP) conformity of IVDs, 113
   FSCAs in, 203
   GHTF, 1–2
   guidelines for stability testing, 99
   HCT/P regulatory approach, 237–239
   HTA systems in, 290–291
   ISO 13485 applicability in, 40t
   IVD classification and regulation, 109, 112
   labeling strategy, 73–75
   legislative and regulatory changes in, 150–153
   local labeling requirements in, 82t
   marketing guidelines and standards, 38, 191–192, 195
   MDSAP and, 148
   NCAR postmarket monitoring, 203
   OMR harmonization, 232
   patent term extension in, 257–258
   postmarket QMS and reporting, 204, 210
   QMS compliance and, 85–88
   reclassification of IVDs in, 117
   registration requirements in, 138
   regulation of cell/device products, 241–242
   regulatory legislation, 232
   regulatory risk summary, 35t
   submission requirements, 34t
   target market approval timelines, 33t
   trade/professional organizations, 225–226t
evidence assessment approach, HTA systems and, 288–289
evidence-based medicine (EBM), 288–289
evidence collection. *See* data integrity
evolutionary software development model, 270
executive business strategy
   development of, 185
   marketing support for decision making, 186
   regional strategy development, 186–187
   regulatory approval costs, 188, 188f
   regulatory barriers and analysis, 187–189
   responsibility with globalization, 62
   segmented target prioritization, 187
expiration date
   in device design and development, 251
   in labeling, 74, 83t
   license renewal and, 144
   regulatory review and, 143
   stability testing for, 98–99

F

Failure Mode and Effect Analysis (FMEA), 207
Failure Mode Effect and Criticality Analysis (FMECA), 207
Fault Tree Analysis (FTA), 207
FD&C Act, §201, device mode of action, 122
FD&C Act, §201(h) and (g)(1), device mode of action, 122–123
FD&C Act, §503(g), primary jurisdiction of combination products, 122
FD&C Act, §510(k)
   admission of patent infringement, 258–259
   approval for changes to device, 143–144
   clinical data requirements, 149
   combination products, 127
   design transfer, 89
   device classifications and, 112
   DHF documentation, 273
   dossier assembly, 137
   dossier documentation, 137
   existing device changes, 90, 208
   market entry and, 148–149
   marketing strategy, 86, 124
   patent infringement and, 258–259
   in patents as Prior Art, 258
   postmarket reporting, 210

postmarket reporting for, 210
  as prior art, 258
  software changes and, 269
  software DHF documentation in, 273
  strategy plan and, 18t, 31, 34t
  substantial equivalence proof, 215–216, 256
FD&C Act, §513
  de novo products, 112
  device classification information, 125
FD&C Act, §522
  PMS studies, 21, 210
  scope of, 204
FDASIA Health IT Report, software regulatory requirements and, 267
Federal Communications Commission (FCC), 267
Federal Food, Drug, and Cosmetic Act (FD&C Act)
  de novo products, 112
  device classification and, 125
  jurisdiction RFD, 124
  Phase 3 510(k) submission, 10
  primary jurisdiction of combination products, 122
  and QSR development, 49
Federal Register
  modification of standards, 176
  new standards from FDA, 170
  Notice 63 FR 9531, standard submission notice, 183
field safety corrective actions (FSCAs)
  harmonized implementation of, 203
  Singapore, 160t
filing submission, 141–142
5-day Report, 128
Food and Drug Administration (FDA)
  Advancing Regulatory Science Initiative, 245
  cloud initiative, 268–269
  CoDx approval of, 116–117
  combination product definition, 121–122
  combination products, 59
  cybersecurity guidance documents, 117
  device classifications by, 112
  device definition, 2–3
  device manufacturing control by, 85–88
  exemption of medical data systems from, 268
  FDAMA, 124
  framework for risk management, 65t, 68–69
  Genomic Working Group, 269
  guidance documents on CoDx, 116
  guidance on human factors, 68
  HCT/P regulatory approach, 237–239
  jurisdiction of combination products, 122
  OCP, 122
  PMS tools, 203
  postmarket regulatory strategy, 201–213

presubmission for IVD performance testing, 116
  presubmission to, 106
  product risk management, 64f
  QMS requirements, 48–49
  Quality System Regulation, 14
  reactive vigilance, 203
  real-time stability studies for IVD reagents, 114
  recognized consensus standard from, 170
  RFD request, 3
  safety and performance guidance, 105
  SMDA and combination products, 122
  social media guidance, 195–196
  See also 21 CFR
Food and Drug Administration Safety and Innovation Act (FDASIA), 267
Food, Drug, and Cosmetic Act (FD&C Act)
  PMS studies, 210
  postmarket data analysis, 2
  See also FD&C Act
France
  advertising and promotion in, 189, 191t, 192–193
  CED implementation, 291
  DRG systems in, 285t–286t, 287–288
  HTA systems in, 290–291
  language requirements for, 79t
  OMR harmonization, 220
  professional trade organizations, 225t
  regulatory agencies in, 221t
Free Sales Certificate (FSC), 140
Freedom of Information Act
  510(k) access and, 258
  RFD decisions and, 125

G

gap analysis
  implementation of ISO 13485, 42
  ISO 14971, 42
gene therapy medicinal product (GTMP), 241–242
general purpose reagents
  IVD reagent regulation, 112
  use with IVDs, 110–111
genome sequencing, 265
Germany
  advertising and promotion in, 189t, 191t, 193
  CED implementation, 291
  DRG systems in, 285t–286t, 288
  evidence assessment harmonization, 290
  HTA systems in, 290–291
  language requirements for, 79t
  professional trade organizations, 225t
  regulatory agencies in, 221t

GHTF/SG5/N7:2012, scientific validity, 113
Global Alert and Response (GAR), 205
Global Harmonization Task Force (GHTF)
   AMDD and, 158
   committees of, 1–2
   design control procedures, 52
   guidance document for STED, 137
   proactive surveillance for, 202
   risk-based classification of IVDs, 154
   See also International Medical Device Regulators Forum (IMDRF)
global market authorization requirements, key concepts of, 1–2
Global Medical Device Nomenclature (GMDN), 3
global produce registrations. *See* product registrations
global regulatory processes, 131–145, 147–155
global regulatory strategy (GRS)
   basic components and plan, 27–36
   cell/device combination product regulation, 237–247
   communication of, 34
   defined, 27
   development recommendations, 35–36
   elements of, 33t
   information gathering, 27–28
      basic components, 28t
      clinical application, 28–29
      current clinical knowledge, 29
      environmental influences, 31–33
      product plan, 28–29
      regulation history, 30–31
      resource availability, 33
      technology and engineering, 30
   regulatory risk summary, 35t
   regulatory submission requirements, 34t
   strategy versus plan, 33–34
   summary presentation of, 35–36
   target market approval timelines, 33t
global technical files, 68–69
globalization
   Axendia report recommendations, 62
   convergent environment, 69–70
   evolution of, 1–2
   evolving technologies, 3
   GLP acceptance, 91–93
   ICT industry, 62
   marketing strategy, 185–197
   medical devices, 2–3
   as new normal for devices, 69
   regulatory dynamics, 3–4
   regulatory processes for, 131–145, 147–155
   risk management planning for, 61–62
Good Clinical Practice (GCP)
   cellular material procurement, 243
   ISO 14155 requirements, 176, 183
   stem cell trials, 244–245
Good Laboratory Practice (GLP)
   elements of, 92t
   nonclinical quality management, 91–93
   noncompliance consequences, 92–93
   QMS development and, 147
   violation examples from, 93t
Good Manufacturing Practice (GMP)
   adoption of, 49
   certificate renewal for registration, 144
   for combination products, 127–128
   HCT/P requirements, 243
   nonclinical laboratory testing and, 101
   product safety, 60
   registration renewals, 144
Good Software Engineering Practices, 265–266
Good Tissue Practices, 239
GOST-R
   certificate and renewals for import, 144–145
   labeling requirements, 82t
Group Purchasing Organizations (GPOs), marketing analysis, 186

H

hardware, testing modification for, 63
harmonization
   advertising and promotion, 191–192
   Asian regulatory focus, 150
   devices in Asia, 232
   EFTA and EU, 232
   EU OMR, 232
   evidence assessment approach, 291–292
   of evidence-assessment of health economics, 290–291
   FDA and MDD alignment, 1
   global regulatory processes, 3–4
   GMDN, 3
   reclassification of IVDs for, 117
   risk management in design and development, 60
   of software, 266
   software standards, 273
   stem cell technology efforts, 245
   TEC and, 60
   Unique Device Identification (UDI), 3
   Z annexes of standards, 153–154
Hatch-Waxman Act, 257–259
Hazard Analysis Critical Control Points (HACCP), 207
hazard and accident analysis, 65
Hazard and Operability Study (HAZOP), 207

Health Canada
   advance consultations on IVDs, 117
   device licenses in, 139
   postmarket requirements, 21, 205
health economics
   evaluation methods for, 290t
   evidence-assessment approach harmonization, 290
   methods and measures for, 289–290
Health Information Technology for Economic and Clinical Health Act (HITECH Act), 268
health information technology (HIT), 262
Health Insurance Portability and Accountability Act (HIPAA), 268
health-related quality of life (HRQL), 289
Health Technology Assessment (HTA), 288–291
Health Technology Assessment international (HTAi), 291
High- Performance Integrated Virtual Environment (HIVE), 269
hospital information systems (HIS), 262
hosting company, 205. *See also* in-country caretaker/agent
human cells, tissues and cellular and tissue-based products (HCT/P), 128, 237–247
human factors
   in device design, 68
   in software development, 266
   usability testing
      assessment in design and use, 67–68
      market assessment and development, 193–194
human use clinical studies, validation of design by, 10
humanitarian device exemption (HDE), 210

I

IAF MD 9:2011, 47
ICH Q1A(R2), 99
ICH Q9, 66–67
IEC 60601, 83t, 170, 172, 174
IEC 62304, 175, 266, 269–270, 272–273
IEC 62366, 68, 174–175, 178
IEC 80001-1:2010, 67
in-country caretaker/agent
   global regulatory processes, 205
   selection of, 142t
in vitro diagnostic device (IVD), 109–119
   analytical testing of, 115
   animal raw materials in reagents, 116
   ASR marketing of, 112
   clinical testing of, 114
   de novo products, 112
   electrical safety for, 116
   EU definition of, 109
   EU regulation of products for, 112
   FDA definition of, 109
   general regulatory requirements, 113
   geographic regional regulatory requirements, 111
   global manufacturing pitfalls, 117–118
   human subject testing, 91
   intended use and indications for, 109–111
   intended use definitions in development, 110
   IVD Regulation (new), 112
   labeling, 73
   lay and professional uses of, 111
   new risk classification for, 154
   performance parameters and testing, 100, 114–116
   performance testing for registration, 114
   presubmissions and consultations on, 117
   reagents for use with, 110–111
   region-specific requirements for, 113
   regulatory classification and pathways, 112–113
   regulatory requirements, 113
   requirements for, 113–114
   RUO and IUO devices, 111
   stability studies for reagents, 114
   stability testing for, 99–100
   stem cell technology and, 239, 241
   target market, 111
   test characteristics for, 110
   trends for, 116–117
   user definitions for, 111
   users defined, 111
In Vitro Diagnostics Directive (98/79/ EC, *IVDD*)
   and AMDD, 160
   EU definition of, 109
   PMS and, 204
   postmarket changes to, 208
   QMS conformance and, 38
   quality management, 38
   registration requirements in EU, 138
incremental software development model, 270
India
   animal research in, 98t
   animal research regulation in, 98t
   labeling requirements, 82t
   language requirements for, 79t
   regulatory risk summary, 35t
   regulatory submission requirements, 34t
   target market approval timelines, 33t
indications for use
   clinical strategy and, 103
   devices changes and, 143–144
   labeling, 83t
   local market considerations, 164
   marketing claims and, 132
   marketing/clinical claims in, 104

mature device changes and, 90
pathway assessment elements and, 16
performance testing strategy, 114
in regulatory strategy, 12, 18t–20t
target market identification by, 111
See also in vitro diagnostic device (IVD)
individual digital healthcare
sensing and monitoring, 3
See also personalized medicine
information communication technology (ICT) industry, 62
information technology
MDDS, 59
medical devices and, 59
informed consent, specimen acquisition and, 115
Infrastructure as a Service (IaaS), 264
inspections in manufacturing, 85–86
Institutional Animal Care and Use Committee (IACUC), 98
instructions for use (IFU)
labeling, 73
and packaging, 76
intellectual property and patents, 249–259
intellectual property (IP)
defined, 249
IP categories in devices, 249–250
medical device IP protection, 250–251
See also patents
intended use
animal study requirements for, 97
biocompatibility and, 94
claimed intended use, 180–181
clinical data support for, 164–165
combination products, 121–122
design control procedures and, 52, 63
device output and, 240, 242
device registration, 159
effects of changes in, 143
FDA definition of, 109
finding standards for medical device, 180
in global strategy, 2
and indications, 217
ISO Standard 18113-1 definition of, 109–110
IVD regulatory strategy and, 109–111
in labeling, 74, 83t
language and, 76
marketing and clinical claims for, 12, 105, 167, 190
patent applications and, 256
performance testing strategy, 114
postmarketing strategy and, 206
product classification, 133

regional or cultural differences in, 68–69, 113, 139, 164
regional strategy and, 186
regulatory classification and pathways, 112
in regulatory pathway, 16t
regulatory strategy and plan elements, 18t–20t, 105
RFD and labeling claims, 125
risk management, 93, 168, 175, 178
small company perspectives for CDT, 6
software and unauthorized changes to, 264
stability requirements and testing, 98–99
standards in regulatory strategy, 169, 173
stem cell POCT processing, 240–241
See also indications for use
International Accreditation Forum (IAF), 41
International Council on Harmonization (ICH)
biotechnology product guidelines, 245
models for risk management, 66
stability testing guideline, 99
International Electrotechnical Commission (IEC) standards, 169, 185. *See also* specific IEC standards
International Health Regulation implementation, 205
international labeling standards. *See* labeling; labeling strategy
International Medical Device Regulators Forum (IMDRF)
ASEAN document availability, 158
device-specific risk management, 66
formation and membership, 1–2
guidance document for STED, 137
guidance documents from, 41
IVD classification by, 112
MDSAP and, 148
postmarket requirements, 205
priorities for medical technology sector, 60
software regulatory alignment, 266
international medical device resources, 230t
International Network of Agencies for Health Technology Assessment (INAHTA), 291
International Organization for Standardization (ISO)
audits for QMS compliance assessment, 45
committee on quality management, QMS 2016 revision, 60–61
compliance assessment, 40
device-specific risk management, 66
IVD intended use definition, 109–110
PMS and compliance, 40
See also specific ISO standards
international partnerships, communications with, 16–17
international registration requests, CDT and, 1–2
International Society for Stem Cell Research (ISSCR)
clinical guidelines, 245

International Society for Stem Cell Research's (ISSCR), with stem cell technologies, 245
international standards, labeling, 73
international trade/professional organizations, 224–227t
interoperability in software systems, 267
Investigational New Drug (IND), stem cell devices, 239
investigational reimbursement. *See* reimbursement
investigational use only (IUO). *See* in vitro diagnostic device (IVD)
Iran, language requirements for, 79t
ISO 8601, date format, 76–77
ISO 9000, postmarket requirements, 204
ISO 9001
    PDCA cycle in, 38
    Quality Management Systems Requirements, 37
ISO 10993
    biocompatibility testing and GLP, 91, 94, 96, 171, 178–179
    biocompatibility testing of devices, 91, 94–96
    biological evaluation of medical device, 178
ISO 13485
    2003 applicability, 38
    2012 harmonization, 38
    2016 feedback process requirement, 57
    2016 management responsibility, 56
    2016 personnel requirements, 56
    2016 product realization, 57
    2016 risk management, 57
    2016 software validation, 56
    2016 transition timing, 56f
    Agile software development and, 272
    certification availability, 38
    cloud compliance strategy, 268–269
    combination with QSR, 148
    EU registration requirements, 140
    exclusions and non-applications and, 38
    jurisdictions of, 40t
    manufacturing/certification for, 85–86, 88
    PMS requirements, 207
    postmarket requirements, 204
    quality management for, 14
    revised standard requirements, 57
    risk management in, 53
    software DHF documentation in, 273
    software QMS, 265
    See also quality management systems (QMS)
ISO 13485, QMS regulatory requirements, 37
ISO 14001, 38
ISO 14155
    clinical investigation and GCP, 176
    clinical investigation of devices, 171, 174, 176
ISO 14971
    2012, risk management, 207
    Agile software development and, 272
    device-specific risk management, 66
    enhanced 2012, 60
    gap analysis, 42
    postmarket requirements, 204
    risk analysis stipulation, 60
    risk management, 176
    risk management defined, 67
    second edition of, 60
    software DHF documentation in, 273
    software risk management, 265
    standard requirements, 60
ISO 15223
    labeling, 77
    symbols in, 74–75, 176
ISO 19011, principles of auditing, 41, 54
ISO 22301, 152–153
ISO 31000, 67
ISO 46001. *See* Quality System Regulations (QSR)
ISO/IEC 17021, QMS certification for devices, 47–48
ISO/IEC 27001, cloud compliance strategy, 268–269
ISO/TR 14969, 38, 41
ISO18113-1, IVD intended use definition, 109–110
IVD Directive, 113
IVD Regulation, 112–113
    CoDx control under, 117
IVDs, 109–119

J

Japan
    animal research in, 98t
    animal research regulation in, 98t
    choosing medical device standards, 180
    Class I devices in market, 139–140, 232
    GHTF, 1–2
    guidelines for stability testing, 99
    ISO 13485 applicability in, 40t
    IVD advance consultations in, 117
    IVD definition, 109
    IVD performance studies in, 113
    IVD regulation in, 112
    labeling requirements, 82t
    language requirements for, 79t
    MDSAP, 148
    Ministerial Ordinance #169, 140
    PAL, 2
    PAL revision, 2
    patent term extension in, 258
    postmarket requirements, 204–205
    Premarket Approval application (*Shonin*), 139

Premarket Certification application (*Ninsho*), 139
Premarket Submission (*Todokede*), 139
real-time stability studies for IVD reagents, 114
regenerative medicine laws, 243
regulatory submission requirements, 34t
target market approval timelines, 33t
trade/professional organizations, 224t
Japanese Medical Device Nomenclature (JMDN code), 140
jurisdiction
combination products, primary, 122
OSMP appeal, 125

K

key opinion leaders (KOLs)
management support by, 193–194
marketing team and, 12–13
as reimbursement stakeholders, 284
Korea
emerging HTA system in, 290
labeling requirements, 82t
language requirements for, 79, 79t
MFDS regulations, 139
stability studies for IVD reagents, 114
type-testing for MFDS registration, 139
See also South Korea
Korean Good Manufacturing Practice (KGMP), 140
Korean Ministry of Food and Drug Safety (MFDS), 82t, 139–140

L

labeling, 53, 73–83
add-on, 78
AMDD and MDD, 160
ASEAN marketing, 190t
CE Mark, 74
cellular materials, 243
change during development process, 8t, 10–11
and changes to medical device, 165
claims and OCP decisions, 125
combination products, 121, 127
content of, 83t
contents, 74–75
control in manufacturing process, 87
COO requirements for, 145
CTD activity and, 23t–24t
culture and language in, 67, 187
Do Not Reuse, 74
DTC marketing, 192
electronic, 75
European, 191t
false/misleading, 105
in global market, 68, 73–74, 132, 137
guidance for, 68
intended use and, 109
ISO format for, 76–77
IVD reagents, 112, 114, 116–117
labeling standards for, 179
language requirements for, 79t–80t
local requirements, 76, 82t, 204
lot number, 74
model number, 75
for nonclinical laboratory testing, 21t
in product development stage, 216
product realization, 157, 166
QMS control for, 53, 56, 90
QSR for integrity, 53
Ref Number, 75
regulatory strategy and plan elements, 18t, 21t
requirements for, 3, 145
in risk management, 64f, 66
social media misinformation and, 195
software for content management for, 277–278
software QSM tools for printing, 276
standards and guidance for, 176
sterile, 74
trade name, 75
UDI and, 74, 266, 278
units-of-measure in labeling, 76
use-by date, 74
during V&V process, 89
validation for device, 67
laboratory developed test (LDT), 112
laboratory information management system (LIMS), 276
language in labeling, 76–77, 79–80t
large company perspectives
CDT activity flow, 25
clinical affairs team member, 13
clinical strategy for, 105
distribution control and, 145
international registration requests, 17
manufacturing, 13
marketing, 12
OEM and QMS, 13
project manager roles, 12
quality assurance and risk management, 14
regulatory interactions of CDT, 19
Latin America
intelligence resources, 233t
medical device markets in, 233
postmarket requirements, 205
regulatory agencies in, 223t
learning management system (LMS), 276

Index 309

leftover specimens, 114–115
legalization of dossier documentation, 137–138
lifecycle management
    CDT in, 5
    in device development, 60
    maximization by patents, 256–257
    of medical devices, 166f
    patent protection during, 251
    postmarket regulatory strategy, 201–213
    risk-based software standard in, 269–270
    SDLC, 272–273
    software development tools, 274f
    software regulation in, 265–266
    stability testing, 98–99
    strategy during, 27
localization, 76, 139

M

maintenance procedures
    ISO 13485:2016, 56
    mitigation strategies and, 62t
Management of Emergency Health Surveillance Information (EVISA), 205
management responsibility
    communication by, 56
    in manufacturing process, 86
    postmarket regulatory strategy, 211
    support of QMS, 49–50
Managing the Risks From Medical Product Use, 68
Manufacturer and User Facility Device Experience (MAUDE) database, 203
manufacturing processes, 85–90
    acceptance activities, 87
    biological safety evaluation by, 96–97
    CAPA processes in, 87
    CDT in, 12–13
    control and validation in, 87
    design and development processes in and, 88–90
    HCT/P requirements, 243–244
    HTA systems and, 291
    for IVDs, 117–118
    labeling control in, 87
    lot or serial identification in, 86–87
    mature device process change, 90
    medical device environment and, 85–86
    modification for conformity in, 182
    nonconforming product handling in, 87
    postmarket regulatory strategy and, 202
    purchasing materials for, 86
    QSR and CGMPs, 86–88
    R&D transfer to, 89

resources for strategy development, 216
    software strategy in, 269–270
Marketing Authorization Application (MAA), 242
Marketing Authorization Holders (MAHs), 232
marketing strategy, 185–199
    abbreviations/disclaimers for, 192–193
    advertising and promotion for, 189–191
    approval changes and times (EU), 189
    commercial strategy for, 132
    distributor/in-country partners, 194
    DTC advertising in Europe, 193
    ethical guidelines for, 191–192
    executive strategy development, 185
    KOL program, 12
    market assessment research for, 186, 193–194
    regional strategy development, 186–187, 189t
    regulatory approval costs, 188
    regulatory barrier assessment, 187–189
    segmented target prioritization in, 186–188
    social media, 195–196
master document list and labeling, 78
materials and services purchase, 62t
Medical Device Amendments, 49
medical device data systems (MDDS), 59
Medical Device Establishment License (MDEL), 139
Medical Device License (MDL), 139
medical device regulatory process, 37–57
Medical Device Reporting (FDA), 207
medical device reporting (MDR), 203
Medical Device Single Audit Program (MDSAP), 148
Medical Device Tracking regulation, 51
Medical Device User Fee and Modernization Act of 2002 (MDUFMA), 122
Medical Device Vigilance Reporting (EU), 207
Medical Devices Directive (93/42/ECC, MDD)
    AMDD comparison, 160
    combination products, 242
    current standards compliance, 207–208
    established markets, 138
    in EU, 150–151
    FDA alignment with, 1
    labeling requirements, 77, 79t
    manufacturing, 85–88
    non-application of ISO 13458, 38
    packaging versus IFU and, 76
    PMS obligations and, 202
    QMS and, 38, 116
    reclassification of IVDs, 117
    strategy elements, 18–19t
    testing acceptance, 7
    tiers of labeling and, 76
    tissue and cell regulation, 239, 241t

Medical Devices: Guidance document (MEDDEV)
    harmonization and, 150
    as intelligence resources, 232
    postmarket changes and, 208
    revision on PMCF, 203
    software regulation, 265
Medical Devices Product Working Group (MDPWG), 158
Medical Devices Regulations (SOR/98-282)
    intelligence resources for, 234t
    language requirements, 82t
    medical device markets in, 221
Medical Imaging & Technology Alliance (MITA), 60
Medical Technology Score Card, 188
Medicare Prescription Drug, Improvement, and Modernization Act of 2003 (MMA), 107
Medicinal Products Directive, 239, 241t, 244
Medicines and Healthcare products Regulatory Agency (MHRA), 29, 222t, 232t
Medicines and Medical Devices Safety Authority (MEDSAFE), 205
Mercado Común del Sur (MERCOSUR), 233
Mexico
    advertising and promotion in, 189t, 192t
    labeling requirements, 82t
    language requirements for, 79t
    regulations in, 233
    regulatory risk summary, 35t
    regulatory submission requirements, 34t
    target market approval timelines, 33t
    trade/professional organizations, 226t
    translation for, 138
Middle East
    intelligence resources, 230t
    medical device markets, 230–231
    regulatory agencies in, 218t
Ministry of Health, Labour and Welfare (MHLW)
    Ministerial Ordinance 169, 38
    postmarket requirements, 204–205
Ministry of Health (MOH), 205
mitigation strategies
    device changes and, 207
    maintenance procedures and, 62t
    for market barriers, 186–187
    materials and services purchase and, 62t
    options in strategy, 167–168
    in regulatory strategy, 32, 62, 153
    risk management, 60, 62t
    standards and guidance for, 175–176
model number, labeling, 75
models/methodology
    for risk management, 63–64
    for software development, 269–270
Monitoring Project on Health Products Marketed in Brazil, 205
Murphy's Law and Corollaries, 67–68

N

National Competent Authority Report (NCAR), 203
National Institute of Standards and Technology (NIST), 268–269
NB-MED/2.12/Rec1, 151
near patient testing (NPT), 111
Netherlands
    DRG systems in, 285t–286t
    harmonization in, 232
    HTA systems in, 290
    language requirements for, 79t
    professional trade organizations, 226t
    regulatory agencies in, 222t
    stem cell products and, 238
new drug application (NDA), 127
New Zealand
    CED implementation in, 291
    dossier assembly in, 137
    language requirements for, 82t
    MEDSAFE regulation, 205
    regulatory agencies in, 220t
    WAND database, 205
Next Generation Sequencing (NGS), 263
Ninsho (Premarket Certification application), 139
nonclinical and laboratory testing, 91–101
    animal models for in vivo testing, 93t, 96t
    animal studies in, 20t, 97–98, 97f
    biocompatibility testing, 93–94
    biological safety evaluation by, 96
    core team activities, 23t
    device stability, 98–99
    GLP in, 91–93
    GMPs and, 101
    IVDs, 99
    labeling for, 21t
    outsourcing of, 100
    risk analysis/management, 93–94
noncompliance, GLP consequences, 92–93
North America
    intelligence resources, 234t
    medical device markets in, 233–234
    regulatory agencies, 223t
Norway
    EFTA harmonization and, 232
    language requirements for, 79t
    regulatory agencies in, 222t

Notified Body (NB)
    CE Mark assessment, 38, 40, 74, 233
    clinical data collection, 149
    combination product assessment, 242
    compliance assessment by, 40, 145
    consultations with, 106, 117, 160
    evaluation of role of, 152
    harmonization in QMS development, 147–148
    inspections and audits by, 85–88, 138–139, 152
    ISO 13485 and, 38
    IVD reviews, 112, 154
    legislative and regulatory changes in, 150–153
    PMCF changes, 151–153
    postmarket device changes and, 90
    premarket submission to, 88
    review for registration, 138

O

obsolescence and design change, 10–11
Office of Combination Products (OCP), 122, 239
Office of Special Medical Programs (OSMP), 125–126
Organization for Economic Cooperation and Development (OECD), 91–92, 288–289
original equipment manufacturer (OEM), 13
OUS studies and, 127
Outermost Regions (OMR) of EU, 232
outside US (OUS), 127
outsourcing
    NB production audits, 154
    nonclinical laboratory testing, 100–101
    risk management in manufacturing, 61
    selection of CRO, 100t

P

packaging of devices, and IFU, 76
Pan American Health Organization (PAHO), GHTF, 1–2
Patent Cooperation Treaty (PCT), 251
patents, 249–259
    Bracco Diagnostics, Inc. v. Shalala, 256
    comprehensive patent portfolio, 252
    device development/commercialization and, 252
    Eli Lilly & Co. v. Medtronic, Inc., 258
    EU patent term extension, 257
    infringement of, 252–255
    maximization of product lifecycle, 256–257
    patentability requirements, 251–252
    PCT applications, 251
    PMOA support by application, 256
    protection offered by, 254–255
    regulatory approval delays in US, 257
    regulatory considerations and, 255–256
    rights assignment by personnel, 259
    SPCs in EU, 257–258
    substantial equivalence claims, 256
    third-party patents and device development, 255
    types and applications of
        design patent, 251
        utility patent, 251
    US term adjustments, 256–257
    See also intellectual property (IP)
patient classification system (PCS), 284–285
patient-reported outcome (PRO), 289
Pediatric Investigation Plan (PIP), 258
performance testing strategy, 114–116
periodic safety update reports (PSURs), 245
peripheral blood stem cells (PBSCs), 240–241
personalized medicine
    data integrity and, 3
    IVDs in, 116
    mobile applications/platforms, 263–264
personnel requirements
    mitigation strategies and, 62t
    risk management participation, 65–66
Pharmaceutical Affairs Law (PAL), 2
Pharmaceutical Medical Device Act (PMD Act), 109
pharmaceutical product/device separation, 2–3
Pharmaceuticals and Medical Devices Agency (PMDA)
    advance consultations on IVDs, 117
    device adverse event reporting, 204–205
    device registration and, 139
pharmacovigilance. *See* adverse event reporting
Pharmacovigilance Report Intake and Managed Output (PRIMO), 203
PIP breast implant scandal, 152
Plan-Do-Check-Act (PDCA)
    iterative cycle, 45f, 46
    in process approach, 38, 38f
Platform as a Service (PaaS), 264
point-of-care (POC), risk management and, 68
point-of care testing (POCT)
    autologous cell therapies, 240
    IVDs, 111
political, economic, social and technological factor (PEST) analysis, 186
postmarket clinical follow-up (PMCF), 152
postmarket regulatory strategy, 201–213
    adverse event/vigilance reporting, 210
    changes after initial release, 208–209
    compliance, 207–208
    compliance and commercialization, 206
    current standards, 207
    customer focus of, 201–202
    desired outcomes of, 210–211

development and execution of, 209
FSCAs in, 203
IMDRF, 205
maintenance/sustaining activities, 203
manufacturer/distributor/importer responsibilities, 205–206
postmarket problem origins, 209–210
postmarket regulatory strategy and, 206
premarket strategy and, 202
proactive surveillance for, 202
reactive vigilance, 203
regional QMS requirements, 204–205
regulatory requirements, 203–204
risk analysis in, 206–207
state-of-the-art principles, 207
postmarket surveillance (PMS)
Directive 2007/47/EC, 150–151
QMS and surveillance, 40
surveillance for design issues, 60
Postmarketing 15-day Alert Report, drug and biological components, 128
postmarketing regulation, 201–213
Pre-Investigational Device Exemptions (IDE), 106
Pre-Investigational New Drug (IND)
drug combination products, 127
FDA program, 106
preapproval inspection (PAI), 85–86
preclinical testing
core team activities, 20t
GLP and, 91
outsourcing of, 100
QMS and, 56
regulatory professionals and, 100
in risk management, 62
validation of design by animal studies, 10
predicate device
510(k) and, 258–259
performance testing strategy, 114, 116
in registration requirements, 138
Premarket Approval (PMA)
application from device manufacturer, 85–86
approval for changes to device, 143–144
for combination products, 127
dossier documentation, 137
postmarket reporting for high risk, 210
stem cell devices, 239
Presubmission (device), combination products, 127
Prevor, 125–126
primary mode of action (PMOA)
in combination products, 122
device classifications and, 256
stem cell technology devices, 239

Principles of Good Laboratory Practice, 91–92
process approach in QMS
ISO 9001 series and, 37
model of, 37f
process standards, 169, 173–175, 180
product development matrix, 186t
product development protocol (PDP), 210
product knowledge portal, 5
product realization
device strategy trends and, 157
GHTF regulatory model, 166f
ISO 13485:2016 and, 57, 174
ISO 14971 and QMS, 42, 166–167, 175
local considerations in, 164
strategy development and, 39–40
traceability and identification, 52
product registration holder, 142
product registrations, local representatives for, 7
Product Regulation Standard (China), 139
product standards, 139, 169
production. *See* manufacturing processes
professional trade organizations, 224–227t
project management
activities of, 11
ad hoc participant designations, 15
quality assurance and risk management, 14
Public Health Service Act (PHS Act)
§351(i) on combination products, 123
§361 (HCT/P product regulation), 238–239
stem cell devices, 239–240
Pure Food & Drug Act, 49

Q

QMS and, 37–57
qualitative test, defined, 110
Quality Management Systems—Medical Devices—Guidance on the Control of Products and Services Obtained from Suppliers, 52, 54
quality management systems (QMS), 37–57
assessing operational system, 44
audits and, 45, 47t–49t
automated tool use in, 276
CDT and, 6–7, 13–14
certification and registration, 46–47, 46t
change management, 165
continuous improvement in, 45–46
customization of, 54–56
defining responsibilities, 43f
Directive EN/ISO 13485, 147–148
documentation hierarchy in, 44, 44f
in GLP, 93t

in-house versus external development, 148–149
implementation of ISO 13485, 40–42
implementation of plan, 43–44
implementation plan, 42–43
implementation team appointment, 41
ISO 9001, 37–38, 38t
ISO 13485, 14, 38–39, 39f
jurisdictions of ISO 13485, 40t
lifecycle approach to regulation, 167f
management system functions, 36
in manufacturing, 85–88
for multi-site organization, 47–48
nonconformity areas in, 55
PDCA cycle in resource management, 38f
postmarket regulatory strategy, 201–213
process approach in, 37–38, 37f
product realization, 57
QMS implementation sample, 42f
QSD and, 140
QSR and, 14, 49, 53–54, 86–88
resources for strategy development, 216–217
risk-based approach to, 56, 60–61. *See also* Quality System Regulations (QSR)
software tools for, 276
strategy for, 147
US FDA system requirements, 48–49
See also Quality System Regulations (QSR)
quality of life (QoL), 289
quality system documentation (QSD), 140
Quality System Regulation (QSR)
   acceptance activities, 51f
   Agile software development and, 272
   CAPA processes in, 50–51
   cloud compliance strategy, 268–269
   combination with ISO 13485, 148
   complaint unit for, 50–51
   design control, 51–52, 51f
   for device manufacturer, 85–86
   DHF in, 51
   document and record control, 50
   FDA exemption of medical data systems from, 268
   ISO 14971-1 standard requirement, 60
   ISO principles in, 48–49
   labeling and packaging controls, 53
   personnel requirements, 50
   postmarket regulatory strategy, 207
   product realization, 57
   QMS development and, 147
   QMS manufacturing requirements, 86–88
   risk analysis stipulation, 60
   risk management in, 53
   software DHF documentation in, 273

supplier audits, 54
traceability and identification, 52–53
vendor quality systems, 54
See also design control procedures; quality management systems (QMS)
quantitative test, defined, 110

R

randomized controlled clinical trial (RCT), 289
raw materials, BSE-free requirements for, 116
RDC 15/2014, 141
RECAST, 117
Ref Number, labeling, 75
regional regulatory agencies, 224–227t
Registered Certified Body (RCB), 139
Regulation (EC) No. 1394/2007, 238–239
regulator's perspective
   ASEAN AMDD, 158
   change management, 165
   regulatory tool kit, 165–168
   strategy for effective regulation, 157–158
   See also regulatory processes; regulatory professionals
Regulatory Affairs Professionals Society (RAPS), 208
regulatory agencies, 218–223
   CDT in authority notification, 10–11
   communications with, 217
   meetings with, 227–229
regulatory convergence
   AMDD and EU MDD, 158–160
   Asian regulatory system focus, 60, 150
   design and development process, 59–60
   TEC, 60
regulatory environment
   approval barrier assessment, 188–189
   third-party perspectives, 147–155
regulatory framework
   automated tools/enterprise systems, 266–267
   environmental influences, 31–32
   lifecycle management and, 166, 168
   MDPWG development of, 158–163
regulatory information management (RIM), 262
regulatory information providers, 229t
regulatory processes, 131–145, 147–155
   accuracy and integrity requirements, 135–136
   AHWP and ASEAN in, 150
   ASEAN submission format consensus, 150
   Authorized Representative, 142
   automated tools/enterprise systems, 266
   Brazilian ABIMED shortcut, 140–141
   changing interpretation of, 151–152
   China, 139

clinical data collection, 136–137, 149
compliance with GMPs, 140
continuous improvement in PMS, 152–153
COO compliance requirements, 145
  in-country caretaker, 205
  customs violations in, 145
data integrity in, 134–135, 136f
device change approval, 143
device classification and, 134
Directive 2007/47/EC, 150
distribution control, 144–145
dossier assembly and documentation, 136–138
dossier review, 142–143
established markets, 138
EU regulatory change examples, 150
  hosting company, 205
import licensing and requirements, 144–145
Korea, 139
localization and, 138–141
market entry strategy, 148–149
MDD and AIMDD effects of, 151
MDSAP and QMS structure for, 148
NB changes in EU, 152
overview of, 131
pathway assessment elements, 16t
pathway assignment for, 256
PMCF changes, 152
post-approval activity, 143
product classification and, 133
QSR and ISO 13485 and, 148
registrations and renewals, 137, 144
regulatory and commercial strategy linkage, 132
regulatory costs and commercial potential, 132–133
RFD process and, 3
risk assessment and management, 132, 153
STED and, 137, 149
strategy and planning for, 131
submission planning and filing, 133t, 141–142
third-party perspectives, 147–155
type-testing in, 139
regulatory professionals
  animal studies and resources for, 99t, 124
  Annex Z implementation, 153–154
  automated tools and, 277–278
  cell/device combination product regulation, 243
  clinical strategy and, 103–104
  collaboration in combination products, 60
  device standards choice and, 177, 180–182
  EU changes to NB and, 152
  evolution of outlook, 149–150
  guidance from ISO 22301:2012, 152–153
  health economics integration in strategy, 291–292
  in-house QMS development, 148
  IVD regulatory requirement identification, 114
  manufacturing responsibilities of, 86–88
  market assessment and development, 193–194
  obtaining ISO 13485 certification, 154
  performance testing strategy, 116
  predicate device testing strategy, 116
  QMS development and, 153
  renewal planning, 144
  review of proposed changes, 143–144
  role and responsibility clarification, 154–155
  software risks and, 274
  standards development or revision and, 183, 208
  training and expertise of, 215
  user proficiency and competency, 163–164
  See also strategy development resources
regulatory risk summary by country, 35t
regulatory submission requirements, 34t
reimbursement, 283–293
  alternative routes for, 287–288
  CED adoption, 291
  changes for device industry, 283–284
  CMS and IDE coverage, 107
  coding systems, 286t
  cost-containment mechanisms and, 291–292
  DRG systems in Europe, 285t
  EBM and HTA, 288–289
  health economics and evaluation of, 289
  market access stakeholders, 284f
  marketing analysis and, 186
  of public health services, 284–285
  US coding systems, 287t
Request for Designation (RFD)
  animal studies and, 124
  combination products, 62, 123–125
  required information for, 124–125
  stem cell technology devices, 239
  timeline for response to, 125
research and development (R&D)
  large company perspectives, 12
  product maintenance, 10–11
  small company perspectives, 11
research use only (RUO). *See* in vitro diagnostic device (IVD)
resource management, PDCA cycle in, 38f
resources for regulatory professionals, 215–235
restriction of the use of hazardous substances (RoHS), 116
return on investment (ROI), 186

risk management
    ALAP versus ALARP, 153
    analysis for, 65–67
    assessment and documentation impact on, 62
    classification by risk level, 138–139
    contingency plans in, 62, 62t
    COSO framework, 67
    design and development process, 59–72
    design transfer for global product, 68
    device classifications and, 112
    early risk management planning benefits, 62–63
    evaluation principles, 94
    failure of, 69
    FDA framework for, 65f, 68–69
    feedback process requirement, 57
    human factors in, 67–68
    ICH guidelines, 66–67
    IEC framework, 67
    IMDF device-specific risk management, 66
    ISO device-specific risk management, 66
    ISO framework, 57, 67
    labeling in, 67–68
    mitigation strategies, 62t
    models for, 63–64
    multi-jurisdictional product technical file, 68–69
    NRC framework for, 66
    personnel participation in, 65–66
    plan for devices, 94
    point-of-care (POC) and, 68
    QMS integration of, 42, 60–61
    risk identification and prioritization, 62
    risk mitigation, 62, 62t
    at root level, 70
    software DHF documentation in, 273
    sources in devices, 94t
    strategies for, 69
    strategy development resources, 216
    TC210, 60–61
    total lifecycle planning for, 62
    trigger point, 62
    See also regulatory risk summary
Roszdravnadzor (Russia), 139–140
"router." *See* device history record (DHR)
Russia
    Declaration of Conformity, 140
    GOST-R certificate term, 144
    IMDRF membership, 1–2
    importing requirements, 144
    language requirements for, 79t
    local labeling requirements, 82t
    local testing-based registration in, 139
    Roszdravnadzor review of device, 140

trade/professional organizations, 224t

S

Safe Medical Devices Act (SMDA), 49, 122
safety and effectiveness data (SSED), 117
scientific validity, 113
semi-quantitative test, 110
shelf life
    defined, 98–99
    device standards choice and, 178
    IVD reagent requirements for, 114
    in IVDs, 114, 117
    stability testing for, 99
    termination (*See* expiration date)
    USP definition of, 99
shipping restriction control software, 144–145
Shonin (Premarket Approval application), 139
Singapore
    animal research in, 98t
    choosing medical device standards, 180
    device registration, 162–163
    language requirements for, 80t
    postmarket requirements, 205
    premarket evaluation system in, 162
    regulation implementation in, 160f
    regulatory framework rollout, 160–162
    risk classifications in, 161t
single-entity combination product, 122
small company perspectives
    audits and, 50
    CDT activity flow, 25
    clinical affairs team member, 13
    clinical strategy for, 105
    CRO, 78
    distribution control by, 144–145
    intended use and CDT, 6
    KOL and clinical team, 13
    manufacturing, 13
    marketing, 12
    OEM outsourcing by, 13
    project manager roles, 11–12
    QMS for start-up, 147
    quality assurance and risk management, 14
    regulatory interactions of CDT, 17, 19
smart medical technology. *See* information technology
social media
    FDA cybersecurity guidance documents, 117
    marketing strategy, 195–196
Software as a Service (SaaS), 264
software development and regulation, 261–281
    §510(k) and existing device changes, 143–144, 269

ACOs, 262
automated tool strategy, 274–278
bioinformatics, 265
cloud compliance strategy, 268–269
cloud computing, 264
COO compliance requirements, 272–273
cybersecurity and data privacy, 264
device interoperability with HIT, 263
DHF documentation in, 273–274
distribution control, 144–145
EMRs, 262
EU regulation of, 265
genome sequencing, 265
harmonized standards for, 273
healthcare environment evolution, 262
HIT and, 262
hospital information systems (HIS), 262
IEC 62304, 172
international regulation of, 265
interoperability standards, 267
for IVDs, 116
lifecycle management tools, 274f
medical device systems and, 261–263, 265
mobile/app and devices, 263–264, 268
models/methodology for, 269–270
policy and procedure strategies for, 278–279
regulatory landscape for, 266
SOUP, 272
telemedicine/mobile applications, 262
testing modification for, 63
US regulation of, 265
validation requirements, 3, 56, 268–269
software of unknown provenance/pedigree (SOUP), 272
somatic cell therapy medicinal product (CTMP), 242
South Africa
language requirements for, 80t
local labeling requirements, 82t
registration requirements in, 111
regulatory agencies in, 219t
regulatory requirements in, 231
trade/professional organizations, 224t
South Korea
cell therapy products from, 238t
Class I devices in market, 139–140
compliance with KGMPs, 140
regenerative medicine laws, 243
registration approvals and GMP renewal in, 144
regulatory agencies, 220t
type-testing for device registration, 139
See also Korea
Spain
DRG system in

DTC marketing in, 193
language requirements for, 79t
marketing promotion in, 189t–190t
regulatory agencies in, 222t
trade organizations, 225
special technology
combination products, 120–130
IVDs, 109–119
software, 261–281
stem cell technologies, 237–247
sponsor
clinical trials database updates by, 229
communication with CRO, 101
device testing and challenge by, 180
FDA presubmissions, 116
labeling information, 82t
maximizing value of device, 250
performance testing strategy, 116
responsibility of, 64f–65f, 105, 179
RFD for exemption, 127
specimen identification, 114–115
stability testing (IVD reagents), 114
stakeholders, risk management involvement, 66
Standard Management Staff (SMS), 176
standard operating procedure in GLP, 93t
standard treatment practice, 29
Standards Council of Canada (SCC), ISO compliance assessment, 40
standards development organization (SDO), consensus standard, 170
standards in regulatory strategy, 169–184
case study examples, 177–179
choosing standards, 177, 180–182
CLSI analytical testing standards, 115
defined, 169, 183
development process for, 177, 182
human and animal tissues, 178–179
nonclinical laboratory testing, 222
proposals of, 176
recognition process for standards, 176–177
recognized consensus standard, 170
risk management in design and development, 60
separation of standards and regulation, 169–170
software interoperability standards, 267
transition periods for revisions, 182
types of standards, 169
Standards Task Group (STG), 176
state-of-the-art principles, 207
stem cell devices, IND application for, 239

stem cell technology, 237–247
   adverse event reporting, 245
   ATMP Regulation and, 238–239
   borderline device regulatory determination, 239
   cell/device combination product regulation, 237
   clinical trials with, 244–245
   currently marketed products, 238t
   EU device classification, 241–242
   EUTCD regulation of, 242
   harmonization efforts, 245
   hospital exemption, 242
   jurisdictions other than US/EU, 243
   periodic safety update reports (PSURs), 245
   pharmacovigilance reporting, 245
   PMS for, 245
   POCT processing, 240
   regulatory routes for, 241t
   starting cellular material in, 243
   tissue processing (US & EU), 238
sterile labeling, 74
strategy
   components of regulation, 27–36
   defined, 103
   labeling strategy, 73–83
   regulatory process, 131–145, 147–155
strategy development resources, 215–235
   blogs and websites, 228t
   clinical processes and studies, 217
   clinical trial databases and registries, 229–230, 229t
   communication
      with regulators, 217, 227, 229
      technical staff and, 217
   conferences and educational programs, 229t, 230
   cross-cultural skills and translation, 227
   documentation in, 216
   intended use and indication assessment, 217
   manufacturing process, 216
   notification services, 230
   personnel, 215
   process and computer system validation, 216
   for product submissions, 220, 223, 227
   professional literature and publications, 228t, 230
   project staff training, 217
   quality system, 216–217
   regulatory agency listing, 218–219t
   regulatory information providers, 229t
   regulatory requirements and strategy, 216–217
   risk management, 216
   software for, 228t, 230
   testing, 216
   time and cost constraints, 217
   trade/professional organizations, 224–227t, 229

study protocol
   animal study element of, 96t
   in GLP, 93t
submissions, filing of, 141–142
Summary Technical Documentation (STED)
   dossier documentation, 137
   in-house versus external development, 149–150
   in risk management, 69
Sunshine Act, 189, 193
Supplementary Protection Certificates (SPCs), 257–258
suppliers
   audits of, 54
   third-party supplier audits, 54
supply chain
   CDT and *ad hoc* participants in, 15
   globalization of, 61, 65
   labeling and, 73
   lifecycle management and, 166
   QMS and, 56
surveillance, postmarket. *See* postmarket surveillance (PMS)
Sweden
   DRG systems in, 285t
   HTA systems in, 290
   language requirements for, 79t
   professional trade organizations, 226t
   regulatory agencies in, 222t
Switzerland
   DRG systems in, 286t
   EFTA harmonization and, 232
   language requirements for, 79t
   professional trade organizations, 225t
   regulatory agencies in, 222t
symbols in labeling, 77
systems development lifecycle (SDLC), 272–273

T

Taiwan, 220t
   advertising and promotion in, 189t–190t
   animal research in, 98t
   animal research regulation in, 98t
   device changes in, 143
   emerging HTA system in, 290
   ISO 13485 applicability in, 40t
   IVD reagent requirements in, 114
   language requirements for, 80t
   local labeling requirements, 82t
   QSD letter/facility license, 140
   TFDA licensing, 140
Taiwan Food and Drug Administration (TFDA), 140
target market approval timelines, GRS and, 33t

technical elements
    clinical trials, 103–108
    design and development process, 59–72
    manufacturing, 85–90
    nonclinical and laboratory testing, 91–101
    standards use, 169–184
technology and engineering, cross-specialty application, 30
test driven development (TDD), 272
Testing-based Product Registration (Russia), 139
Thailand
    advertising and promotion in, 189t–190t
    IVD reagent testing in, 114
    language requirements for, 80t
    RECAST, 117
    regulatory agencies in, 220t
Therapeutic Goods Administration (TGA)
    device regulation by, 138–139
    postmarket requirements, 205
third-party perspectives, global regulatory processes, 147–155
third-party testing, device type-testing (Korea), 139
30-day Malfunction Report, device adverse event/vigilance reporting, 128
3-day Field Alert Report, drug components of, 128
three Rs principles in animal research, 99, 99t
tissue-engineered product (TEP), 241–242
Todokede (Premarket Submission), 139
traceability and identification, 86–87
trade name, 75
trade secret, 250–251
trademark, 250
Transatlantic Economic Council (TEC), 60
"traveler." *See* device history record (DHR)
Tuckman, Bruce, 15–16
Turkey
    CE Mark recognition by, 21t
    dossier translation for, 138
    language requirements for, 79t
    local labeling requirements, 82t
    regulatory agencies in, 222t
type-testing for device registration, 139

U

Underwriters Laboratories (UL), 172
Unique Device Identification (UDI)
    harmonization, 3
    ISO 13485:2016, 57
    in manufacturing process, 87–88
    postmarket reporting, 210
    software regulatory alignment, 266–267

traceability and identification, 52
US-EU industry trade group promotion, 60
United Arab Emirates (UAE)
    common label contents, 73–75, 74f
    consistency across documents, 78
    global, 73–83
    guidance on human factors for, 68
    language requirements for, 77, 80t
    local labeling requirements, 73, 76–77, 82t
    regional and country adaptations, 77–78
    in risk management, 73
    translation cost in, 77
United Kingdom Accreditation Service (UKAS) ISO compliance, 40
United Kingdom (UK)
    animal research in, 98t
    CED implementation, 291
    HTA systems in, 290
    ISO compliance assessment, 40
    language requirements for, 79t
    overseas territory harmonization, 232
    trade/professional organizations, 226t
United Nations (UN), IVD regulation by, 112–113
United States Code, Title 35, 257–259. *See also* intellectual property (IP); patents
United States (US)
    animal research regulation in, 98t
    CED implementation, 291
    CLIA requirements for IVDs, 113
    device classifications in, 112
    establishment registration renewals, 144
    GHTF, 1–2
    HTA systems in, 290
    ISO 13485 applicability in, 40t
    labeling, 73–77
    language requirements for, 79t
    manufacturing environment in, 85–88
    marketing ethical guidelines, 191–192
    MDSAP, 148
    medical device markets in, 233–234
    patent term extension in, 256–257
    postmarket QMS and reporting, 204, 210
    presubmission for IVD performance testing, 116
    QSR, 48–49
    real-time stability studies for IVD reagents, 114
    registration requirements in, 138
    regulation of cell/device products, 237, 239–241
    regulatory risk summary, 35t
    regulatory submission requirements, 34t
    target market approval timelines, 33t
    trade/professional organizations, 226–227t
    UDI implementation, 266–267

US-EU industry trade groups, 60
US National Library of Medicine MEDLINE/ PubMed service, 29
US National Research Council risk management framework, 66
US Patent and Trademark Office (USPTO), 250, 256–257
US Presidential/Congressional Commission on Risk Assessment and Risk Management, 66
use-by date labeling, 74
utility patent, 251

V

validation. *See* verification and validation
vendor quality systems, mitigation strategies and, 62t
Venezuela
    advertising and promotion in, 189t, 192t
    harmonization efforts and, 233
    language requirements for, 80t
    local labeling requirements, 82t
    regulatory agencies in, 223t
verification and validation (V&V)
    comprehensive usability risk, 63
    data integrity verification, 136f
    design validation, 51f, 137
    hazard and accident analysis, 65
    levels of confidence for, 63
    mature device process change, 88–90
    process validation, 53
    product realization, 57
    quality/reliability engineering, 63–64
    scientific validity, 113
    of software, 265–266
    strategic focus in, 63
    strategies for, 64–65
    testing modification for, 63

W

Waterfall software development model, 270
Web Assisted Notification of Devices (WAND), 205
World Health Organization (WHO)
    IMDRF observer status of, 1–2
    IVD regulation by, 112–114
    MDSAP and, 148
    public health emergency network, 205

Z

Z annexes to harmonized standards, 153–154